PRINCIPLES AND PRACTICE
OF STRESS MANAGEMENT

PRINCIPLES AND PRACTICE OF STRESS MANAGEMENT

Edited by

ROBERT L. WOOLFOLK

Rutgers–The State University

and

PAUL M. LEHRER

UMDNJ–Rutgers Medical School

Foreword by Gary E. Schwartz

THE GUILFORD PRESS
New York   London

To Jeffrey and Suzanne, and to Elizabeth

© 1984 The Guilford Press
A Division of Guilford Publications, Inc.
200 Park Avenue South, New York, N.Y. 10003

Printed in the United States of America
Second printing, August 1984

LIBRARY OF CONGRESS CATALOGING IN PUBLICATION DATA
Main entry under title:

Principles and practice of stress management.

  Bibliography: p.
  Includes indexes.
  1. Stress (Psychology)—Prevention. I. Woolfolk, Robert L. II.
Lehrer, Paul M. [DNLM: 1. Stress, Psychological—Therapy. 2.
Relaxation technics. WM 172 P957]
BF575.S75P75 1984   616.89'14   83-5689
ISBN 0-89862-617-X

CONTRIBUTORS

Theodore Xenophon Barber, PhD, Cushing Hospital, Framingham, Massachusetts

Aaron T. Beck, MD, Center for Cognitive Therapy, Department of Psychiatry, University of Pennsylvania, Philadelphia, Pennsylvania

Douglas A. Bernstein, PhD, Department of Psychology, University of Illinois, Champaign, Illinois

Deborah L. Block, BA, Department of Psychology, The Pennsylvania State University, University Park, Pennsylvania

Thomas D. Borkovec, PhD, Department of Psychology, The Pennsylvania State University, University Park, Pennsylvania

Thomas H. Budzynski, PhD, Behavioral Medicine Associates, Englewood, Colorado

Patricia Carrington, PhD, Department of Psychology, Princeton University, Princeton, New Jersey

Steven L. Fahrion, PhD, Voluntary Controls Program, The Menninger Foundation, Topeka, Kansas

Beverly A. Given, BA, Department of Psychology, University of Illinois, Champaign, Illinois

Mark C. Johnson, BA, Department of Psychology, The Pennsylvania State University, University Park, Pennsylvania

Malcolm Lader, MD, Institute of Psychiatry, London, England

Paul M. Lehrer, PhD, Department of Psychiatry, UMDNJ–Rutgers Medical School, Piscataway, New Jersey

F. J. McGuigan, PhD, Performance Research Laboratory, University of Louisville, Louisville, Kentucky

Patricia A. Norris, PhD, Voluntary Controls Program, The Menninger Foundation, Topeka, Kansas

Chandra Patel, MD, Department of Epidemiology, The London School of Hygiene and Tropical Medicine, London, England

Johann M. Stoyva, PhD, Clinical Psychology Division, University of Colorado Health Sciences Center, Denver, Colorado

Robert L. Woolfolk, PhD, Department of Psychology, Rutgers–The State University, New Brunswick, New Jersey

v

ACKNOWLEDGMENTS

We wish to express our gratitude to all those who played a role in the creation of this book. To Gary Schwartz go our thanks for his support of this project and his encouragement of our work over the years. Seymour Weingarten of The Guilford Press has been in every way an exemplary editor. Our own teachers, colleagues, and students have in various ways enabled us to produce this work; there is not space to give individual recognition to each, but our appreciation goes to every one of them. One of us (P. M. L.) was taught the meaning of relaxation by his parents, Samuel and Ethel Lehrer. He wishes to thank Phyllis Lehrer for her continued support, love, and interest. The other (R. L. W.) wishes to thank three women named Woolfolk—Anita, Jane, and Elizabeth—for making life and the writing of books possible.

FOREWORD

Most people who read this book probably already believe that relaxation and related stress reduction techniques can play a useful role, and in some instances an important role, in the treatment of various psychological and physical disorders. Most people who read this book are probably already aware of the fact that relaxation has been part of many traditions and religions and can be found to be practiced in one form or another throughout recorded history. Also, most people who read this book are probably already aware of the fact that systematic research on relaxation and related stress reduction techniques has occurred only within the past six decades.

It is now well recognized that relaxation techniques play a fundamental role in biobehavioral approaches to the treatment and prevention of disease and are hypothesized to play a fundamental role in health promotion as well. Like biofeedback, relaxation and related stress reduction techniques are currently considered to be core techniques in behavioral medicine. In fact, training in concepts and methods of relaxation and in basic and clinical research using relaxation is now typically required of clinicians who adopt a biopsychosocial approach to health and illness.

However, I suspect that many people who read this book are probably not aware of the fact that the present volume is the first comprehensive book ever published devoted solely to theory, research, and applications of relaxation and related stress reduction techniques. In view of the long history of relaxation spanning thousands of years, and the extensive research on relaxation conducted within the past six decades, one might think that there would already exist a spate of comprehensive books covering this area. Given that this is actually not the case, the question arises as to why.

One major reason for the lack of a comprehensive book on this topic may be that few authors have the conceptual, empirical, and clinical scope to conceive and edit such a comprehensive volume. Many researchers and clinicians working in this area tend to focus their efforts on what seems to be their favorite relaxation technique (e.g., progressive muscle relaxation). As a result, there has been a paucity of general theories of relaxation.

Concerning general theories, it is of value to point out that two of the major theories of relaxation, the relaxation response theory of Benson (1975) and the multiprocess theory of Davidson and Schwartz (1976), both emerged simultaneously at the same university (Harvard) and, interestingly, two of the authors (Benson and Schwartz) had previously collaborated on biofeedback research in the treatment of hypertension (Benson, Shapiro, Tursky, & Schwartz, 1971).

It is probably significant that Benson, Davidson, and Schwartz were at various times associated with a unique combination of scholars in Harvard's Department of Social Relations. This interdisciplinary experimental department unfortunately ended in the early 1970s, when the department was dissolved. However, some of the impact of this interdisciplinary experiment continues to the present. One example is the *Consciousness and Self-Regulation* series, edited by Schwartz, Shapiro, and Davidson (Schwartz & Shapiro, 1976, 1978; Davidson, Schwartz, & Shapiro, 1983). Another example is the appearance of the present volume.

The second editor (Lehrer) obtained his doctoral training in clinical psychology in the Department of Social Relations. He was then, as he is today, committed to a multilevel approach to relaxation. This approach spans biology, psychology, sociology, anthropology, religion, and philosophy. He shares this perspective with the first editor (Woolfolk). Woolfolk is unusually sensitive to the theoretical, research, and clinical questions that span these multiple levels of processes, as illustrated in his book with Richardson titled *Stress, Sanity and Survival* (1978).

It is also worth mentioning that the Editor in Chief of The Guilford Press (Seymour Weingarten) was also the senior editor of the *Consciousness and Self-Regulation* series mentioned above. Together, this unique triad (Woolfolk, Lehrer, Weingarten) has the proper mixture of interest, knowledge, and perspective to develop and publish the present volume.

In my opinion, the present volume is a remarkable success. The combination of authors represents a "who's who" of relaxation. Their chapters, on the whole, are "state of science" and "state of the art." The editors have provided an important service for the field by bringing this group of authors together within one set of covers.

However, the editors have done much more than this. In their own chapters they provide a perspective on the whole field that represents the most comprehensive and "creatious" (creative plus cautious) explication

of the theory, research, and clinical applications of relaxation written to
date. They are careful to point out similarities and differences between
various techniques. Further, they propose a general theory that substantially clarifies and extends the synthesis of the relaxation response and
multiprocess theories offered by Schwartz, Davidson, and Goleman
(1978). The authors are quick to distinguish between theoretically versus clinically significant similarities and differences between techniques,
and in the process they make relaxation come alive.

Altogether, this volume deserves to become a classic in the field. I believe it should be required reading for all students of relaxation, be they
just beginning their research and clinical training, or continuing their research and clinical training (the present author included). I was surprised
how much I learned from reading this book. I have little doubt that the
students and colleagues to whom I personally recommend this volume
will also do the same.

For those readers who want to become enriched and enlightened
about relaxation, the present volume is essential reading. Though each
reader will likely find a particular set of chapters and ideas he or she likes
and dislikes, the process of discovering one's own particular set of likes
and dislikes will be quite informative. I suspect that quite a few years will
pass before another volume of this sort is needed. I also suspect that when
this time arrives, a likely candidate will be a second edition of this excellent handbook.

Gary E. Schwartz
Yale University

REFERENCES

Benson, H. *The relaxation response.* New York: Morrow, 1975.
Benson, H., Shapiro, D., Tursky, B., & Schwartz, G. E. Decreased systolic blood pressure
    through operant conditioning techniques in patients with essential hypertension.
    Science, 1971, *173,* 1144–1146.
Davidson, R. J., & Schwartz, G. E. Psychobiology of relaxation and related stress: A multi-
    process theory. In D. Mostofsky (Ed.), *Behavior modification and control of phys-
    iological activity.* Englewood Cliffs, N.J.: Prentice-Hall, 1976.
Davidson, R. J., Schwartz, G. E., & Shapiro, D. (Eds.). *Consciousness and self-regulation:
    Advances in research.* (Vol. 3). New York: Plenum, 1983.
Schwartz, G. E., Davidson, R. J., & Goleman, D. J. Patterning of cognitive and somatic pro-
    cesses in the self-regulation of anxiety: Effects of meditation versus exercise. *Psycho-
    somatic Medicine,* 1978, *40,* 321–328.

Schwartz, G. E., & Shapiro, D. (Eds.). *Consciousness and self-regulation: Advances in research* (Vol. 1). New York: Plenum, 1976.

Schwartz, G. E., & Shapiro, D. (Eds.). *Consciousness and self-regulation: Advances in research* (Vol. 2). New York: Plenum, 1978.

Woolfolk, R. L., & Richardson, F. C. *Stress, sanity and survival.* New York: Sovereign Books, 1978.

CONTENTS

1 CLINICAL STRESS REDUCTION: AN OVERVIEW

ROBERT L. WOOLFOLK AND PAUL M. LEHRER

Psychosocial stress is known to be a contributor to many emotional disorders and somatic illnesses. These include such ostensibly dissimilar conditions as coronary heart disease, anxiety states, ulcerative colitis, cancer, and insomnia. All have been linked either with aversive life circumstances or with psychological variables that predispose the individual to experience chronically elevated levels of emotional and physiological arousal. The growing recognition of the part played by stress in the etiology of many physical and psychological maladies has led to efforts to prevent or treat those stress-related ailments through directly altering the individual's response to stress.

Within the marketplace of applied behavioral science, stress management technology qualifies as a growth industry. Almost everywhere we see evidence of this. Sales of biofeedback equipment are up; courses on how to cope with stress are being offered widely within industry; there is great interest in Eastern traditions such as yoga and meditation; the media abound with programs and articles on how to avoid the hazards of stress. Unfortunately, many of these developments have been accompanied by wildly extravagant claims and by a notable lack of supporting evidence. In the process, "stress" has become a catch-all category, encompassing everything from quantifiable events in the psychophysiology laboratory to the entire scope of human unhappiness.

While all this hoopla and ballyhoo have been occurring, many serious scientists have systematically evaluated the effects of such techniques as meditation, biofeedback, progressive relaxation, autogenic training, and cognitive-behavior modification. Their work has enabled us to begin to estimate the therapeutic potential of many techniques that heretofore have been broadly applied without a firm empirical foundation. For the clinician seeking methods capable of improving clients' abilities to cope with

1

stress, the empirical literature offers great encouragement. A number of stress reduction techniques have been shown to be effective in the treatment of a variety of stress-related symptoms and disorders.

The clinician who turns to the research literature in order to learn therapeutic strategies, however, is inevitably disappointed. The descriptions of the stress management methods contained therein are cursory and terse. Only those already intimately familiar with the procedures under investigation can develop a clear and accurate picture of what therapeutic interventions were or were not employed. Treatments typically are standardized and uniform for all subjects. Frequently the treatments undergo substantial modifications so that a standardized version can be achieved. Stress reduction techniques are also altered to make them shorter, easier to teach, easier to learn, and consistent with control or comparison conditions on such dimensions as length of training or amount of therapist contact.

Because of the presence of experimental controls necessary for the preservation of internal validity (see Borkovec, Johnson, & Block, Chapter 12, this volume), treatment outcome studies do not provide a veridical picture of the clinical practice of stress management. Because of the logical requirements of research designs seeking to isolate causal influences, a single stress management technique commonly would be the only intervention utilized with a particular group of subjects. Overly recalcitrant or disturbed subjects are either screened initially or dropped from the experiment. In clinical practice, they must be dealt with. The exigencies of research methodology often result in random assignment of subjects to the treatment or treatments under investigation, hence making impossible the important determination of interactions among individual difference and treatment factors. Stress problems often interact in complex ways with other problems of living. The standard factorial design is not well suited to an examination of these and other subtleties. The experimental study is predicated on the assumption of the adequacy of statistical significance as an index of therapeutic benefit. It is of course essential for us to demonstrate that differences between control and treatment conditions are unlikely to have occurred as a result of chance factors. For the clinician, however, this evidence is necessary but insufficient. A technique must be clinically powerful enough to justify its use. It must provide sufficient relief of suffering and enhanced ability to cope with life's travails to make it worth the time and effort to employ it. Many of these issues are, in principle, amenable to systematic study by empirical methods. We have few studies, however, that have sought to address these complex and thorny issues. Our best recourse presently is to turn to those practitioners who, from their reflections upon extensive therapeutic experience, have produced the clinical literature in this new field.

It is unlikely that the totality of clinical stress management will ever by captured within a series of empirical investigations. Applications of scientific knowledge to human problems undoubtedly will always contain an element of art. A mistake often made by newcomers to this field is to assume that the scientific status of self-regulation technology obviates the necessity for clinical sensitivity, perspicacity, and wisdom. Although the techniques of stress reduction are typically more standardized than some other therapeutic approaches, the need for inventive clinical dexterity is crucial to their successful use.

Given the multiplicity of available techniques and claims on their behalf, clinicians and students interested in the treatment of stress problems are in need of some device that can serve to enable them both to gain some clinical familiarity with the methods and to make the important discriminations related to their therapeutic use. *Principles and Practice of Stress Management* has been produced in order to provide the practitioner with a single source through which all those approaches to stress reduction that rest on firm empirical footing can be explored and contrasted. This work is designed primarily to serve the clinician rather than the researcher. Although each of our contributors has impressive research credentials, we have asked them to refrain from providing comprehensive and exhaustive surveys of the empirical literature. Such reviews are readily available in the scientific journals.

Our contributors are the consummate artists of their crafts, each a pioneer in his or her respective area. We have commissioned them to make personal statements and to hold in abeyance some of the circumspection and reserve that might characterize their activities as scientists. Our charge to them was to wear their clinical hats—to communicate to their fellow clinicians those aspects of clinical skill, artistry, and wisdom that so often are missing from standard attempts to characterize thera peutic methods. We have asked our contributors to become teachers— to convey not only the readily specifiable, technical aspects of their craft, but also the therapeutic nuances and clinical rules of thumb that often develop only tacitly within a therapist over many years as he or she functions in the complex environment of clinical practice.

We are not detailing the various stress reduction methods that as of this writing have *not* been widely researched. This does not necessarily invalidate them as clinically useful devices; indeed, some of them are used as widely as some of the techniques that we do include, and we use them ourselves. It is just that the researchers have not yet caught up with them.

Included in this group of methods are the Alexander technique (Barlow, 1977), which involves reeducation of posture and of bodily movement in various activities, from sitting in and getting out of a chair to dancing and acrobatics. This method was originally devised by F. M. Alexander, an actor who cured himself of functional aphonia by reeducating his body to become more erect and balanced. It has been used widely by actors, dancers, and musicians to help them in the practice of their arts. It is utilized especially frequently by artists, who like Alexander himself, find themselves unable to perform because of physical problems caused by emotional tension, injury, or stresses caused by misuse of their bodies. The Alexander technique would appear to have particular promise for helping people with orthopedic and vocal problems, and is one of the few techniques that systematically focuses on producing a state of relaxation while the body is in motion. Moshe Feldenkreis (1972) has extended Alexander's work through the inclusion of more physical manipulation. Although these methods border on the disciplines of osteopathy, chiropractic, and physical therapy, we mention them here as stress reduction methods because they do appear to produce relaxation in parts of the body that are under physical stress, and they are taught within a self-regulation framework.

A much more ancient technique with aims similar to the above-mentioned methods is Tai-Chi. Although Tai-Chi is essentially a martial art, it includes large components of Chinese folk medicine, exercise, philosophy, and meditation. The vast majority of people study it for health, relaxation, and exercise rather than as a means of self-defense. It emphasizes balance, muscular relaxation, deep breathing, and mental concentration during a complex series of slow, dance-like movements. A similar discipline, originating in Japan, is Aikido. The Japanese philosophies and disciplines associated with Zen Buddhism have found increasing interest and acceptance in the West. Zen emphasizes mental discipline along with relaxation, and teaches that a "meditative attitude" should permeate all activities of everyday life.

Two recent American methods also deserve comment. Both derive from American psychology and psychophysiology. Charles Stroebel's (1978) "quieting response" is based on psychophysiological literature showing that emotional tension is manifested in facial expressions as well as in anxious cognitions and altered respiration. The technique consists of breathing slowly and deeply, while smiling and reminding oneself to "keep my body out of this." The other technique was derived by Les Fehmi (Fehmi & Fritz, 1980; Fritz & Fehmi, 1982) from his experience with electroencephalographic (EEG) alpha biofeedback. He found that the act of imaginally representing the spatial characteristics of various regions of the body produces increases in alpha waves, as well as a mental "openness" to experience similar to that described by many writings on meditation. He calls his method "open focus" training. It has been applied to the treatment of various emotional and psychosomatic disorders.

In Chapters 2 and 3 of this collection, two versions of the progressive relaxation technique first devised by Edmund Jacobson (1938) are presented. Jacobson originated the method as a treatment for "neuromuscular tension"—a term he uses to cover a variety of emotional and somatic difficulties. Most early applications of the method were in the area that has more recently come to be known as "psychosomatic medicine." Jacobson's original method was later modified and abbreviated by Joseph Wolpe (1958) for use as a "reciprocal inhibitor" of fear in the systematic desensitization procedure. Wolpe's modifications of Jacobson's original technique were subsequently refined and codified in manuals authored by Paul (1966) and by Bernstein and Borkovec (1973). Progressive relaxation is a widely utilized method, perhaps more familiar to psychotherapists than any other stress management method is. Virtually all behavior therapists are familiar with the method, at least in its abbreviated form.

There are some key differences between the classical form of progressive relaxation and the modified version that are rarely appreciated (cf. Lehrer, 1982, for a review). Jacobson originally conceived of his method as a kind of "proprioceptive sensitivity training." As outlined in Chapter 2 of this volume by McGuigan, the patient is taught from the very beginning of training to recognize and to control decreasingly intense levels of muscular tonus. The primary aim is to make the individual able to recognize and eliminate even the most minute levels of tension, to remain as tension-free as possible at all times, and to eliminate unnecessary tension continuously during everyday activities. In the abbreviated method, the emphasis tends to be somewhat less on the awareness of tension and more on the active "production" of relaxation. While the trained Jacobsonian "releases" minute amounts of tension continuously throughout the day, the trainee in the modified method tends to create a relaxed state through the use of tension–release cycles or some other activity that has been paired with sensations accompanying tension release.

A number of other differences between the two methods are nicely illustrated by Chapters 2 and 3. Training in the classical method can be quite lengthy, often requiring many months or even years before full proficiency is acquired. This is not, however, always the case. Therapeutic results have been obtained in as little as one session of training (Jacobson, 1970). The modified technique is rarely lengthy and often is taught in less than 10 sessions. Jacobson also attempts to avoid the use of suggestion, because he feels its effects to be transitory. He believes that the use of suggestion actually impedes the learning of the muscular skills to be acquired. Jacobson does not even tell the trainee *where* to expect a muscle sensation to occur after a muscle contraction. He wants the trainee to discover it by himself or herself, so that the proprioceptive experience will be "real" and not just a product of the therapist's influence. Only one muscle group is addressed in any training session. The therapist may even leave the room between instructions, while the client works alone on becoming familiar with newly discovered muscular sensations and learning how to control them with newly developed muscular skills and sensitivities. It is not necessarily important whether deep relaxation is experienced in the early sessions. Skill development is all. Deep relaxation occurs as skill in the procedures improves. Each muscle is tensed from the outset only to the degree required for the client to identify the "control sensations," or lowest perceptible level of tonus. Subsequently, each muscle is tensed progressively less and less until the trainee is able to recognize minute amounts of tension (Jacobson, 1970).

In their chapter on abbreviated methods of progressive relaxation, Bernstein and Given (Chapter 3) illustrate some of the modern variations on Jacobson's original therapeutic theme. As distinct from Jacobson's technique, all of the major skeletal muscles are addressed in the very first session. The trainee tenses muscles tightly before releasing the tension. The therapist attempts to produce rather deep relaxation in the very first session. More elements of suggestion are used than in the classical method. These include telling the trainee the sensations that may be experienced, choosing a relaxing environment, having the therapist use voice modulation during tension–release cycles, avoiding having the trainee converse during the training itself, and so forth. This method, however, is less suggestive than are procedures derived from hypnosis. In addition to presenting the abbreviated method of progressive relaxation, Bernstein and Given cover such broader clinical issues as assessment, side effects of treatment, and contraindications. These authors view progressive relaxation as only one technique among many possible interventions and advise the use of the other treatment tools in conjunction with relaxation.

In Chapters 4 and 5, we move from the Western disciplines of psychosomatic medicine and behavior therapy to a consideration of methods derived from the Eastern practice of yoga. Yoga has been an integral feature of the Hindu culture for over 2000 years. Elements of that tradition, especially meditation, have recently been appropriated by Western therapists in their efforts to find more effective tools to combat tension and stress. Bolstered by studies indicating the therapeutic potential of Eastern forms of meditation to produce decrements in physiological arousal (Woolfolk, 1975) and improvement in stress-related disturbances (Shapiro & Giber, 1978), clinicians were encouraged to devise Westernized forms of meditation (Benson, 1975; Carrington, 1977; Woolfolk, Carr-Kaffashan, McNulty, & Lehrer, 1976). These methods are the distillation of the meditative procedures themselves, removed from the complex framework of philosophical and religious belief within which they traditionally have been practiced.

In Chapter 4, Patel describes her highly successful treatment program for hypertension—a program that has wide applicability to a variety of stress-based disorders. Patel's program is multifaceted, incorporating muscle relaxation, biofeedback, and meditation, and some yogic philosophical teachings. The most distinctive feature of the program is Patel's adaptation of the eight steps that lead in yoga to the meditative state. These steps constitute a holistic approach to stress management that has been rendered intelligible to Westerners and requires no acceptance of Hindu religious teachings. Patel, nevertheless, does show how her methods derive from Hindu philosophical and religious practice. The chapter is rich with descriptive prose and imagery that convey quite eloquently this clinician's vision of effective treatment.

In Carrington's description of her meditation training program (Chapter 5), we see another example of Westernized meditation. The reader will note that although Carrington originally was dissuaded from using transcendental meditation because of its cultic overtones, she has come to believe that a certain amount of ceremony is essential. Carrington draws upon her thousands of hours of experience in teaching meditation in her discussion of the limitations and side effects of the method. The clinician inexperienced with the occasional psychic discomfort that clients may encounter during training in all forms of relaxation training might pay particular attention to this chapter.

A much misunderstood subject is that of hypnosis and suggestion. Barber (Chapter 6) has ranged widely to present the approach of a consummate clinician for whom methods of suggestion are often the most direct and expedient means of aiding clients in discomfort. His chapter demonstrates how readily the clinician can incorporate uncomplicated techniques from the tradition of hypnosis without becoming a full-fledged hypnotherapist or subscribing to some of the more extravagant claims that are often made for hypnosis. Indeed, he demonstrates that other stress reduction methods all contain some elements of suggestion, and he outlines how these elements can be used most effectively in the treatment of stress disorders. Barber emphasizes the role of client beliefs and the cultivation of a certain "wisdom" regarding the inevitable disappointments of living.

In their chapter on biofeedback as a treatment for stress disorders, Budzynski and Stoyva (Chapter 7) discuss the multidimensional nature of the stress response. The authors provide a usefully detailed description of the requisite biofeedback equipment and a vivid illustration of its use in stress management. Of particular interest is their discussion of secondary gain. This topic has been neglected in the stress literature, although the gains derived from the "sick role" can serve as a significant impediment to the amelioration of stress disorders. Budzynski and Stoyva, like virtually all capable practitioners of biofeedback, do not rely exclusively upon the signals from their machinery. They employ a number of different relaxation techniques in teaching the client to achieve a low-arousal state. The machinery is of primary value as a teaching aid that provides precise and highly structured information to the client concerning the success of his or her self-regulation activities.

A method of relaxation that has often been employed in conjunction with biofeedback is autogenic training. Autogenic training was one of the earliest Western systems of physiological self-regulation. It was developed at the turn of the century by the German physician Johannes Schultz (1953) out of his experiences with hypnosis. This method and its vast international literature is reviewed in English in a work by Wolfgang Luthe (1969). It is essentially a method of autosuggestion, the aim of which is to achieve a state of mental and physiological equilibrium. Although usually this implies a state of deep relaxation, such is not always the case. The technique is also known to produce emotional abreactions and temporary increases in physiological arousal. Tears are not at all uncommon, and they are often regarded as therapeutic. Essential to the success of the method is the development in the client of a state of "passive concentration," a kind of cognitive set analogous to that often described as requisite for meditation, hypnosis, biofeedback training, and progressive relaxation:

"Passive" concentration implies a casual attitude and functional passivity toward the intended outcome of his concentrated activity, whereas "active" concentration is characterized by the person's concern, interest, attention, and goal-directed active efforts during the performance of the task and in respect to the final functional result. (Luthe, 1969, Vol. 1, p. 14)

During the initial stages of autogenic training the trainee assumes a comfortable and balanced sitting position, one that is free from muscular tension. The trainee then begins to suggest to himself or herself certain physical sensations by silently repeating the basic autogenic phrases:

1. My right/left arm/leg is heavy.
2. My right/left arm/leg is warm.
3. My heartbeat is calm and regular.
4. It [the respiratory process] breathes me.
5. My solar plexus is warm.
6. My forehead is cool. (Luthe, 1969)

The beginning autogenic exercises are taught slowly and intensively. Often only one of the above standard exercises is introduced during a given session. The trainee is urged to practice regularly, while observing his or her reactions. The emphasis is on passivity and observation, rather than on "trying" to make a particular sensation occur. Advanced autogenic training includes meditation and visualization training not unlike the methods described in the chapters by Patel and Carrington (Chapters 4 and 5).

Norris and Fahrion (Chapter 8) describe the method of autogenic biofeedback first developed by Elmer and Alyce Green of the Menninger Foundation. This approach to stress management is a blending of biofeedback and autogenic training. The training begins with the use of modified autogenic phrases, imagery exercises, and deep diaphragmatic breathing. These procedures are effectively integrated with machine-generated skin temperature and electromyographic (EMG) feedback. What is most distinctive about this approach is its emphasis on the extensive use of imagery (visual and kinesthetic) and its explicit attempt to provide a blueprint for the client of the psychological orientation underlying therapeutic relaxation. Not surprisingly, the reader will note some parallels with Barber's techniques of hypnotic relaxation, as described in Chapter 6. Another point of contact with other contributions to this volume is the authors' use of abdominal breathing (see Patel, Chapter 4)—a technique that dates back centuries to its appearance in yoga as a form of "pranayama" (breath control).

Beck (Chapter 9) presents a cognitive model of stress. Drawing both from the literature on cognitive-behavior therapy and from his own extensive clinical experience, Beck has fashioned a description of the etiology, operational dynamics, and treatment of stress symptomatology as a cognitive theorist views it. This perspective is an important corrective to a field populated by clinicians who commonly have tended to conceptualize stress more as physiological arousal than as direct results of cognitive appraisal. Beck's discussion of the cognitive treatment methods is highly structured and specific. It contains much material that can be readily incorporated into a multifaceted program of treatment.

The chapter by Lader (Chapter 10) will greatly increase the sophistication of readers not well versed in psychopharmacology. It clarifies such issues as the biochemical action of principal antianxiety drugs, contraindications for drug treatment, and the most recent research findings. Lader gives explicit guidelines for the adjunctive use of medication. These are very helpful in making the often difficult decision as to when a particular patient might profit from supplementary pharmacological treatment.

In Chapter 11, we (Woolfolk & Lehrer) examine the wider context of stress management. Stress management is placed within its larger sociocultural context. An overview is provided of those subtleties and intangibles that are frequently neglected in writings on the treatment of stress, but are necessary for effective treatment. An account is given of such issues as the nature of the client–therapist relationship; client resistance to and/or compliance with treatment regimens; generalization and maintenance of treatment gains; assessment and the individualization of treatment; and the limitations of stress reduction technology. Building upon the various approaches described in this volume, we outline a perspective on the social, moral, and philosophical issues that are often central to individual struggles with the stressful living conditions of modern culture.

Borkovec, Johnson, and Block (Chapter 12) discuss the methodology of stress reduction research. They specify the criteria that must be addressed if the design of an investigation is to be adequate. This chapter is useful both to students who are encountering the research literature on a daily basis and to practicing clinicians attempting to comprehend the basic research in the area. Ideally, the path between the laboratory and the clinic should be a two-way street (Woolfolk & Lazarus, 1979). Researchers need feedback from clinicians who test research prototypes under "battlefield conditions"; clinicians need to have some means of gauging the efficacy of their techniques, apart from their own subjective impressions of what works for them. But a creative dialogue between researcher and clinician can occur only if the clinician/consumer of the research literature is sophisticated enough to evaluate it critically.

In Chapter 13, we (Lehrer & Woolfolk) review the empirical literature in which direct comparisons have been made among stress management techniques. We cover comparisons between and among techniques *across* problems, and we also analyze results of comparative outcome research *within* particular problems (e.g., headache, insomnia). We find that each of the various techniques has specific effects, in addition to a global, undifferentiated relaxation effect. There are a few kinds of problems for which one technique is clearly superior to another, but, for the most part, the effects of the various techniques are similar. Combinations of techniques often produce better results than single techniques do. Also, there is some evidence that particular individuals may be differentially motivated by and attracted to specific techniques.

REFERENCES

Barlow, W. *The Alexander technique.* New York: Knopf, 1977.

Benson, H. *The relaxation response.* New York: Morrow, 1975.

Bernstein, D. A., & Borkovec, T. D. *Progressive relaxation training.* Champaign, Ill.: Research Press, 1973.

Carrington, P. *Freedom in meditation.* New York: Anchor Press, 1977.

Fehmi, L., & Fritz, G. Open focus. *Somatics,* Spring 1980, pp. 24–30.

Fritz, G., & Fehmi, L. *The open focus handbook: The self-regulation of attention in biofeedback training and everyday activities.* Princeton, N.J.: Biofeedback Computers, 1982.

Feldenkreis, M. *Awareness through movement: Health exercises for personal growth.* New York: Harper & Row, 1972.

Jacobson, E. *Progressive relaxation.* Chicago: University of Chicago Press, 1938.

Jacobson, E. *Modern treatment of tense patients.* Springfield, Ill.: Charles C Thomas, 1970.

Lehrer, P. M. How to relax and how not to relax: A re-evaluation of the work of Edmund Jacobson. *Behaviour Research and Therapy,* 1982, *20,* 417–428.

Luthe, W. (Ed.). *Autogenic therapy* (6 vols.). New York: Grune & Stratton, 1969.

Paul, G. L. *Insight versus desensitization in psychotherapy.* Stanford, Calif.: Stanford University Press, 1966.

Schultz, J. *Das autogene training.* Stuttgart: Georg-Thieme Verlag, 1953.

Shapiro, D. H., Jr., & Giber, D. Meditation and psychotherapeutic effects: Self-regulation strategy and altered state of consciousness. *Archives of General Psychiatry,* 1978, *35,* 294–302.

Stroebel, C. *Quieting response training.* New York: BMA Audio Cassettes, 1978.

Wolpe, J. *Psychotherapy by reciprocal inhibition.* Stanford, Calif.: Stanford University Press, 1958.

Woolfolk, R. L. Psychophysiological correlates of meditation. *Archives of General Psychiatry,* 1975, *32,* 1326–1333.

Woolfolk, R. L., Carr-Kaffashan, L., McNulty, T. F., & Lehrer, P. M. Meditation training as a treatment for insomnia. *Behavior Therapy,* 1976, *7,* 359–365.

Woolfolk, R. L., & Lazarus, A. A. Between laboratory and clinic: Paving the two-way street. *Cognitive Therapy and Research,* 1979, *3,* 239–244.

2 PROGRESSIVE RELAXATION: ORIGINS, PRINCIPLES, AND CLINICAL APPLICATIONS

F. J. McGUIGAN

HISTORY[1]

In 1905, Edmund Jacobson, the originator of progressive relaxation, started graduate work in the Department of Psychology at Harvard University. His early studies were investigations of the startle reaction that often occurs to an unexpected loud noise. Continuing these experiments as part of his PhD thesis, he began to train subjects to relax their skeletal musculature and found that, when the subject was well relaxed, no start took place upon the occurrence of a sudden noise. This was the first psychophysiological study of relaxation.

At the 1921 meetings of the American Medical Association, Jacobson introduced concepts and definitions of his approach to "mental" and "physical" maladies, an endeavor that later came to be known as "psychosomatic medicine." Among the results of consequent investigations were his measurements of nervous states in humans and in animals as conditions of muscular tension, and the development of new methods of treatment of nervous and mental maladies through progressive relaxation.

Jacobson began his tenure in the Department of Physiology at the University of Chicago in 1926 and continued it until 1936. There he conducted research on the knee-jerk reflex with A. J. Carlson. He had also been conducting his clinical practice throughout this period of time, but

[1]Portions of this section are adapted from Jacobson (1977).

12

lacked an objective measure of the progress of his patients. With Carlson he found that the amplitude of the knee jerk was a direct measure of the degree of tension, so that as his patients learned to relax, the amplitude of their knee-jerk reflex decreased. This characteristic of using objective measures of degree of relaxation and tension was critical in guiding him in his efforts to develop the most effective method of relaxation that was reasonably possible.

While the knee-jerk reflex served well, it was obviously a cumbersome measure, so that Jacobson attempted to replace it with a more feasible and sensitive measure—that now known as quantitative electromyography. Seeking a device that could record muscle tension levels as low as a fraction of a millionth of a volt, Jacobson found the existing measurement technology to be inadequate. Frustrated in his early attempts to measure minute levels of muscle tension, he was able to enlist the aid of scientists at Bell Telephone Laboratory. With their aid, he invented the integrating neurovoltmeter, with which he was finally able to measure action potentials from muscle groups and from nerves, at levels as low as a microvolt.

This new equipment allowed Jacobson to make some important discoveries about how the mind and body work. He found that, in the relaxed subject, even *thinking* about moving a limb produced tiny muscle flexion in that limb. Such flexions were measurable only in the fully relaxed state, because they are obscured by general muscle tension. Similarly, he found that *all* thought is accompanied by low levels of skeletal muscle activity particularly in the regions of the eyes and/or the speech area.

In sum, Jacobson's research showed that if one wishes to relax the mind and the body, one must relax all of the complexly interacting systems of the body. One does this by directly relaxing the skeletal musculature, whereupon the central nervous system relaxes along with the various components of the autonomic system. Jacobson developed and practiced his method of progressive relaxation over a period in excess of 70 years. Guided by his numerous scientific and clinical studies, he gave the world extremely effective methods for directly controlling the various systems of the body, including mental processes. The methods are based on direct physiological and psychophysiological principles with no "excess baggage"—the methods work through direct muscular control systems, which in principle are amazingly simple. Let us now turn to an exposition of these methods.

THEORETICAL UNDERPINNINGS

Each stressful situation that we meet in everyday life involuntarily evokes the primitive startle pattern in us, whether it be overt or covert. If the startle reaction of covertly rising on the balls of our feet and hunching forward, together with autonomic changes, is prolonged beyond the immediate emergency, a condition of chronic overtension can result. The consistent, excessive covert tightening and bracing of the body, carried out by the skeletal musculature, can constitute a clinically difficult state with which to deal. Physiologically, the chronic contraction of skeletal muscles overdrives the central nervous system; this phenomenon, together with mediating hormonal involvement, increases activity of the autonomic system. This obvious point can be easily demonstrated by voluntarily contracting the muscles and observing the resultant increase of pulse rate and heightened blood pressure among other measures. Prolonged, heightened skeletal muscle tension may result in any of a variety of pathological conditions, such as those of the cardiovascular and gastrointestinal systems.

In learning to control the skeletal musculature, and thence the rest of the body, one must cultivate an ability to make sensitive observations of the internal sensory world (autosensory observation), comparable to the natural, unlearned ability to perceive the external environment. In acquiring heightened internal sensory observation, one primarily learns to recognize a subtle state of tension. Then, for control, one contrasts that tension sensation with the later elimination of tension, which is relaxation. Each major muscle group is systematically contracted in turn, so that the learner can identify the unique tension sensation (the control signal) for that muscle group, and then the tension is released to achieve a state of relaxation. In progressive relaxation, one thus learns to control all of the skeletal musculature, so that any portion thereof may be systematically relaxed or tensed in order to accomplish the individual's immediate purposes. Those familiar with biofeedback might wish to think of progressive relaxation as a method of "internal biofeedback" in which there is mere short-circuiting of the transduced external signals from the muscles. That is, the learner comes to monitor the feedback signal from the muscles internally, instead of observing its representation on a visual readout display or listening to its auditory representation. In progressive relaxation, however, greater emphasis is placed on using the skeletal muscle controls for the purpose of controlling other bodily systems, including those that generate mental processes.

SELF-OPERATIONS CONTROL

The tension sensation is called "the control signal," because it is literally a control for the neuromuscular circuits that carry out the body's activities. To elaborate briefly on this point, it may be noted that when a muscle contracts (tenses), receptors embedded in the muscle are activated. The activation of these receptors generates volleys of neural impulses that are carried to the brain along afferent neural fibers. It is this muscle–neural phenomenon—the generation and transmission of afferent neural impulses—that constitutes the control signal, the local sign of tension. This phenomenon was reported in the early 19th century by the eminent physiologist Sir Charles Bell, and has since been referred to as the "muscle sense of Bell."

The volleys of neural impulses generated when muscles contract are transmitted to the brain, wherein extremely complex central nervous system events result. Following this, neural impulses return to the muscles along efferent neural fibers. When these efferent neural impulses reach the muscles, there is further muscular contraction, resulting in additional neural impulses directed to and from the brain along numerous neuromuscular circuits throughout the body.

The great importance of this concept of neuromuscular circuits for our work, both clinically and scientifically, may be emphasized by noting that these complex circuits to and from the brain reverberate continuously (and rapidly) when driven by the muscle controls. On the other hand, relaxation of the skeletal muscle controls produces a state of rest in the components of these circuits, including the brain itself. By learning internal sensory observation, one can become quite proficient in recognizing control signals, wherever they may occur throughout the skeletal musculature. By practice, those controls may be activated or silenced. *The long-range goal of progressive relaxation is for the body to monitor instantaneously all of its numerous control signals, and automatically to relieve tensions that are not desired.* The body has an amazing capacity to monitor the many neuromuscular circuits that simultaneously function in parallel fashion throughout the body, and automatically, without conscious effort, to identify and to relax unwanted tensions.

The concept of neuromuscular circuits is not new; it is a venerable idea dating from the period of the ancient Greeks. The evolution of the concept can be impressively traced through the writings of early philosophers, through the Renaissance in the research of physiologists and psychologists, and into the very forefront of contemporary scientific thinking.

Some of the most prominent thinkers in history have recognized that the human body functions in terms of information generated and transmitted between the muscular systems and the brain. One of the most influential presentations of this circuit concept was by Norbert Wiener (1948) in his well-known book *Cybernetics*. In greater depth than all others before him, Wiener developed the notion that the body functions according to the engineering principles of feedback circuits, in which information is conveyed from one region of the body to another within servo loops.

The point that skeletal muscle is the controlling system within a neuromuscular circuit by which the body runs itself was quite clearly made in the 19th century by the famous psychologist Alexander Bain (1855) (and repeatedly confirmed in studies since then). The skeletal musculature, Bain said, is *the only system over which a person has direct control*. The skeletal muscles have been referred to as the "voluntary muscles" precisely for this reason; that is, when one wishes to perform an act, one moves one's limbs by systematically contracting and relaxing them. For instance, if a person wishes to go outdoors, he or she commences by putting one foot in front of the other. This point is so obvious that it does not need elaboration. What is not so obvious is that the internal functions of the body are similarly controlled by means of the skeletal muscles, as in increasing and decreasing pulse rate by tensing and then relaxing the muscles of the body. *The essence of self-operations control is to apply these principles to the more subtle functions of the body—to recognize that subtle, covert functions of the body can also be controlled through slight muscle tensions*. As Bain and others have said, the striated muscles are indeed the instrument of the will (for elaboration, see Chapter 6 of McGuigan, 1981).

The applications of progressive relaxation for self-operations control in this way include increased efficiency in programming oneself in one's work (in part, by eliminating tensions that interfere with one's primary purposes, the control of one's blood pressure, the control of one's emotional life, and the control of one's digestive processes). Covert functions of the body also include mental processes, the principal control of which is for clinical purposes. To understand this, let us more generally consider the scientific nature of mind and its component mental events.

A PSYCHOPHYSIOLOGICAL MODEL OF MIND

We can list a variety of functions of the mind by using such terms from the vernacular as "ideas," "images," "thoughts," "dreams," "hallucinations," "fears," "depressions," and "anxieties." But, regardless of the term, all such mental events are generated when selective systems of the body interact through highly integrated neuromuscular circuits. Most mental processes are generated when muscles of the eyes and speech regions tense, whereupon specialized circuits to and from the brain are activated. Other pathways are activated also, including those involving the somatic musculature and the autonomic functions that add emotional tone to mental processes. Perhaps the most extensive documentation for this conclusion is the summary of relevant research for an 80-year period, compiled elsewhere (McGuigan, 1978). The research provides a firm basis for the conclusion that there is muscular contraction in selected regions of the body corresponding to the nature of the mental activity present. For instance, when a person is imagining the Eiffel Tower, localized, vertical electromyographic (EMG) activity in the eye region indicates covert movements as the eyes move upward in imaginal scanning. Imagining hitting a nail on the head with a hammer three times produces three distinct bursts of covert responses in the "hitting" arm, as measured through EMG readings. Conversely, there is no conscious awareness at all when people are well relaxed, as objectively determined by a lack of tension, measured through EMG readings. These experimental findings, confirmed by clinical reports, indicate how people can exercise control over their mental processes by systematically tensing and relaxing controlling components of the skeletal musculature.

In this work we must decidedly discard any suggestion of philosophical mind–body dualism, such as the common-sense notion that the body *expresses* ideas and emotions, or that mental processes are *correlates* of bodily activities. Instead, the paradigm that has the greatest heuristic value is one of strict materialism, in which emotions and other mental components are viewed as *identical* with the energy expended when neuromuscular circuits are activated. We will soon follow up on the clinical significance of this neuromuscular model of mental processes.

THE MEANING AND PURPOSE OF TENSIONS

It is a basic principle of progressive relaxation that *every tension has a purpose—that every tension means something*. This point is obvious in many instances, such as when the hand is raised at the wrist (Figure 2-1). The learner detects the tension in the upper surface of the forearm, and it is readily apparent that the purpose of that tension was simply to raise the hand at the wrist. Similarly, if a person walks out the door, the reason that the person is tensing the muscles of the legs—the meaning of those tensions—is, simply, that the person is walking out the door. What is not

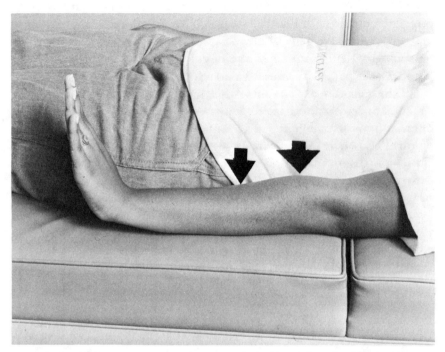

FIG. 2-1. Bending the hand back produces tension in the upper (dorsal) surface of the forearm.

so obvious, and in fact is clinically quite subtle, is the interpretation of tensions present during various kinds of psychiatric difficulties.

At this point, we must distinguish between ''meaning'' and ''process.'' ''Process'' is the manner, the way in which meaning occurs; it is the tension that one observes within one's body. ''Meaning'' designates the significance that a mental act bears for a person; it is the purpose of the tension, the reason that one tenses. In short, ''process'' consists of the muscular contractions present during images and sensations, while ''meaning'' is the content of the thought or other mental processes. The patient, working to control a psychiatric difficulty with the clinician, makes reports in this fashion: He or she first states process, the nature and locality of the tension, and then reports on meaning, the interpretation of those tensions.

After careful training in detecting subtle tensions throughout the body and after careful training in developing the ability to report on the details of one's mental activity, the patient will be able to identify process as subtle tensions, often in unexpected places of the body. The question then to be answered by both clinican and patient working together is this: Why do those localized tensions occur during a given kind of mental activity? By establishing the meaning of the tensions, understanding and control can be better gained over the patient's difficulties.

Consider a case of a lady whose complaints included anemia, chronic constipation, nervous tension with inability to sit quietly, slight dizzy spells during excitement, and a slight discharge from the nose (Jacobson, 1938). She eventually came to be able to state that lately she had been sitting more stiffly and formally. It was explained to her that while learning to relax, such faulty habits can be neglected for a while and the correction can be postponed; however, the immediate question put to her was *why* she had those tensions of sitting stiffly and formally. The patient guessed that the tensions meant that she was determined to maintain proper posture in her back because of a fear of developing a habit of faulty posture. That is, the *purpose* served by maintaining a stiff and formal posture was the prevention of an incorrect everyday posture. She was then informed that there were two ways to do away with such tension: first, on the meaning level, by explaining the reasons why she held herself stiffly and persuading her to change; and secondly, on the process level, by showing her how directly to relax the relevant controlling muscles.

In clinical work, it may be a lengthy process to identify tensions characteristic of the "nervous" condition of the patient, to interpret those tensions, and to deal with them effectively. But the history of clinical progressive relaxation is one of considerable success following this paradigm. For example, the paradigm can also be applied to neurotic states. Thus anxiety can be regarded as a fearful condition represented in the skeletal musculature. Once the clinician can ascertain the meaning of the skeletal muscle representation, it is then possible to relax those critical tensions, whereupon the state of anxiety can be diminished or eliminated. We will return to anxiety later in this chapter.

ASSESSMENT

HOW TO ASSESS FOR USE OF THE METHOD

There are two general purposes of tension control—prophylactic and therapeutic. By learning to relax differentially 24 hours a day, one can increase the likelihood of preventing a tension malady. For a person already victimized, clinical progressive relaxation can often ease or eliminate the condition. After discussing clinical application, we turn to prophylaxis.

Tension maladies fall into two familiar categories. The first consists of such psychological–psychiatric disorders as anxiety, phobias and lesser fears, worries, insomnia, and depressions. The second is often referred to as "psychosomatic illness" and includes such disorders as colitis with accompanying diarrhea and constipation, teeth grinding (bruxism), essential hypertension and coronary heart disease, rheumatological pathologies, chronic fatigue, and such pains as those of headaches and backaches.

The application of clinical progressive relaxation for treating such pathological conditions is to reverse the condition of overtension by relaxing the skeletal muscles. The gradual lengthening of skeletal muscle fibers can result in a state of relaxation, which in turn can produce a state of relative quietude throughout the central nervous system. Consequently the viscera can also relax, as evidenced by a lowering of blood pressure, a reduction of pulse rate, and a loosening of the gastrointestinal tract. In the years since 1908, when Jacobson first started developing progressive relaxation, he provided an abundance of scientific and clinical data that validate this therapeutic application for tension pathologies (e.g., Jacobson, 1938, 1970). Those numerous research studies have effectively guided the development of progressive relaxation as a direct, effective procedure for the treatment of pathological conditions listed therein.

In regard to the clinical application of progressive relaxation for psychiatric difficulties, it has been noted that any interruption of neuromuscular circuits will eliminate thoughts, preventing them from occurring. Some drugs can interrupt neuromuscular circuits, but the most natural way to cause these circuits to be tranquil is to relax tense muscles (a "natural tranquilizer"). Undesired thoughts, such as those of phobias and worries, can be eliminated by relaxing the speech muscles (tongue, lips, jaws, throat, and cheeks, for verbal mental activity) and the eye muscles (for eliminating the visual components of thoughts). By relaxing all of the muscles of the body, all mental processes can be brought to zero. It is not unusual in the early stages of learning progressive relaxation for a learner to report that he or she was unaware of the arm's existence. A student who once made this report was asked why that should be. After a little reflection, he correctly answered that relaxed muscles do not generate control signals, so that, with no neural impulses being transmitted from the arm to the brain, he did not receive information as to where his arm was in space, or even that he had an arm. The next question asked of him was this: What would happen if *all* of the muscles of the body were relaxed? A little further thought led him to the obvious conclusion that a totally relaxed person would be unaware of any aspect of the body and thus unaware of anything. This reasoning has been repeatedly confirmed by reports of totally relaxed individuals who stated that they had been completely "unconscious"—that they had had no thoughts at all.

After patients who have complaints of a mental nature develop a highly cultivated ability to observe internal sensory signals in *all* of the muscle groups, specialized training is given in observing tensions when the patients actually experience their particular complaints. Those muscle tensions are the ones in control of the neuromuscular circuits that generate the unwanted mental acts. By consistently relaxing those covert skeletal muscle components, the tranquility of the neuromuscular circuits can relax away the worry, phobia, or depression.

A large number of human control problems have to do with emotions. Emotions, of course, can be good or bad, and we certainly do not advocate the elimination of all emotions, any more than we do the elimination of all tensions. The goal is to determine rationally when to and when not to be emotional, when to and when not to have given thoughts. One can thus be wisely emotional by wisely tensing. The goal is to learn when to allow emotions to flow freely and when to inhibit them to prevent such wastes as those that occur during temper tantrums. To help patients develop control of emotions, we note that they too are generated when neuromuscular circuits are selectively activated. As patients learn over months of training to control the skeletal musculature in both its tonic and phasic activity, there is diminution of undesired emotions, such as proneness to anger, resentment, disgust, or embarrassment, as has been observed clinically in numerous cases. Conversely, as there is general increased tension, the proprioceptive impulses thereby generated increase emotionality by exciting the central nervous system and the autonomic system. Both the increased and the decreased emotionality are objectively evidenced by the amplitude and latency of patients' reflexes.

Everyday examples of this point are obvious, such as when a saucer is accidentally dropped at a tea party. The excessively tense guest will emit an exaggerated startle reflex with heightened emotionality, while the well-relaxed person may not even blink or interrupt ongoing conversation. Toward the conclusion of progressive relaxation classes, the instructor can drop a large book onto the floor when the students are well into their relaxation period. Seldom is there even a blink of the eye, for the startle reflex is not evoked as long as the students are in that relaxed condition.

This point has been experimentally documented, as in Jacobson's (1938) extensive research on reflexes. He has shown that chronic tonus (sustained tension) of the skeletal muscles increases the amplitude of reflexes and decreases their latency. Conversely, reflexes diminish in amplitude and increase in latency as a patient relaxes. More specifically, reduced tonus of the quadriceps femoris decreases the amplitude of the knee jerk while its latency increases; as there is diminution of tone in the arm muscles, the same thing happens to the flexion reflex; as there is diminution of general skeletal muscle tone, there is a decrease in the involuntary startle reflex. In 1909, Sherrington also made this point when his research established that it is not possible to evoke the patellar tendon reflex in an absolutely toneless muscle. More generally, Sherrington concluded that the appearance of reflexes depends on the presence of tone in the muscles that constitute part of the reflex arc.

To treat an individual who is excessively anxious, we note that often they continually rehearse their griefs, their worries, their difficulties with life. If they can get control of the skeletal muscle tensions that key this internal speech, they can consequently control their emotions and other negative mental processes. These controls occur principally in the eye muscles for visualizing their difficulties and in their speech muscles for verbalizing their problems, though the remaining mass of skeletal musculature also helps to control the mental processes. By thorough training in progressive relaxation, it is possible to gradually change from a condition of continually attending to difficulties and to develop a habit of turning attention away from those issues. One thus becomes better able to verbalize relevant contingencies and to react to problems more rationally. That is to say, instead of reacting reflexively to a difficulty, a trained person can stop and reason about the problem, unless of course it is something like an onrushing truck. (But one needn't worry about such eminent dangers, for relaxation does not reduce inborn tendencies to react instantaneously when genuine dangers appear.) As one becomes relaxed, then, one attends less frequently to disturbing issues, and instead focuses on other matters and becomes less emotionally disturbed about problems. A trained person can stop, relax, and assess a situation, verbalizing, for instance, that "this other person seems to be yelling and screaming at me, and it is to his advantage as well as to mine if I do not yell and scream back." Jacobson (1938) has shown that his patients and experimental subjects have found it impossible to be emotional, or to engage in other mental processes, while simultaneously relaxing.

PREVENTATIVE APPLICATIONS: PRINCIPLES
OF DIFFERENTIAL RELAXATION

When we were first organizing our association, the American Association for the Advancement of Tension Control (now called the International Stress and Tension-Control Association), some delegates suggested the substitution of "reduction" for "control" in the title. This change would have been misleading, because we do not advocate that the human race become vegetables. The term "tension control" is thus to be contrasted with "tension reduction." We simply could not function in life without tensions. The purpose is not to eliminate all tensions, but to control them so that they can be wisely used. In driving an automobile, one should depress the accelerator and steer, but should not grip the wheel excessively, grit the teeth, hunch forward, and attempt to wear out the horn. Those who are untrained in relaxation overtense in such ways until they complain of a stiff neck, a headache, or exhaustion. The efficiently run body of a well-trained person automatically relaxes all of the muscles which are not required for the act being performed. Thus, when one is *differentially relaxed*, there is contraction of *only those muscles necessary for carrying out the purpose at hand, while all others are relaxed*. Furthermore, those muscles that are used are optimally contracted, not excessively so.

Another high-frequency behavior in which differential relaxation can be prophylactic (as well as therapeutic for such patients as those with ulcers) is eating. The eating habits of many people include bizarre, often frantic, eating patterns; such an individual may be hunched over a plate with elbows on the table, eating tools grasped in the hands, tensed legs and torso, and bent shoulders—all as if the eater is ready to leap in animalistic protection of the food, should an adversary momentarily appear. The eating process is often a continuous shoveling of food from plate to mouth, with no interruption of the chewing process. Conversation, if any, is through half-ground food, with particles exuded in the direction of the listener. Common among eating habits is an overtenseness that most assuredly does not contribute to smooth digestion. People should be differentially relaxed when eating in order to enjoy dining as a pleasant process, as well as to help prevent a variety of gastrointestinal difficulties.

A major industry that dispenses a wide variety of products dedicates itself to helping people solve their sleep problems. The complaints of people vary from not getting to sleep when they first get in bed, to waking up during the night and not getting back to sleep. One patient recently reported that he had only about 2 hours of actual sleep over a period of four nights in bed. The consequences of night after night of inadequate sleep can be catastrophic, producing chronic fatigue and inefficient work performance. Nonprescription medicines, opaque blinds for the windows, ear plugs, and covers over the eyes are meant to satisfy complaints that "it's too hot," "too noisy," "too bright," "too cold," and so forth. The effective solution for the insomniac's problem is that people should learn to practice differential relaxation 24 hours a day, which includes sleeping at night! By applying the principles of progressive relaxation, one can carry the habit of automatic relaxation into the sleeping state.

Several other common applications of differential relaxation include those of relaxing while hurrying, of conquering the fear of flying by differentially relaxing on an airplane, of controlling one's own temper, and of learning how to deal with unreasonable people by controlling the tempers of others too. All applications of differential relaxation should be expected to have both prophylactic and therapeutic benefits.

LIMITATIONS AND CONTRAINDICATIONS

Progressive relaxation is appropriately applied for the reduction of everyday tensions, as in differential relaxation, and clinically for the elimination of tension-related syndromes. A more explicit listing of tension maladies that have benefited from progressive relaxation is in Table 10 of *Progressive Relaxation* (Jacobson, 1938). By thus specifying potentially beneficial applications, other applications are probabilistically excluded. These would constitute the limitations of the method. One thus could not expect to use relaxation directly to remove a cancer or to cure a viral infection. At the same time, progressive relaxation can be an adjunctive therapy that can serve to ease a person's discomfort for any malady. The more relaxed a person can be, the less his or her discomfort and pain will be. An excellent application for progressive relaxation is for treatment before and after surgery. The nervous anticipation that the patient experiences can be reduced, and the physical discomfort in the postoperative condition can be diminished. Such conditions, it may be noted, function in vicious circles, such that the more one tenses at discomfort or fatigue, the greater the discomfort and fatigue become; furthermore, the greater the discomfort and fatigue become, the more one tenses. This cycle rapidly produces an escalation in both states, if there is no intervention through progressive relaxation.

As far as contraindications are concerned, I was once asked about them by a world-renowned physician; the question had never before presented itself. As I note in the next section, wherever rest is prescribed, progressive relaxation is appropriate. Whatever contraindications there might be for rest—none really seem to exist, except under emergency conditions—are also applicable for relaxation.

THE METHOD

INTRODUCING THE METHOD TO THE CLIENT

Progressive relaxation begins with the ancient and venerable concept of rest. The physician has long known the value of rest, frequently prescribing it in the form of "bed rest." However, many people instructed to rest simply toss and turn in bed. Mere prescription is not sufficient; the patient may be told *to* rest, but does not know *how* to rest well. Thus, through acquiring habits of effective rest, the learner can possibly prevent the development of a serious tension malady and can certainly learn to use bodily energy with greater efficiency. These points can be explained to the learner, along with the basic physiology of neuromuscular circuits and how they are controlled. Hence, as explained below in "Description of the Method," some effort is made to get the learner to understand the essential nature of tension and relaxation and how these are used to control the body. When relaxation is applied therapeutically, it can be mentioned that clinical progressive relaxation has often helped restore the body to a normally functioning condition—provided, of course, that the tension malady is reversible.

The first step in acquiring tension control is for the learner to recognize the enormity of the task. It is explained that there are some 1030 striated muscles in the human body, and that these comprise almost half of the body weight. The learner is thus provided with a realistic estimate of how far an overly tense individual has to go. A lifetime of injudicious use of such a mass of muscle simply cannot respond to "quick and easy cures" for tension maladies. Just as the learner has spent a lifetime learning how to misuse his or her muscles systematically, it is reasonable to expect that prolonged practice is required to reeducate them. It simply takes time and practice to learn to reverse long-standing maladaptive muscular habits. Fortunately, this cultivation of a state of bodily rest *can* be achieved in much less time than it took to learn to misuse the muscles in the first place.

These are some of the essential points to get across to the beginning learner. To a large extent, the success or failure of the application depends on the learner's self-discipline—on his or her willingness to practice the method each day, 7 days a week, 365 days a year.

THE PHYSICAL ENVIRONMENT AND EQUIPMENT

The physical environment can be varied. Groups have been taught in large rooms such as gymnasiums, dance floors, classrooms, and even a cadaver room (with cadavers removed!). The learners should have something reasonably soft to lie on, such as a thick carpet, gymnasium mats, or their own sleeping bags. In clinical treatment, individual rooms in relative quietude with cots, pillows, and blankets are provided. An adept clinician can treat several patients simultaneously, one in each individual room. But whatever the learning situation, no effort is made to eliminate external distractions *totally*, for the goal is to learn to relax in a "normal" environment, which is at least somewhat noisy. The learner should anticipate any possible distraction during the hour of practice, such as covering the body with a blanket at the start to prevent chiling (since, with successful relaxation, the bodily temperature may fall noticeably).

Ideally, the clinician would want to measure states of tension objectively, electromyographically, throughout treatment. For this, a reasonably sensitive EMG reading is required to confirm the clinical observations of potential progress, and (it may be hoped) the patient's reports of diminishing complaints. Abbreviated tension profiles for a nervous individual and for a relatively relaxed subject are presented in Table 2-1. The table includes a sampling of bodily regions that tense excessively in the one case and are relatively normal in the other. Several other associated psychophysiological measures are also presented; these values have been selected from ongoing research in Jacobson's laboratory. The observations of these two individuals with the naked eye would typically yield traits such as the following for the nervous subject: wrinkled forehead, frown, darting eyes, exaggerated breathing, rapid pulse and respiration, and habits of fidgeting. But even the experienced clinical eye may not properly diagnose an excessively tense individual when such obvious symptoms are absent, and EMG readings may be required.

TABLE 2-1. Tension Profiles of a "Nervous" Subject versus a Normotensive ("Normal") Subject

Measure	Nervous	Normal
Brow EMG (μV)	8.68	2.95
Left-arm EMG (μV)	2.10	.58
Tongue EMG (μV)	5.57	2.75
Right-arm EMG (μV)	3.10	.59
Right-leg EMG (μV)	1.36	.53
Pulse/minute	70	69
Respirations/minute	17	15
Blood pressure (mm Hg)	117/71	96/70

Note. Adapted from Jacobson (personal communication).

THE THERAPIST–CLIENT RELATIONSHIP

In the clinical application of progressive relaxation, it is important to minimize any suggestive influence on the patient. We are all well aware of the suggestive effects that occur because of the placebo effect; that is, *any* method will accomplish something if it instills into the patient the belief that he or she will benefit from its application. Progressive relaxation has been shown to produce definitive physiological changes in the body that are different from those that occur during suggestion (Jacobson, 1938). Consequently, the clinician should avoid suggestion, so that only those psychophysiological changes in the body due to progressive relaxation result. For instance, the clinician should not suggest that the patient's arm is becoming limp; that the patient will feel better after treatment; that the procedure will help the patient to become more tranquil; or that the method will "cure" the patient in any sense of the word. Rather, the goal is for progressive relaxation to lead the patient to become independent of the clinician as much as possible. Thus the hypochondriac who continually seeks reassurance is *not* suggestively reassured. Instead, the patient is trained to detect the tensions present when he or she is discussing his or her maladies and is then instructed to relax those tensions away; this process leads to the patient's reeducation. The teacher then emphasizes to the learner that *he* or *she* is the one who successfully eliminated the tension. Progressive relaxation thus puts the emphasis on the learner, not on the instructor. It is a trial-and-error process that has to be *learned*, step by step, with varying degrees of success and failure. The clinician as a teacher can guide the learner and can aid with critical instructions, even interrupting a patient who is failing to relax with vigorous criticism. Through this process, relaxation, like any other habit, can become permanent and not dependent upon such fleeting variables as suggestion, which may have only short-term effects.

DESCRIPTION OF THE METHOD

The psychological set with which the learner starts is critical. There should be a period in which the patient is to do absolutely nothing at all but learn to relax; he or she should practice in a quiet room, free from intrusion. The session is planned so that practice may be continuous, without interruption from telephones, doorbells, or people entering. Any unnecessary movement such as getting up or fidgeting is prevented, because these added tensions retard the progressive relaxation throughout the period.

The 1030 or so skeletal muscles in the body are formed into groups, so that learners study groups of muscles. The program calls for progressively relaxing the body, moving from one muscle group to the next in a specific order. The learner starts by lying on a couch or bed with arms alongside the body. Only one position is practiced each hour, the tension signal being observed three times in each period. Thus, each practice hour, the learner works with one major muscle group as follows: (1) Identify the control signal, and thereupon (2) "turn off the power" (i.e., give up the tension and let the muscles relax). The key is that one cannot try to relax: *An effort to relax is a failure to relax*! All one does is to discontinue tensing, going "negative," with "power off." Instruction largely consists of preventing the beginner from doing the wrong thing—that is, making an effort to relax.

As the learner searches for the control signal, there may be some uncertainty about what is being sought. Some people identify the control signal immediately, while others have great difficulty. It is very subtle, and only a vague guess as to its location may be sufficient. With repeated practice in observing it, the control signal can become as obvious as a loud noise. The tension sensations that one can eventually detect in the small muscles of the tongue and eyes are perhaps one-thousandth the intensity of those larger ones in the arms.

The first practice sequence (90 days lying down) is as follows: left arm—7 days; right arm—7 days; left leg—10 days; right leg—10 days;

trunk—10 days; neck—6 days; eye region—12 days; visualization—9 days; speech region—19 days. After these positions are practiced lying down, the same positions are practiced again in the same order, but in a sitting position. Repetition is the keynote of progressive relaxation.

To get a better idea of the general plan, observe the positions for the arm in Table 2-2. When the learner starts, the eyes are open for 3 or 4 minutes and then gradually closed (the learner only guesses at the time that elapses). When the eyes have remained closed for another estimated 3 or 4 minutes, the learner bends back the left hand at the wrist steadily, as in Figure 2-1, without fluctuation; there should be no seesawing or wiggling. While bending the hand back with care, the vague, misty sensation in the upper surface of the left forearm, a "tightness," is the signal of tension—the control signal—that the individual is to learn to recognize. As the learner holds position for a minute or two, studying the tension sensation, power goes off for a few minutes. This sequence is repeated two more times on Day 1. On Day 2, the learner bends the left hand forward instead of backward (see Table 2-2), and so on for 14 days, as in McGuigan (1981).

It is to be emphasized that no work is required to turn off the power in the forearm. All one needs to do is to *discontinue* working there; No effort is required. As noted earlier, an effort to relax is a failure to relax. Untrained people often fail to relax because they *work* to relax. In this regard, a learner may assert that he or she *cannot* relax; the point is that he or she *did not* relax. If a learner complains that he or she finds it hard to lie quietly at practice, he or she is confused about what is wanted, for

TABLE 2-2. Practice Program for the Arms

Day	Left arm	Day	Right arm
1	Bend the hand back.	8	Bend the hand back.
2	Bend the hand forward.	9	Bend the hand forward.
3	Relax only.	10	Relax only.
4	Bend the arm at the elbow.	11	Bend the arm at the elbow.
5	Press the wrist down on books.	12	Press the wrist down on books.
6	Relax only.	13	Relax only.
7	Progressive tension and relaxation of the whole arm.	14	Progressive tension and relaxation of the whole arm.

Note. Practice is for one period each day, performing the indicated tension three times at intervals of several minutes. Then go negative for the remainder of each period. Thus, on Day 1, bend the left hand back. On Day 2, bend the left hand forward, and on Day 3 do nothing at all. After 14 days, you are ready to go on to the leg. Adapted from Jacobson (1964).

there has never been an instruction to hold still (holding still is *not* relaxing). It is never "hard" to relax, for "hard" implies effort. If a learner stiffens when requested to relax, he or she is making a task of it, which is not relaxation but only an unsuccessful attempt. When the learner replaces the statement that "relaxing makes me nervous" with the statement that "I am beginning to enjoy it," he or she is making progress.

During each period, the learner uses the *method of diminishing tensions*. For instance, if the learner first raises the hand at the wrist as in Figure 2-1, he or she could raise it not quite as much for the second practice position of that period. Eventually he or she can get to the point of hardly raising the hand off the bed at all, producing a minimum tension to be observed. By diminishing tensions, the neural impulses from and to the muscle group are diminshed too, and there is a furthering of relaxation. Also, one develops greater sensitivity to *very small* muscle contractions. In total relaxation, there is a cessation of impulses along sensory and motor nerves to and from a muscle.

Many people ask, "What shall I think about when I lie down?" They are instructed not to think and not to make the mind a blank. Furthermore, "if you find yourself thinking about anything, merely go off with the power in all the muscle regions on which you have practiced. If the thinking recurs, go negative again, no matter how often. But since you don't yet have control of all of your muscles, do not expect perfection—complete elimination of thought *can* come later if you are diligent."

Also, patients should not think frequently about their symptoms as they continue relaxation training. Signs of progress may appear soon after they start, or there may be a delay, depending upon such matters as how tense they are and what everyday pressures they experience. The essential thing is to practice daily; if they do that, they can expect improvement. Furthermore, they should be aware that learning relaxation skills is like learning any other performance skill: two steps forward and one step back, two steps forward and one step back.

Early in learning, a learner might experience the "predormescent start"—as he or she falls asleep, the trunk and limbs may give a convulsive start, which may awaken him or her. Apparently it takes place in individuals who have been hypertense during the preceding day's activities. It tends to disappear after a restful day but to appear again after exciting experiences. The physiological mechanism may be similar to that of a nervous start, so that it disappears as relaxation progresses.

This section concludes with a brief illustration of progressive relaxation as a method of pain control in treating cardiac patients. In the case

of a patient who has angina, with some difficulty in breathing and difficulty in assuming a prone position comfortably for sleep, the following
technique may be productively applied.

First, start with the patient sitting on the side of the bed, legs off the
side. Carefully assisting the patient onto the bed so as to reduce excess
exertion, help the patient assume a reclining position, with pillows at a
45-degree angle. Then there should be a progressive let-go (power off)
of the legs for several minutes. Next there should be a slow, progressive
let-go of the entire trunk, then of the shoulders and neck, progressing
through the remaining musculature, the forehead, the brow, the speech
musculature. Each instruction is followed by a minute or two of slow, progressive let-go. In this way, the discomfort from the pain and the breathing difficulties can be alleviated with restful sleep.

RESISTANCE, COMPLIANCE, AND MAINTENANCE
OF BEHAVIOR CHANGE

Perhaps half of those individuals who take the first step in learning
progressive relaxation go on to succeed in developing reasonably adequate
control over their bodies, including their mental processes. This estimate
covers a wide variety of potential learners, including patients who come
to the clinic; heterogeneous members of the community in evening
classes; college, medical, and graduate students; and even professionals
who participate in specialized workshops. To explain this difference in
behavior would require a complex research project. Short of that, we can
say that some people have the discipline to see themselves through the
program, while others simply do not. Clearly, the difference cannot be
explained according to the need to relax, for many with the greatest need
have shunned the opportunity immediately after requesting it. For example, a president who had built up a successful company came for treatment of a peptic ulcer. On the second treatment, he confessed that he had
not practiced a single day during the preceding month. His explanation
was that he had spent his life giving other people ulcers and now he re-
sented having to deal with one for himself. It was agreed that further
"treatment" would be a waste of time for all concerned.

Healthy individuals seem to learn more quickly than do patients in
distress. Neurotics, for instance, are distracted, and their learning is thus
prolonged. People who are engaged in cultist activities and fads are especially suggestible and dependent; this makes it more difficult for the

teacher to get them to rely on themselves. They have many bizarre ideas that interfere with their learning to relax, and much time can be lost if the teacher chooses to argue with them. Similarly, people who have excessive faith in the clinician also generally fail to observe tensions for themselves and take longer to relax than do average individuals.

Such illustrations of resistance and failure to comply could be enumerated indefinitely, but the problem is not unique to progressive relaxation. In many spheres of life people behave in a self-destructive fashion, even when they can verbalize the contingencies between their behavioral inadequacies and the consequences thereof. Failure to take prescribed medication for high blood pressure, drug (including alcohol) abuse, and smoking are examples of such self-destructive behaviors. There is often little one can do for individuals who engage in denial processes, such as the hospital nurse who asserted that her cigarette smoking was healthy for her. For those individuals who *can* verbalize the contingencies, perhaps there is some limited hope if they will at least try to discipline themselves in efforts to develop self-operations control—in other words, to enhance their "will power" (McGuigan, 1981).

On the other hand, many of those individuals who have dedicated themselves to daily practice and to accept regular instruction have made amazing progress. A wide variety of symptoms have been alleviated or eliminated with lasting effects, as shown by follow-up testing (Jacobson, 1938, 1970).

CASE EXAMPLE: A CASE OF ANXIETY, EXHAUSTION, AND ACROPHOBIA[2]

Summary. In 1929, an attorney, 32 years old, believed that he had overworked to the point of permanent exhaustion; in his words, "burned out" for life. He was uneasy, irritable, and often dizzy and could not appear in court or drive a car for fear of fainting or other discomfort. His fears kept him from high places. "Reasoning" and "fighting" these "ridiculous" symptoms only made them worse. The symptoms appeared first about 4 or 5 years previously. Instruction in progressive relaxation was begun in 1929 as far as we knew, omitting all reassurance and other "suggestive therapy." Soon he discontinued treatment and went elsewhere; but after several weeks he returned. Gradually with persistence he developed excellence in observation and report on his tension patterns. Voluntarily he acted as

[2]This section is reprinted by permission of Charles C Thomas, Publisher, Springfield, Illinois, from *Modern Treatment of Tense Patients* by E. Jacobson (1970, pp. 91–104).

a subject in electrophysiological studies on mental activities. Action-potential measurements indicated increasing skill in maintaining relaxed states, when lying, when sitting quietly or when reading. He "made it a rule to relax any phobia or disturbing thought-act." In 1931 his symptoms and complaints had diminished; he was able to resume appearances in court and to drive without nervous difficulties. He was discharged in 1931 anxiety-free. Evidently acrophobia was no longer present, for without telling the doctor he moved his law offices to the tower of a high building. Twenty-nine years thereafter he reports that he still practices, although not so regularly as he should. Throughout this period there has been no recurrence of the anxiety, phobias, or other disabilities about which he complained in 1929.

COMPLAINTS

In October of 1929 an exceedingly busy attorney, 32 years of age, was referred by his brother, a physician, for an anxiety state which included fears of heights and of dizziness, general uneasiness and irritability, and headache at the vertex and the occiput. He stated that he had been living at high tension all day long and in his opinion was "burned out" for life. Walking down the street or appearing in court, he was suddenly beset by fears of dizziness, making him feel very uncomfortable. At times he felt as if about to faint, and since he had never fainted, he felt that this was "all ridiculous." "Fighting" the above-mentioned symptoms only had made them worse; he had tried to reason matters out and had tried to relax, he had tried to get his mind off of himself, but all had been in vain. He was particularly concerned because when at court examining a witness, he suddenly began to fear becoming dizzy. In consequence, he had been caused to stay out of court, feeling, however, that sometime he would return.

ONSET

The onset had been 4 or 5 years previously in the middle of a lawsuit when he was confronted with a difficult opposing attorney. At the time he suffered from pain in the left lower portion of his thorax, both subcardially and laterally. He won the case, however, and finally the symptoms disappeared after the use of belladonna plasters and the administration of a tonic. But he had begun to feel anxious about one set of matters, and the anxiety turned gradually to others. His brother, the doctor, had suggested that if he would pay no attention to his symptoms, they would disappear. Accordingly, he had said to himself, "Get your mind off of it. Forget it." This seemed to bring him relief for about 1½ years. Nevertheless, about January 1, 1929, the symptoms insidiously recurred.

PERSONAL HISTORY

Among previous diseases had been influenza during the epidemic of 1920. In May of 1929 he suffered from cystitis following cystoscopy, and since then occasional blood cells had appeared in his urine. As a rule he slept well, but there were exceptions of late when he continued to worry. He was married in 1920 and had two children, a boy and a girl, both well. His parents were well, excepting that his mother was rheumatic and worrisome.

GENERAL EXAMINATION AND CLINICAL LABORATORY TESTS

General examination disclosed a fairly [well-]nourished man looking the age stated. His pulse was regular at the rate of 96 in the sitting posture, while his blood pressure was 130/96. His temperature was 98.6°F. He was 5 feet 7¼ inches and weighed about 157 pounds. General examination revealed a somewhat pendulous abdominal wall but otherwise no significant findings, aside from an extremely lively foot-flexion reflex. Laboratory tests supplied by his brother indicated Wasserman and Kahn reactions negative; basal metabolism, – 12; blood nonprotein nitrogen, 27 mg%; urea nitrogen, 15 mg%; blood sugar, 84 mg%; red blood count, 4,310,000; white count, 6500; hemoglobin, 75% with a color index of 0.8. The differential count fell within normal limits. Fluoroscopy of the chest proved negative. Urine analysis was completely negative aside from a few mucous threads.

INSTRUCTION BEGUN

Instruction in progressive relaxation as outlined in the published text [Jacobson, 1938] was begun in October 1929. At this time, over a 10-year period, I was attempting to rule out from our procedures all use of any form of suggestive therapy, so far as this might be possible. To this end, I tried to avoid not only reassurance to the patient in any possible form, but also unnecessary conversation. I attempted to confine our relationship to instruction in the forms of progressive relaxation appropriate to the patient's needs in my judgment. Accordingly, when the patient asked questions bearing upon the outcome of the instruction, hoping that it might prove favorable, or when he was in doubt that the instruction really applied to his case, I avoided answers that might possibly be interpreted by him suggestively. However, since from the patient's standpoint he was paying fees for a practical result, some of the individuals treated failed to continue with the instruction. Some never even began, for want of assurance that it would help them. The patient whose history and instruction is presented in the present [section] likewise lost confidence after a month or two of instruction, suddenly leaving to go elsewhere for "psychiatric treatment." After 3 weeks of absence with little ado or comment on either side, he returned to complete his course.

I shall omit the early months of instruction, referring the reader to the text mentioned.

November 22, 1929. He has been learning. He states that when emotionally disturbed he localizes the tension patterns and lets them go.

May 3, 9, 1930. Instruction devoted to review of tension patterns in the eyelids and eyeballs. Practice is given in observing tension patterns and going negative upon looking in various directions with eyelids closed and looking from finger to finger with eyelids open.

VISUALIZATION FOUND IMPOSSIBLE DURING COMPLETE EYE MUSCLE RELAXATION

May 13, 1930. He is requested to imagine that he is seeing the fingers held about 10 feet away from his eyes, but at the same time to remain perfectly relaxed. He reports that he finds this instruction impossible to carry out. He finds it necessary to exert effort tensions of the eyes, that is, to look in specific directions, if he is to imagine objects seen. This request and report are typical of our endeavors to secure objective reports from highly trained patients, without leading them to anticipate the answers. Indeed, these autosensory observations with patients have been carried out under strictly controlled methods characteristic of laboratories of experimental psychology.

AUTOSENSORY OBSERVATION DURING EMOTION

May 23, 1930. He mentions fear of being in a high building, but fails to give a clear-cut sensory and imaginal report, evidently not yet prepared to describe his experiences, but losing himself in the emotion. He is given further instruction in observing and in reporting matters of visual imagination of indifferent affect.

May 29; June 3, 13, 1930. He continues to be emotionally disturbed from time to time. Training is devoted to the musculature of speech, with particular reference to steady or static tensions.

July 17, 1930. He states that today he has suffered from phobia of high places. Instruction is given in verbal imagination. As yet he fails to recognize tension patterns in the various muscles of speech and to state their locations.

AUTOSENSORY OBSERVATION DURING UNEMOTIONAL EXPERIENCES

July 18, 1930. He enters the clinic exultant over his personal discovery that attention to the object of fear diminishes the fear. Instruction today begins in the lying posture with the request, "Think of infinity." He fails to report the imaginal, the tension, and other signal patterns, stating only the meaning of his reflection. However, when requested to engage in simple multiplication, as of 14 by 42, he gives a complete report, not only of the meaning but also of the tension pattern. He is given repeated practice in observation of sensory experiences, distinguishing the report thereof from the interpretation or meaning.

ANGER TENSION RELAXED

July 22, 29, 1930. He announces that he now relaxes spells of anger, has been gaining in weight, and, as noted by his family physician, he no longer fidgets as he did formerly upon receiving a hypodermic injection. Upon being requested to describe an experience of phobia, he still engages in the "stimulus error" but to [a lesser] extent than formerly.

September 3, 5, 1930. Differential relaxation is begun, with training devoted to the right arm. He has been at home with a fever of 101°F at times, due to an infection of the right kidney and of the bladder.

October 14, 17; November 10, 21, 1930. Instruction on the limbs is continued in the sitting posture. At times during the period while sitting, he is on the verge of sleep.

EFFICIENCY

December 5, 1930. He asserts that now he does his legal work effectively and without nervous excitement in a manner which he never accomplished previously in his entire life.

December 12, 1930. He complains of tension in the right side of the scalp.[3] After drill in wrinkling of the forehead, he reports relief.

December 16, 23, 1930. Instruction is devoted to the abdomen and back in the sitting posture.

February 13, 1931. He affirms his nerves are greatly improved. At times a little phobia persists, but he is becoming accustomed to observe tension patterns at such moments and to relax them. His brother, the doctor, recently was amazed at his calmness in trying a lawsuit, in contrast with his extreme excitability in former years. Friends who do not know of the instruction which he has been receiving spontaneously say to him that he is a changed man.

PHOBIC TENSION PATTERNS NOW RECOGNIZED AND RELAXED

February 20; March 3, 1931. He states that he has been in very good nervous condition and has been efficient. He makes it a rule to relax any phobia or disturbing thought-act. Instruction concerns brow tensions. He often sleeps during the period.

March 19; April 4, 10, 17, 18, 21, 1931. Repeated practice is given on imagining falling objects of indifferent affect. The purpose here is to teach him [to] observe the pattern of mental processes when any object falls. Thus a first step is taken without him knowing it to lead him to observe what he does in high places when he imagines himself jumping and falling. Thus, without telling him, we proceed in the treatment of acrophobia.

---

[3]He mistakes pull or strain on the scalp for muscular tension.

RETURN OF ABILITY TO TRY CASES

May 1, 2, 14, 29; June 3, 5, 10, 1931. For the first time in years, he tries cases in court without nervous difficulties. His phobia in the court has disappeared. Instruction is devoted to musculature of speech.

RETURN OF ABILITY TO DRIVE AND TO GO ON TRIPS, NO ACROPHOBIA

June 13, 1931. He reports that he has taken for the first time in about 7 years a long drive. Previously fearful, but not knowing why, he now finds that he enjoys [driving]. Previous to present instruction, he dreaded and avoided trying cases outside of Chicago. Recently, in contrast, he has gone on three long trips with no difficulty. Nowadays, he tries cases enjoyably, as previously he met them with dread. The phobia of jumping from high places has been completely absent. Last month was a very difficult time in his business, because large loans for which he was responsible came due at the height of the panic and bank failures of the Great Depression. Nevertheless, he was relaxed and not nervous. He adds that he relaxes concerns about law trials. He no longer argues the legal matters out within himself, but he instead "relaxes the whole thought." Instruction is devoted to tension signals from the tongue and relaxation of tongue muscles.

July 14, 30, 31, 1931. Instruction concerns imagining making various statements. He is still slow to relax to the point where he is ready to observe and report. However, his reports are clear.

September 4, 1931. Instruction is begun on reading while relaxing the left arm so far as possible.

September 8, 18, 22, 25, 29; October 2, 6, 15, 27, 1931. Instruction on reading is continued, while observing tension patterns and learning to relax those not required for the reading in various portions of the anatomy. He fails to report verbal tensions during reading, claiming that there are none, but only visual images and ocular tension patterns. Obviously his training is not yet sufficient, but he is not so informed.

November 6, 1931. His brother-in-law died suddenly. Instruction is devoted to exposing a single printed stimulus word within the instruction to read and get the meaning. At first his reports are confused, for he gives interpretations in place of observations. Finally he begins to report more accurately, as follows: "Ocular tension in seeing the word. Ocular tension in imagining what the word indicates. Tensions in the tongue as in saying the word."

SLIGHT RELAPSE YET PATIENT NOT TOLD WHAT TO LOOK FOR

November 20, 1931. Yesterday he experienced some nervous distress while in court, pleading a lawsuit. Upon relaxing, the unnecessary emotions disappeared. He has been through various trying ordeals. He even ventured for the first time in 10 years to look at a corpse. For 2 months he has failed to report tensions in the organs of speech while reading. Accordingly he is requested to count while reading, employing the method of diminishing tensions. Finally he succeeds in observing the speech tensions. This occurs with no hint from the instructor that he has been omitting anything.

RELAXES DIFFERENTIALLY

December 5, 1931. There have been four deaths in the family which ordinarily would have disturbed him much more, he believes. However, in place of engaging in fears and worries each morning, now he goes to work relaxing and preparing himself to relax during the day. He has found that he does not have to postpone relaxation to the weekend but can relax during the work of each day. Accordingly he is greatly relieved.

DISCHARGED

December 8, 18, 1931. Instruction is given in reading aloud, relaxing so far as possible during this occupation. He is discharged, apparently free from emotional disturbance. Electrical recording has shown excellent technique. He has been a volunteer subject at the University of Chicago, Department of Physiology, for electrical measurement during mental activities. . . .

FREEDOM FROM ACROPHOBIA

Following his discharge in 1931, the phobia of high places had so evidently disappeared that, without suggestion from the doctor, he moved his office to the tower of a very high office building. In his new office, he felt no fear or phobia. In regarding his nervous condition, he considered himself well. He volunteers to act as an experienced observer with skill at tension reduction in the physiological laboratory of the University of Chicago. He practices differential relaxation every day. On some days he fails to lie down, but as a rule after dinner he practices in a lying posture for 45 to 90 minutes. On about one half of these occasions he falls asleep. If he awakens at night and finds himself tense, he locates the tension patterns and relaxes accordingly. Uneasiness no longer is experienced and he no longer shows marked irritability. When engaged in difficult matters, he relaxes so as to avoid becoming irritated. He has no dizziness, no fears and no headaches. His technique shows excellent form.

March 3, 1943. Electrical recording is performed with the eyes open. The right thigh averages little over 0.5 μV. The right biceps averages little over 0.075 μV, with low $\overline{V}$. The right jaw muscles average in neighborhood of 0.2 μV. The eye regions about 3.5 μV. The values are fair for a trained subject, except that variability ($\overline{V}$) is a little high.

August 6, 1945. He reports that for the first time in his life, he has completely lost fear of being in high places. He flew in an airplane and at first was fearful when breathing through tubes of oxygen provided for this purpose, but he used his relaxation technique and enjoyed the flying trip from then on. He relaxes differentially to an extent that is readily appreciated by a professional observer.

PERSISTENT FREEDOM FROM ANXIETY TENSION ALTHOUGH DIFFICULTIES ARE MET

July 22, 1949. He relates that he was "wonderfully well" for many years following the instruction. In 1939 his daughter married and in 1940 she became very unhappy, which was a "terrific jolt" to him. "During that whole year I suffered from worry, hoping that the situation would straighten out." His daughter was operated on for appendicitis and recovered. She joined him for a few weeks only, after which she returned home, since her husband needed her. "This," continued our patient, "took quite a bit out of me." "Then my son was drafted for the war;

usually parents worry about that. In 1940 loose [bowel] movements had occurred once or twice a year and I didn't know what started them. Certain medication overcame any spell promptly. Also I could avert the spells by avoiding raw fruits and vegetables. In 1945 the spells became more intense and frequent. My brother-in-law got me into a business of his own, in which I sunk time and a small fortune. In January 1947 I foolishly let him leave the partnership. Thereafter he enticed the plant manager away, which proved irritating and took my time and interfered with my practice of law. Engineers called in to help the business gave bad counsel with resulting further loss. In December 1947 I sold the business for a pittance."

IRRITABLE COLON

During the summer of 1945, a severe spell of diarrhea was followed by X-ray examination and a diagnosis of duodenal ulcer. The symptoms disappeared after a short period of diet restriction and medication. Since then, there have been only two light spells and one severe spell with burning in the rectum.

PRACTICE NEGLECTED

"It was in the attempt to get rid of nervous disturbance that I sold the plant and returned to more or less regular periods of relaxation, which I had been neglecting, and to which I ascribed alone my lasting improvement. My downfall had been that practice was not regular."

July 25, 1949. A brief refresher course is begun.

July 27, 1949. Roentgenological examination by Dr. James Case indicates negative findings as to duodenal ulcer. The colon, however, is found to be spastic. A similar examination made previously suggested that possibly there had been an early ulcer. At this time, however, he has been relaxing a little more frequently than before and has been able to partake once more of solids.

August 1, 3, 8, 10, 15, 17, 24, 25, 29; September 7, 9, 14, 26; October 10, 1949. Review practice is given on limb tension patterns and relaxation.

1959. His wife writes from her observations in retrospect that through relaxation training he learned "a new way of life."

October 30, 1960. He reports that he has been free from anxiety tension, phobias, fears, and other emotional disturbances these many years. He is able to try lawsuits when and where he desires, [is] able to plead cases at will, and has continued to be generally more relaxed than he had ever been in the decade before he reached the age of 32, when instruction-was begun.

COMMENTS AND REFLECTIONS

I can think of no better way to close this chapter than to quote Jacobson as follows:

Until I see proof I incline in the direction of skepticism. Progressive relaxation, as developed in our laboratory and clinic, was to me a matter of skepticism at every step. Thirty years ago as I went from room to room trying to get individuals with different maladies to relax, I recall saying to myself, "What kind of nonsense is this that you are practicing?" The careful accumulation of data has vindicated the procedure. (1977, p. 123)

ACKNOWLEDGMENTS

I am deeply indebted to Edmund Jacobson for so many things that it would be impossible to list them all here. First and foremost, though, I would specify the innumerable hours and limitless energy that he spent in personally training me in progressive relaxation. More specifically, for this chapter, I am indebted to him for the ideas, the principles, the applications, and in fact, often even for the use of his words, which have become part of my own repertoire.

REFERENCES

Bain, A. *The senses and the intellect.* London: Parker, 1855.

Jacobson, E. *Progressive relaxation* (2nd ed.). Chicago: University of Chicago Press, 1938.

Jacobson, E. *Self-operations control.* Chicago: National Foundation for Progressive Relaxation, 1964.

Jacobson, E. *Modern treatment of tense patients.* Springfield, Ill.: Charles C Thomas, 1970.

Jacobson, E. The origins and development of progressive relaxation. *Journal of Behavior Therapy and Experimental Psychiatry,* 1977, *8,* 119–123.

McGuigan, F. J. *Cognitive psychophysiology: Principles of covert behavior.* Englewood Cliffs, N.J.: Prentice-Hall, 1978. (Now published by Erlbaum, Hillsdale, N.J.)

McGuigan, F. J. *Calm down: A guide for stress and tension control.* Englewood Cliffs, N.J.: Prentice-Hall, 1981.

Sherrington, C. S. On plastic tonus and proprioceptive reflexes. *Quarterly Journal of Experimental Physiology,* 1909, *2,* 109–156.

Wiener, N. *Cybernetics.* New York: Wiley, 1948.

3 PROGRESSIVE RELAXATION: ABBREVIATED METHODS

DOUGLAS A. BERNSTEIN AND BEVERLY A. GIVEN

In a world filled with tension and anxiety, relaxation is a much-sought-after goal. This is true for people in general, but it is especially critical for those whose emotional arousal results in severe subjective distress, overt behavior problems, and damage to various organ systems. Clinicians and researchers seeking nonpharmacological methods for promoting relaxation and combating anxiety have developed a number of useful procedures, the most popular of which is referred to as "progressive relaxation training" (PRT). As noted in the preceding chapter, PRT is not a single method, but a set of techniques that vary considerably in procedural detail, complexity, and length. Our goal in this chapter is to focus attention upon the more abbreviated forms of PRT.

HISTORY

The history of PRT as we now know it originates in the work of Edmund Jacobson in the late 1920s. The course of its development and use in Jacobson's laboratory and clinic is reviewed in the preceding chapter. Jacobson's technique is lengthy and painstaking. The entire training in all muscle groups may require 50 or more sessions over a period of several months or even several years.

A considerably condensed version of PRT was presented by Joseph Wolpe (1958) in the context of his classic work on counterconditioning methods for fear reduction. As is well known, Wolpe based his research upon the concept of "reciprocal inhibition," which suggests that an undesirable emotional response can be suppressed by evoking a stronger incompatible response. The primary treatment package that evolved from this research became known as "systematic desensitization."

43

In systematic desensitization, a phobic response, inappropriate fear, or anxiety is counterconditioned by creating an incompatible state or response in the imagined or "live" presence of the feared stimulus. In most cases, deep relaxation provided a convenient and beneficial state, which appeared to be incompatible with anxiety and which could be induced and maintained while the client learned to tolerate increasingly threatening fear stimuli comfortably (Paul & Bernstein, 1973).

In order to conduct this form of treatment, it was necessary for Wolpe to develop a rapid method for teaching clients to attain a state of deep-muscle relaxation. This he did by modifying and abbreviating Jacobson's PRT procedures. This abbreviated form, which typically requires only six 20-minute training sessions, forms the basis for the brief PRT methods to be presented here.

THEORETICAL UNDERPINNINGS

The theoretical basis of abbreviated PRT methods is essentially similar to that discussed in Chapter 2. Briefly, there is an assumption that anxiety and other emotional states involve subjective, overt behavioral, and physiological components, all of which interact to some degree. For example, when physiological arousal is perceived and labeled as "fear" or "anxiety," the client reports being afraid or anxious or nervous. Such reports and/or the cognitions preceding or accompanying them may act as additional fear-provoking stimuli, which further enhance autonomic arousal. This leads to increased subjective discomfort and even more arousal, in a continuing spiral that may lead to panic, cognitive flooding, or a variety of other behavioral and physiological consequences.

PRT is designed to intervene in this process by providing a way of reducing autonomic arousal. Once this has been accomplished, the client should be more capable of (1) providing meaningful assessment information to the clinician, (2) tolerating fear-provoking stimuli, (3) learning more adaptive alternative responses to such stimuli, and (4) learning or utilizing rational cognitions that help to forestall or eliminate subsequent problematic arousal.

PRT seeks to reduce the autonomic arousal component of anxiety "indirectly" by altering one of its manifestations—namely, skeletal muscle tension. As muscle tension drops, other, less directly accessible aspects of autonomic arousal, such as heart rate and blood pressure, are also lowered. Whether alteration of peripheral muscle tension is sufficient by itself to explain the effects of progressive relaxation training is not entirely clear. For example, it has been argued that central nervous system events, primarily focused attention and pleasant cognitions, may be vital to clinically significant reductions in autonomic arousal (Davison, 1966; Greenwood & Benson, 1977; King, 1980). Thus, when a client learns how to tense and release muscle groups and utilize other relaxation techniques to be described later, he or she is, at the very least, developing a set of voluntary skills that can then be used to reduce maladaptive autonomic arousal and to prevent arousal from reaching a troublesome level in the first place.

It is worth noting that the skills the client learns through PRT represent but one way of achieving a state of deep relaxation. There are many other routes to that state (e.g., biofeedback, hypnosis, and autogenic training), all of which appear to capitalize on similar psychophysiological mechanisms (e.g., Tarler-Benlolo, 1978). Thus, the choice of abbreviated PRT for use in a given clinical situation must be made not because it leads to a relaxed state that is unique, but because it meets the needs of the client and the clinician.

ASSESSMENT

PRT has been successfully used, alone or in combination with other methods, to deal with a wide range of behavior problems in adults and children. These include (but are not limited to) "free-floating anxiety" or general tension, phobias, insomnia, hypertension, asthma, muscle contraction and migraine headache, unassertiveness, hyperactivity, tics, psychogenic seizures, and self-destructive behavior (King, 1980). Underlying the use of PRT in these cases is the judgment that maladaptive levels of autonomic arousal are at least partly responsible for the development and maintenance of the problems that bring the client to treatment. However, recognition of the fact that PRT *can* play a beneficial role in dealing with many diverse human problems must not lead to the conclusion that it *always* will be useful or that it is the treatment of choice for *all* clients whose complaints match those reported in the clinical literature.

On the one hand, it is safe to say that, in the vast majority of cases involving clinical problems similar to those just listed, the use of PRT is probably going to be of some help and is extremely unlikely to do any harm. In the same vein, the time spent in teaching relaxation skills may provide a positive experience for both therapist and client which helps establish a good, task-oriented working relationship. On the other hand, it must be recognized that time spent on PRT for, say, general tension, cannot be spent in working directly with other problems, which in a given case may require immediate attention.

Thus, as is true for any clinical method, the decision to employ abbreviated PRT must be based upon careful assessment of the full range of causal, contributing, maintenance, and complicating factors that may be related to the client's complaints. The information gathered in assessment should determine whether PRT is the intervention of choice, alone or in combination with other treatment modalities (e.g., assertiveness training), or whether the client's problems reflect such factors as basic skill deficits which suggest that other initial interventions would be more appropriate.

The questions outlined below do not comprise an exhaustive list of items to consider in assessment, but they do provide a basic framework for inquiry that can easily be elaborated according to the dictates of each unique situation.

1. *Is there evidence that the client's complaints are related to anxiety, tension, or other aspects of maladaptive emotional arousal?* In some cases, this is a relatively easy question to answer: The client reports being tense and anxious, and there are obvious physiological and behavioral signs that coincide with the subjective experience. In other instances, the emotional arousal may not be the focus of the client's report, nor are there obvious signs that maladaptive arousal is at issue. For example, an adult client may report reduced energy level, lack of motivation, significant absenteeism from work, and mild depression. Though tension or anxiety is not mentioned spontaneously, it may not take much exploration to determine that new job pressures or other events may have threatened, frightened, and stressed the client. Perhaps his or her initial response to the stress involved some obvious tension or anxiety, but by the time help is sought, an avoidance strategy may have been developed to mask the more fundamental problem. As is well known, anxiety may also play a role in the appearance of other escape–avoidance behaviors, such as alcohol or drug abuse, hysterical reactions, and a wide variety of interpersonal conflicts. Other subtle behavioral signs of anxiety can include insomnia, sexual dysfunction, restlessness, irritability, compulsive or stereotyped response patterns, and loss of appetite.

Physiological indicators of maladaptive arousal may include nausea, backache or headache, unusual or irregular bowel activity (or other gastrointestinal problems), genitourinary system problems, hypertension, and a variety of other psychophysiological disorders. Subjectively, anxiety and its consequences may appear in terms of inability to concentrate, loss of memory, confusion, "flooding," or obsessional thoughts.

2. *Is anxiety or tension the primary focus of treatment?* Anxiety may play a significant role in a client's problems, but before choosing PRT as a component of treatment, the clinician should be satisfied that it is an appropriate initial treatment target. It is in regard to this issue that a distinction between "conditioned" and "reactive" anxiety must be made (Paul & Bernstein, 1973). If the client's overarousal has developed (has been "conditioned") primarily through a series of unfortunate learning experiences (e.g., social discomfort stemming from having been threatened by boisterous guests at teenage parties), new learning experiences such as PRT may help alleviate the problem, assuming that the client possesses adequate social skills. However, if the client's fundamental problem primarily involves a *reaction* to punishment brought about by a lack of social skills and/or the presence of maladaptive cognitive habits (e.g., "I'm not as good as these people"), PRT may be of little more than temporary help. In fact, if treatment does not focus upon the development of new cognitive and overt behavioral skills, the disappointing effects of supplemented relaxation procedures could have a negative impact on the client's motivation to continue working with the therapist.

Recognition of the "conditioned versus reactive" dimension requires the clinician to go beyond the client's self-reports of discomfort to look for indications of skill deficits or other problems that may be responsible for overarousal. This can be done in a variety of ways, including interviews with family members, *in vivo* behavioral observations, role playing, and informal observation during routine interviews.

In most cases, the clinician is likely to find that anxiety-related problems have both conditioned and reactive components. The point to keep in mind is that, unless relaxation training is needed as an immediate rapport-building procedure, it may be postponed or eliminated altogether when assessment reveals anxiety that is primarily reactive. If a significant conditioned residue remains after this aspect of the problem is dealt with, relaxation training may then be brought to bear.

3. *Are there organic components in tension-related problems?* It should go without saying that, before choosing progressive relaxation (or any psychologically oriented intervention) to help deal with physical problems apparently brought on by tension, the client should be examined by appropriate medical personnel in order to rule out organic causal factors. This caveat is especially important where the client complains of

"traditional" psychophysiological disorders, such as pain in the head or lower back, cardiac symptoms (such as tachycardia or arrhythmia), asthma, and gastrointestinal difficulties; but it should also be kept in mind when the complaint could have a less obvious organic base. Examples include disorders of memory, concentration, logic or other cognitive functions, depression, irritability, and aggressiveness.

4. *Are there any reasons why the client could not or should not learn relaxation skills?* As noted earlier, in the vast majority of cases, PRT is a benign and pleasant procedure that is extremely unlikely to result in physical or psychological harm to the client. Nevertheless, the clinician considering the use of PRT methods should take care to assure that no past or current physical conditions exist that contraindicate some of the required tension–release cycles. Consultation with the client and his or her physician about this matter is especially important in cases where certain muscles or connective tissues have been damaged or are chronically weak. Similarly, medical advice may suggest that it would be better to focus on strengthening certain muscle groups (e.g., in the lower back) rather than on learning to relax them. In such cases, PRT may still be feasible, but it would have to be modified to delete or alter procedures for problematic muscle groups (see Bernstein & Borkovec, 1973). The same is true in the case of an individual who, as the result of a neuromuscular disability, is incapable of exercising voluntary control over all muscles in the body (see Cautela & Groden, 1978).

Beyond these considerations, the clinician should also assure that the client is both able and willing to (1) maintain focused attention during relaxation training, (2) follow instructions regarding tension–release cycles, and (3) engage in regular home practice between treatment sessions. If serious obstacles to any of these three basic requirements exist, it may be wise to work on eliminating those obstacles before beginning a relaxation program.

THE METHOD

INTRODUCING RELAXATION TO THE CLIENT

Once appropriate assessment has been completed and PRT has been decided upon as a treatment of choice, the method and its specific procedures must be explained to the client in enough detail to promote cooperation and understanding. This presentation should include an explanation of (1) the role that anxiety seems to play in the client's problem and (2) how PRT might be expected to help. The level of discourse and the amount of detail involved in this introductory session should vary from client to client in accordance with individuals' capacities to absorb and integrate the content and concepts involved. At the very least, the clinician should attempt to establish in the client a basic appreciation of how tension is manifested, how it can be reduced, and how that reduction can help alleviate some of the presenting problems. Without such basic understanding, the client's interest in learning and practicing relaxation is not likely to be strong enough to develop useful skills. Most clients find the idea of PRT intrinsically appealing. However, there will be those who continue to express doubts. If the client remains skeptical but is willing to try PRT seriously, the training itself may relieve the skepticism.

Once the client understands and at least provisionally accepts the conceptualization of his or her problems as partly involving maladaptive levels of tension, the clinician can present a more detailed rationale for the choice of abbreviated PRT as a part of treatment. This rationale should provide (1) a brief overview of the history of progressive relaxation; (2) a description of PRT as a method whereby one learns a *skill,* in much the same manner as one learns other skills (such as swimming) that involve muscle control; (3) the stipulation that PRT will require regular practice, so that the client can learn to recognize and control the distinctly different sensations of tension and relaxation; and (4) the clear message that the therapist will not be doing anything *to* the client—rather, that the client will be developing a capability within himself or herself that he or she can then use independently.

A sample rationale is reproduced below.[1] It is given merely as an illustration, not as a script. Each therapist should present this material in his or her own natural style.

The procedures I have been discussing in terms of reducing your tension are collectively called "progressive relaxation training." They were first developed in the 1930s by a physiologist named Jacobson, and in recent years we have modified his original technique in order to make it simpler and more effective. Basically, progressive relaxation training consists of learning to . . . tense and then [to] relax various groups of muscles all through the body, while at the same time paying very close and careful attention to the feelings associated with both tension and relaxation. That is, in addition to teaching you how to relax, I will also

[1]Reprinted by permission of Research Press, Champaign, Illinois, from *Progressive Relaxation Training* by D. A. Bernstein and T. D. Borkovec (1973, pp. 19–20).

be encouraging you to learn to recognize and pinpoint tension and relaxation as they appear in everyday situations, as well as in our sessions here.

You should understand quite clearly that learning relaxation skills is very much like learning any other kind of skill such as swimming, or golfing, or riding a bicycle; thus, in order for you to get better at relaxing, you will have to practice doing it just as you would have to practice other skills. It is very important that you realize that progressive relaxation training involves learning on your part; there is nothing magical about the procedures. I will not be doing anything to you; I will merely be introducing you to the technique and directing your attention to various aspects of it, such as the presence of certain feelings in the muscles. Thus, without your active cooperation and regular practicing of the things you will learn today, the procedures are of little use.

Now I mentioned earlier that I will be asking you to tense and then [to] relax various groups of muscles in your body. You may be wondering why, if we want to produce relaxation, we start off by producing tension. The reason is that, first of all, everyone is always at some level of tension during his waking hours; if a person were not tense to some extent, he would simply fall down. The amount of tension actually present in everyday life differs, of course, from individual to individual, and we say that each person has reached some "adaptation level"— the amount of tension under which he operates day to day.

The goal of progressive relaxation training is to help you learn to reduce muscle tension in your body far below your adaptation level at any time you wish to do so. In order to accomplish this, I could ask you to focus your attention, for example, on the muscles in your right hand and lower arm and then just to let them relax. Now you might think you can let these muscles drop down below their adaptation level just by "letting them go" or whatever, and to a certain extent, you probably can. However, in progressive relaxation, we want you to learn to produce larger and very much more noticeable reductions in tension, and the best way to do this is first to produce a good deal of tension in the muscle group (i.e., [to] raise the tension well above adaptation level) and then, all at once, [to] release that tension. The release creates a "momentum" which allows the muscles to drop well below adaptation level. The effect is like that which we could produce with a pendulum which is hanging motionless in a vertical position. If we want it to swing far to the right, we could push it quite hard in that direction. It would be much easier, however, to start by pulling the pendulum in the opposite direction and then letting it go. It will swing well past the vertical point and continue in the direction we want it to go.

Thus, tensing muscle groups prior to letting them relax is like giving ourselves a "running start" toward deep relaxation through the momentum created by the tension release. Another important advantage to creating and releasing tension is that it will give you a good chance to focus your attention upon and become clearly aware of what tension really feels like in each of the various groups of muscles we will be dealing with today. In addition, the tensing procedure will make a vivid contrast between tension and relaxation and will give you an excellent opportunity to compare the two directly and appreciate the difference in feeling associated with each of these states.

Do you have any questions about what I've said so far?

Instead of memorizing this kind of presentation, the therapist may want to use an outline of the main topics to be covered. This is likely to make the material sound less "canned" (see Bernstein & Borkovec, 1973, pp. 61–62, for a sample outline).

After any questions about the rationale have been answered, the therapist should begin working with the client to develop optimal tension–release procedures for each of the 16 muscle groups that will be the initial focus of training. These groups and a typical tensing strategy for each are presented below:

Muscle Group	*Method of Tensing*
1. Dominant hand and forearm	Make a tight fist while allowing upper arm to remain relaxed
2. Dominant upper arm	Press elbow downward against chair without involving lower arm
3. Nondominant hand and forearm	Same as dominant
4. Nondominant upper arm	Same as dominant
5. Forehead	Raise eyebrows as high as possible
6. Upper cheeks and nose	Squint eyes and wrinkle nose
7. Lower face	Clench teeth and pull back corners of the mouth
8. Neck	Counterpose muscles by trying to raise and lower chin simultaneously
9. Chest, shoulders, and upper back	Take a deep breath; hold it and pull shoulder blades together
10. Abdomen	Counterpose muscles by trying to push stomach out and pull it simultaneously
11. Dominant upper leg	Counterpose large muscle on top of leg against two smaller ones underneath (specific strategy will vary considerably)
12. Dominant calf	Point toes toward head
13. Dominant foot	Point toes downward, turn foot in, and curl toes gently
14. Nondominant upper leg	Same as dominant
15. Nondominant calf	Same as dominant
16. Nondominant foot	Same as dominant

In order to facilitate transfer to the actual training situation, it is generally a good idea to have the client assume a reclining position while these tensing strategies are introduced and attempted. It is also advisable to work on the tension–release cycles for each muscle group in the same order as that to be used in subsequent training. When done in this way, the initial "run-through" can provide a reassuring preview of the procedures to come.

Inevitably some clients will have difficulty achieving tension in the "standard" manner described above. In such cases, the therapist must work with the client to devise alternate methods to achieve significant tension. The client may also find it difficult to tense one muscle group without tensing other groups at the same time. This problem tends to disappear with practice, but the therapist should continue to observe the client and should be ready to provide helpful suggestions and instructions.

Finally, some clients feel self-conscious or silly while tensing certain muscle groups, particularly those involving the face. The therapist can usually put the client at ease by demonstrating all tensing methods before asking the client to try them.

DESCRIPTION OF THE METHOD

Once the relaxation rationale has been presented and discussed, and once a set of muscle-tensing strategies has been agreed upon, a few final instructions should be given. These are presented below in the form a "typical" therapist might employ. Naturally, the specific wording should be adjusted to suit one's own style.

1. I will be instructing you to focus your attention on one muscle group at a time. Please pay attention only to what I am saying and to the sensations you are experiencing in that muscle group, allowing the rest of your body to remain relaxed. I will ask you to tense and relax each of the muscle groups in the same order as we used when we practiced tensing procedures.

2. When I ask you to tense a group, I will say, for example, "Tense the muscles in your forehead by raising your eyebrows, now." "Now" will be the cue word for you to tense the muscles. Do not tense the muscles until I say "now."

3. When I want you to relax a muscle group, I will say "OK, relax the muscles in your forehead." When I say that, let all the tension go all at once, not gradually. This allows the muscles to relax more deeply.

4. I will ask you to tense and relax each muscle group twice. After the second time, I will ask you to signal if the muscle group is completely relaxed. Please signal by raising the index finger on your right hand [whichever hand is visible to the therapist], but do not signal unless the muscles really feel completely relaxed.

5. During the session, try not to move any more than is necessary to remain comfortable. In order to gain the most benefit from relaxation, it is preferable not to move any muscles that have already been relaxed. This prevents tension from reappearing in those muscles.

6. In order to maintain as much relaxation as possible, I am going to ask you not to talk to me during our session unless it is absolutely necessary. We will mainly use your finger signal as a means of communication, and we will talk about how the session went after we finish today. Questions you may have can be discussed after completion of the relaxation.

7. Our session today will take about 45 minutes, so if you would like to use the restroom before we start, please do so.

8. Now I would like to have you remove or loosen any items that may cause discomfort during the session.

9. Do you have any further questions? Is there anything about which you are not clear?

10. OK, get in a comfortable position in your chair—fine. Now please close your eyes and keep them closed during the session. I will dim the lights now to remove any visual stimulation.

At this point, relaxation training can begin. Following the same sequence as the muscle groups presented previously, the therapist should treat each muscle group as follows:

1. Instruct the client to focus attention on the group.

2. Using the predetermined "now" cue, instruct the client to produce tension in that group, repeating the instructions for tensing that group. For example, the therapist may say, "By making a tight fist, tense the muscles in your right hand and lower arm, now." Allow the client to maintain the tension for 5 to 7 seconds while describing the sensations of tension to the client. Use a shorter tension duration for the feet or other muscles where the client may experience cramping.

3. Using the predetermined "relax" cue, instruct the client to relax the muscle group all at once (not gradually) and to attend to the sensations of relaxation. Allow the client to focus on the relaxation for 30 to 40 seconds while giving him or her some relaxation "patter" to highlight the sensations (see example below).

4. Repeat steps 2 and 3. After the second tension–release cycle, allow the client to maintain the relaxation and to focus on the sensations for 45 to 60 seconds.

5. Before moving on to the next muscle group, ask the client to signal if the current muscle group is completely relaxed. If not, repeat the tension and relaxation steps a third time. If the client still does not signal that the group is relaxed, the procedure may be repeated again. However, if relaxation is not achieved in four or five attempts, alternate means for achieving relaxation may be required. One alternative would be to instruct the client to allow those muscles to relax as much as possible while moving on to other groups and to return to them at a later point.

6. When the focus is on the chest, shoulders, and upper back, emphasis on breathing should be introduced as part of the procedure. Instruct the client to take a deep breath and hold it while the muscles are tensed and to exhale when instructed to relax. From this point on, breathing cues

should be included as part of the tension–release procedure for all muscle groups. Specifically, the client should take a breath and hold it while tensing and release the breath upon relaxing the tension. Further, the therapist can incorporate mention of slow, regular breathing into the relaxation "patter."

When these steps are combined, they go something like this:

OK, John, I would like you to focus all of your attention on the muscles of your chest, shoulders, and upper back. And by taking a deep breath and holding it and by pulling your shoulder blades back and together, I'd like you to tense the muscles of the chest, shoulders, and upper back, now. Good, notice the tension and the tightness, notice what the tension feels like, hold it . . . and relax.

Fine, just let all that tension go. Notice the difference between the tension you felt before and the pleasant feelings of relaxation. Just focus all your attention on those feelings of relaxation as they flow into the chest, shoulders, and your back. Just focus on your slow and regular breathing and go right on enjoying the relaxation.

[Tension–release cycle repeated after 30–45 seconds.]

OK, John, I'd like you to signal if the muscles of the chest, shoulders, and upper back are as deeply relaxed as those of the neck (i.e., the previous group). OK, fine, just go on relaxing.

When all 16 muscle groups have been relaxed, the therapist should review each group, reminding the client that these muscles have been relaxed and asking him or her to continue to allow them to relax while attending to the accompanying sensations. The client should then be asked to signal if all the groups are indeed completely relaxed. If the client does not signal, the muscle groups should be named, one at a time, and the client should be instructed to signal when the group or groups that are not totally relaxed are mentioned. A tension–release cycle can then be repeated for these groups. Once again, the client should be instructed to signal if any tension remains. Once a signal of total relaxation is given, the client should be allowed simply to enjoy this totally relaxed state for a minute or two before the session is terminated.

To terminate the relaxation session easily and gradually, the therapist can count backwards from 4 to 1. The client can be asked to move his or her feet and legs on the count of 4, to move hands and arms on the count of 3, to move head and neck on the count of 2, and to open the eyes and sit up on the count of 1. At this point, the therapist should ask open-ended questions such as "How do you feel?" or "How was that?" to encourage the client to discuss the feeling of relaxation and any problems that might have been encountered. If the client does not spontaneously report problems, the therapist should ask whether there were any muscle groups the client had difficulty in relaxing and whether the client has any questions about the procedure. The client should be asked whether any particular aspects of the "patter" helped or hindered relaxation.

If the client feels that some muscles were not well relaxed, it may be necessary for the therapist to suggest an alternate means of tensing those muscles and to incorporate the new method at the next session.

The therapist should arrange for the client to practice relaxation skills twice a day for 15 to 20 minutes each time. The therapist may help the client to decide on appropriate times and places for practice, attending to the same issues as were considered in selecting the location for PRT.

ENVIRONMENTAL FACTORS

Environmental factors can have a marked influence on the effectiveness of relaxation training, especially in the early stages. Factors of particular importance include the location at which training and home practice are conducted, the chair or other furniture the client uses, the client's wearing apparel, and the tone of voice used by the therapist.

The therapist should provide a location for training where there will be a minimum of extraneous stimuli. Particular care should be taken to prevent loud noises or the sound of conversation from reaching the treatment room. A sign should be placed on the door to prevent interruptions. Windows and drapes should be closed, and dim lighting should be used. If the client expresses reservations or feels discomfort in this type of environment, the therapist should discuss and resolve these concerns before proceeding.

If the environmental conditions just described cannot be created for some reason, effective PRT is still possible, though it may progress more slowly than usual. It is also true that relaxation skills may be more helpful to some clients if, once learned, they are practiced under somewhat less than optimal conditions. The assumption is that, if the client can reach and maintain a state of deep relaxation in the face of some distractions, the relaxation skills will be more robust and useful in dealing with *in vivo* stress or imagined stimuli (as in systematic desensitization). An extreme example of this phenomenon is provided by one of our clients who was very successfully trained in progressive relaxation (and subsequently desensitized to performance anxiety) during sessions accompanied by the continuous and occasionally deafening sounds of construction coming from a building site next door.

As to the client's location during training and practice, a good reclining chair is ideal. It should provide full support for the entire body so that, as the skeletal muscles relax, various limbs do not slip off the chair into uncomfortable positions. For some clients, a small pillow may be needed to provide added lower back support or to prevent head turns. The therapist should encourage the client to experiment with a number of chair positions (and body orientations in each) until the best, most comfortably supportive combination is found.

The client should be advised, prior to the first relaxation session, to wear loose-fitting, comfortable clothing during relaxation training and at-home practice. He or she should remove contact lenses or glasses and should remove or loosen other articles (such as shoes, belts, or jewelry) that may cause discomfort.

During PRT, the therapist's voice should initially have a normal, conversational tone, volume, and pace. As the session proceeds, it should become smoother, quieter, and more monotonous. When giving instructions to tense muscles, the voice should have more tension, volume, and speed than when giving instructions to relax. This discrepancy helps to contrast the sensations of tension and relaxation.

THERAPIST–CLIENT RELATIONSHIP

All successful therapeutic endeavors are based, to some degree, upon a good working relationship between client and therapist in which each understands his or her roles and responsibilities. PRT is certainly no exception. While PRT consists of a clear package of techniques, it should be conducted as part of a broader cooperative learning experience for the client, not as the mere dispensation of a "treatment." Indeed, if the therapist focuses entirely upon the *techniques* of relaxation, at the expense of integrating the methods into an overall approach to helping the client in actively dealing with his or her problems, a "medication mentality" may develop. That is, the client may get the idea that the "relaxation exercises" guided by the therapist will, in some independent and mysterious way, solve the problems that are the focus of concern. This point of view may not only detract from the active practice and utilization of PRT, but may cast the therapist in the role of a remote technician who is simply applying a remedial procedure to a malfunctioning organism. As noted earlier, this problem can be prevented in large measure by placing PRT in its proper perspective during the presentation and discussion of the rationale. When this objective is achieved, and especially when generally good rapport exists between client and therapist, PRT is most likely to lead to a beneficial outcome.

A word should also be said about the ways in which PRT can aid in the development of the therapeutic relationship. Abbreviated PRT is often useful early in treatment as a means of helping a very tense or confused client to calm down enough to organize his or her thoughts or discuss emotionally volatile material. One or two sessions of PRT can provide a pleasant experience as part of what had been anticipated to be a very trying therapy enterprise, and, in addition, can be very impressive to the client. Helping a very tense, emotionally overaroused person to reach an unfamiliar state of deep relaxation rapidly may leave the client feeling more confident in the therapist's ability and more willing to "open up" regarding matters that might otherwise have remained private much longer.

This rapport-building aspect of PRT stems not only from the pleasant experiences that it engenders, but also from the fact that it provides an opportunity for the therapist actively and clearly to communicate his or her interest in, caring for, and sensitivity to the client. These things can be conveyed in the care with which the therapist presents and explains PRT, answers questions about it, and expresses optimism about the client's ability to learn and use it. During training itself, a warm, caring attitude can be obviously reflected in the numerous requests for assurance that each muscle group is deeply relaxed and in instructions designed to reassure the client that he or she has no need to do anything but relax. Finally, postsession discussion of progress and problems usually centers upon encouragement for the client's efforts, but perhaps more important, upon minor points of difficulty that the therapist may have detected but that the client may have thought to be too trivial to warrant attention. Recognition that the therapist is truly "tuned in" to what is going on can be a very impressive and beneficial experience for the client.

ASSESSING PROGRESS

In most cases, the client's self-report is the main source of information about the overall success of a program of PRT. Critical positive indicators in these reports include (1) appropriate frequency and regularity of home practice sessions; (2) decreasing time required to reach deep re-laxation; (3) changes in general tension; (4) utilization of relaxation to deal with specific stressors; and (5) general references to satisfaction with the procedures.

Such reports carry added weight when corroborated by changing in-session signs such as the following:

1. Decreased total time to achieve relaxation during training ses-sions.

2. No need to employ more than two tension–release cycles for any muscle group.

3. Increasing depth of relaxation (as indicated by such features as a slack jaw, splayed foot position, slowed relaxation signals, less vigorous signals).

4. Sleep episodes.

5. Absence of gross motor movement.

6. Apparent total relaxation prior to coverage of all muscle groups.

7. Appearance of drowsiness upon termination of session.

COMBINING MUSCLE GROUPS

If, after approximately three formal training sessions (with regular daily practice at home), assessment indicates that the client has become skillful at achieving deep relaxation using 16 muscle groups, a shorter pro-cedure using only seven muscle groups can be introduced.

The 16 muscle groups can be combined into seven groups as follows:

1. Dominant hand, forearm, and upper arm.
2. Nondominant hand, forearm, and upper arm.
3. All facial muscles.
4. Neck.
5. Chest, shoulders, upper back, and abdomen.
6. Dominant upper leg, calf, and foot.
7. Nondominant upper leg, calf, and foot.

These muscles can be tensed by using combinations of the tensing mechanisms prescribed for the 16 groups, or the therapist can work out some alternate means for achieving optimal tension.

The procedure for relaxation with seven muscle groups is the same as that for 16 muscle groups. If the client does not achieve satisfactory relaxation after a week or two with this shorter procedure (and regular at-home practice), the therapist should determine which combined groups are not becoming relaxed, and should temporarily divide these into their original components before resuming use of the seven groups.

The same type of questioning that follows relaxation with 16 groups should be used after relaxation with seven groups in order to encourage the client to express any concerns or questions.

If all goes well, a high level of proficiency in relaxation with seven muscle groups should be attained after about 2 weeks of practice. However, the therapist should assess the client's skill before moving on to the next abbreviating step—namely, four muscle groups. The transition to four muscle groups should be treated in the same manner as the transition to seven muscle groups. The client should be capable of achieving deep relaxation with seven groups before attempting to use this even shorter procedure.

The seven muscle groups are combined into four as follows:

1. Both arms and both hands.
2. Face and neck.
3. Chest, shoulders, back, and abdomen.
4. Both legs and both feet.

Using this four-group procedure, relaxation should take approximately 10 minutes. As with the seven-group method, questioning should follow each relaxation session. It is to be expected that the client will require some practice to achieve deep relaxation using only four muscle groups.

RELEASING TENSION BY RECALL

When the client is capable of achieving deep relaxation using the four-group procedure, relaxation through recall can be attempted. In this procedure, each of the four muscle groups is focused on individually, as before; however, in using recall, the tension stage is eliminated. The client is asked to achieve relaxation by merely recalling the sensations associated with the release of tension. Mastery of this step is essential to the ultimate goal of relaxation training, which is to enable the client to control excess tension as it occurs in "real-life" situations. Obviously, the client will not always be able to stop and run through even a short relaxation procedure every time tension occurs. The use of recall, along with other steps yet to be discussed, should ultimately enable the client to maintain minimum levels of tension in anxiety-provoking situations.

The procedure for teaching relaxation through recall is as follows:

1. Instruct the client to focus on a muscle group (each of the four muscle groups are to be dealt with individually) and to attend to any tension that may be present in that group.

2. Instruct the client to recall the sensations associated with the release of tension.

3. Using the cue word as before, instruct the client to relax the muscle group.

4. Allow the client to focus on the relaxation process for 30 to 45 seconds while making statements to help the client attend to the feelings in the muscles.

5. Ask the client to signal if the muscle group is completely relaxed.

6. If the client signals that relaxation has been achieved, proceed to the next muscle group. If the client has not achieved relaxation, repeat the procedure, once again instructing the client to identify the remaining tension in the muscle group and to focus on releasing that tension.

Taken together, these procedures might sound like this:

OK, Jill, I would like you to focus all of your attention on the muscles of your arms and hands. And I want you to pay close attention to how those muscles feel and notice any feelings of tightness or tension which might be present in those muscles. OK, now just let those muscles relax, just recalling what it felt like when you let all that tension go. Just let that tension go now and allow the muscles of your arms and hands to become more and more relaxed.

[Continue "patter" for 30–45 seconds.]

OK, if the muscles of your arms and hands feel completely relaxed, I'd like you to signal. . . . OK, fine, just go right on relaxing.

If the client experiences a great deal of difficulty achieving relaxation in any group with the recall procedure, it may be necessary to use a tension–release cycle for that group. However, a tensing strategy should be used only for that group and only in the training session. The other groups should be relaxed using recall alone, and the client should try to use recall for all groups when practicing at home. In most cases, relaxation through recall will improve with regular practice.

Termination of the session and questioning is the same for the recall procedures as they have been for previous sessions.

RECALL WITH COUNTING

A "counting down" can be introduced at the end of a recall session, once the recall procedure is a well-established method of achieving relaxation. It should be presented to the client as a simple procedure that will promote even deeper muscle relaxation.

To incorporate counting into the training session, instruct the client to continue relaxing and to allow the relaxation to become deeper with each number as the therapist counts from 1 to 10. The counting should be timed to coincide with the client's exhalations. The therapist should provide some "patter" about the sensations of relaxation between counts. For example, after a signal of complete relaxation as been received, the therapist might say:

OK, as you go right on relaxing, I am going to count slowly from 1 to 10. As I count, I would like you to allow all the muscles in your body to become even more deeply and completely relaxed on each count. Just focus on your muscles as they relax more and more on each count. OK, 1 . . . 2. Let your arms and hands relax even more. 3 . . . 4, focusing on the muscles of the neck and face as they relax. 5 . . . 6, allowing the muscles of the chest, shoulders, back, and abdomen to become even more relaxed. 7 . . . 8, let the muscles in your legs and feet relax more and more. 9 . . . 10, relaxing more and more all through your body.

If the client likes this procedure, he or she can be instructed to sub-vocalize a 1–10 count after relaxation by recall when practicing at home.

COUNTING ALONE

When the client has developed a strong association between counting and relaxation, counting can be used alone to achieve relaxation, both in the consulting room and at home. The counting-alone procedure entails the same basic methods just described, except that the steps for relaxation by recall are eliminated. The therapist merely counts from 1 to 10, timing the counts with the client's exhalations, while presenting brief relaxation "patter" between counts.

Once the counting is finished, the client should be asked to signal if any tension remains. If so, the remaining tension should be identified and released through recall or, in rare cases, through a tension–release cycle.

At this point, the client possesses well-developed skills at relaxation.

Practice may be decreased to once a day, but the client should be encouraged to continue practicing regularly to maintain proficiency.

TIMETABLE

The following timetable for progress in an abbreviated relaxation training program illustrates an ideal case (Bernstein & Borkovec, 1973). Many clients will follow this ideal schedule, but it need not be strictly maintained. Indeed, the pace of progress must be adjusted (especially downward) for clients who are having various kinds of problems in mastering the procedures. There is a corresponding tendency to want to speed things up for clients who are having no trouble, but, in the interest of assuring adequate learning (and with the exception of the recall-with-counting procedure), each step should be employed by the therapist in at least two formal training sessions. The therapist should never proceed to a more advanced step until he or she is satisfied that the one being used is mastered by the client.

Procedure	Session
16 muscle groups, tension–release	1, 2, 3
7 muscle groups, tension–release	4, 5
4 muscle groups, tension–release	6, 7
4 muscle groups, recall	8
4 muscle groups, recall and counting	9
Counting	10

POTENTIAL PROBLEMS

Many problems may appear in the course of relaxation training. In some cases, the therapist may have to find his or her own unique solutions to them. However, some of the more common problems and some workable solutions are given below.

Muscle Cramps

As mentioned previously, cramping may occur in some muscle groups. If this happens, the client should move the affected muscles to alleviate the cramping, while allowing the rest of the body to remain as relaxed as possible. For areas of the body in which the client experiences frequent cramping, alternate tension means should be employed, along with shorter tension periods (e.g., 3–5 seconds). Once the cramp is relieved, the therapist should provide indirect suggestions to help the client regain the previous level of relaxation.

Movement

Frequent gross motor movement during a session may indicate that the client is not relaxing. The client should be reminded not to move any more than is necessary to remain comfortable and not to move any parts of the body that have already been relaxed. The therapist may wish to rephrase the relaxation instructions and present them again. Movement may also represent the presence of a serious problem relating to the client's acceptance of the method being used. If so, this issue should be discussed before proceeding.

Laughter

The client may laugh during relaxation, especially in the first session. This should be ignored unless there is a possibility that the therapist is eliciting the laughter. If the therapist feels this is possible, it should be discussed with the client.

Talking

Talking by the client should be ignored unless the client is reporting a serious problem. It may be necessary to repeat the instructions not to talk.

Muscle Spasms

Clients sometimes experience involuntary muscle spasms during relaxation. If the client seems to be concerned, the therapist should assure the client that such spasms are common, that they indicate the depth of relaxation, and that the client should not try to control them.

Anxiety-Producing Thoughts

If the client reports anxiety-producing thoughts during training, the therapist should first try repeating the instructions to focus only on his or her voice and the sensations experienced in the muscles. The therapist might also increase the amount of "patter" during relaxation; this helps distract the client from unpleasant thoughts. Or the therapist and the client together may decide upon some pleasant imagery that the client can focus on during the session. This imagery can be incorporated in the relaxation "patter."

Sexual Arousal

Especially when the client and therapist are of opposite sexes, the PRT setting and procedure (a dimly lit room, soft voice, pleasant feelings) can have sexual overtones for some clients. The presence of sexual thoughts and consequent arousal can, in most cases, be dealt with routinely as another form of intrusive thinking that may interfere with the relaxation process. The therapist should recognize and accept the problem, while assuring the client that it is unlikely to remain once the focus of attention is fully upon relaxation in the muscles. Naturally, if the problem persists and more substantive interpersonal issues appear to be involved, a more extended discussion outside the context of PRT may be required.

Sleep

Some clients may fall asleep during relaxation. The therapist can determine whether the client is sleeping by first asking the client to signal if relaxed, and then, if no signal is made, by asking the client to signal if not relaxed. Obviously, the client, if awake, would signal after one of these requests. To wake the client, the therapist should gradually increase voice volume, repeating the request for a signal, until the client wakes. The therapist should be careful not to startle the client by making sudden, loud statements.

Coughing and Sneezing

A client's coughing or sneezing may occasionally interrupt the relaxation. Infrequent coughing or sneezing will not usually interfere with the procedure, but, if the client has a cold or other ailment and coughing or sneezing is frequent, the relaxation should probably be postponed. A smoker's cough can be very disruptive to a relaxation session. Since deep breathing can trigger coughing for heavy smokers, the client can be asked to take only shallow breaths during tension, or, alternately, to maintain normal breathing during tension and relaxation.

A CASE EXAMPLE

As noted throughout this chapter, abbreviated PRT can be used alone or in combination with other treatment methods to deal with a broad range of human problems. For purposes of clarity, we have chosen a case example that illustrates the way in which PRT can work as the primary method of intervention in a case where the presenting problems are rather severe but the time available for treatment is artificially short. Had circumstances allowed, a more elaborate, multidimensional treatment program would probably have been preferable, but these same circumstances created a formidable test of the value of abbreviated PRT in isolation.

The client in this case was Mr. N, a professional man in his 50s. He had a wife, two children, and a very "high-pressure" job, which he felt was in large measure responsible for his psychological and physical problems. At the first session, Mr. N described himself as suffering from "chronic tension." He was well aware of the fact that he was "high-strung," irritable, aggressive, and generally difficult to get along with. He was also in considerable pain most of the time as the result of a severe stomach ulcer, which his physician had attributed to stress. For several years, Mr. N had been taking antacids and other prescribed ulcer medication. He also had a supply of prescription tranquilizers, which he took several times each day to combat his chronically high level of general tension.

Mr. N told the therapist that he was planning to move to the East Coast in less than 2 months in order to start a new and even more demanding job. He sought help at this time because he was afraid that the combined stress of the relocation and the new position might be "too much" for him. There was no question of his reassessing the decision to move, so the therapist was faced with the choice of either rejecting the case or seeking to help the client develop some tension reduction skills—namely, through abbreviated PRT.

The latter course was chosen, but only on the condition that the client would agree to a consultation between the therapist and Mr. N's physician about discontinuing the tranquilizer medication. This was more than acceptable to the client and, as it turned out, a long-term goal of the physician, since neither was happy with the idea of an open-ended chemical approach to the problem of tension. (We should add that the therapist was just as unhappy with a narrow and time-limited approach to psychological treatment, but by this time, that issue had been resolved.) The primary purpose in getting the tranquilizing drugs out of the picture was to increase the probability (1) that any relaxation effects observed were a function of PRT; (2) that the client could learn to experience sensations of relaxation fully without interfering drug effects; and (3) that the skills acquired during PRT would not have to transfer to a nondrugged state, with possible loss of potency.

Only five training sessions could be scheduled in the time available before the client's departure, so the sequence of events was compressed somewhat. The therapist's goal was merely to teach the client basic relaxation skills and to bring him to a level of competency with them that might serve to combat general tension. Anything more, such as differential or cue-controlled relaxation (see Bernstein & Borkovec, 1973), was clearly unrealistic under the circumstances. Fortunately, the training sessions went very smoothly. The client was, as one might expect, highly motivated and cooperative. He practiced the procedures faithfully between sessions and, at the fifth session, was able to achieve deep relaxation through the recall method.

Somewhat to the therapist's surprise, but certainly to his delight, the client reported a number of immediate and significant benefits that he attributed to his newly acquired capability for relaxation. The client claimed to be far less generally tense and irritable than before, and he stated that he did not miss his tranquilizers (to our knowledge, he has never resumed their use). In addition, Mr. N said that he was finding it easier to deal with stressful events at work and at home by using relaxation "breaks" at the office and at the end of each day. The reduction in general and specific tension was also accompanied by reports of greatly reduced gastric discomfort. Some combination of increased physical comfort and decreased tension (and, perhaps, the prospect of a job change) created a noticeable improvement in Mr. N's behavior in relation to his family. Specifically, he began to appear less irritable, more understanding and tolerant, and, in general, easier to live with. It seems reasonable to suppose that the changes just described, while not brought about directly by PRT alone, were greatly facilitated by it.

COMMENTS AND REFLECTIONS

After two decades of development, clinical use, and experimental evaluation, abbreviated PRT remains a major component of social learning approaches to behavior change. It is easy to see why this should be the case. The methods involved are relatively simple, straightforward, and easily adapted for use in isolation or along with more elaborate intervention packages of various kinds. Further, clients usually enjoy learning and practicing the procedures and seem to make good use of the skills that evolve.

At the same time, the clinicians and researchers who use and investigate PRT have become more and more sophisticated about it. For one thing, there is far less defensiveness about the method. It is now seen not as a semi-magical method that "makes desensitization work," but as one of several related methods through which autonomic overarousal and maladaptive subjective states can be combated. Accordingly, there is now less emphasis on what is "special" about PRT and more emphasis on how it relates to other relaxation-inducing methods (such as yoga or biofeedback) and what common physiological and cognitive mechanisms might account for all of them (see Tarler-Benlolo, 1978). There also appears to be a less rigid adherence to procedural orthodoxy in PRT. Whereas at one time only certain specific relaxation methods were seen as clinically useful, there is a broadening awareness that a single set of procedures, no matter how carefully developed and presented, may not meet the needs (or may "overtreat" the problems) of all clients. Thus, while "live," client-controlled relaxation methods may be desirable in general (e.g., Borkovec & Sides, 1979), there may be clients and circumstances for which less elaborate procedures may be useful as well (see King, 1980). For example, having the client focus his or her attention during PRT on the physiological sensations of tension and relaxation may be important only for clients reporting certain kinds of problems and might actually decrease the benefits of training in some cases (e.g., Borkovec & Hennings, 1978).

This provides but one illustration of the way in which clinicians and researchers are beginning to turn their attention to individual differences in clients and their problems in the selection of PRT and variations thereof. As another example, it has been suggested that some anxiety or "tension" problems may involve a strong physiological component, while others may incorporate a significant cognitive component, and still others may include both. Relaxation may be more useful in some cases than in others (e.g., Davidson & Schwartz, 1976).

Finally, it should be pointed out that abbreviated PRT, in whatever client-specific form it may be administered, has enjoyed an expansion of applications—not only in terms of the target problems for which it is used, but in the way it is used. Originally suggested as a relatively passive *state* that is incompatible with anxiety, PRT has also been conceptualized during the 1970s as an active coping skill (e.g., Goldfried & Trier, 1974) that the client can bring to bear in handling stressful situations. As before, it is seen as potentially useful alone (e.g., as in cue-controlled relaxation) or as an adjunct to the development and use of more elaborate cognitive coping skills (King, 1980).

As illustrated by the examples in this section, the flexibility and adaptability that are inherent in abbreviated PRT represent two of its most attractive characteristics. These features, when combined with PRT's convenience, clinical utility, and apparent benefits suggest that ever-expanding versions and applications of the original Jacobson and Wolpe methods will be an important part of social learning approaches to human problems for many years to come.

REFERENCES

Bernstein, D. A., & Borkovec, T. D. *Progressive relaxation training.* Champaign, Ill.: Research Press, 1973.

Borkovec, T. D., & Hennings, B. L. The role of physiological attention-focusing in the relaxation treatment of sleep disturbance, general tension, and specific stress reaction. *Behaviour Research and Therapy,* 1978, *16,* 7–19.

Borkovec, T. D., & Sides, J. K. Critical procedural variables related to the physiological effects of progressive relaxation: A review. *Behaviour Research and Therapy,* 1979, *17,* 119–125.

Cautela, J. R., & Groden, J. *Relaxation: A comprehensive manual for adults, children, and children with special needs.* Champaign, Ill.: Research Press, 1978.

Davidson, R. J., & Schwartz, G. E. The psychobiology of relaxation and related states: A multi-process theory. In D. I. Mostofsky (Ed.), *Behavior control and modification of physiological activity.* Englewood Cliffs, N.J.: Prentice-Hall, 1976.

Davison, G. C. Anxiety under total curarization: Implications for the role of muscular relaxation in the desensitization of neurotic fears. *Journal of Nervous and Mental Disease,* 1966, *143,* 443–448.

Goldfried, M. R., & Trier, C. S. Effectiveness of relaxation as an active coping skill. *Journal of Abnormal Psychology,* 1974, *83,* 348–355.

Greenwood, M. M., & Benson, H. The efficacy of progressive relaxation in systematic desensitization and a proposal for an alternative competitive response—the relaxation response. *Behaviour Research and Therapy,* 1977, *15,* 337–343.

King, N. J. Abbreviated progressive relaxation. In M. Hersen, R. M. Eisler, & P. M. Miller (Eds.), *Progress in behavior modification.* New York: Academic Press, 1980.

Paul, G., & Bernstein, D. A. *Anxiety and clinical problems: Treatment by systematic desensitization and related techniques.* New York: General Learning Press, 1973.

Tarler-Benlolo, L. The role of relaxation in biofeedback training: A critical review of the literature. *Psychological Bulletin,* 1978, *85,* 727–755.

Wolpe, J. *Psychotherapy by reciprocal inhibition.* Stanford, Calif.: Stanford University Press, 1958.

4 YOGIC THERAPY

CHANDRA PATEL

HISTORY OF THE METHOD

There has been a gradual shift in the types of health problems facing medical practitioners over the last few decades. With the development of immunization procedures, improved sanitation, and highly effective chemotherapy, a large number of serious infectious diseases have been controlled. On the other hand, problems such as tension headache, migraine, backache, irritability, difficulty in falling asleep, phobia, nerve rash, fatigue, constipation, colitis, hyperacidity, peptic ulcer, coryza, minor allergic problems, chronic bronchitis and other smoking-related respiratory disorders, uncontrolled eating and obesity, alcoholism, hypertension, palpitation, coronary heart disease, enuresis, and sexual problems are commonly presented to all of us who are involved in health care.

In a large number of these behavior- and stress-related disorders, handing out prescriptions is either inappropriate or positively harmful, and yet we continue to prescribe tranquilizers, hypnotics, vitamins, tonics, appetite suppressants, and pain killers for want of better alternatives. The most commonly prescribed group of drugs, the benzodiazepines, produce such tolerance after a few months that they become ineffective except as placebos. The placebo response in most trials of new drugs is 40% or more, which makes us wonder whether it is really necessary to prescribe so many potentially harmful drugs. Iatrogenic conditions are supposed to be one of the commonest problems causing misery and hospital admissions. The patients often seek diagnostic labels or explanations of their symptoms, rather than pain killers or tranquilizers, but because none are available, we prescribe medication as if to hide our ignorance.

On the one hand, there are men and women doing jobs that are not fulfilling or at worst soul-destroying and who need a respectable label of disease to make their absenteeism legitimate. On the other hand, there are men (and, increasingly, women) who work themselves sick because

70

they constantly have to prove their worth to themselves, their companies, or their families. They have to do most things themselves because they are unable to delegate work to their subordinates or cannot tolerate other people's imperfections. They are the products of a materialistic, competitive society that nurtures overexpectation and looks down on the failure to achieve. Then there are the pressures of social disintegration, with the disappearance of the extended family and now the fragmentation of even the nuclear family; family arguments, broken homes, divorces, divided children—multiple-marriage complexes, a newly permissive society, and increased pressure to comply with changing patterns of life are all creating further increases in mental and emotional problems.

People often comfort themselves by indulging in excessive eating, cigarette smoking, alcohol consumption, and prescribed or unprescribed drug taking, with consequent obesity-, tobacco- and alcohol-related diseases, such as arthritis, hypertension, maturity-onset diabetes, varicose veins, chronic bronchitis, lung cancer, coronary heart disease, cirrhosis of the liver, accidents, and drug addiction. When a crisis comes in the form of a heart attack or stroke, a large number of the victims die (often without immediate medical help), while the personal physician is left to cope with the bereaved families or the patients who have survived the attack but are left with considerable physical, psychological, and economic handicaps. It does not require special wisdom to realize that prevention is the only effective answer, that technology is overrated, and that many drugs are totally inadequate if not actually harmful.

However, simply advising people to stop smoking, lose weight, reduce alcohol intake, increase exercise, stop worrying, take things easy, be tolerant of other people, and forget about the things that upset them is not enough. We cannot bully people into healthy behavior. Even when they understand the adverse consequences of unhealthy behavior, they are often unable to change it. Therefore, simple motivation to lose weight or stop smoking is not enough; the patients need more positive help in learning new healthy behaviors. Despite these difficulties, we continue to berate our clients for noncompliance. Such an autocratic approach, requiring complete obedience on the part of the patients, is not in tune with present-day thinking. The maladaptive behaviors are often deeply ingrained habits, and they occur almost automatically, without the person's being aware of them at the time of action. Clients not only need to become aware of their unhealthy behaviors, but also need to create environments that will be more conducive to new healthy behaviors.

The treatment of hypertension with drugs had proved itself of value in moderately severe hypertension, in preventing strokes, heart failure, and uremia, but not myocardial infarction until recently (Breckenridge, Dollery, & Parry, 1970; Veterans Administration Cooperative Study Group on Antihypertensive Agents, 1967, 1970, 1972). The level at which hypertension should be treated is getting lower and lower (Hypertension Detection and Follow-Up Program Cooperative Group, 1979; Management Committee, 1980). It is possible that before long we may have to initiate treatment when the diastolic blood pressure is 90 mm Hg or more. This means starting treatment in a third of the population in middle age and continuing it for the rest of their lives, and we do not yet know what the long-term safety record of this drug treatment will be; the serious side effects of practolol and other drugs previously used must also be considered. Furthermore, we do not know if lifelong drug treatment will be accepted by patients with mild hypertension, especially when compliance in patients with moderately severe hypertension, where the benefits are unquestionable, has been so poor.

It is clear that the time is ripe for developing methods in which we enlist the full participation of patients and make them share in the responsibility of looking after their own health. The methods should be simple, should be pleasant or at least free from side effects, should be effective in alleviating symptoms, should enhance a sense of well-being, should prevent organic damage or complications, and should be relatively inexpensive. In this chapter, the ways in which a specific yogic therapy can play a part in fulfilling these functions are discussed.

"Yoga," meaning union or oneness with life, is part of an ancient Indian culture. It is a personal self-help system of health care and spiritual development. It was developed by Indian wise men and religious leaders (who are called saints in the literature) with the conviction that the cultivation of a healthy mind is necessary for a healthy body. It was not primarily developed to cure the sick, but to awaken spiritual awareness and develop personality integration in healthy people. To that extent, it is preventive rather than curative. It is difficult to date its origin, but it has probably been practiced for thousands of years. Yoga postures have been found engraved on seals dating from 3000 B.C. A distinguished yogi, Patanjali, wrote one of the major textbooks on the subject, which is still considered a classic today (see Johnston, 1970). He described yoga as a means of "controlling the waves of mind." Its meditational discipline is said to help individuals achieve their utmost potential. Paul Brunton (1970), an Englishman who traveled extensively in India to study meditation and yogic mysticism, has stated, "It can bring our bodies nearer the healthy condition which Nature intended them to possess: It can bestow one of modern civilisation's most urgent needs—a flawless serenity of mind" (p. 12).

Through a precise series of postures known as "asanas," people can learn an amazing amount of control over the individual muscles and body movements, and can thus gain suppleness and often relief from musculo-skeletal symptoms. This branch of yoga, called "hatha yoga," is well known in the West. There are other branches, however, that are less well known. The "mantra" or "raja yoga" is concerned with developing the power of the mind. The "gnani yoga" describes intellectual and scientific ways of finding the answers to the mystery of life and the universe. The "karma yoga" encompasses a kind of service in action and encourages services to others. The "bhakti yoga" says that a person can become one with life through devotion and love. The "layakriya yoga" uses the path of sexual relationship to achieve fulfillment. Each branch is supposed to be only one path toward the ultimate aim of achieving personal growth and spiritual development.

This chapter describes the yogic method of meditation as a basis of a behavioral method of stress management. Many of the religious and philosophical connotations have been omitted, and emphasis has been given to scientific principles (although, for completeness, some of the relevant and important religious and philosophical points are discussed).

THEORETICAL UNDERPINNINGS

Before we can appreciate how yogic therapy can be useful in behavior- or stress-related disorders, we need to understand stress and how it affects the body and causes derangement of physiological functions. Throughout this chapter, essential hypertension is used predominantly to illustrate stress-related disorders, as it is the condition I have studied most systematically.

More than 40 years ago, Selye (see Selye, 1956) introduced the concept of "stress" and emphasized that innumerable agents make intense demands on the adaptability of the organism and can cause nonspecific effects—for example, the manifestations of the alarm reaction, with nervous arousal and the discharge of adrenocorticotrophin (ACTH), corticoids, and catecholamines. If the demands are chronic or sustained in nature, it can exhaust the individual to the limits of his or her ability. Stress is difficult to define, because it depends upon how the individual perceives

an environmental situation, how the brain evaluates the information perceived, and, finally, how the body reacts to it. Genetic factors, early
experience, parental influence, and personal and societal expectations all
contribute to the ultimate shaping of the behavior. Stress thus depends
upon how well a person is fitted to cope with his or her environment.
If the person is deficient in coping skills, if the environmental demands
are severe or sustained, or if the physiological responses are acute and
prolonged, the resultant imbalance can lead to strains on the body. To
put it simply, the experience of stress is common to us all, but what varies
is the way in which different individuals react to it and how these reactions are translated into disease or ill health.

Stress is also difficult to measure until it has caused the full manifestations of a disease or measurable indicators of risk (risk factors). A stage is,
therefore, reached wherein it becomes either impossible or only partially
possible to reverse the disease process. By and large, the individual responds to stress by a generalized increase in sympathetic activity, but consistently shows maximal response in only one or two physiological functions, whatever the stress (Engel & Bickford, 1961; Lacey & Lacey, 1958,
1962). It has also been shown that hypertensive or prehypertensive subjects show a greater rise in blood pressure compared with normotensives
in a variety of stressful situations (Brod, Fencl, Hejl, & Zirka, 1959; Innes, Miller, & Valentine, 1959; Schachter, 1957; Shapiro, 1961; Wolf &
Wolff, 1951).

It has generally been accepted that blood pressure rises temporarily
in any individual when a basic response to stress—the defense-alarm reaction or the fight-or-flight response (Cannon, 1941)—is mobilized,
although its relationship to the development of permanent hypertension
is disputed. There is, however, a great deal of evidence suggesting that
frequent rises in blood pressure in a genetically susceptible individual can
lead to resetting of the baroreceptors at a higher level (Kezdi, 1953; Korner, 1971; Kubicek, Kottke, Laker, & Visscher, 1953; McCubbin, Green,
& Page, 1958; Sleight, 1975) and can also lead to structural hypertrophy
of the resistance vessels (Folkow, Hällback, Lundgren, Sivertsson, &
Weiss, 1973; Folkow & Rubinstein, 1966). The research also suggests that
these factors could maintain or perpetuate high blood pressure even in
the absence of initiating factors.

Based on the observations above, I have suggested a hypothetical
pathophysiological model for essential hypertension (Patel, 1976a, 1977).
According to this, blood pressure rises whenever a hypothalamic fight-or-
flight response is mobilized. It is raised either directly through the sympa-

thetic effectors in the heart and blood vessels, or indirectly through the release of various hormones such as catecholamine, the renin–angiotensin–aldosterone system, or the ACTH–cortisol–sodium retention loop. The other signs of this response are erratic breathing, increased muscle tension, increased blood coagulability, increased sweating, mobilization of glucose from the liver, and other metabolic and nervous effects.

If repeated mobilization of this central hypothalamic response could lead to permanent hypertension, probably through baroreceptor and structural vascular alterations, then it is possible that repeated mobilization of an opposing response such as the relaxation response could reduce the intensity of the hypothalamic response and eventually lead to at least partial reversal of one or more of the maintaining factors, and thus to a long-term reduction in blood pressure. This does not really seem a novel idea when one considers the fact that most antihypertensive drugs do act by interfering with the sympathetic nervous system activity at one level or another or by counteracting the effect of other stress-related hormones in some way.

A scheme that incorporates principles of yoga for controlling the intensity of the hypothalamic response consists of the following five steps:

1. The patient is told that the intensity of his or her response depends upon his or her mental evaluation of a particular situation. Audiovisual methods are used to demonstrate appropriate and inappropriate responses in everyday life, as well as realistic and unrealistic fears and aggression. In other words, the patient is made more and more aware of inappropriate responses and is given the know-how to correct them.

2. The patient is taught a simple breathing exercise. Through the use of a simple, rhythmic diaphragmatic breathing exercise, a certain amount of physical and mental calmness can be induced. The exercise can be performed anywhere and in any position without anybody noticing it.

3. The patient is then taught a systematic deep-muscle relaxation. The fact that deep-muscle relaxation reduces the intensity of the hypothalamic response is evident from animal experiments. For example, increase in proprioception through passive movements increases the intensity and degree of rise in blood pressure, while a decrease in proprioception through curarization decreases the intensity and degree of rise in blood pressure when the hypothalamus is electrically stimulated (Gellhorn, 1950, 1964; Hess, 1957; Hodes, 1962). It is thought that the intensity of the response is directly proportional to sensory input to the brain. Perhaps we live in a world today with far too much sensory stimulation, leading to an increased incidence of hypertension. It is assumed that reduction

in sensory input through deep-muscle relaxation, eye closure, and other yogic attitudes can reduce the sympathetic responsiveness of the hypothalamus and eventually lower blood pressure.

4. After a few sessions of breathing exercise and deep-muscle relaxation, a type of mental relaxation is introduced in the form of passive concentration on a visual image and eventually meditation. Whether any of the patients reaches a state of psychological peak experience or the ecstasy of a meditative state is doubtful, but whatever mental calm a patient can get is useful. The regular practice of meditation disciplines the mind to concentrate on a subject or idea. The practical advantages of meditation include gaining problem-solving skills, reducing anxiety as one shuts out irrelevant ideas from the thoughts, and improving the quality of work. Another advantage, which at first may seem paradoxical, is that it prevents sleep. Relaxation is very conducive to sleep through a well-explained neural mechanism (Magoun, 1963). The amount of mental activity introduced by meditation keeps the person mentally alert and yet physically relaxed. In meditation the electroencephalographic (EEG) pattern shows synchronized high-amplitude slow waves *not* passing into the sleep pattern (Wallace & Benson, 1972). Sleep in itself is useful, but the aim of this therapy is to teach people to manage their stress while awake, and this is the reason why attempts are made to avoid having patients fall asleep.

5. The fifth point in the plan is "deconditioning," or integrating the relaxation response into daily activities. It is also known as "meditation in action." It would be useful to know what situations in an individual's life are most productive of hypertension. Then one could desensitize that individual against those situations. In practice, it is not possible to identify these situations for most hypertensive patients. However, we know that the environments of industrialized, urbanized society are particularly important in producing hypertension. We can, therefore, assume that desensitization against certain situations of modern civilization may be beneficial. A person driving a car is asked to take one deep breath and relax at each red traffic light or intersection. The person does the same before answering the telephone or speaking in public, during examinations or interviews, or while waiting for a bus or in a dentist's office. The list is exhaustive and can be made up by an individual to suit his or her requirements. A tiny colored paper disc may be affixed to the person's wrist watch dial, so that every time he or she looks at the watch, it becomes a reminder to relax; we know that time pressure is considered to be one of the important risk factors for coronary heart disease (Friedman & Rosenman, 1974).

Meditation in action can also be seen when a meditator is completely absorbed in whatever he or she is doing at that point—for example, when an artist is painting, a sculptor is sculpting, a dancer is dancing, or a jogger is jogging, with his or her mind so concentrated on the action that he or she becomes completely engrossed. This may be a way of releasing or channeling emotional energy into more productive and creative directions. Those practicing meditation do not necessarily have to pursue higher arts or special leisure-time activities; yogic tradition tells us that people can practice meditation in action during their everyday work, provided they can learn to concentrate on it with body and mind.

In teaching this generalized relaxation response, I also use biofeedback instruments. The most commonly used is the one measuring galvanic skin response (GSR) with sound signals. It is important to realize that the use of biofeedback here is for aiding the relaxation response only, and is therefore not essential to learning. However, it does facilitate learning and serves to give some objective measure of relaxation. The most important objective measure is that of blood pressure; again feedback information of its level to the patient also facilitates learning.

Although hypertension is used here as a model to demonstrate the theoretical reasoning for using a relaxation regimen based on yogic principles, there is no reason why other disease models cannot be used to demonstrate the usefulness of the therapy in many other behavior- or stress-related disorders.

ASSESSMENT

THE PROBLEMS WITH WHICH THE THERAPY IS EFFECTIVE

Yogic methods, including relaxation postures and various types of meditation—including the much-publicized transcendental meditation (TM) and allied techniques, like the relaxation response described by Benson (1977)—have been found to be beneficial in preventing or alleviating several health problems. I am in agreement with Benson that elements common to these various practices include a quiet environment, decreased muscle tension, a passive attitude, and a repetitive mental device. To these I might add another essential ingredient: regular practice. If differences exist between different therapies—and, judging from different results obtained in different studies, differences indeed seem to exist—then they are more likely to be quantitative than qualitative.

Yogic techniques have most commonly been evaluated in essential

hypertension, and some of the studies suggest real benefits (Benson, Rosner, Marzetta, & Klemchuk, 1974; Benson & Wallace, 1972a; Datey, Deshmukh, Dalvi, & Vineker, 1969; Patel, 1973, 1975a; Patel & North, 1975;
Peters, Benson, & Peters, 1977; Stone & De Leo, 1976), although the long-
est follow-up has only been 1 year (Patel, 1975a). Zamarra, Besseghini, and
Wittenberg (1977) studied 16 patients with angina and found substantial
improvement in exercise tolerance. Benson, Alexander, and Feldman
(1975) showed decreased premature ventricular contractions (PVCs) in
eight out of 11 patients with established ischemic heart disease who practiced the relaxation response. However, reduction was significant during sleep only. The clinical significance of this is not yet known. Lown
and Verrier (1976) reported on the usefulness of regular meditation in conjunction with antiarrhythmic drugs in a man who had frequent attacks
of ventricular arrhythmia, including ventricular fibrillation when psychologically provoked.

Yogic therapy has also been found to be a useful adjunct in the treatment of bronchial asthma (Honsberger & Wilson, 1973a, 1973b; Wilson,
Honsberger, Chiu, & Novey, 1975) with significant reduction in airway
resistance as well as subjective improvement. Other areas in which yogic
meditation techniques have shown encouraging results are insomnia (Miskiman, 1977a, 1977b; Woolfolk, Carr-Kaffashan, McNulty, & Lehrer,
1976); stuttering (McIntyre, Silverman, & Trotter, 1974); headaches (Benson, Klemchuk, & Graham, 1974); drug abuse, including heroin, alcoholism, and cigarette smoking (Benson, 1969; Benson & Wallace, 1972b;
Patel & Carruthers, 1977; Shafii, Lavely, & Jaffe, 1974, 1975); anxiety state
(Nidich, Seeman, & Seibert, 1977); and the management of stress (Carrington, Collings, Benson, Robinson, Wood, Lehrer, Woolfolk, & Cole, 1980;
Patel, 1975b).

LIMITATIONS AND CONTRAINDICATIONS

The yogic method is not obviously applicable to all hypertensive patients. Some may find the time commitment, personal responsibility, and
religious or mystical aspects of yogic meditation unacceptable. The last
objection is, however, rare when the religious aspect is omitted and yoga
is presented as a relaxation therapy incorporating scientific principles of
meditation only. For some patients, despite adherence to instructions, the
therapy will be inadequate or ineffective. However, other psychological
benefits may make its practice a worthwhile pursuit, together with appro-

priate pharmacological measures. Some hypertensive patients respond dramatically, and they usually turn out to be those who practice it regularly and who report successful achievement of subjective relaxation (Seer & Raeburn, 1980). Studies that can predict which types of patients are most likely to succeed are badly needed.

Relaxation–meditation techniques, if practiced as prescribed, are quite safe for most people. However, some cases of psychosis have been reported when meditation is practiced for very extensive periods (which is specifically contraindicated for most people), similar to those cases developing from prolonged sensory deprivation (Benson, Beary, & Carol, 1974). Wolpe (1958), from his vast experience with relaxation therapy, reported that some patients became depressed or experienced unpleasant thoughts. The therapy is, therefore, contraindicated in depressive or psychotic patients. Some patients with a past history of injury may complain of pain at various sites (Luthe, 1969), but this in itself is not an indication that such patients should withdraw from the therapy.

Although the emphasis is on self-help, the patient can only be expected to share in the responsibility with his or her personal clinician. Hypertensive patients are asymptomatic until complications, which are often catastrophic, occur. Thus there is a need for constant supervision and assessment by medically qualified personnel. It must, therefore, be understood by all patients and those who care for them that patients who are referred to yoga or meditation centers for training must be simultaneously under continuing medical care. Better still would be for the clinicians to learn these techniques. Even if the patients or other health care personnel have learned to measure blood pressure, this in itself is not sufficient, and periodic checks for other signs and symptoms of organic dysfunction are vital.

THE METHOD

INTRODUCING THE METHOD TO THE CLIENT

A brief explanation of the what, the why, and the how of yogic meditation is given to each client before he or she starts practicing it. It is not necessary to tell everything to every patient, but it is necessary for an inquiring client to know about yoga in some depth. How much one tells to a particular client depends upon the therapist's judgment and knowledge of the client's educational, literary, and spiritual background and of his or her curiosity about esoteric techniques. A number of meditational techniques are described here, and, again, not all of them should be introduced at the same time.

Meditation and contemplation have been a part of the practice of most religions in both East and West. However, with the decline in religious observance in recent years and the increasing secularization of society, a vacuum has been left. Religious practices not only provided the individual with periods of quiet in a peaceful environment and a great deal of emotional support from community members and religious leaders, but also with the faith and belief that "someone is watching over me and will take care of me." In modern times, the emphasis of society has shifted more toward material, social, and academic achievements, but the greater competitiveness and faster pace of life deprive the individual of the ability to adapt to stress. The practice of yogic meditation may be one way to fill the vacuum left by the decline of religious observance without requiring submission to the rituals and beliefs of a particular religion. By providing an antidote to daily stress, yoga may help individuals to preserve health and function more effectively. The effects of yoga have been studied clinically, and the scientific rationale for incorporating the wisdom that has been developed through centuries of practice and teaching of yoga remains empirical.

Just as the body needs rest after a hard day's work, the mind needs rest, too, but many people do not know how to get that rest. If a person does not get sleep for two nights running, how tired that person feels! So it is understandable that frequent frustrations, aggravations, and disappointments, which are so common in daily life, exhaust people mentally and prevent them from getting the best out of their mental capacity. In fact, brain researchers say that most people are using only 10–15% of their potential mental capacities. If people want to exploit more of their mental capacities to become more happy and more fulfilled, then their lives must include a balance of mental exercise, mental rest, and relaxation. There are reasons to believe that a practice that incorporates principles of meditation will restore this balance and allow the mind to recuperate and regenerate. The only thing that is surprising is that wise men over 2000 years ago had thoughts of such needs and developed a program with such profound effects.

Just as an arrow pulled back on a bow gets more force and momentum, the mind pulled back during the practice of meditation gathers more mental energy and creativeness. But how does an individual pull back his or her mind? Some great poets, writers, and saints stumble on the technique almost by accident, as it were, and these gifted people can go in and out of a meditative state very quickly. It has been recorded, for example, that the great poet William Wordsworth used to look at the fire while sitting in an armchair to reach this state of creativeness. Another poet, Alfred Lord Tennyson, just used to repeat his own name! Enid Blyton, the author of many children's books, simply used to close her eyes and see all the characters dramatizing each story in her mind's eye. However, most of us have to proceed step by step. According to yogic meditation, the average individual has to go through eight steps before he or she can reach a condition that is described as a state of fulfillment, a state of illumination. The eight steps in yogic meditation are (1) "yama"; (2) "niyama"; (3) "asanas," or physical postures; (4) "pranayama," or breath control; (5) "pratyahara," or sensory withdrawal; (6) "dharna," or mental concentration; (7) "dhyana," or contemplation; and, finally, (8) "samadhi," or the meditative state.

The first two steps, yama and niyama, are dos and don'ts. They simply advise people to conduct their everyday lives in a moral and peaceful manner; they consist of a moral code comparable to the Ten Commandments. An individual does not become wise just by listening to a sermon or by reading a book without making real efforts. If people want their friends and families to be useful and kind, then they must be useful and kind themselves; if they want their homes to be cheerful and beautiful, then they must be cheerful in them and bring beautiful things into them. A person who cultivates the habit of being kind, compassionate, loving, and forgiving will be rewarded by similar surroundings. The most important ingredient of success is faith. In faith a person believes, not only with the brain but with the soul and body. If individuals submit themselves fully to the will of nature, then all-powerful nature begins to work for them. In order for people to benefit from meditation, they must surrender themselves completely to the process of meditation. They should not be skeptical; they should not doubt their abilities or criticize their difficulties. A person meditating should have no conflict in the mind. This is important not only for successful meditation, but also for successful living.

Asanas, or physical postures, involve learning to control, regulate, and become aware of one's physical existence. During the various exercises, inhaling, exhaling, or pausing bears a certain relationship to the sequence of body movements. One is required to give complete mental attention to each movement. The exercises are also isotonic, involving the contraction of one group of muscles while relaxing or stretching the opposite group of muscles. Conversely, isometric or calisthenic exercises involve contraction of all the groups of muscles at the same time; this, in fact, has been shown to produce a sharp (although temporary) rise in blood pressure and heart rate.

The fourth stage is pranayama, or regulation of breathing. When people are excited, their breathing becomes deeper and faster. When they are tense, their chest walls become rigid and they breathe very shallowly, only using the upper parts of the lungs. By slow but deep abdominal and rhythmical breathing, a person can achieve a certain amount of physical and mental calmness. According to yoga, "prana" is an energy or life force, which serves as a link between the physical and mental level of existence; breath is a vehicle for prana. Our present scientific knowledge does not tell us very much about this prana—whether it is the life-giving oxygen people carry with their breathing, or whether it is some yet unidentified element we do not know. However, we do know that the way in which people breathe reflects their physical, mental, and emotional state. Anger, fear, and depression all have their characteristic breathing patterns. For example, a child may hold his breath in a temper tantrum until he or she gets cyanosed. An hysterical state is characterized by overbreathing; a depressed person shows frequent sighing; an angry person's breathing is very erratic.

In the fifth stage of pratyahara, or sensory withdrawal, the beginner is advised to lie down on the floor, on a couch, or in a reclining chair, with an empty stomach and bladder, and to relax every muscle of the body while keeping the eyes closed. Relaxation is carried out in a particular sequence, starting with the lower limbs and gradually working up to include the upper limbs, shoulders, back, chest, abdomen, neck, face, and scalp, always giving full attention to the particular part being relaxed. This state of sensory withdrawal causes a dramatic reduction in proprioception and is of particular physiological interest as far as correcting high blood pressure is concerned.

In the sixth stage of dharna, or concentration, the person gradually begins to narrow down the focus of attention, so that the mind becomes more restful and concentrated. By giving voluntary concentration to a subject, not only is the person able to see and think about it with great clarity, but the mind also brings into the field of consciousness all the different ideas in memory associated with the subject. This has many practical implications. It trains the mind to concentrate on one subject at a time, and the person is able to find a solution to any problem because the mind is flooded with all the relevant ideas and facts.

The seventh stage, that of dhyana, or contemplation, is a deeper state of concentration, in which the mind becomes sharply focused. The mind has a tendency to wander, so techniques are devised to help it to become steadier through concentration upon an object of contemplation. The objects that can be used for contemplation are infinite: a flower, a blank wall, a candle flame, one's own breath, or an idea. One may close the eyes and listen to various sounds—for example, a word or phrase called a "mantra," repeated mentally, or a suitable piece of music. Most of us have probably seen in a concert hall, when a great piece of music is being played, how the audience is being held in a trance.

Dhyana is an intimate and compelling process. The mind that holds an idea in turn becomes held by it. We do know that if people constantly tell themselves that they are failures or are inferior to others, they eventually come to believe themselves. This power of the subconscious is used to build character and desirable traits and to weed out undesirable characteristics and emotions. As individuals see themselves to be in possession of a desired trait over and over, they begin to express the thought in actions, and eventually the new image becomes a fixed part of their characters.

The final stage of yogic meditation is samadhi, or the meditative stage. The object of mental focusing is to narrow the awareness to a fine point so that it eventually breaks through to a higher, more intense plane of consciousness. This is a state during which the mind is said to transcend the ordinary plane of awareness; it is described as a state of greatest silence, greatest joy, and greatest peace—the moment of illumination and a great spiritual experience. Words cannot describe it because the vocabulary for it does not exist. It is a journey one must make alone. It is an experience one does not share with anybody.

To this extent, meditation cannot be completely separated from the spiritual aspect or divinity. But then, people cannot separate themselves from divinity; everyone has within himself or herself a spark of divinity. Without that there would be no love, no kindness, no give-and-take. Of course, we now live in a scientific age; in order to believe anything, we have to subject it to the most stringent physical, chemical, and medical tests before we can say what it is. Although we have started to measure the effect of yogic meditation on blood pressure and various other parameters, it is clear that we have not yet located the mind, the soul, the conscious, or the subconscious, and so we are a long way from detecting how meditation actually affects them. We simply do not know how to measure peace or harmony, love or kindness, or joy or serenity—let alone the conscious and the subconscious.

Some obvious benefits of meditation, such as lower blood pressure, better sleep, or greater efficiency at work, are only blind pockets on the path of meditation leading to liberation. Even meditation itself, according to Pantanjali and Buddha, is only a tool to be used until there is no longer any need for it.

THE PHYSICAL ENVIRONMENT AND EQUIPMENT

If possible, the individual should meditate in a room or a corner of a room set aside for the practice. This corner should be kept as simple and bare as possible; it should not be used for any other purpose. It should be warm, quiet, and as free from distraction as possible. It is easy to get distracted in the beginning, although, with practice, one learns to practice meditation almost anywhere. Preliminary stages of breathing exercise and relaxation can be practiced lying down, or sitting up in a comfortable armchair.

Time to practice is just as important in the early stages. It is better to practice twice a day, at least 1½ hours after a light meal. A person who has just eaten a meal may become drowsy; a person who is hungry will be distracted, too. The best time for the first practice is in the morning before the day's work begins, with the second practice soon after arrival home from work. That way, the person starts the day fresh and relaxed and then releases the tension of the day in order to enjoy the evening. Again, it is better to keep the times regular. Normally, 15–20 minutes per session is sufficient, although the individual's schedule or inclination must be considered. It is better to practice 10 minutes, if that is all that the day's schedule will allow, than to miss a session.

There are times when beginners will feel that they have no time to practice, or that they are bored and that it will not matter if they do not practice now and again; but if they can discipline themselves to practice despite these pulls, they will make better progress, for it allows them to see how their thoughts imprison them and impose limits on them, and how they can overcome them.

Beginners can practice on their own or in a group. Group meditation has certain advantages: The others in the group become a support system; the resistance to meditation and the urge to stop meditating and get up because of boredom or tension are controlled in a group. It is also the experience of meditators that somehow the depth of meditation is more profound when it is practiced in a group, as though vibrations from each participant create an atmosphere that allows intense meditation.

THERAPIST–CLIENT RELATIONSHIP

The therapist must be involved in teaching meditative techniques and should not merely tell beginners to learn themselves. The objective of this is to develop a favorable attitude in the beginners toward learning. This involves teaching the importance of the topic as well as the substance of it; helping to get the best use of what has been learned; recognizing when beginners are going astray and then bringing them back to the learning path and influencing them to learn more; and, most important of all, influencing beginners' attitudes in such a way that they continue to use their skills after the training is over.

The clients must be told explicitly what they are supposed to learn. If the objectives are stated in vague terms, they are difficult if not impossible to achieve. It is true that sometimes a client may learn unintentionally or accidentally, just as a pupil may learn things the teacher is not teaching under certain circumstances. However, if we compare placebo effects to unintentional learning, then intentional teaching makes learning more than a random phenomenon.

The object of instruction is to facilitate the form of behavior that will be used continuously after the training is completed. This is likely only if the clients develop a favorable attitude toward the behavior taught. Things disliked are often forgotten. Repeated failures also mean that the clients involved are likely to think less highly of themselves, and they will try to avoid the entire subject that has come to signify such a shrinking of self-esteem. Clients should be complimented following each successful attempt, while failure should be played down.

The therapist must provide guidance for learning in a variety of different communication modes, depending on which mode suits the individual client. This is a point where even the best-organized program on a teaching machine cannot replace a human being. The teacher and the pupil together negotiate the meaning of the learning as it is transferred from one very private set of thoughts, concepts, skills, and attributes, to another individual's short- and long-term memory.

The instruction should take place at a level that is within the comprehension of the individual subject. It is useless to spend time explaining all the complicated mechanisms of the electronic biofeedback equipment and the underlying physics principles of the various brain-wave patterns that may emerge during meditation to a person who can barely read and write. On the other hand, a highly intelligent and skeptical client wants to know the logic of the advocated behavior before he or she will practice it sincerely. In my experience, the average client wants to know more than therapists generally realize. The capacity to perform varies widely among individuals, and the task of reaching the goal should be paced accordingly.

Some therapists are more skilled in the establishment of in-depth communication with their clients than others are. Some clients may seem impossible to communicate with. By and large, raising clients' self-esteem and expectations in proportion to their capacity to perform enhances learning. These points must be taken into consideration while choosing an appropriate feedback instrument, setting its target, and engaging in all other verbal and nonverbal communications, if unnecessary frustrations in both therapists and clients are to be avoided. Learning and communication flourish when the self-esteem of the patient is raised; the knowledge of success and eventual mastery of the technique further raises his or her self-esteem. Thus learning and communication are inextricably integrated and lead to a cumulative beneficial effect.

The therapist's or researcher's attitude to teaching is also very important. It is easy for a researcher, busy in controlling many variables and recording unbiased data, to overlook the human aspect of the doctor–patient relationship. While pursuing the science of technology and statistical analysis, the art of medicine should not be forgotten.

It must also be remembered that even an ideal relationship cannot be a complete substitute for the depth of scientific knowledge required in a therapist. In treating hypertensive patients by yogic meditation as a form of behavior modification, the therapist must have in-depth knowledge of the etiology, pathophysiology, and current management of hypertension; the psychology of the doctor–patient relationship; biofeedback principles, practice, and mechanisms; the philosophy of yoga and its scientific validation (and the logical explanation for the use of any other specific techniques); and so on. Without this interdisciplinary knowledge of various fields, he or she cannot inspire confidence in patients and hence be effective as a therapist.

One cannot learn to drive an automobile by merely reading an instruction book, although such a book may be an important aid in learning to drive. In the same way, merely connecting a patient to a biofeedback instrument or reading about a behavior modification technique is not enough in bringing about learning, no matter how sophisticated the instrument or how precise the instruction book may be. In order to teach driving, the instructor must not only teach driving techniques, but also demonstrate driving and finally prove that the student has in fact learned to drive. This implies that the instructor must have the knowledge of driving, just as teachers of mathematics or history must have adequate knowledge of their subjects.

We must also recognize the universal fact that the people sometimes learn more from imitation. The research on modeling tells us that if we want to maximize approach tendencies toward a subject in students or clients, so that they really want to learn, then we must behave the way we want our students or clients to behave. If we are teaching relaxation, this means not only that we must know how to relax, but that our entire attitude should be relaxed. If we are teaching meditation, we must know the art of meditation ourselves.

DESCRIPTION OF THE METHOD

In the early stages, breathing exercises and deep-muscle relaxation can be practiced in a reclining position. Once the art of profound physical relaxation is mastered, the client can practice later stages of meditation sitting up, particularly if relaxation makes him or her very drowsy. Traditionally, meditation is practiced in a lotus position, which allows the head, neck, and spine to remain in a straight line and yet prevents one from falling asleep. However, this position or any other is not essential to the practice of meditation. For hypertensive patients, the fourth stage of pranayama and the fifth stage of pratyahara are so important that I encourage beginners to recline; this may sound strange to many experts on meditation, but then it may sound strange to them that it is a goal-directed meditation—and a short-term goal at that (the lowering of high blood pressure)!

Therapist's Verbal Instructions for Pranayama (Breathing Exercise) and Pratyahara (Deep-Muscle Relaxation)

Make sure that your head, neck, and trunk lie in a straight line. Keep your legs slightly apart with the heels pointing inward and your toes pointing outward. Bring your hands down by your side, a little away from the thighs. Turn your palms upward and bend your fingers slightly. If you are using a reclining chair, there is often not enough space to stretch out your arms and you may find that actually turning the palms upward is less comfortable. Under these circumstances, use any position that feels comfortable to you. Close your eyes and make sure your teeth are not clenched.

Now you are going to practice a simple breathing exercise. Pay total attention to the practice of each step. For example, pay attention to the breathing movements; feel each inhalation and exhalation. Even listen to your breathing sounds and feel the difference in the temperature of the air you are inhaling and exhaling. Very slowly, fill your lungs, starting at the diaphragm right up to the top of your chest, and then slowly breathe out.

After three or four deep breaths, allow your breathing to become normal and regular. Breathe in and out very gently and rhythmically. Don't force your breathing. Don't try deliberately to make it slow. Just keep to your own rhythm. Breathe in and out gently and evenly.

Now you are consciously going to relax each part of the body as I name it. "Relaxation" means complete absence of activity or movement in that part of the body, since "movement" means that some muscles are contracting. It is also the opposite of holding any part rigid. Make mental contact with the part of the body you are relaxing. By doing this you can discover the interlinking of the body and the mind—how they are connected and how one can affect the other.

Now take your mind to the right foot. Relax the toes, instep, heel, ankle, knee, calf, thigh, and hip. Feel all the muscles becoming relaxed and limp. Hold your attention to the feelings of relaxation in the muscles of your right leg and relax as deeply as you can. Become aware of every muscle, nerve, joint, and tissue in your right leg relaxing.

Now take your mind to the left foot. Relax the toes, instep, heel, ankle, knee, calf, thigh, and hip. Just relax. Let all the tension ease away and feel the sensation of relaxation in all the muscles of your left leg. Feel every muscle, nerve, joint, and tissue in your left leg relaxing.

Now become aware of your right hand. Relax the fingers, thumb, palm, wrist, forearm, elbow, upper arm, and shoulder. Feel every muscle in your right arm relaxing and becoming limp. Relax as deeply as you can. Hold your attention to the sensation of relaxation in your right arm. Become aware of every muscle, tissue, nerve, and joint in your right arm relaxing.

Now become aware of your left hand. Relax the fingers, thumb, palm, wrist, forearm, elbow, upper arm, and shoulder. Let all the tension drain away from the muscles. Feel the sensation of relaxation and limpness in every muscle of your left arm. Feel every muscle, tissue, nerve, and joint in your left arm relaxing.

Now bring your concentration to the base of your spine. Work your way up the spine, vertebra by vertebra, relaxing each vertebra into the floor and the muscles on either side of the spine. Feel the back merging with the floor. Now relax the muscles of your upper back. Release all the tension from them. Relax your neck. Let all the muscles in your neck relax completely—first the front of the neck and then the back of the neck. Let your head rest gently and feel all the muscles in the back of your neck relaxing. Just let them go and keep on letting them go.

Now concentrate on your chin. Relax it. Now relax your jaw. Let it drop slightly so that your teeth are slightly apart and the lips are just touching. Relax your tongue. Now your cheeks—feel them relaxing. Relax the muscles around your eyes and feel them becoming heavy and very relaxed. There are no tensions in the eyes, in the muscles around your eyes. They are in a state of complete relaxation. Now relax your forehead. Just let all the tension release from the muscles of your forehead. Feel all the muscles in the face relaxing. There is no tension in your facial muscles at all. Now relax your scalp. Feel the relaxation in the muscles around your head.

Now relax your chest. And every time you breathe out relax a little more; let your body sink into the floor, a little more each time. Let all the muscles, nerves, and organs in your chest relax completely. Now relax the muscles of your stomach. Let all the muscles, nerves, and organs in your stomach relax completely.

Now your body is completely and totally relaxed. Keep your body relaxed and concentrate your mind on your breathing. Feel the air going in and warm air coming out.

Therapist's Instructions on Preparing the Mind for Meditation

As you sit or lie there, either you may want to fall asleep, or your mind begins to wander. Falling asleep can be avoided by sitting up, but how do you prevent yourself from thinking—bringing up memories and fantasies, creating or solving problems? Just thinking is not meditating. In order to keep from getting lost in thinking, just let the thoughts come and go. Don't get attached to any of the thoughts. Let them just float by without any question, judgment, or agitation. Just sit back as it were and observe the thoughts that come and go.

When a bird flies it does not disturb the wind in the sky; when a fish swims in the ocean, it does not leave any track in the water. Let noise, thoughts, or any distractions come and go without causing any whirlpool in your mind. Let your mind become like the sky or the ocean. Just allow your thoughts and distractions to pass by without analyzing them. If you notice yourself getting caught, don't get angry or frustrated, because your attention will get caught many times. Each time, just bring your attention back very gently but firmly to the state of unattached observer.

Meditation Techniques: Choosing the Right One

In the introduction to the chapter, it is mentioned that the objects and methods of meditation can be many. Because of widespread use and advertisement, many people believe that mantra meditation is the only transcendental meditation. This is not so. All types of meditation, if practiced appropriately and sufficiently, can lead to a state that transcends the limits of ordinary awareness. However, each emphasizes a different quality, and it is important for the client to choose a method that he or she feels comfortable with, that is in harmony with his or her interests and personality, and that flows along with his or her natural inclination.

Sometimes a client needs to work with more than one method. If the client learns one or more methods, they can be integrated later according

to his or her need. If institutes or gurus teaching meditation expect that
clients must take a vow to remain loyal and attached to them forever,
or that the method they teach is the best technique, then it is better to
avoid them; if they need a pledge from clients, then they cannot liberate
them, and liberation is the ultimate goal of meditation. Changing from
one method to another is not a weakness; neither is staying on with the
first method if a client feels it is the right one for him or her. Clients should
be guided by their inner feelings. However, they should give a method
a reasonable trial before abandoning it as unsuitable.

Simple Meditation on Breathing. One simple exercise for bringing
awareness to a single subject is concentration on breathing. After the client
has regulated breathing and relaxed the body as described, either sitting
or reclining with the eyes closed, he or she should fix attention on the
breath as it enters and leaves the nostrils. The entire focus should be on
the nostrils, noting full passage of each inhalation and exhalation from
the beginning to the end. The client should feel the sensations of the air
going in and out. These sensations may change from that of a dull feather
to itching to intense pressure or to countless other feelings; there is no
right or wrong way. The client should simply be aware of the breathing
and keep his or her attention on it. If the client has difficulty in keeping
the focus fixed, he or she might try counting 1 on the inhalation and 2
on the exhalation. If the mind still wanders off, the client should just bring
it back without getting agitated about it.

Mantra Meditation. A word, a name of God, a verse from a hymn,
or a prayer is known as a mantra when it is repeated over and over again.
It is an effective way of concentrating the mind. In yoga, certain Sanskrit
words qualify as mantras, such as "Ram" or "Shyam," which are names
of God. "Aum" or "Om" is considered to be the basic sound or the basis
of everything in yoga. According to the ancient scripture, "All that is past,
present, and future is truly Om." All that is beyond this conception of
time is also Om. Tibetan Lamas and Buddhists from China, Japan, and
Indonesia also interpret Om similarly. An instrument called a tonoscope,
which can be used to visualize sound in three dimensions, shows that the
letter O spoken into a microphone produces a perfectly spherical pattern.
Thus Om has some interesting significance. It is also worth noting that
Christians and Jews say "Amen" and Muslims "Amin." The mantra could
be a short phrase like "Aum Namah Shivaya," meaning "Oh God! I bow
to you." One can find several natural mantras, and the client can choose
one according to his or her faith and inclination (e.g., "Lord Jesus Christ,
have mercy on me"). Healing prayers rely on such repetitive sounds for

their fundamental effect. However, it is not necessary to have a mantra with religious connotations. The client can repeat a simple neutral word, such as "relaxed" or "one" or "harmony."

The idea is to set up one thought, one wave that repeats over and over again. All the client should be thinking of consciously is the mantra. In this way, he or she becomes intimate with the sound of the mantra and begins to surrender or merge into it. Again the mind will wander off and distracting thoughts will come, but the client should not get frustrated and say "This is hopeless" or "It won't work with me." He or she should not get disturbed by doubts, discomforts, boredom, or apparent failures, but should learn to watch them instead. Sometimes repeating the mantra with the beads of a rosary is helpful in keeping the attention fixed. As soon as the mind wanders off, the activity of the hand or the touch of a bead reminds the client of the mantra. The rhythm becomes more compelling as the body works in harmony with the mind. With practice, the client will notice that the quality of the mantra changes. When the mind is calm, the mantra will feel subtle and delicate. When the mind is agitated, the mantra will feel strong and coarse. Whatever happens, the client should just keep repeating the mantra and let it make him or her more and more still.

The power of sound waves will be apparent when we consider how modern technology has been able to harness high-frequency sound waves in diagnostic and therapeutic ultrasonic machines. Sound-wave therapy uses as its basic principle the fact that each cell or tissue in the body has its own vibrating frequency, which may be modified by sound waves. Plants seem to grow better when exposed to music than when exposed to random everyday noise (Watson, 1973). Of course, sound waves can have both good and bad effects; hence, care is required in choosing a mantra.

Experiential Meditation. Nature is the easiest object of contemplation, and therapists and clients can devise meditations in which the clients draw their surroundings into their being through their senses until they inspire and lead the clients into a quiet and peaceful state. Therapists can use the following as examples:

1. Visit a meadow, sit under a tree, and just look at the beautiful green fields.

2. After you have mowed the lawn, sit in your own backyard and savor the smell of fresh-cut grass.

3. Listen to the music of the ocean or a waterfall. Just forget yourself while you continue to listen. Let the intensity of the sound fill

your head, and then your whole body, until you vibrate with it.

4. Keep watching the shadow of a boat while you row.

5. Hold an apple in your hand. Feel its shape and texture, examine its color in detail, smell it. Then close your eyes and just capture all you have seen and felt.

6. Taste the wind. What does it carry? Salt from the sea, perhaps, or the clean essence of pines on faraway mountains?

7. Lie in sun-drenched golden sands and relax until you feel completely limp, as if you are a rag doll with no tension at all.

8. Watch the raindrops falling on the ground. Try to see a rainbow in each drop.

9. While you are washing the dishes, look at the many colors of the suds. Feel them caressing your fingers.

Clients can devise countless ways of meditation. Sometimes meditation just happens if a client is in the right state of mind—when there is a spaciousness in existence such that the client is just lost, not holding on to the experience. It just flows through the client when he or she becomes the experience. It is in these moments of life that there is joy, peace, harmony, tranquility, and unity. There is no longer separation; there is a kind of reverie.

Both therapists and clients should read books on meditation and spiritual practices by those who are liberated and attuned to higher states of consciousness. After reading one good book, I often feel a kind of inner peace that lasts as long as a month or two.

Devotional Meditation. Contemplating, praying, thinking religious thoughts, and singing and chanting devotional songs with outflowing love and compassion are devotional meditative practices. Whether the faith involved is Christian or Hindu, Jewish or Buddhist, Jain or Muslim, the important thing for religious persons is the belief that God loves them no matter how bad or good they are, absolutely unconditionally, and that they return this love in a compassionate, unjudging way and open themselves up more and more, to the point that compassion, love, warmth, and patience all radiate from them. They recognize divinity within themselves and feel love for all people.

These are some of the ways in which people begin to meditate. This is a guide for beginners only. As clients practice, they may feel that the goals are very limited. They will then have to seek more profound methods and teachers or gurus, but it is not necessary to have a guru to start meditating. What has been described as "concentration" or "contemplation" is not a meditative state, but a path that can take people to the threshold of the meditative state, which lies beyond words and beyond the boundaries of the ego-self. However, for ordinary working people, what has been described here is sufficient to bring and restore health.

RESISTANCE, COMPLIANCE, AND MAINTENANCE OF BEHAVIOR CHANGE

Resistance

People are often afraid to take up meditation because they fear that it will make them neglect their responsibilities and their duties to their families. Meditation is not an escape from social responsibility or a defense against the problems of life. Neither is it a withdrawal from life, although such withdrawal may occur temporarily when a meditator seeks solitude purposely. In fact, meditation leads practitioners to a deeper appreciation of their relationship to their families, friends, nation, and the world. Meditators play their role in society just as other people do, only more compassionately, more effectively, with more clarity and less attachment or selfishness. They do not have to be politicians or protesters, if that is not their style, but meditation does not prevent them from doing so. Gandhi fought social injustice and yet led a spiritual life. He was an effective leader, and yet his last words were the name of God. Meditation changes the way its practitioners tackle problems, not the problems themselves. By keeping their mental state balanced and undisturbed, they prevent damage not only to themselves, but also to others.

Sometimes people feel disappointed because they do not get what they had expected from meditation. Others describe all kinds of experiences during their meditation practice—feelings of floating or levitation, having visions, leaving their bodies and being somewhere else, and many other experiences. If clients (especially beginners) have never had such an experience, they may feel that they are not "doing it right." They may get bored or begin to doubt the benefit of meditation. On the other hand, clients may get worried because they feel too energetic or too lazy, or feel tingling in some part of the body. Some clients may experience pain in some parts of the body. These are only distractions; if clients just watch them calmly, they will go away. There is no cause for concern. I have not come across anyone in whom unusual experiences have persisted, good or bad, especially if the amount of time one meditates daily is kept to the limit prescribed. If clients practice many hours, they may feel disoriented or get distracted by some symptoms. When this happens, such clients should just cut down the amount of time they spend on meditation practice. If clients do not experience anything special, that is all right, too. No two people are the same. Meditators cannot predict what experiences they have, and they cannot judge the depth of meditation from the quality or quantity of these experiences.

Sometimes people fear losing their control, identity, will, or even friends. They may fear that something will happen that will change them, or that someone will ridicule them. Ram Dass (1978) says:

Such fears will grab at you and influence you to stop meditation. Examine these fears; be open to them. But don't worry; they will pass. . . . Understand that, like all the other feelings meditation brings you—confusion, pleasure, pain, excitement, boredom—your fears too will pass. (p. 180)

I must say that in my experience of several hundred hypertensive patients, I have not come across any side effects that have necessitated a patient's withdrawing from the practice.

Motivating symptomless hypertensive patients to comply with the time-consuming practice of relaxation and meditation is potentially difficult, since immediate reward, such as relief from pain, is absent. Without regular practice, long-term success cannot be achieved. However, the following have been found useful:

1. The concept of self-control of autonomic functions appeals to many. This innate desire must be exploited by providing a sense of mastery in clear terms.

2. The therapist can give a description of some biofeedback experiments in animals, ending with a well-known phrase popularized by the pioneer of biofeedback, Neal Miller: "If rats can do it, surely the humans can do it." This forms a helpful preparatory talk that not only fascinates patients, but makes them readier to accept a challenge. Many almost cannot wait to begin the training.

3. If there is a choice between lifelong drug medications for hypertension or modification of behavior, most patients will opt for the latter. This could apply to patients with borderline hypertension. A patient with severe hypertension who is already on antihypertensive medication would probably be willing to try this behavior therapy if it meant that his or her drug requirement can be reduced by a significant degree. For patients

whose blood pressure is not well controlled on drugs, the therapy could be offered as an alternative to increasing the drug dosage, with a high probability of acceptance. These patients do not need to be told about the side effects of antihypertensive drugs; they already know them.

4. A general educational program to increase patients' understanding of their disease and possible treatments is very useful. This is necessary for all patients with all types of disorders and for all modes of treatment, and is expected of all physicians today by most patients; the program should form an important component of effective medical care in general. For hypertensive patients, it should include an explanation of pathophysiology, the causes and consequences of hypertension, the benefits of lowering blood pressure, details of the treatment available, and rationales for the specific treatment offered. Many patients will want to help themselves if the physician takes the trouble to explain how they can play their part.

5. An increased sense of participation by patients in the management of their conditions ensures extraordinarily high cooperation in most cases. Asking patients for their opinions regarding their drug schedules in relation to their blood pressure, for example, increases their sense of participation and the responsibility they are prepared to take in the management of their hypertension.

6. There are a number of additional side benefits associated with relaxation–meditation therapy—for example, improved quality of sleep, improved interpersonal relationships, a decrease in the number of headaches, better anxiety management, and a general sense of well-being. Whenever they occur, they should be used as an opportunity to reinforce motivation for long-term application of the learned behavior.

Compliance

Studies have shown that despite the willingness of patients to comply, they often fail to adhere to the advocated therapeutic behavior. This has been amply demonstrated in drug intervention studies (Joyce, 1962). Elaborate education about hypertension itself has proved of limited value for hypertensive patients (Sackett, Gibson, Taylor, Haynes, Hockett, Roberts, & Johnson, 1975). However, simple basic information about the disease process and its appropriate management should form a part of the comprehensive educational program, and if carried out by the clinician personally, it also helps consolidate clinician–patient relationships. Information about the regime itself is more likely to be retained if dispensed in small quantities (Epstein & Lasagna, 1969; Joyce, Capla, Mason, Reynolds, & Mathews, 1969) and aided by an audiovisual presentation (Boyd, Covington, Stanaszck, & Coussons, 1974; Clinite & Kabat, 1976; Dicky, Mattar, & Chudzek, 1975) that is within the patient's comprehension (Ley, Jain, & Skilbeck, 1976).

The clinician's relationship with his or her patients is also important. It has been shown that a warm and empathic manner of the clinician, his or her genuine interest and concern for the patients, the patients' active participation in their health care, and social interaction between clinician and patient are important (Crisp, 1970; Korsch & Negrete, 1972).

Maintenance of Behavior Change

Maintaining therapeutic behavior over a long period is a real dilemma in any chronic illness that does not produce immediate disabling symptoms. The secret of success is not in the mysteries of meditation or other therapeutic behaviors, but in the long-term adherence to intervention strategies. This requires real effort on the part of the clinician during the training period to see that the new habits are ingrained into the mental scheme of the patients. The patient must be convinced of the necessity to maintain the therapeutic behavior, which should be simple, enjoyable, and nondemanding. The therapist and the client must work together initially to find ingenious ways of integrating the new behavior into situations of everyday life.

The objectives of integrating relaxation–meditation therapy into the daily routine are twofold:

> 1. Blood pressure reductions or other therapeutic changes are maintained throughout the day.
> 2. The necessity for daily time-consuming practice sessions may be reduced, or at least partially compensated for, when there is a lack of adherence.

When a patient uses frequent daily occurrences in his or her environment, such as answering telephones, waiting at red traffic lights, or looking at a wrist watch, as reminders to relax, he or she is not only reducing the number of daily practice sessions needed, but is also reducing the impact of stressful environments. Meditation in action, discussed earlier, is one of the ways of integrating the benefits of meditation into daily life.

Regular follow-up by the same clinician or therapist is also important. These follow-up sessions can be used for checking blood pressure or other dependent variables; to discuss problems that might be having deleterious effects and their possible solutions; to interact socially and thus to consolidate the clinician–patient relationship; to reinforce therapeutic behavior by raising the self-esteem of those who have successfully maintained lower blood pressure or other therapeutic changes; and to exert gentle pressure on those who might be slipping away from the therapeutic path. Follow-up sessions can also be used as booster training sessions if necessary.

In my program, each patient is given a cassette tape that provides step-by-step instructions in the practice of breathing exercises, deep-muscle relaxation, and meditation; they return the cassette only at the end of the training period of 6–8 weeks, having weaned themselves off it. If blood pressure is elevated at follow-up, or if a patient has stopped practicing, a booster session not only will act as a retraining session, but will also reveal whether the therapy is becoming ineffective or inadequate with that patient. If necessary, a small dose of an antihypertensive drug may be added at this stage. Those patients who have stopped or reduced medications previously are so highly motivated to maintain changes that they do not need much persuading to get back to practicing the therapeutic behavior.

Self-monitoring of blood pressure can be very useful in maintaining behavior change. If a diabetic patient can be trusted to test his or her urine and adjust the insulin dose accordingly, I see no reason why a hypertensive patient cannot be trusted to check his or her blood pressure and adjust the therapeutic behavior accordingly. The patient soon learns which events elevate his or her blood pressure, and thus can learn appropriate handling of these events, especially if they cannot be avoided.

In spite of careful considerations of all the points discussed, we know very little about long-term maintenance of therapeutic behavior. This is an area that needs systematic evaluation.

THE EVIDENCE OF EFFICACY

PILOT STUDY

In a pilot study, 20 patients who had been known to be hypertensive for at least a year and whose conditions were controlled on antihypertensive medications were treated by the relaxation–meditation behavior modification program. A similar number of hypertensive controls were matched from the age and sex register kept in the same general practice under the United Kingdom's National Health Service (Patel, 1973, 1975a). Patients in the treatment group attended three times a week for half-hour training sessions. The training was enhanced by the use of the GSR biofeedback instrument. Patients in the control group also attended the same number of sessions, but were simply asked to lie down without being given any training in a behavioral program. The number of blood pressure measurements were kept the same in both groups.

Baseline blood pressure was averaged from 18 measurements made during three separate attendances. Final blood pressure was averaged from 24 measurements made during the final four sessions. If blood pressure was reduced to normal in any individual during the program, a reduction was made in the dosage of antihypertensive drugs until the pressure was satisfactorily controlled. In the treatment group, during a 3-month trial period, five patients stopped their drugs altogether; a further seven patients showed reductions in drug intake ranging from 33 to 66% of initial levels. In a further four patients, no reduction was made in the amount of drugs taken, but their blood pressure was better controlled; while in the remaining four patients, the therapy did not make any material change in the level of blood pressure, although in one patient almost daily attacks of migraine stopped altogether. In addition to this reduction in medications, mean systolic and diastolic blood pressures were reduced by 20 and 14 mm Hg, respectively ($p < .001$). In the control group, the mean reductions in systolic and diastolic pressures were .5 and 2.0 mm Hg (not significant). The drug requirement did not change in the control group.

All the patients were followed up monthly for 12 months. Except for some minor changes, both blood pressure and drug reductions were maintained in the treated group. In some patients who stopped practicing relaxation, blood pressure started to go up. However, with restarting the practice, blood pressure came down again. The lesson learned during this follow-up study was the clear importance of motivating these patients for a lifetime of practicing and integrating relaxation behavior into their daily activities.

RANDOMIZED CONTROLLED STUDY

Because of the fairly impressive results of the pilot study, it became important to conduct a randomized controlled study (Patel & North, 1975). To avoid any subjective or objective bias, all blood pressure measurements were made by an experienced nurse, using a random-zero sphyg-momanometer (Wright & Dore, 1970).

A total of 34 patients known to be hypertensive for at least 6 months, who had original diastolic blood pressure of at least 110 mm Hg and whose conditions were controlled with antihypertensive medications or other measures, were randomly allocated to groups after the baseline blood pressure for each was established. The baseline blood pressure was an average of nine measurements taken during three separate sessions. The patients in each group attended twice a week for 6 weeks. The patients in the treatment group were given biofeedback-aided training in relaxation and meditation. They were also given education in stress management. The patients in the control group were asked to lie down and engage in whatever they thought was relaxation. After this 6-week trial period, each patient was followed once every 2 weeks for 3 months. All blood pressures taken during these follow-up sessions were averaged as the final pressure. The drugs were kept constant.

The results showed a small but significant reduction in systolic and diastolic pressures in the control group (8 and 4 mm Hg, respectively). However, the reductions were much larger in the treatment group (26 and 15 mm Hg, respectively) and the differences between the groups were highly significant ($p < .005$). At 2 months after the last follow-up, patients were recalled. Results at this visit showed that blood pressures in the control group had gone back to their original levels, while most of the reductions in the treatment group were maintained. It would seem that the results in the control group demonstrated the placebo effect in the sense that they lasted as long as placebo factors were operating, whatever they might have been.

By chance, random allocation had not divided patients into two equal groups. The study was extended in the second phase, during which the behavior modification program was offered to the control group over a period of 6 weeks; both systolic and diastolic blood pressures were reduced to levels close to those of the group that was previously treated.

BEHAVIORAL METHODS IN REDUCING
THE EFFECT OF STRESS

Blood pressure rises as a result of physical, emotional, or painful stimuli in everyone. The rise is more acute and prolonged in hypertensive patients. The pressure load on the left ventricle and vessel walls is an integrated average pressure over long periods; therefore, the cumulative benefit of reductions in magnitude as well as in duration of pressor responses is obvious.

A total of 32 hypertensive patients were randomly allocated into treatment and control groups (Patel, 1975b, 1977). All the patients were subjected to two experimental stressors—an exercise and a cold-pressor test—and these were repeated 6 weeks later. During this period, the patients in the treatment group were trained in the behavior modification program outlined earlier. The patients in the control group were given the attention placebo, also as described earlier.

The results showed significant reduction in the magnitude as well as the duration of pressure rises in the treatment group, compared with the control group.

BIOCHEMICAL EVIDENCE

The question of whether the claimed reduction in blood pressure due to the relaxation–meditation behavioral program lasts only while the measurement is being made or endures outside the laboratory when the patient is either not relaxing or not thinking about blood pressure cannot be answered definitely, unless 24-hour ambulatory monitoring is conducted. This can at present be done reliably only by an intraarterial method (Bevan, Honour, & Stott, 1969), and it is hard to justify such an invasive procedure when it cannot be claimed to have a potential life-saving value for the participating patient. However, the claim can be supported by other corroborative biochemical evidence.

Stone and De Leo (1976) showed a reduction in plasma dopamine beta-hydroxylase as well as furosemide-stimulated plasma renin activity in hypertensive patients who practiced Zen meditation. However, their study sample was small, highly selected, and not properly controlled. My colleagues and I have studied the effect of the outlined behavioral program on serum cholesterol and other lipids, plasma renin activity, and plasma aldosterone.

In a pilot study involving 14 hypertensive patients (Patel, 1976b), the results over a 6-week period showed a reduction in average systolic pressure from 171 to 148 mm Hg and in average diastolic pressure from 103 to 85 mm Hg. The mean cholesterol was reduced from 242 to 217 mm per 100 ml ($p < .001$). Of 14 patients, 13 showed some decrease. However, this was an uncontrolled study.

In another pilot study (Patel & Carruthers, 1977), four groups of subjects were studied. A normotensive group of 18 subjects acted as the control group; another normotensive group of 18 subjects was treated by the biofeedback–relaxation–meditation behavior modification program; a group of 22 hypertensives and a group of 18 current smokers were similarly treated. The results showed significant reduction in blood pressure in all the treated groups, with no significant change in the control group. Plasma cholesterol, triglycerides, and free fatty acids were reduced in some but not all subjects in the treated groups, with no change in the control group. Cigarette smoking was dramatically reduced. However, the smokers were volunteers who wanted to give up smoking, and there are dangers in extrapolating results from a volunteer group to the smoking population in general.

In a recent large intervention study of multiple risk factors, a group of 204 patients with two or more risk factors (blood pressure 140/90 or more, serum cholesterol 6.3 mmol/liter or more, and current cigarette smoking of 10 or more cigarettes per day) were randomly allocated (Patel, Marmot, & Terry, 1981) to treatment and control groups. The results showed significantly greater reduction in systolic and diastolic blood pressure in the treatment group at 8 weeks, and these differences between the groups were maintained at an 8-month follow-up ($p < .001$). In a subsample ($n = 52$), there was a significant reduction in plasma renin activity and plasma aldosterone in the treated group compared with the control group at 8 weeks ($p < .025$), but not at 8 months. Similarly, plasma cholesterol was reduced significantly in the high-risk treated group compared with the control group at 8 weeks, but not at 8 months. The number of smokers who attempted to reduce or stop smoking, as well as the reduction in the number of cigarettes smoked per day, was significantly greater in the treatment group compared with the control group, both at 8 weeks and at 8 months (Patel, Marmot, Terry, Carruthers, & Sever, 1979).

CORONARY HEART DISEASE RISK: PREDICTION

Assuming that greater reductions in blood pressure, cigarette smoking, and cholesterol achieved by this therapy would reduce mortality from coronary heart disease, we can calculate the potential reduction in mortality using the multiple-logistic function from the London Whitehall Study (Marmot, Rose, Shipley, & Hamilton, 1978). The reduction in the predicted risk of death from coronary heart disease at 8 weeks was 21%

greater, and at 8 months it was still 18% greater, in the group that was treated by the behavior modification program outlined.

COMMENTS AND REFLECTIONS

It is easy to evaluate a new drug using a double-blind technique. It is not possible to use this method to evaluate behavioral treatment when a patient is expected to change his or her behavior consciously and deliberately. By using a random-zero sphygmomanometer and a trained nurse to measure blood pressure, researchers can reduce bias but cannot claim to have eliminated it. At least four studies have tried to solve the problem that patients may show reduced blood pressure only while the measurement is being made. Blackwell, Bloomfield, Gartside, Robinson, Hanenson, Magenheim, Nidich, and Zigler (1976) showed good correlation between changes in blood pressure taken at home and blood pressure taken in the clinic. Kristt and Engel (1975) demonstrated drops in pressure in both home and clinic settings. Using the Halstead category subtest as an independent measure of generalization of effects, Kleinman, Goldman, Snow, and Korol (1977) argued that improvements on the Halstead subtest that correlated with improvements in blood pressure are proof that blood pressure was being reduced in other settings as well. Changes in plasma cholesterol, plasma renin activity, and aldosterone (Patel *et al.*, 1981), which were determined blindly, increase the confidence that the blood pressure reductions reported in this chapter might be genuine and not merely artifacts of measurement or short-term reactions to measurement. However, biochemical or hormonal changes occurred for the short term only.

It would seem from the results above that the mechanisms of short-term blood pressure reductions might be different from those involved in their long-term maintenance. It is a common experience of clinicians that blood pressure control becomes easier with time in many hypertensive patients, and that when antihypertensive medications are withdrawn, it often takes weeks or months before blood pressure rises again. A partial reversal of some of the factors responsible for maintaining and perpetuating hypertension, as discussed in the hypothesis and shown in some animal and human experiments (Folkow *et al.,* 1973; Vaughan Williams, Hassan, Floras, Sleight, & Jones, 1980), and the persistence of the reversal by the limited practice of relaxation–meditation therapy, might be responsible for long-term reduction in blood pressure. If these comments are logical, it also suggests that we have gone a long way toward proving the hypothesis.

Given the potential hazards of long-term antihypertensive medications, behavior therapy should be preferred as a first-line approach for patients with mild hypertension (diastolic pressure in the range of 90–105 mm Hg). According to the Hypertension Detection and Follow-Up Program Cooperative Group (1979), this group constitutes approximately 70% of hypertensive patients.

The program used and advocated in this chapter is effective in the medium term, although its long-term effectiveness cannot yet be claimed. Lowering of blood pressure, serum cholesterol, and cigarette smoking by this behavioral method does not necessarily mean that morbidity and mortality will be reduced, although such reductions should be the logical outcome.

REFERENCES

Benson, H. Yoga for drug abuse. *New England Journal of Medicine*, 1969, *281*, 1133.

Benson, H. Systemic hypertension and the relaxation response. *New England Journal of Medicine*, 1977, *296*, 1152–1156.

Benson, H., Alexander, S., & Feldman, C. L. Decreased premature ventricular contractions through the use of relaxation response in patients with stable ischaemic heart disease. *Lancet*, 1975, *ii*, 380–382.

Benson, H., Beary, J. F., & Carol, M. P. The relaxation response. *Psychiatry*, 1974, *37*, 37–46.

Benson, H., Klemchuk, H. P., & Graham, J. R. The usefulness of relaxation response in the therapy of headache. *Headache*, 1974, *14*, 49–52.

Benson, H., Rosner, B. A., Marzetta, B., & Klemchuk, H. Decreased blood pressure in pharmacologically treated hypertensive patients who regularly elicited the relaxation response. *Lancet*, 1974, *i*, 289–292.

Benson, H., & Wallace, R. K. Decreased blood pressure in hypertensive subjects who practiced meditation. *Circulation*, 1972, *45*(Suppl.), 516. (a)

Benson, H., & Wallace, R. K. Decreased drug abuse with transcendental meditation· A study of 1862 subjects. In C. J. D. Zaraforgetis (Ed.), *Drug abuse: Proceedings of the International Conference*. Philadelphia: Lea & Febiger, 1972. (b)

Bevan, A. T., Honour, A.J., & Stott, F. H. Direct arterial pressure recording in unrestricted man. *Clinical Science*, 1969, *36*, 329–344.

Blackwell, B., Bloomfield, S., Gartside, P., Robinson, A., Hanenson, I., Magenheim, H., Nidich, S., & Zigler, R. Transcendental meditation in hypertension: Individual response pattern. *Lancet*, 1976, *i*, 223–226.

Boyd, J. R., Covington, T. R., Stanaszck, W. F., & Coussons, R. T. Drug defaulting: I. Determinants of compliance. *American Journal of Hospital Pharmacology*, 1974, *31*, 362–364.

Breckenridge, A., Dollery, C. T., & Parry, E. H. O. Prognosis of treated hypertension. *Quarterly Journal of Medicine*, 1970, *39*, 411–429.

Brod, J., Fencl, V., Hejl, Z., & Zirka, J. Circulatory changes underlying blood pressure elevation during acute emotional stress (mental arithmetic) in normotensive and hypertensive subjects. *Clinical Science,* 1959, *18,* 269–279.

Brunton, P. *A search in secret India.* London: Rider, 1970.

Cannon, W. R. The emergency function of the adrenal medulla in pain and the major emotions. *American Journal of Physiology,* 1941, *33,* 356–372.

Carrington, P., Collings, G. H., Benson, H., Robinson, H., Wood, L. W., Lehrer, P. M., Woolfolk, R. L., & Cole, J. W. The use of meditation–relaxation techniques for the management of stress in a working population. *Journal of Occupational Medicine,* 1980, *22,* 221–231.

Clinite, J. C., & Kabat, H. F. Improving patient compliance. *Journal of the American Pharmaceutical Association,* 1976, *16,* 74–76.

Crisp, A. Therapeutic aspects of the doctor/patient relationship. *Psychotherapy and Psychosomatics,* 1970, *18,* 12–33.

Datey, K. K., Deshmukh, S. N., Dalvi, C. P., & Vineker, S. L. "Shavasan": A yogic exercise in the management of hypertension. *Angiology,* 1969, *20,* 325–333.

Dicky, F. F., Mattar, M. E., & Chudzek, G. M. Pharmacist counseling increases drug regimen compliance. *Hospitals,* 1975, *49,* 85–88.

Engel, B. T., & Bickford, A. F. Response specificity: Stimulus–response and individual response specificity in essential hypertensives. *Archives of General Psychiatry,* 1961, *5,* 478–489.

Epstein, L. C., & Lasagna, L. Obtaining informed consent: Form or substance. *Archives of Internal Medicine,* 1969, *123,* 682–688.

Folkow, B., Hällback, M., Lundgren, Y., Sivertsson, R., & Weiss, L. Importance of adaptive changes in vascular design for establishment of primary hypertension: Studies in man and in spontaneously hypertensive rats. *Circulation Research,* 1973, *32–33*(Suppl. 1), 2–16.

Folkow, B., & Rubinstein, E. H. Cardiovascular effects of acute and chronic stimulations of the hypothalamic defense area in the rat. *Acta Physiologica Scandinavica,* 1966, *68,* 48–57.

Friedman, M., & Rosenman, R. *Type A behavior and your heart.* New York: Knopf, 1974.

Gellhorn, E. The influence of curare on hypothalamic excitability and the electroencepalogram. *Electroencephalography and Clinical Neurophysiology,* 1958, *10,* 697–703.

Gellhorn, E. Motion and emotion: The role of proprioception in the physiology and pathology of emotion. *Psychological Review,* 1964, *71,* 457–472.

Hess, W. R. Hypothalamus and vegetative autonomic function. In J. R. Hughes (Ed.), *Functional organization of diencephalon.* New York: Grune & Stratton, 1957.

Hodes, R. Electroencephalographic synchronization resulting from reduced proprioceptive drive caused by neuromuscular blocking agents. *Electroencephalography and Clinical Neurophysiology,* 1962, *14,* 220–232.

Honsberger, R. W., & Wilson, A. F. The effect of transcendental meditation upon bronchial asthma. *Clinical Research,* 1973, *21,* 278. (a)

Honsberger, R. W., & Wilson, A. F. Transcendental meditation in treating asthma. *Respiratory Therapy: Journal of Inhalation Technology,* 1973, *3,* 79–80. (b)

Hypertension Detection and Follow-Up Program Cooperative Group. Five-year findings of the Hypertension Detection and Follow-Up Program: I. Reduction in mortality of persons with high blood pressure, including mild hypertension. *Journal of the American Medical Association,* 1979, *242,* 2562–2571.

Innes, G., Miller, W. M., & Valentine, M. Emotion and blood pressure. *Journal of Medical Science,* 1959, *105,* 840–851.

Johnston, C. *The book of the spiritual man: An interpretation.* London: Stewart & Watkins, 1970.

Joyce, C. R. B. Patient co-operation and the sensitivity of clinical trials. *Journal of Chronic Diseases,* 1962, *15,* 1025–1036.

Joyce, C. R. B., Capla, G., Mason, M., Reynolds, E., & Mathews, J. A. Quantitative study of doctor/patient communication. *Quarterly Journal of Medicine,* 1969, *38,* 183–194.

Kezdi, P. Sinoaortic regulatory system: Role in pathogenesis of essential and malignant hypertension. *Archives of Internal Medicine,* 1953, *91,* 26–34.

Kleinman, K. M., Goldman, H., Snow, M. Y., & Korol, B. Relationship between essential hypertension and cognitive functioning: II. Effects of biofeedback training generalize in non-laboratory environment. *Psychophysiology,* 1977, *14,* 192–197.

Korner, P. I. Neural cardiovascular control and hypertension. *Journal of the Royal College of Physicians,* 1971, *5,* 213–221.

Korsch, B. M., & Negrete, V. F. Doctor–patient communication. *Scientific American,* 1972, *227,* 66–74.

Kristt, D. A., & Engel, B. T. Learned control of blood pressure in patients with high blood pressure. *Circulation,* 1975, *51,* 370–378.

Kubicek, W. G., Kottke, F. J., Laker, D. J., & Visscher, M. B. Adaptation in pressor–receptor reflex: Mechanisms in experimental neurogenic hypertension. *American Journal of Physiology,* 1953, *175,* 380–382.

Lacey, J. I., & Lacey, B. C. Verification and extension of the principle of autonomic response-stereotypy. *American Journal of Psychology,* 1958, *71,* 50–72.

Lacey, J. I., & Lacey, B. C. The law of initial value in the longitudinal study of autonomic constitution: Reproducibility of autonomic responses and response patterns over a four year interval. *Annals of the New York Academy of Sciences,* 1962, *98,* 1257–1290.

Ley, P., Jain, V. I., & Skilbeck, C. E. A method for decreasing patients' medication errors. *Psychological Medicine,* 1976, *6,* 599–601.

Lown, B., & Verrier, R. L. Neural activity and ventricular fibrillation. *New England Journal of Medicine,* 1976, *294,* 1165–1170.

Luthe, W. *Autogenic therapy* (6 vols.). New York: Grune & Stratton, 1969.

Management Committee. The Australian Therapeutic Trial in Mild Hypertension. *Lancet,* 1980, *i,* 1261–1267.

Magoun, H. W. *The waking brain* (2nd ed.). Springfield, Ill.: Charles C Thomas, 1963.

Marmot, M. G., Rose, G., Shipley, M., & Hamilton, P. J. S. Employment grade and coronary heart disease in British civil servants. *Journal of Epidemiology and Community Health,* 1978, *32,* 244–249.

McCubbin, J. W., Green, J. H., & Page, I. M. Baroreceptor function in chronic renal hypertension. *Circulation Research,* 1958, *4,* 205–210.

McIntyre, M. E., Silverman, F. H., & Trotter, W. D. Transcendental meditation and stuttering: A preliminary report. *Perceptual and Motor Skills,* 1974, *39,* 294.

Miskiman, D. E. Long term effects of the Transcendental Meditation Program in the treatment of insomnia. In D. W. Orme-Johnson & J. T. Farrow (Eds.), *Scientific research on the Transcendental Meditation Program: Collected papers* (Vol. 1). Rheinweiler, West Germany: Maharishi European Research University Press, 1977. (a)

Miskiman, D. E. The treatment of insomnia by the Transcendental Meditation Program. In D. W. Orme-Johnson & J. T. Farrow (Eds.), *Scientific research on the Transcendental Meditation Program: Collected papers* (Vol. 1). Rheinweiler, West Germany: Maharishi European Research University Press, 1977. (b)

Nidich, S., Seeman, W., & Seibert, M. Influence of the Transcendental Meditation Program on state anxiety. In D. W. Orme-Johnson & J. T. Farrow (Eds.), *Scientific research on the Transcendental Meditation Program: Collected papers* (Vol. 1). Rheinweiler, West Germany: Maharishi European Research University Press, 1977.

Patel, C. H. Yoga and biofeedback in the management of hypertension. *Lancet,* 1973, *ii,* 1053–1055.

Patel, C. 12-month follow-up of yoga and biofeedback in the management of hypertension. *Lancet,* 1975, *i,* 62–65. (a)

Patel, C. Yoga and biofeedback in the management of "stress" in hypertensive patients. *Clinical Science and Molecular Medicine,* 1975, *48*(Suppl.), 171S–174S. (b)

Patel, C. *Biofeedback-aided behavioural methods in the management of hypertension.* Unpublished MD thesis, University of London, 1976. (a)

Patel, C. Reduction of serum cholesterol and blood pressure in hypertensive patients by behaviour modification. *Journal of the Royal College of General Practitioners,* 1976, *26,* 211–215. (b)

Patel, C. H. Biofeedback-aided relaxation and meditation in the management of hypertension. *Biofeedback and Self-Regulation,* 1977, *2,* 1–44.

Patel, C., & Carruthers, M. Coronary risk factor reduction through biofeedback-aided relaxation and meditation. *Journal of the Royal College of General Practitioners,* 1977, *27,* 401–405.

Patel, C., Marmot, M. M., & Terry, D. J. Controlled trial of biofeedback-aided behavioural methods in reducing mild hypertension. *British Medical Journal,* 1981, *282,* 2005–2008.

Patel, C. H., Marmot, M., Terry, D. J., Carruthers, M., & Sever, P. *Coronary risk factor reduction through biofeedback aided relaxation and meditation.* Paper presented at the 52nd annual scientific meeting of the American Heart Association, Anaheim, California, November 1979.

Patel, C. H., & North, W. R. S. Randomised controlled trial of yoga and biofeedback in the management of hypertension. *Lancet,* 1975, *ii,* 93–95.

Peters, R. K., Benson, H., & Peters, J. M. Daily relaxation response breaks in a working population: II. Effects on blood pressure. *American Journal of Public Health,* 1977, *67,* 954–959.

Ram Dass, B. *Journey of awakening: A meditator's guidebook.* New York: Bantam, 1978.

Sackett, D. L., Gibson, E. S., Taylor, D. W., Haynes, R. B., Hockett, B. C., Roberts, R. R., & Johnson, A. L. Randomised clinical trial of strategies for improving medication compliance in primary hypertension. *Lancet,* 1975, *i,* 1205–1207.

Schachter, J. Pain, fear and anger in hypertensives and normotensives. *Psychosomatic Medicine,* 1957, *19,* 17.

Seer, P., & Raeburn, J. M. Meditation training and essential hypertension: A methodological study. *Journal of Behavioural Medicine,* 1980, *3,* 59–73.

Selye, H. *The stress of life.* New York: McGraw-Hill, 1956.

Shafii, M., Lavely, R. A., & Jaffe, R. Meditation and marijuana. *American Journal of Psychiatry,* 1974, *131,* 60–63.

Shafii, M., Lavely, R. A., & Jaffe, R. Meditation and the prevention of alcohol abuse. *American Journal of Psychiatry,* 1975, *132,* 942–945.

Shapiro, A. P. An experimental study of comparative responses of blood pressure to different noxious stimuli. *Journal of Chronic Diseases,* 1961, *13,* 293–311.

Sleight, P. Baroreceptor function in hypertension. In C. Berglund, L. Hansson, & L. Werko (Eds.), *Pathophysiology and management of arterial hypertension.* Mölndal, Sweden: A. Lindregn & Sons, 1975.

Stone, R. A., & De Leo, J. Psychotherapeutic control of hypertension. *New England Journal of Medicine,* 1976, *294,* 80–84.

Vaughan Williams, E. M., Hassan, M. O., Floras, J. S., Sleight, P., & Jones, V. J. Adaptation of hypertensives to treatment with cardioselective and non-selective beta-blockers: Absence of correlation between bradycardia and blood pressure control and reduction in slope of QT/RR relation. *British Heart Journal,* 1980, *44,* 437–487.

Veterans Administration Cooperative Study Group on Antihypertensive Agents. Effects of treatment on morbidity in hypertension: I. Results in patients with diastolic blood pressures averaging 115 through 129 mm Hg. *Journal of the American Medical Association,* 1967, *202,* 1028–1034.

Veterans Administration Cooperative Study Group on Antihypertensive Agents. Effects of treatment on morbidity in hypertension: II. Results in patients with diastolic blood pressures averaging 90 through 114 mm Hg. *Journal of the American Medical Association,* 1970, *213,* 1143–1152.

Veterans Administration Cooperative Study Group on Antihypertensive Agents. Effects of treatment on morbidity in hypertension: III. Influence of age, diastolic pressure and cardiovascular disease. *Circulation,* 1972, *45,* 991–1004.

Wallace, R. K., & Benson, H. The physiology of meditation. *Scientific American,* 1972, *226,* 84–90.

Watson, L. *Supernature: The natural history of the supernatural.* London: Hodder & Stoughton, 1973.

Wilson, A. F., Honsberger, R., Chiu, J. T., & Novey, H. S. Transcendental meditation and asthma. *Respiration,* 1975, *32,* 74–80.

Wolf, S., & Wolff, H. G. A summary of experimental evidence relating life stress to the pathogenesis of essential hypertension in man. In E. T. Bell (Ed.), *Hypertension.* Minneapolis: University of Minnesota Press, 1951.

Wolpe, J. *Psychotherapy by reciprocal inhibition.* Stanford, Calif.: Stanford University Press, 1958.

Woolfolk, R. L., Carr-Kaffashan, L., McNulty, T. F., & Lehrer, P. M. Meditation training as a treatment for insomnia. *Behavior Therapy,* 1976, *7,* 359–365.

Wright, B. M., & Dore, C. F. A random zero sphygmomanometer. *Lancet,* 1970, *i,* 337–338.

Zamarra, J. W., Besseghini, I., & Wittenberg, S. The effects of the Transcendental Meditation Program on the exercise performance of patients with angina pectoris. In D. W. Orme-Johnson & J. T. Farrow (Eds.), *Scientific research on the Transcendental Meditation Program: Collected papers.* Rheinweiler, West Germany: Maharishi European Research University Press, 1977.

5 MODERN FORMS OF MEDITATION

PATRICIA CARRINGTON

HISTORY OF THE METHOD

Modern forms of meditation, simplified and divested of esoteric trappings and religious overtones, possess some unique therapeutic properties. This chapter presents ways in which these noncultic techniques can be applied in clinical practice.

Meditation is a mental device that limits stimulus input by directing attention to a single unchanging or repetitive stimulus. It is usually practiced seated, in a quiet environment. The object of the meditator's attention may be a mentally repeated sound, the breath, or any number of other appropriate focal points. When his or her attention wanders, he or she is directed to bring it back to this attentional object in an easy, unforcing manner.

While a basically simple procedure, meditation has been used by numerous societies throughout recorded history to alter consciousness in a way that has been perceived as deeply beneficial. Traditionally, its benefits have been defined as spiritual in nature, and meditation has constituted a part of many religious practices. Recently, however, simple forms of meditation have been used for stress management with excellent results.

Contributing to the rising interest in the meditative techniques is the fact that these techniques are related to the biofeedback techniques (which also emphasize a delicately attuned awareness of inner processes) and to the relaxation methods used in behavior therapies. In addition to providing deep relaxation, however, the meditative disciplines appear to assist the client in an area peripheral to many other therapeutic interventions—the fostering of communication between the client and his or her own self, *apart from* his or her interpersonal environment. In a world where inner enrichment from any source is scarce, many clients hunger for a more profound sense of self than is implicit in merely "getting along with others." Such people seek an awareness of their identity as *being* (as distinct from identity as *doing*). The inner communion of meditation offers a means of fulfilling this need, thus promising to heal an aspect of the psyche that may be as needful as any other presently identified. The use of meditation along with other forms of therapy may therefore be an inevitable accompaniment of the trend currently seen in the behavioral sciences toward encompassing more and varied aspects of life.

NONCULTIC METHODS

Of all the Westernized forms of meditation, transcendental meditation (TM) is the most widely known and extensively studied to date. More accurately described as "transitional" rather than modern, because it retains certain cultic features such as the "puja" (Hindu religious ceremony), TM is taught by an organization that does not permit mental health practitioners to assume an active role in its clinical management (unless they are TM teachers). Despite its popularity with segments of the general public, therefore, the TM method has been relatively little used in clinical settings.

Among the clinically oriented meditation techniques, "clinically standardized meditation" (CSM) (Carrington, 1978) and "respiratory one method" (ROM) (Benson, 1975) have been the most widely used to date. These techniques were devised with clinical objectives in mind and are strictly noncultic. The methods differ from each other in several important respects, however.

A trainee learning CSM selects a sound from a standard list of sounds (or creates one according to directions) and then repeats this sound mentally, without intentionally linking the sound to the breathing pattern or pacing it in any structured manner. CSM is thus a relatively permissive meditation technique and may be subjectively experienced as almost "effortless." By contrast, when practicing ROM, the trainee repeats the word "one" (or another word or phrase) to himself or herself mentally, while at the same time intentionally linking this word with each exhalation. ROM is thus a relatively disciplined form of meditation with two meditational objects—the chosen word *and* the breath. ROM thus requires more mental effort than CSM and may appeal to a different type of person.

Other modern methods of meditation have also been used in some clinical settings, but they are less standardized and thus depend more heavily on individual expertise and the personality of the instructor. These less commonly used forms are not discussed here, although their usefulness in the proper hands is not to be negated.

THE PHYSIOLOGY OF MEDITATION

All of the simplified meditation techniques—including the transitional form, TM—have in common the fact that they rapidly bring about a deeply restful state that possesses certain well-defined characteristics.

Research has shown that during meditation, body and mind typically enter a state of profound rest. Oxygen consumption can be lowered during 20 to 30 minutes of meditation to a degree ordinarily reached only after 6 to 7 hours of sleep (Wallace, Benson, & Wilson, 1971); heart and respiration rates typically decrease during meditation (Allison, 1970; Wallace, 1970); and forearm blood flow and forehead skin temperatures increase (Ritterstaedt & Schenkluhn, as cited in Kannellakos, 1974), suggesting a shift toward parasympathetic dominance. Electrical resistance of the skin also tends to increase markedly during meditation (Wallace, 1970), suggesting a lowering of anxiety at this time, while a sharp decline in the concentration of blood lactate may occur (Wallace *et al.,* 1971).

During the meditative state, the electroencephalograph (EEG) shows an alert–drowsy pattern with high alpha and occasional theta wave patterns, as well as an unusual pattern of swift shifts from alpha to slower (more sleep-like) frequencies and then back again (Das & Gastaut, 1957; Wallace *et al.,* 1971). These findings suggest that meditation may be an unusually fluid state of consciousness, partaking of qualities of both sleep and wakefulness and possibly resembling the hypnogogic or "falling-asleep" state more than any other state of consciousness. A number of studies have also shown that the physiology of meditation differs from that of ordinary rest with eyes closed and from most hypnotic states (Brown, Stewart, & Blodgett, as cited in Kanellakos, 1974; Wallace, 1970; Wallace *et al.,* 1971).

It appears, therefore, that during meditation deep physiological relaxation, somewhat similar to that occurring in the "deepest" non-rapid-eye-movement (REM) sleep phase, occurs in a context of wakefulness. Wallace *et al.* have thus termed meditation a "wakeful, hypometabolic state" (Wallace *et al.,* 1971) and Gellhorn and Kiely call it "a state of trophotropic dominance compatible with full awareness" (Gellhorn & Kiely, 1972).

When practiced regularly, meditation also appears to alter behavior occurring outside of the meditative state itself, with both clinical and research evidence suggesting that a number of beneficial changes may take place in people who meditate. These changes are described later, when clinical indications for meditation are discussed.

THEORETICAL UNDERPINNINGS

Several theories have been proposed concerning the manner in which meditation operates to effect change. The four most widely accepted are presented below.

GLOBAL DESENSITIZATION

There is an interesting similarity between the situation occurring during a meditation session and that occurring during the technique of systematic desensitization used in behavior therapy (Carrington & Ephron, 1975; Goleman, 1971). In the latter process, increasingly greater increments of anxiety (prepared in a graded hierarchy) are systematically "counterconditioned" by being paired with an induced state of deep relaxation. If the treatment is successful, presentation of the originally disturbing stimulus ceases to produce anxiety.

In meditation, awareness of the meditative "focus" (the mantra,[1] the breathing, a candle flame, or whatever) becomes a signal for turning inward and experiencing a state of deep relaxation. Simultaneously, the meditator maintains a permissive attitude with respect to thoughts, images, or sensations experienced during meditation. Without rejecting or unduly holding onto these thoughts, he or she lets them "flow through the mind" while continuing to direct attention to the focal point of the meditation.

This dual process—free-flowing thoughts occurring simultaneously with a repetitive stimulus that induces a state of calm—sets up a subjective state in which deep relaxation is paired with a rapid, self-initiated review of an exceedingly wide variety of mental contents and areas of ten-

---

[1] A resonant sound used for purposes of meditation. In the modern forms of meditation the mantra is most often repeated silently, by thinking.

sion, both verbal and nonverbal. As thoughts, images, sensations, and amorphous impressions drift through the mind during meditation, the soothing effect of the meditative focus appears to neutralize the disturbing thoughts. No matter how unsettling a meditation session may feel, a frequent response of meditators is that they discover that upon emerging from meditation, the "charge" has been taken off their current concerns or problems.

Do the modern forms of meditation "work," then, merely because they are a form of systematic desensitization? Such a reductionist point of view would seem to overlook certain important differences between these approaches. In systematic desensitization, therapist and patient work together to identify specific areas of anxiety and then proceed to deal with a series of single isolated problems in a sequential, highly organized fashion. During meditation, the areas of anxiety to be "desensitized" are selected by the responding organism (the meditating person) in an entirely automatic manner. At this time, the brain of the meditator might be said to act like a computer programmed to run certain material through "demagnetizing" circuits capable of handling large amounts of data at one time. We might conceptualize subsystems within the brain scanning vast memory stores at lightning speed during the meditative state, with the aim of selecting those contents of the mind that are most likely to be currently tolerated without undue anxiety. For these reasons, meditation would seem to operate with a considerably wider scope than systematic desensitization, although for exactly this reason, it may lack the clinical precision of the latter.

BLANK-OUT

Ornstein (1972) has proposed that mantra meditation (or other forms of "concentrative" meditation in which stimulus input is intentionally limited) may create a situation similar to that occurring when the eye is prevented from continuously moving over the surface of the visual field, but is instead forced to view a constant fixed image without recourse to scanning. When an image is projected onto a contact lens placed over the retina, the lens can follow the movement of the eye so that the image becomes stabilized in the center of the visual field. Under such conditions, the image soon becomes invisible; without constantly shifting his or her eyes to different parts of the perceived image, the subject apparently cannot register the object mentally. At this point, which Ornstein refers to as "blank-out," prolonged bursts of alpha waves may be recorded in the occipital cortex.

It seems, therefore, that the central nervous system is so constructed that if awareness of any sort is restricted to one unchanging source of stimulation, then consciousness of the external world may be turned off, and the individual may achieve a form of mental blank-out. Since mantra meditation involves continuously recycling the same input over and over, it may result in a blank-out effect, which in turn has the effect of temporarily clearing the mind of all thoughts. The after effect of blank-out may be an opening up of awareness, a renewed sensitivity to stimuli. After meditation, some meditators seem to experience an innocence of perception similar to that of the young child who is maximally receptive to all stimuli.

Although Ornstein does not address himself to the therapeutic implications of the blank-out effect, it is evident that at the least such a phenomenon might break up an unproductive mental set, thus giving the meditator the opportunity to restructure his or her thoughts along more productive lines. This could result in a fresh point of view on emotional problems, as well as on other aspects of life. Also, becoming more open to direct sensory experience may in itself be valuable in a world beset by problems deriving from overemphasis on cognitive activity. The enlivened experiencing following meditation (often described by meditators as "seeing colors more clearly," "hearing sounds more sharply," or "sensing the world more vividly") may in fact be a prime reason for the antidepressive effects of meditation.

EFFECTS OF RHYTHM

In mantra meditation, where a lilting sound is continuously repeated, rhythm is an obvious component. But rhythm also plays a role in all other forms of meditation, as the inner stillness involved allows the practicer to become profoundly aware of his or her own bodily rhythms. In the unaccustomed quiet of the meditative state, one's own breathing may be intimately sensed, the pulse rate may be perceived, and even such subtle sensations as the flow of blood through the veins are sometimes described as emerging into awareness. Some meditative techniques even use bodily rhythms as their object of focus, as when the Zen meditator is instructed to concentrate on his or her own natural, uninfluenced breathing.

This rhythmic component of meditation may be a major factor in inducing calm. Rhythm has universally been used as a natural tranquilizer; virtually all known societies use repeated sounds or rhythmic movements to quiet agitated infants, for example. The world over, parents have rocked children gently, hummed lullabies to them, recited nursery rhymes, repeated affectionate sounds in a lilting fashion, or bounced the children rhythmically on their laps, with an intuitive awareness of the soothing effects of such rhythmic activities on the children's moods. Similarly, in the psychological laboratory, Salk (1973) demonstrated that neonates responded to a recorded normal heartbeat sound (played to them without interruption day and night) by greatly lessened crying, as compared to a control group of infants who were not exposed to the sounds, and also by gaining more weight than the controls.

If contacting deep biological rhythms in oneself is a prominent component of meditation, then regular meditation might be expected to exert a deeply soothing effect. One might, so to speak, gain considerable stabilization from returning periodically to a source of well-being (in meditation), from which one could draw strength in order to deal more effectively with an outer environment whose rhythms are, more often than not, out of phase with one's own.

SHIFT IN HEMISPHERIC DOMINANCE

Research suggests that during meditation a greater equalization in the workload of the two cerebral hemispheres may occur (Banquet, 1973). Verbal, linear, time-linked thinking (processed through the left hemisphere, in the right-handed person) seems to be lessened during meditation as compared to the role it plays in everyday life, whole holistic, intuitive, wordless thinking (usually processed through the right hemisphere) comes more to the fore. The therapeutic effects derived from meditation may reflect this relative shift in hemispheric dominance.

Restrictive moral systems are for the most part transmitted verbally, with much role modeling dependent on verbal imitation. Ameliorative effects of meditation on self-blame, a clinically relevant benefit of this technique, might be explained by this basic shift away from the verbal mode during meditation. Minimizing verbal–conceptual experience (yet still remaining *awake*) may afford the individual temporary relief from self-derogatory thoughts, as well as from excessive demands on the self that have been formulated through internal verbalizations. Having obtained a degree of relief from these verbal injunctions *during* the meditative state, the meditator may find himself or herself less self-critical when returning to active life—the reduction in the strength of self-criticism having generalized from the meditative state to the life of action.

There are therefore a number of theoretical reasons why meditation might be of benefit in clinical practice. I now turn to the identification of those clinical conditions that have been shown to respond to the technique.

ASSESSMENT

CLINICAL CONDITIONS RESPONDING TO MEDITATION

Based on research and clinical reports, a substantial body of knowledge has accumulated concerning the usefulness of meditation in clinical practice. The discussion that follows summarizes the major findings in this area.

Reduction in Tension–Anxiety

In research where the effects of meditation on anxiety have been measured, results have consistently shown anxiety to be sharply reduced in a majority of subjects after they commenced the practice of meditation (Carrington, 1977). Accordingly, Glueck (1973), in a study conducted with a group of psychiatric inpatients, found that dosages of psychotropic drugs could be greatly reduced after these patients had been meditating for several weeks; in a majority of cases, sedatives could also be reduced or eliminated in these patients.

The quieting effects of meditation, however, differ from the effects brought about by psychotropic drugs. While the relaxation brought about by drugs may slow the person down and cause grogginess, the relaxation resulting from meditation does not bring with it any loss of alertness. On the contrary, meditation seems, if anything, to sharpen alertness. Groups of meditators have been shown to have faster reaction times (Appelle & Oswald, 1974), to have better refinement of auditory perception (Pirot, 1978), and to perform more rapidly and accurately on perceptual–motor tasks (Rimol, 1978) than nonmeditating controls.

Meditation may therefore be indicated where anxiety is a problem, and can often be used productively in place of tranquilizers or as a supplement to drug treatment.

Improvement in Stress-Related Illnesses

Many stress-related illnesses have proven responsive to meditation. Research has shown meditation to be correlated with improvement in the breathing patterns of patients with bronchial asthma (Honsberger & Wilson, 1973); in decreased blood pressure in both pharmacologically treated and untreated hypertensive patients (Benson, 1977; Patel, 1973, 1975); in reduced premature ventricular contractions in patients with ischemic heart disease (Benson, Alexander, & Feldman, 1975); in reduced serum cholesterol levels in hypercholesterolemic patients (Cooper & Aygen, 1979); in reduced sleep-onset insomnia (Miskiman, 1978; Woolfolk , Carr-Kaffashan, McNulty, & Lehrer, 1976); in amelioration of stuttering (McIntyre, Silverman, & Trotter, 1974); and in reduction of symptoms of psychiatric illness (Glueck & Stroebel, 1975), among other effects. Meditation may thus be a useful intervention in a wide variety of stress-related illnesses.

Increased Productivity

Meditation may bring out increased efficiency by eliminating unnecessary expenditures of energy; a beneficial surge of energy is often noted in persons who have commenced the practice. This can manifest itself variously as a lessened need for daytime naps, increased physical stamina, increased productivity on the job, increased ideational fluency, the dissolution of writer's or artist's "block," or the release of hitherto unsuspected creative potentials. Meditation may therefore be useful when it is desirable to increase a client's available energy and/or when a client is experiencing a block to productivity.

Lessening of Self-Blame

A useful by-product of meditation may be increased self-acceptance, often evidenced in clients as a lessening of unproductive self-blame. A spontaneous change in the nature of the meditator's self-statements—from self-castigating to self-accepting—suggests that the noncritical state experienced during the meditation session itself can generalize to daily life. Along with the tendency to be less self-critical, the meditator may show a simultaneous increase in tolerance for the human frailties of others, and there is often concomitant improvement in interpersonal relationships. Meditation may therefore be indicated when a tendency toward self-blame is excessive or where irrational blame of others has become a problem.

Antiaddictive Effects

A series of studies (Benson & Wallace, 1971; Shafii, Lavely, & Jaffe, 1974, 1975) have shown that, at least in persons who *continue* meditating for long periods of time (usually for a year or more), there may be a marked decrease in the use of nonprescription drugs, such as marijuana, amphetamines, barbiturates, and psychedelic substances (e.g., LSD). Many long-term meditators, in fact, appear to have discontinued use of such drugs entirely. Similar antiaddictive trends have been reported in ordinary cigarette smokers and abusers of alcohol as well (Shafii, Lavely, & Jaffe, 1976). Meditation may therefore be useful for a patient suffering from an addictive problem, particularly if that problem is in its incipient stage.

Mood Elevation

Both research and clinical evidence indicate that people suffering from mild chronic depression or from reactive depression may experience distinct elevation of mood after commencing meditation (Carrington, Collings, Benson, Robinson, Wood, Lehrer, Woolfolk, & Cole, 1980). People with acute depressive reactions do not generally respond well to meditation, however, and are likely to discontinue practicing it (Carrington & Ephron, 1975). Meditation therefore appears indicated in mild or chronic depressive reactions, but not in acute depressions.

Increase in Available Affect

Those who have commenced meditating frequently report experiencing pleasure, sadness, anger, love, or other emotions more easily than before. Sometimes they experience emotions that have previously been unavailable to them. Release of such emotions may occur during a meditation session or between sessions, and may be associated with the recovery of memories that are highly charged emotionally (Carrington, 1977). Meditation is therefore indicated where affect is flat, where the client tends toward overintellectualization, or where access to memories of an emotional nature is desired for therapeutic purposes.

Increased Sense of Identity

Meditation may increase "psychological differentiation." Persons possessing a high degree of psychological differentiation are said to be inner-directed rather than outer-directed; to be better able to use their own selves as reference points when making judgments or decisions; to have a clear sense of their separate identity; and to be aware of needs, feelings, and attributes that they recognize as their own, distinct from those of others. Such persons have been termed "field-independent." Persons with a less developed sense of separate identity—those who tend to rely on external sources for definition of their attitudes, judgments, sentiments, and views of themselves—have been termed "field-dependent."

When meditators have been tested for field dependence–independence before learning to meditate, and then retested several months later, studies from several different laboratories have shown changes in the direction of greater field independence following the commencement of the practice of meditation (Hines, as cited in Carrington, 1977; Pelletier, 1978). Such studies suggest that a fundamental change in the person's perception of his or her own self may take place as a result of meditation.

Consistent with the research on field independence, meditating clients frequently report that they have become more aware of their own opinions since commencing meditation; that they are not as easily influenced by others as they were previously; and that they can arrive at decisions more quickly and easily. They may also be able to sense their own needs better, and thus may become more outspoken and self-assertive and more able to stand up for their own rights effectively.

One result of the increased sense of identity fostered by meditation may be marked improvement in the ability of a meditator to separate from significant others when such separation is called for. Meditation can thus be extremely useful in pathological bereavement reactions, or where an impending separation (threatened death of a loved one, contemplated divorce, upcoming separation from growing children, etc.) presents a problem.

Meditation is therefore indicated where separation anxiety is a problem. Since it is particularly useful in bolstering the inner sense of "self" necessary for effective self-assertion, it may also be helpful as an adjunct to assertiveness training.

Lowered Irritability

The meditating person may become markedly less irritable in his or her interpersonal relationships within a relatively short period of time after commencing meditation (Carrington *et al.*, 1980). Meditation thus appears indicated where impulsive outbursts or chronic irritability is a symptom. This recommendation includes cases of organic irritability, since preliminary observations have shown meditation to be useful in increasing overall adjustments in several cases of brain injury (Glueck, 1973).

HOW TO ASSESS FOR USE OF THE METHOD

A few attempts have been made to identify personality characteristics of the meditation-responsive person. The bulk of these studies have used nonclinical populations, however, and their criteria for "responsiveness to meditation" have not been relevant to problems involved in clinical assessment. The only area of *clinical* improvement that has been experimentally addressed in an attempt to identify its correlation with personality factors is anxiety. Beiman, Johnson, Puente, Majestic, and Graham (1980) noted that the more "internal locus of control" that participants reported prior to learning meditation, the greater were their reductions in anxiety as measured by the Fear Survey Schedule; and Smith (1978) found that reductions in trait anxiety following meditation training were moderately correlated with two of Cattell's Sixteen Personality Factor Inventory (16-PF) factors: "autia" (preoccupation with inner ideas and emotions) and "schizothymia" (steadiness of purpose, withdrawal, emotional flatness, and "coolness"). However, Carrington *et al.* (1980), studying employee stress in a large corporation, found no significant correlations between any of the 16-PF factors (including anxiety) measured at pretest, and subsequent drops in symptomology as measured by the Revised 90-Item Symptom Checklist (SCL-90–R), a validated self-report inventory.

At this point, therefore, the research is too inconclusive to permit us to predict which clients will respond to meditation by means of standard personality tests. There has, however, been an attempt to identify predictive personality variables correlated with successful meditation practice on a theoretical basis. Davidson and Schwartz (1976) have suggested that relaxation techniques have varied effects, depending on the system at which they are most directly aimed. They categorize progressive relaxation as a "somatically oriented technique," because it involves learning to pay closer attention to physiological sensations, particularly muscle tension; while they categorize forms of meditation in which a word or sound is internally repeated as "cognitively oriented techniques," since repeating a word (i.e., the mantra) presumably blocks other ongoing cognitive activity. In support of this, Schwartz, Davidson, and Goleman (1978) report questionnaire data showing that meditation produces greater decreases in cognitive symptoms of anxiety than does physical exercise, while the latter appears to produce greater decreases in somatic anxiety symptoms.

On the basis of the Davidson–Schwartz hypothesis, some clinicians have felt justified in advising meditation for clients who show symptoms of cognitive anxiety, and in advising physiologically oriented techniques such as progressive relaxation or autogenic training for those who show symptoms of somatic anxiety. While this criterion has the advantage of offering the therapist clear-cut guidelines, the empirical support for cognitive–somatic specialization remains at best insubstantial (see Lehrer & Woolfolk, Chapter 13, this volume).

To assess for the suitability of meditation for a particular client, a clinician may do well to start out by determining whether this client shows one or more of the meditation-responsive symptoms or difficulties. The following is a summary checklist of these primary indicators of meditation:

- Tension and/or anxiety states
- Psychophysiological disorders
- Chronic fatigue states
- Insomnias and hypersomnias
- Abuse of "soft" drugs, alcohol, or tobacco
- Excessive self-blame
- Chronic low-grade depressions or subacute reaction depressions
- Irritability, low frustration tolerance
- Strong submissive trends, poorly developed psychological differentiation, difficulties with self-assertion
- Pathological bereavement reactions, separation anxiety
- Blocks to productivity or creativity
- Inadequate contact with affective life

• A need to shift emphasis from client's reliance on therapist to reliance on self (of particular use when terminating psychotherapy)

If the therapist determines that the client possesses the requisite pathology for use of meditation, he or she should recognize that other modalities may also be used for treating these same symptoms. At this point, therefore, the decision to employ meditation becomes a practical one. The following are some of the factors that may guide this decision:

1. *Self-discipline.* The degree to which the client has a disciplined life style may be an important factor to consider when deciding on meditation as a stress management technique. Meditation requires less self-discipline than do most other methods currently used for stress control. The technique itself can usually be taught in a single session, with the remainder of the instruction consisting of training in practical management of the method. Unlike some other techniques, meditation does not require the memorization and carrying out of any sequential procedures. It does not even require the mental effort involved in visualizing muscle groups and their relaxation, or in constructing "calm scenes" or other images. The modern forms of meditation are simple one-step operations that soon become quite automatic. They are therefore particularly useful for those clients who may not be willing to make a heavy commitment in terms of time or effort, or in situations where relatively rapid results are desired.

2. *Self-reinforcing properties.* For many clients, the peaceful, drifting mental state of meditation is experienced as unusually pleasurable, a "vacation" from all cares. This self-reinforcing property of meditation makes it especially appealing to many clients. Other things being equal, a modern form of meditation is more likely to be continued, once experienced, than are the more focused relaxation procedures. Therefore, when motivation to continue with a program for stress management is minimal, meditation may be an especially useful strategy.

3. *Contraindication for clients with excessive need to control.* Clients who fear loss of control may equate meditation with hypnosis or forms of mind control, and may thus be wary of learning the technique. If they do learn it, they may experience the meditation as a form of punishment, a surrender, a loss of dominance, or a threat to a need on their part to manipulate others; they may soon discontinue the practice unless therapeutic intervention brings about a sufficient change in attitude. Such overly controlling clients may prefer a more "objective" technique that they can manage through conscious effort (e.g., by tensing and relaxing muscles, dealing with biofeedback hardware, etc.). The response of a client to the clinician's initial suggestion that he or she learn meditation

will often be the deciding factor—those clients who fear loss of control from meditation will usually indicate this and will respond negatively to the suggestion that they learn the technique.

LIMITATIONS OF THE METHOD

Tension–Release Side Effects

Like all techniques used to effect personality change, meditation has its limitations. One of these is the stress–release component of meditation, which must be understood if this technique is to be used effectively. Particularly in the new meditator, physiological and/or psychological symptoms of a temporary nature may appear during or following meditation. These have been described elsewhere (Carrington, 1977, 1978) and appear to be caused by the release of deep-seated nonverbal tensions. Their occurrence can be therapeutically useful, provided the therapist is trained in handling them properly; however, too rapid a release of tension during or following meditation can cause difficulties and discouragement in a new meditator and may result in a client's backing off from meditation or even abandoning the practice altogether. For this reason, careful adjustment of meditation time and other key aspects of the technique must be made if this modality is to be used successfully. Such adjustments can usually eliminate problems of tension–release in short order; accordingly adjustment of the meditation to suit each practicer's individual needs is central to such modern forms of meditation as CSM.

Rapid Behavior Change

Another potential problem in the use of meditation stems from the rapidity with which certain alterations in behavior may occur. Some of these changes may be incompatible with the life style or defensive system of the client. Should positive behavioral change occur before the groundwork for it has been laid (i.e., before the client's value system has readjusted through therapy), an impasse can occur, which must then be resolved in one of two ways: (1) The pathological value system must be altered to incorporate the new attitude brought about by the meditation; or (2) the practice of meditation must be abandoned. If the meditator facing such an impasse has recourse to psychotherapy to work through the difficulties involved, this usually allows the individual to continue productively with meditation and make use of it to effect a basic change in life style.

Some of the ways in which meditation-related behavioral changes may threaten a client's pathological life style are as follows:

1. Meditation may foster a form of self-assertion that conflicts with an already established neurotic "solution" of being overly self-effacing. The tendency toward self-effacement must then be modified before meditation can be accepted into the person's life as a permanent and beneficial practice.

2. Meditation tends to bring about feelings of well-being and optimism which may threaten the playing out of a depressive role that may have served an important function in the client's psychic economy.

3. The deeply pleasurable feelings that can accompany or follow a meditation session can cause anxiety. For example, clients with masturbation guilt may unconsciously equate meditation (an experience where one is alone and gives *oneself* pleasure) to masturbation, and thus may characterize it as a "forbidden" activity.

4. Meditation can result in an easing of life pace, which may threaten to alter a fast-paced, high-pressured life style that is used neurotically as a defense or in the service of drives for power, achievement, or control. Clients sensing that this may happen may refuse to start meditating in the first place—or, if they start, may quickly discontinue the practice—unless these personality problems are treated.

5. The client may develop negative reactions to the meditation process, or to a meditational object of focus such as a mantra. Some individuals view meditation initially as being almost "magical." When they are inevitably forced to recognize that the technique varies in its effectiveness according to external circumstances, or according to their own mood or state of health, they may then become angry and quit the practice unless the clinician can help them modify their irrational demands.

Fortunately, such complications as these do not occur in all meditating patients. Often meditation assists the course of therapy in such a straightforward fashion that there is little necessity to be overly concerned with the client's reaction to it.

CAUTIONS

1. An occasional person may be hypersensitive to meditation, so that he or she needs much shorter sessions than the average. Such a person may not be able to tolerate the usual 15- to 20-minute sessions prescribed

in many forms of meditation and may require drastic reductions in meditation time before benefiting from the technique. Most problems of this sort can be successfully overcome by adjusting the meditation time to suit the individual's needs.

2. Overmeditation can be dangerous. On the theory that "If one pill makes me feel better, taking the whole bottle should make me feel exceptionally well!," some clients may, on their own, decide to meditate 3 or 4 hours (or more) per day instead of the prescribed 15–20 minutes only once or twice a day. Just as with a tonic or medicine, meditation may cease to have beneficial effects if it is taken in too heavy doses, and may become detrimental instead. Release of emotional material that is difficult to handle may occur with prolonged meditation; in a person with an adverse psychiatric history, the commencement of meditation training has been known to precipitate psychotic episodes (Carrington, 1977; Lazarus, 1976). Although it is not certain that overmeditation will lead to such serious results in relatively stable people, it is probable unwise for any person to enter into prolonged meditation sessions, except in special settings (such as a retreat) where careful supervision is available.

The fact that meditation may be a tonic and facilitator when taken in short well-spaced dosages, but may have an antitherapeutic effect when taken in unduly prolonged sessions, is essential to consider when reviewing a psychiatric case history where any form of meditation has previously been practiced by a client. Certain forms of meditation currently promoted by "cults" *demand* up to 4 hours of daily meditation from their followers—an important factor to note when assessing some of the "brainwashing" effects frequently reported by ex-members of these cults.

3. Meditation may enhance the action of certain drugs in some clients. Requirements for antianxiety and antidepressive drugs, as well as antihypertensive and thyroid-regulating medications, should therefore be monitored in patients who are practicing meditation. Sometimes the continued practice of meditation may permit a desirable low-dosage treatment of such drugs over more prolonged periods, and occasionally may permit the discontinuance of drug therapy altogether.

To avoid such difficulties as these, meditation should therefore be practiced in moderation, with the meditator following instructions in a reliable meditation training program. Full training in the management and adjustment of the technique, not just instruction in *how* to meditate, is essential in the clinical use of meditation.

THE METHOD

Optimal use of meditation in a clinical setting depends on teaching the client to manage the technique successfully—a consideration that can easily be overlooked. Unless routine problems that arise during the practice of meditation are handled, the likelihood of obtaining satisfactory compliance is poor. If the technique is regulated to meet the needs of the particular client, however, compliance is often excellent.

It is doubtful if meditation can ever be taught effectively through written instructions, since correct learning of the technique relies on the communication of the "meditative mood"—a subtle atmosphere of tranquility best transferred through nuances of voice and tonal quality. Meditation can be taught successfully by means of tape recordings, however, provided the latter effectively convey this elusive meditative mood (i.e., that they are not "cold" or "mechanical" in nature) and that the recorded teaching system is sufficiently detailed in terms of the information it conveys, so that the trainee is instructed in handling minor problems that may arise before the technique becomes truly workable.

The CSM method (which incorporates the ROM method as an alternate form of meditation) teaches meditation through cassette tapes and a programmed instruction text and comprises a total training program in the management of meditation. Because of these advantages, the following discussion on method is confined to CSM. Some of the points made, however, can be applied to any of the modern meditation methods.

The following discussion covers some of the ways in which CSM may be introduced to a client.

INTRODUCTION OF THE METHOD

Clinicians are in a strategic position to introduce the idea of learning CSM to their clients. This is best done by referring to specific difficulties or symptoms that a client has previously identified. Simply mentioning research that suggests that meditation may be useful for these problems is often all that is needed to motivate the client to learn the technique.

To forestall misunderstandings, however, several aspects of the CSM method are useful to mention when the subject of meditation is first introduced. The clinician will want to indicate that this form of meditation is strictly noncultic in nature. Clients with religious convictions will not want their beliefs violated by competitive belief systems and can be relieved to learn that CSM is a "scientifically developed" form of meditation. In addition, clients who are uncomfortable with seemingly unconventional interventions will also benefit from being reassured about the noncultic nature of the method.

The clinician will also want to emphasize that the technique is easily learned, since one of the most prevalent misconceptions about meditation is the notion that it requires intense mental concentration. Most people are reassured by the knowledge that a modern technique such as CSM does not require forced "concentration" at all, but actually proceeds automatically once it has been mastered. The clinician should also routinely check on the client's knowledge about and/or previous experience with meditation in order to clear up any further questions about the method.

The preliminary discussion between therapist and client is typically brief, but certain clients may need to be introduced to meditation in a more planned manner. "Type A" clients, for example, may resist learning meditation (or any other relaxation technique) because the idea of "slowing down" threatens their life style, which is often hectic and high-pressured. When recommending CSM to a Type A person, therefore, a useful strategy is to indicate that the time that this person will take out of his or her day for meditation practice is likely to result in increased efficiency. Much research suggests that this is so, and Type A individuals are typically achievement-oriented.

Type A or extremely active people can also be helped to accept meditation by being informed that they can break up their practice into a series of what have been termed "minimeditations" (Carrington, 1978). These are short meditations of 2 or 3 minutes (sometimes only 30 seconds) in duration, which can be scattered throughout the day. Frequent minimeditations may be much more compatible to an impatient, driven sort of person than longer periods of meditation may be (although these can be used too), and they have the advantage of helping the client reduce transient elevations in stress levels *as these occur.*

A final strategy useful when recommending meditation to Type A or exceedingly active persons can be to inform them that they can use CSM while simultaneously engaged in some solitary sport that they may already practice and enjoy. Meditation can be successfully combined with solitary, repetitive physical activities such as jogging, walking, bicycling, or swimming, and this practice may be a salutary one. Benson, Dryer, and

Hartley (1978) have shown, for example, that repeating a mantra mentally while exercising on a stationary bicycle can lead to increased cardiovascular efficiency.

THE PHYSICAL ENVIRONMENT AND EQUIPMENT

CSM is usually taught by means of three cassette recordings and a programmed instruction workbook, but instruction in the technique can also be carried out in person where indicated.

With the recorded training, the client is introduced to the principles of meditation by an introductory tape played before instruction per se is undertaken. Later (usually on another day), the client listens to the actual instruction recording under quiet conditions in a room arranged to certain specifications. During the instruction session, the trainee repeats his or her mantra out loud in imitation of the instructor and meditates silently "along with" the latter. Subsequently, he or she fills out a post-intruction questionnaire and completes the instruction session by listening to the other side of the tape, which directs meditation practice for the next 24 hours.

On the following day the trainee listens to another tape, which discusses potential problems involved in meditation practice, and plays the final tape of the series 1 week later. The latter prepares the trainee for a permanent practice of meditation. During the week's training period, the trainee works with the programmed instruction text to master the details of his or her meditation practice and to adjust the technique to suit his or her personal needs. The clinician may also assist in making clinically relevant adjustments of the technique.

Most clients learn CSM in their homes (or hospital rooms), making their own arrangements for a suitable instruction environment. Where clients are taught on the premises of the clinician (usually so that the latter can immediately advise on adjustment of the technique), the clinician makes available a quiet, uncluttered room where the client can be alone while learning. This room typically contains a comfortable straight-backed chair and some visually pleasant object such as a plant or vase upon which the trainee can gaze when entering and exiting from meditation. The arrangements are simple but must be carefully observed for maximum effect.

THERAPIST–CLIENT RELATIONSHIP

Once the clinician has selected meditation as the intervention of choice, he or she must then decide whether to teach CSM by means of the recordings or in person. Factors influencing this decision typically center on special requirements of the client.

When weighing the factors involved, the following advantages of recorded instruction should be noted:

1. Learning the technique in his or her home or domitory room facilitates the client's generalization of the meditative response to the living situation; this helps to prevent problems that can occur when instruction is given in person in a setting outside the home. In the latter instance, trainees frequently complain that their subsequent meditation sessions are never "the same as" or "as good as" their initial learning session—a factor that may adversely affect compliance.

2. Learning the technique alone, through his or her own efforts, fosters the client's reliance on *self* as an initiator of the practice.

3. Replaying the recordings at intervals reinforces the meditation practice. The recordings may also be used to reestablish the meditation routine after the client has temporarily ceased to practice it.

4. The client's family or friends can also learn to meditate from the recordings. Their subsequent involvement in the practice (plus the fact that on occasion they may meditate together with the client) can lend substantial support and improve compliance.

5. Certain clients are embarrassed at the idea of speaking the mantra out loud or sitting with eyes closed in anyone else's presence. Such clients find learning by tape preferable.

There are some situations where tape-recorded instruction is not suitable, however. Clients experiencing severe thought disturbances or other clinical symptoms that make it difficult for them to learn from a recording require personal instruction in the technique. Similarly, non-English-speaking clients, those who belong to a subculture that uses highly idiomatic speech, clients too physically ill to concentrate on a recording, or those who may have a natural antipathy to learning from recordings will also need to be instructed in person. There is a standardized procedure for teaching CSM by means of personal instruction.

People who have successfully used other meditation techniques often make excellent instructors of CSM, since almost all meditation techniques have a number of points in common. Even those trained in some of the more concentrative forms of meditation have been able to teach the non-concentrative, permissive approach of CSM after first learning the technique themselves and practicing it for several months prior to teaching it. Personal experience with this *particular* meditative technique is essential, in order that the prospective instructor understand the basic permissiveness of the technique.

Trainees receiving personal instruction first select a mantra from a list of 16 mantras in the workbook. They are instructed to choose the one that sounds most pleasant and soothing to them, or to make up a mantra according to simple instructions. The mantras used in this method are resonant sounds (often ending in the nasal consonants "m" or "n") that have no meaning in the English language, but that, in pretesting, have been shown to have a calming effect on many people. Such sounds as "Ah-nam," "Shi-rim," and "Ra-mah" are among those used.

After the trainee has selected a mantra, training is conducted in a peaceful setting removed from any disturbances that may detract from the "meditative mood." The instructor walks quietly, speaks in low tones, and typically conveys by his or her behavior a respect for the occasion of learning meditation.

When teaching meditation, the instructor repeats the trainee's mantra out loud in a rhythmical manner to demonstrate how this is done. The trainee then repeats the mantra in unison with the instructor, and finally alone. He or she is next asked to "whisper it" and then simply to "think it to yourself" silently, with eyes closed.

Instructor and trainee then meditate together for a period of 10 minutes, after which the trainee remains seated for a minute or two with eyes closed, allowing the mind to return to "everyday thoughts." The trainee is then asked to open his or her eyes very slowly.

At this point the instructor answers any questions the trainee may have about the technique and corrects any misconceptions, then leaves the room so that the trainee can meditate alone for a stated period of time (usually 20 minutes). The experience of meditating on one's own is included in order to "wean" the trainee as soon as possible from dependency on the instructor's presence when meditating.

Immediately following the first meditation session, the trainee completes a postinstruction questionnaire and reviews his or her responses with the instructor. In the postinstruction interview, procedures for a home meditation practice are clarified, and instructions are given for the trainee's meditation program for the next week. The trainee is then apprised of possible "tension–release side effects" (Carrington, 1978) and is taught how to handle these, should they occur.

Individual follow-up interviews are later held at intervals, or group meetings are scheduled where new meditators can gather to share meditation experiences, meditate in a group, or pick up new pointers on handling any problems that may arise in their practice. These trainees then learn to adjust their technqiues to suit their own individual needs and life styles.

Whatever the method of instruction (recorded or in person), close clinical supervision of the meditation practice is strongly advised. A careful follow-up program ensures much greater participation in a continued program of meditation.

RESISTANCE, COMPLIANCE, AND MAINTENANCE OF BEHAVIOR CHANGE

Problems of resistance have been discussed under "Limitations of the Method." Compliance and maintenance of behavior change are now considered.

Compliance

Researchers have found compliance with the modern forms of meditation to be about 50% among adults in a typical community, with about half of those who learn to meditate discontinuing the practice within 3 years of having learned it, and an even larger number cutting down to once instead of twice a day, or to only occasional use of the practice (Carrington, 1977).

Several problems emerge when we try to evaluate the existing compliance figures, however. The trend has been to define "compliance" as "regular daily practice" of the meditation technique in question, a viewpoint undoubtedly influenced by the TM organization's firm conviction that twice-daily practice is necessary in order to obtain benefits from meditation. Some recent findings cast doubt on the necessity of daily meditation for all people, however, and suggest that the degree of compliance that is necessary to produce benefits may be an individual matter.

When my colleagues and I (Carrington *et al.,* 1980) studied the use of two modern meditation techniques (CSM and ROM) in a working population self-selected for symptoms of stress, we found that after 5½ months of practicing meditation, these subjects showed highly significant reductions in symptoms of stress as measured by the SCL-90–R, in comparison with controls. However, when the groups were broken down into (1) "frequent practicers" (subjects who practiced their technique several times a week or more), (2) "occasional practicers" (subjects who practiced it once a week or less), and (3) "stopped practicers" (subjects who no longer practiced their technique), the results were unexpected. Although SCL-90–R improvement scores for stopped practicers and controls did not differ (as might be expected), no differences in degree of symptom improvement were found between frequent and occasional practicers when the scores for these two groups were compared, contrary to our expectation. Nevertheless, when frequent and occasional practicers were collapsed into a single "practicers" group, and stopped practicers and controls into a single "nonpracticers" group, the difference in degree of symptom reduction between these two groups was highly significant. As long as subjects practiced at all, then they were likely to show improvement in symptoms of stress. When they did not practice, they were unlikely to improve more than controls.

The finding in this study—that frequent practice appears unnecessary to produce symptomatic improvement—disagree with those in several studies using the TM technique. The latter studies have reported positive effects of frequent (as opposed to occasional) practice of meditation on neuroticism (Ross, 1978; Tjoa, 1978; Williams, Francis, & Durham, 1976), trait anxiety (Davies, 1978), autonomic instability (Orme-Johnson, Kiehlbauch, Moore, & Bristol, 1978), intelligence test scores (Tjoa, 1975), and measures of self-actualization (Ross, 1978). However, the Carrington *et al.* findings are in agreement with research that has reported no differences between frequent and occasional practicers with respect to anxiety reductions (Lazar, Farwell, & Farrow, 1978; Ross, 1978; Zuroff & Schwarz, 1978).

It should be noted that several differences exist between the above-mentioned study with the employee group and those studies using the TM technique that did not show effects for frequency of practice. All but one of the TM investigations were conducted with subjects who had signed up to learn TM at training centers. These subjects were not selected for high initial stress levels (although in some cases perceived stress may have played a role in their decision to learn meditation). It is therefore unlikely that they were under the same degree of stress as the employees in the Carrington *et al.* study, who had been self-selected for this variable and whose initial SCL-90–R scores fell at the edge of the clinical range. Possibly when stress symptoms approach clinical levels, even a moderate amount of meditation, or the use of meditation when needed, is sufficient to achieve sharp reductions in symptomatology. When the initial stress levels are close to the norm, however, it may be necessary to practice meditation more frequently in order to reduce symptoms to a still lower level.

Another factor differentiating the employee study from the others is that teachers of the TM technique prohibit the use of minimeditations, which they consider harmful to proper meditation practice. In the employee study, however, strong emphasis was laid upon the use of minimeditations in addition to full meditation sessions, and the effectiveness of this teaching was demonstrated by the fact that at the end of 5½ months, 88% of the employees who had learned meditation reported that they were using minimeditations. Minimeditations may therefore have exerted a leveling effect, causing a blurring of expected distinctions between frequent and occasional practicers.

Although frequency of practice could not predict stress reduction in the employee study, this should not be taken to mean that frequent practice of a meditation technique is not valuable. For some subjects in the study, regular daily practice may have been necessary for them to acquire noticeable benefits. Realizing this, such people may have developed the habit of meditating frequently. Other subjects, however, may have found it unnecessary to practice their technique more than a few times a week to obtain noticeable symptom improvement.

It is also not presently known whether frequent practice will *in time* produce beneficial changes in some practicers who do not report benefits from frequent practice during the first 6 months; whether physiological (as opposed to psychological) measures respond to occasional practice as well as they do to frequent practice; or whether effective control of a maladaptive form of behavior (e.g., drug addiction) requires the frequent practice of meditation in order to alter this behavior.

Research findings such as those described above, coupled with clinical reports on the benefits of using meditation on a contingency basis (and/or of using frequent minimeditations), suggest the wisdom of reconsidering our present criteria for compliance. This might serve to lessen some of the current confusion in the field. For example, in the Carrington *et al.* study, using "practicing at all" (whether frequent or occasional) as the criterion for compliance, 81% of the CSM subjects and 76% of the

ROM subjects were still "practicing" their respective technique at the end of 5½ months. However, using "frequent practice only" as the criterion for compliance, 50% of the CSM subjects and 30% of the ROM subjects were "practicing" their techniques by the end of this time. Which figures are the "true" ones?

Spontaneous comments offered by subjects in the Carrington *et al.* study (on a postexperimental questionnaire) may offer some clues. When these comments were examined in relation to frequency of practice, analysis revealed that more occasional practicers than frequent practicers were using their techniques for strategic purposes (i.e., as needed); that more frequent practicers than occasional practicers made strong positive statements about the benefits derived from their technique; and that only occasional practiers qualified their statements about their benefits (e.g., "Under extreme pressure in my department, I don't feel as tensed up, but don't find meditation as beneficial as I had hoped" or "I think there has been some possible effect"). The tentative statements of many of the occasional practitioners attest to the "in-between" quality of their evaluative statements, as opposed to the certainty that characterized those of the frequent practicers.

We might summarize the findings to date, then, by saying that the effects of frequency of practice are only partially known. While frequency may not play a major role in symptom reduction per se for certain patients (although it may for others), it may be positively related to perceived benefits in other areas such as personal growth, and seems clearly related to the degree of enthusiasm subjects experience for their technique.

In a practical sense, therefore, it would seem wise to encourage regularity of practice in a client wherever possible, without being unduly alarmed if that client should shift from meditating regularly to using the technique for strategic purposes only, or to relying heavily on minimeditations. The deciding factor should be the degree of benefit that the client is deriving from the practice. If, in the estimation of the clinician, this factor remains satisfactory, then even if the client meditates only occasionally or uses only minimeditations, his or her decision to employ the technique in this manner should be supported.

Also relevant to compliance is the manner in which meditators stop practicing. In the Carrington *et al.* study, the timetable for quitting in the stopped practicers was revealing. The practice of meditation appears to have stabilized markedly within the first 3 months. One-third of the stopped practicers reported that they had abandoned their technique within the first *2 weeks* after having learned it; another 27% reported that they abandoned it after between 2 and 6 weeks; and still another 37% reported having abandoned it after between 6 weeks and 3 months. Only one subject had abandoned the technique between 3 and 5½ months (during the final 2½ months of the study).

It would seem, therefore, that during the first 3 months of their practice, a more or less permanent stand was taken by these trainees with respect to continuation of their meditation practice. Thereafter, while a trainee might shift from frequent to occasional practice (or back again), he or she was extremely unlikely to stop practicing entirely. This timetable of attrition strongly suggests that once meditation has been successfully adopted and practiced for a period of several months, it may become a permanent coping strategy that can then be called upon by a trainee when he or she has need of it—in short, that the strategic use of meditation is not likely to be abandoned.

It has also been observed that meditators may stop practicing meditation temporarily for a variety of reasons. These "vacations" from meditation appear to be a normal part of the practice for many people and are not evidence of noncompliance. It is important, therefore, that the clinician not label a cessation of meditation practice as "dropping out" until such a fact has been proven correct. The client should be helped instead to understand that such "vacations" can be normal occurrences, and that meditators frequently return to their regular practice later on with renewed enthusiasm. In CSM, reuse of the meditation instruction recording by the client is recommended as a useful means of reinstating the meditation practice after having taken a break from it.

The clinician should also be aware that even if a client eventually abandons his or her technique, this is not necessarily a negative sign. Recent reports from a corporate program using CSM at New York Telephone suggest that after an extended period (e.g., 1 year or more) of successful meditation practice, some people may no longer need to practice meditation on a formal basis, because its benefits have been incorporated into their life style.

One telephone company employee reported that he no longer needed to meditate, because he had begun to spend his lunch hour eating by the fountain in the courtyard where he worked, "just watching the water rise and fall." He described this as so peaceful that afterward "I feel better for the rest of the day." He typically spent 20 minutes watching the fountain, but before he learned to meditate (approximately a year earlier), "I would never have thought of such a thing, because then I was always in a hurry, even when I had a lunch break." When asked whether his experience of gazing into the fountain had any features in common with meditation, he replied that although this had not occurred to him before, actually the two processes were "exactly the same, except that I don't think the mantra when I watch the fountain."

Similar reports from other long-term meditators, now being collected at New York Telephone, suggest that formal meditation may be phased out by some clients as a meditative approach to life is phased in. Such people appear to have substituted their own meditation equivalents for formal meditation sessions. This is by no means the case with all meditators, however. A sizable number of people need to continue with the formal practice of meditation indefinitely in order to maintain the beneficial changes brought about by the use of the technique.

Maintenance of Behavioral Change

As noted above, the maintenance of behavioral change is substantial and may be closely linked with compliance in some, but not necessarily in all, instances. However, cases have occasionally been reported where after several years of meditation, meditators have ceased to notice any more benefits accruing from their practice. Since these have all been anecdotal reports, it is unclear whether the people involved were actually no longer benefiting from their meditation practice, or whether benefits were still occurring but were not perceived because the meditators' tension levels had been reduced for so long a time. In clinical practice, an empirical test can be applied in the event of reports of diminished benefits. The client can be asked to stop practicing meditation for a stated period of time; if cessation of meditation brings no change in the clinical condition, or if it results in a beneficial change, then meditation (at least as originally learned and practiced) may have outgrown its usefulness for the client. Substitution of another variant of meditation, if this is desired, is sometimes useful at this point and can result in a revival of beneficial effects in some cases.

The reasons for these occasional apparent habituations to the method are unclear, as are the causes of reports of certain meditators' having experienced adverse effects after having practiced their techniques for prolonged periods of time. While the latter problem can usually be brought under control by proper readjustment of the meditation routine, discontinuance of the practice is in order where it cannot.

CASE EXAMPLE

Training in meditation was recommended for a middle-aged female client, because her chronic tension headaches had consistently resisted all forms of intervention, even though her other psychosomatic symptoms (e.g., gastric ulcer and colitis) had abated with therapy.

After she commenced meditation, this client's headaches worsened for a period of about a week (temporary symptom acceleration is not unusual following commencement of meditation) and then abruptly disappeared; the patient remained entirely free of headaches for 4 months (for the first time in many years).

During this period, however, she noticed personality changes that disturbed her and that she attributed to meditation. Formerly self-sacrificing and playing the role of a "martyr" to her children, husband, and parents, she now began to find herself increasingly aware of her own rights and impelled to stand up for them, sometimes so forcefully that it alarmed her. Although she was apparently effective in this new self-assertion (her adolescent sons began to treat her more gently, making far fewer scathing comments), other members of her family commented that she was no longer the "sweet person" that she used to be, and the client soon complained that "meditation is making me a hateful person."

At the same time this client also noticed that she was no longer talking compulsively—a change for which she received favorable comments from others, but which bothered her because she was now able to sense the social uneasiness that had been hidden beneath her compulsive chatter. She related this tendency to remain quieter in social situations directly to meditation, since it was more apt to occur soon after a meditation session. Unable to assimilate the personality changes noted, the client stopped meditating, despite the fact that her tension headaches then returned.

It was necessary at this point in therapy to trace the origins of this client's need to be self-effacing before she could consider reinstating the practice of meditation. In doing so, it was discovered that her competition with an older sister was at the root of much of her difficulty in this respect. This sister had been considered a "saint" by their parents, while the client had always been considered a troublesome, irritating child. During her childhood she had despaired at this state of affairs; but in her adolescence, she developed an intense compulsion to become more "saintly" than her exalted sister, although this often meant total sacrifice of her own wishes or needs to those of others. Even the simple pleasure of a meditation session seemed to this client to be a self-indulgence out of character for so "self-sacrificing" a person.

After working on these problems in therapy, and after some role playing with respect to positive forms of self-assertion, the client finally agreed to resume daily meditation. It was soon discovered, however, that the meditative process was once again pushing her toward self-assertion at too rapid a rate for her to handle. The therapist then suggested that she reduce her meditation to *once weekly*. Her meditation session was to take place only at the start of each therapy session, and the therapist was to meditate *with the client* at these times, giving tacit support to the client's right to independence and self-assertion and serving as a role model in terms of acceptance of a meditation practice in one's life.

These weekly joint meditative sessions proved extremely productive; the client described her sessions with her therapist as being "deeply restful," pleasurable, and constructive. Since her emotional responses to each meditation session could be promptly dealt with in the discussion that followed, guilt over self-indulgence was prevented from occurring. With this approach, the client's headaches again disappeared, and she began to experience personality changes typical of regular daily meditators, such as marked enrichment of a previously impoverished fantasy life. She repeatedly stated, however that this weekly meditation session was all she could "take" of meditation at one time without feeling "pounded" by it.

In this moderate dose, the client appeared well able to assimilate the changes in self-concept brought about by meditation, and the client–therapist relationship was used to enhance the effectiveness of the meditation through the joint meditation sessions.

As this case illustrates, the use of other forms of therapy along with meditation can be crucial in certain instances to the success of the technique. In most cases, however, meditation contributes to the patient's therapeutic progress with few if any complications.

COMMENTS AND REFLECTIONS

A note of caution seems appropriate at this point. Although it is clearly desirable to be clinically oriented in one's approach to meditation training, this need not be defined as making the instruction of the technique impersonal in nature. The clinician should be aware that, in a zeal for objectivity, he or she could inadvertently "throw the baby out with the bath water."

The attitude of quiet respect and the peaceful surroundings that have traditionally accompanied the teaching of meditation may have something important to teach us. They cannot, it seems, be lightly dispensed with without losing something essential to the meditative process. Properly taught, meditation can be a compelling subjective experience. To hand a client a sheet of instructions and tell him or her to "go home and meditate," therefore, is likely to result in a serious loss in terms of the importance the client will attach to learning the meditation, as well as to deprive him or her of a role model to demonstrate the subtle meditative mood.

Following the old adage, "easy come, easy go," those taught meditation in an abbreviated fashion and without attention to the conveying of the delicate mood inherent in this practice are apt to treat meditation casually and may soon discontinue its practice. When field-testing versions of the CSM recorded instructions, I discovered, for example, that clients' compliance increased in direct proportion to the inclusion in later versions of informal, "personal," mood-setting recordings. Similarly, when giving personal instruction in meditation, clinicians are advised to give careful attention to the setting and the mood that accompany the teaching of meditation. The instruction need not reflect any belief system, but it should be pleasant, peaceful, and in some sense rather special in nature. Learning meditation is an important moment in an individual's life. If it is treated as such, the entire practice takes on a new and deeper meaning.

A somewhat related issue is the tendency of some clinicians to view meditation as so "simple" that it can be taught in one session merely by imparting the technique itself, and that the client can then be left to his or her own devices. While the actual technique can indeed be taught in a single session, this does not mean that a successful practice of meditation has been established by doing this. The latter requires that a number of changes be made in the trainee's daily routine, that individual regulation of the technique be provided, and that knowledge of ways to handle problems that may arise in meditation practice be taught. Without full training in the *management* of meditation, learning the technique alone can be detrimental, in that it may lead a trainee to believe that he or she is not a likely candidate for meditation (because he or she may have run into some problems with its practice), when in fact this may not be the case at all.

The clinician who recommends meditation to a client must therefore be careful to supply complete training in all the practical aspects of the technique. Only in this manner can he or she insure that the method will have the best opportunity to be successful. Imparted with full respect for both its inherent ease *and* the problems involved in teaching it, meditation can be a potent tool for personality change—one that greatly enlarges the clinician's repertoire.

REFERENCES

Allison, J. Respiratory changes during the practice of transcendental meditation. *Lancet*, 1970, *7651*, 833–834.

Appelle, S., & Oswald, L. E. Simple reaction time as a function of alertness and prior mental activity. *Perceptual and Motor Skills*, 1974, *38*, 1263–1268.

Banquet, J. Spectral analysis of the EEG in meditation. *Electroencephalography and Clinical Neurophysiology*, 1973, *35*, 143–151.

Beiman, I. H., Johnson, S. A., Puente, A. E., Majestic, H. W., & Graham, L. E. Client characteristics and success in TM. In D. H. Shapiro & R. N. Walsh (Eds.), *The science of meditation*. Chicago: Aldine, 1980.

Benson, H. *The relaxation response*. New York: Morrow, 1975.

Benson, H. Systemic hypertension and the relaxation response. *New England Journal of Medicine*, 1977, *296*, 1152–1156.

Benson, H., Alexander, S., & Feldman, C. L. Decreased premature ventricular contractions through use of the relaxation response in patients with stable ischaemic heart disease. *Lancet*, 1975, *ii*, 380.

Benson, H., Dryer, T., & Hartley, H. L. Decreased CO_2 consumption during exercise with elicitation of the relaxation response. *Journal of Human Stress*, 1978, 38–42.

Benson, H., & Wallace, R. K. Decreased drug abuse with transcendental meditation: A study of 1,862 subjects. *Congressional Record*, 92nd Congress, First Session, Serial #92-1. Washington, D.C.: U.S. Government Printing Office, 1971.

Carrington, P. *Freedom in meditation*. New York: Anchor Press/Doubleday, 1977.

Carrington, P. *Clinically standardized meditation (CSM) instructor's kit*. Kendall Park, N.J.: Pace Educational Systems, 1978.

Carrington, P., Collings, G. H., Benson, H., Robinson, H., Wood, L. W., Lehrer, P. M., Woolfolk, R. L., & Cole, J. W. The use of meditation–relaxation techniques for the management of stress in a working population. *Journal of Occupational Medicine*, 1980, *22*, 221–231.

Carrington, P , & Ephron, H. S. Meditation as an adjunct to psychotherapy. In S. Arieti (Ed.), *New dimensions in psychiatry: A world view*. New York: Wiley, 1975.

Cooper, M. J., & Aygen, M. M. A relaxation technique in the management of hypercholesterolemia. *Journal of Human Stress*, 1979, *5*, 24–27.

Das, N. N., & Gastaut, H. Variations de l'activité électrique du cerveau, du coeur, et des muscles squelletiques au cours de la méditation et de l'extase yogique. *Electroencephalography and Clinical Neurophysiology*, 1957, *6*(Suppl.), 211–219.

Davidson, R., & Schwartz, G. The psychobiology of relaxation and related states: A multiprocess theory. In D. I. Mostofsky (Ed.), *Behavior control and the modification of physiological activity*. Englewood Cliffs, N.J.: Prentice-Hall, 1976.

Davies, J. The Transcendental Meditation Program and progressive relaxation: Comparative effects on trait anxiety and self-actualization. In D. W. Orme-Johnson & J. T. Farrow (Eds.), *Scientific research on the Transcendental Meditation Program: Collected papers* (Vol. 1). Livingston Manor, N.Y.: Maharishi European Research University Press, 1978.

Gellhorn, E., & Kiely, W. F. Mystical states of consciousness: Neurophysiological and clinical aspects. *Journal of Nervous and Mental Disease,* 1972, *154,* 399–405.

Glueck, B. C. *Current research on transcendental meditation.* Paper presented at Rensselaer Polytechnic Institute, Hartford Graduate Center, Hartford, Conn., March 1973.

Glueck, B. C., & Stroebel, C. F. Biofeedback and meditation in the treatment of psychiatric illness. *Comprehensive Psychiatry,* 1975, *16,* 302–321.

Goleman, D. Meditation as a meta-therapy: Hypothesis toward a proposed fifth state of consciousness. *Journal of Transpersonal Psychology,* 1971, *3,* 1–25.

Honsberger, R. W., & Wilson, A. F. Transcendental meditation in treating asthma. *Respiratory Therapy: The Journal of Inhalation Technology,* 1973, *3,* 79–80.

Kanellakos, D. (Ed.). *The psychobiology of transcendental meditation.* Menlo Park, Calif.: W. A. Benjamin, 1974.

Lazar, Z., Farwell, L., & Farrow, J. T. The effects of the Transcendental Meditation Program on anxiety, drug abuse, cigarette smoking, and alcohol consumption. In D. W. Orme-Johnson & J. T. Farrow (Eds.), *Scientific research on the Transcendental Meditation Program: Collected papers* (Vol. 1). Livingston Manor, N.Y.: Maharishi European Research University Press, 1978.

Lazarus, A. A. Psychiatric problems precipitated by transcendental meditation. *Psychological Reports,* 1976, *10,* 39–74.

McIntyre, M. E., Silverman, F. H., & Trotter, W. D. Transcendental meditation and stuttering: A preliminary report. *Perceptual and Motor Skills, 1974, 39,* 294.

Miskiman, D. E. Long-term effects of the Transcendental Meditation Program in the treatment of insomnia. In D. W. Orme-Johnson & J. T. Farrow (Eds.), *Scientific research on the Transcendental Meditation Program: Collected papers* (Vol. 1). Livingston Manor, N.Y.: Maharishi European Research University Press, 1978.

Orme-Johnson, D. W., Kiehlbauch, J., Moore, R., & Bristol, J. Personality and autonomic changes in prisoners practicing the transcendental meditation technique. In D. W. Orme-Johnson & J. T. Farrow (Eds.), *Scientific research on the Transcendental Meditation Program: Collected papers* (Vol. 1). Livingston Manor, N.Y.: Maharishi European Research University Press, 1978.

Ornstein, R. *The psychology of consciousness.* San Francisco: W. H. Freeman, 1972.

Patel, C. H. Yoga and bio-feedback in the management of hypertension. *Lancet,* 1973, *ii,* 1053–1055.

Patel, C. H. 12 month follow-up of yoga and bio-feedback in the management of hypertension. *Lancet,* 1975, *i,* 62–64.

Pelletier, K. R. Effects of the Transcendental Meditation Program on perceptual style: Increased field independence. In D. W. Orme-Johnson & J. T. Farrow (Eds.), *Scientific research on the Transcendental Meditation Program: Collected papers* (Vol. 1). Livingston Manor, N.Y.: Maharishi European Research University Press, 1978.

Pirot, M. The effects of the transcendental meditation technique upon auditory discrimination. In D. W. Orme-Johnson & J. T. Farrow (Eds.), *Scientific research on the Transcendental Meditation Program: Collected papers* (Vol. 1). Livingston Manor, N.Y.: Maharishi European Research University Press, 1978.

Rimol, A. G. P. The transcendental meditation technique and its effects on sensory–motor performance. In D. W. Orme-Johnson & J. T. Farrow (Eds.), *Scientific research on the Transcendental Meditation Program: Collected papers* (Vol. 1). Livington Manor, N.Y.: Maharishi European Research University Press, 1978.

Ross, J. The effects of the Transcendental Meditation Program on anxiety, neuroticism, and psychoticism. In D. W. Orme-Johnson & J. T. Farrow (Eds.), *Scientific research on *the Transcendental Meditation Program: Collected papers* (Vol. 1). Livingston Manor, N.Y.: Maharishi European Research University Press, 1978.

Salk, L. The role of the heartbeat in the relations between mother and infant. *Scientific American,* 1973, *228,* 24–29.

Schwartz, G., Davidson, R., & Goleman, D. Patterning of cognitive and somatic processes in the self-regulation of anxiety: Effects of meditation versus exercise. *Psychosomatic Medicine,* 1978, *40,* 321–328.

Shafii, M., Lavely, R. A., & Jaffe, R. D. Meditation and marijuana. *American Journal of Psychiatry,* 1974, *131,* 60–63.

Shafii, M., Lavely, R. A., & Jaffe, R. Meditation and the prevention of alcohol abuse. *American Journal of Psychiatry,* 1975, *132,* 942–945.

Shafii, M., Lavely, R. A., & Jaffe, R. D. Verminderung von zigarettenrauchen also folgc transzendentaler meditation (Decrease of smoking following meditation). *Maharishi European Research University Journal,* 1976, *24,* 29.

Smith, J. Personality correlates of continuation and outcome in meditation and erect sitting control treatments. *Journal of Consulting and Clinical Psychology,* 1978, *46,* 272–279.

Tjoa, A. Increased intelligence and reduced neuroticism through the transcendental meditation program. *Gedrag: Tijdschrift voor Psychologie,* 1975, *3,* 167–182.

Tjoa, A. Some evidence that the transcendental meditation program increases intelligence and reduces neuroticism as measured by psychological tests. In D. W. Orme-Johnson & J. T. Farrow (Eds.), *Scientific research on the Transcendental Meditation Program: Collected papers* (Vol. 1). Livingston Manor, N.Y.: Maharishi European Research University Press, 1978.

Wallace, R. K. Physiological effects of transcendental meditation. *Science,* 1970, *167,* 1751–1754.

Wallace, R. K., Benson, H., & Wilson, A. F. A wakeful hypometabolic state. *American Journal of Physiology,* 1971, *221,* 795–799.

Williams, P., Francis, A., & Durham, R. Personality and meditation. *Perceptual and Motor Skills,* 1976, *43,* 787–792.

Woolfolk, R. L., Carr-Kaffashan, K., McNulty, T. F., & Lehrer, P. M. Meditation training as a treatment for insomnia. *Behavior Therapy,* 1976, *7,* 359–365.

Zuroff, D. C., & Schwarz, J. C. Effects of transcendental meditation and muscle relaxation on trait anxiety, maladjustment, locus of control, and drug use. *Journal of Consulting and Clinical Psychology,* 1978, *46,* 264–271.

6 HYPNOSIS, DEEP RELAXATION, AND ACTIVE RELAXATION: DATA, THEORY, AND CLINICAL APPLICATIONS

THEODORE XENOPHON BARBER

Hypnotic induction procedures typically include two kinds of suggestion: (1) suggestions for deep relaxation and (2) suggestions intended to enhance responsiveness to subsequent suggestions. Following the completion of the preliminary hypnotic induction procedure, two additional types of suggestion are often administered: (3) test suggestions for limb heaviness, hand numbness, age regression, posthypnotic behavior, and so on, and (4) indirect and direct therapeutic suggestions for losing weight, ameliorating depression, stopping smoking (e.g., "The desire to smoke will decrease day by day as your determination to live with full health and enjoyment increases"), and so forth. In this chapter, I focus on only one of these sets of suggestions—the suggestions for deep relaxation; the other three types of important suggestion that are also found in hypnotic situations (responsiveness-enhancing suggestions, test suggestions, and indirect and direct therapeutic suggestions) are discussed only peripherally.[1]

SUGGESTIONS FOR DEEP RELAXATION

At least since the 1840s (Braid, 1843/1976), suggestions for deep relaxation have comprised a large proportion of the statements that have been typically included in hypnotic induction procedures (Edmonston, 1981).

[1]Hypnosuggestive approaches to therapy usually emphasize both the suggestions for relaxation and the indirect and direct therapeutic suggestions. In this chapter, I am focusing on only one of the two major aspects of hypnosuggestive therapy (the relaxation suggestions);

Although the phrasing of the deep relaxation suggestions has varied over the years, due to cultural changes and to changes in conceptions of hypnosis (Ellenberger, 1970), they have been used by virtually all hypnotists in the great majority of their hypnosis sessions (Edmonston, 1981). At the present time, hypnotists differ in the way they word their suggestions for deep relaxation and also in the number of deep relaxation suggestions they include in their hypnotic procedures; nevertheless, there appears to be a specifiable pattern to the deep relaxation suggestions.

Suggestions for deep relaxation, as used in modern hypnotic inductions, typically follow a pattern somewhat as follows:

Close your eyes and take a deep breath. As you breathe out slowly, you feel all the tensions leaving. Letting go of tensions, worries, frustrations, and becoming more and more calm, at ease, deeply relaxed. Floating on a soft, cushiony cloud [or lying on a pleasant beach, feeling the warm sand and the sun] . . .[2] more and more comfortable, tranquil, serene, relaxed . . . Breathing slowly and gently. Thoughts slowing down . . . Time slowing down, lots of time, so much time . . . Mind and body slowing down. Arms relaxing, legs relaxing, face relaxing, body and mind relaxing. Warm and comfortable . . . At peace, calm, more and more relaxed and drowsy . . . moving slowly, calmly down [an escalator] and becoming more and more deeply relaxed . . . Peaceful, quiet, drifting, floating, deeper and deeper relaxed.

Why have these kinds of suggestions for deep relaxation received so much emphasis in hypnotic situations? It appears that implicitly, if not always explicitly, hypnotists have recognized that their induction procedures aim to produce a state that, although historically labeled "hypnosis" (the Greek word for "sleep"), can more appropriately be labeled "deep relaxation"—a state of calmness, "letting go," and awayness in which the relatively passive subject has reduced his or her motoric, cognitive, and physiological activity. As Edmonston (1981) has recently shown in a thorough survey, typical hypnotic inductions that focus on suggestions of relaxation often succeed in their aim; that is, many subjects report that they are relaxed in body and mind, and they show an associated reduction in respiratory rate, skin conductance, electrodermal spontaneous activity, and other psychophysiological indexes of arousal. In fact, Edmonston's (1981) review indicates that even when hypnotic

---

[1] discuss the other major aspect (indirect and direct therapeutic suggestions) in other communications (e.g., Barber, 1979b, 1982).

[2] The series of three dots (. . .) indicates a pause, not a deletion, in the presentation of the suggestions.

induction procedures include both relaxation suggestions and other types of suggestions that tend to alert the subject, both the subjective and psychophysiological effects of the hypnotic inductions are nevertheless usually similar to those of other relaxation procedures, such as progressive relaxation and transcendental meditation.

It should be noted that although suggestions for deep relaxation are at times useful, they are not necessary to elicit a high level of responsiveness to test suggestions for hand levitation, arm rigidity, age regression, analgesia, negative or positive hallucinations, amnesia, posthypnotic behavior, and so forth. In a small proportion of subjects who have special "hypnotic abilities," a very high level of responsiveness to test suggestions can be elicited without any preliminaries whatsoever (Wilson & Barber, 1981, 1983). A high level of response can also be elicited in a substantial proportion of subjects by task-motivational instructions, by instructions to imagine vividly those things that will be described, and even by instructions to be very alert (Banyai & Hilgard, 1976; Barber, 1969, 1970; Barber, Spanos, & Chaves, 1974; Barber & Wilson, 1977; Ludwig & Lyle, 1964).

If suggestions for deep relaxation are not necessary for attaining a high level of responsiveness to suggestions, which is usually seen as the major goal of hypnosis, why then are they so often used by hypnotists? There are at least eight major reasons why deep relaxation suggestions are very often used in hypnotic situations: (1) They define the situation as "hypnosis." (2) They are "easy" suggestions that most subjects can "pass." (3) They can help reduce critical and analytical thinking. (4) They can change the situation so that imagining and fantasizing is appropriate. They can also provide a "calm mind," which has several important uses: (5) thinking through solutions to life problems; (6) mentally practicing tasks or performances such as delivering a speech or taking a test; and (7) mentally rehearsing overcoming addictions, such as smoking and alcoholism. Finally, (8) they can help produce peace of mind or calmness, which is useful for overcoming stress-related disorders, such as migraines, headaches, asthma, insomnia, and hypertension. I now discuss in turn each of these eight uses of deep relaxation suggestions in hypnosis situations.

USING DEEP RELAXATION SUGGESTIONS TO DEFINE THE SITUATION AS "HYPNOSIS"

Suggestions for deep relaxation implicitly define the situation to the subjects as "hypnosis." Many individuals come to hypnotherapists because their (erroneous) conceptions of hypnosis lead them to believe that hypnosis is a uniquely powerful tool; even when they are given potentially potent therapeutic suggestions, they will not accept that they are in a potent situation if they have not been exposed to a preliminary procedure that they view as an hypnotic induction. Since suggestions for deep relaxation are accepted by virtually all clients as an hypnotic induction, they are at times used by hypnotherapists to define the situation to their clients (and also to themselves) as hypnosis and to capitalize on their clients' (and also their own) positive excitement and expectancies about hypnosis (Barber *et al.,* 1974; Goldstein, 1981; Stanton, 1979). (Of course, defining the situation as "hypnosis" by utilizing a deep relaxation procedure, or in any other way, can also backfire among clients who have not volunteered for hypnotherapy and/or among those who have negative attitudes and fearful expectations toward what they conceive of as hypnosis.)

DEEP RELAXATION SUGGESTIONS AS "EASY" SUGGESTIONS THAT ENHANCE RESPONSE TO LATER SUGGESTIONS

Another implicit or latent function of deep relaxation suggestions derives from a general principle: If individuals are first given easy suggestions that they can experience, they are more likely to expect that they will also experience the later suggestions; consequently, they may be more at ease with and more likely to pass the subsequent suggestions (Barber & DeMoor, 1972; Weitzenhoffer, 1953). Suggestions for deep relaxation are "easy" suggestions that are experienced by a high proportion of subjects (Wilson & Barber, 1978). Consequently, by receiving suggestions for deep relaxation first, as part of the hypnotic induction procedure, individuals generally find themselves experiencing what is suggested, and they presumably say to themselves such things as "It's working," or "It's easy to experience what the therapist suggests," and thus they have more positive expectancies that they will experience subsequent suggestions.

USING DEEP RELAXATION SUGGESTIONS TO ENHANCE RESPONSIVENESS BY REDUCING CRITICAL, ANALYTICAL THINKING

A third goal of the suggestions for deep relaxation is more "official" or explicit: to enhance clients' responsiveness to subsequent suggestions by guiding them to become calm, relaxed, less critical and analytical, and less concerned about time, place, and person. If a client does not have negative attitudes or fears about hypnosis, the suggestions for deep relaxation are usually successful in enhancing the subject's responsiveness (Barber, 1969; Weitzenhoffer & Sjoberg, 1961). However, it should also be noted that heightened response to suggestions can also be elicited by procedures that do not lead to relaxation—for example, laying on of hands à la Mesmer (Barber, 1981b); exhortative instructions to use one's mind creatively and to think and imagine the suggested effects (Barber & Wilson, 1977); and talking to subjects in a way that is personally meaningful or engrossing to them, or using surprise techniques that grab their attention (Barber, 1981a; Erickson, 1980).

USING DEEP RELAXATION SUGGESTIONS TO CHANGE THE SITUATION SO THAT FANTASY IS APPROPRIATE

A fourth goal of suggestions for deep relaxation is to change the situation from a reality-oriented, more or less formal social interaction to one where fantasy, primary processes, and a kind of role playing are appropriate (Fromm, 1979; Sarbin & Coe, 1972). For instance, after administering suggestions for deep relaxation, the hypnotherapist feels more at ease in administering, and the client generally feels more at ease in receiving, such suggestions as "I would now like to speak to your Inner Mind" (Francuch, 1981), or "I now wish to speak to your unconscious mind" (Erickson, 1980), or "It is now 1673" (suggestions for "past-life" regression), or "It is A.D. 2112" (suggestions for age progression). Also, since suggestions for deep relaxation change the situation to one that is more "loose," more informal and less rigid, the hypnotherapist can now more easily advance (and the subject can more easily accept) suggestions to free-associate more easily, to proffer new or creative ideas, and to interrelate with others present in a more "loose" or informal manner. For instance, when clients in insight-oriented therapy who are expected to free-associate are having an unproductive "dry" period in which "nothing comes to mind," the therapist might consider first giving suggestions for deep relaxation and then suggesting, "Now that you are relaxed . . . calm . . . at peace . . . thoughts will flow more freely . . . you will speak more easily . . . ideas and feelings will come to mind and you will find yourself talking about them in a smooth, free-flowing way" (Wolberg, 1948). Similarly, in group therapy, when the group has reached a relatively unproductive period, the therapist can suggest to the group members and to himself or herself that they all are relaxing deeply; immediately upon completion of a series of relaxation suggestions, the therapist could suggest, "After we open our eyes in a few moments, we will continue to feel at ease, at peace, calm, and relaxed, and we will be able to talk with each other more freely and relate with each other more easily and empathically."

It is important to note that suggestions for deep relaxation can be used for this purpose—that is, to change the situation to one where fantasy and a kind of role playing are appropriate—even when the clients do *not* become especially relaxed. Perhaps more important for this purpose than the actual degree of relaxation is the clients' *belief* that they are now in a different situation wherein they can behave and experience in more "loose," fantasy-related, and play-like ways. This is somewhat analogous to a situation where alcoholic beverages are served (or where individuals believe they have received alcohol in their beverages even when they have not); because of their beliefs about alcohol, they now feel more free to converse, to laugh, and to have fun or be silly, even before there is sufficient time for any alcohol in the beverages to take effect (Marlatt, 1979).

USING DEEP RELAXATION (A "CALM MIND") FOR WORKING ON LIFE PROBLEMS

Suggestions for deep relaxation are also at times given in hypnotic situations in order to foster the solving of life problems. This fifth function is based on the premise that at least some decisions or problems can be approached and solved more easily and satisfactorily when a person is experiencing deep calmness. When the suggestions for deep relaxation appear to have produced a state of calmness, the hypnotherapist may say to the client: "Now that you are calm, at peace, tranquil, relaxed [or in hypnosis], you will be able to see new facets and new approaches to a life problem [or to an issue or decision to be made]. As you now work on the problem by yourself with a calm, relaxed, peaceful mind during the next [10] minutes, you will come up with new ideas, insights, and creative solutions."

This approach can also be used to help clients stop worrying during their daily lives. For instance, I instruct the clients to put aside worries deliberately during the day and to set aside about 15 minutes in the evening, when they first listen to a 7-minute cassette tape I have made for them composed of deep relaxation suggestions. While relaxed, calm, and at ease, they are to take one problem in their lives (e.g., a financial or work problem or a problem in interpersonal relations with children, spouse, parents, coworkers, etc.) and let themselves feel and experience the problem in a new way, with new ideas, insights, and viewpoints on how they can best deal with it. This procedure benefits clients in two ways: It minimizes worrying during the day, and it also provides a calm, productive situation for thinking through a life problem.

USING DEEP RELAXATION (A "CALM MIND") FOR MENTALLY REHEARSING TASKS AND PERFORMANCES

In hypnotic situations, suggestions for deep relaxation also have a sixth function: While relaxed, the client can mentally rehearse carrying out tasks and performances that can be accomplished most effectively when the person is calm instead of tense or "uptight" (Barber, 1979c). For instance, after receiving suggestions for deep relaxation, a client who is to give a speech in public may be asked to rehearse his or her talk mentally while continuing to experience tranquility. More specifically, the client may be given suggestions for deep relaxation and then told, "Continue to feel calm and at peace as you picture yourself or feel yourself walking to the speaker's stand, as you pause and look at the audience, and as you begin speaking. Now hear yourself calmly and smoothly speaking each word as you practice the talk [while remaining deeply relaxed]." Similarly, student clients may be asked to remain deeply relaxed as they see or feel themselves at their desks preparing to study and as they begin to read and become more and more engrossed in the study material (Barber, 1979a; Donk, Knudson, Washburn, Goldstein, & Vingoe, 1968). While in a state of deep relaxation, student clients may also be guided to a mental rehearsal of taking an examination while remaining calm and at ease and allowing the information and material they have learned to flow easily and smoothly from the unconscious (Stanton, 1977). Athletic or sports performances—running, bowling, tennis, football, baseball, weight lifting—can also be mentally rehearsed immediately after the client has received suggestions for deep relaxation. It appears likely that these kinds of procedures, which have been used by a large number of investigators, are useful to the extent that they reduce performance anxiety; by repeatedly practicing the performance while deeply relaxed, the client may be able to extrapolate the feeling of calmness and to minimize anxiety and worry prior to and during the performance.

USING DEEP RELAXATION (A "CALM MIND") FOR REHEARSING OVERCOMING ADDICTIONS

Deep relaxation suggestions have a seventh function in hypnotic situations: They are used to produce a high level of tranquility which is useful for mentally rehearsing changing addiction behaviors such as smoking, overeating, or overindulgence in alcohol (Barber, 1979b). After receiving suggestions for deep relaxation, the clients are guided to feel themselves in particular situations where they typically have a desire to smoke, or to overeat, or to drink alcoholic beverages and then are guided to imagine and feel themselves calm, relaxed, and at ease in each situation with no desire to smoke, to overeat, or to drink alcohol. This "hypnotic desensitization" procedure is continued until the client has rehearsed calmly avoiding the addiction behavior in all situations in which it is likely to occur.

USING DEEP RELAXATION SUGGESTIONS FOR REDUCING STRESS AND TENSION

Suggestions for deep relaxation have also been used in hypnosis situations simply to produce a state of deep relaxation. The deep relaxation that is aimed for, the "tropotrophic response" (Hess, 1954) or the "relaxation response" (Benson, Beary, & Carol, 1974), has been used by hypnotherapists for over a century to reduce stress and tension, especially in individuals with stress-related or psychosomatic ailments such as migraine, headache, asthma, insomnia, or hypertension. During the 1800s, hypnotic treatment for ailments of this type typically consisted simply of suggesting to patients that they would become "deeper and deeper relaxed . . . drowsy, sleepy, going into a relaxed, hypnotic state" (Bernheim, 1886/ 1957; Liebeault, 1889). In fact, Wetterstrand's (1897) practice of hypnotherapy with stress-related and psychosomatic ailments consisted solely of suggesting over and over to the hospitalized patients continually every few hours for a period of days or even weeks that they would remain deeply relaxed, calm, and at peace. The patients would get up from bed briefly to eat and to relieve bodily needs, but otherwise they remained in bed while receiving continual suggestions to relax deeply. Wetterstrand reported that this prolonged hypnotic deep relaxation had marked effects in relieving a wide variety of illnesses that we would now label hysterical and psychosomatic.

Although modern hypnotherapists do not use Wetterstrand's pro-longed relaxation treatment, they commonly suggest deep relaxation to their stressed patients and then suggest that they continue practicing the relaxation procedures by themselves at home. I describe the modern hypnotic relaxation procedures in detail later in this chapter.

A CASE ILLUSTRATING THE MANY USES OF DEEP RELAXATION SUGGESTIONS IN HYPNOTIC SITUATIONS

The major contention of this chapter, up to this point, has been that hypnotherapists use deep relaxation suggestions for a variety of implicit and explicit purposes. I now present a case of very brief (one-session) hypnotherapy that concretely illustrates this contention. (After presenting the case illustration, I turn to the second major contention of the chapter—namely, that deep relaxation and "active relaxation" suggestions, as used in modern hypnotherapy, are useful for the treatment of stress-related or psychosomatic disorders such as migraine, headaches, asthma, insomnia, and hypertension.)

This case involves Joe R, a 22-year-old man who had married very recently and found himself impotent with his wife, even though he had functioned satisfactorily in previous sexual situations with other women. A few days after his marriage, after he had attempted and failed at intercourse several times, he came to me for help, because he had heard that I used hypnosis in therapy and he believed that hypnosis could quickly alleviate his problem. After he and I had talked for about 35 minutes, it became clear that the underlying problem was a type of performance anxiety.

Joe and his bride, Mary, were the same age, lived in the same small town, and had had a speaking acquaintance during their high-school years. When Mary was 20, she was married for a relatively short time (less than a year) to Zack, who had been the star football player on their hometown high-school team. Zack was 6 feet 4 inches tall, weighed about 250 pounds, and was powerfully built. In contrast, my client, Joe, was short and thin. After talking to Joe for about 35 minutes, it became clear that (1) Joe and Mary were excited about each other, loved each other, and were very happy to be married; but that (2) when Joe was in bed with Mary, he was self-conscious—instead of focusing on Mary, on loving, on the erotic, the sexual, and the exciting, he was focusing on his "deficiencies" and thinking to himself that Mary was viewing him as "not built like a man" in comparison with her ex-husband. The task for the remainder of the session was to attempt to guide Joe in such a way that later, when he was in sexual situations with Mary, he would shift his thoughts away from himself and his "deficiencies" and toward Mary, to his feelings of love for her, and to the erotic and sexually exciting.

My quickly formulated therapeutic plan was first to present a series of deep relaxation suggestions to Joe so that (1) he would accept that hypnosis was being used in his treatment (and thus would be confirmed in his expectations and beliefs that hypnosis could cure him); (2) he would experience the relatively easy-to-experience suggestions for relaxation and would thus feel that "hypnosis was working"; (3) he would relax and become more calm and at ease with me and with the therapeutic situation; (4) he would become less "reality-oriented" and thus more ready to accept the instructions that I would give him during the session to imagine, to fantasize, and to rehearse mentally an ideal sexual situation; (5) he would become more receptive to the somewhat unusual therapeutic suggestions that I would give him during and at the end of the session; and (6) he would be able to transfer some of the feelings of calmness that he would experience during the session to actual sexual situations that he would experience with Mary later.

I informed Joe that we would now use hypnosis. However, I also informed him that when hypnosis is used therapeutically—for example, to cure a sexual problem—it differs in a very important way from the hypnosis that is seen on the stage, in movies, or on TV. I stated that hypnosis is helpful in therapy when it helps clients feel deeply calm, relaxed, at ease, and at peace. I also stated that in therapeutic hypnosis clients are conscious; for instance, they hear the therapist's words clearly and may also hear outside noises, but they are not concerned about such extraneous matters because they are so relaxed, calm, and at ease. The aim of this introduction was to obviate the basic misconception that I find in virtually all individuals who come to me for hypnosuggestive therapy—namely, that they will be "put under" and be rendered unconscious and unaware of what is "done to them" or what they are told during the hypnotic session. A second reason why I introduced hypnosis in this way was because the suggestions for deep relaxation that I would give him actually aimed to produce exactly what I said—feelings of deep calmness, relaxation, and peace.

I next suggested to Joe that we both close our eyes and let ourselves feel calm. After a few moments I continued:

Let's take a deep breath, and as we breathe out slowly, we feel all the tensions leaving . . . Take another deep breath, and as we breathe out slowly we feel calm . . . at ease . . . at peace . . . waves of deep calmness . . . waves of deep peace and relaxation flowing through our body and mind . . . lots of time . . . so much time . . . more and more time . . . feeling so good . . . floating . . . at peace . . . deep waves of calmness and tranquility . . . deeply relaxed . . . deep peace flowing calmly and gently through every muscle, organ, and cell . . . absolutely calm . . . waves of deep relaxation . . . lots of time . . . so much time . . . feeling so good . . . deep peace . . . deeper and deeper relaxation.

After suggesting deep relaxation and calmness for about 7 or 8 minutes, I began to interblend suggestions for feeling good, alive, strong, and healthy:

Mind calm . . . deeply calm and at peace . . . and feeling so good . . . so healthy . . . and strong . . . with peace of mind . . . waves of calm health and energy . . . mind at peace . . . feeling so good . . . so good to be alive . . . waves of calm strength and health flowing smoothly and peacefully through mind and body.

The intent of these additional suggestions, as soon becomes clear, was to prepare Joe to feel calm and yet healthy, vital, and strong when in a sexual situation with Mary.

Next, we moved into the "fantasy rehearsal" or "mental rehearsal" phase, in which I guided Joe to see himself focusing on sexually exciting, erotic loving with Mary:

You feel yourself now with Mary . . . you feel so good . . . loving . . . close . . . flowing . . . so close to Mary . . . touching . . . feeling calm . . . so good . . . so calm, relaxed, strong, healthy . . . touching . . . hugging close and warm . . . loving . . . vibrant, healthy . . . so alive . . . enjoying . . . deep calmness . . . close and warm and touching . . . feeling so good.

After guiding Joe in this way for a few minutes, I said to him, "Now you take over." He understood my request perfectly well; slowly, with pauses, he verbalized his ongoing fantasy: "I am moving my fingers slowly around Mary's thigh . . . buttocks . . . hugging . . . kissing . . . entering . . ." He continued with long pauses to describe an exquisite sexual experience, apparently basing his fantasy on his sexual experiences prior to his marriage and his hopes and imaginings of what could take place with Mary.

After several minutes Joe concluded his fantasy; while he was sitting back quietly on the reclining chair with his eyes closed, I gave him "posthypnotic suggestions" in a modern form:

When you're with Mary you can feel like this . . . calm . . . relaxed . . . at peace . . . feeling so good . . . so alive . . . with lots of time . . . flowing . . . with waves of health and strength and energy . . . able to touch . . . and hug . . . and hold . . . and feel . . . enjoying . . . loving.

The "posthypnotic suggestions" were my way of telling Joe that, when he was with Mary, he could let himself feel at ease and calm; feel that there was lots of time; feel good about himself and Mary and about being alive; and, instead of thinking about himself and his performance, focus on what was important in the situation—the loving, the sexual, the exciting, the erotic—and let his body do what it would do naturally.

Joe telephoned the next day and stated that everything was "great" and that the sexual encounter with Mary was quite similar to the one he had imagined in my office. A follow-up telephone call on my part, about a year later, confirmed that their sexual relations continued at a high level. Of course, this was not a difficult case—Joe and Mary loved each other, and Joe had previously experienced satisfactory sexual relations—and he could have been helped relatively quickly by many approaches. The reason for presenting this uncomplicated case here is because it illustrates the first major theme of this chapter—namely, that suggestions for deep relaxation serve many functions in hypnotic situations.

Let us turn now to the second major theme of this chapter: the usefulness of deep relaxation and "active relaxation" suggestions in the hypnosuggestive treatment of stress-related disorders.

HYPNOTHERAPEUTIC TREATMENT OF MIGRAINE COMBINING DEEP RELAXATION WITH "ACTIVE RELAXATION"

A series of studies reviewed by Mitchell and White (1977) and by Adams, Feuerstein, and Fowler (1980) indicates that in individuals with a predisposition to migraine, the migraine headaches are typically precipitated by "negative" thoughts and feelings (negative emotions), such as resentment or anger, associated with life events perceived as stressful (Bakal, 1975; Bihldorf, King & Parnes, 1971; Henryk-Gutt & Rees, 1973; Mitchell, 1969; Mitchell & Mitchell, 1971; Selby & Lance, 1960). Henryk-Gutt and Rees (1973), for instance, asked migraine patients to observe for a period of 2 months both their emotional state and any other associated events coinciding with the onset of migraine. Although the patients were frequently distracted by the onset of the migraine and had difficulties in carrying out the assignment, they nevertheless were able to associate 54% of the migraines with emotional stress. Other studies, reviewed by Harrison (1975), indicate that unexpressed anger may be the most common emotion related to the onset of migraine. These and other data suggest the hypothesis that reducing negative emotions by using hypnosuggestions for deep relaxation and "active relaxation" (maintaining equanimity during ongoing daily activities) may reduce the severity and frequency of migraine. This hypothesis was supported in earlier studies by Meares (1967, p. 31) and Harding (1967), and in a more recent investigation carried out in London (Anderson, Basker, & Dalton, 1975; Basker, Anderson & Dalton, 1978).

Anderson, Basker, and Dalton conducted their study with 47 new patients who met strict criteria for migraine (e.g., unilateral recurrent throbbing headaches preceded by a visual or other sensory aura and present for at least 1 year). The patients were randomly assigned to two treatments: Half were to be treated by hypnotic suggestions emphasizing deep relaxation and "active relaxation," and half were to receive the drugs that were typically prescribed for migraine in that medical setting. Four physicians worked on the project, and each treated half his patients with the hypnotic procedures and half with the drug therapy. The patients on drug therapy were seen by the physicians once per month for 12 months and were asked to take 5-mg doses of prochlorperazine (Stemetil) four times daily during the first month and thereafter twice daily. They were also provided with ergotamine to be taken at the first sign of migraine. Patients assigned to the hypnosis treatment were also seen monthly for a year. During the first part of the year, they participated in at least six sessions in which they were exposed to hypnotic procedures, which were comprised of (1) repeated suggestions for deep relaxation, followed by (2) suggestions that the patients would be less tense, anxious, and apprehensive, and more energetic and happier (Hartland, 1965). Next, the patients were instructed and shown how to give themselves daily suggestions of deep relaxation ("self-hypnosis"). They were also instructed to give themselves suggestions for "active relaxation" whenever they first felt the beginning of a migraine, without necessarily closing their eyes and sitting down; at the first indication of a migraine, they were to massage their foreheads lightly and repeat silently to themselves suggestions such as "Becoming more and more calm . . . more and more comfortable . . . I feel the comfort spreading."

As Table 6-1 shows, 43% of the patients treated by the hypnotic relaxation procedures reported no migraine headaches during the last 3 months of the project, as compared to 13% treated by drugs. Also as shown in Table 6-1, the average number of migraines dropped markedly under the hypnotic treatment but not under the drug treatment, and the number of

TABLE 6-1. Hypnosuggestive Therapy versus Drug Therapy of Migraine

Outcome	Hypnosuggestive therapy (n = 23)	Drug therapy (prochlorperazine and ergotamine) (n = 24)
Median number of migraines each month		
6 months prior to therapy	4.5	3.3
First 6 months of therapy	1.0	2.8
Second 6 months of therapy	0.5	2.9
Number of patients with incapacitating attacks		
6 months prior to therapy	13	10
First 6 months of therapy	4	13
Second 6 months of therapy	5	14
Patients reporting no migraines during last 3 months of therapy	10 (43%)	3 (13%)

patients suffering very severe, incapacitating attacks of migraine decreased markedly in the hypnotic group but did not drop at all (in fact, went slightly up) in the drug group.

Since individuals receiving the hypnotic therapy apparently received more unique, intense, and close attention from their physicians than did those receiving the drug therapy, they probably had a stronger tendency to overemphasize the success of their treatment. Keeping this reservation in mind, we can interpret the results as follows: Ostensibly useful procedures that can be added to the armamentarium of all therapists who treat migraine include (1) suggestions for deep relaxation given first in the office and then practiced daily at home; (2) positive suggestions for reduced anxiety and apprehension and for heightened well-being; and (3) instructions to use "active relaxation" in daily life, especially when experiencing the first signs of migraine. Research would be useful here to determine whether these three components are equally useful in minimizing migraine, or whether one is significantly more useful than the others.

The study described above focused almost exclusively on treating migraines by training patients in deep relaxation and "active relaxation" in a hypnotic context. In another recent study, Andreychuk and Skriver (1975) included in their hypnotic treatment of migraine both suggestions for deep relaxation and direct suggestions for reducing the migraine pain. They reported that the hypnotic treatment reduced the frequency, duration, and intensity of the migraines over the 10-week treatment period, but not more so than two other comparison treatments that also aimed to produce relaxation—namely, an alpha biofeedback treatment, and a skin temperature biofeedback treatment that was combined with autogenic phrases (self-suggestions for calmness and relaxation).

In an earlier study, Basker (1970) taught deep relaxation (which he called "autohypnosis") to 28 migraine patients and also gave them positive suggestions to feel more competent, assertive, happy, and so forth, plus direct suggestions for control of blood flow to the cranium. A follow-up of the patients, which varied for different patients from about 1 year to 3 years, indicated that 16 of the 28 (57%) had experienced complete remission of their migraines.

Migraines have also been reduced in frequency, duration, and intensity by various other procedures that aim to produce a state of deep relaxation. These include thermal biofeedback (Johnson & Turin, 1975; Wickramasekera, 1973); thermal biofeedback together with progressive relaxation and/or together with autogenic phrases for calmness and relaxation (Blanchard, Theobald, Williamson, Silver, & Brown, 1978; Sargent, Green, & Walters, 1972); progressive muscle relaxation (Hay & Madders, 1971; Lutker, 1971); transcendental meditation (Benson, Malvea, & Graham, 1973); and a combination of muscle relaxation and transcendental meditation (Warner & Lance, 1975).

If an individual prone to migraines can learn to maintain calmness and peace of mind (an outlook that is not worried, not irritated, not frustrated, and not bothered), it is highly likely that his or her headaches will be markedly reduced, if not totally alleviated. However, there is no reason to believe that hypnotic training in deep relaxation and active relaxation, or training in other relaxation procedures such as biofeedback and progressive relaxation, is maximally effective in producing a generalized calmness and equanimity. In fact, it appears likely that the equanimity of clients can be maximized by using a variety of therapeutic procedures in addition to training in relaxation.

A pertinent investigation is that done by Mitchell and White (1977). These investigators treated their migraine patients over a period of 48 weeks by training in several relaxation procedures (progressive muscle relaxation, mental relaxation, and self-desensitization), supplemented by instructions to the clients to practice deep relaxation daily and also to practice active relaxation whenever they became aware of negative thoughts, feelings, or emotions. This treatment was associated with a 55% reduction in migraine frequency at a 60-week follow-up (compared to a 4% reduction for control patients who merely self-recorded the frequency of their headaches). However, a more marked 83% reduction in migraine frequency was found in a group of patients who received training in all of the relaxation procedures mentioned above, *plus* training in additional behavioral and cognitive–behavioral procedures such as thought stopping, time out for worry, assertion training, imaginal modeling, *in vivo* desensitization, and rational thinking.

In summary, the data indicate that hypnosuggestive procedures, such as suggestions for deep relaxation to be practiced daily and self-suggestions for active relaxation to be used at the first sign of migraine, are useful in migraine therapy, but that the hypnotherapeutic procedures should be part of a broader armamentarium of useful approaches that are presently available.

MULTIDIMENSIONAL HYPNOTHERAPEUTIC APPROACH TO TENSION HEADACHES

Individuals who often have tension headaches usually have difficulties in coping with life problems and tend to have many negative thoughts and feelings (negative emotions) such as anxiety, worry, anger, loneliness, and depression (A. P. Friedman, 1972; Harrison, 1975; Martin, 1978; Ziegler, 1978). Since relaxation training can increase feelings of calmness and reduce negative emotions, it can generally be expected to have an ameliorative effect on tension headaches. This hypothesis has been confirmed in a rather large number of studies, which have shown that procedures that aim to produce deep relaxation (e.g., training in progressive muscle relaxation, electromyographic or EMG biofeedback, and hypnotic induction focusing on suggestions for deep relaxation) are generally effective in reducing the frequency and intensity of tension headaches below the levels found with placebos or with a no-treatment control (Chesney & Shelton, 1976; Cox, Freundlich, & Meyer, 1975; Daniels, 1976, 1977; Epstein, Abel, & Webster, 1976; Fichtler & Zimmerman, 1973; Haynes, Griffin, Mooney, & Parise, 1975; Tasto & Hinkle, 1973). Although there are problems in drawing strong conclusions from these studies—for example, the reduction in headaches may have been partly due to the relaxation training's changing the clients' expectancies that they could control their headaches, or to their now interpreting their unchanged headaches as less severe—I can nevertheless agree with Blanchard, Ahles, and Shaw (1979), who carefully reviewed the data, that the "regular practice of some form of relaxation" is a useful approach in the treatment of head-aches.

The important goal, however, is not "muscle relaxation" per se (as some of the earlier work in this area would lead us to believe), but peace of mind, equanimity in the face of situations perceived by others as stressful, and reduction in anxiety, anger, and other negative emotions (Meares, 1967; Philips, 1978; Rachman, 1968). It is, of course, possible for a person to be calm, not worried, at peace, and so on, while simultaneously tensing many muscles—witness, for example, a champion long-distance runner who is continually tensing virtually all muscles while running with equanimity. On the other hand, a person may have virtually all muscles very relaxed and yet may be very frightened, worried, and mentally far from relaxed—witness a person who has been exposed to a muscle-paralyzing drug, such as curare. In fact, if muscle relaxation were especially important, then muscle-relaxing drugs should be especially efficacious in headache therapy; unfortunately, this is not the case (Ostfeld, 1962).

A major aim of a multidimensional approach to the treatment of tension headaches should be to help clients "relax" in a much broader sense —that is, to maintain calmness, peace of mind, and "active relaxation" throughout their daily lives, especially when situations are encountered that tend to arouse negative emotions.

The beginnings of a multidimensional hypnosuggestive approach to the treatment of headaches has been presented by Field (1979), who worked with 17 long-term headache patients, each of whom had previously undergone drug therapy for chronic headaches over many years. The patients were given suggestions for deep relaxation and were encouraged to practice the relaxation at home. Other procedures in the armamentarium of the hypnotherapist (e.g., age regression and scene visualization) were used to uncover attitudes and emotions that underlay the headaches. Suggestions aimed to enhance assertiveness and to heighten self-confidence were also used to help the patients handle life problems more efficiently and with more equanimity. Field reported that after four or five therapy sessions, 5 of the 17 patients (29%) showed total alleviation of their long-standing headaches, and an additional 29% showed marked reduction in the frequency of headaches. Field concluded that in treating tension headaches therapists should utilize a broad armamentarium, including a variety of hypnosuggestive procedures, which aim to enhance personal adjustment by reducing negative attitudes and emotions.

It appears that cost-effective treatments of headaches will be maximized when therapists are able to select, from a large number of potentially useful approaches, those procedures that can help a specific client

(Turin, 1981). These approaches may include insight-oriented procedures for uncovering the client's long-standing attitudes and cognitions that underlie present problems; cognitive-behavior therapy procedures, which aim to change the client's self-defeating methods for handling life problems; and hypnosuggestive procedures, which aim to heighten the client's self-esteem and to help him or her maintain calmness and serenity in daily life. To help readers of this chapter incorporate some of the hypnosuggestive procedures into their approaches, I now present my general methods for treating headaches. Since the aim is to highlight the hypnosuggestive procedures, I present these procedures in detail, and I only mention peripherally other procedures I also use that derive from other therapeutic approaches.

The preliminary procedures in my approach to tension headaches include consultation with a physician to exclude brain tumor, subarachnoid hemorrhage, allergies, dietary deficiencies, and other medical causes for headaches; also included is a thorough interview to reconstruct the patient's life history and headache history, with special emphasis on problems pertaining to self-esteem, self-confidence, and interpersonal relations. In the first treatment sessions, I try to attain four goals: to explain to clients how negative thoughts and feelings of resentment, anger, guilt, and self-criticism are related to the onset of headaches; to help them become aware of subtle signs that a headache is beginning; to guide them to look for past and present associations between negative emotions and the beginning of headaches; and to sensitize them to situational cues that trigger negative thoughts and feelings, which in turn can precipitate headaches (Holroyd & Andrasik, 1978; Holroyd, Andrasik, & Westbrook, 1977).

Also early in the treatment, I explain to the clients that headaches can be minimized when they are able to remain calm and avoid negative emotions as they face the day-to-day problems of life. I also explain that they can begin to proceed toward learning to live with equanimity by first practicing deep relaxation and "active relaxation." Since most of my clients come to me for hypnotherapy, I define the deep relaxation procedures as "self-hypnosis"; for those who do not come for hypnosis, I call the same procedures, with equal validity, "deep relaxation."

I then give suggestions for deep relaxation to each client while he or she reclines comfortably on a lounge chair with eyes closed. These suggestions, which are individualized for each client, typically include such phrases as "taking a deep breath and letting all the tensions go . . . relaxed . . . calm . . . deep peace . . . letting go . . . lots of time . . . waves of relaxation, peace, and calmness moving into every cell, every tissue, every muscle . . . deep, deep calmness." While giving the suggestions to the client, I let myself experience the suggested calmness, and I thus present the suggestions slowly and calmly; in fact, peace and calmness are imbedded in the tone, pacing, pauses, and meaning of each word. Also, while giving these suggestions, I simultaneously make a cassette audiotape recording (which usually extends over a period of about 7 to 12 minutes).[3] I give the tape recording to the client and instruct him or her to use it at home. Typically, the client is asked to listen to the tape and to relax deeply every evening immediately before or after supper; also at another specified time earlier in the day; and, if possible, whenever signs are detected of an incipient headache. Further procedural details are also worked out with the client (e.g., how to listen to the tape alone in a quiet room and how to set oneself to relax deeply without falling asleep).

During the next therapy session, the client's utilization of the cassette tape and the effectiveness of the suggestions are discussed. Toward the end of this session, I often present the client with a revised set of deep relaxation suggestions, which take into account the client's comments regarding the original suggestions. These revised suggestions are also recorded on audiotape, and the client is asked to listen to them at home during the forthcoming week.

Overlapping with the home practice of deep relaxation, I begin to guide the client to use active relaxation. Although clients have been previously instructed to find an isolated place in which to practice deep relaxation whenever they experience the beginnings of a headache, it is also acknowledged that headaches often begin in situations from which people cannot escape. Clients are told that when they become aware of a beginning headache while they are working, interacting with others, or engaging in other activities during the day, they can reinstate a feeling of calmness and peace of mind that can abort the headache by subvocally saying to themselves and feeling the meaning of "cue words," such as "at ease," "relaxed," "lots of time," "take it easy," "peace," "centered," and so on. The instructions for active relaxation are usually worded along the following lines:

Whenever you feel the slightest sign of what may be the beginning of a headache, or when you begin feeling frustrated, angry, irritated, nervous, or bothered, and it is not possible to leave the situation and to relax deeply, then repeat silently

[3]With the exception of those cassette tapes that are to be used before the client goes to sleep, the tapes end with statements such as these: "In a few moments you will open your eyes and feel refreshed . . . feeling good . . . alert . . . so alive . . . Opening your eyes while feeling alert, refreshed, very awake."

to yourself "cue words" such as "calm" and "centered" and let yourself feel calm and centered as you continue with the task you are performing. By shifting to feelings of calmness, you will remove the conscious or unconscious negative thoughts and feelings that bring on the headache.

Mental rehearsal is then used in the office to practice active relaxation. Clients are asked to close their eyes and to picture or feel themselves in situations that are likely to be followed by a headache or that tend to produce anger, resentment, guilt, feelings of worthlessness, or the like. When clients signal—for instance, by a small finger movement—that they feel themselves in the situation (which can vary from being stuck in a traffic jam to being rejected by a significant person), they are told, "Now feel yourself saying to yourself, 'Calm . . . relaxed . . . flowing with the situation' and picture and feel yourself calm and relaxed [in the situation]."

The above procedures—practice of deep relaxation and of active relaxation—are imbedded in a broader context. One facet of this broader context is the work performed by the client and myself in delineating and analyzing the way the client has approached and is approaching life problems, as well as the ways in which these approaches are determined by his or her specific life experiences. These discussions often involve step-by-step analysis of how the client has handled particular past and is handling particular present problems, plus such procedures as hypnotic age regressions to probe the early background of the problems.

In addition, the broader context includes utilization of suggestions to provide a philosophical context for "flowing with" the problems of life, and also suggestions that aim to raise the client's self-esteem. To teach my clients to "relax" in the most meaningful sense—to be able to meet the major and minor problems of life with equanimity—I have found it necessary to expend much effort in gently guiding them to develop a broader philosophy of life. I next discuss my philosophical hypnosuggestive approach to "flowing with the problems of life," and then I discuss my philosophical hypnosuggestive approach to raising self-esteem.

PHILOSOPHICAL CONTEXT FOR FLOWING WITH LIFE PROBLEMS

To place the active relaxation in the broader context, I discuss with the clients their "philosophy of living," and I gently try to guide them to accept a broader philosophy, which is based on four tenets that I now describe. Whenever appropriate, I also make audiotapes that present the philosophy of living in a way that is acceptable to the client (Barber, 1978). (When making the audiotapes in the office, the client is told that I will now employ philosophical hypnosis; he or she is then given suggestions for relaxation, followed by statements that suggest a more useful philosophy of life.)

The major tenets of this philosophical approach for coping with the difficulties of life are as follows:

1. For every human being, life has undesirable aspects. Aging and death are inevitable for me and you and every person we care about. Also, either we or people we love will experience birth defects, paralysis, blindness, deafness, major physical and mental illnesses, severe pain, bodily disfigurement, and many other very undesirable happenings. Every human being will also experience other unwanted events, such as loss of a job or loss of financial security; rejection by parents, lovers, children, or friends; unsavory encounters with others (parents, siblings, spouses, children, friends, coworkers) who are not the way "we want them to be"; and encounters with many undesirable external events (ranging from inclement weather or traffic jams to wars or a world in turmoil). The first and most essential facet of wisdom and ability to live happily is *fully to accept at a very deep level* that life inevitably has problems and that virtually every day we will encounter events and behaviors from others that we do not like at all and that we wish would never occur. When we deeply accept the fact that in living we will sooner or later encounter major undesirable events and also daily unwanted happenings, we meet the problems of life philosophically, with the thought and feeling that "This is a happening that I do not like at all but it is part of life—one of the many undesirable events that I and every other human being will experience in our lives." This philosophical attitude, which is found in those who have attained wisdom and the ability to live at a high level, is quite different from the implicit philosophy adopted by the great majority of individuals. When encountering their daily quota of unwanted happenings, most people magnify the undesirable aspects by refusing to accept deeply that life has problems, and by repeating to themselves such statements as, "It can't be . . . it shouldn't be . . . I can't stand it . . . This can't be happening to me [or my children, spouse, parents, friends, etc.] . . . It isn't fair . . . I'm going to scream . . . " (Ellis, 1962).

2. As stated above, the first principle of wisdom is the deep acceptance that life has major undesirable events and daily unwanted difficulties. The second principle of wisdom is to accept deeply and calmly the immediate difficulty as one of life's undesirable events that happens

to face us now, by stating calmly to ourselves, "I have this undesirable happening now in my life. Can I change it for the better, and, if so, how?"

3. The third principle of wisdom is to realize deeply that we cannot change many things we do not like. We cannot change any event that has already occurred. We cannot change what we have already said or done, or what has happened to us or to people we care about. Also, we can influence only some events that will occur from now on, and then only to a certain degree. We can influence the interpersonal situations and the tasks that we encounter in our lives by thinking and planning ahead, so that we can interrelate with others and perform our tasks and jobs with as much preparation and equanimity as possible. We can influence the happenings in our lives very little if at all for the better by directly trying to change others. Since many difficulties in life are related to the behavior of other people, individuals often try to surmount their problems by attempting to change the behaviors of others. In fact, almost everyone tries to change the attitude and behaviors of significant individuals in their lives by directly or indirectly criticizing them, telling them what they should or should not do, and subtly trying to make them feel guilty, incompetent, inferior, and unlikable. These approaches may change the behaviors of significant others superficially—they may comply to avoid the criticisms or negative reinforcements—but it does not change the attitudes and understandings that underlie their actions, and it is very likely to elicit resentment and hostility (Skinner, 1953).

4. The fourth major principle of wisdom is that we can improve our life situations by (a) thinking ahead calmly so that we can encounter people and situations with preparation and serenity; (b) changing ourselves so that we are more accepting, nonjudgmental, compassionate, and loving toward ourselves and others; (c) emphasizing the positive aspects and the positive potentials of ourselves and others; (d) modeling for others (showing them what they can be by our example); and (e) when others look up to us and wish to learn from us, talking to them and gently guiding them in an accepting and loving way.

The above principles are directly implemented and practiced in the hypnotic situation. Clients choose a specific problem facing them now, such as a financial problem, a health problem, or a problem in interrelating with others (such as a boss, a coworker, a parent, or a spouse). Next, the clients are given suggestions for deep relaxation for about 7 minutes, and then are given suggestions to see themselves handling the problem situation with wisdom and maturity—that is, accepting deeply that life has problems, including this specific problem; calmly deciding whether this is one of the many life difficulties that cannot be changed directly or whether there are steps that can be taken to improve the situation; calmly deciding what steps can be taken; and then calmly rehearsing mentally the actions that will be executed later with equanimity. The client is also given a cassette tape of the instructions to take home and to use at specified times as an aid in relaxing deeply and applying the four principles to immediate life problems.

A HYPNOSUGGESTIVE APPROACH FOR ENHANCING "RELAXATION" (EQUANIMITY) BY RAISING SELF-ESTEEM

Virtually all clients who come for therapy have low self-esteem; they feel they are more or less unattractive, unlovable, incompetent, unexciting, unappealing, dull, and so on. This negative self-image is a very serious hindrance in attempting to help the client relax in the most meaningful sense—facing the day-to-day events of life with equanimity. There appears to be a threshold level of positive self-regard that is necessary to enable clients to utilize active relaxation in everyday life. Some of the hypnosuggestive procedures that I use to help clients raise their levels of self-esteem include the following:

1. First, I look for and emphasize all of the manifest and latent positive characteristics that I can observe about the client. I am always able to find many such attributes, and I sincerely tell the client about them at intervals in our discussion, using statements such as the following:

- You have done so much [or worked so hard or struggled so much] in your life.
- You have been able to overcome so many difficulties [misfortunes, illnesses, rejections, deaths of loved ones].
- You have helped many people in your life.
- You did well in a very difficult situation.
- You really care about people.
- You have much empathy and love for others that you have not been able to express.
- You are a kind person.
- You have so much that you haven't begun to use—so much more love, so much more competence, so much more ability to be at ease, to enjoy life, to live fully.

In addition to interspersing these kinds of statements in our discussions, I also include them as suggestions in the hypnosuggestive procedures; for example, after the client has been given repeated suggestions of deep relaxation, he or she may be given a series of suggestions on various topics, interspersed with suggestions that "Starting now, you can begin to focus more on your strengths and positive aspects . . . you can become more aware of your ability to overcome obstacles . . . your caring and love for people . . . your growing ability to be at ease and to enjoy life," and so on.

2. A second hypnosuggestive approach that aims to enhance self-esteem derives from the fact that clients with low self-regard have typically been criticized by parents or other significant individuals in their early lives, and they have incorporated the criticisms into their self-images. In the therapy sessions, we trace back the destructive criticisms the clients have received from parents, siblings, or other important people ("You're dumb, stupid, ugly, clumsy, rotten, no good," etc.). After we have uncovered some or many of the origins of the low self-esteem, I proceed as follows in a hypnosuggestive session. I first give to the client (and indirectly to myself) suggestions for deep relaxation and then, when the client and I are both relaxed with eyes closed, I speak to the client from my "inner self"—for instance, somewhat as follows:

We understand now why you have felt you were unattactive, unintelligent, and not likable. It is clear now that your mother had a tremendous amount of resentment and anger and was unable to love you or anyone else because of her own father, who degraded her and made her feel totally unlikable and worthless. It's clear that you were too young to understand why your mother constantly put you down and screamed at you and made you feel there was something wrong with you. You can now see how your negative feelings about yourself were due to negative suggestions you received constantly from your mother, who was negative about everything and everyone because of her own misery. Now you can begin breaking through the negative suggestions you have received, you can begin coming out of the negative hypnosis you have been in for so many years, and you can begin to be your true self that has been held down for so long. You can see more and more clearly that as long as you were negatively hypnotized and believed you were stupid, ugly, and no good, you reacted to events and people around you in a nonconfident, afraid way, which tended to confirm your own beliefs. You can now begin to let go of these negative suggestions and begin to be your true self, realizing more and more each day that you are a good, kind, loving, and lovable person. Each day you can become less and less afraid, more and more at ease, more and more able to enjoy life and to be your true self.

3. As part of the hypnosuggestive approach to raising self-esteem, I make additional cassette tapes for the clients (cf. Barber, 1978, 1979a, 1979b). These tapes, which are made when the client and I are in my office, begin with suggestions for deep relaxation, followed by specific suggestions that aim directly or indirectly to enhance self-esteem by guiding the clients to focus on their underlying strengths, virtues, and positive

qualities. The clients are asked to listen to the cassette tape at home once a day during the forthcoming week, to let themselves relax deeply, and to let the ideas "go deep in your mind." Although these tapes are individualized for each client, they typically emphasize positive aspects of the client that have been neglected or suppressed and that can be released and expanded. Examples of the kinds of suggestions that are included in the hypnosuggestive tapes are as follows:

You have much caring and concern and love for others that you hold down and keep within you . . . You can begin now to let out these good feelings . . . allowing the kind, caring, good feelings to flow out to others . . . you can begin more and more to be your true self as you release your warmth and empathy toward others.

Starting now, you can be more and more aware of your true self that is being released, and you can stop criticizing yourself. . . . You can stop blaming yourself for what you did that you should not have done or what you did not do that you should have done, and you can forgive yourself as you forgive others . . . you can be as kind to yourself as you are to others . . . as loving to yourself as you are to others . . . you can stop criticizing and blaming yourself, and you can be free—free, more and more, to be your true self.

Starting now, you can more and more allow yourself to be the person you can be . . . appreciating again and grateful again to be able to see, to hear, to smell, to touch, to be alive . . . appreciating again as if it's your first day on earth, as if you've never felt the sun before, never heard a bird sing, never smelled a flower before . . . Grateful to be able to touch the rain and a stone, to hear the laughter of children and the sound of the sea, to smell the grass and appreciate tasty food, to see the colors of the earth and the stars . . . Appreciating again the strength and power in your body . . . Feeling the energy and health vibrating and flowing through your being . . . Feeling again the excitement and enthusiasm and the feeling of aliveness that has been suppressed for so long . . . more and more ready to enjoy, to have fun, to play and laugh and sing . . . More and more feeling good to be you and to be alive.

HYPNOSUGGESTIVE RELAXATION PROCEDURES IN THE TREATMENT OF ASTHMA

Asthma is characterized by spasms of the bronchial musculature with oversecretion of viscid mucus, resulting in "wheezy" breathing. Although there are many complexities in the etiology of asthma (Alexander, 1981; Weiner, 1977), there is convincing evidence that in at least some asthmatics, attacks are provoked both by allergen inhalation and also by situations that arouse negative emotions (Dekker & Groen, 1956). The relationship between negative emotional reactions and the onset of asthma suggests that hypnosuggestive procedures aiming to produce a feeling of calmness in situations that precipitate asthmatic attacks, or when the individual first becomes aware of the onset of wheezing, should have a beneficial effect on at least some asthmatics. This hypothesis has been tested in a number of studies, of which Collison's (1975, 1978) recent work may serve as the clearest example.

Collison worked with 121 asthmatics who were referred to him by other physicians for hypnosuggestive therapy, either because there were psychological factors associated with their asthma or because it was important to reduce their need for steroid medication. The hypnosuggestive therapy, which apparently extended over a variable period of weeks or months, included suggestions for deep relaxation, suggestions for increased self-confidence, and posthypnotic suggestions for continued relaxation and the ability to remain calm and cope well in life situations. In addition, the patients were taught self-hypnosis, which was comprised of self-suggestions for calmness, ease, and self-confidence. Collison also stated that he used at least two additional hypnosuggestive procedures (discussions of problems under hypnosis, and age regression to uncover early traumatic factors).

The results were as follows: 21% of the patients were relieved of asthma by the hypnosuggestive procedures; they were asymptomatic during a follow-up that extended more than 1 year. An additional 35% of the patients were clearly helped by the treatment—"improved at least 50%"—even though they were not cured. The asthmatic symptoms were not alleviated significantly in the remaining 44% of the patients, but about half of these reported subjective benefits in general well-being from the hypnosuggestive treatment. (Unfortunately, Collison did not take objective measurements of lung function.)

Since it is clear that some asthmatic patients benefit much more than others do from hypnosuggestive procedures, important data in Collison's report pertained to the type of patients who were helped the most. Collison reported that the greatest degree of improvement was found in the younger patients with psychological problems but less severe asthma, who were able to respond well to the suggestions for deep relaxation (hypnosis).

Other therapists utilizing hypnosuggestive procedures (focusing primarily on deep relaxation during the hypnotic session and on the practice of deep relaxation and active relaxation during daily life) have reported that the procedures are generally effective in producing both subjective and objective improvement in a minority of patients, including at times complete remission of asthma (Brown, 1965; Edgell, 1966; Edwards, 1960; Maher-Loughnan, 1970; Maher-Loughnan & Kinsley, 1968; Maher-Loughnan, MacDonald, Mason, & Fry, 1962; McLean, 1965; Meares, 1967, pp. 109–111; Moorefield, 1971; H. White, 1961). In a representative study by Edwards (1960), six patients who had been admitted to a hospital for treatment of severe asthma were seen for hypnosuggestive therapy. Over a series of sessions, Edwards exposed each patient to a hypnotic induction procedure, comprised primarily of suggestions for deep relaxation, followed without interrruption by forceful suggestions that the asthma would gradually disappear. Five of the six patients were followed for more than a year, when they were questioned about their subjective improvement and assessed for objective improvement by measuring respiratory functions. Of the six patients, four had subjectively complete remission of their asthma, and in two of these the remissions were also objectively complete.

As might be expected, other types of relaxation procedures have also been shown to be helpful in treating asthma. For instance, in less severe asthmatics, the same degree of increase in peak expiratory flow measures was found with training in Jacobson's progressive muscle relaxation, with training in progressive relaxation combined with EMG frontalis biofeedback, and also with simple direct instructions to relax (Davis, Saunders, Creer, & Chai, 1973). Scherr, Crawford, Sergent, and Scherr (1975) found that, as compared to 22 untrained asthmatic controls, 22 asthmatic children who were trained in relaxation with the aid of EMG frontalis biofeedback showed an increase in peak expiratory flow, a reduction in number of asthmatic attacks, a decrease in number of infirmary visits, and a reduction in steroid use. A significant effect in helping asthmatics has also been shown in other studies that have taught variations of transcendental meditation (Wilson, Honsberger, Chiu, & Novey, 1975) and Jacobson's progressive relaxation (Alexander, 1972; Alexander, Cropp, & Chai, 1979; Alexander, Miklich, & Hershkoff, 1972; Phillip, Wilde, & Day, 1972; Sirota & Mahoney, 1974).

Although various types of relaxation procedures are useful in the treatment of asthma, it is clear that, with rare exceptions, the illness requires a *multidimensional* psychosocial approach to supplement sophisticated medical procedures. In addition to training in deep relaxation and active relaxation, the psychosocial therapy should also focus on enhancement of self-esteem, social skills training, problem-solving procedures, and more general insight training for understanding and dealing with life problems.

I would surmise, however, that hypnosuggestive procedures (and other psychosocial procedures) may help the asthmatic more than they have heretofore if greater emphasis is placed on utilizing either deep relaxation or active relaxation procedures *at the first indication* of respiratory difficulties. When asthmatics begin to experience bronchial spasms, they become anxious, and the "snowballing" effect of the anxiety further constricts the bronchioles (Spiegel & Spiegel, 1978, p. 226). By using either deep relaxation or an active relaxation procedure (e.g., covertly repeating to oneself that one feels "relaxed . . . calm . . . at peace . . . ") *at the first signs of respiratory difficulties*, the asthmatic may be able to shift away from the anxious thoughts and feelings—and thus to minimize or abate further constriction of the bronchioles.

HYPNOSUGGESTIVE RELAXATION PROCEDURES IN THE TREATMENT OF INSOMNIA

Insomnia is a multifaceted complaint that may include one or a combination of the following components: (1) a long delay in falling asleep, (2) frequent awakenings during the night, (3) early-morning awakening, and (4) feelings of fatigue and dissatisfaction with sleep upon awakening (Price, 1974).

In middle age and old age, the problem usually lies in frequent awakenings during the night and early-morning awakenings. In younger individuals, the major problem is typically difficulty in falling asleep, which may be related to worry, anxiety, ruminating over problems, and fears of "letting go." Most sleep problems seem to be related to chronic worry and ruminative activity, which may be exacerbated by additional worry regarding inability to sleep or to get sufficient sleep (Hauri, 1975). A series of studies reviewed by Youkilis and Bootzin (1981) indicate that insomniacs tend to be characterized in personality studies as anxious, depressed, neurotic, and introverted. However, although insomnia may have originally derived from anxiety or depression, it may later be maintained by a new set of factors. Also, treatments that successfully reduce or even eliminate insomnia (to be discussed below) may not significantly change the symptoms of anxiety or depression (Nicassio & Bootzin, 1974).

As Youkilis and Bootzin (1981) noted in a useful review of the research, insomnia is a much more complex problem than is at times assumed. For instance, the sleep problem at times lies in a deficiency in "deep" (Stage 4 slow-wave) sleep, rather than an overall shortage in the amount of sleep; some individuals get a sufficient amount of sleep, but are oversensitive to periods of awakening that occur during the night; some individuals are satisfied with 5 or 6 hours of sleep, whereas others are not satisfied with 7 or 8. Another important consideration in understanding the problem arose in a sleep laboratory study with representative insomnia patients who complained that they slept little and required 1 or 2 hours to fall asleep; nearly 50% of these individuals fell asleep relatively rapidly in the laboratory and slept relatively well, according to electroencephalographic (EEG) criteria of sleep (Dement, 1972, pp. 81–83).

Other difficulties in sleeping are due to sleep apnea (a disorder in which the sleeper stops breathing for about 30 seconds and awakens); to nocturnal myoclonus (in which the muscles of the lower leg jerk during sleep and arouse the sleeper); to physical illnesses such as duodenal ulcers, arthritis, and cancer; and to overuse of caffeine, alcohol, and "sleeping pills."

All sleep medications have serious problems. The barbiturates are associated with such problems as deaths from overdose, buildup of tolerance to the drug, hangover effects, and disturbances in an important part of the sleep cycle (rapid-eye-movement or REM sleep) during both drug administration and withdrawal. The nonbarbiturate benzodiazepine hypnotics such as nitrazepam (Mogadon) and flurazepam (Dalmane) become ineffective after a few weeks of use, can disturb REM sleep, and have disturbing withdrawal effects (Kales & Kales, 1973; Karacan & Williams, 1971). The over-the-counter medications, which rely on some form of antihistamine, often produce drowsiness, but they also produce undesirable side effects and are typically found to be no more effective than a placebo is in improving sleep (Kales, Tan, Swearingen, & Kales, 1971).

Since present-day drugs are generally ineffective and often counterproductive in the treatment of insomnia, researchers have sought new methods that might help the sleep-deprived patient. During recent years, two kinds of useful procedures have been developed—"stimulus control instructions," and a set of procedures that aim to produce deep relaxation and calmness. Let us glance briefly at each in turn.

A new approach to the treatment of insomnia has been labeled as "stimulus control instructions" by its developer (Bootzin, 1972). These instructions aim to strengthen the stimuli or cues for falling asleep and to separate them clearly from the stimulating cues that are associated with other activities. The "stimulus control instructions" that are given to the insomnia patient include the following ideas:

Lie down to sleep *only* when you are sleepy; with the exception of sexual activity, do not use your bed for anything except sleep (i.e., no reading, watching television, eating, or worrying in bed); if unable to sleep in 10 minutes, get up and do other things (work, read, etc.) and return to bed when ready to sleep; set an alarm and get up at the same time each morning; and do not nap during the day.

Several controlled evaluations of these "stimulus control instructions" indicate that they can produce substantial improvement in time for the patient to fall asleep (Bootzin, 1977; Lawrence & Tokarz, 1976; Tokarz & Lawrence, 1974; Zwart & Lisman, 1979). The average improvement in sleep-onset latency in the six studies was 71% (Bootzin & Nicassio, 1978). There is evidence to indicate that these instructions are useful, primarily because they disrupt tossing and turning in bed and the related worries, ruminations, and other bothersome thoughts that prevent the person from sleeping (Zwart & Lisman, 1979).

Since difficulties in falling or staying asleep are commonly associated with anxiety, worry, and ruminating activity, it appears likely that the difficulties would be alleviated if the patient could be helped to relax and attain relative calmness and peace of mind. This hypothesis has been tested in a large number of studies and has been found to be generally valid. A series of studies reviewed by Bootzin and Nicassio (1978) and Borkovec (1979) have shown that a brief form of Jacobson's progressive relaxation (involving the systematic tensing and relaxing of major muscle groups throughout the body) is more effective in alleviating insomnia than are placebo control and no-treatment conditions. Progressive relaxation training has proved helpful for college students with moderate insomnia (e.g., Borkovec, Kaloupek, & Slama, 1975; Haynes, Woodward, Moran & Alexander, 1974; Steinmark & Borkovec, 1975) and also for chronic insomniacs with severe sleep problems (e.g., Lick & Heffler, 1977; Nicassio & Bootzin, 1974). This improvement has been demonstrated both with daily sleep diaries (e.g., Borkovec et al., 1975; Nicassio & Bootzin, 1974) and with EEG laboratory assessments (e.g., Borkovec, Grayson, O'Brien, & Weerts, 1979; Borkovec & Weerts, 1976; Freedman & Papsdorf, 1976; Haynes, Sides, & Lockwood, 1977). A series of studies have also shown that two additional procedures aiming to produce deep relaxation and peace of mind—meditation and autogenic training—are as helpful for insomnia patients as is Jacobson's progressive muscular relaxation (e.g., Nicassio & Bootzin, 1974; Woolfolk, Carr-Kaffashan, McNulty, & Lehrer, 1976). Furthermore, three studies found that EMG frontalis biofeedback and progressive muscular relaxation were both more helpful in alleviating insomnia than the control condition was, but that they did not differ significantly from each other (Freedman & Papsdorf, 1976; Haynes et al., 1977; Nicassio, Boylan, & McCabe, 1976).

In brief, four kinds of relaxation-oriented procedures (progressive relaxation, meditation, autogenic training, and EMG biofeedback) are useful for insomnia, but the degree of improvement is usually limited. The average reduction in time needed to fall asleep associated with training in relaxation is less than 50% (Bootzin & Nicassio, 1978). For instance, the severe insomniacs exposed to progressive relaxation training by Nicassio and Bootzin (1974) still required about an hour to fall asleep at the end of the study, even though the time they needed to fall asleep was reduced by 44%.

Since traditional hypnotic induction procedures and self-hypnosis procedures are comprised almost exclusively of suggestions for deep relaxation, we might expect that such procedures would be as effective as other relaxation procedures are in reducing insomnia. This conjecture was confirmed by Borkovec and Fowles (1973), who assigned 37 college students with difficulties in sleeping to one of three treatment groups: progressive muscular relaxation; hypnotic induction comprised of suggestions for deep relaxation; and self-relaxation. The subjects were exposed to their assigned treatment in three sessions a week apart, and also practiced their particular procedure at home twice a day for 10 minutes each time. The treatments were also compared with a no-treatment control group (10 subjects) on a daily questionnaire that assessed sleep latency time, number of awakenings, and restfulness of sleep. In comparison with the no-treatment control, all three treatments resulted in a significant reduction in the number of times the subjects awakened during the night and in how rested they felt in the morning. Progressive muscular relaxation and the hypnotic procedure comprised of repeated suggestions for deep relaxation were equally effective in reducing the amount of time needed to fall asleep.

Graham, Wright, Toman, and Mark (1975) presented data indicating that self-suggestions for deep relaxation may be more effective in reducing sleep latency and amount of time asleep when subjects are told they are being taught "systematic relaxation" rather than "self-hypnosis." Four other recent studies found that hypnotic procedures comprised primarily of deep relaxation suggestions are useful for insomnia (Barabasz, 1976; Basker, Anderson, & Dalton, 1979; Nuland, 1975; Stanton, 1975). In a controlled study, Stanton (1975) randomly assigned 30 students with insomnia to one of three groups: hypnosis, progressive muscle relaxation, or placebo. All groups were exposed to six therapy sessions. The hypnosis group received suggestions for deep relaxation, suggestions to visualize relaxing scenes, and additional suggestions such as "More relaxed . . . pleasantly tired . . . allowing your whole body to relax . . . feeling of heaviness . . . drowsier." During the study, the subjects recorded their own sleep latencies and nocturnal awakenings. Stanton reported his results in terms of an insomnia index, which was the product of minutes to fall asleep multiplied by the number of awakenings. The hypnosuggestive treatment was the most effective: The insomnia index was 2.8 for the base level, 2.2 for the placebo treatment, .98 for progressive muscle relaxation, and .31 for the hypnosuggestive treatment.

Basker *et al.* (1979) studied the insomnia-reducing effects of nitrazepam, a placebo, and autohypnosis. Eighteen patients aged 16 to 70, with insomnia of 3 months' to 22 years' duration, were randomly allocated to receive a double-blind treatment consisting of either nitrazepam for 2 weeks followed by placebo for 2 weeks, or, vice versa, placebo first followed by nitrazepam. During the Weeks 5 to 8, the patients continued to receive the same tablets as they had during Weeks 1 to 4 and, in addition, during Weeks 5 and 6, were taught autohypnosis (apparently consisting of repeated self-suggestions of relaxation, drowsiness, and sleep). The patients continued using autohypnosis during Weeks 7 and 8, and also in Weeks 9 and 10, by which time all tablets had been withdrawn.

The placebo and nitrazepam did not differ in their effects on the four sleep measures: time needed to go to sleep, hours of sleep, quality of sleep, and after-sleep feelings of tiredness or alertness. The time taken to go to sleep was less while practicing autohypnosis than when receiving either nitrazepam or placebo. Autohypnosis was generally effective, regardless of whether or not a tablet was taken as well. The patients slept more hours with autohypnosis; an average of more than 6 hours of sleep per night was attained by 82% of the patients when practicing autohypnosis alone, 70% of those receiving nitrazepam alone, and 41% of those receiving the placebo. With regard to the quality of sleep (as restless, normal, etc.), 94% of the patients reported normal sleep when practicing autohypnosis alone, as compared to 40% with nitrazepam and 30% with placebo. With regard to after-sleep feelings of tiredness or alertness, only 12% were tired after autohypnosis, as compared to 40% with nitrazepam and 47% with placebo. Although conclusions from the study should be guarded, because the autohypnosis could not be counterbalanced with the drug treatments and the outcome measures were derived only from the patients' own reports, the study suggests that autohypnosis may have a powerful ameliorative effect on insomnia.

Although hypnotic procedures focusing on deep relaxation are useful in treating insomnia, more effective treatments would probably include suggestions for deep relaxation as only one aspect of a broader based approach. Nuland (1975) reported enthusiastically on the effectiveness of a broader approach, which includes the following nine dimensions: specifying the precise nature of the sleep problem; helping clients deal with the stresses, tensions, and anxieties that underlie the insomnia; prescribing a drug such as imipramine (Tofranil) for depressed clients; instructing clients to use Bootzin-type "stimulus control instructions" (e.g., not to go to bed until sleepy); instructing clients to maintain relaxing mental activities and to avoid caffeinated beverages, alcohol, and large meals before bedtime; explaining to clients that since calmly resting in bed is about as restorative as sleep per se, they should not worry about whether or not they are asleep at night; exposing clients (in the formal hypnosuggestive sessions) to suggestions of deep relaxation and suggestions that they will sleep soundly when they go to bed; showing clients how to use self-hypnosis, (i.e., how to picture themselves in the most pleasant and relaxed surroundings, feeling more and more calm, relaxed, and drowsy); and, finally, showing clients how to practice autogenic training exercises focusing on feelings of heaviness and warmth.

Although Nuland did not present precise figures, he reported that (1) the above procedures relieved the sleep problem in the majority of his insomnia patients; (2) the milder cases responded surprisingly quickly; and (3) with very few exceptions, the procedures removed the distress associated with insomnia, and, with the relief of distress, the patients' sleep was improved.

It appears that the procedures listed above, plus additional procedures delineated by other workers, can be utilized in various combinations to construct more effective individualized treatments for patients. For instance, other procedures that promise to be useful, at least for some patients, include (1) all-night sleep recordings to verify the sleep deficiencies and to rule out sleep apnea, nocturnal myoclonus, and narcolepsy; (2) practice in identifying maladaptive thoughts interfering with sleep, and practice in formulating and using more useful thoughts; and (3) identifying factors or events discriminating nights with good sleep from nights with poor sleep (Thoresen, Coates, Kirmil-Gray, & Rosekind, 1981). Additional procedures that I have found effective for some insomnia patients include (1) making individualized cassette tapes for the patients, which slowly and calmly for about 10 minutes present suggestions of relaxation, peacefulness, and drowsiness—suggestions that they are to listen to immediately before or after they go to bed at night; and (2) instructing the more fantasy-prone patients (Wilson & Barber, 1981, 1983) to become immersed in a pleasant fantasy when they have difficulties sleeping (immersion in fantasy while lying quietly in bed at times moves, by a smooth transition, into sleep).

It appears that useful procedures for treating insomnia provide clients with alternatives on which to focus, other than their sleep-preventing concerns, worries, and ruminative thoughts. For instance, progressive relaxation procedures provide the alternative of focusing on the feelings of muscle tension and relaxation (Borkovec, 1979); typical meditation procedures instruct the patient to focus on a mantra such as "Om"; hypnosuggestive procedures provide the alternative of focusing on the ideas and feelings of "relaxed . . . calm . . . at peace"; autogenic training procedures provide the alternative of focusing on feelings of warmth, heaviness, and regular respiration; and "stimulus control instructions" explicitly guide the patient to focus on almost anything except worrisome thoughts. It appears that a parsimonious theory of insomnia reduction can be formulated in terms of providing alternatives for reducing sleep-preventing thoughts.

HYPNOSUGGESTIVE RELAXATION PROCEDURES IN THE TREATMENT OF HYPERTENSION

After a thorough review of available data, Weiner (1977) concluded that there are many roads to hypertension; it can be brought about by disturbances in any of the large number of systems that regulate blood pressure. Despite the complexities in the predisposition to, initiation of, and sustaining factors in high blood pressure, it appears likely that stress reactivity plays an important role in some phases of the disease in at least some patients. In borderline, labile hypertension, for instance, the increased cardiac output appears to be produced by sympathetic stimulation of the heart (Weiner, 1977, p. 182). In fact, as Harrell (1980) has pointed out, borderline hypertension resembles the blood pressure rise that is an immediate concomitant of stress, in that there is an increase in cardiac activity, a reduction in baroreceptor sensitivity, and a mediation by the sympathetic nervous system in both cases. Also, the sympathetic nervous system may play a role in maintaining elevated blood pressure via its direct influence on blood volume. Most important, the sympathetic nervous system's response to stress may be exaggerated in individuals with a predisposition to hypertension, and the repeated transient, exaggerated elevations in blood pressure may produce structural thickening of the arteries, which may be responsible for permanent hypertension (Folkow, Hällback,

Lundgren, Silvertsson, & Weiss, 1973; Folkow & Rubinstein, 1966).[4] These and other considerations (Weiner, 1977) suggest that procedures aiming to reduce "sympathetic arousal" by producing calmness, equanimity, and relaxation may reduce hypertension, provided that it has not yet resulted in structural thickening of the arteries. At least, as Kaplan (1980) has concluded in a medically oriented review, four nondrug interventions should be tried before using drugs to combat hypertension: reduction of salt intake, reduction in weight, increase in exercise, and enhanced relaxation or reduction in reactivity to stress.

Modest reductions in blood pressure have been associated with various types of relaxation treatments (Blanchard & Miller, 1977; Jacob, Kraemer, & Agras, 1977), including mantra meditation (20 minutes twice daily for 6 months) (Benson, Rosner, Marzetta, & Klemchuk, 1974), galvanic skin response (GSR) biofeedback together with mantra meditation (see Patel, Chapter 4, this volume), abbreviated Jacobson's progressive relaxation (Shoemaker & Tasto, 1975), and autogenic training (Luthe, 1972). After reviewing the data in this area, Blanchard and Miller (1977) concluded that when practiced regularly, on virtually a daily basis, these treatments typically result in a modest reduction in blood pressure of 10–15 mm Hg.

A study of Deabler, Fidel, Dillenkoffer, and Elder (1973) suggests that hypnosuggestive procedures should be part of the armamentarium for treatment of hypertension. In this study, six individuals with high blood pressure, who were not receiving medication for their hypertension, served as a control group; they simply returned to the medical setting seven times to have their blood pressure recorded. Fifteen hypertensive individuals were assigned to the experimental (hypnosuggestive) treatment; six of these were not receiving medication for their elevated blood pressure, and the remaining nine were on stabilized antihypertensive medication. These 15 patients participated in eight or nine treatment sessions, comprised of abbreviated Jacobson's progressive muscular relaxation followed by a hypnotic procedure consisting exclusively of suggestions for deep relaxation. The patients were also instructed in self-hypnosis to be used outside the medical setting. During the hypnosuggestive procedure, some of the patients showed a reduction of 40 mm Hg in systolic pressure and 20 mm Hg in diastolic pressure. The overall results were presented separately for

[4]Folkow and Neil (1971) also propose another mechanism: The restriction of renal circulation that is associated with repeated acute elevations in blood pressure gives rise to a release of renin–angiotensin–aldosterone, which is followed by salt and water retention. Salt retention, in turn, gives rise to chronic hypertension.

the patients who did not receive hypertensive drugs and those who continued their drug treatment during the study. By the end of the study (eight or nine sessions), the no-drug group showed, during suggested deep relaxation, an average reduction of 17% in systolic pressure and 19% in diastolic pressure. At the end of the study, the drug group showed, during deep relaxation, a reduction of 16% in average systolic pressure and 14% in average diastolic pressure. (The patients in the control group did not show significant changes in blood pressure.) The authors stated that the vast majority of the patients in the hypnosuggestion group reported improvement in their hypertensive symptoms as a consequence of using muscular relaxation and hypnotic deep relaxation, including reduced time needed to fall asleep at night, deeper sleep, reduction in frequency and intensity of headaches, and decreased anxiety.

H. Friedman and Taub (1977, 1978) found, at a 6-month follow-up, that seven hypnosuggestive sessions consisting of repeated suggestions for deep relaxation were associated with an average reduction of 12% in diastolic pressure and 11% in systolic pressure. Although these investigators also utilized a biofeedback group and a no-treatment control group and found that the hypnosuggestion group showed larger reductions in blood pressure, no conclusions can be drawn from these data because of failure to assign the patients to the treatments at random (apparently the most responsive subjects were assigned to the hypnosuggestive treatment).

The above studies suggest that hypnosuggestive procedures focusing virtually exclusively on suggestions for deep relaxation are associated with a reduction in blood pressure. Another recent study by Case, Fogel, and Pollack (1980) indicates that hypnosuggestive procedures that do *not* aim to produce deep relaxation should not be expected to reduce hypertension. These investigators found no reduction in blood pressure in 16 mildly hypertensive patients who were instructed to practice 6 to 10 times per day for 4 months a brief exercise consisting of allowing the left arm to levitate as a signal to enter a trance state, and to concentrate on the need to relax and to respect and protect their bodies.

The hypnosuggestive procedures were used in a very restricted sense in the above-mentioned studies. I would conjecture that a more marked effect on hypertension would be observed if we (1) teach clients both deep relaxation and active relaxation; (2) conduct insight-oriented therapy to uncover the historical roots of clients' approach to problems; (3) utilize hypnosuggestive procedures to help enhance clients' self-regard and to guide them to a deeper philosophy of life; (4) teach clients deep relaxation for calmly thinking through solutions to immediate problems; and (5) expose clients to additional behavioral and cognitive–behavioral procedures, including thought stopping, assertive training, and training in problem solving.

HYPNOSIS, RELAXATION, AND BEYOND

This chapter develops two themes. The first theme is that suggestions for deep relaxation are used in many ways in hypnotic situations. Their "official" use is to produce "hypnosis" or "trance," in the sense of an awayness or withdrawal from active daily concerns, with an associated readiness to experience those things that are suggested. Suggestions for deep relaxation are also used more or less "officially" in hypnotic situations to produce and maintain a state of tranquility while the client mentally rehearses forthcoming tasks and solutions to life problems. "Unofficially," suggestions for deep relaxation are used in hypnotic situations in order (1) to define the situation as "hypnosis" and thus to capitalize on both the clients' and the therapists' positive expectancies and excitement about hypnosis; (2) to enhance clients' expectancies that they can experience forthcoming suggestions because they have already experienced the relatively easily experienced (relaxation) suggestions; and (3) to change the formal therapeutic situation so that it is more "loose" and more conducive to fantasy, primary processes, and a kind of role playing. An implicit contention behind this delineation of the various "official" and "unofficial" uses of deep relaxation suggestions in hypnotic situations is to demonstrate that such situations are complex and multidimensional and have many subtle, often unnoticed aspects. The more we understand heterohypnotic situations, the more we see that the two individuals involved are relating in complex ways; that the communications from the hypnotist have many levels of meaning; and that a single set of suggestions can often have many different aims (Field, 1972).

The second theme of this chapter is that hypnosuggestive procedures focusing on deep relaxation and active relaxation are useful in the treatment of stress-related or psychosomatic disorders such as migraine, tension headache, asthma, insomnia, and hypertension. Several subtle themes also are present in this discussion: (1) Many of the studies lacked important controls, and it was not clear to what extent the effectiveness of the relaxation procedure was due to relaxation per se and to what extent it was due to associated variables such as the excitement, positive expectancies, and special efforts that were part of the hypnotic situation; (2) the hypnosuggestive relaxation procedures were more helpful with some clients than with others; and (3) the usefulness of the procedures appears to depend on many variables, including how, when, and under what conditions they are presented. Also, hypnosuggestive procedures focusing on deep relaxation and active relaxation have not been shown to be generally more effective than other procedures (such as progressive muscular relaxation, autogenic training, meditation, and various kinds of biofeedback) that have similar aims. In fact, it appears that individual differences are very important here; individuals with certain kinds of characteristics may "fit" one type of relaxation procedure and be "misfits" with another. For instance, it may be preferable to use progressive muscular relaxation or EMG biofeedback with individuals who manifest a high degree of muscle tension, show an external locus of control (Ollendick & Murphy, 1977), or have little ability to imagine and to become "absorbed" (Qualls & Sheehan, 1981). Vice versa, it may be more appropriate to use more "cognitive-based" approaches such as hypnosuggestions, autogenic training, and meditation (Davidson & Schwartz, 1976) with individuals who are more philosophical, and also with those who are more imaginative and fantasy-prone (and are thus good hypnotic subjects) (Wilson & Barber, 1981, 1983).

Although the goal of "relaxation" can be approached in various ways, therapists should acknowledge more often that the goal is not muscular relaxation per se, but a new level of being that is characterized by peace of mind. Although training in muscle relaxation may be useful at times in the preliminary phase, the end desired is virtually always the equanimity or tranquility that is associated with a marked reduction of negative feelings or emotions, such as anger, resentment, guilt, and fear. By instructing clients to practice deep relaxation, we hope that they can experience what it is like to be without worries and negative feelings. We also hope that the clients will generalize to "real life" the feelings of well-being and tranquility that they attain during deep relaxation. However, instead of assuming that the feeling of serenity will be extrapolated to active living, we try to enhance its extrapolation by asking clients to practice active relaxation—that is, we ask them to practice, while deeply relaxed, mentally rehearsing being in real-life stress situations and coping calmly and successfully.

However, attainment of true relaxation—that is, equanimity or peace of mind—involves far more than the ritualized practice of stereotyped procedures. It involves movement toward a "higher" or, at least, a different state of consciousness, characterized by "detachment" in the sense of accepting that life has unwanted happenings and not demanding that the world be made to please us. The attainment of relaxation in the most important sense has a dimension that has been emphasized by Eastern spiritual approaches—living fully in the present moment instead of in the past or future, and thus excluding worry and negative emotions (J. White & Fadiman, 1976, pp. 252–253).

Attaining equanimity requires much more than the practice of muscle relaxation or the practice of deep relaxation; it also requires effective therapy to help clients leave behind their self-defeating behaviors by overcoming their feelings of incompetence, unworthiness, guilt, and unlovableness. This requires an individualized, step-by-step, multidimensional approach that utilizes psychoanalytically oriented procedures together with behavioral and cognitive–behavioral procedures to increase self-understanding, enhance self-esteem, and build a new philosophical outlook. This, in turn, requires exceptional therapists who are not only highly skilled and caring individuals, but also models of tranquility and equanimity.

ACKNOWLEDGMENTS

The ideas in this chapter were formulated in a series of hypnosis and self-hypnosis workshops conducted for Proseminar in 1980 and 1981. I am indebted to Sheryl C. Wilson for critical comments pertaining to the chapter.

REFERENCES

Adams, H. E., Feuerstein, M., & Fowler, J. L. Migraine headache: Review of parameters, etiology, and intervention. *Psychological Bulletin*, 1980, *87*, 217–237.

Alexander, A. B. Systematic relaxation and flow rates in asthmatic children: Relationship to emotional precipitants and anxiety. *Journal of Psychosomatic Research*, 1972, *16*, 405–410.

Alexander, A. B. Asthma. In S. N. Haynes & L. Gannon (Eds.), *Psychosomatic disorders: A psychophysiological approach to etiology and treatment*. New York: Praeger, 1981.

Alexander, A. B., Cropp, G. J. A., & Chai, H. The effects of relaxation training on pulmonary mechanics in children with asthma. *Journal of Applied Behavioral Analysis*, 1979, *12*, 27–35.

Alexander, A. B., Miklich, D. R., & Hershkoff, H. The immediate effects of systematic relaxation training on peak expiratory flow rates in asthmatic children. *Psychosomatic Medicine*, 1972, *34*, 388–394.

Anderson, J. A. D., Basker, M. A., & Dalton, R. Migraine and hypnotherapy. *International*

Journal of Clinical and Experimental Hypnosis, 1975, *23*, 48–58.

Andreychuk, T., & Skriver, C. Hypnosis and biofeedback in the treatment of migraine headache. *International Journal of Clinical and Experimental Hypnosis*, 1975, *23*, 172–183.

Bakal, D. A. Headache: A biopsychological perspective. *Psychological Bulletin*, 1975, *82*, 369–382.

Banyai, E., & Hilgard, E. R. A comparison of active–alert hypnotic induction with traditional relaxation induction. *Journal of Abnormal Psychology*, 1976, *85*, 218–224.

Barabasz, A. F. Treatment of insomnia in depressed patients by hypnosis and cerebral electrotherapy. *American Journal of Clinical Hypnosis*, 1976, *19*, 120–122.

Barber, T. X. *Hypnosis: A scientific approach*. New York: Van Nostrand Reinhold, 1969.

Barber, T. X. *LSD, marihuana, yoga and hypnosis*. Hawthorne, N.Y.: Aldine, 1970.

Barber, T. X. *Positive suggestions for effective living and philosophical hypnosis*. Medfield, Mass.: Medfield Foundation, 1978. (Cassette tape)

Barber, T. X. *Hypnotic and self-hypnotic suggestions for study-concentration, relaxation, pain control, and mystical experience* Medfield, Mass.: Medfield Foundation, 1979. (a) (Cassette tape)

Barber, T. X. *Hypnotic suggestions for weight control and smoking cessation*. Medfield, Mass.: Medfield Foundation, 1979. (b) (Cassette tape)

Barber, T. X. Training students to use self-suggestions for personal growth: Methods and word-by-word instructions. *Journal of Suggestive–Accelerative Learning and Teaching*, 1979, *4*, 111–128. (c)

Barber, T. X. Innovations and limitations in Erickson's hypnosis. *Contemporary Pscyhology*, 1981, *26*, 825–827. (a)

Barber, T. X. Medicine, suggestive therapy, and healing. In R. J. Kastenbaum, T. X. Barber, S. C. Wilson, B. L. Ryder, & L. B. Hathaway (Eds.), *Old, sick, and helpless: Where therapy begins*. Cambridge, Mass.: Ballinger, 1981. (b)

Barber, T. X. Hypnosuggestive procedures in the treatment of clinical pain: Implications for theories of hypnosis and suggestive therapy. In T. Millon, C. J. Green, & R. B. Meagher, Jr. (Eds), *Handbook of clinical health psychology*. New York: Plenum, 1982.

Barber, T. X., & DeMoor, W. A theory of hypnotic induction procedures. *American Journal of Clinical Hypnosis*, 1972, *15*, 112–135.

Barber, T. X., Spanos, N. P., & Chaves, J. F. *Hypnosis, imagination, and human potentialities*. New York: Pergamon Press, 1974.

Barber, T. X., & Wilson, S. C. Hypnosis, suggestions, and altered states of consciousness: Experimental evaluation of the new cognitive–behavioral theory and the traditional trance-state theory of "hypnosis." *Annals of the New York Academy of Sciences*, 1977, *296*, 34–47.

Basker, M. A. Hypnosis in migraine. *British Journal of Clinical Hypnosis*, 1970, *2*, 15–18.

Basker, M. A., Anderson, J. A. D., & Dalton, R. Migraine and hypnotherapy. In F. H. Frankel & H. S. Zamansky (Eds.), *Hypnosis at its bicentennial: Selected papers*. New York: Plenum, 1978.

Basker, M. A., Anderson, J. A. D., & Dalton, R. Insomnia and hypnotherapy. In G. D. Burrows, D. R. Collison, & L. Dennerstein (Eds.), *Hypnosis 1979*. New York: Elsevier–North Holland, 1979.

Benson, H., Beary, J. F., & Carol, M. P. The relaxation response. *Psychiatry*, 1974, *37*, 37–46.

Benson, H., Malvea, B. A., & Graham, J. R. Physiologic correlates of meditation and their clinical effect in headache: An ongoing investigation. *Headache*, 1973, 13, 23–24.

Benson, H., Rosner, B. A., Marzetta, B., & Klemchuk, H. Decreased blood pressure in pharmacologically treated hypertensive patients who regularly elicited the relaxation response. *Lancet*, 1974, *i*, 289–292.

Bernheim, H. *Suggestive therapeutics.* Westport, Conn.: Associated Booksellers, 1957. (Originally published, 1886.)

Bihldorf, J. P., King, S. H., & Parnes, L. R. Psychological factors in headache. *Headache,* 1971, *11,* 117–127.

Blanchard, E. B., Ahles, T. A., & Shaw, E. R. Behavioral treatment of headaches. *Progress in Behavior Modification,* 1979, *8,* 207–247.

Blanchard, E. B., & Miller, S. T. Psychological treatment of cardiovascular disease. *Archives of General Psychiatry,* 1977, *34,* 1402–1413.

Blanchard, E. B., Theobald, D. E., Williamson, D. A., Silver, B. V., & Brown, D. A. Temperature biofeedback in the treatment of migraine headaches. *Archives of General Psychiatry,* 1978, *35,* 581–588.

Bootzin, R. R. A stimulus control treatment for insomnia. *Proceedings of the American Psychological Association,* 1972, *4,* 395–396.

Bootzin, R. R. Effects of self-control procedures for insomnia. In R. B. Stuart (Ed.), *Behavioral self-management: Strategies and outcomes.* New York: Brunner/Mazel, 1977.

Bootzin, R., & Nicassio, P. Behavioral treatments of insomnia. In M. Hersen, R. Eisler, & P. Miller (Eds.). *Progress in behavior modification* (Vol. 4). New York: Academic Press, 1978.

Borkovec, T. D. Pseudo (experiential)-insomnia and idiopathic (objective) insomnia: Theoretical and therapeutic issues. In H. J. Eysenck & S. Rachman (Eds.), *Advances in behavior research and therapy* (Vol. 2). London: Pergamon Press, 1979.

Borkovec, T. D., & Fowles, D. C. Controlled investigation of the effects of progressive and hypnotic relaxation on insomnia. *Journal of Abnormal Psychology,* 1973, *82,* 153–158.

Borkovec, T. D., Grayson, J. B., O'Brien, G. T., & Weerts, T. C. Treatment of pseudo-insomnia and idiopathic insomnia via progressive relaxation with and without muscle tension–release: An electroencephalographic evaluation. *Journal of Applied Behavior Analysis,* 1979, *12,* 37–54.

Borkovec, T. D., Kaloupek, D., & Slama, K. The facilitative effect of muscle tension in the relaxation treatment of sleep disturbance. *Behavior Therapy,* 1975, *6,* 301–309.

Borkovec, T. D., & Weerts, T. C. Effects of progressive relaxation on sleep disturbance: An electroencephalographic evaluation. *Psychosomatic Medicine,* 1976, *38,* 173–180.

Braid, J. *Neuropnology, or the rationale of nervous sleep considered in relation with animal magnetism.* New York: Arno Press, 1976. (Originally published, 1843.)

Brown, E. A. The treatment of asthma by means of hypnosis as viewed by the allergist. *Journal of Asthma Research,* 1965, *3,* 101–119.

Case, D. B., Fogel, D. H., & Pollack, A. A. Intrahypnotic and long-term effects of self-hypnosis on blood pressure in mild hypertension. *International Journal of Clinical and Experimental Hypnosis,* 1980, *28,* 27–38.

Chesney, M. A., & Shelton, J. L. A comparison of muscle relaxation and electromyographic biofeedback treatments for muscle contraction headache. *Journal of Behavioral Therapy and Experimental Psychiatry,* 1976, 7, 221–225.

Collison, D. R. Which asthmatic patients should be treated by hypnotherapy? *Medical Journal of Australia,* 1975, *1,* 776–781.

Collison, D. R. Hypnotherapy in asthmatic patients and the importance of trance depth. In F. H. Frankel & H. S. Zamansky (Eds.), *Hypnosis at its bicentennial: Selected papers.* New York: Plenum, 1978.

Cox, D. J. Freundlich, A., & Meyer, R. G. Differential effectiveness of relaxation techniques and placebo with tension headaches. *Journal of Consulting and Clinical Psychology,* 1975, *43,* 892–898.

Daniels, L. K. The effects of automated hypnosis and hand warming on migraine: A pilot study. *American Journal of Clinical Hypnosis*, 1976, *19*, 91–94.

Daniels, L. K. Treatment of migraine headache by hypnosis and behavior therapy: A case study. *American Journal of Clinical Hypnosis*, 1977, *19*, 241–244.

Davidson, R. J., & Schwartz, G. E. The psychobiology of relaxation and related states: A multi-process theory. In D. I. Mostofsky (Ed.), *Behavior control and modification of physiological activity*. Englewood Cliffs, N.J.: Prentice-Hall, 1976.

Davis, M. H., Saunders, D. R., Creer, T. L., & Chai, H. Relaxation training facilitated by biofeedback apparatus as a supplemental treatment in bronchial asthma. *Journal of Psychosomatic Research*, 1973, *17*, 121–128.

Deabler, H. L., Fidel, E., Dillenkoffer, R. L., & Elder, S. The use of relaxation and hypnosis in lowering high blood pressure. *American Journal of Clinical Hypnosis*, 1973, *16*, 75–83.

Dekker, E., & Groen, J. Reproducible psychogenic attacks of asthma: A laboratory study. *Journal of Psychosomatic Research*, 1956, *1*, 58–67.

Dement, W. C. *Some must watch while some must sleep*. San Francisco: W. H. Freeman, 1972.

Donk, L. J., Knudson, R. G., Washburn, R. W., Goldstein, A. D., & Vingoe, F. J. Toward an increase in reading efficiency utilizing specific suggestions: A preliminary approach. *International Journal of Clinical and Experimental Hypnosis,* 1968, *16*, 101–110.

Edgell, P. G. Psychiatric approach to the treatment of bronchial asthma. *Modern Treatment*, 1966, *3*, 900.

Edmonston, W. E., Jr. *Hypnosis and relaxation: Modern verification of an old equation*. New York: Wiley, 1981.

Edwards, G. Hypnotic treatment of asthma: Real and illusory results. *British Medical Journal*, 1960, ii, 492–497.

Ellenberger, H. F. *The discovery of the unconscious: The history and evolution of dynamic psychiatry*. New York: Basic Books, 1970.

Ellis, A. *Reason and emotion in psychotherapy*. New York: Lyle Stuart, 1962.

Epstein, L. H., Abel, G. G., & Webster, J. S. Self-managed relaxation in the treatment of tension headaches. In J. D. Krumboltz & C. E. Thoreson (Eds.), *Counseling methods*. New York: Holt, Rinehart & Winston, 1976.

Erickson, M. H. *The collected papers of Milton H. Erickson on hypnosis* (E. L. Rossi, Ed.) (4 vols.). New York: Irvington Publishers, 1980.

Fichtler, H., & Zimmerman, R. R. Changes in reported pain from tension headaches. *Perceptual and Motor Skills*, 1973, *36*, 712.

Field, P. Humanistic aspects of hypnotic communication. In E. Fromm & R. E. Shor (Eds.), *Hypnosis: Research developments and perspectives*. Chicago: Aldine–Atherton, 1972.

Field, P. B. *Stress reduction in hypnotherapy of chronic headaches*. Paper presented at the annual meeting of the American Psychological Association, New York, September 2, 1979.

Folkow, B., Hällback, M., Lundgren, Y., Silvertsson, R., & Weiss, L. Importance of adaptive changes in vascular design for establishment of primary hypertension: Studies in man and in spontaneously hypertensive rats. *Circulation Research*, 1973, *32–33* (Suppl. 1), 2–16.

Folkow, B., & Neil, E. *Circulation*. New York: Oxford University Press, 1971.

Folkow, B., & Rubinstein, E. H. Cardiovascular effects of acute and chronic stimulations of the hypothalamic defence area in the rat. *Acta Physiologica Scandinavica*, 1966, *68*, 48–57.

Francuch, P. D. *Principles of spiritual hypnosis*. Santa Barbara, Calif.: Spiritual Advisory Press, 1981.

Freedman, R., & Papsdorf, J. D. Biofeedback and progressive relaxation treatment of sleep onset insomnia. *Biofeedback and Self-Regulation*, 1976, *1*, 253–271.

Friedman, A. P. Treatment of headache. *International Journal of Neurology*, 1972, *9*, 11–22.

Friedman, H., & Taub, H. A. The use of hypnosis and biofeedback procedures for essential hypertension. *International Journal of Clinical and Experimental Hypnosis*, 1977, *25*, 335–347.

Friedman, H., & Taub, H. A. A six-month follow-up of the use of hypnosis and biofeedback procedures in essential hypertension. *American Journal of Clinical Hypnosis*, 1978, *20*, 184–188.

Fromm, E. The nature of hypnosis and other altered states of consciousness: An ego psychological theory. In E. Fromm & R. E. Shor (Eds.), *Hypnosis: Developments in research and new perspectives* (2nd ed.). Hawthorne, N.Y.: Aldine, 1979.

Goldstein, Y. The effect of demonstrating to a subject that she is in a hypnotic trance as a variable in hypnotic interventions with obese women. *International Journal of Clinical and Experimental Hypnosis*, 1981, *29*, 15–23.

Graham, K. R., Wright, G. W., Toman, W. J., & Mark, C. B. Relaxation and hypnosis in the treatment of insomnia. *American Journal of Clinical Hypnosis*, 1975, *18*, 39–42.

Harding, C. H. Hypnosis in the treatment of migraine. In J. Lassner (Ed.), *Hypnosis and psychosomatic medicine*. New York: Springer-Verlag, 1967.

Harrell, J. P. Psychological factors and hypertension: A status report. *Psychological Bulletin*, 1980, *87*, 482–501.

Harrison, R. H. Psychological testing in headache: A review. *Heachache*, 1975, *13*, 177–185.

Hartland, J. The value of "ego-strengthening" procedures prior to direct symptom-removal under hypnosis. *American Journal of Clinical Hypnosis*, 1965, *8*, 89–93.

Hauri, P. *Psychology of sleep disorders: Their diagnosis and treatment*. Paper presented at the 83rd annual meeting of the American Psychological Association, Chicago, August 1975.

Hay, K. M., & Madders, J. Migraine treated by relaxation therapy. *Journal of the Royal College of General Practitioners*, 1971, *21*, 664–669.

Haynes, S. N., Griffin, P., Mooney, D., & Parise, M. Electromyographic biofeedback and relaxation instructions in the treatment of muscle contraction headaches. *Behavior Therapy*, 1975, *6*, 672–678.

Haynes, S. N., Sides, H., & Lockwood, G. Relaxation instructions and frontalis electromyographic feedback intervention with sleep onset insomnia. *Behavior Therapy*, 1977, *8*, 644–652.

Haynes, S. N., Woodward, S., Moran, R., & Alexander, D. Relaxation treatment of insomnia. *Behavior Therapy*, 1974, *5*, 555–558.

Henryk-Gutt, R., & Rees, W. L. Psychological aspects of migraine. *Journal of Psychosomatic Research*, 1973, *17*, 141–153.

Hess, W. R. *Diencephalon: Autonomic and extrapyramidal functions*. New York: Grune & Stratton, 1954.

Holroyd, K. A., & Andrasik, F. Coping and self-control of chronic tension headache. *Journal of Counseling and Clinical Psychology*, 1978, *46*, 1036–1045.

Holroyd, K. A., Andrasik, F., & Westbrook, T. Cognitive control of tension headaches. *Cognitive Therapy and Research*, 1977, *1*, 121–123.

Jacob, R. G., Kraemer, H. C., & Agras, W. S. Relaxation therapy in the treatment of hypertension. *Archives of General Psychiatry*, 1977, *34*, 1417–1427.

Johnson, W. G., & Turin, A. Biofeedback treatment of migraine headache: A systematic case study. *Behavior Therapy*, 1975, *6*, 394–397.

Kales, A., & Kales, J. Recent advances in the diagnosis and treatment of sleep disorders. In G. Usdin (Ed.), *Sleep research and clinical practice*. New York: Brunner/Mazel, 1973.

Kales, J., Tan, T. L., Swearingen, C., & Kales, A. Are over-the-counter sleep medications effective? Allnight EEG studies. *Current Therapeutic Research*, 1971, *13*, 143–151.

Kaplan, N. M. The control of hypertension: A therapeutic breakthrough. *American Scientist*, 1980, *68*, 537–545.

Karacan, M., & Williams, R. L. Insomnia: Old wine in a new bottle. *Psychiatric Quarterly*, 1971, *45*, 274–288.

Lawrence, P. S., & Tokarz, T. *A comparison of relaxation training and stimulus control.* Paper presented at the annual meeting of the Association for Advancement of Behavior Therapy, New York, 1976.

Liebeault, A. A. *Le sommeil provoqué et les états analogues.* Paris: 1889.

Lick, J. R., & Heffler, D. Relaxation training and attention placebo in the treatment of severe insomnia. *Journal of Consulting and Clinical Psychology*, 1977, *45*, 153–161.

Ludwig, A. M., & Lyle, W. H., Jr. Tension induction and the hyperalert trance. *Journal of Abnormal and Social Psychology*, 1964, *69*, 70–76.

Luthe, W. Autogenic therapy: Excerpts on applications to cardiovascular disorders and hypercholesteremia. In J. Stoyva, T. X. Barber, L. V. DiCara, J. Kamiya, N. E. Miller, & D. Shapiro (Eds.), *Biofeedback and self-control 1971.* Chicago: Aldine–Atherton, 1972.

Lutker, E. R. Treatment of migraine headache by conditioned relaxation: A case study. *Behavior Therapy*, 1971, *2*, 592–593.

Maher-Loughnan, G. P. Hypnosis and autohypnosis for the treatment of asthma. *International Journal of Clinical and Experimental Hypnosis*, 1970, *18*, 1–14.

Maher-Loughnan, G. P., & Kinsley, B. J. Hypnosis for asthma—a controlled trial: A report of the Research Committee of the British Tuberculosis Association. *British Medical Journal*, 1968, *iv*, 71–76.

Maher-Loughnan, G. P., MacDonald, N., Mason, A. A., & Fry, L. Controlled trial of hypnosis in the symptomatic treatment of asthma. *British Medical Journal*, 1962, *2*, 371–376.

Marlatt, G. A. Alcohol use and problem drinking: A cognitive–behavioral approach. In P. C. Kendall & S. D. Hollon (Eds.), *Cognitive–behavioral interventions: Theory, research, and procedures.* New York: Academic Press, 1979.

Martin, M. J. Psychogenic factors in headache. *Medical Clinics of North America*, 1978, *62*, 559–570.

McLean, A. F. Hypnosis in "psychosomatic" illness. *British Journal of Medical Psychology*, 1965, *38*, 211–230.

Meares, A. *Relief without drugs: The self-management of tension, anxiety and pain.* Garden City, N.Y.: Doubleday, 1967.

Mitchell, K. R. The treatment of migraine. An exploratory application of time-limited behavior therapy. *Technology*, 1969, *14*, 50–55.

Mitchell, K. R., & Mitchell, D. M. Migraine: An exploratory treatment application of programmed behaviour therapy techniques. *Journal of Psychosomatic Research*, 1971, *15*, 137–157.

Mitchell, K. R., & White, R. G. Behavioral self-management: An application to the problem of migraine headaches. *Behavior Therapy*, 1977, *8*, 213–221.

Moorefield, C. W. The use of hypnosis and behavior therapy in asthma. *American Journal of Clinical Hypnosis*, 1971, *13*, 162–168.

Nicassio, P., & Bootzin, R. A comparison of progressive relaxation and autogenic training as treatments of insomnia. *Journal of Abnormal Psychology*, 1974, *83*, 253–260.

Nicassio, P., Boylan, M, & McCabe, T. *Progressive relaxation, EMG biofeedback, and biofeedback placebo in the treatment of insomnia.* Paper presented at the 16th meeting of the Inter-American Society of Psychology, Miami, 1976.

Nuland, W. The evaluation and treatment of insomnia. In L. Unestahl (Ed.), *Hypnosis in the seventies.* Orebro, Sweden: Veje Forlag, 1975.

Ollendick, T. H., & Murphy, M. J. Differential effectiveness of muscular and cognitive relaxation as a function of locus of control. *Journal of Behavior Therapy and Experimental Psychiatry*, 1977, *8*, 223–228.

Ostfeld, A. M. *The common headache syndromes: Biochemistry, pathophysiology, therapy.* Springfield, Ill.: Charles C Thomas, 1962.

Phillip, R. L., Wilde, G. J. S., & Day, J. H. Suggestion and relaxation in asthmatics. *Journal of Psychosomatic Research*, 1972, *16*, 193–204.

Philips, C. Tension headache: Theoretical problems. *Behaviour Research and Therapy*, 1978, *16*, 249–261.

Price, K. P. The application of behavior therapy to the treatment of psychosomatic disorders: Retrospect and prospect. *Psychotherapy: Theory, Research, and Practice.* 1974, *11*, 138–155.

Qualls, P. J., & Sheehan, P. W. Electromyograph biofeedback as a relaxation technique: A critical appraisal and reassessment. *Psychological Bulletin*, 1981, *90*, 21–42.

Rachman, S. The role of muscular relaxation in desensitization therapy. *Behaviour Research and Therapy*, 1968, *6*, 159–166.

Sarbin, T. R., & Coe, W. C. *Hypnosis: A social psychological analysis of influence communication.* New York: Holt, Rinehart & Winston, 1972.

Sargent, J. D., Green, E. E., & Walters, E. D. The use of autogenic feedback training in a pilot study of migraine and tension headache. *Headache*, 1972, *12*, 120–124.

Scherr, M. S., Crawford, P. L., Sergent, C. B., & Scherr, C. A. Effect of biofeedback techniques on chronic asthma in a summer camp environment. *Annals of Allergy*, 1975, *35*, 289–295.

Selby, G., & Lance, J. W. Observations on 500 cases of migraine and allied vascular headache. *Journal of Neurology, Neurosurgery, and Psychiatry*, 1960, *23*, 23–32.

Shoemaker, J. E., & Tasto, D. L. The effects of muscle relaxation on blood pressure of essential hypertensives. *Behaviour Research and Therapy*, 1975, *13*, 29–43.

Sirota, A. D., & Mahoney, M. J. Relaxing on cue: The self regulation of asthma. *Journal of Behavior Therapy and Experimental Psychiatry*, 1974, *5*, 65–66.

Skinner, B. F. *Science and human behavior.* New York: Macmillan, 1953.

Spiegel, H., & Spiegel, D. *Trance and treatment: Clinical uses of hypnosis.* New York: Basic Books, 1978.

Stanton, H. E. The treatment of insomnia through hypnosis and relaxation. *Terpnos Logos*, 1975, *3*, 4–8.

Stanton, H. E. Test anxiety and hypnosis: A different approach to an important problem. *Australian Journal of Education*, 1977, *21*, 179–186.

Stanton, H. E. The hypnotherapeutic placebo. In G. D. Burrows, D. R. Collison, & L. Dennerstein (Eds.), *Hypnosis 1979.* New York: Elsevier–North Holland, 1979.

Steinmark, S., & Borkovec, T. Active and placebo treatment effects on moderate insomnia under counterdemand and positive demand instructions. *Journal of Abnormal Psychology*, 1975, *83*, 157–163.

Straus, R. A. *Strategic self-hypnosis.* Englewood Cliffs, N.J.: Prentice-Hall, 1982.

Tasto, D. L., & Hinkle, J. E. Muscle relaxation treatment for tension headaches. *Behaviour Research and Therapy*, 1973, *11*, 347–349.

Thoresen, C. E., Coates, T. J., Kirmil-Gray, K., & Rosekind, M. R. Behavioral self-management in treating sleep-maintenance insomnia. *Journal of Behavioral Medicine*, 1981, *4*, 41–52.

Tokarz, T., & Lawrence, P. *An analysis of temporal and stimulus factors in the treatment of insomnia.* Paper presented at the 8th annual meeting of the Association for Advancement of Behavior Therapy, Chicago, 1974.

Turin, A. C. *No more headaches! Practical, effective methods for relief.* Boston: Houghton Mifflin, 1981.

Warner, G., & Lance, J. W. Relaxation therapy in migraine and chronic tension headache. *Medical Journal of Australia*, 1975, *4*, 298–301.

Weiner, H. *Psychobiology and human disease.* New York: Elsevier–North Holland, 1977.

Weitzenhoffer, A. M. *Hypnotism: An objective study in suggestibility.* New York: Wiley, 1953.

Weitzenhoffer, A. M., & Sjoberg, B. M. Suggestibility with and without "induction of hypnosis." *Journal of Nervous and Mental Disease*, 1961, *132*, 204–220.

Wetterstrand, O. G. *Hypnotism and its application to practical medicine.* New York: Putnam, 1897.

White, H. Hypnosis in bronchial asthma. *Journal of Psychosomatic Research*, 1961, *5*, 272–279.

White, J., & Fadiman, J. (Eds.). *Relax.* New York: Confucian Press, 1976.

Wickramasekera, I. Temperature feedback for the control of migraine. *Journal of Behavior Therapy and Experimental Psychiatry*, 1973, *4*, 343–345.

Wilson, A. F., Honsberger, R., Chiu, J. T., & Novey, H. S. Transcendental meditation and asthma. *Respiration*, 1975, *32*, 74–80.

Wilson, S. C., & Barber, T. X. The Creative Imagination Scale as a measure of hypnotic responsiveness: Applications to experimental and clinical hypnosis. *American Journal of Clinical Hypnosis*, 1978, *20*, 235–249.

Wilson, S. C., & Barber, T. X. Vivid fantasy and hallucinatory abilities in the life histories of excellent hypnotic subjects ("somnambules"): Preliminary report with female subjects. In E. Klinger (Ed.), *Imagery* (Vol. 2, *Concepts, results, and applications*). New York: Plenum, 1981.

Wilson, S. C., & Barber, T. X. The fantasy-prone personality: Implications for understanding imagery, hypnosis, and parapsychological phenomena. In A. A. Sheikh (Ed.), *Imagery: Current theory, research, and applications.* New York: Wiley, 1983.

Wolberg, L. R. *Medical hypnosis* (2 vols.). New York: Grune & Stratton, 1948.

Woolfolk, R., Carr-Kaffashan, L., McNulty, T., & Lehrer, P. Meditation training as a treatment for insomnia. *Behavior Therapy*, 1976, *7*, 359–365.

Youkilis, H. D., & Bootzin, R. R. A psychophysiological perspective on the etiology and treatment of insomnia. In S. N. Haynes & L. Gannon (Eds.), *Psychosomatic disorders: A psychophysiological approach to etiology and treatment.* New York: Praeger, 1981.

Ziegler, D. K. Tension headache. *Medical Clinics of North America*, 1978, *62*, 495–505.

Zwart, C. A., & Lisman, S. A. Analysis of sleep control treatment of sleep-onset insomnia. *Journal of Consulting and Clinical Psychology*, 1979, *47*, 113–118.

7 BIOFEEDBACK METHODS IN THE TREATMENT OF ANXIETY AND STRESS

THOMAS H. BUDZYNSKI AND JOHANN M. STOYVA

INTRODUCTION

In this chapter, we explore the use of biofeedback in the context of stress management. After a brief definition of "biofeedback," we next provide some history and theory of the technique. This effort is limited to the types of biofeedback most often considered when anxiety relief and/or stress management is the goal.

In general, biofeedback systems operate by detecting changes in the biological environment and, by means of visual and auditory signals, notifying the patient of these changes. The patient, using this precise and immediate information, engages in trial-and-error strategy testing in order to make the signals change in the desired direction. With the biofeedback as a guide, the patient in relatively short order learns how to control the biological response system from whence the biofeedback signals originate. With additional training, the patient is gradually weaned away from the biofeedback; having now calibrated the subtle internal events corresponding to the biological system in question, he or she can maintain control without the biofeedback.

The object of such training is to achieve control over biological systems that have been operating in a maladaptive fashion and have been beyond conscious control. The term "maladaptive" implies that the system has been operating over a range of functioning that contributes to inefficiency at the very least and to stress-related disease at the worst.

Biofeedback training really involves three stages (Budzynski, 1973). The first stage is *awareness* of the response that is maladaptive. Through the biofeedback, the client learns that certain thoughts as well as bodily events influence the response in question. Next, the client learns to *con-*

trol the response guided by the biofeedback signal. Finally, the client learns to *transfer* the control into everyday life situations.

It should be noted that biofeedback does more than guide patients to correct strategies for bringing their biology into a proper range of functioning. Perhaps its most important contribution is the instillation in patients of an increased belief in their ability to control events in their lives.

As soon becomes clear, the control issue is rapidly assuming a role of increasing importance in the area of psychoimmunology. But first, let us go back a relatively short time in order to trace the beginnings of biofeedback as it was applied to anxiety and stress management.

HISTORY OF THE METHOD

ELECTROENCEPHALOGRAPHIC AND ELECTROMYOGRAPHIC FEEDBACK

In 1966, Kamiya's technique of controlling the alpha electroencephalographic (EEG) rhythm by means of a feedback tone to indicate the presence of the alpha rhythm was already well known on the West Coast. In the same year, Neal Miller was exciting the participants of a Moscow colloquium with his results of recent animal studies, showing that certain autonomic responses could be operantly conditioned.

Later that year we built an alpha EEG feedback device. It had occurred to us that the pleasant, tranquil, relaxing characteristics of the "alpha state" as reported by Kamiya (1969) could be used to counter anxiety in the behavior therapy procedure known as "systematic desensitization." We reasoned that with the feedback device we first could teach patients to produce more alpha. Then we could ask them to visualize themselves in anxious or stressful situations. As the amount of alpha diminished, we could stop the visualization and allow the patients to "recover" the alpha state using the feedback tone.

The approach did in fact result in a highly successful desensitization of a patient with a severe thanatophobia (Budzynski & Stoyva, 1973). Desensitization was completed in four sessions. A 14-year follow-up indicated no return of the anxiety. To our knowledge, this was one of the first applications of electronic biofeedback in a psychotherapy setting.

Subsequent investigation into the possibilities of using alpha EEG feedback as an adjunct to behavior therapy caused us to conclude that surface electromyographic (EMG) feedback might be more useful in teaching patients to relax. We then developed one of the first EMG feedback devices for this purpose in 1967. It incorporated the constant reset level integrator used by Sainsbury and Gibson in their studies of surface EMG (Sainsbury & Gibson, 1954). Our device took the output of the integrator, a series of pulses, and converted it to a digital readout at selected intervals. The device also provided two types of auditory feedback, in addition to a three-level vertical-array visual display. (It is interesting to note that the original prototype is still in use in our research laboratory.)

From the beginning, our goals—first with the alpha EEG and then with surface EMG feedback—were to facilitate the development of relaxation ability, as well as to provide an objective indicator of depth of relaxation. Much of the initial research with surface EMG feedback was focused on the use of the forehead musculature as a sensor site. Earlier research by Sainsbury and Gibson (1954), Malmo (1975), Goldstein (1972), Reinking and Kohl (1975), and Leaf and Gaarder (1971) had indicated that the frontalis or frontal EMG was a useful indicator of anxiety, tension, or arousal.

We next began to work with anxious patients. The first few of these were individuals who had been unable to learn to relax with the brief Wolpe–Jacobson training usually provided by behavior therapists. Some others were patients who thought they could relax but were surprised to see that their levels of tension in selected muscles were quite high.

We discovered that without biofeedback, patients would often show an increase of tension throughout a systematic desensitization session, even while reporting that they were still relaxed (Budzynski & Stoyva, 1973). Often this took the form of an inability to recover the relaxed state after the first or second visualization of a scene from the "fear hierarchy." Not knowing that they were still tense, the patients would typically report relaxation between visualizations, and thus the desensitization would proceed with the patients' level of tension escalating. With the EMG feedback device, we were able to monitor the exact level of muscle tension in selected muscles. Moreover, the patients could use the feedback to relax quickly.

We began a series of case studies of circumscribed phobic anxiety and chronic, pervasive anxiety. Not too surprisingly, we found that, as a rule, the more chronic pervasive anxiety cases required approximately twice as many biofeedback relaxation and systematic desensitization sessions as did those cases of circumscribed anxiety (Budzynski & Stoyva, 1975).

A number of other studies later provided support for the application of frontal (frontalis) EMG biofeedback to anxiety disorders. Raskin, Johnson, and Rondestvedt (1973) found that this type of biofeedback training, in combination with daily practice of relaxation, was moderately useful for patients suffering from severe chronic anxiety. Their 10 patients had been troubled by severe symptoms for 3 years or more. Previous therapeutic efforts, including tranquilizers and psychotherapy, had not been successful. After training to a criterion of 2.5 μV peak to peak or less on frontal EMG, one patient showed a dramatic reduction of all anxiety symptoms; three others found the training to be useful in controlling previously intolerable situational anxiety. Of the six patients who also had insomnia, five improved in this regard. In addition, three of the four patients who had headache conditions showed decreased headache activity. It should be pointed out, however, that it is not enough simply to teach people to relax in quiet settings; they also must be taught to *transfer* this skill to everyday life situations (Budzynski, 1973).

Another study (Canter, Kondo, & Knott, 1975) compared frontal EMG feedback to progressive relaxation with 28 patients diagnosed as suffering from anxiety neurosis and as having complaints of muscle tension and insomnia, in addition to a high level of anxiety. Both EMG feedback and progressive relaxation training produced significant decreases in frontal EMG activity. However, EMG feedback was found to be generally superior in producing an associated diminution in anxiety symptoms.

Townsend, House, and Addario (1975) contrasted frontal EMG feedback with group psychotherapy as a treatment for chronically anxious patients. In the group receiving EMG feedback, there were significant decreases in EMG levels, mood disturbance, trait anxiety, and to a lesser extent, state anxiety. These changes were not seen in the group receiving psychotherapy.

An interesting result was obtained by Hiebert (1981). Reporting on his carefully done dissertation, Hiebert noted that frontal EMG biofeedback alone was more effective in reducing anxiety than when it was combined with systematic desensitization or cognitive monitoring. In fact, the training with frontal EMG feedback reduced anxiety better than cognitive monitoring or a high-expectancy discussion-group format.

Perhaps one of the most intriguing studies of chronic, free-floating anxiety compared frontal EMG feedback to Valium (Lavallée, Lamontagne, Pinard, Annable, & Tétreault, 1977). The 40 outpatients were randomly assigned to one of four groups: EMG feedback and Valium, EMG feedback and Valium placebo, EMG feedback placebo and Valium, and both placebos. The results showed that during treatment, frontal EMG and Valium were additive in reducing muscle tension. Although all active treatment groups reduced their anxiety, Valium-treated patients (with or without feedback) did less well than other subjects did in measures of anxiety, adjuvant medication usage, and home practice. In general, the results showed that frontal EMG feedback training without Valium had a more prolonged therapeutic effect for chronically anxious patients than did Valium alone. This anxiety study is of some importance, because it compared frontal EMG biofeedback with the most popular antianxiety drug, Valium, and the biofeedback training produced better results.

Shortly after we had begun our work with anxious patients, we entered into a parallel effort to apply frontal EMG biofeedback to tension headache. Our pilot observations (Budzynski, Stoyva, & Adler, 1970) were later confirmed by a larger controlled study (Budzynski, Stoyva, Adler, & Mullaney, 1973). Since it is generally agreed that tension or muscle contraction headache is produced by sustained contraction of the musculature of the head and neck, we were not surprised to find that these patients did benefit from biofeedback training in forehead relaxation. Considering the fact that estimates of the incidence of tension headache are in the area of 100 million in the United States (Budzynski, 1979), we feel that this is an important application.

MULTIPLE FEEDBACK

Even though we carried out the bulk of our early work on anxiety with only the EMG feedback as an aid, other forms of biofeedback were being brought into the clinical setting in the early to mid-1970s. These new forms of biofeedback included the galvanic skin response (GSR), sometimes known as the electrodermal response (EDR), which is the skin's emotional sweating response; and thermal feedback, reflecting peripheral skin temperature. EEG equipment also appeared on the market. Some clinics preferred to work with this brain-wave biofeedback in order to relax patients.

Our early rationale for using only the EMG feedback was that deep relaxation of the musculature should, theoretically, "pull" all of the autonomic responses in the direction of decreased sympathetic and increased parasympathetic responses. It was the case, however, that some individuals could show low EMG levels and still report that they felt anxious. In almost all of these instances, they would show a high EDR or a low peripheral temperature or both. Apparently some anxious patients can have fairly low muscle tonus, although they are probably in the minority. Nevertheless, we began to use the EDR feedback and thermal feedback to augment the EMG.

Mixer systems allowed these various forms of feedback to be presented singly or in combinations through the headphones to the patient. Now the shaping of low arousal could be carried out in a definitive fashion. The therapist could monitor all three response systems (some monitored heart rate and EEG as well), and could feed back whatever appeared to be the most responsive system(s).

A well-trained patient can control all three responses, even when imagining anxious or stressful situations.

BIOFEEDBACK IN THE PSYCHOTHERAPY SETTING

In 1972, one of us (Budzynski, 1973) established a private clinic in order to combine biofeedback with more traditional therapies for the treatment of anxiety and stress-related disorders. A systems approach was devised that incorporated training of three basic response systems. This required the use of not only EMG feedback, but other forms, such as thermal and EDR feedback. The latter two, reflecting autonomic activity, contributed to a complete program of training that was sequenced according to certain criteria (Budzynski, Stoyva, & Peffer, 1980).

A home training program of cassette tapes was developed in order to provide a motivating sequence of relaxation training and systematic desensitization.[1] Adaptations of progressive relaxation and autogenic training were combined with a generalized form of systematic desensitization. The biofeedback simply accelerated and refined the basic skills provided by the home practice program.

The last 10 years have seen an integration of the biofeedback training (often done by a technician now) with the behavioral therapies and psychotherapy, in order to deal more effectively with factors such as secondary gain and unconscious motivation.

BIOFEEDBACK AND SYSTEMATIC DESENSITIZATION

We have noted earlier that much of our early work with EMG biofeedback was focused on relaxing the patient prior to the behavior therapy procedures known as "systematic desensitization" (Wolpe, 1958). Since this procedure involves the counterconditioning of anxiety with relaxation, we felt that EMG biofeedback could be used, first, to aid the patient

[1]The Home Relaxation Cassette Tape Program is available from Hice Enterprises, Ltd., 6460 E. Yale CD 161, Denver, Colorado 80222.

in achieving the skill of relaxation, and second, to act as a monitor of depth of relaxation during the subsequent desensitization.

A number of researchers have shown that an anxious patient typically shows elevated levels of muscle tension, particularly during an anxiety episode (Jacobson, 1938; Malmo, 1975); Martin and Grosz (1964), for example, found that when various emotions were hypnotically suggested to a group of psychiatric patients, their arousal indicators changed in the expected direction. When told they were anxious, the patients showed increases in heart rate and muscle tension over that of the "relaxed" condition. In fact, the researchers noted that the most consistent measure was that of muscle tension.

Obviously, not all anxious patients are muscle responders, but even for those who are not, the relaxation of major muscle groups appears to dampen the activity of the sympathetic nervous system (SNS), thus producing a shift toward a lower arousal, characterized by parasympathetic dominance (Gellhorn, 1964; Germana, 1969; Hess, 1954; Luthe, 1969; Obrist, Webb, Sutterer, & Howard, 1970). Since the state of anxiety, and for that matter stress, is characterized by heightened sympathetic tone, it is reasonable to assume that procedures that shift autonomic dominance from the SNS toward the parasympathetic nervous system (PNS) would be effective techniques for coping with stress or anxiety.

A possible neurophysiological basis for the effects of muscle relaxation was advanced by Gellhorn (1964). In commenting on a number of animal studies that dealt with autonomic–somatic relationships, Gellhorn noted that "a reduction or inhibition of proprioceptive impulses through blocking of the neuromuscular junction reduces sympathetic and increases parasympathetic discharges, and also reduces the state of cortical excitation: synchronous potentials and behavior indicate that sleep has been induced. . . . These experiments are believed to represent a physiological model of the mechanism by which abnormal states of emotional tension are alleviated through various forms of 'relaxation therapy' " (p. 468).

Now that we had a rationale for muscle relaxation, we turned our efforts toward the desensitization phase.

DESENSITIZATION WITH ELECTROMYOGRAPHIC FEEDBACK

We first monitored EMG levels of patients undergoing systematic desensitization. In the typical behavior therapy situation, the patient is given brief training in a modified form of Jacobson's progressive relaxation. He or she is then expected to produce this relaxed condition in the face of scenes from the anxiety hierarchy. The demand characteristics of the average therapy setting, however, encourage the patient to report that he or she is relaxed after a reasonable period of time, whether this is actually true or not. Moreover, we found that patients will almost always show a rise in tension just before they are presented with the first hierarchy scenes. Often, too, once aroused by a particular hierarchy visualization, they have difficulty returning to relaxed levels again. Without objective monitoring of their physiology, the arousal level of such patients may be an unknown quantity.

The EMG biofeedback served as a guide to fast, successful relaxation, and as an accurate monitor of tension level during the desensitization. A patient could use it after each visualization to return to a relaxed baseline condition. The therapist, watching the biofeedback display, would know when to signal the patient to start the next visualization.

PERVASIVE ANXIETY TECHNIQUE

With cases of generalized or pervasive anxiety, it is often difficult for a patient to discover which stimuli actually trigger the anxiety. We have found the frontal (or forehead) EMG can be a sensitive indicator of subtle increases in anxiety in generally relaxed patients. A patient who has initial training in relaxation is simply told to let his or her thoughts wander while receiving feedback. If the tone suddenly rises in pitch, the patient knows that the thought coincident with, or just preceding, the rise in tone is arousing in nature. He or she next attempts to put the thought out of mind and relax, lowering the feedback tone. After this, the patient reintroduces the thought and tries to keep the tone low while doing so. This visualize–relax sequence is repeated until the patient can think of the thought without a rise in tension. At this point he or she allows the thoughts to wander again, repeating the sequence with the next arousing thought.

RECOVERY TRAINING

We also developed a procedure to ensure better transfer of the desensitization to real-life situations. It had been noticed that even though patients could complete a hierarchy successfully, they might still be unsure of their ability to handle a sudden buildup of anxiety in an unusual circumstance. If patients could learn to recover from small anxiety increases in the clinic, perhaps they could transfer the skill more confidently.

The procedure involves the generation of easily tolerated anxiety stimulations through exaggerated visualization of the last hierarchy scene. The scene is imaged until the patient reports feeling anxious. At this point the biofeedback is introduced, and the patient uses it to guide himself or herself back to a relaxed state. This sequence is repeated until the patient can recover in roughly 15 to 20 seconds. At this point, the patient usually feels more confident about controlling anxiety if it should occur in a real-life situation.

THEORETICAL UNDERPINNINGS

A notable characteristic of those disorders variously called "psychosomatic," "functional," or "stress-related" is not only that there is some aberrant physiological response, but that the condition has developed gradually over the years. We are rarely born with such afflictions—consider, for example, ulcers or essential hypertension. In view of this and similar evidence, we assume that there is an important learning component in stress-related and psychosomatic disturbances. Not only is there a gradual evolution of such disorders, but they appear to be closely related to the struggles and coping endeavors of everyday life. If we assume that learning plays a part in these disorders, then it becomes reasonable to employ learning techniques to change the maladaptive learning that has occurred.

The matter of exactly which kind of learning is involved is still unsettled. One point of view involves a straightforward instrumental learning model. For example, little Johnny reports, "My stomach hurts." Not only is there much fuss made over him, but he avoids the arithmetic exam as well! However, in our situation, the operant model does not readily account for the common observation that, when the individual reacts to threat or challenge, multiple integrated physiological reactions are brought into play. Not just one system is active; many are active at the same time. The conception we utilize for our stress management patients postulates a cortical triggering of the defense-alarm reaction. This involves not only physiological and behavioral components, but cognitive ones as well.

Our approach, like that of many engaged in stress management, involves a sequence of interventions, and is based on a conceptual framework that divides the individual's response to stress into two alternating parts: a phase of active coping efforts, and a rest phase (Stoyva & Anderson, 1982). Patients with stress-related symptoms show many signs of being excessively in the active coping phase. There is evidence of high sympathetic activity and high arousal in one or more systems, as in the anxious patient; there are complaints of tension and of inability to "unwind" or relax when it is appropriate to do so. There are complaints of disturbed sleep. The patient may be irritable and short-tempered. Type A behavior is often prominent, and catecholamine levels are likely to be elevated (Frankenhaeuser, 1978).

In our view, the individual's endeavors at adaptation may be regarded as consisting of an alternation between active coping efforts and a rest phase. This alternation is reflected at many levels of psychological and physiological organization. In the striate muscle system, there is an alternation between muscular contraction (involved in active coping efforts) and muscular relaxation, an alternation integral to the operation of this system. In the autonomic nervous system (ANS), there is a division into two great branches—the SNS, which acts to support high energy utilization and vigorous physical activity; and the PNS, which acts to promote digestion, sleep, and the rebuilding of energy sources.

Stress and anxiety share the common factor of a dominance of the sympathetic branch of the ANS. Does this have anything to do with stress-related disorders? A noted psychophysiologist has presented evidence for this view. Wenger and colleagues studied the resting autonomic patterns of nearly a thousand young, healthy Air Force cadets during World War II. Wenger then developed a scoring system by which each cadet was given an estimate of autonomic balance called the $\bar{A}$ score (Wenger & Cullen, 1972). This score was a composite of the scores obtained on each of seven physiological variables reflecting autonomic functioning. Low $\bar{A}$ scores meant apparent SNS dominance. The cadets' scores formed a normal distribution by which Wenger could compare groups with various disorders. He found, for example, that most psychosomatic patients produced low $\bar{A}$ scores, indicating an apparent SNS dominance in the resting state.

Approximately 15 years after the cadet study, Wenger sent out questionnaires to the former cadets. The questionnaire was designed to allow a determination of which disorders, including mental problems, had been developed by the formerly healthy cadets. He found that those individuals who had low $\bar{A}$ scores (apparent SNS dominance) reported the greatest incidence of stress-linked disorders. It appears that those individuals who show a resting autonomic pattern characterized by SNS dominance are more prone to stress disorders. Wenger's findings suggest that training in decreased SNS tone might act as a preventive program.

Even in the neuroendocrine system, there are probably periods of activation and nonactivation—as, for example, in the case of hormone responses to various stressors (Mason, 1972). Moreover, an interlocking series of experiments by Frankenhaeuser (1978) at the University of Stockholm indicate that the neuroendocrine system in humans is highly reactive to perceived stress. In particular, situations demanding a marked degree of active coping efforts generate large increases in catecholamine levels, with adrenalin output being especially responsive. Again, at the experiential level, there are marked differences between periods of active effort and times of tranquility.

Coping behaviors can be of two general types—those that are effective and therefore adaptive, and those that are ineffective and maladaptive. Recent studies, most of them with laboratory animals, have indicated that some types of stressors appear to weaken the immune defense system, while other types can actually strengthen this system (Sklar & Anisman, 1981). For example, one study (Visintainer, Volpicelli, & Seligman, 1982) compared the ability of three groups of rats to reject implanted cancer tumors. The rats experienced inescapable, escapable, or no electric shock. Only 27% of the rats receiving yoked inescapable shock rejected the tumors, whereas 63% of those receiving escapable shock rejected the tumors. The no-shock control group rejected the tumors at a 54% rate. The researchers concluded that these results imply that lack of control over stressors reduces tumor rejection and decreases survival.

The factor of perceived control in coping with stress appears to be of great importance in determining the effects of a given stressor on our immune defense. Stern, McCants, and Pettine (1982) asked volunteers to fill out a Schedule of Recent Life Events (SRLE) and an illness inventory. In addition to checking the recent life events that were applicable to them, the volunteers were asked to rate whether or not at the time of the events they felt that their occurrence was under their control or not. Moreover, they rated each event for perceived stressfulness. The results showed that uncontrollable events were rated as more stressful: The correlation between illness and controlled events was only .076 and not statistically significant, whereas the correlation was .590 between uncontrollable events and illness, and this was significant. Earlier, Stern and Berrenberg (1977) had demonstrated that frontal EMG biofeedback training *increased* perception of control. It may be possible that biofeedback training enhances immune defense by means of this increased perception of control.

To summarize our argument: Patients with psychosomatic or stress-linked disorders are likely to show signs of high physiological arousal in one or more systems—they are strongly or excessively engaged in the active coping mode. They also show evidence of being deficient in the ability to shift from the coping to the rest mode, and thus they feel a lack of control. It may also be hypothesized that this defect in the ability to shift to a rest condition is the principal reason why various relaxation procedures have so often proved useful in the alleviation of stress-related symptoms. Moreover, it should be noted that as stress management is generally practiced, various procedures for enhancing voluntary control over relaxation figure prominently in the first phase (Stoyva & Anderson, 1982).

We also find it useful to divide the coping phase and the resting phase further into three main levels of observation—a physiological one, a behavioral one, and an experiential one (as indexed by verbal report). Such a tripartite conceptualization helps the therapist to be attuned to the complex and multidimensional nature of the individual's stress response.

If we examine the various procedures commonly utilized in stress management, it can be noted that they reflect the multidimensional nature of the stress response. Some techniques, such as relaxation training and biofeedback, emphasize modification of physiological reactions. Others focus on cognitive changes—the self-statements approach and imagery techniques, for example. In others, such as in assertiveness training and social skills learning, behavior change is emphasized.

In actuality, the clinical work presently under way in stress management already reflects the three-systems conceptualization of the stress response. We think it is of value, however, to state the idea formally. It encourages the therapist to ask: In which system or systems has the patient's stress reaction gone awry? Similarly, during treatment, we would want interventions to be addressed to the task of changing the maladaptive coping response. For example, if misperceptions and distorted beliefs seem to be the main problems, cognitive interventions would be in order; if physiological arousal appears excessive, relaxation training or biofeedback would be initiated. Lastly, we would wish to know whether any change in the maladaptive response has in fact occurred, and whether it has persisted. In other words, the conception proposed here would be relevant not only to diagnosis and treatment, but to the assessment phase of stress management as well. We believe that a three-systems approach to stress management will act to produce a more sophisticated approach to the area, since it encourages us not to overlook important aspects of the stress response in favor of some single-track strategy.

It is also important to note that the various indications of stress may be discrepant from one another. For example, a Type A individual may indicate verbally that he or she feels "just fine" during stressful situations, yet at the same time may show a powerful physiological reaction. Another individual may say that he or she is relaxed, but may show very high EMG levels compared to normal. At the very least, such information suggests hypotheses to the therapist concerning the processes at work in such patients' stress reactions. It also makes for a more comprehensive treatment approach. Thus, in relaxation training, we remain slightly skeptical if there is just the verbal report of relaxation; we want the physiological indications of relaxation as well.

In the remainder of this chapter, we describe feedback procedures as they have evolved in our laboratory and clinic since we initiated work in 1966. Most of our stress management procedures fall within the framework of the coping–rest model. Generally, our emphasis is first on procedures addressed to the rest phase; the later ones aim at a reshaping of maladaptive coping efforts.

ASSESSMENT

Biofeedback training is used in two general ways in a clinical setting: first of all, as a method of teaching self-regulation of physiological skills in order to *prevent* stress disorders; and second, to teach the patient already suffering from a stress disorder to alleviate or eliminate the condition by adjusting relevant physiological response systems back within the normal range of functioning.

The efficacy of biofeedback is demonstrated best in those individuals who seem to be unable to relax even when they consciously attempt to do so. Such people are often relatively unaware of the level of tension (stress) that they habitually manifest. Without this awareness of inner tension, these individuals are often unsuccessful at attempts to relax with nonbiofeedback approaches. The inherent objectivity of the biofeedback allows these people to develop this awareness.

Our decision as to whether to use biofeedback training or some other therapeutic intervention is dependent upon several factors:

1. *Does the patient show a maladaptive physiological response pattern?* We can determine this by the use of the PSP (Psychophysiological Stress Profile), which involves physiological monitoring of the patient

while he or she (a) relaxes, (b) is subjected to serial 7s (a mathematics task), and (c) recovers by relaxing a second time (Budzynski *et al.,* 1980; Budzynski & Peffer, 1980).

2. *Are the symptoms longstanding, or did they result from some very recent, single incident?* Long-term disorders almost always are accompanied by chronically heightened arousal in the skeletal muscle or autonomic systems, or both. Chronic "bracing" of this sort is eliminated with biofeedback training. Even short-term symptoms, however, may be reflective of a long-term bracing coupled with a recent, severe stress situation.

3. *Does the symptom appear to be a conversion reaction?* If so, biofeedback may not be the therapy of choice.

4. *Does the patient exhibit moderate to severe depression?* We would use cognitive therapy rather than biofeedback in this case.

5. *What are the antecedents of the symptoms?* If we can identify these triggering stimuli, we can modify or perhaps eliminate them. Such stimuli can be cognitions, internal sensations or external events.

6. *What are the consequences of the symptoms?* Often patients are subtly rewarded for their symptoms. This can take form of interest, pity, being taken care of, or, in some cases, monetary settlements for on-the-job injuries or illnesses. Perhaps a more common factor is the reinforcement of the symptom because of its avoidance capability. Does the patient go home from work or perhaps not even go to work if the symptom appears? Is he or she able to avoid going to parties or having sex?

These associations must be delicately determined in order for a thorough program to be designed.

THE PSYCHOPHYSIOLOGICAL STRESS PROFILE

Many biofeedback or behavioral medicine clinics use a type of diagnostic procedure that involves physiological monitoring of relevant responses as the patient is first relaxed, then presented with a mild stressor (usually mental arithmetic), and finally recovers from the stress (Budzynski *et al.,* 1980).[2]

At Behavioral Medicine Associates, we have used the PSP for over 4 years to determine the profile of the patient (i.e., the order of responsiv-

---

[2]PSP criteria establishment and monitoring are accomplished with equipment from Bio-Feedback Systems, Inc., 2736 47th Street, Boulder, Colorado 80301. The bandpass of the EMG units is 100–1000 Hz.

ity of his or her systems to stress). Most patients will produce a profile of heightened EMG and cool hands. A smaller percentage, usually generalized anxiety cases, will show heightened EDR activity.

The PSP thus provides data from a number of response systems under the three conditions—relaxation, stress, and recovery. Maladaptiveness is indicated by responses that fall outside the normal range of responding. Thus, maladaptiveness can be seen in the magnitude of the response and in the slope of the recovery period.

It is interesting to observe that it is in the recovery phase where most anxious or stress-disordered patients show maladaptiveness. Apparently it is difficult for them to recover to a relaxed baseline after being stimulated.

Data gathered from individuals who present no history or evidence of mental or physical disorders have allowed us to develop a "normal" PSP with which to compare individual patients. These data are being collected in identical fashion at our clinic and at the Biofeedback Laboratory of Lilian Rosenbaum at Georgetown University Family Center.

All new patients are given the PSP after the initial interview. Their responses are compared to relaxed-level criteria for the EMG sites, as well as for thermal and EDR feedback. If the PSP result shows that they meet or are quite close to these criteria on all responses, then we would move to systematic desensitization or some other form of therapy.

Eventually, with a large enough n in each group, we will be able to compare the normal group with groups suffering from anxiety, tension headache, migraine, labile essential hypertension, depression, and other disorders. For example, a large group of tension headache patients ($n = 64$) produced a significantly higher level of frontal (forehead) EMG than the normal group ($n = 110$) in all three phases of the PSP (Budzynski, 1981).

DISORDERS TREATED IN BIOFEEDBACK SETTINGS

Certain disorders are treated routinely in most biofeedback clinics. At Behavioral Medicine Associates, we see patients for tension headache, common and classic migraine, insomnia, Raynaud's disease, irritable bowel, colitis, cardiac rehabilitation, temporomandibular joint (TMJ) problems, anxiety, tinnitus, certain forms of muscle rehabilitation, and a variety of pain syndromes. However, research in the applications of biofeedback to epilepsy, learning disorders, and diseases such as multiple sclerosis and muscular dystrophy is at a stage preliminary to routine clinical practice.

QUANTIFICATION OF SYMPTOMS

It has been our experience that a patient progresses faster when he or she is involved in keeping a daily record of symptoms. Consequently, if the symptoms can be coded in pain levels, frequency, and type, we instruct the patient in these quantification procedures (Budzynski *et al.*, 1980). When such data are graphed, the trends can be seen clearly. Both patient and therapist gain much from this extra effort.

LIMITATIONS AND CONTRAINDICATIONS

Biofeedback training is not much help as a crisis intervention, although dramatic results sometimes occur rapidly in certain types of pain problems, due to muscle spasm relief.

In cases of reported *constant* vascular headaches, especially where all medications have failed, we would suspect a psychogenic head pain. Psychotherapy would be more appropriate.

Hysterical and conversion reaction symptoms do not usually respond to biofeedback unless parallel psychotherapy is successfully resolving the unconscious conflict.

Therapists should use caution if giving biofeedback to insulin-dependent diabetics. The sudden relaxation may result in a greatly decreased need for insulin. The training should be done under careful medical supervision.

SECONDARY GAIN

Biofeedback training may need to be delayed in the therapy schedule if there is evidence of strong secondary gain. Since biofeedback is a self-regulation procedure, its success is dependent upon the patient's desire first to learn in the clinical setting, and then to apply the skill in daily life. If secondary gain is present, the motivation to learn and apply the self-regulation skills will be lacking, and progress will be minimal. Therefore, we attempt to determine the type and degree of secondary gain in the initial interview. Once the antecedents and consequences of the symptoms are defined, it is possible to institute change procedures.

For example, one of our patients avoided social situations by developing migraine headaches. An analysis of the patient's experience in social situations revealed that she felt inadequate with regard to small talk. She feared that she sounded ignorant when she attempted to speak. We found out that she read very little and did not watch the news on TV. The patient was encouraged to join an interesting book club, to subscribe to *Time* magazine, and to watch the news on TV each night. Soon she was able to converse with others at social gatherings. At this point, she made good progress with the biofeedback training and showed a dramatic reduction in migraine headaches soon afterward.

If secondary gain is not detected, it may manifest itself as a reluctance on the part of the patient to do homework exercises; as a continuing report of symptoms, even though the biofeedback monitoring indicates an ability to relax deeply; or as a seeming inability to acquire relaxation skills.

THE METHOD

INTRODUCING THE METHOD TO PATIENTS

A critical, but often neglected, aspect of biofeedback training is explaining the procedure to patients. If the patients lack a clear understanding of how and why biofeedback might be useful for their anxiety disorders, then not much benefit can be expected to accrue. For example, they are unlikely to see the point of engaging in much home practice. As Frank (1961) has pointed out in his discussion of psychological therapies, there must exist a shared assumptive framework between the patient and the therapist. There should be a mutual understanding as to what the problem is and why the proposed course of treatment is likely to be helpful.

Briefly, we explain to patients in a conversational way that their anxiety is a type of stress reaction—one that has become excessive and maladaptive. The aim of the program is to alter this maladaptive stress reaction. Fundamentally, the stress (and anxiety) response is an energization reaction in which a whole cluster of processes are set in motion. Muscles become tense, heart rate and blood pressure increase, and stored glycogen is released into the blood, as are many hormones. The physiological activities associated with rest and digestion diminish. This emergency reaction is one we all possess; it is a basic survival response.

What becomes a problem, however, is that some individuals react too strongly. Small or moderate amounts of anxiety help us to meet challenges and to get things done. But the brain often gets a person into trouble; it may, because of the person's life history, begin to interpret all sorts of events and situations as threats. In other words, the interpretive activity of the brain leads to frequent, and sometimes crippling, triggering of the stress (anxiety) reaction. Since the stress reaction is very powerful, and involves many systems, various symptoms may appear in addition to anxiety; elevated blood pressure, migraine and tension headache, duodenal ulcers, skin irritations, sleep disturbances, and irritable bowel syndrome. We believe that anxiety, like most psychophysiological disturbances, can be conceptualized as a disorder of adaptation.

At this point, a good justification for biofeedback relaxation training can be developed. The fundamental idea, by now supported by a wealth of evidence (Budzynski & Stoyva, 1973; Stoyva & Anderson, 1982; Stoyva & Budzynski, 1974), is that the effects of profound relaxation are generally opposite to those produced by psychological stress (and anxiety). The bodily systems supporting active effort slow down, and the individual begins to feel more calm. Patients first learn to relax with feedback, then without it. Acquiring this skill entails much independent, individual practice. Other interventions such as systematic desensitization are added later. This last procedure enables patients to think about, and later to confront, situations that previously caused them severe anxiety. As with relaxation training, the patients first practice in the clinic, then practice their new skills in the real-life anxiety situations troubling them.

The basic principles of biofeedback are explained as follows:

The main idea of biofeedback is to use instruments to tell you what is happening inside your own body—and to tell you immediately. For example, is my pulse rate going up or down? With biofeedback instruments, we can tell at once.

What's happening with your muscle tension? In order to find out, we place sensors over the muscle we are interested in. The sensors pick up the tiny electrical signals generated by the muscles. Through your headphones you'll learn that when you tense the muscle you hear a high-frequency sound. As soon as you relax, the tone frequency goes down. In other words, the tone tells you instantly if you're going in the right direction. Is the muscle tensing or relaxing? Let the tone be your guide. We've used this on a lot of people now, and it helps them to relax a lot faster.

Some patients know little or nothing about biofeedback. For them, a fairly full explanation is important. In particular, they must know how biofeedback training can be helpful for anxiety. Other individuals may have heard of biofeedback, but may have invested it with magical expectations. Here it is important to clarify what can be expected and to set realistic treatment goals.

As already indicated, we find it useful to convey the idea that a patient's anxiety is part of an excessive stress reaction. This helps place the symptom(s) in a wider and somewhat reassuring perspective—moderate amounts of anxiety are adaptive and normal; large amounts are not. Again, the term "stress," despite its scientific ambiguity, is one readily comprehended by the average individual. On the other hand, if a patient hears that the problem is "psychosomatic," he or she often misinterprets this to mean, "They think it's all in my head."

THE PHYSICAL ENVIRONMENT AND EQUIPMENT

Biofeedback devices range in size from the tiny ¼-inch liquid crystal temperature dots to large physiographs or computers connected to input–output peripherals. However, the majority of biofeedback therapists use stereo-size separate components. Typically they will have in their training rooms one or two EMG units, one thermal unit, and one EDR unit. A mixer unit is of value, since it greatly simplifies the coordination of several types of feedback. The mixer allows the presentation of one or more combinations of auditory feedback. "Pink noise" (pleasant "white noise") is available as a background sound. Tape-recorded instructions or the trainer's voice can be mixed in with feedback if so desired.

The physical environment of most biofeedback clinics ranges from the Victorian home of the San Francisco Biofeedback Clinic to the traditional medical office. Some therapists prefer to use a one-room system, in which a therapist will be present in the room with a patient and the equipment. Other therapists prefer a two-room arrangement, wherein the patient sits back in a recliner chair in a semidarkened, quiet room. The trainer and equipment are in the next room. There is constant voice communication between patient and trainer if desired.

We have used both of these systems over the years and have concluded that patients learn faster in the two-room system if they have some initial difficulty relaxing in the presence of another person. Since this is often the case with individuals suffering from stress-related disorders or anxiety, we prefer the two-room approach. At Behavioral Medicine Associates, we employ both a one-room and a two-room setting. The one-room setting is used for patients who have overcome their initial difficulty of relaxing in the presence of another.

In the case of group training in stress management, the smaller, inexpensive temperature sensors are most often used. Almost any setting can be employed, although it is useful to ensure that each participant can lie down or at least sit comfortably for the relaxation practice.

THERAPIST–PATIENT RELATIONSHIP

As with all psychological therapies, the biofeedback treatment of anxiety requires a relationship of trust and confidence. Such a relationship can be fostered by the following:

1. *As mentioned above, the therapist should explain how biofeedback and related procedures can be useful in the treatment of anxiety.* This explanation becomes strongly convincing as the patient begins to benefit from his or her relaxation training. One of us (Stoyva) employs autogenic exercises right from the outset for the home practice phase of relaxation training (Stoyva, in press). Surprisingly, patients often report some reduction in anxiety with even the very first autogenic exercise, "My right arm is heavy," which is practiced in brief episodes five to seven times daily. Budzynski, on the other hand, starts patients out with the first of the six-phase home training cassette tapes.

2. *The therapist should specify treatment goals.* Patients are reassured and given confidence in the therapist when they realize that reliable step-by-step procedures are available for the management and reduction of their anxiety. However, in the case of the disturbances that are more difficult to treat, such as generalized anxiety, agoraphobia, or multiple sources of anxiety, we emphasize that the program will involve a lot of time; that it may require the use of several different procedures; and that their anxiety will probably not vanish completely, but will be reduced and made more manageable. It is also worth noting that biofeedback per se will not help a great variety of medical problems, relationship problems, marital difficulties, character disorders, or psychoses. Such a disclaimer is especially important in the case of patients harboring magical expectations. Subsequent disappointments are minimized, and the ground is set for a long-term relationship of honesty and mutual respect.

3. *The therapist should cultivate a sense of mastery in the patient.* This factor is prominent not only in biofeedback and self-regulation therapies, but probably in all psychological therapies (Strupp, 1970). A feeling of mastery can be promoted by arranging a success experience early in the program; biofeedback lends itself well to such an endeavor. Gen-

erally, we commence biofeedback training with a muscle group that is easy
to relax, such as the forearm extensors. But, should relaxation of the right
arm prove difficult, we will shift the feedback site to the other arm. Relaxation can nearly always be accomplished at one or the other of these sites
(Budzynski *et al.,* 1980). Even a modest success, especially on a task
deemed relevant to the disorder, acts as a definite source of encouragement for the anxious patient. A sense of mastery, and a sense that one
can regain control of oneself and one's life, is set in motion.

4. *The therapist should be a sympathetic listener.* As in other therapies, the process of listening allows for reassurance of feelings and encouragement to continue with the program. Typically, an excellent time
to interact with the patient is immediately after the feedback portion of
the session, a task generally occupying 10 to 20 minutes. At this time, the
patient is likely to be more communicative, and may bring up matters not
previously discussed. We generally begin by asking which relaxation strategies were helpful and which were not (as indicated by the feedback tone).
Then we inquire as to how the home practice went this last week and
whether there were any difficulties. This question often leads to a discussion of current life stress: pressures on the job, difficulties with supervisors or subordinates, problems with children, financial difficulties, self-
doubts with regard to performance challenges, difficulties in making an
important life transition, and social and marital problems. Clearly, biofeedback and relaxation training can be only of limited help for this array of difficulties—though often they help individuals to feel better rested
and give them a sense of having more energy to devote to active coping
efforts (active problem solutions).

5. *The therapist should ask about home practice.* In each session, as
noted above, we inquire as to how the home practice of the relaxation
has been going. Training difficulties are explored and suggestions for coping with them may be offered (Stoyva, 1979). These inquiries let patients
know of our continuing concern with their problems and emphasize the
importance of changing behavior outside the clinic setting. Similarly, with
systematic desensitization, the patients are encouraged to face the feared
situations as the clinic phase of desensitization is successfully accomplished.

6. *Termination is generally accomplished by spacing the sessions
further apart.* This allows patients to realize they can function independently; yet there is still some contact with the therapist should difficulties
arise.

DESCRIPTION OF THE METHOD

Initial Training

Given that biofeedback is indicated by virtue of the intake evaluation and the PSP results, we proceed with technician-directed training. Each patient will have sensors attached for monitoring forearm extensor EMG, frontal EMG, finger temperature, and EDR. These sensors are all easily applied in less than 3 minutes. Patients are told how the sensors function to pick up the small biosignals of the various responses.

Preliminary training in lower abdominal breathing helps patients begin to relax. Since they have been using the first tape of the six-phase home training series for a week or so, the patient has already developed some awareness of muscle tension. This awareness will be refined in this first biofeedback session.

The technician leaves the room after this initial breathing practice. Outside now with the equipment, he or she establishes voice contact with the patient, who is reclining in a comfortable chair. The initial voice interchange assures that the trainer is outside and can hear the patient.

At the beginning and end of each biofeedback session, several data points are taken. These serve to inform the trainer as to the level of the responses without feedback. As training progresses, the levels will approximate those obtained during the feedback itself.

The patient is then presented with feedback, usually from the forearm extensor, since this muscle is ordinarily easy to control. As the patient practices increasing and decreasing the muscle tension, he or she is told that there are two modes of attending to this task (lowering arousal). One way is called "active striving" and is the way most people have been taught to learn. It involves conscious, active focusing on the task. This mode does not work toward the attainment of low muscle tension or decreased autonomic tone. The more successful mode has been labeled "passive volition." It involves a sort of "letting go." Strangely enough, the very act of not trying allows patients to succed at controlling these response systems in the relaxed direction.

After this get-acquainted period, the patient is asked to practice letting go and to listen to the biofeedback for guidance. This is a stage of strategy testing, with the biofeedback providing fast and reliable indications of whether a given strategy is working. It is during this session that patients first may realize the connection between thought and physiological responding. They are often amazed that a seemingly benign thought could effect a change in one or more of the monitored response systems.

When the patient becomes successful at lowering the tension in the arm, the gain or sensitivity of the feedback loop is increased. This means the patient will now be required to manifest an even lower level of EMG in order to lower the tone. These changes of gain are always reported to the patient before the change is made.

The patient will progress from forearm extensor EMG to frontal EMG feedback when he or she can demonstrate a low level of EMG even without feedback. The sequencing of biofeedback training is detailed elsewhere (Budzynski *et al.*, 1980).

Multiple-Feedback Application

When the patient reaches criterion on forearm extensor EMG (2.5 vV peak to peak), we shift to frontal EMG biofeedback. Often a change of attention from a first, relaxed response to a second, not yet relaxed response causes the first response to move in the direction of higher arousal. For this reason, a visual form of feedback is fed back from the first response system, simultaneous to the second-system biofeedback, which is auditory. The two distinct biofeedback forms make it easier for the patient to maintain the first system in a relaxed state as passive volition is "focused" on the second system.

When mastery of the second system, frontal EMG, is demonstrated by meeting the criterion of 2.5 μV peak to peak while simultaneously holding the forearm EMG at a low level, the patient can progress to the third system, which is hand temperature. In the relaxed condition, with relatively low SNS tone, the skin of the hands and feet will show temperatures greater than 90°F. This is our criterion for relaxation in the peripheral skin temperature system. Thermal feedback can be employed to help the patient reach this criterion. Sequencing to this third system often allows us to drop off the feedback from the first system (the forearm EMG). Although patients can learn to control three systems simultaneously, we prefer to use one or two at any given time during relaxation training. Later, during the systematic desensitization phase, the patient will often be monitoring three systems at once.

Criteria are more difficult to establish with EDR, since too low a level can indicate a flatness of affect or inhibition of emotion. From our normal group we have determined that a level between .5 and 2.5 μmhos is ideal. A high EDR (greater than 10 μmhos) is often seen in individuals with generalized anxiety.

Home Practice

The six-phase home stress management program is synchronized to the biofeedback training. Initial training in muscle tensing and relaxing, in order to develop an awareness of muscle tonus, is followed by autogenic-like training in control of low muscle tonus and peripheral warmth. A third phase of the relaxation training specializes in the facial musculature and establishes a cognitive conditioned stimulus for relaxation production. The final phase is a generalized systematic desensitization.

An interesting note: Our follow-up questionnaires reveal that, should symptoms return after completing biofeedback training, patients fall back on daily use of the tapes to banish the symptoms.

Systematic Desensitization

If the patient has completed relaxation training and has met our criteria for mastery of these responses, and yet has difficulty in real-life situations, we use the systematic desensitization procedure described earlier. Over the years, since our work with EMG feedback, we have added thermal and EDR feedback to this procedure. As we present scenes from the fear or stress hierarchy, we watch all indicators for signs of disruption of the relaxed state. The scene is terminated if one or more of the responses changes significantly in the direction of heightened arousal. Between visualizations, the triple feedback is used by the patient to return to baseline levels.

Recovery training, as noted earlier, is employed after the systematic desensitization to ensure that the patient is able to recover after generation of an anxiety pattern.

The pervasive anxiety technique (PAT) is used with the multiple feedback to identify anxiety sources or stressors not known to patients with generalized symptoms.

Alternative Procedures

Biofeedback is of little use if the factor of secondary gain looms large. If this can be so identified, steps can be taken to offset its value. Behavior and cognitive modification can be used to instill adaptive behaviors, so that the patient need not employ symptoms as a way of receiving reinforcement or avoiding situations. For example, a young black woman was promoted to a position as a purchasing agent. Her headaches increased dramatically after the promotion. A behavioral analysis revealed that she was stressed by a flood of salespeople who, taking advantage of her inexperience, bombarded her with sales pitches all through the day. We taught her to bring order to this chaos by demanding that all salespeople have scheduled appointments. Her headaches declined to the low baseline level.

Behavioral methods are used not only to enhance assertiveness, but to build more adaptive coping behaviors in all areas of life.

Biofeedback in Stress Management Training for Groups

Up to this point, we have described procedures that are used with one patient at a time. More recent applications, however, include the use of simplified forms of biofeedback in group settings. This type of training is made possible through the use of inexpensive biofeedback devices, such as various forms of liquid crystal temperature sensors or small GSR units.

Larger and more expensive pieces of biofeedback equipment can be used in a group setting, with a few clients role-modeling relaxing or hand-warming behavior with the aid of the equipment. These larger units can also be employed for brief (3- to 5-minute) monitoring and feedback from each participant. This last procedure gives each participant information about EMG, EDR, and skin temperature levels. At the end of the group training, these same units can be used for "after" measures.

The smaller, inexpensive liquid crystal sensors allow each participant to monitor hand temperature during training and even outside the training setting. The temperature-sensing rings are attractive and provide an accurate measure of finger temperatures over a range of 67–97°F.[3]

At Behavioral Medicine Associates, we combine didactic lecture–slide presentations with relaxation training experience. Cognitive coping skills are sharpened as well. Systematic desensitization is taught so

---

[3]Temperature-sensing rings are available from Hice Enterprises, Ltd., 6460 E. Yale CD161, Denver, Colorado 80222.

that participants can use this procedure after developing their relaxation ability. The six-phase cassette program is the basic training of the course.

RESISTANCE, COMPLIANCE, AND MAINTENANCE OF BEHAVIOR CHANGE

Most patients follow instructions for daily homework and charting of symptoms. If they have difficulty in so doing, we suspect some resistance to a program of getting well. Perhaps the patient's family is unconsciously attempting to return him or her to the "sick" role in order to preserve the dynamic balance created around such a role. If so, family therapy is employed.

More often, resistance is the result of an early script that could be expressed by the old adage, "An idle mind is the devil's workshop." Many patients with Type A behavior patterns fall into this category. A careful probing of the thoughts and feelings generated during homework relaxation practice usually reveals this resistance to the patient. Once he or she is aware of the script, the patient can counter it each time with a thought such as "This relaxation allows my body to repair itself."

Compliance is enhanced by a careful blend of positive expectation and regular attention to the charting and home relaxation efforts. Patients often need to be reminded that acquisition of biofeedback skills requires daily practice, just as golf or tennis does.

Maintenance of behavior change appears to be enhanced primarily by the development of effective "transfer skills." Most of these are brief relaxation or cognitive techniques. For example, in the fifth phase of the home training program, the silent phrase "I am calm" is made a conditioned stimulus for the relaxation response. After being paired with the deep relaxation developed by this training, simply thinking the phase can produce relaxation. Frequent practice in daily situations is necessary in order to establish this habit.

The patient must learn to become aware of maladaptive thoughts, behavior, and physiology so that coping skills can be applied. We have found it useful to have patients place small pieces of brightly colored tape on their watches, steering wheels, telephones, and wherever else their gaze tends to fall (Budzynski, 1973). Each time a patient notices the tape, he or she checks for maladaptiveness in the three systems. If it is present, the patient uses an appropriate coping technique.

Finally, patients are encouraged to come back for booster sessions at 3-, 6-, and 12-month intervals.

CASE EXAMPLES

TENSION HEADACHES

Of all the stress disorders treated with biofeedback, tension headache typically requires the fewest number of sessions, ranging from 5 to 15.

John C was a 36-year-old geologist who reported daily tension headaches. The intake information revealed that he began having them after receiving a promotion 3 years before to a position of greater responsibility. Although he enjoyed the job, John realized that the headaches were worsening. He preferred not to take medication for the pain.

In the short space of 6 weeks, and with only five frontal EMG biofeedback sessions, John managed to rid himself of the headaches. A good scientist, he practiced outside the clinic twice daily and carefully charted the headache pain. John quickly became aware of rising muscle tension and was able to use the "I am calm" thought to relax himself.

TEMPOROMANDIBULAR-JOINT
HEAD PAIN

Molly J, a 54-year-old typist, came to us with severe lancinating headaches. They appeared to be related to stress at work. The headaches typically occurred on days when a great deal of typing was required. When we measured the masseter EMG as she typed, we made an interesting discovery. At typing speeds up to 45 words per minute, there was no particular increase in EMG; however, above this speed, the EMG began to build. Apparently, she had developed the habit of clenching her teeth as she typed at high speeds.

While receiving EMG feedback from the masseter, she learned to type at high speeds while keeping her jaw relaxed. A total of four biofeedback sessions was required for total elimination of the headaches.

GENERALIZED ANXIETY

Because of the pervasiveness of this disorder, it is difficult to treat. Charles M was a 37-year-old businessman who displayed an exaggerated startle response as a young boy. He remembered being anxious in high school, especially when he had to give a speech in front of a class. During college years, the anxiety manifested itself primarily at social events. However, it began to worsen when he began his first job after graduation. At work, he was expected to make presentations at the main plant and at remote locations as well. Gradually the anxiety generalized from these situations to all social events, even with small groups of close friends. Just before seeking help, he became unable to travel even for short distances.

Charles was put through a long (26-session) period of biofeedback training. He slowly began to control his physiology, especially the very high EDR (roughly 20 μmhos). Cognitive therapy helped him to be aware of maladaptive thoughts and enabled him to substitute more realistic thought processes. The PAT was used to identify specific anxiety sources, and he subsequently received eight sessions of systematic desensitization.

Although he is not totally free of travel anxiety, Charles now fulfills travel obligations at work. His social anxiety is alleviated to the point where he and his wife can host small parties of fellow employees and supervisors. To keep down arousal, Charles regularly practices twice each day with the cassette tape program.

LABILE ESSENTIAL HYPERTENSION

This disorder, so common in our society, is seen often in biofeedback clinics. Many of our patients are commercial airline pilots, who must demonstrate blood pressures in the normal range every 6 months during their flight physicals. In most instances, these individuals are in good physical condition, although they manifest high blood pressure when this is measured. Training is straightforward in most instances.

Bill K was a 37-year-old pilot for one of the major airlines. His pressure measured approximately 150/90 when initial readings were taken. He would have to sit quietly for some time before the pressure would edge below 140/90. Over the years, his pressure had been slowly climbing. He decided that he had to do something or he would be out of a job. Bill re-

ceived 12 sessions of biofeedback and faithfully followed the home practice program. At the completion of the relaxation training, he underwent
systematic desensitization for the fear of having his blood pressure measured by a professional. On his next physical, the reading was 130/82.

TENSION AND ANXIETY

Bob W, a 26-year-old black office worker, reported feelings of severe
tension and anxiety and an inability to "wind down." Additional symptoms were occasional migraine headaches and fragmented sleep, as well
as somewhat elevated blood pressure. In his case, physiological monitoring showed that his relaxation skills were quite good, even at the beginning. The important thing was to encourage him to use them, in addition
to teaching him to identify the sensations he felt when he relaxed well.
With Bob, physiological monitoring was valuable in guiding the course
of treatment, in tailoring the program to his individual needs, and in convincing him that the training regime was pertinent to his symptom picture. As Bob began to integrate the transfer skills into his daily life, his
blood pressure decreased to normal levels, the migraine headaches were
eliminated, and his sleep greatly improved.

AGORAPHOBIA

David G, a 41-year-old artist, suffered from agoraphobia and various
other types of anxiety. During feedback training, we noted that his hand
temperature was low (about 75°F). David was trained in a combination
of biofeedback and autogenic training, which aided greatly in reducing
his anxiety. For his posttreatment home practice, he was given a temperature ring accurate to half a degree Farenheit. This simple feedback device proved to be useful in guiding and maintaining his subsequent home
practice efforts. David was able to generalize his skill at hand warming into
all areas of his life. He reported an increased feeling of control as the ring
provided daily proof of his ability.

CONCLUSION

As can be seen from these examples, biofeedback helps to pinpoint
the problem and in tailoring interventions focused on altering the aberrant response. It should also be emphasized that biofeedback provides a

number of strategies for application in case of training difficulties. More-over, in the case of nonbiofeedback approaches to relaxation, the fact that a patient is having problems in relaxation may well go unrecognized.

COMMENTS AND REFLECTIONS

We note at the beginning of this chapter that the issue of controllability is beginning to play an important role in the management of stress and the alleviation of stress disorders. Evidence from the new research area known as "psychoimmunology" has underscored the danger of a belief that one is out of control, that life pushes one from pillar to post. Both animal and human studies indicate that most chronic stress, especially if it is perceived to be uncontrollable, appears to weaken the immune de-fenses (Budzynski & Sparks, in press; Crofton, Budzynski, & Ross, in press).

Biofeedback, on the other hand, is marvelously suited to the shap-ing of the belief that indeed one can control aspects of one's life. In the very first session, the biofeedback device provides objective evidence that the individual is controlling factors that had up to that point appeared to be uncontrollable. For reasons as yet unknown, this small evidence of ability to exercise control or self-control is generalized to many other areas of one's life.

Biofeedback does more than simply instill a sense of control. Its pre-cise guiding function allows people to alter stress patterns in the direc-tion of the resting or recuperative mode. In this sense, biofeedback may help to maintain the immune defenses by reducing the hormonal products of stress that can produce immunosuppression.

Future research may demonstrate a more direct link between biofeed-back training and immune competence. For now, we must be satisfied with the significant contribution of biofeedback in the areas of anxiety and stress disorders.

REFERENCES

Budzynski, T. Biofeedback procedures in the clinic. Seminars in Psychiatry, 1973, 5, 537–547.
Budzynski, T. H. Biofeedback strategies in headache treatment. In J. V. Basmajian (Ed.), Bio-feedback: A handbook for clinicians. Baltimore: Williams & Wilkins, 1979.
Budzynski, T. PSP data: Tension headache vs. normal. Unpublished data, 1981.
Budzynski, T., & Peffer, K. Biofeedback training. In I. L. Kutash & L. B. Schlesinger (Eds.),

Handbook on stress and anxiety. San Francisco: Jossey-Bass, 1980.

Budzynski, T. H., & Sparks, T. F. Toward a behavioral oncology: Stress response, brain lateralization and the psychophysiology of cancer. In S. Gross & S. Garb (Eds.), *Humanism and science in cancer research and treatment.* Boulder, Colo.: Westview Press, in press.

Budzynski, T., & Stoyva, J. Biofeedback techniques in behavior therapy. In N. Birbaumer (Ed.), *Neuropsychologie der Angst (Reihe Fortschritte der Klinishen Psychologie,* Bd. 3). München: Urban & Schwarzenberg, 1973.

Budzynski, T., & Stoyva, J. EMG-Biofeedback bei unspezifischen und spezifishen Angstzustanden. In H. Legewie & L. Nussett (Eds.), *Biofeedback-Therapie: Lernmethod in der Psychosomatic, Neurologie und Rehabilitation (Fortschritte der Klinischen Psychogie,* Vol. 6). München: Urban & Schwarzenberg, 1975.

Budzynski, T. H., Stoyva, J. M., & Adler, C. S. Feedback-induced muscle relaxation: Application to tension headache. *Behavior Therapy and Experimental Psychiatry,* 1970, *1,* 205–211.

Budzynski, T. H., Stoyva, J. M., Adler, C. S., & Mullaney, D. J. EMG biofeedback and tension headache: A controlled outcome study. *Psychosomatic Medicine,* 1973, *35,* 484–496.

Budzynski, T. H., Stoyva, J. M., & Peffer, K. E. Biofeedback techniques in psychosomatic disorders. In A. Goldstein & E. Foa (Eds.), *Handbook for behavioral interventions: A clinical guide.* New York: Wiley, 1980.

Canter, A., Kondo, C. Y., & Knott, J. R. A comparison of EMG feedback and progressive muscle relaxation training in anxiety neurosis. *British Journal of Psychiatry,* 1975, *127,* 470–477.

Crofton, K., Budzynski, T., & Ross, R. *The healthy Type A.* New York: Summit Books, in press.

Frank, J. D. *Persuasion and healing.* Baltimore: Johns Hopkins University Press, 1961.

Frankenhaeuser, M. Psychoneuroendocrine approaches to the study of emotion as related to stress and coping. In H. E. Howe & R. A. Deihstbier (Eds.), *Nebraska Symposium on Motivation.* Lincoln: University of Nebraska Press, 1978.

Gellhorn, E. Motion and emotion. *Psychological Review,* 1964, *71,* 457–472.

Germana, J. Central efferent processes and autonomic–behavioral integration. *Psychophysiology,* 1969, *6,* 78–90.

Goldstein, I. B. Electromyography: A measure of skeletal muscle response. In N. S. Greenfield & R. A. Sternbach (Eds.), *Handbook of psychophysiology.* New York: Holt, Rinehart & Winston, 1972.

Hess, W. R. *Diencephalon: Autonomic and extrapyramidal functions.* New York: Grune & Stratton, 1954.

Hiebert, B. A comparison of EMG feedback and alternative anxiety treatment programs. *Biofeedback and Self-Regulation,* 1981, *6,* 501–506.

Jacobson, E. *Progressive relaxation* (2nd ed.). Chicago: University of Chicago Press, 1938.

Kamiya, J. Operant control of the EEG alpha rhythm and some of its reported effects on consciousness. In C. T. Tart (Ed.), *Altered states of consciousness.* New York: Wiley, 1969.

Lavallée, Y. J., Lamontagne, Y., Pinard, G., Annable, L., & Tétreault, L. Effects of EMG feedback, diazepam and their combination on chronic anxiety. *Journal of Psychosomatic Research,* 1977, *21,* 65–71.

Leaf, W. B., & Gaarder, K. R. A simplified electromyographic feedback apparatus for relaxation training. *Journal of Behavior Therapy and Experimental Psychiatry,* 1971, *2,* 39–43.

Luthe, W. (Ed.). *Autogenic therapy* (6 vols.). New York: Grune & Stratton, 1969.

Malmo, R. B. *On emotions, needs, and our archaic brain.* New York: Holt, Rinehart & Winston, 1975.

Martin, I., & Grosz, H. J. Hypnotically induced emotions. *Archives of General Psychiatry,* 1964, *11,* 203–213.

Mason, J. W. Organization of psychoendocrine mechanisms. In N. S. Greenfield & R. A. Sternbach (Eds.), *Handbook of psychophysiology.* New York: Holt, Rinehart & Winston, 1972.

Obrist, P. A., Webb, R. A., Sutterer, J. R., & Howard, J. L. The cardiac–somatic relationship: Some reformulations. *Psychophysiology,* 1970, *6,* 569–587.

Raskin, M., Johnson, G., & Rondestvedt, J. W. Chronic anxiety treated by feedback-induced muscle relaxation. *Archives of General Psychiatry,* 1973, *28,* 263–267.

Reinking, R. H., & Kohl, M. L. Effects of various forms of relaxation training on physiological and self-report measures of relaxation. *Journal of Consulting and Clinical Psychology,* 1975, *43,* 595–600.

Sainsbury, P., & Gibson, J. F. Symptoms of anxiety and tension and the accompanying physiological changes in the muscular system. *Journal of Neurological and Neurosurgical Psychiatry,* 1954, *17,* 216.

Sklar, L., & Anisman, H. Stress and cancer. *Psychological Bulletin,* 1981, *89,* 369–407.

Stern, G. S., & Berrenberg, J. L. Biofeedback training in frontalis muscle relaxation and enhanced belief in personal control. *Biofeedback and Self-Regulation,* 1977, *2,* 173–182.

Stern, G. S., McCants, T. R., & Pettine, P. W. Stress and illness: Controllable and uncontrollable life events' relative contributions. *Personality and Social Psychological Bulletin,* 1982, *8,* 140–145.

Stoyva, J. M. Guidelines in the training of general relaxation. In J. V. Basmajian (Ed.), *Biofeedback: A handbook for clinicians.* Baltimore: Williams & Wilkins, 1979.

Stoyva, J. Guidelines for cultivating general relaxation: Biofeedback and autogenic training combined. In J. V. Basmajian (Ed.), *Biofeedback: Principles and practice for clinicians.* Baltimore: Williams & Wilkins, 1983.

Stoyva, J., & Anderson, C. A coping/rest model of relaxation and stress management. In L. Goldberger & S. Breznitz (Eds.), *Handbook of stress: Theoretical and clinical aspects.* New York: Free Press–Macmillan, 1982.

Stoyva, J. M., & Budzynski, T. H. Cultivated low arousal—an antistress response? In L. V. DiCara (Ed.), *Recent advances in limbic and autonomic nervous systems research.* New York: Plenum, 1974.

Strupp, H. Specific versus nonspecific factors in psychology and the problem of control. *Archives of General Psychiatry,* 1970, *23,* 393–401.

Townsend, R. E., House, J. F., & Addario, D. A comparison of biofeedback-mediated relaxation and group therapy in the treatment of chronic anxiety. *American Journal of Psychiatry,* 1975, *132,* 598–601.

Visintainer, M. S., Volpicelli, J. R., & Seligman, M. E. P. Tumor rejection in rats after inescapable or escapable shock. *Science,* 1982, *216,* 437–439.

Wenger, M. A., & Cullen, T. D. Studies of autonomic balance in children and adults. In N. S. Greenfield & R. A. Sternbach (Eds.), *Handbook of psychophysiology,* New York: Holt, Rinehart & Winston, 1972.

Wolpe, J. *Psychotherapy by reciprocal inhibition.* Stanford, Calif.: Stanford University Press, 1958.

8 AUTOGENIC BIOFEEDBACK IN PSYCHOPHYSIOLOGICAL THERAPY AND STRESS MANAGEMENT

PATRICIA A. NORRIS AND STEVEN L. FAHRION

HISTORY OF THE METHOD

Over the past two decades, evidence has accumulated that conscious, voluntary regulation of the autonomic nervous system is possible, and that in many instances such self-regulation has positive health benefits.

"Autogenic training," a system of psychosomatic self-regulation that was developed in Germany at about the turn of the century, permits the gradual acquisition of autonomic control (Schultz & Luthe, 1969). This control is not active; rather, it develops out of a "passive concentration" through which the trainee intends to move toward certain effects (e.g., relaxation) and yet remains detached as to his or her actual progress. The point of focus of his or her concentration is on visual, auditory, and somatic imagery that is employed to induce specific physiological changes, such as hand warmth or muscle relaxation.

"Biofeedback training" is a rubric applied to a collection of techniques that may be useful in accelerating psychosomatic self-regulation. Physiological activity is monitored, and visual and auditory instruments are used to show the patient what is happening in bodily functions that are normally unavailable to awareness. Control of a wide variety of physiological parameters has been demonstrated, and seems limited only by the opportunity to monitor the level of function in a physiological system consciously; by the possibility of providing continuous feedback on that level; and by the expectation of success on the part of the patient (Leeb, Fahrion, & French, 1976).

"Autogenic biofeedback training" (Green, Green, Walters, Sargent, & Meyer, 1975) represents an integration of these two self-regulatory techniques that provides a methodology combining the best features of

220

AUTOGENIC BIOFEEDBACK 221

each and has wide-ranging applications in medicine, psychology, and education.

Autogenic biofeedback training may be somewhat unusual in the sense that the goal, conscious acquisition of physiological self-regulation, was conceived of prior to the development of the specific methodology required to aid acquisition of self-regulatory skills. Elmer Green, a physicist, and his wife, Alyce—cofounders and developers of autogenic biofeedback treatment methods—decided to pursue their interest in the development of human awareness and volition in order to develop ways of teaching people to become conscious of, and to learn voluntary control of, normally unconscious processes, both physiological and psychological. Elmer Green developed a plan, in the Research Department of the Menninger Foundation, to study the control of unconscious processes through their physiologic correlates in the autonomic nervous system. Gardner Murphy, Director of Research at the Menninger Foundation, was open to and interested in this line of inquiry.

With Murphy's encouragement, a proposal was prepared, and a government grant to fund this biofeedback research was obtained from the National Institute of Mental Health in 1967. The study, Voluntary Control of Internal States (Green, Ferguson, Green, & Walters, 1970; Green, Green, & Walters, 1970b), concerned the training of college students, with the aid of feedback, simultaneously (1) to reduce the level of muscle firing in the forearm as an indication of striate relaxation (Green, Walters, Green, & Murphy, 1969); (2) to increase hand temperature as an indication of autonomic relaxation (Luthe, 1965); and (3) to increase the density of alpha rhythm in the EEG record as an indication of central nervous system relaxation (Kamiya, 1968). From that project, the first biofeedback research to be funded by the federal government, the Voluntary Controls Program of the Menninger Foundation, was generated. The word "biofeedback" was actually not invented until the founding meeting of the Biofeedback Research Society 2 years later.

In 1966, prior to the research mentioned above, Elmer Green had observed in one subject a strong relationship between relief from a migraine headache and vasodilation in the hands (correlated with a temperature increase in the hands of 10°F in 2 minutes). This observation was made during the course of investigations by the Greens. To elucidate how these concepts and mechanisms interrelate, the Greens initially studied the physiological correlates of autogenic training (changes in vasodilation, muscle activity, heart rate, brain waves, etc.) in the Psychophysiology Laboratory of the Menninger Foundation. The discovery led directly to the first integration of autogenic training and simultaneous feedback of the consequent psychophysiological changes.

Upon hearing of the migraine incident, the wife of one of the Greens' colleagues in the research department, who suffered from migraine headaches, asked if she could be "trained" out of migraine. After cautioning that no positive results could be promised, Elmer Green explained the limbic–hypothalamic–pituitary rationale described below, gave her an autogenic biofeedback temperature training session, and loaned her one of the just-constructed temperature trainers. As so often happens in the development of a new treatment modality, this first patient was a great success. Although she had previously experienced an incapacitating headache almost every week, after a month of hand temperature training she had the migraine problem under control, and she eliminated entirely her dependence on headache medication. She remained headache-free during 10 years of follow-up.

Subsequently, Joseph Sargent, Chief of Internal Medicine at the Menninger Foundation, heard of the headache control trials and asked for a demonstration. This led to Sargent's initial research in relief of migraine with biofeedback training (Sargent, Green, & Walters, 1972).

At the same time that the Greens' research in self-regulation of the autonomic nervous system was being designed, two other investigators, unknown to each other, were also doing work in the area: John Basmajian, at Emory University in Atlanta, was investigating the use of feedback to teach college students to gain voluntary control over the firing of single motor units, and Joe Kamiya, at the University of Chicago, was teaching college students to gain voluntary control of states of consciousness through brain-wave training for increase of alpha production. Self-regulation was an idea whose time had come.

A number of research reports and conceptual papers describing autogenic biofeedback training began to emerge on a variety of topics, including deep relaxation (Green *et al.*, 1969), voluntary control of internal psychological and physiological states (Green, Ferguson, Green, & Walters, 1970; Green, Green, & Walters, 1970b), self-regulation and healing (Green, Green, & Walters, 1971a), creativity (Green, Green, & Walters, 1971b), migraine headaches (Sargent *et al.*, 1972), and anxiety–tension reduction (Green, Green, & Walters, 1973). By the middle 1970s, other investigators began to use autogenic techniques combined with biofeedback, both clinically and experimentally, but few reports appeared until after 1975.

A recent (June 1982) survey of the literature found autogenic training papers outnumbering autogenic biofeedback papers by 15 to 1. A total of 33 papers either describe autogenic biofeedback training as part of a clinical treatment package ($n = 27$), or compare autogenic training with biofeedback as separate training modalities ($n = 6$). These papers vary markedly in sophistication of design and conceptualization, in the use of experienced versus untrained therapists, in whether an adequate number of training sessions were used to obtain a clinical result, in the populations from which subjects were drawn, and in the depth of physiological relaxation achieved. These differences make comparison of results problematic at best. Clinical cases demonstrating efficacy of autogenic biofeedback training include treatment of writer's cramp (Akagi, Yoshimura, & Ikemi, 1977), pain due to causalgia (Blanchard, 1979), migraine headache (Boller & Flom, 1979; Fahrion, 1977; Sargent *et al.*, 1972), dysmenorrhea (Dietvorst & Osborne, 1978), angina pain (Hartman, 1979), collagen vascular disease (Keefe, Surwit, & Pilon, 1981), and blood pressure (Green, Green, & Norris, 1979; McGrady, Yonker, Tan, Fine, & Woerner, 1981; Sedlacek, 1979).

In our experience, these published reports represent only a small indication of the extent of clinical work in which autogenic biofeedback training is in use. Clinical seminars in the use of these techniques began at the Menninger Foundation in 1971, and several thousand professionals have attended them to date. Subsequently, many of these individuals have incorporated autogenic biofeedback into their clinical practice.

Autogenic biofeedback training has also had an impact on other than clinical areas. It has been used in educational settings with emotionally handicapped children (Walton, 1979), with normal children (Engelhardt, 1976), with incarcerated prisoners (Norris, 1976), in personal growth (Leeb *et al.*, 1976), and in other health, physical exercise, and sports applications.

THEORETICAL UNDERPINNINGS

All the neuromechanisms involved in voluntary self-regulation of the autonomic nervous system have not yet been delineated, but it is clear that the limbic–hypothalamic–pituitary axis is an essential part. The classic paper of Papez (1937), "A Proposed Mechanism of Emotion," laid the groundwork for an understanding of biopsychological factors, and additional work has elaborated Papez's position (Brady, 1958). The work of Penfield and Heath in exploring tumor boundaries, in which brain areas were probed with depth electrodes in conscious patients, has demonstrated that limbic stimulation results in the experience of emotion and sensory perception. MacLean coined the phrase "visceral brain" for the limbic system (MacLean, 1955), and others have referred to it as the "emotional brain," but the important point is that emotional states are reflected in, or correlated with, electrophysiological activity in the limbic system. It seems that the limbic system is the major responder to psychological stress, and that chronic psychological problems can manifest themselves in chronic somatic processes through numerous interconnections between the limbic system and autonomic and hormonal control centers in the hypothalamus and pituitary gland.

It may be possible to bring under some degree of voluntary control any physiological process that can be continuously monitored, amplified, and displayed. This is implied by the psychophysiological principle that as we postulate it, affirms: "Every change in the physiological state is accompanied by an appropriate change in the mental–emotional state, conscious or unconscious; and conversely, every change in the mental–emotional state, conscious or unconscious, is accompanied by an appropriate change in the physiological state" (Green, Green, & Walters, 1970a). From a theoretical point of view, when coupled with volition, this principle makes self-regulation possible. But how can knowledge about what is going on inside the skin make possible the self-regulation of what are usually "involuntary" physiological processes? A cybernetic model of the underlying neurological and psychological principles is described below (Green & Green, 1977).

Figure 8-1 is a highly simplified representation of processes that occur in the voluntary and involuntary neurological domain, and simultaneously in the conscious and unconscious psychological domain. The upper half of the diagram represents the normal domain of conscious processes—that is, processes of which we normally have awareness when we wish it. The lower half of the diagram represents the normal domain of unconscious processes. The normal neurological locus for conscious processes seems to be the cerebral cortex and the craniospinal apparatus. The normal locus for unconscious processes appears to be in the subcortical brain and in the autonomic nervous system.

Electrophysiological studies show that every perception of outside-the-skin (OUTS) events (see the upper left box of Figure 8-1) has associated with it (Arrow 1) electrical activity in both conscious and unconscious structures, those involved in emotional and mental responses. The boxes labeled "emotional and mental response. . . " have been placed on the

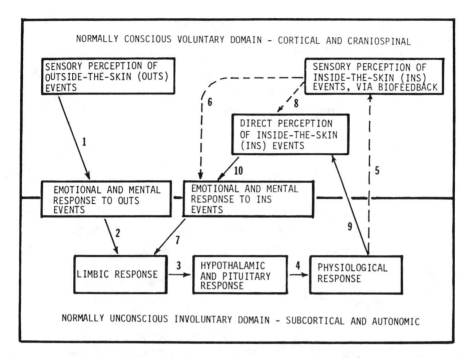

FIG. 8-1. Simplified operational diagram of "self-regulation" of psychophysiological events and processes. Sensory perception of OUTS events, stressful or otherwise (upper left box), leads to a physiological response along Arrows 1 to 4. If the physiological response is "picked up" and fed back (Arrow 5) to a person who attempts to control the "behavior" of the feedback device, then Arrows 6 and 7 come into being, resulting in a "new" limbic response. This response in turn makes a change in "signals" transmitted along Arrows 3 and 4, modifying the original physiological response. A cybernetic loop is thus completed, and the dynamic equilibrium (homeostasis) of the system can be brought under voluntary control. Biofeedback practice, acting in the opposite way to drugs, increases a person's sensitivity to INS events, and Arrow 8 develops, followed by the development of Arrows 9 and 10. External feedback is eventually unnecessary, because direct perception of INS events becomes adequate for maintaining self-regulation skills. Physiological self-control through classical yoga develops along the route of Arrows 7–3–4–9–10–7, but for control of specific physiological and psychosomatic problems, biofeedback training seems more efficient.

midline of the diagram, divided by our horizontal center line into conscious and unconscious parts in order to show their two-domain nature. The next box, called "limbic response," is placed entirely in the "unconscious" section of the diagram, though some neural pathways lead from limbic structures directly to cortical regions, implying that "information" from limbic processes can reach consciousness.

Of major significance to a proper rationale is the fact that the limbic system is connected by many pathways, represented by Arrow 3, to the central "control panel" of the brain, the hypothalamus. Though the hypothalamus weighs only about 4 grams, it regulates a large part of the body's automatic neural machinery; in addition, it controls the pituitary gland. The pituitary, the so-called "king gland" of the body, is at the top of the hormonal hierarchy, and its action precipitates or triggers changes in other glandular structures. With these concepts in mind, it is easy to see how news from a telephone message could cause a person to faint, or to have a sudden surge of high blood pressure. The perception of OUTS events leads to limbic–hypothalamic–glandular responses, and, of course, physiological changes are the inevitable consequence.

If a physiological change from the box at the lower right in Figure 8-1 is "picked up" by a sensitive electrical transducer and displayed to the person on a meter (Arrow 5) or made audible by a tone in order to feed back physiological information, then there ensues (Arrow 6) a "new" emotional response, a response to normally unconscious inside-the-skin (INS) information. The new emotional response is associated with a "new" limbic response (Arrow 7). It combines with, or replaces, or modifies, the original limbic response (Arrow 2). This new limbic response in turn develops a "new" pattern of hypothalamic firing and pituitary secretion, and a "new" physiological state ensues. Thus, a biocybernetic control loop is completed as a result of providing the conscious cortex with information about normally unconscious INS processes. Closing the biocybernetic loop bridges the normal gap between conscious and unconscious processes, voluntary and involuntary processes.

In learning voluntary control of normally unconscious processes, we do not become directly aware of the neural pathways and muscle fibers involved, any more than we become aware of what cerebral and subcerebral nerves are involved in hitting a golf ball. But, as in the case of hitting the golf ball, when we get external objective feedback we can learn to modify the internal "set-up" so as to bring about changes in the desired direction.

With the advent of biofeedback, certain previously existing distinctions between the voluntary and involuntary nervous system, and between conscious and unconscious processes, are being eroded. Conscious control of the autonomic nervous system (once conceptualized to be unconscious and involuntary) is as possible as conscious control of the muscular system is, and it takes place in much the same way. In picking up a pen the intent is conscious, and visual and proprioceptive feedback are utilized to carry out the activity (consciously or unconsciously). The mechanism whereby the activity is carried out is unconscious; the cortical decision, the visual and motor coordination, and the messages from the visual and motor cortexes to spinal ganglia, to motor neurons, and thus to contracting muscles are unconscious; and the result, the pen in hand, is conscious—at least to some extent—and is always available to consciousness.

In the same way, the intent to warm one's fingers is conscious, and visual feedback provided by a temperature trainer is utilized initially to carry out the activity. The mechanism whereby this vasodilation is accomplished (cortex to limbic system to hypothalamus–pituitary, with accompanying neurohormonal changes in the autonomic nervous system) is unconscious, and the result, the change on the meter or the sensation of warmth, is once again conscious or available to consciousness, like the pen in hand. Initially, of course, the result is made conscious through the use of sensitive physiological monitoring and feedback. Through this process certain autonomic nervous system activity, as well as striate, craniospinal activity, can come under conscious, voluntary control.

It is useful to focus attention especially on Arrows 5, 6, 7, 8, 9, and 10 of Figure 8-1. Biofeedback information, along Arrow 5 and then Arrow 6, is often not needed for more than a few weeks. Biofeedback is not addictive, it seems, because voluntary internal control is established, rather than dependence on an external agency. In this, biofeedback differs considerably from drugs. Dosages of many drugs often need to be increased as time goes by in order to overcome the body's habituation. With biofeedback, however, sensitivity to subtle internal cues is increased, rather than decreased. This increased sensitivity, indicated by Arrow 8, is an essential step in closing the internal cybernetic loop, so that the need for feedback devices is only temporary. Eventually the ability to regulate autonomic activity without the aid of machinery can be developed (Green & Green, 1973).

Visualization is an important part of autogenic feedback training. "Making mental contact with the part" (of the body to be regulated) is one of the most interesting concepts in autogenic training. It is clear that consciousness is implicit in learning, and top athletes, musicians, and performers of all kinds have reported that conscious "visualizations" (which may be visual, auditory, and/or kinesthetic) are essential to correct learning and performing. Animal research has clearly demonstrated that perceptual stimuli may result in physiological and behavioral changes. There is, for example, the often-cited case of the stickleback fish that responds to an orange truck parked across the street from its aquarium with the same physiological changes (mating behavior) that would normally be elicited by the orange underbelly of a female fish nearby, because the truck subtends the same angle on the retina (Dobzhansky, 1951).

In humans visualizing events, imagining sources of stimulation can create as great a physiological response as the actual experience of the event can. For many, the image of squeezing lemon juice under the tongue produces increased salivation as effectively as actually doing so does; the physiological effects of sexual fantasies and visual stimulation are well known; advertisers are well aware of the connections between images created and eventual behavior. Whereas animals are regulated almost entirely by the environment, humans are regulated by the environment *as perceived by them*, and by their own inner fantasies, visualizations, images and expectancies; humans can thus regulate themselves by choosing appropriate visualizations and expectations of desired goals.

ASSESSMENT

HOW TO ASSESS FOR USE OF THE METHOD

Autogenic biofeedback therapy, described in detail below, is widely useful in the treatment of stress-related disorders, including such problems as classical and common migraine headache (Sargent *et al.*, 1972), tension headache (Budzynski, Stoyva, & Adler, 1970), mixed tension–vascular headache (Fahrion, 1977), idiopathic essential hypertension (Green *et al.*, 1979), primary idiopathic Raynaud's disease (Taub & Stroebel, 1978), irritable bowel syndrome, peptic ulcer, and cardiac arrhythmias.

Autogenic biofeedback therapy is also appropriate as an adjunctive treatment for other disorders where stress may play a part in causing or exacerbating the problem. In neuromuscular rehabilitation with problems of paresis and spasticity following trauma or stroke, for example, autogenic biofeedback training may be used to reduce the impact of the stresses associated with the disability, to improve circulation to damaged areas in the interests of healing, and to restore or improve function in areas affected by paresis. Autogenic biofeedback has also been found useful for self-regulation training in instances of tic, blepharospasm, Bell's palsy, and torticollis. Autogenic biofeedback therapy may play an important adjunctive role in reducing symptoms and stress while potentiating other medical treatments in such illnesses as cancer, diabetes, and multiple sclerosis.

Psychological dysfunctions ameliorated by autogenic biofeedback therapy include such stress-related disorders as agoraphobia, neurotic depression, impulse disorders (anger, acting out), and other generalized stress syndromes with no underlying organicity—for all of which, in non-psychiatric medical settings, Valium or other palliatives are often prescribed. Autogenic biofeedback therapy and physiological monitoring also constitute a useful adjunct to desensitization psychotherapy.

We have found that autogenic biofeedback training can be accommodated to any age group; we have treated people from ages 4 through 89 with equally good success. Autogenic biofeedback training can also be accommodated to a wide range of intelligence levels, and has been used with positive results with retarded children (French, Leeb, & Fahrion, 1975).

At another level, assessment proceeds according to psychophysiological considerations, and the initial session as a whole may be seen as an opportunity for both therapist and patient to assess the appropriateness of this treatment approach. Initial physiological levels for most patients coming to a therapists's office for the first time provide a sample that represents some degree of the stress response. Then, as the patients go through the relaxation procedures of the first session, the therapist observes the patients' levels and flexibility of response: To what extent are the patients *able* to relax at the outset? Thus the initial evaluation and demonstration proceeds simultaneously.

With this information, the therapist can inform a patient about the observed response, and ask, based on this sample of what the training will involve, whether the patient wishes to proceed. This "self-selection" approach permits the patient to provide truly informed consent for the treatment, an ideal that is all too often missing in practice in most medical treatment.

LIMITATIONS AND CONTRAINDICATIONS

This treatment approach fails, when it does, primarily due to lack of motivation on the part of the patient. Consistent (daily) effort is required to practice psychophysiological control until normal homeostatic functioning is restored. Thus, while we are presently observing 90% of our medicated patients with essential hypertension develop the ability to maintain normal blood pressures while eliminating all antihypertensive medications, those who fail are those who do not learn physiological control (indexed by objective criteria), or those who, having developed such control, do not practice the five to seven times per week required to initially make a significant change in their stress-related problems. Later, patients are able to *maintain* their gains with only infrequent formal practice, as average before-practice hand and foot temperatures increase through experience of the self-regulatory exercises.

While there are no known contraindications to the application of these techniques in themselves, patients with psychosomatic and psychophysiological stress disorders—if they are taking medication with major systemic effects such as antihypertensive or thyroid medication, or insulin— may become overmedicated as they make progress in the acquisition of these self-regulatory skills, with the consequent neurohormonal changes and physiological improvements. Close monitoring of such physiological change in relation to medications is a necessity to prevent possible overmedication and its consequences, and to be sure reductions in medication levels are made when appropriate. This is always done in cooperation with, and at the order of, such patients' managing physicians.

Individuals who have been highly stressed and who become very relaxed physiologically may also find themselves in much better touch with emotion-laden unconscious processes. This discharge phenomenon actually represents a part of the therapeutic action of autogenic biofeedback, but if it should become temporarily overwhelming for the patient, the therapist may wish to recommend that the patient engage in several short sessions (5 minutes or less) during the day, rather than in one or two longer sessions, until this process settles itself. With some more severely disturbed patients, the therapist may find it necessary to conduct all the experiential processes with the patients in the office at first. We have observed that stress management therapy with seriously disturbed patients often takes much longer, particularly in instances of high levels of psychoactive medications; that it may have definite but only limited beneficial effects; and that, in a few instances, it may not persist beyond the treatment period.

It is important to recognize in this regard that if a patient is able to maintain a relaxed physiology in the face of this discharge of emotion-laden thoughts and images, a kind of naturalistic desensitization process ensues, and autogenic abreaction and neutralization are facilitated. At any rate, this phenomenon does not represent a contraindication for the experienced therapist so much as a technical problem to be dealt with in the psychotherapeutic process.

THE METHOD

INTRODUCING THE METHOD TO THE CLIENT

While there is considerable variability in the procedures used by various practitioners in teaching voluntary control of autonomic processes, those that are described here are fairly typical. At the beginning of psychophysiological therapy, each medically symptomatic patient should have his or her medical records reviewed, and/or should have a further medical examination to establish the diagnosis and to assure that any appropriate medical treatment that may be required in addition to the psychophysiological therapy will be recommended or provided.

That the variability in concepts among the various practitioners using biofeedback contributes to a rather wide range of procedures and results can be seen from an examination of the literature. With respect to the role of awareness in biofeedback, for example, the paradigms under which biofeedback is used range from ''Biofeedback training has nothing to do with awareness'' to ''Biofeedback training *is* awareness training.'' The latter position is implicit in autogenic training, a procedure that mobilizes intention and volition; it is the position of the founders of autogenic biofeedback therapy, as well as of clinicians who think of biofeedback in terms of self-regulation and voluntary control rather than conditioning.

The philosophy under which autogenic biofeedback is used in treatment has an impact on all aspects of the method, and is the determining factor in such aspects of treatment as the introduction of the method to the client and the nature of the client–therapist realtionship. In our practice, we place great emphasis on engendering in the client a clear understanding of the basic mechanisms of stress and anxiety, of self-regulation concepts, of principles underlying psychosomatic illness and psychosomatic health (Green, Green, & Walters, 1970b), and of the rationale for the methods to be employed. To this end, we frequently employ audiovisual aids (graphs, diagrams, films, and videotapes) and assigned reading, as well as a variety of experiential exercises to familiarize patients with their own mind–body coordination.

From the beginning of therapy, we make it clear to patients that the essence of self-regulation of *any* kind is proper visualization. This is true of all acquired skills, from executing a pole vault or a cartwheel to playing the piano, as well as in the learning of autonomic self-regulation. The neurological rationale described above is provided to patients, and every effort is made to "demystify" the topic of mind–body coordination, and to foster a mental set within which physiological self-regulation is easier to learn. We hypothesize that understanding the rationale underlying treatment engages both hemispheres of a client's brain in the therapeutic process; the left cortex, appreciating the rational and practical nature of neurological self-regulation, enhances (or at least does not interfere with) the right cortex in creating appropriate visualizations. Each patient participates in goal setting and in developing the treatment program, and is in every sense a coparticipant in the treatment process.

THE PHYSICAL ENVIRONMENT AND EQUIPMENT

Training sessions typically occur in a standard office environment with, at a minimum, a reclining chair for the patient, a nearby table for the equipment, and comfortable seating space for the therapist. The office setting should be pleasant and conducive to relaxation, rather than sterile and emotionally cold. Office temperatures ideally will be well stabilized, and perhaps somewhat warmer than usual (72–74°F), and/or a light blanket should be available to cover the patient during the early phases of training. The office should be quiet and softly lighted, without fluorescent lights to create electrical artifacts that are difficult to filter out. These ideal conditions are facilitative in early training, particularly with patients who are tense, anxious, and in pain. Later in training, it is important for patients to accomplish relaxation in any environment.

Commercially available biofeedback equipment is commonly used; this may vary markedly in complexity, from inexpensive thermometers to multiplexed multichannel microcomputers for data collection and display. Minimal equipment would include simple, stand-alone electronic thermal and electromyographic (EMG) biofeedback units, plus a digital integrator to average data over variable time intervals. In general, the expense of equipment is largely determined by its sensitivity, by the complexity of its data processing, and by the variety of its feedback displays.

No comprehensive literature currently exists to compare the effects of these equipment parameters in training, but clinical observation suggests that individual clients may prefer one or another form of feedback display, and that it is useful to follow these preferences in so far as this is possible. The fact that patients seem to learn self-regulation with many different feedback regimens suggests that these aspects of training are relatively unimportant, as long as the feedback is immediate, continuous, and reasonably pleasant in character.

Some therapeutic advantage may actually accrue from the use of simpler, less expensive equipment, in that it is less likely to suggest to the patient that the equipment itself will "do something to" the patient, rather than simply serving as an electronic mirror. This assures that the mere presence of the equipment will be less likely to induce short-lived, counterproductive placebo effects that may produce initial confusion in the process of learning self-regulatory skills. Simpler equipment is also less subject to "down time," an important consideration for the practicing clinician, since the expense of more complicated units may also inhibit acquisition of backup equipment. Thermal and EMG biofeedback units, together with breathing exercises and other adjunctive strategies, can accomplish symptom alleviation or removal and can increase psychosomatic health in any and all of the patients seen. More specific training can often be facilitated using other feedback modalities, such as electroencephalographic (EEG), electrodermal response (EDR), electrocardiographic (ECG), sphygmomanometer, and goniometer feedback. These physiological measures may be used both for skills training and for objective measurement of other psychophysiological behaviors being treated.

THE THERAPIST–CLIENT RELATIONSHIP

Since autogenic biofeedback therapy emphasizes self-regulation, much importance is placed on the client's assuming and/or maintaining self-responsibility for his or her stress responses, healing process, and state of wellness. This necessitates several strategies of approach, which differ from those of many other therapies. First, the relationship is not an authoritarian one; rather, it is a healing partnership in which the client participates fully. Patients are not simply passive receivers of health care, but, rather, active participants in a teamwork approach between therapist and patient. To this end, no information is withheld from any patient. Patients are fully informed of their condition, their physiological parameters and measurements, and the nature of their progress through the treatment process. As part of increasing self-awareness, we encourage patients to know everything possible about themselves and their conditions. If appropriate, X-rays, blood tests, and other medical findings are shared with clients, and these may help form the basis of the visualizations employed.

Effective therapists are generally acute observers. This is an invaluable skill for biofeedback practitioners as well, and is even more invaluable as a skill to pass on to patients—an ability to become an "observer of the self" maximizes choice and is a central part of self-regulation.

DESCRIPTION OF THE METHOD

In a typical case, a major portion of the initial appointment is spent developing rapport with the client, taking a clinical data history from the client's point of view, and introducing the concept of biofeedback training. Particular emphasis is placed on explaining the rationale described above for the way in which biofeedback is applied to the client's specific disorder; that is, what body functions are being measured and how the normalization of these functions can help to alleviate the symptoms. The client may be shown several graphs or other relevant data of successful training outcomes of similar patients, with the intent of inducing a sense of hopefulness and positive expectancy about the treatment process. Patients with psychophysiological disorders have typically undergone a variety of different treatments without successful results, and often feel somewhat hopeless or skeptical about the prospects of improving their condition.

At the outset of training, the client is monitored for baseline levels of skin temperature and forehead muscle tension at least, and frequently EDR and other parameters are also evaluated. Since the initial training is usually performed with the patient reclining in a chair, the baseline data is also taken in this position in our practice. Each physiological function is monitored and the data recorded, first over a few minutes of baseline and then during the relaxation experience, which together provide an index of the stress level. Some clinicians do initial diagnostic evaluations with stressors administered as well. While this provides useful information for research and outcome measures, these advantages may be offset by the initial "message" to the client that is implicit in such a procedure.

In addition to the physiological assessment, our diagnostic evaluation includes psychological measures. Each patient completes a Spielberger State–Trait Anxiety Scale, a Cornell Medical Index, and a Personal Orientation Inventory at the beginning of treatment and again at termination. The test results are generally shared and discussed fully at the end of treatment. Occasionally other psychological measures may also be administered.

In a typical first training session, as soon as the baseline data are taken, the trainee is oriented to the training process with remarks such as the following:

At this point I'm going to give you some autogenic training phrases, and I want you to say each phrase over and over to yourself. Your attitude as you do this is quite important. This is the kind of thing where the more you try to relax, the less it will happen. So the best approach is to have the intention to warm and relax, but to remain detached about your actual results. Since everyone can learn voluntary control of these processes, it is only a matter of time until you do, and therefore you can afford to be detached about the results. Secondly, saying the phrases is good because it keeps them in mind, but it is not enough. The part of the brain that controls these processes, the limbic system, doesn't understand language well, so it is important to translate the content of the phrase into some kind of image. One of the phrases is "My hands are heavy and warm." If you can actually imagine what it would feel like if your hands did feel heavy or if they did feel warm, that helps to bring on the changes that we are looking for. Or use a visual image; imagine that you are lying out on a beach in the sun, or that you are holding your hands over a campfire. Whatever works for you as a relaxing image, and a warmth-inducing image, that's the thing to use, but the imaging itself is important. Finally, if you simply trust your body to do what you are visualizing it as doing, then you will discover that it will.

The modified autogenic training phrases adapted by Alyce Green, including the "mind-quieting" phrases she developed (see Figure 8-2), are then administered for approximately 20 minutes. During the first autogenic biofeedback experience, only verbal feedback is typically given, because direct instrument feedback may induce performance anxiety at this stage, and because verbal feedback facilitates the focus of attention on internal awareness. The therapist observes the physiological response on the instrument and either provides verbal feedback for improvement in hand temperature between the autogenic phrases, if indicated, or records impressions for sharing at the conclusion of the experience. The client might be told, "You are beginning to get warmer," and "You're now warming more rapidly," as these events occur. The client is given encouragement and reinforcement. The therapist paces the phrases to correspond to the client's actual physiological changes; it is important for the client to be given sufficient time between phrases to be able to repeat each phrase slowly to himself or herself at least three times.

Toward the end of the first session, auditory or visual feedback may be introduced. Various instruments provide different forms of feedback, but the most widely used is either an analog or digital meter, or a tone that decreases in pitch as the hands warm. Another sensitive and useful

Trainee's Initials _____   Date _____

Initial Temperature_____

Meter Reading (at the
start of each phrase)   Phrases

left	right	
		1. I feel quite quiet.
		2. I am beginning to feel quite relaxed.
		3. My feet feel heavy and relaxed.
		4. My ankles, my knees, and my hips feel heavy, relaxed, and comfortable.
		5. My solar plexus, and the whole central portion of my body, feel relaxed and quiet.
		6. My hands, my arms, and my shoulders feel heavy, relaxed, and comfortable.
		7. My neck, my jaws, and my forehead feel relaxed. They feel comfortable and smooth.
		8. My whole body feels quiet, heavy, comfortable, and relaxed.
		9. Continue alone for a minute.
		10. I am quite relaxed.
		11. My arms and hands are heavy and warm.
		12. I feel quite quiet.
		13. My whole body is relaxed and my hands are warm, relaxed and warm.
		14. My hands are warm.
		15. Warmth is flowing into my hands; they are warm, warm.
		16. I can feel the warmth flowing down my arms into my hands.
		17. My hands are warm, relaxed and warm.
		18. Continue alone for a minute.
		19. My whole body feels quiet, comfortable, and relaxed.
		20. My mind is quiet.
		21. I withdraw my thoughts from the surroundings, and I feel serene and still.
		22. My thoughts are turned inward, and I am at ease.
		23. Deep within my mind I can visualize and experience myself as relaxed, comfortable, and still.
		24. I am alert, but in an easy, quiet, inward-turned way.
		25. My mind is calm and quiet.
		26. I feel an inward quietness.
		27. Continue alone for a minute.
		28. The relaxation and reverie is now concluded, and the whole body is reactivated with a deep breath and the following phrases: "I feel life and energy flowing through my legs, hips, solar plexus, chest, arms and hands, neck and head . . . The energy makes me feel light and alive." Stretch.

Final Temperature _____

FIG. 8-2. Autogenic biofeedback training phrases.

form of feedback is a tone that increases in pitch as the *rate* of warming increases.

In concluding the first training period, the therapist and client discuss the experience and the homework exercises to be practiced daily between office visits. The therapist informs the client that positive results are likely, provided that two criteria are met: (1) The client must perform hand-warming exercises every day until symptoms are overcome, and must be able finally to sustain a hand temperature of at least 95.5°F for 10 minutes or more; and (2) the client must be able to increase hand temperature at a rate of at least 1°F per minute. (These criteria are perhaps somewhat more stringent than those currently used by most biofeedback practitioners, but their achievement has been observed to be essential if the best clinical results are to be obtained and maintained over time.)

In addition to the more formal practice, we also encourage our clients to experiment with the equipment. We may say something like, "This equipment is yours to use for the time being, so have fun with it; let the scientist within you out. If you are watching TV, it is interesting to see what your hand temperature does during the news, during a comedy, or during tender or frightening moments. It might be enlightening to see what happens to your hand temperature if you have a difficult phone call to make . . . do your hands get cold? Can you keep them warm or make them warm? You may want to check this response during any opportunity to explore your own physiological functioning, so let your imagination be your guide."

A thorough description of all the specific training methods is beyond the scope of this chapter. A description of the aims of autogenic biofeedback therapy will suffice to provide a guideline for clinical work and all its ramifications and applications.

In autogenic therapy, as developed by Schultz and Luthe, the first four standard exercises are these:

1. Heaviness (associated with neuromuscular quietness)
2. Warmth (associated with autonomic quietness)
3. Cardiac regulation
4. Respiration

These exercises are considered mandatory as preparation for, and to optimize the effectiveness of, "organ-specific formulae" (Schultz & Luthe, 1969).

In the development of autogenic biofeedback therapy, we have followed a similar paradigm. In order for visualization, intentional formulas, and specific physiological training to be most effective, the client first learns to achieve a quiet body, quiet emotions, and a quiet mind. To that end, the threefold autogenic biofeedback training phrases (see Figure 8-2) were developed by the Greens to help initiate these states, and can be used with any or all of the training modalities, although they are customarily introduced at the outset with thermal training for vascular relaxation and sympathetic deactivation.

Also, to achieve these ends (quiet body, quiet emotions, quiet mind), training proceeds generally in the following order: First, emotional quietness is approached by thermal training, and is achieved when criterion levels of hand warming are met. At the second or third session, breathing exercises are introduced, and corrective exercises are given if necessary to switch the patient from thoracic to diaphragmatic breathing. The goals of the breathing exercises are these:

1. To establish deep diaphragmatic breathing.

2. To extend the breathing cycle until the breathing rate during relaxation is gradually reduced, over a period of weeks, to a maximum of three–four times per minute.

3. To develop awareness of gasping and holding of breath as a means of blocking feelings, and awareness of rapid shallow breathing at times of anxiety and/or daily life stress.

4. To learn to exhale, let go, and breathe slowly and deeply as an instant destressing technique.

Practice of both thermal training and breathing exercises is continued daily. Some attention must be paid to integrating the practice into the daily life of the client, and homework practice is considered imperative in facilitating a generalization of training skills.

Another technique we have found to be especially useful is one we have dubbed "constant instant practice." When some mastery of physiological self-regulation is demonstrated (e.g., when a temperature of 95°F or more is reached in the hand a number of times, or a deeply relaxed EMG level is attained), the patient is told to practice the process of constant instant practice for 1 week, with the following guidelines:

Repeat to yourself as often as possible a brief phrase indicating the change you want to occur—for example, "My hands are warm and my muscles relaxed." The primary goal is to become relaxed, so if you forget for a while, don't be concerned, just think, "Good, I remembered now." But bearing this in mind, the more often you do it the better—100 times is better than 50. So every time you come to a stop sign, every time you sit down, stand up, use the phone, or start or end any activity, simply think of the phrase and the accompanying sensation briefly, without interference in whatever you are doing, without performance anxiety, without checking to see if anything is happening—simply, over and over, generate the feeling and let go.

We have found with the majority of our patients that this practice consolidates the training, is especially facilitative of the transfer of training, and helps to establish the new homeostatic balance.

The patient may practice briefly two or more times a day. Once a day, at the conclusion of a practice session, a short report of the training session is made (see Figure 8-3). This report is an invaluable part of the awareness enhancement, as the patient tunes in to physical sensations, emotions, and thoughts and fantasies that accompany relaxation. We have observed that psychotherapeutic gains are made by almost every individual learning pe-·ripheral temperature regulation. The realization on the part of a patient that he or she can control some internal processes that were thought involuntary is a recognition always accompanied by a self-image change and an enhanced sense of self-mastery. Over a period of time, both physical and mental well-being are enhanced, as relaxation and self-regulatory skills are transferred to everyday life.

Next, a quiet body is further enhanced by EMG feedback (commonly introduced in the first or in an early session) and by general relaxation training, until criterion levels of deep relaxation are reached and can be maintained for at least 10 minutes.

Often these three steps are sufficient to produce a quiet mind, as well as physical and emotional quietness. If the "quiet mind" condition has not already been met, EEG alpha and theta training may reduce mental stress and aid in the achievement of mental quietness.

This training—the "core" of autogenic biofeedback training and the sine qua non of our stress management training—precedes specific visualizations and training, whether the disorder being treated is agoraphobia, cancer, arthritis, multiple sclerosis, or any of the commonly occurring stress disorders.

RESISTANCE, COMPLIANCE, AND MAINTENANCE OF BEHAVIOR CHANGE

Once patients' gains through daily deep relaxation have been achieved and consolidated, in many instances they may begin to taper off the daily practice. This may be achieved by warming only on days on which the

TEMPERATURE FEEDBACK TRAINING QUESTIONNAIRE

Your initials _____ Date _____ Time of Day _____

Where did you practice? _____ Starting Skin Temperature _____

Highest Temp. Increase in Degrees F. _____

Were you able to feel the following internal changes?

a.	Warmth	Definitely	Moderately	Slightly	Not at All
b.	Flushing	Definitely	Moderately	Slightly	Not at All
c.	Throbbing/Pulsating	Definitely	Moderately	Slightly	Not at All

How did the training session seem?

Were you able to relax? YES   NO   If not, what seemed to interfere?

Physical sensations that occured.

Emotional feelings that occurred.

Thoughts, fantasies, and imaginings.

Did your mind wander at all? YES NO   If so, A LOT   MODERATELY   SLIGHTLY

Did you have any tendency to fall asleep (or get drowsy)? YES   NO

Did you have any dream-like experiences or mental pictures? YES   NO

a.   If so, did these experiences occur in a particular way?   VISUAL   AUDITORY   SPATIAL

                                                                                      TOUCH (PRESSURE)   SMELL   TASTE

b.   If so, were you aware of these experiences all of a sudden (very quickly) or in a gradual way?   SUDDEN   GRADUAL

Was there anything that you particularly liked or did not like about this training session?

Further experiences you would like to share, or remarks you would like to make (if necessary please use reverse side of this sheet).

FIG. 8-3. Daily report form for enhancing psychophysiological self-awareness during home practice.

hands are cool to begin with, or only every other day. The symptoms are monitored during this process, and symptomatic regression is an indication of need to increase the daily practice once again; otherwise, practice may be reduced and eliminated, except for very stressful periods.

The trainee continues to send the symptom report cards to the therapist for the next few months after treatment is concluded. If it appears from these reports that the trainee is experiencing difficulties, or if he or she does not send in the cards, the therapist telephones the individual to inquire about progress and to recommend whatever modifications in training methodology seem appropriate. As a routine procedure, the therapist telephones each trainee after several months for a follow-up evaluation.

CASE EXAMPLE

The case example we present here, though complex, has been chosen precisely because it affords an opportunity to illustrate several aspects of autogenic biofeedback therapy. We discuss a patient treated simultaneously for two major stress disorders: cancer and essential hypertension.

It is beyond the scope of this chapter to describe in detail all the elements of our protocol for the adjunctive treatment of patients with cancer and immune system disorders. The treatment program is multifaceted, and it is probably not possible or even useful to ascribe relative value to the various components, due to their synergistic nature. Yet in our clinical experience, the autonomic self-regulation gained through autogenic biofeedback procedures is the most synergistically powerful element of the entire package. Autogenic biofeedback training mediates stress reduction; aids visualization; enhances the psychotherapeutic process; reduces the adversity and probably potentiates the effectiveness of the concurrent medical treatment (chemotherapy, radiation, and surgery); and facilitates physical exercise.

Autogenic biofeedback can thus play a significant role in the adjunctive treatment of patients with cancer and other immune system disorders and catastrophic illnesses. In working with cancer patients, we follow a wellness model. Our protocol is designed to help patients restore and/or maintain the greatest level of health possible, with the rationale that cancer will have less chance to survive in a healthy, optimally functioning body. To this end, we use a "whole person" approach. The major elements of the program are these:

1. Acquisition of relaxation skills.
2. Psychotherapy, including exploration of will to live, past and present stressors, and self-image.
3. Nutritional counseling.
4. Exercise, including breathing exercises.
5. Goal setting and play: Participating as fully as possible in living, enjoyable activities, and productivity constitutes a "vote for life."
. 6. Visualization and imagery of the specific healing process.

A comprehensive wellness program, but also a straightforward stress management program based on biofeedback-assisted relaxation, can have significant impact on the lives and well-being of cancer patients. It is well to remember that there is often a triple stress associated with cancer: the stress that may have contributed to cancer's developing in the first place: the stress of having cancer; and the stress associated with surgery, chemotherapy, and radiation. The capacity to cope with stress through learned self-regulation can reduce pain and the need for pain medication, ameliorate unpleasant side effects of treatment and potentiate its positive effects, and enhance immune competence. From a human perspective, self-regulation increases feelings of mastery and well-being, increases coping, and enhances the quality of life.

Louis B is a 60-year-old successful self-employed businessman who was referred for autogenic biofeedback and psychophysiological therapy as an adjunctive treatment for metastatic carcinoma of the prostate. He had a diagnosed adenocarcinoma of the prostate, Stage C, and had been treated with a high dose of radiation therapy, concluding 18 months prior to the first appointment. Seventeen months prior to autogenic treatment, there was no evidence of active neoplasm, along with evidence of good recovery from the acute effects of radiation therapy. His blood pressure was observed to be elevated, and he was medically referred for further evaluation of this problem.

Three months later, Mr. B experienced some diffuse ache in the back and extreme tiredness. One month later, he continued to experience increasing tiredness and loss of libido, as well as frontal headaches, and he was started on hydrochlorothiazide, 50 mg per day. After another two months, he began to experience an ache in the lumbar spine, which gradually became constant. Radiological data acquired three weeks later revealed multiple areas of osteoblastic bone metastases, including the lumbar spine, pelvis, ribs, right femur, right tibia, right and left scapulae, and sternum. He was started on diethylstilbestrol (DES), but was not given further radiation. His physicians, at that time, expected that he would suffer increasing pain and would soon begin experiencing paralysis.

Mr. B was brought to the first interview by his son, a social worker who works with cancer patients in a hospice program. During the first session, the patient quietly shared his feelings of hopelessness and helplessness, as well as his fears and expectations about his condition and the treatment he was undertaking. The therapist presented a rationale for treatment, including research findings and clinical evidence that substantiate the value of our psychophysiological adjunctive treatment for cancer patients (Ader, 1981; Bahnson, 1981; Bahnson & Kissen, 1966; Burish & Lyles, 1981; LeShan, 1977; Rosch, 1979; Stoll, 1979).

The patient and his son then viewed a film on our work with essential hypertension (Hartley, 1981), which presents a rationale, describes the method of treatment, and presents the successful results, including the comments of a number of patients. Viewing this film created a critical incident in the therapeutic process: Mr. B burst into tears and confessed that he had been feeling like a helpless bystander, and that he had believed there was nothing he could do on his own behalf to make a difference in his health; but seeing and hearing the previously successful patients describe their results had awakened him to the possibility that his own situation was not hopeless, and that he could be an active participant in the therapeutic processes.

Mr. B was then introduced to thermal biofeedback and breathing exercises and began daily home practice of these immediately, with the aid of a small electronic digital thermometer. These exercises began to help him with pain control during the first week of practice. He was then hospitalized for implantation of a ureteral shunt; he reported practicing both autonomic relaxation and breathing during this time with good results, further reinforcing his sense of ability to control some psychophysiological processes. Although it was never stated explicitly, at this time it was the understanding of Mr. B and his family that his physicians believed he had only a matter of weeks to live.

By the end of the first month of weekly 1-hour sessions, Mr. B could invariably warm his hands to 96–97°F, and was ready to begin warming his feet. We regularly teach patients with essential hypertension to warm the feet, as this is associated with significant drops in blood pressure in our clinical experience; in addition, it was expected that this would be beneficial for Mr. B, since he had extensive metastases in the lower half of his body.

Despite his excellent success at hand warming, Mr. B had great difficulty warming his feet during the first 2 months. To begin with, his feet
would often start in the high 70s (degrees Fahrenheit) and cool 2–3°F
while his hands were warming as much as 22°F, depending on their initial
level. It is worth noting that he first succeeded in raising his foot temperature into the 90s in the middle of the coldest part of winter, and a month
later, he was achieving this level of foot temperature virtually every day.

Patients with essential hypertension are asked to obtain a home blood
pressure monitor and to assume responsibility for taking their pressures
every day. During the first week that Mr. B was taking his pressure daily
before and after relaxation, his weekly average before relaxing was 177/97
mm Hg, and ranged up to 198/98. Figure 8-4 shows the weekly averages
of his prerelaxation blood pressure readings over 31 weeks of training.
Weekly averages for our Medication Index (M) (Green *et al.*, 1979) and

FIG. 8-4. Reductions in blood pressure, Medication Index, and Severity Index experienced
by patient Louis B during psychophysiological training.

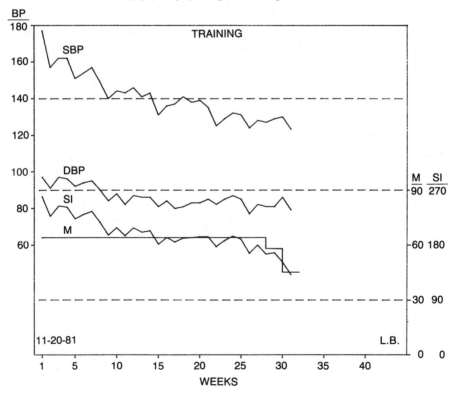

our Severity Index (SI) are also shown. The Severity Index represents a weighted combination of systolic and diastolic pressures and the Medication Index, and thus provides a way of tracking overall improvement in a medicated patient.

During the first month of therapy, Mr. B also had a nutrition consultation with our physician; suggestions were made for a low-fat, low-sugar, high-fiber diet that stressed natural foods, whole grains, and raw fruit and vegetable juices. Vitamins and minerals, including C, A, B-complex, iron, and zinc were prescribed, but no digestive enzymes or special dietary additions were considered necessary for this particular patient. Mr. B brought his wife to this consultation, and both of them have been following this diet enthusiastically ever since. At about this time Mr. B began walking a mile or more each day before breakfast, and maintained a higher activity level throughout the day; for example, he would often take the stairs instead of an elevator. He frequently expressed amazement at how pain-free he was becoming and at how well he was sleeping.

Very early in therapy, a program of visualization was initiated, basically following the Simonton method (Simonton, Matthews-Simonton, & Creighton, 1978). This was a central focus of treatment with this patient; but since it is not the primary focus of this chapter, the interested reader is encouraged to explore other literature on these visualization techniques (Achterberg & Lawlis, 1978, 1980; Children of the Center for Attitudinal Healing, 1978; Maltz, 1974; Samuels & Samuels, 1975, Shorr, 1974). In essence, the patient develops a visualization that includes his or her immune system, particularly the white cells; the cancer; and any chemotherapy or radiation he or she may be receiving. Furthermore, the patient is encouraged to develop associated kinesthetic imagery—the feeling that the immune system battle with the cancer cells is taking place inside his or her body; that the white cells are powerful against the cancer and protective of the healthy cells; that the chemotherapy is also powerful against the cancer cells; that the healthy cells are more impervious, repair themselves faster, and cooperate in the battle by reflecting or diverting the chemotherapeutic substances administered only to the cancer cells; and that the cancer cells are weak and are losing the battle.

The patient is encouraged to visualize the cancer being destroyed and the battle being won each time he or she practices this exercise—not because the immune system can eliminate the tumor in one session, but because visualizing it in this manner constitutes a *blueprint* that expresses the *intentionality* underlying the completed process. The visualization process is carefully monitored through discussions, guided imagery, and drawings.

During the course of treatment, Mr. B's first sessions with the therapist were spent in thermal training in developing awareness of related physical, emotional, and mental events correlated with autonomic relaxation, as well as awareness of associated imagery and insights. One or two sessions were spent on the mechanics of taking and recording blood pressure, and in giving the breathing exercises and their rationale. Also during this time, transfer of training of these new autogenic skills was focused on in every session. Mr. B was found to have fairly low muscle tension levels and was able to relax to criterion levels at the outset, so EMG training was not necessary.

Major emphasis during the sessions was on the psychotherapeutic process and was frequently wide-ranging, covering not only the imagery and insights that arose from the relaxation and visualization themselves, but also past life events, present life stressors, triumphs and accomplishments, and family concerns. Other family members were invited to certain sessions in which these relationships were explored.

During the entire course of therapy, Mr. B continually experienced improvements in his blood pressure and in his cancer-related symptoms. Blood pressure decreases were gradual but steady. On the average, he has been able to reduce both his systolic and diastolic blood pressure approximately 10 mm Hg during relaxation. The pain he initially experienced in his back, hips, and legs gradually decreased, and he became pain-free. He began sleeping better, had a better appetite, and felt more trim and fit. His co-workers and his family both noticed that he was more relaxed and easygoing, and was better able to cope with daily irritants, deadlines and other stressors.

At the present time Mr. B has reduced his hypotensive medication by approximately a third, and his blood pressures are continuing to come down; currently they average 128/82 on reduced medication. On the basis of previous clinical experience, it is expected that he will be able to reduce the hypotensive medications by about one dose every 2 weeks until he is medication-free and normotensive.

A recent bone scan carried this addendum, dated 5/7/82: "Compared with 9/5/81, the scan of 5/7/82 shows considerable diminished osseous activity involving spine and ribs. This would suggest a favorable response to recent therapy."

Realistically, no claims can be made for the role of autogenic biofeedback training and psychophysiological self-regulation in the diminution of Mr. B's cancer. Mr. B, however, is a person who is participating in life and in gaining health, who feels competent, who is reducing hypertension and medications as well as cancer activity, and who is enjoying an enhanced quality of life.

REFLECTIONS AND COMMENTS

Many authors have focused on the nonspecific elements that all psychotherapies appear to share, including a confiding and emotionally charged relationship, and a treatment rationale that is confidently conveyed and is accepted by both patient and therapist. These are important in the process of autogenic biofeedback training as well. There must be communication of new conceptual and experiential information through percept, example and the process of self-discovery, a strengthening of the patient's expectation of help, the provision for success experiences, and the facilitation of the arousal of one's emotions (Frank, 1971). Despite these commonalities, striking contrasts also occur among various therapies, especially when cross-cultural comparisons are made.

Even within the domain of relaxation-based therapies, quite different rationales appear to underlie the different procedures. Lehrer, Atthowe, and Weber (1980) have pointed out that, with progressive relaxation, the focus is on achieving very deep levels of muscular relaxation, which may lower physiological activation in general; while the rationale of autogenic training is to allow the body to reestablish a state of healthy homeostasis through states of deep relaxation and abreactive emotional discharges.

Karasu (1977) has classified the three predominating themes in the development of psychotherapies as dynamic, behavioral, and experiential. This is very similar to the categorization of psychotherapies by Ikemi as psychoanalytic, behavioral, and autogenic self-regulatory (Ikemi & Aoki, 1976; Ikemi, Nakagawa, Suematsu, & Luthe, 1975). Indeed, Karasu (1977, p. 852) sees autogenic training as an experiential psychotherapy, but places biofeedback training as represented by the Greens in the behavioral category. His examples, among others, of the three therapeutic themes include the following: (1) *dynamic*—classical psychoanalysis (Freud), analytical psychology (Jung), character analysis (Horney), ego analysis (Klein), and biodynamic therapy (Masserman); (2) *behavioral*—reciprocal inhibition therapy (Wolpe), modeling therapy (Bandura), rational-emotive therapy (Ellis), reality therapy (Glasser), and biofeedback training (Green); and (3) *experiential*—existential analysis (Binswanger), client-centered therapy (Rogers), psychoimagination therapy (Shorr), experiential therapy (Gendlin), and autogenic training (Luthe).

Based on an examination of Karasu's description of the thematic dimensions of these psychotherapeutic categories (1977, p. 853), operant conditioning biofeedback does fit the behavioral paradigm, whereas the Greens' autogenic biofeedback fits the experiential dimension most closely, but combines features of behavioral and also dynamic dimensions.

Behavioral therapies seek, as their primary concern, to reduce anxiety. Behaviorists see pathology as the product of maladaptive learned habits, and they conceive of health as an increased ability to take action or perform—a state enhanced by direct learning, conditioning, systematic desensitization, and shaping. Experiential therapies have as their primary concern a reduction in alienation. The source of pathology is seen as existential despair, fragmentation of self, and lack of congruence with one's experiences, and health is conceived of as actualization of potential, self-growth, authenticity, and spontaneity, through immediate experiencing.

An examination of the research literature indicates that biofeedback is used in both behavioral and experiential contexts. Further, it is gradually becoming clear that when biofeedback is applied in a conditioning context, the learning of self-regulatory skills proceeds less effectively than when biofeedback is seen as a method to enhance awareness (Brown, 1978; Green & Green, 1977; Lynch, Thomas, Paskewitz, Malinow, & Long, in press); this perhaps accounts for some of the marked variability in results reported in the biofeedback research literature.

Autogenic biofeedback training as developed by the Greens is an experiential psychotherapy arising in the context of humanistic existentialism; it derives from the basic concept that humans have innate regulatory mechanisms that, if given the chance, can restore the brain and body processes to optimal homeostatic conditions. Its concept of pathology includes both human loss of possibilities and fragmentation of self (experiential), and learned maladaptive habits (behavioral). Its concept of health emphasizes actualization of potential, self-growth, authenticity, and spontaneity (experiential); symptom removal and anxiety reduction (behavioral); and an increase in ego strength, particularly a more positive self-image and field independence (dynamic). The treatment model is educational, but it takes place in a partnership alliance, an egalitarian existential relationship between therapist and client. This therapy thus emphasizes self-regulation, self-actualization, choice as responsibility, an authentic client–therapist relationship, and awareness. Behavioral techniques such as symptom charting, shaping, and systematic desensitization are used as appropriate, but the therapeutic context is not primarily behavioral, since (1) the locus of control for improvement is seen to reside inside the client, not inside the dispenser of reinforcements, and since (2) awareness is considered to be the prime requisite for higher levels of integration.

From this standpoint, it is important to emphasize that the therapeutic goal in autogenic biofeedback training is to maintain and promote desirable levels of functional harmony, rather than simply to reduce anxiety by relaxing deeply. Along with improvements in physiological functioning, a higher-order personality integration often does occur, together with increased empathy, creativity, and productivity.

What stands in the way of these therapeutic improvements is not just chronic, homeostasis-disturbing physiological activation of the autonomic and muscular systems as a result of stress, but also habitual, functionally fragmented patterns of afferent and efferent corticolimbic activity. It is these disturbed psychophysiological patterns ("automatizations," in psychoanalytic terminology) that are corrected ("deautomatized") by the normalizing, self-repair functions and facilitated by autogenic discharge ("abreaction"), thereby overcoming the restricted capacity for self-regulation. This self-neutralizing process seems to be facilitated and stabilized by the patient's insight into the previous antihomeostatic reaction patterns and distorted conditioning; such insight helps to avoid repetition of the same failures (Ikemi et al., 1975).

Luthe (1965) has contrasted the ergotropic nature of active concentration with trophotropic functional change resulting from passive concentration on autogenic formulas. He has also discussed the potential specificity of the physiological effect of visualization through the use of organ-specific formulas. These would seem essential features of the method, as embodied in the psychophysiological principle that affirms, "Every change in the physiological state is accompanied by an appropriate change in the mental–emotional state, conscious or unconscious; and conversely, every change in the mental–emotional state, conscious or unconscious, is accompanied by an appropriate change in the physiological state "(Green, Green, & Walters, 1970b).

While the initial training in autogenic biofeedback training is oriented toward attaining states of deep relaxation, physiological studies of the passive concentration state of autogenic training have revealed an increased density of 15- to at least 20-cycle-per-second EEG activity, together with concurrent slow-wave activity density (Degossely & Bostem, 1977). Fischer (1978–1979) interprets these data as indicating that the passive concentration state represents not only a state of relaxation, but a state of arousal as well. Focused attention and the increased awareness of formerly unconscious events occurring during relaxed states are both a part of the process of effective autogenic biofeedback training. This unusual state, then, appears to share characteristics with both the vigilant rapid-eye-movement (REM) dreaming state and the hypoaroused relaxed waking state. Therapeutically, it enables detached introspection concerning the exciting and possibly traumatic material emerging from the unconscious (Fischer, 1978–1979).

Similar observations were made in the Greens' studies of imagery and states of consciousness associated with creativity. Their first studies focused on normal, healthy subjects and used biofeedback methods to explore the relation between specific internal states, or states of consciousness, and specific brain-wave patterns. They found theta waves to be associated with a deeply internalized (vigilant) state and with a quieting of the body, emotions, and thoughts, thus allowing usually "unheard or unseen things" to come to consciousness in the form of hypnogogic imagery (Green & Green, 1977).

There has been increasing interest in examining similar psychophysiological correlates of meditation. Fischer (1978–1979) likens the altered state of consciousness that accompanies autogenic training to Theraveda Buddhist meditation. In order to adapt the system for research in states of consciousness, and to shorten the learning time associated with autogenic training, the Greens combined "the conscious self-regulation aspect of yoga and the psychological method of autogenic training with the modern instrumental technique called physiological feedback" (Green, Green, & Walters, 1970a).

Benson, Beary, and Carol (1974), who adapted their methods for achieving the relaxation response from transcendental meditation, note that the physiological states thus achieved resemble those achieved through autogenic training, hypnosis, Zen, yoga, and other meditative techniques. Bostem and Degossely (1978) described, using spectral analysis of EEG data, the progressive spread of a dominant alpha band all over the scalp during autogenic training. These findings are very similar to those of Banquet (1973) in his spectral analysis of EEG during meditation. Fehmi (1978) has also observed a global high-amplitude, high-density alpha state brought about by a spatial-imagery meditative task and enhanced by EEG biofeedback.

Levine (1976) developed a sophisticated method for analyzing EEG correlates of meditation-induced altered states of consciousness, which has not yet been comparatively applied to states associated with other meditative procedures and with autogenic biofeedback training. Using this technique, Orme-Johnson, Clements, Haynes, and Badaoui (1977) found a significant correlation between the subjective experience of meditation and bilateral frontal lobe coherence. Frontal coherence in the alpha band was associated with increased indexes of creativity (ideational fluency on the Torrance Novel Uses Test), while frontal coherence in the theta band was associated with increased flexibility of concept formation. Interestingly, global coherence (all frequencies) increased with wakefulness and progressively decreased during sleep stages, with minimum coherence in Stage 4 sleep. Based on the studies mentioned above, we speculate that autogenic biofeedback produces the same global coherence associated with wakefulness, while inducing deep autonomic and muscular relaxation; this may provide a fruitful direction for future research.

Other cerebral changes have also been noted. Mathew, Largen, Dobbins, Meyer, Sakai, and Claghorn (1980) report cerebral blood flow increases accompanying self-regulated hand warming. (This finding supports the Greens' original hypothesis regarding the mechanism of improvement in migraine headache activity with hand warming.) Since blood flow in the brain is correlated with increased metabolic activity, these results again substantiate the dual nature of the autogenic state—simultaneously concentrated and relaxed, creating ideal conditions for passive volition.

Recent improvements in measurement techniques, together with new paradigms encompassing expanded conceptual frameworks of human psychological functioning, are leading to new understandings of the communalities underlying different healing and meditative states. The Greens' early observation that "if there is such a thing as psychosomatic illness, there must be such a thing as psychosomatic health," moves beyond the elimination of disease toward a greater actualization of the human potential. Self-regulation for physical and emotional well-being etches a new image of the human being as volitional, well and strong, self-affirmative and self-responsible.

More than a decade ago, Green, Green, and Walters (1971a) expressed the hope that, with

the resurgence of interest in self-exploration and in self-realization, it will be possible to develop a synthesis of old and new, East and West, prescience and science, using both yoga and biofeedback training as tools for the study of consciousness. . . . Much remains to be researched, and tried in application, but there is little doubt that in the lives of many people a penetration of consciousness into previously unconscious realms (of mind and brain) is making understandable and functional much that was previously obscure and inoperable. (p. 8)

The synthesis of concept and technique continues, while, at a practical level, many people have begun to experience the healing and personally integrative consequences of unifying mind and body.

REFERENCES

Achterberg, J., & Lawlis, G. F. *Imagery of cancer.* Champaign, Ill.: Institute for Personality and Ability Testing, 1978.

Achterberg, J., & Lawlis, G. F. *Bridges of the bodymind.* Champaign, Ill.: Institute for Personality and Ability Testing, 1980.

Ader, R. (Ed.). *Psychoneuroimmunology.* New York: Academic Press, 1981.

Akagi, M., Yoshimura, M., & Ikemi, Y. A clinical study of the treatment of writer's cramp by biofeedback training. *Behavioral Engineering,* 1977, *4,* 45–50.

Bahnson, C. B. Stress and cancer: The state of the art. *Psychosomatics,* 1981, *22,* 207–220.

Bahnson, C. B., & Kissen, D. M. (Eds.). Psychophysiological aspects of cancer. *Annals of the New York Academy of Sciences,* 1966, *125,* 773–1055.

Banquet, J. P. Spectral analysis of the EEG in meditation. *Electroencephalography and Clinical Neurophysiology,* 1973, *35,* 143–151.

Basmajian, J. V. Control and training of individual motor units. *Science,* 1963, *141,* 440–441.

Benson, H., Beary, J. F., & Carol, M. P. The relaxation response. *Psychiatry,* 1974, *37,* 37–46.

Blanchard, E. B. The use of temperature biofeedback in the treatment of chronic pain due to causalgia. *Biofeedback and Self-Regulation,* 1979, *4,* 183–188.

Boller, J. D., & Flom, R. P. Treatment of the common migraine: Systematic application of biofeedback and autogenic training. *American Journal of Clinical Biofeedback,* 1979, *2,* 63–64.

Bostem, F. & Degossely, M. Spectral analysis of alpha rhythm during Schultz's autogenic training: A tentative approach to rapid visualization. *Electroencephalography and Clinical Neurophysiology,* 1978, *34*(Suppl.), 181–190.

Brady, J. The paleocortex and behavioral motivation. In H. Harlow & Woolsey (Eds.), *The biological and biochemical bases of behavior.* Madison: University of Wisconsin Press, 1958.

Brown, B. Critique of biofeedback concepts and methodologies. *American Journal of Clinical Biofeedback,* 1978, *1,* 10–14.

Budzynski, T. H., Stoyva, J. M., & Adler, C. S. Feedback-induced muscle relaxation: Application to tension headache. *Journal of Behavior Therapy and Experimental Psychiatry,* 1970, *1,* 205–211.

Burish, T. G., & Lyles, J. N. Effectiveness of relaxation training in reducing adverse reactions to cancer chemotherapy. *Journal of Behavioral Medicine,* 1981, *4,* 65–78.

Children of the Center for Attitudinal Healing. *There is a rainbow behind every dark cloud.* Millbrae, Calif.: Celestial Arts, 1978.

Degossely, M., & Bostem, F. Autogenic training and states of consciousness: A few methodological problems. In W. Luthe & F. Antonelli (Eds.), *Proceedings of the 3rd World Congress, ICPM, Pozzi, Rome,* 1977, *4,* 18–25.

Dietvorst, T. F., & Osborne, D. Biofeedback-assisted relaxation training for primary dysmenorrhea: A case study. *Biofeedback and Self-Regulation,* 1978, *3,* 301–305.

Dobzhansky, T. *Genetics and the origin of species* (3rd ed.). New York: Columbia University Press, 1951.

Engelhardt, L. J. *The application of biofeedback techniques within a public school setting.* Paper presented at the Seventh Annual Meeting of the Biofeedback Society of America, Colorado Springs, Colorado, 1976.

Fahrion, S. L. Autogenic biofeedback for migraine. *Mayo Clinic Proceedings,* 1977, *52,* 776–784.

Fehmi, L. EEG biofeedback, multi-channel synchrony training and attention. In A. A. Sugarman & R. E. Tarter (Eds.), *Expanding dimensions of consciousness.* New York: Springer, 1978.

Fischer, R. Healing as a state of consciousness: Cartography of the passive concentration stage of autogenic training. *Journal of Altered States of Consciousness.* 1978–1979, *4*, 57–61.

Frank, J. Therapeutic factors in psychotherapy. *American Journal of Psychotherapy*, 1971, *25*, 350–361.

French, D., Leeb, C. S., & Fahrion, S. *Biofeedback hand temperature training in the mentally retarded.* Paper presented at the Sixth Annual Meeting of the Biofeedback Society of America, Monterey, California, 1975.

Green, E. E., Ferguson, D. W., Green, A. M., & Walters, E. D. *Preliminary report on the Voluntary Controls Project: Swami Rama.* Topeka, Kansas: Voluntary Controls Project, The Menninger Foundation, 1970. (Mimeograph)

Green, E. E., & Green, A. M. Regulating our mind–body processes. *Fields within Fields . . . within Fields,* Winter 1973, pp. 16–24.

Green, E., & Green, A. *Beyond biofeedback.* New York: Delacorte Press, 1977.

Green, E. E., Green, A. M., & Norris, P. A. Preliminary observations on a new non-drug method for control of hypertension. *Journal of the South Carolina Medical Association,* 1979, *75*, 575–586.

Green, E. E., Green, A. M., & Walters, E. D. *Psychophysiological training for inner awareness.* Paper presented at the conference of the Association for Humanistic Psychology, Miami, 1970. (a)

Green, E. E., Green, A. M., & Walters, E. D. Voluntary control of internal states: Psychological and physiological. *Journal of Transpersonal Psychology,* 1970, *2*, 1–26. (b)

Green, E. E., Green, A. M., & Walters, E. D. *Biofeedback for mind–body self-regulation: Healing and creativity.* Paper presented at the symposium, "The Varieties of Healing Experience," De Anza College, Cupertino, California, 1971. (a)

Green, E. E., Green, A. M., & Walters, E. D. *Psychophysiological training for creativity.* Paper presented at the meeting of the American Psychological Association, Washington, D.C., 1971. (b)

Green, E. E., Green, A. M., & Walters, E. D. Biofeedback training for anxiety tension reduction. *Annals of the New York Academy of Sciences,* 1973, *233*, 157–161.

Green, E. E., Green, A. M., Walters, E. D., Sargent, J. D., & Meyer, R. G. Autogenic feedback training. *Psychotherapy and Psychosomatics,* 1975, *25*, 88–98.

Green, E. E., Walters, E. D., Green, A. M., & Murphy, G. Feedback technique for deep relaxation. *Psychophysiology,* 1969, *6*, 371–377.

Hartley, E. *Hypertension: The mind–body connection.* Cos Cob, Conn.: Hartley Film Foundation, 1981. (Film)

Hartman, C. H. Response of anginal pain to hand warming. *Biofeedback and Self-Regulation,* 1979, *4*, 355–357.

Ikemi, Y., & Aoki, H. Comprehensive psychosomatic training for internists (at university level). *Dynamische Psychiatrie,* 1976, *9*, 287–299.

Ikemi, Y., Nakagawa, T., Suematsu, H., & Luthe, W. The biologic wisdom of self-regulatory mechanism of normalization in autogenic and oriental approaches to psychotherapy. *Psychotherapy and Psychosomatics,* 1975, *25*, 99–108.

Kamiya, J. Conscious control of brain waves. *Psychology Today,* 1968, *1*(11), 55–60.

Karasu, T. B. Psychotherapies: An overview. *American Journal of Psychiatry,* 1977, *134*, 851–863.

Keefe, F. J. Surwit, R. S., & Pilon, R. N. Collagen vascular disease: Can behavior therapy help? *Journal of Behavior Therapy and Experimental Psychiatry,* 1981, *12*, 171–175.

Leeb, C. Fahrion, S., & French, D. Instructional set, deep relaxation and growth enhancement: A pilot study. *Journal of Humanistic Psychology,* 1976, *16*, 71–78.

Lehrer, P. M., Atthowe, J. M., & Weber, E. S. P. Effects of progressive relaxation and autogenic training on anxiety and physiological measures, with some data on hypnotizability. In F. J. McGuigan, W. E. Sime, & J. M. Wallace (Eds.), *Stress and tension control*. New York: Plenum, 1980.

LeShan, L. *You can fight for your life: Emotional factors in the causation of cancer*. New York: M. Evans, 1977.

Levine, P. H. The coherence spectral array (COSPAR) and its application to the study of spatial ordering in the EEG. *Proceedings of the San Diego Biomedical Symposium*, 1976, *15*, 237–247.

Luthe, W. *Autogenic training*. New York: Grune & Stratton, 1965.

Lynch, J. J., Thomas, S. A., Paskewitz, D. A., Malinow, K. L., & Long, J. M. Interpersonal aspects of blood pressure control. *Journal of Nervous and Mental Disease*, in press.

MacLean, P. D. The limbic system ("visceral brain") in relation to central gray and reticulum of brain stem. *Psychosomatic Medicine*, 1955, *17*, 355–356.

Maltz, M. *The magic power of self-image psychology*. New York: Simon & Schuster, 1974.

Mathew, R. J., Largen, J. W., Dobbins, K., Meyer, J. S., Sakai, F., & Claghorn, J. L. Biofeedback control of skin temperature and cerebral blood flow in migraine. *Headache*, 1980, *20*, 19–28.

McGrady, A. V., Yonker, R., Tan, S. Y., Fine, T. H., & Woerner, M. The effect of biofeedback-assisted relaxation training on blood pressure and selected biochemical parameters in patients with essential hypertension. *Biofeedback and Self-Regulation*, 1981, *6*, 343–353.

Norris, P. A. *Working with prisoners, or, there's nobody else here*. Topeka, Kansas: Voluntary Controls Program, The Menninger Foundation, 1976. (Mimeograph)

Orme-Johnson, D. W., Clements, G., Haynes, C. T., & Badaoui, K. Higher states of consciousness: EEG coherence, creativity, and experiences of the sidhis. In D. W. Orme-Johnson & J. T. Farrow (Eds.), *Scientific research on the Transcendental Meditation Program: Collected papers* (Vol. 1). Rheinweiler, West Germany: Maharishi European Research University Press, 1977.

Papez, J. W. A proposed mechanism of emotion. *Archives of Neurology and Psychiatry*, 1937, *28*, 725–743.

Rosch, P. J. Stress and cancer: A disease of adaptation? In J. Toche, H. Selye, & S. B. Day (Eds.), *Cancer, stress, and death*. New York: Plenum, 1979.

Samuels, M., & Samuels, N. *See with the mind's eye*. New York: Random House, 1975.

Sargent, J. D., Green, E. E., & Walters, E. D. The use of autogenic feedback in a pilot study of migraine and tension headaches. *Headache*, 1972, *12*, 120–125.

Schultz, J. H., & Luthe, W. *Autogenic therapy* (Vol. 1, *Autogenic methods*). New York: Grune & Stratton, 1969.

Sedlacek, K. Comparison between biofeedback and relaxation response in the treatment of hypertension. *Biofeedback and Self-Regulation*, 1979, *4*, 259.

Shorr, J. E. *Psychotherapy through imagery*. New York: Intercontinental Medical Book Corporation, 1974.

Simonton, C., Matthews-Simonton, S., & Creighton, J. *Getting well again*. Los Angeles: J. P. Tarcher, 1978.

Stoll, B. (Ed.). *Mind and cancer prognosis*. New York: Wiley, 1979.

Taub, E., & Stroebel, C. F. Biofeedback in treatment of vasoconstrictive syndromes. *Biofeedback and Self-Regulation*, 1978, *3*, 363–373.

Walton, W. T. The use of a relaxation curriculum and biofeedback training in the classroom to reduce inappropriate behaviors of emotionally handicapped children. *Behavioral Disorders*, 1979, *5*, 10–18.

9 COGNITIVE APPROACHES TO STRESS

AARON T. BECK

COGNITIVE MODEL OF STRESS

COGNITIVE STRUCTURING

The individual's construction of a particular situation may be likened to taking a snapshot. In taking a photograph, the individual scans the relevant environment and then decides which aspect he or she wants to focus on. The photograph reduces a three-dimensional situation to two dimensions and consequently sacrifices a great deal of information (for example), and also introduces a certain amount of distortion into the system. The specific *settings* (lens, focus, speed) have an enormous influence on the type of picture that will be obtained. Depending on the type of lens (wide-angle or telephoto), for example, breadth is sacrificed for detail, or vice versa. In addition, certain aspects are highlighted at the expense of others, and the relative magnitudes and prominence of particular features are distorted.

In addition, there is blurring or loss of detail due to inadequate focusing or too rapid exposure; moreover, the use of filters further influences the salience and coloring of particular features.

Similarly, in conceptualizing a particular event, the cognitive set influences the "picture" obtained by an individual: Whether the mental image or conception is broad, skewed, or narrow, clear or blurred, accurate or distorted depends on the *existing cognitive settings*. The existing cognitive set determines which aspects are to be magnified, which minimized, and which excluded. It is probable that a person takes a series of "pictures" before making a final conceptualization. The first "shot" of an event provides data regarding the *nature* of the situation—for example, whether it is likely to be pleasant, neutral, or noxious.

255

The discussion that follows is restricted to a consideration only of those reactions that may lead to stress. This "first shot" of an event provides feedback that either reinforces or modifies the preexisting cognitive set. An initial impression is formed on the basis of scanty data and is important in that it indicates the general nature of the situation—specifically, whether it directly affects the individual's vital interests. It should be noted that the first impression (first "shot") is especially important because, unless modified or reversed, it determines (influences) the direction of subsequent steps in conceptualization of and total response to the situation. If the individual judges the situation to be affecting his or her vital interests, he or she shows what I call a "critical response." The critical response which is of particular importance in the development of stress reactions, may be viewed as including two types of reactions.

One type of critical response is the "emergency response." The response is activated when the individual perceives a threat to his or her survival, domain, individuality, functioning, status, or attachments—that is, attack, depreciation, encroachment, thwarting, abandonment, rejection, or deprivation. Another type of critical response occurs when the individual perceives an event as increasing or facilitating self-enhancement—attainment of personal goals, exhibitionism, or receiving admiration.

An essential feature of the critical response is that it is egocentric. Through a sequence of cognitive processing, the situation is conceptualized in terms of "How does it affect me?" The immediate interests of the individual are central in the conceptualization, and the details are selected and molded (or distorted) to provide a meaningful answer to that question. The kinds of conceptualizations in the critical response tend to be global and to include a limited number of dimensions. The primitive forms of the conceptualization correspond to primitive content—physical danger, predation, social bonding, and so forth. Data that are not considered relevant to the particular content are excluded. Generally, the critical response tends to be overly inclusive: Some events that in reality are not related to issues of personal identity, survival, or self-enhancement are perceived as though they are relevant.

For our present purpose, let us assume that the first impression of a situation is "noxious." This appraisal activates a particular mode (assembly of "schemas"), which is used to refine the classification of the stimulus situation.

The initial impression of a situation fits into the category of "primary appraisal" (Lazarus, 1966). If the primary appraisal is that the situation is noxious, successive "reappraisals" are made to provide preliminary answers to a series of questions:

1. Is the noxious stimulus a threat to the individual or his or her interests?
2. Is the threat concrete and immediate, or abstract, symbolic, and remote?
3. What is the content and magnitude of the threat?
   a. Does it involve possible physical damage to the individual?
   b. Is the threat of a psychosocial nature—for example, disparagement or devaluation?
   c. Does the threat involve violation of some rules that the individual relies on to protect his or her integrity or interests?

At the same time that the nature of the threat is being evaluated, the individual is assessing his or her resources for dealing with it. This assessment, labeled "secondary appraisal" by Lazarus, aims to provide concrete information regarding the individual's coping mechanisms and ability to absorb the impact of any assault.

The final picture or construction of the noxious situation is based on an equation that takes into account the amount and the probabilities of damage inherent in the threat as opposed to the individual's capacity to deal with it (the "risk–resources equation"). These assessments are not cool, deliberate computations, but to a large degree are automatic. The equation is based on highly subjective evaluations that are prone to considerable error; two individuals with similar coping capacities might respond in a vastly different manner to the same threatening situation.

If the risk is judged to be high in relation to the coping resources available, the individual is mobilized to reduce the degree of threat through avoidance or escape ("flight reaction"); preparing for defense, or self-inhibition ("freezing"). If the individual judges the threat to be low in relation to available coping mechanisms, he or she is mobilized to eliminate or deflect the threat ("fight reaction").

Another type of critical response occurs when the stimulus situation is perceived as potentially self-enhancing. For example, a person is challenged or invited to compete for a prize. The person then makes rapid evaluations of the desirability of the goal, his or her capacity for reaching it, and the "costs" to him or her in terms of expenditure of time, energy, and sacrifice of other goals. These factors may be reduced to a cost–benefit ratio analogous to the risk–resources ratio. The final construction of the stimulus situation determines whether the person accepts the challenge or invitation, and, consequently, whether or not the person becomes mobilized to attain the goal.

The processes involved in the critical response tend to present not only a one-sided but also an exaggerated view of the stimulus situation, because of the exclusionary and categorical nature of the thinking at this primitive level. The processes involved in the critical response are automatic, involuntary, and not within awareness.

The conceptualization presented above is compatible with theories of information processing advanced by other authors. As pointed out by Bowlby (1981), current studies of human perception show that before a person is aware of seeing or hearing a stimulus, the sensory inflow coming through the eyes or ears has already passed through many stages of selection, interpretation, and appraisal. During the course of this process, a large proportion of the original inflow has been excluded. The reason suggested by Bowlby for this extensive exclusion is that "since the channels responsible for the most advanced processing are of limited capacity, they must be protected from over-load to insure that what is most relevant gets through and that the less relevant is excluded." The selection of inflow is under central control. Although this processing is done at extraordinary speeds, and almost all of it is outside awareness, much of the inflow is nonetheless carried to a very advanced stage of processing before being excluded.

In the ordinary course of a person's life, the criteria applied to sensory inflow that determine what information is to be accepted and what is to be excluded reflect what appears to be in the person's best interests at any one time. Thus, when a person is hungry, information regarding food is given priority, whereas other information that might ordinarily be useful is excluded. "Yet, should he or she perceive danger, priorities would quickly change so that inflow concerned with issues of danger and safety would take precedence and inflow concerned with food be temporarily excluded. This change in the criteria governing what inflow is to be accepted and what excluded is effected by evaluating systems that are central to the cognitive organizations" (Bowlby, 1981).

The first principle in the cognitive model of stress reactions, thus, is this: *The construction of a situation (cognitive set) is an active, continuing process that includes successive appraisals of the external situation and the risks, costs, and gains of a particular response. When the individual's vital interests appear to be at stake, the cognitive process provides a highly selective conceptualization.*

MOBILIZATION TO ACTION

Of course, not all stimuli are interpreted as noxious, and not all psychophysiological reactions are "fight" or "flight." Depending on the kind of appraisal, a host of different reactions may be stimulated by a given situation. The variety of impulses that are stimulated may range from a wish to engage in some recreational activity to a desire to undertake a dangerous mission. These reactions have a common theme: The individual is mobilized to engage in some kind of action. For a variety of reasons, he or she may not yield to the desire, wish, or drive—but the mobilization has a powerful effect, nonetheless. Recent writings have emphasized the emotional response to a stressful stimulus but have largely neglected the importance of the motivational response.

If a person is activated to perform a particular behavior, the directing force may be labeled a "behavioral inclination." The behavioral inclinations, or action tendencies, constitute one type of motivation. Another class of motivations is concerned with "receiving" rather than "doing" and includes wishes for love, praise, or approval, or the appetitive wishes. The intensity of the behavioral inclination is reflected in the degree of arousal. If the behavioral inclination is not translated into action, then the individual remains in a state of arousal for a period of time, even though the instigating stimulus is no longer present.

At the same time that an individual is aroused to action, he or she may experience an affective response. For example, people who believe they are in a dangerous situation generally experience subjective anxiety as well as a desire to escape; if they judge that other people are mistreating them, they are likely to experience anger as well as a desire to attack. Similarly, people may experience feelings of excitement as they prepare to engage in a competitive sport.

In each case, the "behavioral inclination" represents the catalyst to action. The affective response occurs independently of the behavior (although these two phenomena are often fused in technical as well as popular concepts). Both the behavioral inclination and the affective response stem from the individual's conceptualizations of the situation and are related to each other only insofar as they are both related to the cognitive structuring of the situation. It should be noted that a behavioral inclination may be aroused with minimal or no evidence of an emotional response. Persons exposed to a sudden dangerous situation (e.g., an impending automobile collision) may react to avert the danger without experiencing subjective anxiety.

The mobilization of the individual for action is the key to under-standing stress reactions. If the arousal is intense and is not dissipated by action, then the individual is prone to experience some degree of stress. The stress is manifested by an interference with the normal functioning of the organism. The term "stress" is applied to the response of the or-ganism and not to the external stimulus. The stimulus that sets up the chain of events leading to this dysfunctional reaction is labeled the "stressor." Depending on the conceptual process, the stressor may be regarded as either "trivial" or "overwhelming" by an observer. Similarly, an observer may regard the individual as "underreacting" or "overreacting" to the stimulus situation.

Thus, the second principle of the cognitive model is as follows: *The cognitive structuring of a situation is responsible for mobilizing the organism' to action. If the mobilization is not adequately discharged, it forms the precursor to a stress reaction.*

DISTINCTION BETWEEN BEHAVIORAL INCLINATIONS AND EMOTIONS

The popular concept of emotions—which is also reflected to some de-gree in psychoanalytic theory—revolves around the notion that these phe-nomena are like a fluid or reservoir. When the internal hydraulic system reaches a certain level, it builds up a pressure for overt expression. Ac-cording to the same metaphor, the suppression of certain emotions such as anger can lead to a wide variety of ills, ranging from headache to hyper-tension. By the same token, it has been stated that the free and open ex-pression of emotions such as anger or sadness can relieve the psycho-somatic disorders.

The question naturally arises: How do we know that people are sup-pressing or expressing their emotions? Let us take the example of angry people, who may stamp their feet, yell, shout epithets, or physically attack persons whom they regard as adversaries. They may state that they have been unjustly injured and that they are going to "get even" with the other persons. According to the conventional notions, we would label the ob-served behavior as "anger" or as an "angry reaction." Further reflection, however, forces us to raise questions about this notion. Are we actually seeing in the observed behavior a manifestation of some endopsychic pro-cess other than emotion? When we see an individual shake a fist and express condemning words, it seems more logical to infer that we are seeing the direct expression of a *motivation* (behavioral inclination), rather than the expression of an emotion. (As a matter of fact, an individual can play-act this scenario without feeling angry at all.)

If we question individuals who are behaving in this way, they may explain that they are "blowing off steam" or "expressing angry feelings." Similarly, people who have tightened their muscles in an attempt to prevent themselves from engaging in antagonistic behavior are likely to explain this behavior as "bottling up my feelings." (Note once again the use of a fluid metaphor to refer to feelings.) If we ask such persons, "What would you like to do?," they may respond with a description of a series of actions, such as "I would like to punch him in the nose . . . I would like to humiliate him . . . I'd like to make him feel the way I feel." If we inquire about such individuals' feelings, they may describe them in terms of "anger swelling up inside me." They believe that if they could release (and thus reduce) the anger, they would feel better. Suppose such an individual does scold the offender, and that person then apologizes. The individual feels better and is no longer angry. This sequence of events, thus, appears to be consistent with the person's notions regarding the release of anger: He or she felt angry; expressed the anger; is no longer angry; and feels better. Thus, the person "demonstrates" to his or her own satisfaction that the problem lay in "suppressing my anger."

Does this experience really confirm the validity of the conventional notions regarding the expression of emotions? Let us examine the earlier phase of the process, when an individual feels "anger bursting out all over." When we analyze the situation, we might question whether the person is transforming the anger into overt behavior or whether he or she is simply carrying out an *inclination* to act against the adversary. The second formulation—that what we are observing are the effects of an impulse to scold, berate, or attack the other person—seems more plausible, because it does not require the notion of some "transmutation" of an emotion in behavior, and fits in general with our idea that goal-directed physical activity is preceded by a wish, drive, or impulse (behavioral inclination). According to this formulation, the behavioral inclination—not the emotional response—is involved in the mobilization for action.

The third principle of the cognitive model is this. *Overt behavior stems directly from the mobilization of impulses, drives, or wishes (behavioral inclinations). The emotional experience is parallel to the behavioral inclination and is not a determinant of overt action.*

STRUCTURAL ORGANIZATION

The foregoing discussion lays the foundation for discussing the priority of the conceptual processes in stress reactions. The way the cognitive organization processes the information determines the behavioral inclination and affect. The behavioral inclination, in turn, activates the overt behavior. Thus, we can conceive of a chain of events proceeding from the environmental event to the cognitive processing system (controlling cognitive constellation) to the action-arousing system (behavioral inclination), to the motoric system, and finally to the observable actions. Concomitantly, the controlling cognitive constellation may activate the affect-arousing system.

The role of the cognitive organization in processing information has been described previously (Beck, 1967, 1976). Briefly, the organization is composed of systems of structural components—namely, "cognitive schemas." When an external event occurs, specific cognitive schemas are activated and are used to classify, interpret, evaluate, and assign a meaning to the event. In normal functioning, the schemas that are activated are relevant to the nature of the event. A series of adjustments occur so that the appropriate schemas are "fitted" to the external stimulus. The final interpretation of an event represents an interaction between that event and the schemas.

The thematic content of the cognitive schemas determines the nature of the affective response and of the behavioral inclinations. Thus, if the content is relevant to danger, then a wish to flee and the feeling of anxiety are experienced. The theme of personal encroachment stimulates anger and the wish to attack. The perception of receiving desired interpersonal "supplies" (such as love) may stimulate feelings of affection and the desire to approach the other person. Perceived disapproval on the other hand produces sadness and often the desire to avoid the other person.

Our view of an individual's interactions with his or her environment, thus, must include a consideration of certain durable characteristics of the individual's personality. These include not only the relatively stable cognitive schemas, but also other personality structures that are relevant to instigating affect and behavior. (In our schematic representation, these structures are integrated with the cognitive structures to form a triad.) In metaphorical terms, we may visualize the cognitive schemas as energized initially and then energizing the motivational, motoric, and affective schemas. In order to make this formulation complete, we should postulate a feedback loop, with data from the motivational and affective schemas being routed back to the cognitive schemas.

The central role of the cognitive structures is expanded in this formulation to include not only energizing the other structures, but also controlling and modulating them. Whether an impulse will be expressed in overt behavior is dependent on the controlling cognitive constellation. The following example illustrates the sequence: An individual, confronted with a possible assault by another person, structures the situation as noxious, and consequently becomes mobilized to attack. The impulse to attack will be transformed into actual behavior, unless the individual decides that counterattack is unwise and that the impulse to do so should be inhibited.

Translating the foregoing example into structural terms, I propose that the activation of the cognitive constellation leads ultimately to the activation of the motor apparatus, which "prepares for action." The feedback to the cognitive schemas triggers a new signal—namely, to control or inhibit action. The result of this interaction is that the organism is mobilized for action, but is prevented by internal controls from carrying it out. It should be noted that the controlling signal does not deactivate the mobilization, which persists. This formulation suggests the need for postulating a system of controls whose functions range from blanket inhibition to sensitive modulation of the impulses. (In a later section, I discuss how modifications in the cognitive constellation can facilitate "demobilization.")

It should be noted that although affect may be stimulated, it has no role in the mobilization for action. Moreover, although the individual may inhibit the inclination to attack, he or she nonetheless experiences anger. Similarly, if the individual carries out the hostile inclinations, he or she also experiences this affect. Furthermore, he or she will continue to experience both the inclination and the affect until there is some modification in the controlling cognitive constellation. This modification, which is discussed below in "Cognitive Therapy of Stress Reactions," results from procedures such as changing the dominant conceptualizations and shifting the cognitive focus.

The fourth principle, thus, is as follows: *Depending on the content of the cognitive constellation, the behavioral inclination may be a desire to flee, attack, approach, or avoid; the corresponding affect would be anxiety, anger, affection, or sadness. The responses can be regarded as organized into structures, with primacy assigned to the controlling cognitive constellation, which activates and controls the behavioral inclinations and the affective response.*

COGNITIVE STRESS AND THINKING DISORDERS

Under ordinary conditions, the activation of the cognitive–behavioral–affective configuration does not cause any particular problems. In fact, the configuration can be viewed as the mechanism for producing the wide range of normal emotions and normal behavior. Under certain circumstances, however, the primitive, egocentric cognitive system is activated (Beck, 1967, pp. 281–290). This activation is likely to occur when the individual perceives that vital interests are at stake. Specific idiosyncratic cognitive schemas become hyperactive if the resultant behavioral and affective mobilization is sufficiently intense or prolonged; distress, conceptual distortions, cognitive dysfunctions, and frequently disturbance of physiological functions such as appetite and sleep are produced.

Although depression, anxiety, and hostility have at times been included in discussions of stress reactions (e.g., Holroyd, 1979), the cognitive organization per se has rarely been singled out as the "target organ" (Beck, 1964, 1976).

Conceptual Distortions

In stress reactions, deviations in the thinking process play a major role. The stress-prone individual is primed to make extreme, one-sided, absolutistic, and global judgments. Since the appraisals tend to be extreme and one-sided, the behavioral inclinations also tend to be extreme. For example, a hostility-prone employer may be primed to react to a relatively minor error by an employee as though it was "criminal negligence," and consequently will be inclined to attack him or her. A person who is prone to have fear reactions may interpret an unfamiliar noise as the firing of a revolver or an earthquake, and will have an overpowering urge to escape. A depression-prone individual may interpret a humorous comment as a rejection and will want to withdraw.

As I have previously pointed out, conditions such as depression have conventionally been regarded as "affective disorders," pure and simple, and cognitive difficulties have been ignored or glossed over (Beck, 1963). Nonetheless, we observe in those conditions a generalized thinking disorder that we attribute to the dominance of the "primitive cognitive system" (Beck, Rush, Shaw, & Emery, 1979, pp. 14–15). Disordered individuals tend to personalize events that are not relevant to them and to interpret their experiences in global, categorical, absolutistic terms. These misconstructions of reality are detectable in the various cognitive distortions, such as polarization, selective abstraction, overgeneralization, and arbitrary inference. Some of these characteristics have been described in the psychoanalytic literature under the concept of "primary-process thinking."

In the primitive mode of thinking, the complexity, variability, and diversity of human experiences are reduced to a few crude categories. In contrast, mature cognition ("secondary-process thinking") integrates stimuli into many dimensions or qualities, is quantitative rather than categorical, and is relativistic rather than absolutistic.

Cognitive Disorganization

The sequential flow of adaptive thinking is disrupted by "mental symptoms" such as preoccupation, perseveration, difficulty in concentration, and forgetfulness, especially in severe stress. A salient feature of these symptoms is the loss of volitional control over the thinking process. Perhaps even more striking is the disruption of crucial cognitive functions such as objectivity and reality testing (see Caplan, 1981).

Impairment of Voluntary Control

It is interesting to note that the characteristics of the primitive cognitive organization are also reflected in the systems relevant to behavioral inclinations, control, and affect. Thus, the content of the impulses tends to be more extreme, and the mechanisms of control also show a dichotomous character. Just as the individual's capacity to "fine-tune" cognitive responses is impaired, so his or her modulation of behavioral inclinations deteriorates into a "choice" between total inhibition and no control at all.

For example, the hostility reaction might be manifested by an inclination to respond to an insult with a violent counterattack and by a reduced control over the impulse. The depressed person has strong regressive desires, such as staying in bed and avoiding constructive action; he or she also has attenuated control over these inclinations. The fearful person has exaggerated impulses to escape from "noxious" stimuli; he or she experiences "overcontrol" (inhibition) of assertiveness and "undercontrol" of the wish to escape.

Another feature of cognitive stress or strain is the relative diminution of what has been described in the psychoanalytic literature as "secondary-process thinking" (Beck *et al.*, 1979, p. 15). Thus, stressed individuals lose, to varying degrees, their capacity to observe their "automatic thoughts" (cognitions) objectively, to reality-test them, and to adjust them to reality. Furthermore, the idiosyncratic cognitions are often so intense that such individuals have difficulty in "turning them off" and shifting their focus to other topics. The processes relevant to reality testing and control have been categorized in the psychoanalytic literature as ego functions.[1]

Erosion of Cognitive Functions

It seems likely that the erosion of "secondary-process" functions is a combination of the preemption of the cognitive organization by the hyperactive idiosyncratic schemas and of "mental fatigue" (depletion of the resources for energizing secondary-process schemas). After long periods of sleep loss or hard mental work, there seems to be not only a weakening of secondary-process thinking, but also a loosening of controls over impulses. These functional impairments are manifested in the phenomena of low stress tolerance.

What situations are likely to lead to the hyperactivity of the idiosyncratic cognitive schemas and impairment of "secondary-process" functions? Generally, either overwhelming traumatic events (such as an unexpected death in the family or a near-fatal accident) or intermittent or chronic, insidious stressors (such as continuous low-grade danger, repeated thwarting or defeats, or continual rejecting behavior from a spouse) lead to cumulative stimulation of the schemas relevant to loss, danger, or rejection, and a concomitant drain on secondary-process functions. It should be noted that different people have different sensitivities, so that situations that are stressful for one person may be innocuous for another person (see Principle 7, below).

A consequence of the hyperactivity of the idiosyncratic schemas is that they become relatively "autonomous": The conceptualization and ruminations are far less under the influence of external stimuli than of internal factors.

In the normal state, the cognitive organization fluctuates—in an adaptive way—between being predominantly "reactive" (i.e., activated and directed by environmental stimuli), "proactive" (forcing environmental stimuli into a preformed mold), and "detached" (walled off from environ-

---

[1]A more complete description of the cognitive organization with specific reference to "primary-process" and "secondary-process" thinking is presented elsewhere (Beck, 1983).

mental stimuli). Thus, a person watching a horror film is predominantly reactive; a door-to-door salesman attempting to sell a product and a child building a mud castle are proactive; and a person daydreaming or thinking through the details of a plan is detached. In severe psychopathology, the ability to shift flexibly from one mode to another is greatly reduced. The individual is "stuck" in one of the modes. Thus, the fearful person stamps each environmental event as dangerous and ruminates about catastrophes; the hostile person indiscriminately labels others' behaviors as encroaching on him or her; the manic person perceives his or her reflected glory in environmental events.

The fifth principle is this: *The stressors lead to a disruption of the normal activity of the cognitive organization. In addition to erosion of the ability to concentrate, recall, and reason, and to control impulses, there is a relative increase in primitive (primary-process) content.*

COGNITIVE CONSTELLATIONS AND SPECIFIC SENSITIVITIES

Granted that there are commonalities in the form of the thinking disturbance in the various stress disorders, how do we account for differences in the content? Why is one person prone to react to life experiences with chronic hostility, another with depression, and a third with severe or chronic anxiety? People differ not only in the type of response to stressors, but also in the kind of stressors to which they overreact. Thus, they are likely to demonstrate an individualized hypersensitivity to specific stressors and to experience a specific pattern of responses. The differences in the types of susceptibility and response patterns may be attributed to differences in cognitive organization, and, in many cases, to differences in personality.

The previous section has described how flaws in thinking are associated with stress. However, it has left unanswered the question as to why these cognitive dysfunctions are evoked by some situations and not by others. The construct, "specific sensitivity," first described by Saul (1947) as "specific emotional vulnerability," applies to the individual's predilection to overreact to certain highly specific situations (specific stressors). My theoretical formulation postulates that the individual has a number of "sensitive" areas, and that when a given situation impinges on one of these areas, he or she is prone to respond cognitively in the kind of relatively crude, categorical form characteristic of "primary-process cognition.'' The idiosyncratic cognitive response sets in motion the motivational systems that may lead to stress.

To illustrate the concept of specific sensitivity, let us take a commonplace example. A young man was bitten by a dog as a child. From that time on, he has responded with anxiety to the sight of *any dog*, to the sound of a dog barking, or even to the picture of a dog. Any stimulus relevant to a dog elicits the thought, ''It will bite my leg off,'' and generally an image of the leg being severed at the calf. He then experiences anxiety and a wish to flee. Thus, the young man reacts to an innocuous stimulus as though it were dangerous. The specific stressor in this case is any dog, and the specific cognitive response is automatic, stereotyped, and undifferentiated. Even though he ''knows'' at one level (the mature cognitive system) that there is no danger, the primitive cognitive system is prepotent for as long as the stimulus is present. Since the reaction disappears after the stimulus is removed, this case would be considered a ''simple phobia'' and would not be regarded as a stress reaction (unless the exposure was prolonged or intense enough to produce a residual dysfunction).

In order to illustrate how a specific sensitivity predisposes an individual to a stress reaction, let us consider the case of a middle-aged man with intense chronic anxiety. The episode of anxiety started shortly after his brother died of a heart attack. He began to have pains in his chest. From that point on, he has been acutely aware of changes in his breathing or heart rate and any perceptible sensations in his chest—all of which make him believe that he is having a heart attack and lead to chest pain (due to splinting of the intercostal muscles), anxiety, and a desire to rush to the hospital. He has a similar reaction when he hears of anybody dying of a heart attack. This case qualifies as a stress reaction, because the psychophysiological effects last after exposure to a stimulus and are represented in continued dysfunctional thinking (''I am in danger of dying''), impaired concentration, chronic feelings of discomfort, and increased heart rate.

This anecdote illustrates how a person responds selectively (fear reaction) to an initial stressor (his brother's death) with hypersensitivity to any stimuli suggestive of coronary disease. The hypersensitivity can be understood in terms of the predominance of a cognitive constellation relevant to the danger of ''instant death.'' This constellation remains prepotent, so that most internal stimuli are scanned for signs of an impending heart attack. Moreover, even external stimuli relevant to the concept of heart attack (such as news of a friend's having a coronary episode) are capable of activating or intensifying his fear.

In summary, the case can be formulated in terms of three constructs:

1. Specific stressor = Stimuli relevant to heart attack.
2. Specific response = Fear of sudden death.
3. Specific dysfunctions = Preoccupation, chest pain, tachycardia.

A wide variety of sensitivities and response patterns may exist. People with a sensitivity to the same stressor may have notably different response patterns; others may have the same type of response, but to dissimilar stimuli. For example, two students studying together may react strongly when they hear a loud noise, such as the backfiring of a car—one with hostility, the other with fear. The first regards the noise as an encroachment; the other perceives it as a danger—namely, gunfire.

Other people might show the same type of response (e.g., fear of bodily damage or death) to quite different stimuli, such as the sight of blood or a barking dog. It is therefore expedient to categorize stress reactions in terms of the cognitive response (fear, hostility, depression) rather than the specific stimulus.

A further word is indicated to explain how a particular cognitive constellation is formed and how it contributes to the specific sensitivity. In the course of development, individuals gradually form a number of concepts ("schemas") about themselves and their world. As these concepts are structuralized, they become embedded in a cluster of related memories, meanings, assumptions, expectations, and rules, which the individuals utilize to process incoming data and to mobilize themselves into action. The related schemas (Beck, 1964) may be so broad and pervasive across situations that they may comprise a major dimension of personality type. On the other hand, the schemas may be relatively narrow and applicable only to a highly specific set of stimuli. If a concept (schema) was formed under stressful conditions, it may assume the characteristic structures of the "primitive cognitive system" (primary-process thinking): rigid, global, categorical, and absolutistic.

To illustrate a primitive concept, let us take the example of the young man who was bitten by the dog. According to the theory I am proposing, the severity of the trauma was responsible not only for the formation of an extremely negative memory of the dog, but also of an extreme unidimensional, undifferentiated construction of the category "dog." The primitive concept has a content such as "All dogs are dangerous." When this schema is activated, dogs are appraised according to only one dimension: not whether they are large or small, frisky or passive, shaggy or smooth-skinned, but whether they are dangerous or safe. Since the schema is categorical and absolutisitc, the specific appraisal excludes the notion "safe." Hence the cognitive response to the sight of any dog is uniform: "This dog is dangerous." This response occurs even when the dog is objectively harmless, geographically remote, or safely chained. Associated with the concept are a number of assumptions and expectations, such as "If it comes closer, it will bite me," and "I won't be able to ward off the attack." Furthermore, several rules (imperatives), such as "You must get to a safe place," "Get ready to be attacked," and "Freeze!" are derived from the concept. Of course, when the primitive schema is not invoked, the individual is capable of responding realistically to the category "dog" (mature cognitive system).

To return to the sequence, any dog is automatically labeled as "dangerous." Since the young man does not believe he has the resources to deal with the danger and believes that the "risk" is high, he experiences the typical fear reaction described previously:

1. He has the expectation of being attacked.
2. He does not believe he can safely counterattack or repel the attack.
3. He becomes mobilized to flee.

If flight does not appear possible, he may "freeze" in order to reduce the probability of the attack, and also to prepare his body to sustain the impact of the expected attack. Concomitantly, he will experience anxiety. "Freezing" may be an anachronistic response stemming from the assumption that a still, silent object will blend into the environment (like an opossum) and thus will not be subject to attack. When freezing occurs in interpersonal encounters, of course, it is highly maladaptive.

It is important to recognize that when a concept or schema is highly structuralized and hypervalent, the power of mature thinking to reality-test the construction, make discriminations, and correct the distortion is greatly diminished. Nonetheless, it is possible in psychotherapy to counterbalance the primitive concept by helping the patient to strengthen and to apply realistic, flexible, multidimensional concepts (secondary-process thinking). As becomes clear later, the task of psychotherapy is much more difficult when the individual has a large assembly of broad primitive concepts organized around a single major theme relevant to a large proportion of his or her experience, such as interpersonal relations.

The sixth principle, thus, is as follows: *Specific primitive cognitive constellations are "chained" to specific stimuli. This pairing constitutes the specific sensitivity of a given individual and prepares the way for inappropriate or excessive reactions. Since people vary widely in their specific sensitivities, what is a stressor for one person may be a benign situation for another.*

STRESS AND PERSONALITY

It may not be difficult to understand how a person can react excessively to a highly specific type of stimulus. However, it is puzzling to observe that certain individuals overreact in a relatively uniform way to a wide variety of apparently dissimilar situations. As we get to know such persons better, we find that most of the situations fit into a pattern. Thus, one individual may react with fear and inhibition when making requests, making a phone call, asking directions, associating with strangers, or traveling alone—in other words, whenever there is any conceivable risk of rejection or isolation. Another person will react with hostility in situations demanding conformity to social norms or institutional requirements. These observations suggest that such people are governed by certain broad expectations and conceptions that they carry with them into every situation. The situations are found to have a common thread—namely, a similar individualized meaning to the person.

In some cases, the individualized meanings seem to pervade every interaction. In structural terms, it appears that a few schemas whose content is relevant to this individualized meaning are activated by the diverse situations.

To illustrate the formulation regarding broad pervasive concepts, we can return to the anecdote of the student who becomes hostile when he hears a loud noise while he is studying. In reviewing his reaction to a multitude of varied life situations, we find that he is extremely sensitive to any characteristic of the situation that represents an incursion on his "life space" or an impediment to his goals. He becomes hostile if interrupted while talking, studying, or daydreaming. He is intolerant of being crowded by other people in restaurants, elevators, or conference rooms. He prefers to sit near the exit in theaters or other public places. He reacts strongly against formal rules, orders, and restrictions. He insists on "leaving his options open" and may, for example, break off a love relationship rather than accept a limitation on his freedom of action.

This individual has a host of related concepts that are applied to all interpersonal as well as impersonal relationships. These are organized into a value system whose theme is fulfillment through action, expression of individuality, and preservation of autonomy. (In contrast, the sociotropic person is oriented to receiving, togetherness, and dependency.) Thus, even minimal encroachment on this system elicits cognitions such as "He is interfering with me," "He is pushing me around," "He is crowding me," "She is trying to trap me," "I am boxed in." These extreme ideas occur, respectively, in interactions as diverse as someone expressing an interest in his work; asking him to participate in a group project; asking personal questions; or expressing love and affection. Situations such as those listed above that might elicit, respectively, gratitude, cooperativeness, friendliness, or affection in other people stir up hostility in this individual.

I have previously described this set of characteristics in proposing that "autonomous depressions" tend to occur in people who would be rated high on the personality dimension of individuality and low on sociality. Such individuals may experience depression if blocked from achieving their goals (Beck, 1983). I have applied the label "autonomous personality" to characterize this "type" of person.

These "autonomous" individuals' conception of other people is slanted toward sensitivity to interference, intrusion, coercion, or restraint. The relevant concept is associated with assumptions and expectations such as "In order to reach my objective, I must do it myself," "If other people interrupt me, I won't be able to do what I have to," "I need breathing space in order to survive," "Since the strong prey on the weak, I must appear strong in every interaction." Some individuals of this type may show exorbitant reactions even when the noxious situation is impersonal or physical (e.g., crawling through a narrow tunnel). For example, a "war hero," who had received many decorations for bravery in World War II, experienced a crippling (and demoralizing) anxiety attack when he attempted to crawl through a large cylinder in an amusement park. The possibility of being immobilized in the cylinder threatened his notion of his autonomy, upon which his concept of his identity was based. He could not tell even his best friend about his emotional reaction, because he was afraid of being ridiculed. It is of interest to note that this paratrooper's heroic exploits had centered around "escaping" from closed-in environments: He had shown extraordinary daring in *jumping* out of aircraft behind enemy lines and in *breaking out* of prison camps.

Clinical observations and some preliminary systematic investigation suggest that the two dimensions of personality are clinically and empirically useful for purposes of exposition. The two dimensions are described in terms of the type of individual who would score high on one and low on the other. The "autonomous type" is an individual whose personality is disproportionally weighted with characteristics of individuality or who would be rated high on individuality and relatively low on sociality; the "socially dependent type" is one who has excessive weight on sociotropism or sociality.

"Individuality" refers to an individual's investment in freedom of action, independence, and mobility. The motif of this cluster is "doing." The sense of well-being for such persons depends on preserving the integrity and autonomy of their domain; on having unrestricted freedom of choice, action, and expression; on directing their own activities; on being free from outside encroachment, restraint, pressure, or interference; and on attaining meaningful goals through action.

"Sociality" or "sociotropism" refers to a person's investment in positive interchange with other people. The motif of this cluster is "receiving." This cluster includes passive, receptive wishes such as the desire for acceptance, intimacy, understanding, support, and guidance, and feedback from other people for purposes of validation of beliefs and behavior. Such individuals are dependent on these social inputs not only for the gratification that they bring, but also as a means of motivating and directing their own behavior and helping them to modify ideas and behaviors in order to receive more social approval and avoid social disapproval.

Recent clinical studies suggest that two types of depression are associated with these two dimensions of personality. Individuals who are high on one of the dimensions have a different set of symptoms and vulnerabilities than do those who score high on the other dimensions (Beck, 1983). I have observed that the "autonomous type" of person is more prone than the "socially dependent" type to experience acute or chronic hostility, claustrophobia, anorexia nervosa, and "endogenous depression." The sociotropic type of person is more likely to experience "reactive depression," anxiety, and agoraphobia. From the description of the individual types, we can conclude that the autonomous type is more sensitive to restraint, encroachment, and defeat, the sociotropic type is more susceptible to rejection, abandonment, and deprivation.

The difference in the two personality types may be understood in terms of the differing sets of rules, expectancies, and imperatives incorporated in their cognitive organizations. The rules governing the behavior of the autonomous personality include, "I must fight for my rights," "I must not let people get in my way," "I should push people away if they start to crowd me," "I mustn't let a person get away with crossing me." The application of these rules mobilize such individuals to fight their way out of situations that symbolize traps to them; to attack people who appear to restrain, coerce, or encroach on them; and to resort to flight if fighting is not possible. If the individuals are overmobilized or are unable to "demobilize" through action, then they are prone to experience stress reactions.

This personality type illustrates how an individual may have a sensitivity to a wide range of stimuli. Such persons may be vulnerable to stress reactions unless they can arrange their social or impersonal environments in such a way as to protect their privacy and independence and insure the attainment of their goals. Such individuals may compensate for their sensitivities in their customary life situations, but are traumatized when their environment is radically changed—for example, when they are inducted into the Army, get married, are jailed, or are thwarted or demoted in their jobs.

The origin of this particular cognitive organization differs from one person to another, but a typical case might show the following background: An active, action-oriented child strikes out against boundaries set by parents, teachers, and even peer groups. He or she forms a concept of parents and other authority figures as obstructionistic and coercive. It seems to the child that the more he or she presses against the boundaries, the more rigid and constraining they become. The child's concern about threats to his or her freedom and autonomy spreads to his or her entire social and physical environment. If this individual's life situation restricts freedom of mobility, expression, and choice, he or she is susceptible to stress reaction.

A traveling salesman, for example, began to experience anxiety attacks after his engagement. For several years after marriage, he was depressed and complained that his wife had trapped him into the marriage and then cemented him in by having several children. He attributed his lack of advancement in his career to the necessity to restrict his sales territory to the immediate area. The patient had volunteered for active duty during the Korean War. Shortly after his induction, he had begun to experience great hostility toward all of his officers. These reactions had continued until he was discharged for severe chronic headaches. It was clear that his psychological problem stemmed from his extremely low threshold for any type of restriction on his mobility and freedom of action.

The second cluster of personality patterns revolves around the dimension of sociality. When the sociotropic structure is particularly prominent, it is useful to think in terms of the "socially dependent type" as analogous to the autonomous type. This type of person is exquisitely sensitive to rejection, exclusion, separation, and "abandonment." He or she believes that "Life is not meaningful without love," "I can't live unless I have people around who care," "If a person is unkind to me, there is something wrong with me." Since this type has been described extensively elsewhere (Beck, 1983), I do not elaborate further here.

The typical background of an individual dominated primarily by sociotropic patterns would be as follows: As a child, this individual was driven to receive affection, nurturance, and praise. Although the mother was a "giving" person, older siblings whom the child admired tormented and rejected him or her. The hypersensitivity to rejection that resulted undermined the child's receiving full acceptance into his or her peer group. From adolescence on, the individual has "felt like a loner," and although he or she may have achieved the symbols of success—prestige in a career and a devoted family—he or she has continually sought praise and reassurance and is hypersensitive to rejection and separation.

The seventh principle, thus, is this: *Differences in personality organization account for some of the wide variations in individual sensitivities to stressors. Thus, the autonomous and sociotropic personality types differ in the type of stressors to which they are sensitive. The occurrence of a stress reaction, thus, is contingent to a large degree on specific vulnerabilities related to personality.*

STRESS SYNDROMES

When the schemas have been overstimulated for long enough to produce the symptoms of a well-defined disorder, the term "syndrome" may be applied to designate the triad consisting of the cognitive constellation, behavioral inclination, and affect.

There are a variety of syndromes involved in the stress reaction; only three are described at this point. A characteristic of all the syndromes is that once the cognitive constellation becomes overactive, it tends to select and process stimuli that are congruent with it, a process described by Mahoney (1982) as "feed-forward." As a result of extracting only congruent stimuli, the cognitive constellation continues to be hyperactive or becomes more active. Thus, individuals who are fixated on ideas of personal danger are likely to scan their environment for signs of potential harm and to misread innocuous events as dangerous. Consequently, the notion of imminent harm becomes progressively greater. Similarly, the tendency of depressed patients to direct their attention to negative events and to misinterpret or blot out positive events intensifies their negative constructions of their experience. The same vicious cycle may be observed in acute hostile reactions. As hostile individuals misinterpret successive events as challenges or affronts, they are more likely to interpret subsequent neutral occurrences in the same way.

In the "hostility syndrome," individuals are hypersensitive to any events that suggest restraint, interference, assault, or encroachment on their domain (Beck, 1976, pp. 64–75). They may, for example, respond to even gentle suggestions with the idea that they are being controlled, and they are thus stimulated to "counterattack." As indicated earlier, any threat to the domain may evoke the hostility "fight" reaction if such individuals place a higher premium on attacking—or counterattacking—than on the possible risks or costs. The affect associated with hostility reactions may range from mild irritation to intense anger or rage. A key component in the hostility syndrome, therefore, is these individuals' belief that they have the resources to oppose or punish the presumed restrictions, encroachments, or affronts. Unlike individuals with the fear or depressive syndromes, they are not concerned about their inability to negate adverse reactions to their aggressive behavior.

In the "fear syndrome," individuals are hyperreactive to any situation that represents danger to them. Their state of arousal is manifested by a desire to flee to a safe place or to inhibit any behavior that does not ostensibly facilitate reducing the danger. This inhibition, manifested by "freezing," "choking up," or "blocking," is anachronistic and, indeed, generally increases the danger; it is related to a total focusing on the danger and an automatic blotting out of any other cognitions, including coping strategies. It is seen most frequently in interpersonal situations such as public speaking, taking tests, or initiating social contacts. While some aspects of this automatic inhibition may have had adaptive value in earlier stages of evolution of the species, it is maladaptive in contemporary life. Thus, the disorder is best viewed in terms of an activation of an anachronistic mechanism of defense, rather than as a "neurotic" reaction. Since the emotion associated with this fear syndrome is anxiety, the subsyndromes are generally referred to as "public-speaking anxiety," "test anxiety," or "social anxiety." Although the syndromes are named after the associated affects, they could be labeled more precisely according to the nature of the cognitive constellation—for example, "public-speaking fear," "fear of being tested," or "social fear."

The "depression syndrome" is more complex than the two previously described syndromes and consists of a variety of possible cognitive constellations, behavioral inclinations, and affects. The relationship of the controlling cognitive constellation to the characteristic affects has been described previously (Beck, 1967, 1976). In brief, the prevailing cognitive constellation in depression has a content relevant to sense of loss, thwarting, or defeat and is reflected in negative attitudes toward the self, the future, and external events. The cognitive schemas become prepotent and activate tendencies to withdraw, give up, and become passive. These tendencies may become accentuated because of the "deenergizing" or inhibition of the drives toward goal-directed activity.

Suicidal impulses are directly derived from hopelessness, which is a component of the cognitive constellation. Since hopelessness and the derivative suicidal wishes occur in conditions other than depression, these particular psychological phenomena should not be considered to be exclusive properties of the depressive syndrome.

The eighth principle, thus, is as follows: *Each of the stress syndromes (such as hostility, anxiety, and depression) consists of hyperactive schemas with an idiosyncratic content specific for that syndrome. Each syndrome comprises a specific controlling cognitive constellation and the resultant behavioral inclinations and affect.*

THE "INTERNAL STRESSOR"

We can observe that individuals may develop typical stress reactions when there are no external conditions to account for them. In such cases, the origin of the stress may be internal and consist of such phenomena as the demands the individuals place on themselves, their repetitive self-nagging, and their self-reproaches.

A stereotype of one kind of person prone to this form of self-stressing is the "typical" hard-driving business person or scientist. Such persons set high goals and drive themselves and others in order to achieve them. Their outward behavior reflects their system of goals and beliefs, which leads to a constant state of tension. Although there may be no objective evidence of pressure from the outside, such patients' occupations present problems for them because of the way they perceive their work.

Since they regard each specific task as a major confrontation, they are continually driving, nagging, and pressing themselves. Their self-imposed psychological stress is accompanied by overloading of one or more of their psychophysiological systems.

The excessive momentum behind the work drive may be such persons' chronic concern that they will not reach their goals, or that they or their subordinates will make costly errors. These "worried achievers" react to each new task with strong doubts. They exaggerate the importance or the difficulty of a task (faulty cognitive appraisal) and underestimate their capacity to deal with it (also a faulty cognitive appraisal). Not only do they magnify the obstacles to completing a task, but they also exaggerate the consequences of failure. They may, for example, visualize a chain of events leading to bankruptcy whenever the outcome of a particular financial venture is uncertain. These individuals are predisposed to excessive tension, because they exaggerate not only the dire *consequences* of falling short of their goals, but also the *probability* of these consequences occurring.

These "irritable achievers" are also in a continuous state of tension because of what they conceive of as unnecessary obstacles in the path toward their goal. They are prone to experience hostility toward their coworkers or subordinates whenever their systems fail to operate at maximum efficiency. Alternatively, they will reproach themselves savagely if they perceive that they have been inefficient or negligent. The system may be so important that the "end" becomes more important than the means.

Thus, the ninth principle is this: *The principal stressor may be internal, with no apparent referent in the outside world. The assumption that the only road to fulfillment is through total success is intrinsic in achievement-oriented persons prone to stress reactions.*

RECIPROCAL INTERACTION MODEL OF STRESS

In the discussion up to this point, I have regarded the patterning of stress reactions in terms of the responses of single individuals to external stimuli. For purposes of convenience, I have not dealt with the way in which individuals may develop stress reactions in response to complicated interrelationships with other people in their environment.

Stress does not occur in a vacuum. When we look at the interpersonal relations of stressed individuals, we realize that their behavior evokes responses from other people, which are fed back to them and stimulate further responses in them. Ordinarily, interpersonal responses are modulated in such a way as to minimize the amount of friction among people, and also the degree of disturbance within individuals. Thus, people operate as though they have a kind of "thermostat" that regulates their behavior. When these adjustments in behavior do not occur in an adaptive way, the stage is set for stress in individuals and/or in the persons with whom they are interacting (see Lazarus, 1981).

Cognitive–Behavioral Interactions

A more comprehensive reciprocal or interactional model demands the inclusion of cognitive structuring. Thus, an individual structures a particular situation with another person in a specific way. The individual's structuring of the situation will lead to a particular behavior. His or her behavior is interpreted in a specific way by the other person, who then manifests a behavioral response to this interpretation. Thus we get a continuous cycling of cognition→behavior→cognition→behavior.

For example, Bob thinks that it would be nice to do something with Harry and makes a request for Harry. Harry reacts to the overt behavior (the request) with his own idiosyncratic interpretation—"He is making an unwarranted demand"—and starts to criticize Bob for his "demandingness." Bob responds to this critical behavior with the interpretation, "He is treating me unfairly. I would certainly fulfill *his* request. I can't let him get away with this." He then verbally counterattacks.

Harry responds cognitively with the notion, "This guy is useless to me; I might as well write him off," and tells Bob, "Look, we just can't get along. Why don't we call the whole thing off?" Bob's cognitions then run something like this: "Harry is being unreasonable. He regards me as a pushover. I can't let him get away with it, or other people will think they can push me around." Bob then becomes overmobilized for further attack. At this point, what he says will be insufficient to restore his mobilization to a baseline level. Consequently, the state of overmobilization persists for a period of time.

This kind of overmobilization is the immediate factor in producing stress. If sustained and repeated over a long enough period, the individual's reactions may move from a heightened activity in the neuroendocrine system to specific physiological dysfunctions.

The Egocentric Mode

As pointed out previously, when people consider their vital interests to be at stake, they are likely to shift into the egocentric mode. The egocentric mode organizes present, past, and future situations or events predominantly in terms of how they affect the individuals' own vital interests. Since such individuals are focused on the meanings of the events to them, the meanings of other persons are not part of their phenomenal field. Even when they attempt to view situations from the standpoints of other persons, they will—as long as they are in the egocentric mode—come up with interpretations that are heavily laden with the meanings the events have for *them.*

In interpersonal relations, clashes are likely to occur when each individual is operating solely within the egocentric mode. Even though an individual may have no desire to hurt—and, indeed, may even want to help—his or her egocentricity places a burden on the other person and ultimately on himself. A clash is inevitable when both individuals view things according to their highly personalized formulations. Their constructions of their own behavior and that of the other person's behavior will inevitably lead to a conflict of interest.

The stressful nature of interactions is well illustrated in the form of the widely recognized frictions that develop in marital relations. The stressful interactions derived from marital conflict serve as a model to exemplify the mutually reinforcing nature of stressors.

A couple demonstrated completely different cognitive sets in the following situation: The wife asked the husband to stay home with her on a particular night because she felt sick. He refused, because he had already committed himself to spend the evening with a business colleague. They then slipped into such a screaming match that each started to think seriously about getting a divorce.

On explanation, it became apparent that each partner was not only viewing the disagreement in egocentric terms but was "catastrophizing." The wife's thoughts were these: "If he won't do this small favor for me, how can I count on him when I have a major problem? It shows I can't count on him for anything." The husband's interpretation was this: "She is completely unreasonable. She won't give me any freedom. She looks for any excuse to keep me home. If I have to give in, I can't survive."

This anecdote illustrates several charcteristics of the egocentric mode. First, neither person was aware of the meaning conveyed by his or her behavior to the spouse. Second, each believed that his or her interpretation of the event was so valid that its reasonableness should be apparent to anybody. The wife, for example, was convinced that her husband's noncompliance with minor requests proved that she would not be able to rely on him for help when she needed it. The husband believed that compliance with the "small request" would place him in a straitjacket. Third, because the egocentric mode precludes the possibility of integrating crucial interpersonal feedback, that is, understanding the spouse's perspective, each individual was prone to attempt maladaptively to force the spouse to accept his or her frame of reference. The result was that each partner became frozen in his or her own perspective.

It is interesting that the egocentric mode tends to highlight certain dominant personality patterns. In the preceding example, the husband, who had a strong autonomous bent, needed to maintain a certain freedom of action in his relationships. His specific vulnerability was "being tied down." The wife, on the other hand, had a strong sociotropic–dependent pattern, and consequently was especially sensitive to being left alone. A continued abrasion of the sensitive areas could lead to stress in either or both partners.

The therapeutic approach in this case would consist of "decentering" (to use Piaget's term) each individual's perspective, and facilitating his or her awareness of the mate's perspective. This procedure would require delicate handling by the therapist, because the perspective of one or both partners might be relatively idiosyncratic and might be regarded by the other spouse as either "unreasonable" or "ridiculous."

Framing

When people view other people with whom they are in conflict, they tend to make an appraisal, not only of the others' behavior, but of the other persons themselves. Generally, the type of actions that people consider to be most typical of these others or most salient in terms of their interaction with them are transformed into images or concepts of the other individuals. For example, somebody who is regarded as acting deviously will emerge in an image as a "sneak" or "cheat." In the preceding example, the husband pictured his wife as a demanding, needy, rigid person, the wife visualized the husband as a self-centered, insensitive, undependable person.

"Framing" consists of focusing on some characteristic one attributes to another person and portraying this individual in such a way that this attribute dominates the picture of that person. The term "frame" is applied to the specific image or concept of an individual with whom one is in conflict.

The frame not only reduces a highly complex individual to a few negative character traits, but manufactures additional elements to flesh out the image (which inevitably is a distortion or caricature of the other person). It is possible to have more than one frame of another person: A wife may see her husband at one time as kind and generous, and at other times as selfish and rejecting. The wife in this instance becomes sensitized to certain types of behavior, which she correlates with the negative attributes. When a particular instigating event occurs, the frame that is anchored to that type of stimulus is aroused. For example, whenever the husband places a priority on *his* interests, the wife is prone to visualize him as a bully.

Polarization

As the couple in the "framing" example discuss their opposing wishes, they become increasingly angry at one another. Moreover, as their discussion progresses, they take more extreme, inflexible, opposing positions. We see two interacting phenomena—"external polarization" (moving further apart in their expressed opinions) and "internal polarization" (thinking more negatively of each other).

Their view of each other becomes increasingly more negative until it is finally hardened into a specific frame. The view is expressed also in a vague image, which may be verbalized as follows:

Husband: She is weak, demanding, incapable of helping herself. She is mush, a weakling.
Wife: He is insensitive, ruthless, rejecting, inconsiderate.

The negative constructions by the husband lead him to withdraw more. This behavior in turn is "processed" cognitively by the wife as rejection and abandonment, and leads her to become more dependent, clinging, scolding—and ultimately depressed. He structures her depressed behavior as a manipulation to induce guilt and force him to comply. Thus, he wants even more to be free of her.

The cognitive processing by each person takes on the characteristics of a thinking disorder of the neuroses: extreme unrealistic evaluations of the other person, selective abstraction of data consistent with the "frame" each person has imposed on the other, ablation of favorable data by inattention or forgetting, misinterpretation of the other's behavior, and attribution of unworthy motives to explain the other's behavior.

To describe the phenomena of the interaction, the model must be expanded still further. The cognitive structuring does not lead directly to overt behavior. Interposed between the cognitive process and behavior, there is the motivational component labeled "behavioral inclination." The behavioral inclination emerges from the cognitive constellation in the form of a wish to scold, demand, complain, withdraw, and punish. The overt behavior (speech) of one spouse is consequently tinged with phrases, inflections, and tones that connote disapproval and devaluation of the other spouse.

The tenth principle is as follows: *Stressful interactions with other people occur in a mutually reinforcing cycle of maladaptive cognitive reactions. Specific mechanisms such as the egocentric cognitive mode, framing, and polarization lead to increased mobilization and consequently to stress.*

THE UNITARY PSYCHOPHYSIOLOGICAL SYSTEM

An individual may show the same type of response, regardless of whether the noxious stimulus is physical or abstract (psychosocial): The person responds in much the same way to a psychosocial challenge, threat, or injury as he or she does to an actual physical confrontation or attack (see Wolff, 1950).

To illustrate, let us examine one of these "real-life dramas." A man was shoved in a ticket line by somebody wanting to move the line along. As he felt the pressure on his back, he became mobilized to counterattack: His voluntary muscles became tense, and he experienced an increase in heart rate and blood pressure as he braced himself to push back the offender. Now consider a situation in which one of his coworkers was pressing him to speed up his work. The individual experienced *the same type of physical pressure across his back* as when he was shoved in line. Moreover, he felt the same wish and bracing of his muscles to push away his coworker.

The crucial observation is that our protagonist became mobilized to counteract the challenge in the same fashion (voluntary nervous system, autonomic nervous system) when he was "pressured" to do something he did not want to do as when he was threatened with or subjected to physical pressure from an adversary. Although it may be conceded that there might be some adaptational benefit in preparing to defend oneself against physical encroachments (such as being shoved), there seems little benefit from this total kind of physical mobilization when an adequate response would be a verbal statement employing only the muscles of articulation: "Leave me alone," "Get off my back," "I don't want to do it."

Why do people who are confronted with minor psychosocial challenges respond unnecessarily with a mobilization of the fight–flight apparatus when their conscious desire is simply to utter a few words? Certainly, the total mobilization is at best superfluous and at worst self-destructive. It seems that even though humans are generally well trained to respond overtly in an appropriate "civilized" way to minor challenges, they are nontheless the victims of an inherited primitive response system. Although they may have a well-functioning system of controls to keep the primitive responses in check, they nonetheless have to contend continually with being mobilized for aggressive action far in excess of the demands of the real situations.

If our protagonist is "attacked" verbally—say, by somebody insulting him—he may experience an urge to strike the offender just as though he has been attacked physically. These examples indicate that there is an equivalence between the abstract, verbal stimulus and the concrete physical stimulus. The initial response to both psychosocial or physical transgressions is identical: Each elicits an impulse to counterattack physically. Irrespective of the concreteness or symbolic nature of the transgression, there is a basic physical response.

It is easy to confirm the observation that individuals who have hostile reactions generally experience tightening of their shoulder, arm, back, or leg muscles, even though they may not be aware of the "behavioral inclination" to use these muscles against an adversary. With introspection, individuals who are retaliating verbally may recognize a concomitant impulse to strike their adversaries. In the disorders characterized by chronic muscular tension, it is important to determine whether individuals are experiencing this kind of behavioral inclination to defend themselves or to counterattack.

The reactions of the fear syndrome are analogous to those of the hostility syndrome. The noxious stimulus may be a threat of psychological injury (e.g., betrayal) or of physical injury (e.g., being stabbed in the back). Such persons may respond verbally, for example, by shouting, "How can you do this to me?" *and* physically by an impulse to protect themselves or to flee. The typical reactions of the voluntary and the autonomic nervous systems occur, irrespective of whether the fear is of an abstract (e.g., psychosocial) injury or a concrete (physical) injury. Such individuals become mobilized for self-protection or flight, irrespective of the abstractness or concreteness of the danger.

The similarities in response to either a psychosocial or a physical stimulus suggest the presence of a generalized meaning that encompasses both types of stimulus. In the hostile reaction, the generalized meaning occurs in the form of an idea such as "That person is transgressing against me." In the fear reaction, the meaning assumes a general form such as "I am in danger of having a damaging experience."

An encroachment on or danger to the physical integrity of an individual would appear logically to be more serious than a transgression or threat to an individual's psychological status. This notion is exemplified in the old saw, "Sticks and stones will break my bones, but words will never hurt me." Despite the common-sense utility of such a saying, the *meaning* of a verbal assault is so close to that of a physical assault that the same cognitive and motor systems are activated in response to each stimulus.

This formulation suggests that in our "civilized" society, the symbolic meanings of countless social interactions are continuously arousing us to fight, defend, or flight. It seems plausible that, since we rarely allow this arousal to be transformed into physical action, our voluntary and autonomic nervous systems are continuously overloaded. Beyond a certain point, this overloading leads to a stress reaction.

The eleventh principle, thus, is this: *An individual experiences an inclination to respond physically, although the stimulus may be psychosocial or symbolic and although ultimate overt behavior is verbal. The mobilization for "fight–flight" involves the same cognitive–motoric systems, irrespective of whether the level of meaning of a threat or challenge is "physical" or psychosocial.*

COGNITIVE THERAPY OF STRESS REACTIONS

RELIEF OF SYMPTOMS

To understand the cognitive approach to treatment of stress reactions, let us take a commonplace example and see how this problem would be approached.

Mr. A is a hard-driving businessman who has hypertension, headaches, and a sleep disturbance. Every day he leaves his house early—at 7 A.M.—in order to avoid the heavy traffic. However, by the time he arrives at his office half an hour later, his face is red, he is perspiring, his pulse is racing, and he has a headache. What has happened in the interim?

The following scenario is elicited. Although Mr. A believes that he has simply been driving his car to work, it is apparent that he himself *has been driven* by forces that he is only dimly aware of. Practically every second of his trip, he is engaged in sequences of confrontations and challenges with other drivers. The competitive struggle leads him to cut in and out of lanes and to attempt to get the jump on the other drivers at stop signals. He believes that the other drivers are similarly trying to beat him, and he is impelled to counterattack if one of them does get an advantage.

Aside from his competitive reactions, Mr. A has his own goal of making the best possible time. He reacts to any loss of momentum as though he were blocked by a major barrier. He mentally or orally attacks a slow driver who impedes forward progress. He regards it as a personal defeat if he does not beat out a signal before it turns red.

It is apparent that Mr. A—far from simply traveling to work—has been engaged in a kind of survival course. His maneuverng has not been a game, but rather a series of fierce encounters. He is mobilized for aggressive physical action, as manifested by his muscular tension, increased blood pressure, and increased heart rate. Since he has no opportunity to transform the mobilization into action, by the time he reaches the office his muscles are taut and he is coiled, prepared to strike. However, there is no opportunity to engage in the kind of physical action that would facilitate "demobilization." Moreover, since his cognitive set revolves around the notion of "attack," he is prone to interpret further encounters in terms of this construct, and then to remain in a state of mobilizaton.

If we take this example as the prototype of a stress reaction, let us consider how the cognitive approach can be applied to alleviate his symptoms.

Rationale

The first step in the management of stress reactions is the application of the principles outlined in the first part of this chapter to understanding the case. The case needs to be formulated in terms of the theoretical framework, and then the appropriate strategies and techniques can be developed and utilized.

The basic model that provides the rationale for the treatment is that certain idiosyncratic cognitive patterns become hyperactive and lead to overmobilization of the voluntary nervous system and autonomic nervous system. Concurrently, the system of buffers and adaptive functions (objectivity, perspective, reality testing) becomes strained and is progressively less effective in counteracting the dominance of the controlling cognitive constellation. The direct result of the overmobilization may be experienced in terms of the "syndromes" (e.g., anxiety reaction or hostility reaction) or psychosomatic disorders. In the latter disorders, the physical effects are observable in dysfunction of specific systems or organs (musculoskeletal, cardiovascular, gastrointestinal, etc.).

The overall aim of therapy is to reduce the hyperactivity of the controlling cognitive constellations and to shore up the adaptive functions. An initial direct approach is to reduce the exposure to situations that serve as stressors (i.e., that serve to increase or maintain the stimulation of controlling cognitive constellations). An example of environmental modification would be for a harassed worker to take time away from the job or to stop driving to work. As the overactivity of the cognitive constellation is reduced, there is not only a reduced mobilization of the neuromuscular–endocrine system, but also a relative increase in the adaptive functions, particularly objectivity and perspective. As the individual's total involvement in the immediate work-related stimuli is reduced, the person is then able to reflect upon his or her reactions, recognize overreactions, test some of his or her conclusions, and adopt a broader view regarding his or her realistic problems. When this approach is systematized, the specific cognitive techniques are used: identifying automatic thoughts, recognizing and correcting cognitive distortions, and identifying the broad beliefs and assumptions that underlie the hyperactive constellations.

Clarifying and Defining the Problem

It is important to recognize that although we might label Mr. A's symptoms manifestations of a "stress reaction," environmental stressors—as we generally conceive of them—are not present. If we think simply in terms of external factors, we are hard put to explain why Mr. A experiences his trip as more stressful than the other drivers do. In order to give him an understanding of his problem, we need to encourage him to examine the internal factors: his thoughts, impulses, and feelings. It is especially important to grasp the workings of the "internal stressor" (Principle 9).

Understanding the Meanings. Mr. A needs to become aware, first of all, that his driving has surplus meanings. He is not fully conscious of how he is driven to fight off the other drivers, nor does he see the connection between his combativeness on the road and his symptoms. By preparing himself to observe his attitudes and reactions, he is enabled to make the crucial observations during his next trip. Once he is prepared to observe, he can delineate the pattern of challenge, confrontation, and competition, as well as his reactions to any difficulty as though it were a major barrier. He is able to see that he has layered a heavy web of meanings onto the relatively easy task of driving his car to work. This overload of meanings (and their association with primary-process thinking) leads to the over-mobilization manifested in his stress symptoms: increased heart rate, increased blood pressure, and headache. Moreover, he can see the carryover of these cognitive patterns; throughout his working day, he reacts to each encounter as though he is engaged in hand-to-hand combat.

Recognizing Egocentrism and Cognitive Distortions. One of the most important characteristics for Mr. A to detect is his own egocentrism. He views all events as though he were the central character in a drama; the behavior of all the other characters has meaning only insofar as he relates it to his own "vital interests." He personalizes events that are essentially impersonal, and perceives confrontations and challenges when others are conducting their own lives oblivious of him. The egocentric mode can be viewed as responsible for Mr. A's way of interpreting events in terms of factors such as survival, and attaching extreme negative labels to other drivers.

Once Mr. A understands the problem, he can understand the rationale for various therapeutic maneuvers. To summarize, the steps in formulating the case and understanding the problem are as follows: First, Mr. A must recognize that crucial components of stress are *internal* (i.e., idiosyncratic meanings are attached to events). Second, he must pinpoint the overall idiosyncratic meaning (e.g., that he is prepared for combat). Third, he must focus attention on the overmobilization (muscular tension with vegetative sensations). Fourth, he must connect the meaning ("combat") with the behavioral inclination ("beat them out") and the affect (anger, etc.). Finally, he must recognize how "vital interests" are injected into mundane situations because of the egocentric frame of reference.

Increasing Objectivity

"Objectivity" refers to the capacity of individuals to examine their thinking, motivations, and behavior as though they were disinterested observers. It is essential that patients attain "distance" from their reactions, so that they can look at their experiences as phenomena rather than be totally absorbed by them. Then they may be able to recognize that their thoughts and conclusions are inferences, not facts—that their beliefs are derived from an internal process and are not pure images of external reality. They would consequently realize that, since their cognitive processes are fallible, they may have been accepting misinterpretations, distortions, and exaggerations as "truth." Further, they can observe that the laws and rules that they apply to themselves and others are not immutable, natural laws (like the laws of gravity and thermodynamics), but are often arbitrary and self-defeating.

With increasing objectivity they can recognize that the meanings and significances of events are "man-made" and do not occur independently in nature. Although they do not voluntarily attach irrelevant and self-defeating meanings to events, it is possible to undo the meaning-assignment—to strip away the excess baggage from events.

It is worth emphasizing that simply taking a history and asking the "right" questions increases objectivity (and perspective). As a therapist probes for meanings, a patient spontaneously begins to question the validity of his or her conclusions and to see the symptoms "in a new light."

Increasing Perspective

"Gaining perspective" refers to individuals' expanding the frames by which they judge events, themselves, and others. The expanded frame of reference facilitates seeing an event in a broader vista. By applying a calibrated measurement, individuals can obtain a more relative concept of magnitude, seriousness, and duration. In contrast, people who have lost perspective think in absolute terms—as though the present instance is of utmost importance and will go on forever.

With increasing perspective, Mr. A can see that beating other drivers and getting to work fast is relatively unimportant—not a life and-death struggle—and can further realize that the encounter with other drivers is time-limited and not a part of a continuous war. The conceptualizations involved in a broader perspective are far more complex and involve many more kinds of shading than those derived from the narrow egocentric frame of reference.

Expanding boundaries means not only processing more information, but also forming conceptualizations that are more heterogeneous and contain contradictory elements. For example, other people may simultaneously feel friendly toward Mr. A and wary of him; they have a blend of positive and negative characteristics. Moreover, his beliefs are becoming more dimensional and less absolutistic. Thus, he introduces uncertainty into his belief that other drivers are out to get him.

Moreover, he extends the concept of time so that an upsetting incident does not preempt his view of the past and the future, but is just a point on a time continuum. The increasing *time perspective* helps to reduce the exaggerated significances.

Shifting or Damping Cognitive Set

The crucial element in facilitating demobilization of the neuroendocrine system is changing the cognitive set. Each time Mr. A goes out to his car, a specific cognitive set is induced—that is, his view of his world shifts from a relatively peaceful, harmonious outlook during breakfast to an expectation of confrontation and competition. Since this cognitive set is not fixed, it is possible to change it. All of the techniques listed below involve his changing from a combative to a noncombative "frame of mind."

The cognitive set is the final product of the network of associated attitudes, expectations, memories, and meanings that are activated by a given situation. This set may be induced by specific situations, such as Mr. A's trip to work, or it may be relatively stable across all situations, as when a person is depressed. In the earlier portion of this chapter, I apply the term "controlling cognitive constellation" to designate the basic cognitive structures (schemas) that are reflected in the cognitive set. Although the structures are out of awareness, the individual has access to the content represented in the set. Changing the cognitive set may be achieved by changing the nature of the environmental stimuli, by transferring attention to a different set of stimuli, or by subjecting the content of the set to logical and empirical analysis.

The cognitive set induced by specific stimuli may also be conceptualized as consisting of a composite of primary and secondary appraisals. Thus, therapeutic work may be directed toward modifying the conception of threat or challenge ("primary appraisal") or toward the evaluation of coping resources ("secondary appraisal"). The validity of the primary and secondary appraisals is tested by subjecting them to a series of questions: What is the evidence of a threat? How serious is it? What coping resources are available? The individual also can reduce exaggerated threats through "coping self-statements" (Ellis, 1962; Goldfried, 1977; Meichenbaum, 1977; Novaco, 1975; Turk, Meichenbaum, & Genest, 1983).

Environmental Change. Since the stimuli from driving in traffic lead to the arousal of a specific combative pattern, another mode of travel might eliminate this source of stimulation. For example, if Mr. A takes the train to work, he is removed from the specific situation that led to the mobilization. A person who is overinvolved in the demands or obligations of business or family might seek a "change of scenery" by taking a vacation.

Diversion. Mr. A can attempt to shift his attention away from the other drivers, from thinking about competition, and so on. Thus, the therapist might suggest that he focus on listening to an audiotape or to the radio, or observe features of his environment to which he had been oblivious. The diversion vitiates the power of the cognitive set and thus reduces the frequency and intensity of Mr. A's hostile inferences regarding confrontations and challenges.

Relaxation. Using a technique such as Edmund Jacobson's progressive relaxation (1938) may serve several purposes. By training Mr. A to relax during his journey, it is possible that there may be a damping down of the physiological arousal—as Jacobson claims. Furthermore, relaxation sessions during the day may also lower the level of arousal.

Beyond the obvious purposes of relaxation, it is probable that this procedure helps to modify the cognitive set. Certainly, focusing on relaxing the muscles can divert Mr. A from his overvigilant attention to the other drivers. In addition, the instruction by the therapist to relax conveys a powerful meaning, such as "Things are not as serious as I make them out to be," "I can just sit back and take it easy," "It's not desirable to keep driving myself." Since the motive force behind the tension is the drive to *action*, the assignment to relax activates cognitive structures relevant to *inaction* and *passivity*.

Cognitive Restructuring and Reality Testing

The techniques of cognitive modification are aimed at improving a patient's way of processing information and, consequently, his or her grasp of reality. Take, for example, Mr. A's notion that the other drivers are trying to beat him out or to obstruct his progress. A series of questions could be raised: (1) What is the evidence for this conclusion? (2) Is there evidence that contradicts this conclusion? (3) Are there alternative explanations for their presumed hostile behavior?

The joint inquiry between therapist and patient has been labeled "collaborative empiricism" elsewhere (Hollon & Beck, 1979). The technique consists of framing a conclusion as a hypothesis, which is then jointly investigated. By assuming an investigative role, the therapist encourages the patient to view his or her ideas as conclusions or inferences to be examined, rather than as beliefs to be defended. The approach has the benefit of increasing the patient's objectivity and reality testing—functions previously ascribed to the "secondary process."

For example, after Mr. A has been asked to look for evidence either consistent with or contradictory to his notion that the other drivers were trying to beat him out (or obstruct him), he may report the following incident: "There was a truck ahead of me. I thought it was deliberately trying to block me. So I gunned my engine to pass it. Then I noticed the driver was busy talking to his buddy and didn't even notice me." By looking for evidence, he can recognize that, far from engaging in a battle with him, the drivers of other vehicles are not even aware of him. This observation not only can correct a misconception, but can also help shake his egocentric perspective—a process I call "decentering." His discovery that his attribution of malicious intent was wrong fits into the concept of "disattribution." The cognitive techniques of examining the evidence, looking for alternative explanations, and disattribution have been described in detail in previous writings (Beck, 1963; Beck *et al.,* 1979).

Recognizing and Correcting Dysfunctional Cognitions. Patients with stress reactions show the kinds of deviations in information processing and logical thinking that have been described previously in terms of depression, anxiety, disorders, and hostility reactions (Beck, 1963, 1976). These deviations appear to be manifestations of primary-process patterns of thinking and a relative reduction of secondary-process thinking.

Mr. A can gradually become aware of his thoughts and impulses while driving. Each time he is able to identify these cognitions, he can increase his objectivity toward them. Some of the categories are these:

1. *Projections:* "They think I am a pushover."
2. *Exaggeration:* "I'll never get to work at this rate. . . . This bottleneck is awful."
3. *Imperatives:* "I must get to work as fast as I can," "I can't let him think he can get away with edging me out," "I must show him," "I must not allow myself to be jammed in."
4. *Negative attributions:* "They are deliberately trying to cut me off."
5. *Punitive wishes:* "I will show him how stupid he is by cutting in front of him."

The step after noting and recording a particular cognition is to evaluate it logically. For example, the therapist may ask Mr. A for the evidence that other drivers are deliberately trying to impede his progress. The homework assignment may be to test this hypothesis on his next trip by observing other drivers more closely.

Special Cognitive Problems. In addition to the therapeutic techniques listed earlier (examining the evidence, disattribution, decentering, etc.), specific techniques are important to counteract some of the characteristics of primitive or "primary-process" thinking.

"Premature closure" can be counteracted by asking patients to train themselves to record their immediate conclusions and then to attempt to postpone acting on the conclusions until they have had a chance to review the bases for the conclusion. Some patients develop a real skill in carrying on an internal debate, in lieu of immediately accepting the validity of a conclusion.

"Absolutistic" or "dichotomous" thinking can be approached by inducing patients to introduce a scale into their appraisal of situations. For example, a student who had acute diarrhea before exams reported that he had just undergone a "horrible" experience. He and I then had the following interchange:

> *Therapist:* On a 100-point scale, how bad was it?
> *Patient:* About 100.
> *Therapist:* What was the worst experience you ever had?
> *Patient:* When my grandfather died.
> *Therapist:* If that rated 100, how would you rate yesterday's experience?
> *Patient:* Oh, I guess about 60.

The patient then went on to say that it could be "horrible" if he did not do well on a test the next day.

> *Therapist:* How horrible could it be?
> *Patient:* About 100%
> *Therapist:* If your grandfather's death was 100, how bad would this be?
> *Patient:* About 40, I guess.

This technique tends to give a patient a greater sense of proportion and a sense that unpleasant events are relative and not absolute. This technique, indeed, reduces the magnitude of the perceived stressor by enabling the patient to view events in terms of degrees of severity, rather than in absolute terms. In actuality, much of the patient's thinking does include perspective, relativism, and dimensionality. The aspects of secondary-process thinking are overridden, however, by the narrow, egocentric, absolutistic categories of primary-process thinking when the individual perceives that his or her vital interests are at stake.

Typical dichotomous thinking is manifested in the patient's framing inferences in terms of success–failure, liked–disliked, happy–sad. Since the patient has a tendency to set a relatively high standard for an event to be rated in terms of having succeeded, been liked, or felt happy, he is particularly vulnerable to the risk of experiencing "failure," "dislikes," or "unhappiness." The student with fear of exams reported the following:

> *Patient:* I feel terrible today.
> *Therapist:* Why?
> *Patient:* I feel like a failure . . . I really blew the exam.
> *Therapist:* What do you think you got?
> *Patient:* A really bad score.
> *Therapist:* 50, 60, 70?
> *Patient:* 80, I guess.
> *Therapist:* Does that mean you failed?
> *Patient:* No, but I didn't do as well as I wanted.
> *Therapist:* What did you want?
> *Patient:* At least a 90.
> *Therapist:* So anything less than a 90 is a failure:
> *Patient:* Sounds silly, but I guess that's right . . . OK, I didn't blow it, but I wish I had done better.

The "seriousness" attached to anticipated adverse events can be approached in a way illustrated in the following example of the same student before an exam:

> *Patient:* I feel like jumping out of my skin. . . . If I fail this exam, I don't know what I'll do.
> *Therapist:* What could be a failure?
> *Patient:* Anything less than 80 . . .
> *Therapist:* Imagine you got a 70. What do you visualize would happen?
> *Patient:* I'd flunk out. My parents would be disappointed. My classmates would cut me up.
> *Therapist:* Why don't you rate the probabilities?
> *Patient:* I guess I would not flunk out. I've got too many A's for

that. My parents would be disappointed if I did. The other kids wouldn't cut me up, but their opinion of me would go down.

This belief interchange was powerful enough to undercut the seriousness of the possible consequences. There was a durable effect, in that the student became less fearful and was less prone to diarrhea prior to exams.

STRUCTURAL CHANGE

The description of Mr. A's driving patterns as a hypothetical case covers only one aspect of the actual case history of Mr. A. The treatment plan already described is one designed primarily to produce "symptom relief." That result, which is no small achievement in itself, is often attained in 5 to 10 interviews. Since this type of relief is dependent on a shift in cognitive set, the improvement may not be durable if there has been no fundamental change in the cognitive organization. I find, however, that many patients need—and often want—more substantial and more lasting change, so that they are less vulnerable to future stress reactions. In addition, the more basic work is important to improve interpersonal relations and overall satisfactions. Structural change consists not only of modifying the habitual cognitive errors (arbitrary inferences, personalization, framing, polarization, etc.), but of modifying the inappropriate meaning-assignment system and the underlying organization of rules, formulas, assumptions, and imperatives.

In conducting a cognitive analysis of a case, it is useful to elicit a broad range of dysfunctional attitudes and behaviors and to specify the circumstances or situations in which they are typically evoked. These data can then be organized or grouped according to the thematic content or some other form of patterning. In treating Mr. A, for example, I was able to list a host of distinctive dysfunctional behaviors and attitudes. (This list, incidentally, is applicable to many individuals who are prone to develop depression—see Beck, 1983—or myocardial infarction.)

In the following description, I present additional details of Mr. A's life that indicated a need for more work than simply the treatment of his disturbance in driving. After giving more details of his case history, I present an organization of the data in terms of the specific situations (stressors) that elicited dysfunctional responses, and in terms of his specific vulnerabilities. This "situational analysis" then provides the basis for a structural analysis" of his personality.

Case History and Analysis

Mr. A, a 45-year-old businessman, had been referred for psychotherapy for hypertention and chronic tension in all his muscles. The referring therapist, who was highly experienced in the utilization of relaxation techniques and biofeedback, made the referral because these approaches had been only mildly effective in this case.

On interview, the patient was extremely restless and unable to sit still; he asked whether he could move around. He then paced the floor for the first part of the interview. He said that he got little enjoyment out of life, although he was successful in his business and (as was confirmed later) had a happy marriage and a good relationship with his children. He complained that he was unable to relax at home and that he and his wife had to take frequent vacations in order for him to have a period of rest and relaxation. He also reported having had a serious case of depression.

In the course of therapy, the case was analyzed in terms of significant factors that appeared to combine to produce his symptoms.

Specific Stressors. The stress situations involved specific "ordinary" business events. These circumstances produced a strong reaction in Mr. A. The kind of of events that upset him were (1) the initiation of a new contract, project, or account; and (2) any action by one of the employees that impeded his progress in any way. Taking on a new project added substantially to the feeling of pressure he chronically experienced. Further, he interpreted anything less than optimum efficiency on the part of one of his employees as "negligence" and he would experience hostility to that employee. Since he considered it unwise to scold his employees, he carried a constant load of hostility. Thus any performance below his standards (mistakes, delays, etc.) would contribute to the stress he experienced.

Specific Vulnerability. It was apparent that Mr. A was hypersensitive to a variety of events that would only minimally disturb other people:

1. If asked to do something, he would feel "put upon." This reaction was due to his perceiving additional tasks as making his burden unbearable.

2. Any limitation of his freedom of action made him feel "locked in" or "trapped." Thus, unpleasant sensations occurred, whether the limitation was physical or psychological.

3. He was sensitive to any interference in his goal-directed activity. If somebody interrupted him while he was working, he would feel furious at the other person. The same reaction occurred when somebody impeded his progress when he was driving. He reacted badly to being in crowds, finding that a door was locked or difficult to open, being told that a rule prohibited a certain course of action, or being asked to finish a project before he was ready.

Rules and Imperatives.

1. Mr. A placed a very high value on his standards and goals, and thus was driven to meet his highly valued standards and to achieve his objectives at all costs. He was intolerant of any obstacles, delays, or detours.

2. Just as when driving to work, he was constantly pressing toward a goal and was continually monitoring his progress toward meeting the goals.

3. Since he attached too much significance to the goals, he regarded each activity as a do-or-die matter. He was chronically over-mobilized.

4. Simple procedural matters were elevated to the rank of major substantive matters. Thus, he became excessively upset by unexpected problems that could readily be solved.

5. Minor mistakes by himself or his other workers were labeled as monstrous misdeeds.

6. Problems *had* to be solved as soon as possible. If there was no immediate solution to a problem, he believed he was faced with a disaster.

7. The reason that he became impatient, restless, and uncomfortable was that his goal attainment was mobilized and he could not demobilize it. Hence, he was impelled to work toward a particular objective even when there was nothing to be done at a given time.

An Analysis of Cognitive Organization . The patterning of rules, expectancies, and imperatives comprises a substantial component of what has been traditionally included in the concept of personality structure. This patterning determines to a large degree the nature of a person's cognitive responses, motivations, affect and behavior. The therapy of the "structural" problems can, for purposes of convenience, be divided into certain topical areas. These areas then become the targets for intervention. Three areas were of special importance in Mr. A's structural modification. These were (1) his egocentricity, (2) his system of rules and regulations, and (3) his punitiveness. The first two areas are crucial in most cases requiring personality change.

"Vital Interests" and Egocentricity

Importance of Meanings. Why are the "vital interests" so ubiquitous? Why do individuals react so strongly to events that a disinterested observer would consider trivial? Psychological problems may arise when an event is somehow connected with a central core of meaning that involves fundamental elements—self-enhancement, self-protection, escape, nurturance, and so on. It could be speculated that these elemental meanings take on particular force because they are derived from more primitive concepts and motivations, such as those involved with predatory behavior, protection against attack, and kinship attachments. Irrespective of the possible anthropological or developmental roots, our vital interests seem to involve the kind of primitive thinking that one might expect to be precursors to "primitive impulses."

Since each business activity was connected with a core construct (survival, self-enhancement), then each activity had exaggerated importance to Mr. A. Thus even a trivial matter such as having sharp pencils available to him was invested with the same kind of meaning and degree of seriousness as the availability of capital to carry out one of his ventures. He would become almost as distressed over not finding a sharp pencil or paper on his desk as he would be if he found that part of his bank account had been encumbered by a lien.

On exploration, it was discovered that behind his overreaction to the kind of "trivial" occurrence such as not having a pencil available was his heavy investment in his "system." Any imperfection in the workings of his organization meant a breakdown in the system. Therefore the line of reasoning would go something like this: "If I can't count on my staff to have something available that is so tangible and easy to attend to as pens and pencils, how can I count on them for something really important?" In brief, any event that weakened his confidence in the efficient operation of his employees led to a complete loss of confidence in the system. The resulting sense of being let down led to his experiencing anger and a wish to punish the offenders. At a previous time, when he was going into a depression, the chain of mental events had led him to believe that he was going bankrupt as a result of the system breaking down.

Now let us review some of the meanings of "success" to this individual in order to understand why making money was of such a "vital interest."

1. Financial success, according to Mr. A's system of rules and formulas, was a way of gaining the respect of other people in the same line of business. Thus, making money was a source of gratification. However, it had a far more important meaning than this, in that it afforded him a sense of protection against the disdain of other people and also against destitution. Because of early childhood experiences with the contempt of older siblings, he had a continual expectation of being ridiculed. Thus, whenever there was any question of loss of financial security, he began to experience anxiety and to visualize the contempt of his business associates. When he had been depressed, he had thought that the loss of money would lead to destitution and thus to death, because he would not be able to afford medical treatment.

2. Mr. A's sense of confidence depended upon the tangible evidence of success. When he did well on a business deal, he would think, "I am successful. I am really bright." If he did not do well, he would think, "I am stupid." Apparently he had not built up any solid core of self-esteem that would be relatively insensitive to fluctuations in his cash flow.

3. It was very important to Mr. A to be able to provide an adequate standard of living for his family. He took great pride in the material satisfactions that his family had, but always had a nagging sense that he would "lose everything" if his business went under. His dichotomous thinking was evident in his considering his business (and himself) as either a success or a failure; there was nothing in between.

The therapy consisted of unraveling each of these meanings and then subjecting them to scrutiny. It was possible, first of all, to expose the dichotomous thinking so that Mr. A could start to make evaluations in terms of *varying degrees* of success (or failure). Then we were able to assess the probabilities of his being considered unworthy by his family and friends if he should indeed show a financial slippage.

Egocentric Mode. Mr. A was able to recognize that he was making his judgments from an egocentric frame of reference. For example, he had decided that people would ridicule him if he failed. He had not, however, considered their reactions from *their* frame of reference. When he was asked to try to determine their frame of reference, he was able to see that he had not even taken into account that they might react differently from the way that he automatically expected. He and I were particularly successful in demonstrating his egocentricity in his expectation that his wife would lose respect for him. When he spoke to her about his financial problems, he was able to see that her frame of reference was completely different from that which he had projected onto her. Specifically, what mattered to her the most were qualities other than his ability to provide the material comforts. He was subsequently able to generalize from this demonstration of his egocentric notions to other situations in which he showed a similar degree of egocentric thinking (e.g., suicidal wishes).

Another point that we were able to explore successfully was that he defined "competence" only in terms of the outcome of his most recent ventures. Even if he had been successful a dozen times in his business ventures, a slight financial loss on the 13th venture would mean that he was incompetent. This example again demonstrated a type of egocentricity, in that he appraised his financial acumen solely in terms of the outcomes of his most recent ventures, rather than on the basis of the long-range results of his specific skills. Moreover, he had not taken into account that the outcomes of his ventures were to a large extent determined by factors such as fluctuations in the market, changes in the economy, and information about particular investments that he had not known at the time. He came to recognize that the business cycle was subject to numerous oscillations that he could not predict and that he had no control over. Thus, he came to recognize that a downturn in the economy that affected everybody in his industry was more likely to be the cause of financial problems than a deficiency in his acumen was.

System of Formulas, Rules, and Regulations

Mr. A operated according to a complex set of rules, formulas, injunctions, and prohibitions. He applied these rules to himself and to others in his employment. Thus, the rules or the system were the instrument for (1) reaching his goals and (2) protecting himself against destitution, disgrace, and death.

As pointed out previously, if a rule was broken, Mr. A was prone to catastrophize. The underlying theme seemed to be this: "If a rule is broken a little bit, then all rules could be broken a lot." When a rule was broken, he would react just as strongly when no damage was done as if there actually was damage. For instance, if he did not receive a message promptly, he would react almost as strongly if no harm resulted as he would if he lost an account because of the delay.

It is also notable that when the pressure would build up, the formulas would become more rigid. When upset, Mr. A adopted the formula that, if he was not very strict with his employees, there could be a serious loss. This concept showed dichotomous thinking. His employees were either "careful" or "totally negligent." He either could control them well, or they were completely uncontrolled. His firm either ran smoothly, or it was chaotic. Thus he needed absolute control to insure his security.

"Personalizing the System." As our discussions continued, it became apparent that Mr. A's system had become an end in itself. He was less fixated on the probable outcomes of deficiencies than on the imperfections themselves. It appeared that the means had become more important than the end. In the course of time, it became apparent that he had identified himself with his system. For example, when he was having some remediable difficulty in the operations of the organization, he experienced feelings of paralysis.

Expectations. Because of Mr. A's overinvestment in the system, he tended to "ride herd" over his employees, an approach that probably engendered a certain amount of resentment and possibly of passive resistance on their part. It is notable that his demands and expectations of himself were just as stringent as those he imposed on his employees. Thus he would become concerned at any error in judgment that he made. The reason for this was that he saw this as a harbinger of the slide down the road to disaster. A single stone rolling down the hill indicated that an avalanche was about to come. Partly as a result of the presumed disastrous consequences of mistakes, he rarely made mistakes, but he was continually under the impression that "he might make a fatal error."

The therapeutic approach to this psychological problem was to ask Mr. A to list his expectations of the key individuals in his organization. Then he was asked to rate their performance periodically. If a person's performance was below his rational expectations, then he could revise them or decide whether he was willing to assume the risk of further imperfections in that individual's work. If, on the other hand, the imperfections were what he had anticipated, he could use his observation to counteract his unreasonable expectations.

We found that his discovery of an inefficiency was generally followed by a catastrophic thought ("The whole organization will fall apart"). The therapeutic work of decatastrophizing consisted of making "predictions" each time he discovered an error and then reviewing the predictions and the outcome several weeks later.

Notions of Causality. Mr. A had primitive notions of causality in reference to business problems. If anything went wrong, then a particular person was to blame. Just as he expected himself to have total knowledge of all the factors necessary to making a decision, he expected the same from his staff. His underlying theme was "I do not expect anything more from them than from myself." It was important in terms of the therapy to demonstrate to him that he indeed expected too much of himself—that he was not the only determinant in the outcome of his ventures. Similarly, his staff would not be the sole causes of the success or failure of any enterprise. In fact, as he explored the situation further, he recognized that many factors other than simply judgment were causes of the fate of the ventures.

Punitiveness

Since Mr. A was prone to attribute accountability, responsibility, and causality to both himself and his staff, he was constantly prepared to punish the offending party when something went wrong. Typically, he would conduct an investigation when there was any "foul-up" and would feel a strong urge to come down hard on the offending party. It should be pointed out that he was aware that he could not continually badger his staff, so that a good part of the time he had hostile reactions to the staff, but did not express them.

The reasons behind this punitive attitude had to do with the following:

1. Since his "vital interests" were at stake, it meant that any offense by the staff struck at the heart of these interests. This caused pain and raised a desire to retaliate because of the pain that had been caused him.

2. Part of the punitiveness was to "teach them a lesson" so as to prevent a recurrence.

3. A related concept was that he needed to punish members of the staff periodically in order to "tighten the reins."

It is notable that much more hostility was engendered as a result of rules being broken than as a result of any real damage being done. Because of the importance of the rules to Mr. A, he was continually vigilant to make sure that they were followed closely. Thus he would check his secretary's work to make sure that there were no mistakes in punctuation, and he would monitor the arrival and departure times of the employees to make sure that they were not cheating. Because of this overvigilance, he did indeed perceive a fair number of infractions, and as a result was hostile about these.

SUMMARY

1. The construction of a situation (cognitive set) is an active, continuing process that includes successive appraisals of the external situation and the risks, costs, and gains of a particular response. When the individual's vital interests appear to be at stake, the cognitive process provides a highly selective conceptualization. The cognitive structuring of a situation is responsible for mobilizing the organism to action. If the mobilization persists substantially beyond realistic demands, it forms the precursor to a stress reaction.

2. Overt behavior stems directly from the mobilization triggered by activated cognitive structures. Depending on the content of the cognitive constellation, the behavioral mobilization will be directed toward flight, attack, approach, or withdrawal. The concomitant affect would be respectively anxiety, anger, affection, or sadness.

3. Specific primitive cognitive constellations are "chained" to specific stimuli. This pairing constitutes the specific sensitivity of a given individual and prepares the way for inappropriate or excessive reactions. Since people vary widely in their specific sensitivities, what is a stressor for one person may be a benign situation for another.

4. The stressors lead to a disruption of the normal activity of the cognitive organization. Deviations in the thinking process occur as a result of the stress. When vital interests are at stake, the primitive, egocentric cognitive system is activated and the individual is primed to make extreme, one-sided, absolutistic, and global judgments. Further, there is a loss of volitional control over thinking processes and a reduced ability to "turn off" intense, idiosyncratic cognitive schemas. There is a reduction in the ability to concentrate, recall, and reason.

5. Differences in personality organization account for some of the wide variations in individual sensitivities to stressors. Thus, the autonomous and sociotropic personality types differ in the type of stressors to which they are sensitive. The occurrence of a stress reaction, consequently, is contingent to a large degree on specific vulnerabilities related to personality.

6. Each of the stress syndromes (such as hostility, anxiety, and depression) consists of hyperactive schemas with an idiosyncratic content specific for that syndrome. Each syndrome comprises a specific controlling cognitive constellation and the resultant behavioral inclinations and affect.

7. The principal stressor may be internal with no apparent referent in the outside world. The assumption that the only road to fulfillment is

through total success is intrinsic in achievement-oriented persons prone
to stress reactions.

8. Stressful interactions with other people occur in a mutually reinforcing cycle of maladaptive cognitive reactions. Specific mechanisms
such as the egocentric cognitive mode, framing, and polarization lead to
increased mobilization and consequently to stress.

9. An individual responds physically, although the stimulus may be
psychosocial or symbolic and although ultimate overt behavior is verbal.
The mobilization to "fight–flight" involves the same cognitive–motoric
systems, irrespective of whether the level of meaning of a threat or challenge is "physical" or psychosocial.

10. The cognitive approach to the treatment of stress reactions focuses on reducing the hyperactivity of the controlling schemas and supporting the adaptive functions. The patient is encouraged to examine the
internal factors—thoughts, impulses, and feelings—contributing to the
stress response. The patient also identifies the meanings he or she has assigned to events that are connected to both behavioral activation and affect. Cognitive techniques such as identifying automatic thoughts, recognizing and correcting cognitive distortions, and identifying broad beliefs
and assumptions that underlie cognition are used to clarify the problems.

11. Through a process of collaborative empiricism, the cognitive therapist and the patient frame the patient's conclusions as hypotheses which
are investigated and tested by increasing both objectivity and perspective.
Logically evaluating dysfunctional cognitions leads to shifts in thinking,
with the ultimate goal being structural change. Structural change may
come about through the analysis of specific stressors and vulnerabilities,
rules, and imperatives which have governed the person's responses. Structural change, then, extends beyond modifying habitual cognitive errors
to the underlying organization of rules, formulas, assumptions, and imperatives which misclassify events as threatening.

REFERENCES

Beck, A. T. Thinking and depression: 1. Idiosyncratic content and cognitive distortions. *Archives of General Psychiatry,* 1963, *9,* 324–333.
Beck, A. T. Thinking and depression: 2. Theory and therapy. *Archives of General Psychiatry,* 1964, *10,* 561–571.
Beck, A. T. *Depression: Clinical, experimental, and theoretical aspects.* New York: Hoeber,
1967.
Beck, A. T. *Cognitive therapy and the emotional disorders.* New York: International Universities Press, 1976.

Beck, A. T. Cognitive therapy of depression: New perspectives. In P. Clayton (Ed.), *Depression*. New York: Raven Press, 1983.

Beck, A. T., Rush, A. J., Shaw, B. F., & Emery, G. *Cognitive therapy of depression*. New York: Guilford Press, 1979.

Bowlby, J. *Cognitive processes in the genesis of psychopathology*. Invited Address to the Biannual Meeting of the Society for Research in Child Development, Boston, April 1981.

Caplan, G. Mastery of stress: Psychosocial aspects. *American Journal of Psychiatry*, 1981, *138*, 413–420.

Ellis, A. *Reason and emotion in psychotherapy*. New York: Lyle Stuart, 1962.

Goldfried, M. R. The use of relaxation and cognitive relabeling as coping skills. In R. B. Start (Ed.), *Behavioral self-management: Strategies and outcomes*. New York: Brunner/Mazel, 1977.

Hollon, S. D., & Beck, A. T. Cognitive therapy of depression. In S. D. Hollon & P. C. Kendall (Eds.), *Cognitive–behavioral interventions: Theory, research, and procedures*. New York: Academic Press, 1979.

Holroyd, K. A. Stress, coping and the treatment of stress. In S. R. McNamara (Ed.), *Behavioral approaches to medicine*. New York: Plenum, 1979.

Jacobson, E. *Progressive relaxation*. Chicago: University of Chicago Press, 1938.

Lazarus, R. S. *Psychological stress and the coping process*. New York: McGraw-Hill, 1966.

Lazarus, R. S. The stress and coping paradigm. In C. Eisdorfer, D. Cohen, A. Kleinman, & P. Maxim (Eds.), *Conceptual models for psychotherapy*. New York: Spectrum, 1981.

Mahoney, M. Psychotherapy and human change processes. In J. H. Harvey & M. P. Parke (Eds.), *Psychotherapy research and behavior change*. Washington, D.C.: American Psychological Association, 1982.

Meichenbaum, D. H. *Cognitive-behavior modification: An integrative approach*. New York: Plenum, 1977.

Novaco, R. *Anger control: The development and evaluation of an experimental treatment*. Lexington, Mass.: D.C., Health, 1975.

Saul, L. J. *Emotional maturity*. Philadelphia: J. B. Lippincott, 1947.

Turk, D. C., Meichenbaum, D., & Genest, M. *Pain and behavioral medicine: A cognitive–behavioral perspective*. New York: Guilford Press, 1983.

Wolff, H. G. Life stress and bodily disease—a formulation. In *Life stress and bodily disease: Proceedings of the Association for Research in Nervous and Mental Disease, December 2 & 3, 1949, New York*. Baltimore: Williams & Wilkins, 1950.

10 PHARMACOLOGICAL METHODS

MALCOLM LADER

INTRODUCTION

Stress is an ubiquitous experience in modern life and is taking its toll. Levels of anxiety and tension have increased, and many stress-related diseases, such as hypertension and myocardial infarction, have risen markedly in incidence. "Stress" refers to major environmental demands that require behavioral and physiological adjustment. "Stress response" refers to those adjustments. But stress is more than just major environmental stimuli. The attitude of a person toward those stimuli is of paramount importance. What constitutes an overwhelming stress for one person may be dismissed as a nugatory perturbation of another.

The reduction of stress comprises three elements:

1. The environmental stresses can be physically altered. For example, an airport can be relocated in a sparsely populated area.
2. The stressed person's attitudes can be changed: An overwhelmed executive promoted beyond the level of his or her competence can opt out of the rat race.
3. The behavioral and physiological responses of the body can be damped down by relaxation and related techniques or by chemical means.

The last-mentioned method—"chemical means"—constitutes pharmacological methods of management. Many self-administered drugs reduce stress responses, the cardinal examples being cigarette smoking and tobacco (although it must be emphasized that the use of these may fulfill needs other than simply stress response reduction). However, I confine my discussion in this chapter to the use of medication prescribed by a medically qualified professional under the understanding that the person taking the medication should benefit.

Because prescribing is the physician's prerogative, the medical model of illness has been applied to stress responses. Various syndromes have been described and remedies suggested. Examples include "effort syndrome," "hyperventilation syndrome," and "irritable colon syndrome." All these and similar syndromes affecting almost every system of the body are probably part of a general stress response, and remedies specific to just one bodily system are inappropriate. The growing realization of this by the medical profession is reflected by the steady increase in the prescription of general stress-reducing remedies—namely, the antianxiety drugs. These drugs are being increasingly prescribed for general stress responses, with the rationale that the symptoms complained of by the patient are part of a general stress response characterized by emotional overarousal. Damping down the emotional overresponsiveness, runs the reasoning, will result in a lessened stress response in the bodily systems underlying the symptoms.

Be that as it may, the prescribing of the major group of antianxiety drugs, the benzodiazepines, has increased rapidly. Use of the older drugs, mainly the barbiturates, has diminished, but not as much as benzodiazepine use has increased. By 1972, diazepam (Valium) was the most frequently prescribed drug in the United States. Its close analogue, chlordiazepoxide (Librium), was the third most often prescribed. Over 70 million prescriptions were filled for these two agents at a cost of over $200 million. These comprised over half of all the prescriptions for psychotropic drugs (Blackwell, 1973). In a survey in the Oxford region of the United Kingdom in 1977, diazepam accounted for over 4% of all prescriptions, making it the most frequently prescribed drug (Skegg, Doll, & Perry, 1977).

The majority of prescriptions for benzodiazepines are written by nonpsychiatrists—in particular, by family physicians, orthopedic specialists, gynecologists, general physicians, and pediatricians. Lasagna (1977) reviewed such benzodiazepine usage in nonpsychiatric practice and found that tranquilization was the major desired action. Nevertheless, voices have been raised against this "benzodiazepine bonanza" (Tyrer, 1974).

The patterns of benzodiazepine usage vary somewhat from country to country (Balter, Levine, & Manheimer, 1973). The United States and the United Kingdom are about in the middle of the league, with 14% of the adult population reporting tranquilizer use at some time during the year prior to the survey. Figures for Belgium and France are higher than average; those for Italy and Spain are lower than average. Usage among females is about twice that of males. Usage goes up with age in females but is not age-related in males. Usage is higher in the lower social classes in females.

SYNDROMES OF ANXIETY

Before describing the drugs that alleviate stress responses and the ways such drugs are used, it is useful to outline the syndromes involved. In general, pharmacological methods of stress management are directed toward symptom relief, the cardinal symptom being anxiety. The medical practitioner confronted by a patient with symptoms typical of a stress response— palpitations, tension headache, gastric discomfort, or whatever—will try to elicit general anxiety as a central psychological symptom. He or she may then attempt to relate the symptom pattern, onset, duration, and other factors to one of the usually recognized anxiety syndromes.

Anxiety is a subjective feeling of uneasiness and apprehension about some undefined threat in the future. The threat is often physical, with intimations of bodily harm or of death, or psychological, with threats to self-esteem and well-being. The subjective feeling is diffuse, inchoate, and ineffable, and the indefinable nature of the feeling gives it its peculiarly unpleasant and intolerable quality. If the threat can be identified and is appropriate in nature and magnitude to the emotion evoked, the feeling is generally termed "fear." If the threat is disproportionate, the feeling produced is termed "anxiety" (Lewis, 1967). The essential element in the evocation of anxiety is its disproportionate nature vis-à-vis the cause. But such anxieties are still normal in that the response is understandable in terms of the putative cause. When the response is undeniably exaggerated, the anxiety syndrome is generally dubbed "neurotic" (Clancy & Noyes, 1976). Internal factors in the individual are important; the anxiety reflects an interaction between the predisposition in the patient and the external event. This predisposition is more than the person's attitude to the external event that turns it into a stress. The factor may be deeply embedded in the person's personality structure, and the interaction between personality and event may take place at a symbolic level. This makes the ensuing anxiety even more disturbing than normal anxiety, because its sources are baffling to the patient. Often he or she will search around despairingly for causes for the disabling symptoms, and may be mistaken in his or her attributions.

Of course, not everyone with anxiety seeks medical help. A survey carried out in the United Kingdom suggested that about one in three of the adult population suffers from anxiety, anxiety-related symptoms, or acute stress responses during the course of each year. This incidence was about the same in a carefully planned "new town," a commuter suburb, and a decaying inner-city area (Taylor & Chave, 1964). A survey using a self-rating scale of anxiety came up with similar results: About 30% of a representative sample of adults gave scores in the clinically anxious range. About a third of the sample had consulted their family practitioners at some time concerning anxiety or stress-related problems, about half of these during the year prior to the interview (Salkind, 1973). In the United Kingdom, less than 5% of a sample of adults are referred for the opinion of a psychiatric specialist, and these patients are generally the more severely or the more chronically ill, or those with personality or social problems.

The factors that lead one anxious person to seek advice while another struggles stoically on without help are complex. Personal tolerance is obviously important, as is the attitude of the doctor toward mental illness. But the definition of "clinical anxiety" is operational: The person seeks medical advice and assumes the mantle of a "patient" when the anxiety becomes too severe, too pervasive, or too persistent for the person to tolerate.

Further distinctions can be made. One is between "state anxiety" and "trait anxiety" (Zuckerman, 1976). "State anxiety" refers to anxiety at a particular point in time; "trait anxiety" implies an enduring personality predisposition, the anxious temperament (Spielberger, 1972). The factors underlying a high level of trait anxiety are unclear, but genetic, developmental, and emotional learning factors are all important to differing extents in different people. The clinical version of state anxiety is the person who is normally calm, but under stress develops anxiety symptoms for which he or she seeks help. Clinical trait anxiety is recognized in the form of a person of an anxious disposition who, as stresses begin to mount, finds lifelong worries becoming increasingly unbearable. Typically, the two syndromes are found in conjunction, with external events interacting with the anxious temperament to produce an anxiety state that fluctuates in response to the external events.

Anxiety may be "free-floating"—that is, present fairly constantly and diffuse in nature—or "situational" (phobic), when panics are elicited by certain situations, often social, or particular objects. The two types often coexist, with a background level of free-floating anxiety being made worse in certain situations. The patient soon learns to avoid the anxiety-provoking situations, but is baffled by the apparently spontaneous, background anxiety.

Finally, an almost infinite variety of symptom patterns can be found in anxious patients (Tyrer, 1976). A useful division is the distinction between psychological and physiological symptoms (Hamilton, 1959). The former includes ineffable feelings of foreboding and vague apprehensions, irritability, and fears of cancer or of death. The latter can relate to almost any organ system in the body. Palpitations, tremor, and gastrointestinal symptoms are the most common. A diffuse anxiety state with mainly psychological symptoms can become more focused as time goes on, with respect both to the precipitants and to the predominant symptoms. In other instances, the anxiety starts as a monosymptomatic condition that preoccupies the patient more and more until a state of hypochondriasis occurs.

ANTIANXIETY DRUGS

DEFINITIONS

The term "sedative" originally meant a drug able to allay or assuage anxiety, to calm. More recently it has come to imply feelings of drowsiness or torpor, a state originally called "oversedation" and traditionally attributed to the barbiturates and older drugs, such as the bromides and chloral. To replace the term "sedative," the term "tranquilizer" has been introduced in an effort to distinguish in the prescriber's mind between the older drugs and the newer compounds, particularly the benzodiazepines. This distinction is largely spurious, as, apart from safety in overdose, benzodiazepines have many points in common with the barbiturates, and should be allocated to the same drug class. Sometimes the word "tranquilizer" is qualified by the adjective "minor" to distinguish these drugs from the "major tranquilizers" or antipsychotic drugs. But there is nothing "minor" about the extent of usage of the benzodiazepines (Skegg *et al.,* 1977), nor in the symptom relief they afford the truly anxious.

The terms "antianxiety drug" and "anxiolytic" are also in vogue; these terms underline the chief, but by no means the sole, use of these drugs. Table 10-1 lists the chief antianxiety drugs (by both generic and trade names) and their usual dosages.

HISTORY

The use of anxiety-allaying drugs goes back to Neolithic times, to the discovery that grape juices or grain mashes could be fermented to make drinks with definite psychotropic properties. Opium derivatives were known in the Middle and Far East and to the ancient Greeks. Other herbal remedies were discovered, but opium and alcohol remained the main-

TABLE 10-1. Antianxiety Drugs

Generic name	Trade name	Usual dose range (mg/day)
Barbiturates		
Phenobarbital	Luminal	30–120
Amobarbital	Amytal	100–200
Secobarbital	Seconal	100–200
Propanediols		
Meprobamate	Miltown	800–2000
	Equanil	800–2000
Tybamate	Tybatran	750–2800
Antihistamines		
Hydroxyzine	Vistaril	75–400
Diphenhydramine	Benadryl	75–300
Benzodiazepines		
Chlordiazepoxide	Librium	15–100
Diazepam	Valium	5–40
Oxazepam	Serax	30–120
Clorazepate	Tranxene	15–60
Prazepam	Centrax	20–60
Lorazepam	Ativan	1–6
Tricyclic antidepressants		
Doxepin	Sinequan	75–225
	Adapin	75–225
Amitriptyline	Elavil	75–225
β-Adrenoceptor antagonists		
Propranolol	Inderal	30–240

stays of therapy until the last century; they were used as anesthetics, to quiet disturbed patients, to allay anxiety, and to induce sleep.

In the 19th century, the developing chemical industry produced simple inorganic and organic compounds. Bromides were introduced as anticonvulsants and as sedatives and became widely used. Their limited effectiveness, cumulative toxicity, and potential for abuse became apparent by the 1930s. Even so, 20 or 30 years later, some mental hospitals still routinely screened all newly admitted patients by estimating serum bromide levels to detect the occasional bromide-induced toxic state.

Anesthetics such as ether and chloroform, and sedatives such as chloral hydrate and paraldehyde, were developed in the 19th century. Chloral hydrate, in more acceptable solid formulations, still has some therapeutic usefulness; however, paraldehyde is unpleasant to take, is liable to be abused, and may induce psychotic states.

The last of the important 19th-century sedatives were the barbiturates. Many different compounds were introduced: the ultra-short-acting (e.g., anesthesia-inducing agents such as thiopentone), short-acting (e.g., quinalbarbitone, known as secobarbital in the United States), medium-acting (e.g., butabarbital), and long-acting (e.g., phenobarbital). As with the bromides, over 50 years elapsed before the disadvantages of the barbiturates became apparent. Side effects of drowsiness, tolerance to therapeutic effects, dangers when taken in overdose, and physical and psychological dependence (with consequent dangerous withdrawal syndromes) led to a growing dissatisfaction with these drugs ("Action from the CRM: Barbiturates," 1980).

The scene was thus set for the phenomenal short-lived success of meprobamate. This drug was developed from mephenesin, which was a muscle relaxant with its primary action on the spinal cord; however, it was too short-acting to be of much clinical utility. Meprobamate is longer-acting and was introduced as the first of the modern tranquilizers (Berger, 1963). Unfortunately, its advantages over the barbiturates proved illusory. It was still dangerous in overdosage and likely to be associated with dependence. Skin reactions to it were rather frequent. It is still used as a sedative and a muscle relaxant, and finds its widest application in combination with an analgesic in the management of painful muscle and joint injuries. Tybamate is a drug similar to meprobamate, but short-acting. Its dependence liability is supposedly low. Other nonbarbiturate hypnotics and sedatives were developed, including glutethimide, methyprylon, and ethchlorvynol. The eager acceptance of these drugs reflected growing dissatisfaction with the barbiturates, but in turn these barbiturate substitutes proved disappointing.

THE BENZODIAZEPINES

HISTORICAL INTRODUCTION

The discovery of the benzodiazepines provides a typical example of accidental discovery of a psychotropic substance (Ayd & Blackwell, 1970). In the 1930s, Sternbach, an industrial chemist in Poland, became interested in some complex organic chemicals (Cohen, 1970). Twenty years later, then working for Roche Laboratories in the United States, he decided to reinvestigate these compounds, with a particular interest in determining any intrinsic biological activity. Forty such derivatives were tested and found to be inert, but eventually a compound proved to have biological activity. It had a profile of activity in animals similar to that of meprobamate, but with many times the potency. This compound, chlordiazepoxide, was found to have the chemical structure of a 1:4-benzodiazepine. Well over a thousand benzodiazepines and related compounds have been synthesized, with diazepam the most widely used of all. Much is known of the structural requirements for pharmacological activity.

The benzodiazepines have been very successful drugs commercially. It is hardly surprising that many drug companies have invested much time, effort, and funds in the search for better drugs of this class. However, differences among the benzodiazepines have not proved very substantial. The main differences relate to the pharmacokinetics of the various drugs.

PHARMACOKINETICS

"Pharmacokinetics" refers to the way in which the body deals with the drug—the absorption, distribution, metabolism, and elimination of the drug. For the prescriber, two aspects of the pharmacokinetics of the benzodiazepines are important: namely, the speed of onset of action and the duration of action (Shader & Greenblatt, 1977). The speed of onset of action depends on the mode of administration and the penetration time to the brain. Thus, diazepam is rapidly absorbed when taken orally and enters the brain quickly. It can thus be used to give prompt relief of acute panic states. Given intravenously, it is the treatment of choice for stopping repeated epileptic fits. By contrast, oxazepam is slowly absorbed and takes some time to penetrate the brain. Clorazepate takes a little longer than diazepam. Lorazepam is also rapid in its entry to the brain and can be used intravenously as premedication. Diazepam is relatively slowly absorbed after intramuscular injection (Hillestad, Hansen, Melsom, & Drivenes, 1974).

The metabolic half-lives of the benzodiazepines also vary greatly. The crucial compound is N-desmethyldiazepam (nordiazepam), the major metabolite of diazepam. It has psychotropic activity as a tranquilizer. Its half-life is very long, typically over 100 hours. Consequently, it cumulates over the first month of treatment, reaching higher plasma and body concentrations than the parent compound, diazepam (Mandelli, Tognoni, & Garattini, 1978). N-Desmethyldiazepam is also the major metabolite of clorazepate, medazepam, prazepam, ketazolam, and to some extent chlordiazepoxide. Consequently, the clinical actions of these drugs will be very similar, because they share this common and major metabolite. Switching from one to another of these compounds during pharmacotherapy is likely to be unproductive.

Clobazam, a 1:5-benzodiazepine, also has a long-acting metabolite, N-desmethylclobazam. In contrast, lorazepam, oxazepam, and temazepam have half-lives of about 12 hours. This means that they tend not to accumulate much, as the body eliminates most of the dose each time. These compounds are appropriate for allaying acute, short-lived anxieties and for use as hypnotics. Triazolam is even shorter-acting, its half-life being less than 4 hours. Flurazepam, the most popular hypnotic in the United States, has a similarly short half-life, but it has an active metabolite or metabolites with a prolonged action. It is thus rather inappropriate as an hypnotic unless sedation during daytime is also required (Greenblatt, Shader, & Koch-Weser, 1975). Nitrazepam, an hypnotic widely used in Europe, has a moderately long half-life of about 30 hours, so it tends to accumulate on repeated use as a nightly hypnotic.

BASIC PHARMACOLOGY

The mode of action of the benzodiazepines, as with other tranquilizers, was obscure until recently. It now seems that the benzodiazepines potentiate the actions of the neurotransmitter, γ-aminobutyric acid (GABA). This compound is involved in about 40% of all synapses and is believed to be inhibitory both presynaptically and postsynaptically. Thus, any drug potentiating this most ubiquitous of inhibitory neurotransmitters would be expected to have widespread actions in damping down neuronal activity. The mechanism of the potentiation is unclear. Benzodiazepines do not act directly on GABA receptors. Specialized binding sites with a high affinity for benzodiazepines have been identified throughout the brain. The natural neurotransmitter that acts on those receptors has not yet been identified. Some benzodiazepine receptors are not in close affinity to GABA receptors, so more than one mechanism of action may be involved. Barbiturates do not bind to the benzodiazepine receptors, but have a less specific action on ionic mechanisms in synaptic membranes.

As a consequence of these widespread inhibitory effects, benzodiazepines can alter the turnover of other neurotransmitters, such as noradrenalin and 5-hydroxytryptamine (serotonin). The main sites of action of the benzodiazepines are as follows:

1. The spinal cord, where presynaptic and postsynaptic inhibition results in muscle relaxation.

2. The brain stem, which probably accounts for the anticonvulsant effects of most benzodiazepines.

3. The cerebellum. Ataxia is a common adverse effect of high doses of benzodiazepines, and this could be mediated via cerebellar mechanisms.

4. Limbic and cortical areas, particularly those concerned with emotional integration and responses. It is possible that arousal systems from the reticular formation to limbic and cortical areas are inhibited by benzodiazepines.

There are some minor differences among the benzodiazepines with respect to their pharmacodynamic profiles of action. Diazepam is more anticonvulsant than chlordiazepoxide. Clobazam has much less effect on muscle relaxation than diazepam does, when these are given in clinically equal antianxiety doses. Clobazam also produces much less psychomotor impairment than diazepam does (Hanks, Lader, & Lawson, 1978). Lorazepam seems particularly sedative and is potent in producing amnesia after intravenous use or after large doses given by mouth.

CLINICAL PHARMACOLOGY

The depressant effects of a single dose of benzodiazepine can be detected in normal subjects by means of objective tests of intellectual, cognitive, and psychomotor performance (e.g., Lader, Curry, & Baker, 1980). At low doses, subjective changes such as drowsiness or torpor may be undetectable, despite objective impairment (McNair, 1973). However, in the clinical context with anxious patients and with repeated dosing, impairment of functioning is much more difficult to detect. Although some studies have demonstrated a lowering of performance after the first dose, such decrements have generally disappeared by the end of a week or two of repeated usage, and may even have been replaced by improvements in functioning relative to pretreatment levels. Part of the explanation relates to the well-known impairment of performance produced by high levels of anxiety. All kinds of tasks—perceptual, cognitive, psychomotor, intellectual—are performed badly by anxious patients. The mechanisms whereby mental functioning is impaired in anxiety are complex; they include problems with attention and concentration, preoccupation with anxiety, competing responses, inability to inhibit irrelevant information, and so on. The addition of a tranquilizer further depresses performance, especially if the dose is substantial. However, as the antianxiety effects build up and the patient becomes calmer, he or she functions better: The improvement in performance related to the lessening of anxiety first equals and then surpasses the direct drug-related impairment of performance.

A second mechanism concerns tolerance. There is evidence that physiological changes, such as the induction of fast-wave activity in the electroencephalograph (EEG), wane over time due to a direct tissue tolerance in the brain. That is, the response systems in the brain become less sensitive to the drug. Such tolerance would also be expected to occur with respect to drug effects on psychological functioning. Despite the extensive long-term usage of the benzodiazepines, few studies have evaluated the chronic effects of these drugs. It is not clear whether therapeutic effects are maintained for longer than a few weeks, nor whether any changes in psychological functioning can be detected.

CLINICAL USES

The benzodiazepines have supplanted the barbiturates almost entirely, for the following reasons:

1. The benzodiazepines are more effective than the barbiturates (e.g., Lader, Bond, & James, 1974). Many controlled trials have shown the therapeutic superiority of the benzodiazepines over a placebo, and many others have shown that benzodiazepines are generally better than the barbiturates with respect to both the quality and the quantity of improvement in anxiety- and stress-related symptoms.

2. The benzodiazepines have fewer and less severe side effects than do the barbiturates. Drowsiness and psychological impairment is less with the benzodiazepines than with the barbiturates, when each is given in effective antianxiety doses. Idiosyncratic responses such as rashes are more common with the barbiturates.

3. The benzodiazepines are much safer in overdosage than the barbiturates. Twenty times the usual hypnotic dose of a barbiturate will produce coma and can kill; the equivalent dose of a benzodiazepine merely produces deep sleep.

4. The benzodiazepines are less likely than the barbiturates to induce

dependence. In general, this is true with respect to escalation of dose, high-dose dependence, and drug-seeking behavior, but mild physical dependence on the benzodiazepines may be relatively common.

5. Metabolic interactions with other drugs are frequent with the barbiturates but infrequent with the benzodiazepines. For example, it is inadvisable to combine an antidepressant such as amitriptyline with a barbiturate, because the barbiturate will accelerate the liver metabolism of the antidepressant so that therapeutic levels cannot be attained. Such an interaction does not occur with a benzodiazepine.

The main use of the benzodiazepines is in the symptomatic management of anxiety and stress-related conditions (Greenblatt & Shader, 1974a, 1974b, 1974c). The indications are wide, but the common factor is the symptom of anxiety (Blackwell, 1973; Lasagna, 1977). There seems little degree of choice among the benzodiazepines in terms of effectiveness. Hundreds of trials have compared one benzodiazepine with another; the earlier ones generally used chlordiazepoxide as the standard treatment, while the more recent ones have settled on diazepam as the standard. Differences have been marginal, provided that flexibility of dosage has been allowed so that inappropriate dosages are avoided.

Antianxiety medications are difficult to assess (Solomon & Hart, 1978). Anxiety states and stress responses vary greatly in their natural history; some subside rapidly over a few weeks, while others become protracted and chronic for no apparent reason. The latter patients tend to be referred to psychiatric outpatient departments, because they present major treatment problems and because it is time-consuming to attempt to identify any factors perpetuating the chronic anxiety. Such patients tend to respond relatively poorly to standard antianxiety medication. Observations on patients in family practice gives a more encouraging impression of antianxiety drugs than does assessment of psychiatric clinic patients, especially if the observations are uncontrolled or unsystematic, because of the high rate of spontaneous remission (Hesbacher, Rickels, Rial, Segal, & Zamostien, 1976)

The initial choice of a benzodiazepine should take into account the temporal pattern of the anxiety state. A benzodiazepine with a long half-life, such as diazepam or clorazepate, is appropriate if the anxiety levels are high and sustained. Because of the long half life, twice-daily or once-nightly dosage is sufficient. Even so, some patients prefer more frequent dosages, because they can detect the sedative effects following each dose and are reassured by them. For episodic anxiety, shorter-acting compounds such as lorazepam can be used, taken 30 minutes or so before entering the anxiety-provoking situation. If the panic attack has already started, lorazepam can still be given and will exert a fairly prompt action, aborting the panic attack. Some patients are reassured by carrying some lorazepam or a similar compound for just such an eventuality. Oxazepam is also short-acting, but its absorption rate is too slow for emergency use of this type.

Many patients report increases in anxiety on the background of an already raised anxiety level. In these cases, the most appropriate drug, from the point of view of its pharmacokinetics, is diazepam. A proportion—perhaps a half—of the daily dose can be given before the patient goes to bed. This acts as an hypnotic because of its rapid absorption and transient peak levels. During the day, the long half-life of diazepam and its major metabolite, N-desmethyldiazepam, ensures a background antianxiety effect. Superimposed on this, small doses of diazepam can be given during the day as required. Shorter-acting drugs can also be prescribed in this way, but divided doses are necessary.

However, the largest use for short-acting benzodiazepines is in the management of insomnia, especially that related to stress and anxiety. The essential criterion for an hypnotic where daytime sedation is not required is that it should not accumulate on repeated dosage during the course of treatment. To this end, its half-life should not exceed 8–10 hours on average. Triazolam has a very short half-life; that of temazepam is about 8–10 hours; but those of nitrazepam and flurazepam (and their metabolites) are too long to meet this criterion. In many patients with insomnia, daytime sedation is appropriate, as the insomnia is but one symptom in a response to stress. As mentioned earlier, diazepam may be given both to act as a nighttime hypnotic and as a daytime sedative.

Other uses for which the short-acting benzodiazepines are appropriate are as preoperative medication and as deep sedation for minor operative procedures such as dentistry. The drugs render the patient calm, conscious, and cooperative, yet anterograde amnesia may be total for the operation or procedure. Benzodiazepines are also in great vogue as skeletal muscle relaxants in the management of acute conditions such as tetanus and trauma and of chronic conditions such as the relief of spasticity and athetosis in patients with neurological illnesses (Cazort, 1964). Benzodiazepines can be used as adjuncts to various types of relaxation therapy, especially where the patient is very tense and anxious and is unable even to commence relaxation. Diazepam or lorazepam can be administered by mouth 30–60 minutes before the relaxation therapy session, or, in the more severe cases, by careful and slow intravenous injection. Benzodiazepines have also been advocated in the management of alcohol withdrawal. However, there is cross-tolerance and sensitivity between alcohol and the benzodiazepines, as well as the danger that dependence may be transferred from alcohol to the benzodiazepine.

UNWANTED EFFECTS

The most common unwanted side effects of the benzodiazepines are tiredness, drowsiness, and torpor, these being most marked within the first 2 hours after large doses. Drowsiness is complained of most frequently during the first week of treatment and then wanes and disappears, probably because of a tolerance effect. Accordingly, patients should be warned of the potential side effects of any prescribed benzodiazepine. The dosage should initially be cautious until the effects of the drug can be gauged. In particular, patients should be advised not to drive a vehicle during the initial adjustment of dosage. If driving is essential for their livelihood, very small doses should be used initially, and these should be increased under close supervision until symptom relief is obtained or adverse effects begin to occur. Once the optimal dosage has been determined, there is less danger of interference with mechanical skills such as driving or operating dangerous machinery. Judgment may also be impaired during the first week or two of drug treatment, so important decisions should be deferred.

As with most depressant drugs, the effects of alcohol can be markedly potentiated (Linnoila, Mattila, & Kitchell, 1979). Patients must be warned not to drink alcohol when taking benzodiazepines, either chronically or intermittently. In particular, the combination of alcohol and a benzodiazepine may profoundly impair ability to drive, even when the patient has been taking the benzodiazepine for some time (Linnoila & Häkkinen, 1974).

Patients taking benzodiazepines may show paradoxical behavioral responses. Such phenomena include increased aggression and hostility (Gaind & Jacoby, 1978); uncharacteristic criminal activities, such as shoplifting; sexual improprieties or offenses, such as importuning or self-exposure; and excessive emotional responses, such as uncontrollable giggling or weeping. This phenomenon is by no means confined to the benzodiazepines; alcohol provides a cardinal example of a drug that may be associated with uncharacteristic, aggressive, or criminal behavior. With the benzodiazepines, paradoxical reactions are most common during the first 1 or 2 weeks of treatment or following dosage increases. Often such reactions subside spontaneously, but if they do not, dosage adjustment, usually downward, is generally successful. Hostile and aggressive feelings often baffle a patient, who fails to attribute them to the drug he or she is taking. It is wise to question patients routinely about any unexplained emotions that may be troubling them.

Administration of benzodiazepines can cause respiratory depression in patients with respiratory problems such as chronic bronchitis and emphysema. The respiratory center in the brain becomes less sensitive to arterial carbon dioxide, which thus builds up. This is a particular problem after intravenous administration of benzodiazepines, with diazepine seeming more hazardous than lorazepam. Some studies suggest that lorazepam might even stimulate, rather than depress, the respiratory center.

Other side effects include excessive weight gain, skin rash, impairment of sexual function, menstrual irregularities, and (rarely) blood abnormalities. Benzodiazepines should be avoided during pregnancy, especially during the first 3 months, but claims that diazepam is associated with a higher-than-normal incidence of cleft lip with or without cleft palate in the fetus have not been sustained in large-scale retrospective surveys (Hartz, Heinonen, Shapiro, Siskind, & Slone, 1975). Benzodiazepines pass readily into the fetus and have been suspected of causing respiratory depression in the newborn. Benzodiazepines also pass into the mother's milk and can oversedate the baby, so breast feeding should be discontinued if a benzodiazepine is prescribed for the mother.

OVERDOSE

Overdose with the benzodiazepines is common, but deaths are mercifully rare (Greenblatt, Allen, Noel, & Shader, 1978). Although fatal overdose statistics contain deaths attributed to benzodiazepines alone, many such attributions are suspect. Often, other drugs or alcohol have been taken. Only in children and the physically frail, especially those with respiratory problems, are the benzodiazepines hazardous. Typically, a person who takes an overdose, say 100 mg of diazepam, becomes drowsy and falls into a deep sleep. A few develop rigidity or twitching of limbs or a skin eruption. Sleep lasts 24–48 hours, but patients are generally rousable. Plasma benzodiazepine concentrations are often high on hospital admission, and are still very high when the patient wakes up and seems conscious and oriented. This presumably reflects major acute tolerance to the depressant effects of the drug.

DEPENDENCE

Dependence on benzodiazepines is a controversial subject (Palmer, 1978), but, in view of the widespread use of these drugs, urgent studies are needed to establish the extent and the nature of any dependence on the benzodiazepines.

Tolerance has been mentioned earlier, and acute tolerance both at normal dose and at overdose occurs (Allgulander, 1978). However, relatively few patients escalate their dosage to levels so high that the prescriber suspects that dependence has developed. One estimate puts the risk of dependence arising in the therapeutic context (as opposed to polydrug abuse) at less than one case per 50 million patient-months of use (Marks, 1978). When escalation does occur, each elevation of dosage seems to be related to a temporary increase in stress. Most people increase their intake of antianxiety medication under these circumstances, but reduce the dose once the crisis is past. A few patients maintain their increased dose and increase the dose still further when the next stress supervenes. No definite features characterize such patients, except that they may have previously abused alcohol or a barbiturate. Tolerance with escalation of dose is not due to the body's metabolizing the drug at an increasingly rapid rate, because plasma concentrations of benzodiazepines are abnormally high in patients taking excessive doses.

Tolerance to clinical effects in patients who take moderate doses of benzodiazepines for long periods of time is less easy to establish (Covi, Lipman, Pattison, Derogatis, & Uhlenhuth, 1973). If medication is withdrawn, symptoms appear, often resembling those for which the benzodiazepine was originally prescribed (e.g., anxiety, tension, insomnia, trembling, palpitations, and sweating). This is sometimes taken as evidence that the anxiety has merely been kept under control by the drug and that the symptoms have reemerged when the drug has been withdrawn, rather than evidence that a true withdrawal syndrome is ensuing (Rickels, Downing, & Winokur, 1978).

A definite withdrawal syndrome has been described in patients who have escalated their dose of benzodiazepine and have been on a high dose for a long time. After long-acting benzodiazepines such as diazepam are stopped, withdrawal symptoms usually do not develop until about the sixth day but may be delayed for 10–14 days. The onset is quicker in patients discontinuing shorter-acting benzodiazepines such as lorazepam. The mildest symptoms are anxiety, tension, apprehension, dizziness, insomnia, and anorexia. More severe physical dependence is manifested by withdrawal symptoms of nausea and vomiting, tremor, muscle weakness, and postural hypotension. Occasionally, hyperthermia, muscle twitches, convulsions, and confusional psychoses may occur (Fruensgaard, 1976). The management of benzodiazepine withdrawal is to lower the dose over 2–4 weeks and to rely on supportive psychotherapy to help the patient over the worst of the withdrawal period, which usually lasts about 2 weeks. Substitution of an antipsychotic drug such as chlorpromazine is not advisable, because the convulsive threshold is lowered. Propranolol, the β-adrenoceptor antagonist, may help, especially if tremor is extreme.

Recently, evidence has been adduced to suggest that patients on normal therapeutic doses (i.e., up to 30 mg per day of diazepam or equivalent) who report difficulty in discontinuing their drugs develop a full-blown withdrawal syndrome if their drugs are stopped. On withdrawal, affective and perceptual changes occur, identical in nature, extent, and severity to those experienced in patients discontinuing high doses. That these phenomena are not the original anxiety returning is evidenced by several sets of observations. First, the anxiety level gradually subsides over 1–2 weeks, despite the fact that no other medication is being given. If the original anxiety had returned, it would be expected to be maintained at high levels. Secondly, perceptual changes uncharacteristic of anxiety are almost invariable. They include abnormally high sensitivity to light and sound, a feeling of unsteadiness (as if on board a ship), and oversensitivity of touch. Some of these symptoms persist for a while but eventually disappear. Thirdly, patients feel physically ill during the withdrawal period, as if suffering from a severe bout of influenza. This, also, is untypical of anxiety and stress responses.

These observations were made on patients who had already experienced difficulty discontinuing their medication and were thus highly selected. Few studies have attempted to determine the incidence of withdrawal problem in unselected patients. One estimate is that about 5% of anxious patients starting therapy with a benzodiazepine will eventually experience withdrawal symptoms. Another estimate is that patients who have been on a benzodiazepine for a year or more will have an incidence of withdrawal symptoms of about 30%. Thus, the longer a patient is maintained on a benzodiazepine, the greater the chance of a withdrawal syndrome on discontinuation of the drug. However, it may be that patients become dependent quite quickly, experience withdrawal symptoms when they try to stop, and therefore continue with their medication. Few comparative data are available, but it is probable that all benzodiazepines have the property of producing dependence and that there is little choice among them in this respect. Lorazepam may give rise to more difficulties than diazepam (Tyrer, 1980a).

OTHER ANTIANXIETY DRUGS

ANTIPSYCHOTIC DRUGS

Antipsychotic drugs (neuroleptics) such as chlorpromazine, thioridazine, and trifluoperazine have been advocated in the treatment of anxiety. The suggested dose is quite low, typically below half of the usual antipsychotic dose. Even at this low dosage, the antipsychotic drug may be poorly tolerated by the anxious patient, because autonomic side effects such as dry mouth and dizziness too closely resemble his or her own symptoms. Even more upsetting are extrapyramidal symptoms such as restlessness and mild parkinsonism, with paucity of voluntary movements and a coarse tremor. Such unwanted effects are usually uncommon at the low doses used. More worrisome is the possibility of tardive dyskinesia, a disorder characterized by repetitive sinuous or jerky movements of the tongue, mouth, face, or limbs. This condition may supervene after months or years of treatment and may persist despite discontinuation of therapy. A few cases have been described even at the low dosage of antipsychotic drugs used. However, there is a spontaneous incidence of orofacial dyskinesia, especially in the elderly, so the relationship to drug therapy is not always firmly established. Whereas the risk of tardive dyskinesia may be justifiable in a severely psychotic schizophrenic patient who without medication would be uncontrollable, it is doubtful whether the treatment of anxiety should be attended by any such risk. The possibility of tardive dyskinesia has led to a marked decrease in the prescribing of antipsychotic medication, especially in the United States.

The chief advantage of antipsychotic drugs in the management of anxiety is that dependence on these drugs is virtually unknown. Accordingly, the chief indication for their use is in patients with histories of dependence on other drugs that depress the central nervous system, such as alcohol or the barbiturates. Dosage should be cautious, and careful observations should be made to establish whether any therapeutic benefit is accruing. Extrapyramidal signs should be carefully sought, and if they are detected the dose should be lowered, because there may be a danger of the eventual development of tardive dyskinesia.

TRICYCLIC ANTIDEPRESSANTS

Several of the tricyclic antidepressants, such as amitriptyline, doxepin, and mianserin, have useful secondary sedative properties. They are the treatment of first choice in depressed patients with anxiety or agitation. They are not appropriate for patients with primary anxiety states. However, the distinction between primary depressive and primary anxious illnesses is not always easy, especially in milder cases as encountered in general practice. If a patient with anxiety fails to respond to simple antianxiety treatment, the possibility of an underlying depressive illness should be seriously considered.

Fixed combinations of tricyclic antidepressants with tranquilizers or antipsychotic medication have been formulated and marketed. They have little to commend them: Their convenience as a single medication is outweighed by the prescriber's loss of flexibility of symptom management.

MONOAMINE OXIDASE INHIBITORS

Monoamine oxidase inhibitors are used to treat atypical depressives but are controversial; some psychiatrists use them routinely, but others avoid their use as attended by too many side effects. Some patients with phobic anxiety respond very well to full doses of phenelzine or tranylcypromine, but "free-floating" anxiety is not usually helped. It is doubtful whether these drugs have any place in the management of stress responses.

β-ADRENOCEPTOR ANTAGONISTS

Many different bodily symptoms in patients with anxiety states are mediated by the sympathetic nervous system (Lader, 1974). In particular, palpitations, tremor, and gastrointestinal upset are related to overactivity of β-adrenergic sympathetic neurons. Consequently, blockade of this activity by means of β-adrenoceptor antagonists might be expected to help patients with anxiety, especially those with the above symptoms. Many trials have been carried out in the last 15 years, especially in the United Kingdom, using various β-blockers (Tyrer, 1980b). The results have consistently indicated that only those symptoms mediated by the beta division of the sympathetic nervous system are helped by administration of drugs such as propranolol or sotalol. Somatic symptoms, such as headache, that are not mediated that way or general psychological symptoms are not usefully improved. Whether a patient finds relief on a β-blocker depends on his or her symptom profile. Patients with predominant complaints of palpitations, trembling, and diarrhea are often much improved. Even so, the improvement may be limited to those symptoms alone, and general anxiety symptoms may be unchanged.

Occasional patients may be made worse by β-blockers. Some phobic patients use their somatic symptoms such as palpitations or tremor as signals that they are approaching a phobic situation, which they then avoid. β-Blockage results in loss of those signals, which may result in phobic patients' unknowingly extending themselves into a phobic situation.

β-Adrenoceptor antagonists may be combined with a benzodiazepine in an attempt to attenuate the symptoms, peripherally by preventing their mediation and centrally by lowering arousal. Such combinations have to be established in each individual case by trial and error.

β-Adrenoceptor antagonists should not be used in patients with any history of asthma, and a cardiologist's advice should be sought for those with heart disease. A test dose, say 20 mg of propranolol, should be administered to detect any undue sensitivity of the patient, as shown by the pulse slowing below 60 beats per minute at rest. If no sensitivity is found, the dose can be started at 20 mg four times a day and increased over the course of a week or two to 40 mg four times a day. The resting pulse rate should be monitored and used as an endpoint. Dosage should be maintained at that needed to keep the pulse rate at normal levels. This is usually not more than 160–200 mg per day in divided doses.

At these dose levels, the drug is predominantly acting peripherally on symptom mechanisms. Some β-blockers enter the brain readily, some slowly. Depressant effects can be detected but are usually minimal. The lack of psychological impairment makes these drugs a useful choice in people undergoing acute but transient stress reactions with palpitations, tremor, or diarrhea as the prime symptom, but in whom clarity of mental functioning must be maintained. Students taking examinations provide a good example of this type of patient.

MANAGEMENT OF ANXIETY STATES AND STRESS RESPONSES

CONCEPTUAL MODEL

It is useful to have in mind some comprehensive conceptual scheme of anxiety and stress response when dealing with patients. One such model regards anxiety as the interaction between external stresses and an internal predisposition. A state of overarousal results. The internal predisposition results from the genetic makeup and previous learning experiences of the individual. It contains a symbolic element that may exaggerate or distort the person's perception of the external events. Thus, stress is seen as a threat, and anxiety is part of the stress response.

In addition to a model for the genesis of anxiety, it is useful to have a conceptual framework within which to set methods for lessening the anxiety. Excessive anxiety interferes with the patient's ability to cope with his or her own anxiety. He or she loses mastery over the symptoms, and this loss of control in itself constitutes a further stress. Nonpharmacological methods of therapy, such as biofeedback or relaxation, may be rendered ineffective at these excessively high anxiety levels because the person cannot attend to or concentrate on the instructions or the techniques. Psychotherapy may be impractical with a highly anxious person and may even worsen the patient's symptoms. In order to control the anxiety sufficiently for other therapies to become feasible and effective, antianxiety drugs may be used, preferably as a temporary expedient.

TAKING THE HISTORY

Particular attention should be paid to the following points:

1. The apparent precipitants of the present attack should be sought. Care is needed in evaluating the patient's spheres of functioning in the home, at work, and in the community. Patients are often confused by their symptoms and search for easy explanations. They may attribute their symptoms to spurious stresses. A problem produced by the illness may be transposed in time to antedate the symptoms. Thus an effect is misinterpreted as a cause. A good informant can be invaluable in establishing the factors contributing to an anxiety state.

2. The patient's previous personality should be assessed, with special reference to the customary level of anxiety and methods of coping with previous stresses.

3. The family history may be important, especially if other family members have suffered from anxiety or other neurotic disorders.

4. The patient's current social support—for example, the quality of the marriage—often influences the type of treatment recommended and the response to that treatment.

5. The symptom profile should be carefully established. Which symptoms particularly upset the patient, and what significance does he or she invest them with? It is important to determine whether somatic or psychological symptoms predominate. The degree of interference with personal and social functioning should be ascertained.

6. The pattern of the anxiety should be recognized. It may be constant or episodic; it may be related to particular situations or bafflingly unpredictable. It sometimes helps for the patient to keep a fairly detailed diary of anxiety attacks so that the pattern can be established.

7. Response to previous treatment should be inquired into. Patients who have found alcohol helpful tend to respond well to prescribed tranquilizers.

8. Finally, the patient's expectations should be evaluated. A patient may be reluctant to admit to needing help. In particular, he or she may insist that the symptoms are physical and that therefore there must be something physically amiss. Recognition of psychological problems is an important step in instituting appropriate and effective treatment. A person with lifelong high trait anxiety may entertain the unreal expectation of a miracle cure that will make him or her into a phlegmatic stoic. Or a person with an acute stress response may desperately believe that he or she is suffering from a chronic mental illness. And does the patient expect to be given tranquilizers? If so, does he or she have confidence in them?

DRUG THERAPY

When to Use Drugs

The fundamental dilemma faced by the therapist is whether the benefits of antianxiety medication outweigh the risks of dependence, the "medicalizing" of an essential interpersonal or environmental problem, the probable facile resort to drugs in future episodes, and so on. The main criterion for giving drugs is that the anxiety is so severe as to hinder the patient's coping with both the anxiety and the underlying problems. Very often it is an acute severe anxiety that requires pharmacological treatment, so that the drugs tide the patient over a week or two of distress until the basic problems can be tackled, or while the patient adapts to or is reeducated to cope with insoluble problems. For example, sedation after a tragic and sudden bereavement is appropriate, but a routine administration of anxiolytics after a long-expected death in the family is not. Control of symptoms by prompt and vigorous treatment enables the patient to regain mastery over his or her own symptoms—to reestablish confidence in himself or herself, with the ability to approach difficulties realistically. Although most acute anxiety states subside spontaneously, a few become chronic if the symptoms are allowed to persist unabated for more than a week or two. If the anxiety symptoms are closely related to stress, they will usually subside as the stress lessens.

When tranquilizers are given to help combat stress responses, the patients must be warned that the drugs will be given for a limited period. They must agree to cooperate when the time comes to discontinue medication, even if they then think that their stress responses have not fully subsided. There is little justification in continuing tranquilizers for more than a month in patients suffering from acute stress responses. The aim should be to establish nonpharmacological methods of treatment as soon as possible, so that drug withdrawal can be expedited.

A more difficult situation concerns more prolonged neurotic episodes of anxiety. Drug administration will be over a longer time scale than that with acute stress responses, and the risk of developing dependence is correspondingly that much greater. Again, the criteria should be the severity of the anxiety and the distress it causes the patient. If the anxiety interferes with everyday functioning, handicapping the patient in some way, tranquilizers should be seriously considered. Such episodes usually peter out after weeks or months. In the younger patient, maturation is often accompanied by better coping responses and mastery of anxiety. The general tendency is for the symptoms to lessen. The prescriber must reassess the patient from time to time to see whether reduction in dosage and eventual discontinuation of drugs is possible.

The most complex decision concerns the patient with lifelong personality-bound anxiety who reacts to every change in circumstance, however minor, as if it were a major stress. Here the anxiety constantly permeates the person's existence. Every decision is an agony of doubt, every departure from routine a source of apprehension, every encounter with a stranger a signal for panic. It is essential to establish whether the patient functions better on drugs with respect to interpersonal, social, occupational, and leisure activity and also derives some symptom relief. If this benefit can be established, then long-term, even indefinite medication can be justified. To withhold tranquilizers in these circumstances is to make a moral rather than a medical judgment.

Choice of Drug

Many of the factors relevant to the choice of a drug have been discussed earlier. β-Adrenoceptor antagonists should be considered if somatic symptoms are paramount. Depressive states with anxiety are common, and sedative tricyclic antidepressants are then appropriate.

Among the tranquilizers, the benzodiazepines are deservedly the most popular drugs. Among the benzodiazepines, pharmacokinetic differences, as discussed earlier, provide some basis for a rational choice. Most patients do not have marked preferences among the benzodiazepines, but some are able to distinguish long-acting from shorter-acting compounds and may prefer one or the other.

Dosage Schedules

The keynote for treatment should be flexibility, to accommodate the individual needs of the patient. If repeated daily doses of a short-acting drug are used, it is helpful for the patient to keep a daily log of drug usage in relation to stressful circumstances. This facilitates the adjustment of the dosage that the patient needs, and also increases his or her feeling of participation in a therapeutic process, rather than being merely a passive recipient of medication.

The rule for establishing dosage is to balance the best clinical response against the patient's ability to tolerate any side effects. The longer-acting drugs are easier to stabilize in this respect. Despite the rationale of usage based on the pharmacokinetics of the various benzodiazepines, too rigid an adherence to dosage schedules can be unproductive. Thus, one patient may manage well on one dose of clorazepate at night, another on a minuscule dose of diazepam several times a day, a third on twice-daily lorazepam. Yet another may take hypnotic drugs in small doses during the day.

Duration of Therapy

The question of the duration of therapy has also been touched on earlier. Short courses of treatment are usually appropriate in patients undergoing symptomatic responses to stress. As remission is very likely, treatment should be planned in terms of 2–4 weeks. The patient should not be allowed to persist with marginally effective treatment. Either it must be withdrawn and something else tried, or the dose must be increased. Some patients with recurrent episodes of anxiety keep a store of tranquilizers handy and are adept at reverting to them for a short course of treatment during a crisis. Disapproval of such action only leads to such patients' taking the drugs clandestinely.

Drug Discontinuation

Withdrawal is best carried out over a few weeks, especially when dosage has been high or treatment prolonged. The patient should be seen frequently during the days after withdrawal.

Response to Treatment

Anxiety itself and somatic complaints are the symptom areas most sensitive to tranquilizer effects. Depressive symptoms occasionally respond, but obsessional symptoms are usually refractory to tranquilizers. Interpersonal sensitivity, such as a patient's feelings being easily hurt, is also unresponsive. Psychotherapy is more appropriate for patients with excessive sensitivity.

Predictors of Response

These predictors, as derived by Rickels and his coworkers, are set out in Table 10-2. Obviously some of these factors, such as a patient's educational level, cannot be altered by the physician. Others can be modified and will result in a better treatment response. Thus, establishment of good rapport with the patient and explanation of symptom mechanisms and the expectations from treatment do much to ensure the success of that treatment, pharmacological or nonpharmacological.

CONCLUSIONS

Drug treatment must be an adjunct to other forms of anxiety reduction and to general management of anxious patients. Drugs can be very helpful when anxiety levels are so high that they interfere with all forms of anx-

TABLE 10-2. Predictors of Improvement with Benzodiazepines

Patient	Physician	Illness and treatment related	Presenting psychopathology
Employed	Good prognosis	Acute duration	Less severe obsessive–compulsive
More educated	Feels comfortable with patient	Diagnosis of anxiety or mixed anxiety–depression	Less severe interpersonal sensitivity
Treated in family practice	Feels comfortable prescribing drugs	None or few previous drugs	Less severe depression
Expects drug treatment		Good response to previous drugs	More severe anxiety
Knows problems are emotional		No concurrent medical illness	
Married		Precipitating stress present	
Female without menopause or hysterectomy		Side effects (primarily sedation) present at 2 weeks	

Note. Reprinted by permission of Plenum Publishing Corporation, New York, from "Antianxiety Drugs: Clinical Use in Psychiatry" by K. Rickels, R. W. Downing, and A. Winokur. In L. L. Iversen, S. D. Iversen, and S. H. Snyder (Eds.), *Handbook of Psychopharmacology* (1978, p. 423).

iety reduction. In general, benzodiazepines are the drugs of choice and are usually effective, provided that the choice of drug is careful and the dosage is flexible.

REFERENCES

Action from the CRM: Barbiturates. *Drug and Therapeutics Bulletin,* 1980, *18,* 9–11.

Allgulander, G. Dependence on sedative and hypnotic drugs: A comparative clinical and social study. *Acta Psychiatrica Scandinavica,* 1978 (Suppl. 270).

Ayd, F. J., & Blackwell, B. (Eds.). *Discoveries in biological psychiatry.* Philadelphia: J. B. Lippincott, 1970.

Balter, M. B., Levine, J., & Manheimer, D. I. Cross-national study of the extent of anti-anxiety/ sedative drug use. *New England Journal of Medicine,* 1973, *290,* 769–774.

Berger, F. M. The similarities and differences between meprobamate and barbiturates. *Clinical Pharmacology and Therapeutics,* 1963, *4,* 209–231.

Blackwell, B. The role of diazepam in medical practice. *Journal of the American Medical Association,* 1973, *225,* 1637–1641.

Cazort, R. J. Role of relaxants in the treatment of traumatic musculoskeletal disorders: A double-blind study of three agents. *Current Therapeutic Research,* 1964, *6,* 454–458.

Clancy, J., & Noyes, R. Anxiety neurosis: A disease for the medical model. *Psychosomatics,* 1976, *17,* 90–93.

Cohen, I. M. The benzodiazepines. In F. J. Ayd & B. Blackwell (Eds.), *Discoveries in biological psychiatry.* Philadelphia: J. B. Lippincott, 1970.

Covi, L., Lipman, R. S., Pattison, J. H., Derogatis, L. R., & Uhlenhuth, E. H. Length of treatment with anxiolytic sedatives and response to their sudden withdrawal. *Acta Psychiatrica Scandinavica,* 1973, *49,* 51–64.

Fruensgaard, K. Withdrawal psychosis: A study of 30 consecutive cases. *Acta Psychiatrica Scandinavica,* 1976, *53,* 105–118.

Gaind, R. N., & Jacoby, R. Benzodiazepines causing aggression. In R. N. Gaind & B. L. Hudson (Eds.), *Current themes in psychiatry.* London: Macmillan, 1978.

Greenblatt, D. J., Allen, M. D., Noel, B. J., & Shader, R. I. Acute overdosage with benzodiazepine derivatives. *Clinical Pharmacology and Therapeutics,* 1977, *21,* 497–514.

Greenblatt, D. J., & Shader, R. I. *Benzodiazepines in clinical practice.* New York: Raven Press, 1974. (a)

Greenblatt, D. J., & Shader, R. I. Benzodiazepines: Part I. *New England Journal of Medicine,* 1974, *291,* 1011–1015. (b)

Greenblatt, D. J., & Shader, R. I. Benzodiazepines: Part II. *New England Journal of Medicine,* 1974, *291,* 1239–1243. (c)

Greenblatt, D. J., Shader, R. I., & Koch-Weser, J. Flurazepam hydrochloride. *Clinical Pharmacology and Therapeutics,* 1975, *17,* 1–14.

Hamilton, M. The assessment of anxiety states by rating. *British Journal of Medical Psychology,* 1959, *32,* 50–55.

Hanks, G. W., Lader, M. H., & Lawson, D. H. (Eds.). Clobazam. *British Journal of Clinical Pharmacology,* 1978, 7 (Suppl. 1).

Hartz, S. C., Heinonen, O. P., Shapiro, S., Siskind, V., & Slone, D. Antenatal exposure to meprobamate and chlordiazepoxide in relation to malformations, mental development, and childhood mortality. *New England Journal of Medicine,* 1975, *292,* 726–728.

Hesbacher, P. T., Rickels, K., Rial, W. Y., Segal, A., & Zamostien, B. B. Psychotropic drug prescription in family practice. *Comprehensive Psychiatry*, 1976, *17*, 607–615.

Hillestad, L., Hansen, T., Melsom, H., & Drivenes, A. Diazepam metabolism in normal man: I. Serum concentrations and clinical effects after intravenous, intramuscular, and oral administration. *Clinical Pharmacology and Therapeutics*, 1974, *16*, 479–484.

Lader, M. The peripheral and central role of the catecholamines in the mechanisms of anxiety. *International Pharmacopsychiatry*, 1974, *9*, 125–137.

Lader, M. H., Bond, A. J., & James, D. C. Clinical comparison of anxiolytic drug therapy. *Psychological Medicine*, 1974, *4*, 381–387.

Lader, M. H., Curry, S., & Baker, W. J. Physiological and psychological effects of clorazepate in man. *British Journal of Clinical Pharmacology*, 1980, *9*, 83–90.

Lasagna, L. The role of benzodiazepines in nonpsychiatric medical practice. *American Journal of Psychiatry*, 1977, *134*, 656–658.

Lewis, A. Problems presented by the ambiguous word "anxiety" as used in psychopathology. *Israel Annals of Psychiatry and Related Disciplines*, 1967, *5*, 105–121.

Linnoila, M., & Häkkinen, S. Effects of diazepam and codeine, alone and in combination with alcohol, on simulated driving. *Clinical Pharmacology and Therapeutics*, 1974, *15*, 368–373.

Linnoila, M., Mattila, M. J., & Kitchell, B. S. Drug interactions with alcohol. *Drugs*, 1979, *18*, 299–311.

Mandelli, M., Tognoni, G., & Garattini, S. Clinical pharmacokinetics of diazepam. *Clinical Pharmacokinetics*, 1978, *3*, 72–91.

Marks, J. *The benzodiazepines: Use, overuse, misuse, abuse.* Lancaster, England: MTP Press, 1978.

McNair, D. M. Antianxiety drugs and human performance. *Archives of General Psychiatry*, 1973, *29*, 609–617.

Palmer, G. C. Use, overuse, misuse, and abuse of benzodiazepines. *Alabama Journal of Medical Sciences*, 1978, *15*, 383–392.

Rickels, K., Downing, R. W., & Winokur, A. Antianxiety drugs: Clinical use in psychiatry. In L. L. Iversen, S. D. Iversen, & S. H. Snyder (Eds.), *Handbook of psychopharmacology.* New York: Plenum, 1978.

Salkind, M. R. *The construction and validation of a self-rating anxiety inventory.* Unpublished doctoral dissertation, University of London, 1973.

Shader, R. I., & Greenblatt, D. J. Clinical implications of benzodiazepine pharmacokinetics. *American Journal of Psychiatry*, 1977, *134*, 652–656.

Skegg, D. C. G., Doll, R., & Perry, J. Use of medicines in general practice. *British Medical Journal*, 1977, *ii*, 1561–1563.

Solomon, K., & Hart, R. Pitfalls and prospects in clinical research on antianxiety drugs: Benzodiazepines and placebo—a research review. *Journal of Clinical Psychiatry*, 1978, *39*, 823–831.

Spielberger, C. D. Anxiety as an emotional state. In C. D. Spielberger (Ed.), *Anxiety: Current trends in theory and research* (Vol. 1). New York: Academic Press, 1972.

Taylor, L., & Chave, S. *Mental health and environment.* London: Longmans, 1964.

Tyrer, P. The benzodiazepine bonanza. *Lancet*, 1974, *ii*, 709–710.

Tyrer, P. *The role of bodily feelings in anxiety.* London: Oxford University Press, 1976.

Tyrer, P. Benzodiazepine dependence and propranolol. *Pharmaceutical Journal*, 1980, *225*, 158–160. (a)

Tyrer, P. Use of β-blocking drugs in psychiatry and neurology. *Drugs*, 1980, *20*, 300–308. (b)

Zuckerman, M. General and situation-specific traits and states: New approaches to assessment of anxiety and other constructs. In M. Zuckerman & C. D. Spielberger (Eds.), *Emotions and anxiety: New concepts, methods, and applications.* Hillsdale, N.J.: Erlbaum, 1976.

11 CLINICAL APPLICATIONS

ROBERT L. WOOLFOLK AND PAUL M. LEHRER

The proliferation of techniques of clinical stress management has given rise to many questions about their range of application and their relation to more traditional forms of psychotherapy. There are, additionally, specific clinical issues that arise for the practitioner who employs this recently developed psychotechnology to intervene in stress-related disorders. Among these issues are the nature of the client–therapist relationship; client resistance to and/or compliance with treatment regimens; generalization and maintenance of treatment gains; assessment and the individualization of treatment; the wider sociocultural context of treatment; and the limitations of stress management technology. In the pages that follow, we examine these and other issues that arise in the clinical practice of stress management.

Clinical stress management consists of two crucial components, technique and art. Each is necessary; neither is sufficient to benefit the wide array of diverse problems and individuals the therapist encounters. As in all spheres of human endeavor, it is easier to give a precise and comprehensive account of technique than it is to transmit the subtleties and intangibles that seem to differentiate the clumsy practitioner from the therapeutic virtuoso. One of the goals of this collection has been the exposition of that clinical art. So too, in this chapter, an effort is made to go beyond technique to describe certain common denominators that characterize the artful application of stress management methods.

Underlying clinical stress management is the assumption that palpable gains can be achieved by the client in the absence of fundamental personality change or characterological transformation. At its base, clinical stress management does not rest on psychodynamic assumptions. The "working through" of unconscious conflicts having their roots in the psychic past of the patient is not seen as having much utility. Nor is it assumed, in the manner of the Rogerians, that a warm, empathic, genuine client–therapist relationship is sufficient to produce therapeutic progress.

Clinical stress management is a form of *direct* treatment. Its aim is the identification and amelioration of symptoms deriving from pathological stress through training the client in methods that are relatively standardized and replicable. Of all the systems of psychotherapy with which it might be compared, clinical stress management is probably closest in its outlook and orientation to behavior therapy. Insight is achieved within an explanatory framework that is present-centered and that generates coping activities. Insight for the sake of insight is not a primary goal, although self-understanding that leads to implications for self-regulation is pursued vigorously. The activities of the therapist are somewhat task-oriented and problem-centered. As with behavior therapy, the therapeutic core of the procedures of clinical stress management consists of empirically tested techniques that have some palpable impact on debilitating stress disorders.

But the clinician whose view of the complexity of the client's life situation is blinded by enthusiasm for the precision and elegance of a simple technical intervention is a poor therapist. The techniques described in this anthology are nothing more than useful tools. Not one of them, nor their entire aggregation, is a panacea. Nor do they constitute collectively a comprehensive system of therapy adequate for the treatment of every stress-plagued client. The treatment of stress-related symptoms solely through direct technical intervention is often insufficient to achieve substantial amelioration.

The clinician who is to be successful in treating a wide array of stress problems not only must be conversant with the latest stress reduction technology, but also must understand how the client's life style, social environment, and world view can generate or compound stress problems. A deeply ingrained pattern of hostility and time urgency, excessively high achievement needs untempered by any philosophical perspective, or fundamental conflict among life goals can lie at the root of stress disorders. Factors such as these must be given careful therapeutic attention in any effective program of stress management. Without a careful evaluation of the whole person to be treated—his or her goals and aspirations, style of life, and the social context in which he or she functions—stress management methods cannot be utilized for maximum benefit.

Although significant improvement in stress disorders can occur entirely as the result of technical intervention, often more fundamental changes in attitudes, beliefs, goals, values, and life style are necessary if stress is to be coped with effectively. The challenging task of the clinician treating stress disorders is to utilize the available armamentarium of stress management strategies while at the same time remaining a therapist—realizing that each individual is unique and may require a unique solution to his or her stress problems. The client's personality or style of life are often inextricably bound up with stress and discomfort. When this is the case, changes of a more fundamental sort are indicated. Without such more basic alterations in the way the client lives, stress management may even be counterproductive. It could be utilized to make tolerable and thereby to sustain the very dysfunctional patterns of behavior that are the most appropriate targets of treatment.

CLIENT–THERAPIST RELATIONSHIP

For some clinicians, one of the great attractions of the forms of treatment presented in this book may be that they represent a technology—a specifiable body of techniques, along with seemingly clear-cut formulas for their application. Contrasted with the improvisational and ephemeral nature of other forms of psychotherapeutic intervention, techniques of stress management sometimes appear objective and very robust. They do not seem so much to succeed either as a function of the personality and skill of the therapist or of the quality of the client–therapist relationship.

Certainly it is true that the techniques of clinical stress management are not inevitably embedded in the dynamics of the client–therapist interaction, as are those of some other forms of therapy. Because the patterns of communication between client and therapist tend to be somewhat more highly structured than in other approaches to intervention, the roles available for the client to assume in therapy are not as numerous as in more conventional forms of therapy that frequently seek to create some ambiguity in the client–therapist relationship. The technology of stress management can be taught quite effectively without explicitly examining such issues as transference and countertransference or exploring in depth the client's feelings toward the therapist.

From the fact that the client–therapist relationship is not the focus of treatment, however, it does not follow that this relationship is unimportant to the success of treatment. On the contrary, the evidence we have suggests that, far from being an impersonal discipline to which the therapist is essentially superfluous, the successful treatment of stress disorders requires an effective working relationship between client and therapist. In a recent review of the literature on progressive relaxation, Borkovec and Sides (1979) determined that therapist-administered training in progressive relaxation was typically more effective than audiotaped instruction. Lehrer (1982) reviewed the very recent literature on this topic and concluded that, for progressive relaxation, live training is necessary if acquired ability to lower physiological arousal during training sessions is to generalize to the outside activities of the client. In Chapter 13, we provide a more thorough discussion of this issue. Studies that have found weak effects for meditation training have typically employed training procedures involving minimal therapist contact (cf. Woolfolk, Lehrer, McCann, & Rooney, 1982, for review). With regard to the important issue of adherence to treatment, the evidence suggests that adherence is enhanced when the therapist is warm and empathic (Blackwell, 1976; Dunbar & Stunkard, 1979). Taub (1977) found that a warm interaction with the experimenter is necessary for laboratory subjects to learn to increase their finger temperatures through biofeedback.

The therapist may play many roles over the course of treating the individual's stress problems. The therapist is, of course, inescapably cast in the role of the expert; the therapist does in fact possess a specific kind of expertise, namely a storehouse of knowledge concerning the relationship of various coping activities to the reduction of stress. The therapist also has the ability to teach the client how to cope more effectively, and thus acts much as a teacher or a coach. The therapist is also a role model. Although we are aware of the logical fallacy involved in concluding that a therapist must *necessarily* be coping effectively with stress in his or her own life in order to be able to teach others how to do so, we find, in practice, that this most often is the case. The therapist is also a source of social reinforcement and punishment. Toughness and the ability to confront are necessary ingredients in clinical stress management as in other therapeutic transactions, but most often kindness, support, and empathy are called for. Although we discourage the formation of friendships between client and therapist that extend beyond the consulting room, because of the potential for introducing too much complexity into the client–therapist relationship, we believe that the therapeutic relationship has the potential to become an authentic and caring encounter.

In surveying the chapters of our expert contributors, the following descriptors of the therapeutic relationship have emerged:

- Budzynski and Stoyva: "The therapist is a sympathetic listener."
- Patel: "The teacher and the pupil together negotiate the meaning of learning."
- Barber: "Therapists who are not only highly skilled and caring individuals but also models of tranquility and equanimity."

- Beck: "The therapist encourages the patient to view his or her ideas as conclusions or inferences to be examined rather than beliefs to be defended."
- Carrington: "A subtle atmosphere of tranquility."
- Norris and Fahrion: "A healing partnership in which the client participates fully."
- Bernstein and Given: "Encouragement for the client's effort."
- McGuigan: "The clinician as a teacher can guide the learner."

The picture that emerges from these descriptions is that of a therapeutic relationship in which the therapist is an authority but not authoritarian—a supportive teacher who fashions a partnership, a cooperative problem-solving liaison with the client.

ASSESSMENT AND THE INDIVIDUALIZATION OF TREATMENT

Stress management techniques are generally appropriate for the vast array of maladies, both psychological and physical, that are either precipitated or maintained by physiological or cognitive arousal and its emotional, autonomic, muscular, and behavioral concomitants. Some of the most common of these are anxiety states, phobias, asthma, migraine and tension headaches, insomnia, essential hypertension, bruxism, backaches, chronic fatigue, anger, and gastrointestinal disorders.

When a therapist is presented with a client who seems to be a potential candidate for some form of stress management training, there are a number of diagnostic decisions to be made. These are addressed in the following set of questions that should be answered by the clinician before embarking upon a program of stress management:

1. *Is the client psychotic?* In most cases the presence of delusions, hallucinations, thought disorder, or inappropriate affect rules out the use of stress management techniques. Under no circumstances should methods of clinical stress management constitute the primary treatment modality for an individual with psychotic symptomatology. Although some forms of stress management (most particularly meditation) have been utilized with psychotic and borderline psychotics (Glueck & Stroebel, 1975), this is questionable policy outside of a closely supervised hospital environment. Most individuals so classified lack the capacity for the sustained concentration required by self-regulation procedures. Although self-regulation procedures are among the most benign of interventions, there have been some isolated reports of relaxation techniques' precipitating psychotic

episodes in patients with a history of severe disturbance (see Carrington, Chapter 5, this volume).

2. *Is the client severely depressed?* Cases of mild depression whose linkage to life stress is immediate can profit from various stress management techniques (see Lehrer & Woolfolk, Chapter 13, this volume). But severe depression, that labeled "Major Depressive Episode" in the third edition of the *Diagnostic and Statistical Manual of Mental Disorders* (DSM-III)—characterized by a constellation of severe dysphoria, sleep disturbance, poor appetite, fatigue, anhedonia, feelings of worthlessness, and suicidal ideation—is another matter entirely. Severe depression is unlikely to be aided by treatment that targets stress and arousal. It requires a psychological treatment (Beck, Rush, Shaw, & Emery, 1979), a pharmacological treatment, or a combination of the two (Gelenberg & Klerman, 1978) designed to eliminate the depression. Because of the risk of suicide, it is crucial that severely depressed individuals not be assigned to training in stress management unless their depression is concurrently being carefully monitored and treated more comprehensively.

3. *Does the client's stress problem have an organic basis?* Because of the close relationship between stress and physiological processes, the therapist treating stress disorders will occasionally be confronted with problems that have some organic basis. Furthermore, because of the demonstrated ability of psychological stress to produce deleterious changes in somatic processes, individuals beset by psychological stress may have already experienced some organic consequences. A medical examination should therefore be a routine accompaniment of treatment in stress management. One problem with using stress management procedures to treat organically based disorders without prior medical screening is that therapy may result in enough symptomatic improvement to cause the client to delay obtaining the necessary medical treatment. In the case of the classic psychosomatic problems, such as irritable colon or back pain, a consultation should be sought with a physician specializing in the organ area of concern. Deficits in cognitive functions should dictate a neuropsychological assessment.

4. *Does the client suffer from other problems of living that would make it unlikely that he or she could successfully carry out a program of stress management?* Stress management training requires that the individual be able to carry out assignments reliably between sessions. It also presupposes that the client is stable enough to assume a rather substantial degree of responsibility for implementing the coping strategies learned in therapy. A multitude of factors, ranging from a fear of loss of control

experienced when attempting relaxation procedures to the presence of continual marital conflict that undermines home practice, may preclude such assumptions. It is up to the skillful therapist to identify and, if appropriate, to remedy such obstacles before proceeding to attempt more direct corrective intervention with the client's stress problem. Assuming that the questions listed above have been answered satisfactorily, the therapist is faced then with the decision of which technique to employ. Unfortunately, the empirical literature offers little guidance here. The comparative outcome studies have shed some light on this question. At this stage, the empirical literature favors the view of stress management techniques as having rather general and overlapping effects, especially when utilized by a clinical population as part of a total program to cope more effectively with stress (see Lehrer & Woolfolk, Chapter 13, this volume; Woolfolk *et al.*, 1982). Carefully controlled studies of responses to laboratory stress have suggested that there may be important differences in the impact of different stress management methods (Davidson, 1978; Davidson & Schwartz, 1976). But the clinical implications of these studies are far from clear (cf. Chapter 13, this volume), and it remains for future investigations to uncover advantages in efficacy that may be inherent in the use of a given technique with a particular stress problem.

It should be noted that some conditions may be exacerbated by relaxation training. For example, in diabetics the need for insulin may be decreased, and there have been rare reports of resulting insulin shock among persons taking insulin supplements. A few paradoxical increases in blood pressure in about 2–3% of cases in autogenic training have been observed (Luthe & Schultz, 1969). Thus, in treating hypertensives with relaxation methods, blood pressure should be monitored carefully.

RESISTANCE, COMPLIANCE, GENERALIZATION

Of all the issues that bedevil therapists involved in treating stress disorders, perhaps none are more perturbing than those of client noncompliance. Stress management techniques are effective when employed, but only *if* employed. Unfortunately, a rather large percentage of clients troubled by stress fall into one of two categories: (1) those reluctant or unwilling to attempt a program of stress management, and (2) those who begin such a program but fail to persist in their efforts over time.

All of the methods of stress management outlined herein require the active participation of the client outside of the therapeutic sessions, both

in daily home practice and in the direct application of the methods of self-regulation in the stressful environment of daily life. Deep relaxation and peace of mind are often readily obtained in the somewhat tranquil and protected confines of the consulting room. In order for these states to generalize to the outside world, much work must be done by the client outside the therapeutic sessions.

Having effective techniques avails us little if our clients do not invest the homework time and effort required to learn how to apply the methods effectively to the stresses that confront them. The following recommendations are based on our own clinical experience and that of numerous colleagues.

CLIENT SELF-RESPONSIBILITY

The sine qua non of all therapies that require the treated individual to perform acts between therapeutic sessions is the proposition that the client is solely responsible for taking the insights and skills acquired in therapy and translating these to everyday life. In the therapies of self-regulation, the responsibility of the client for his or her own learning is fundamental. The client must understand that stress management is a learned skill that must be practiced religiously during the early phases in order to be acquired with any degree of proficiency; it is analogous in this regard to various athletic or artistic pursuits. The client must understand that the gains to be derived from stress management techniques are proportional to the amount of practice one engages in. As with any program of salutary activities, such as jogging, one derives the benefits only if one performs the requisite activity. "It doesn't work if you don't do it" is a message that must be communicated unambiguously to clients prior to beginning their training in stress management.

AN INFORMED CLIENT

Although it is neither feasible nor desirable to make the client an expert in the biochemical, physiological, and psychological dimensions of stress, a small amount of education can go a long way toward instilling in the client a sense of informed participation in the project of his or her own stress management. A basic model of stress and a rationale for why this particular treatment is valuable in combating stress can both inspire

confidence in the method and lend some increased sense of purpose to the sometimes tedious activities required of the client. All reasonable questions related to stress should be answered, provided the therapist is not confronted with the occasional obsessional client who seems to prefer a seminar on stress to treatment for it. An open therapist, possessed of minimal defensiveness, is likely to be one with whom problems related to practice can be discussed fruitfully.

A COMPATIBLE TECHNIQUE

In order to gain the active participation of the client, the therapist should strive to match the client with a stress management method that holds some appeal for the client. In cases where the client comes into treatment with some clear preference or distaste for one or more methods, the task of the therapist is facilitated. The client can be exposed initially to several stress management techniques through short handouts, videotaped examples of training, or a brief *in vivo* demonstration. Initial client attraction for a particular method, however, may diminish after actual experience with it. Under no circumstances should a client continue to practice any method of stress control that is experienced as aversive more than very infrequently.

MODIFIED TECHNIQUES

Individual adjustments in practice schedules, in frequency of meetings with the therapist, and in the techniques themselves are desirable. This kind of individual tailoring is essential to therapeutic efficacy. The essential directive is to get the client regularly and systematically doing something that will alleviate excessive stress. In meditation, for example, some people find the standard 20-minute, twice daily routine unworkable. We have found that variations in this routine do not vitiate the benefits of meditative practice. A recent study (Carrington, Collings, Benson, Robinson, Wood, Lehrer, Woolfolk, & Cole, 1980) found the same self-reported benefits from relaxation and meditation among those subjects whose practice schedules departed from the standard routine as were observed for subjects who practiced as prescribed. Similarly, although meditation techniques derived from yoga are practiced with the eyes shut, some people have great difficulty keeping their eyes closed. Meditating with the eyes open or half-open not only seems an effective alternative, it has the centuries-old Zen tradition to suggest it as a legitimate alternative. While some rather high degree of expertise with a technique may be necessary to make effective adjustments, this is the essence of therapeutic artistry. Adjustments in the standard methods, however, do necessitate that the careful attention paid by the therapist to the evaluation of therapeutic progress must be augmented so that no loss of efficacy occurs. Combining techniques can also be a useful variation. In Chapter 13, we review evidence showing that combinations of techniques with slightly different therapeutic benefits or motivational properties are more effective for a variety of conditions than is using a single technique.

SCHEDULING, PLANNING, AND REHEARSAL

One of the common errors made by therapists is to send clients away from their first training sessions having spent no time discussing the particulars of how the clients will incorporate the routines of practice into daily life. The investment of a few moments of time to anticipate possible obstacles and to schedule the routines of the first weeks of practice can yield considerable therapeutic benefits. It is extremely useful to have a client make a commitment to a specific place and time for each practice session and to schedule the time and place on his or her weekly calendar. Practice must be accorded a high enough priority by clients that they understand that it will be carried out always, except in the event of an emergency. Having clients imagine themselves actually relaxing in the environment they have chosen can identify potential difficulties. Each client should be asked about possible aspects of the chosen time and place that may interfere with the prescribed activities.

A frequent therapeutic mistake is to train a client in some stress management method such as progressive relaxation and then simply to inform the client to use the technique whenever he or she is under stress. This kind of haphazard approach is doomed to failure. Once the client has become reasonably skilled at one or more stress management techniques, the client and therapist must anticipate specific recurrent stresses in the client's life and begin to practice the utilization of the technique under these conditions. Using either imagery or role playing to generate some approximation of the stressful situation, the client can rehearse coping efforts in the therapy session itself. Subsequent *in vivo* practice should be planned systematically, and its effects should be evaluated. Eventually these predictable stressors will become cues to initiate coping efforts. Chapter 13 reviews the empirical literature on the importance of giving clients specific training in how to utilize stress management in coping with stressful real-life situations.

FAMILY INVOLVEMENT

Opposition from significant others can scuttle the most artfully engineered program of stress management. Conversely, the supportive involvement of family members in a program of behavior change can have a positive impact on its success. A cooperative spouse can benefit a client's coping efforts in a number of ways. He or she can serve as a buffer between the client and family demands during practice times, can provide the support and encouragement that can aid a program of stress management immensely, and can provide the therapist with an additional source of information concerning the client's progress. Without some prior preparation, the client's embarking on a comprehensive program of stress management may be disruptive to stable patterns of family dynamics and may result in high emotional costs to the client. A short meeting with the client's spouse, for example, can be of great utility in enlisting cooperation and in giving the therapist access to a quasi-objective external observer of the client's activities.

MONITORING OF PROGRESS

The therapist must make some systematic effort to evaluate clients' progress. This should include not only some evaluation of clients' proficiencies with the techniques of stress management, but also monitoring of the clients' target symptoms and improvements. Client self-monitoring can be of great benefit in this regard, although the therapist must realize that self-monitoring is subject to client noncompliance just as stress management efforts are.

A therapist should never give a client therapeutic homework without subsequently checking to see that it has been done and assessing the impact of the intervention. Failure to follow up an intervention in this fashion communicates to the client that the assignment was unimportant and that no consequences follow its lack of completion. An active, involved therapist who is keeping track of the client's activities outside treatment not only is better able to guide the conduct of therapy, but also communicates a high level of commitment to the client and implants in him or her a sense of accountability to the therapy process.

In this same vein, the scheduling of "booster sessions" at intervals of 3 and 6 months following termination has some useful effects. Such sessions can serve as incentives to continue utilization of the tools acquired in clinical stress mangement. These sessions are also useful in "troubleshooting" and "fine-tuning" the client's coping skills.

APPROPRIATE EXPECTATIONS

In order to take stress reduction methods seriously enough to learn and practice them, clients need reasonably high expectations that the methods will help them (for a further discussion of this issue, see Chapter 13, this volume). All too often, however, clients with stress problems enter therapy with unrealistically high expectations. They seek rapid miracle "cures" that will in a brief period of time forever rid them of the debilitating effects of psychosocial stress. Inordinately lofty hopes of this kind are always met with disappointment. Stress is the recurring result of daily transactions with the social and physical environment. It is not analogous to a disease for which a cure is possible. Clients should be prepared by their therapists to expect eventually to manage stress rather than to eradicate it. The learning of coping skills is rarely a rapid process free of setbacks. Therapists should prepare clients to expect these setbacks and to realize that progress toward more effective coping is never a smooth and steady process.

The self-regulation strategies described in this volume are no panacea. The stress of life is unavoidable. We cannot completely escape it in this existence. Training in stress management offers the hope of eliminating some significant fraction of the pain, tension, and discomfort that result from excessive emotional and physiological arousal. Coping with stress is a lifelong effort for those of us in postindustrial society. The effort is never entirely successful. A certain amount of discomfort, uncertainty, and tragedy are inevitable aspects of living. Indeed, if it were possible to completely eliminate psychosocial stress, it would mean that most freedom, ambition, passion, loyalty, caring, and commitment to higher ideals also would vanish from human experience. Thus the promotion of some philosophical acceptance of the inevitable stress of life is a recommended accompaniment to training in stress management. More is said about this last point in subsequent sections.

STRESS: THE PSYCHOSOCIAL CONTEXT

The client receiving treatment for stress-related symptomatology, being a member of species *Homo sapiens*, is perhaps above all else a social being. The quality of the client's participation in his or her social environment determines his or her level of stress and ability to withstand it.

Numerous studies strongly indicate the significance that the immediate social millieu holds for health and well-being. Animal research has shown rather graphically that "societal disruptions" induced through the alteration of group size produce dramatic increases in pathology, even when other aspects of the environment are held constant (Ader, Kreutner, & Jacobs, 1963; Calhoun, 1962). Cassel (1974) has noted the similar social circumstances associated with such rather diverse maladies as tuberculosis, schizophrenia, alcoholism, multiple accidents, and suicide:

Common to all these people is a marginal status in society. They are individuals who for a variety of reasons (e.g., ethnic minorities rejected by the dominant majority in their neighborhood; high sustained rates of residential and occupational mobility; broken homes or isolated living circumstances) have been deprived of meaningful social contact. (p. 474)

Major alterations in social circumstances can produce deleterious effects on mental and physical well-being. The extensive research on life change has shown a consistent relationship between negative life change requiring social readjustment and both physical and mental symptomatology (Dohrenwend & Dohrenwend, 1974; Rahe, 1975). Individuals who move from stable rural communities to industrialized urban environments where cultural norms are inconsistent with their own values manifest large elevations in blood pressure (Eyer, 1975). In a series of investigations, Syme and his colleagues found higher rates of coronary heart disease in people manifesting high residential and occupational mobility than in more stable populations (Syme, Hyman, & Enterline, 1965). Christenson and Hinkle (1961) discovered that managers whose family backgrounds and educations had prepared them poorly for the demands of managerial life had higher incidences of physical disease and psychopathology than did a sample of age-matched managers whose preparation for executive life had been more complete.

The individual's susceptibility to stress-related symptomatology is a direct function of the social support received from the environment. Social support derives from meaningful ties to other individuals, groups, and the larger community. Such connections to other people and institutions may both reduce the likelihood of stressful events and alter the significance of those events to the individual. Presumably, meaningful participation in social relationships provides direct psychological benefits that may serve to buffer the effects of stressors (Cobb, 1976).

The absence of supportive interpersonal relationships seems to reduce individuals' ability to withstand the adverse effects of stress. Gore (1978) found that the elevated serum cholesterol, increased depression, and higher incidence of stress-related illness were all reduced in men who had supportive marriages, ties to their extended families, and involvement with peer groups. Widowers have been found to have death rates from three to five times higher than married men of the same age for every cause of death (Kraus & Lilienfeld, 1959). The recent death of a spouse is associated with higher death rates during the first 6 to 12 months of bereavement, and also with more symptoms of autonomic arousal and more hospital admissions (Minter & Kimball, 1980). A study of the relation of social support to illness (Berkman & Syme, 1979) showed that mortality was inversely related to each of four measures of social involvement: marriage, close friends and relatives, church membership, and informal and formal group associations. The ability of social support systems to reduce psychosomatic symptoms and enhance mental health has been shown in a number of investigations (Lin, Simeone, Ensel, & Kuo, 1979; Pinneau, 1976; Williams, Ware, & Donald, 1981).

The effects of life stress are moderated by social support. A study by Nuckolls, Cassel, and Kaplan (1972) found that women who had high life change scores during pregnancy had fewer complications when they also benefited from strong relationships with family and friends. In a study of reaction to occupational stress (LaRocco, House, & French, 1980), it was discovered that social support beneficially modified the relationship between perceived job stress and health. In a series of studies, Turner (1981) found a positive relationship between social support and psychological well-being; this relationship was strongest under conditions of high stress.

Lazarus and Cohen (1977), in what may be the most adequate model of stress available, describe "stress" as a transaction between the individual and the environment. Implicit in this definition is the notion that psychological factors mediate the impact of stressors and that stress is a function of the meaning of the stressor to the perceiver. Woolfolk and Richardson (1978) have described the active role played by the individual in the construction of stressful experience. Under this formulation of "stress," the individual is not a passive recipient in stressful transactions between the person and the environment, but may generate stress through maladaptive beliefs, attitudes, and patterns of action.

Certain psychological or life style factors seem both to create chronic emotional arousal and to predispose the individual to illness. On the basis of observations of a sample of 185 men over almost four decades, Vaillant (1979) concluded that chronic anxiety, depression, and emotional maladjustment predicted early aging, as defined by an irreversible decline in the health of subjects. A further conclusion was that "positive mental health significantly retards irreversible midlife decline in physical health" (p. 1253). The voluminous literature on the coronary-prone behavior pattern ("Type A") has established in prospective studies a predictive relationship between the Type A classification and subsequent coronary heart disease. Some recent research has established a link between hostility and subsequent heart disease. Matthews, Glass, Rosenman, and Bortner (1977) found that anger items from the standardized interview measure of Type A significantly discriminated men who later developed coronary heart disease from a group that remained disease-free. Williams, Haney, Lee, Kong, Blumenthal, and Whalen (1980) found that psychometrically assessed hostility was a significant predictor of coronary artery occlusion among patients who underwent diagnostic coronary arteriography. Data from the Framingham Heart Study (Haynes, Feinleib, & Kannel, 1980) indicate that among women Type A behavior, suppression of hostility, tension, and anxiety were predictors of future coronary heart disease.

In a fascinating set of studies, Kobasa and her colleagues (Kobasa, 1979; Kobasa, Maddi, & Courington, 1981) present evidence supporting a prophylactic effect against life stress for a constellation of attributes they label the "hardy personality style." "Hardiness" is characterized as an "amalgam of cognition, emotion, and action" that facilitates "transformational coping" with life stress. It consists of three components: "commitment" (as opposed to alienation), "control" (as opposed to powerlessness), and "challenge" (as opposed to threat). Hardy persons believe life to be meaningful; feel that they can influence the course of events; and believe change to be normal, inevitable, and a challenge to growth. Research supporting Kobasa's thesis has come from studies showing that high levels of life change are less damaging to individuals whose locus of control is highly internal (Johnson & Sarason, 1978) and to high "sensation seekers" (individuals who tend to seek out novel situations and high levels of stimulation) (Smith, Johnson, & Sarason, 1978). Cooley and Keesey (1981) recently have found that various scales of the Myers–Briggs Type Indicator also moderate the effects of life change. They report that physical illness is more closely associated with life change for the Introvert, Thinking, and Sensing types.

One's world view seemingly has important ramifications for the degree to which one copes effectively with stress. Marshaling an impressive body of evidence in his recent review of the stress literature, Antonovsky (1979) has suggested that a "sense of coherence," a "generalized, long-lasting way of seeing the world and one's life in it," is critical to the maintenance of good health. Antonovsky's "sense of coherence" is similar to Kobasa's notion of "hardiness" and is defined as

a global orientation that expresses the extent to which one has a pervasive, enduring though dynamic feeling that one's internal and external environments are predictable and that there is a high probability that things will work out as well as can reasonably be expected. (p. 123)

Antonovsky is careful to point out that a "sense of coherence" is not isomorphic with a "sense of control." Many events in life are both uncontrollable and unfavorable. A sense of coherence requires a "solid capacity to judge reality" so that one can accept the inevitable. A recent study by Suls and Mullen (1981) suggests that undesirable events were more highly correlated with subsequent illness when their controllability was uncertain than when subjects perceived the events as totally uncontrollable. The acceptance of the inevitable may, in fact, serve a critical coping function. Reinhold Niebuhr expressed this approach to coping so eloquently that it has been adopted by Alcoholics Anonymous (1975) as its motto: " . . . grant me the strength to change what I can, the courage to bear what I cannot, and the wisdom to know the difference."

THE PROBLEM OF STRESS IN ITS SOCIOCULTURAL AND EXISTENTIAL CONTEXT

The stressors, diets, toxins, and activity patterns of industrialized urban life take their toll on our minds and on our bodies. Diseases such as coronary heart disease, hypertension, and colitis, which are rare among primitive peoples, are our chief causes of death and disability. A major reason for the rise of the degenerative physical diseases, as well as the high levels of psychological distress in contemporary Western culture, may well be the chronic stress of modern life. That stress is inescapable. No matter what we do, we are unable to avoid it entirely.

Why, we might ask, is stress such a problem in contemporary society? Were there not terrible happenings and awful circumstances that troubled our ancestors, just as our current frustrations and tribulations beset us? Clearly, premodern life was and is (in contemporary unmodernized societies) very difficult. Wars, pestilence, and dangers from the elements have undoubtedly produced emotional arousal throughout human history. Yet there are key differences in the sociocultural environment that can foster a kind of unremitting tension in modern individuals—a level of stress that is chronic, as opposed to the episodic stressors that are more characteristic of less complicated societies. The modern world is different from that of the past—fundamentally, qualitatively. These differences provide some important clues to the capacity that contemporary culture seems to have for the creation of high levels of stress and tension in its citizens.

One of the distinctive features of modernization is the ordering of life by the clock and a large increase in time-pressured work. Caplan, Cobb, French, Harrison, and Pinneau (1975) found that machine-paced assembly workers reported more somatic complaints and anxiety than did assemblers who were not machine-paced. Levi and his colleagues (Levi, 1972) reported that piecework pressure produced increases in noradrenalin levels and in blood pressure. Tax accountants show substantial increases in serum cholesterol when working under the pressure of deadlines (Friedman, Rosenman, & Carroll, 1958).

As Alvin Toffler (1970) and various other observers have pointed out, not only is modern society an ever-changing panorama, but also the rate of that change is ever-increasing. Many of the implications of this condition are rather straightforward. The individual is constantly required to make adjustments to a varying sociocultural matrix. We have earlier reported how such social disruptions can elevate levels of stress. In the areas of job skills, interpersonal relationships, management of personal finances, and sex roles, to name just a few, such rapid and fundamental changes have occurred that old assumptions are in constant need of revision.

Three hundred years ago, it was possible for one individual, Leibniz, to know everything worth knowing. Forty years ago, it was possible for one individual to span the entire fledgling field of psychology. But today the knowledge explosion makes it impossible for one person to possess a significant fraction of the pertinent information even in a small area of the discipline of psychology. And the pool of knowledge is growing every day. Professionals who are not inclined toward voracious reading within their specialties are soon out of date, their knowledge obsolete. Life is a little that way for all of us. We must keep changing, continually adapting to a world that transforms itself more rapidly each day. We must move faster and faster just to maintain our places.

The women's liberation movement and its effects on society provide an excellent illustration of the stress-producing effects of rapid social change. Both men and women, socialized by a culture that accepted certain stereotypic views of the sexes, suddenly found themselves playing a game in which many of the rules had been changed. What had seemed the "natural" order of things was turned on its head as women reversed the repressive and destructive effects of the old rules. Women achieved many more options and undoubtedly eliminated many frustrations related to their previously restricted opportunities, but with new opportunities came new pressures and responsibilities. For many women, it was no longer good enough to stay home and raise a family. To preserve one's dignity, a job, a career, was necessary. Many women launched careers without adequate preparation—preparation that only years of a certain kind of socialization could provide. They were attempting to compete in what was still a "man's world," full of unwritten rules that were poorly understood by them. Meanwhile, males were finding that much of their taken-for-granted power was being stripped from them. Families were altered as women began demanding to exercise options formerly reserved for males. These changes affected almost every aspect of relations between the sexes, from matters as trivial as whether males should open doors for females to those as substantive as the nature of marriage in a nonsexist society.

One important effect of industrialization and modernization is that of dramatically enhancing the freedom and material well-being of individuals. The removal of many of the economic and social barriers to individual growth and self-expression presents the modern individual with a dazzling array of choices, as well as an awesome set of responsibilities. Compare the situation of a contemporary individual with that of one growing up in rural America 100 years ago. A century ago, the individual had few significant options. He or she would follow in the footsteps of the same-sexed parent, becoming either a farmer or a farm wife. A marriage to a youth from the area would be followed by a rather predictable life, characterized by conformity to a pattern of values and a life style to which there were no known alternatives. Today we choose our own careers, our circle of friends, our place of residence, and, perhaps most critical, our own values. We must make decisions on a multitude of issues that have been given or fixed in prior eras. We decide everything from whether to alter our appearances through dieting, exercise, or cosmetic surgery to what religion, if any, to follow. We are able to create for ourselves the rules that will govern our marriages or to decide what our sexual orientations will be. Very little is set, fixed, taken for granted. In the absence of some generally agreed-upon set of values or beliefs that provides practical wisdom to guide the making of choices, too many options can be difficult to bear. The great French sociologist, Emile Durkheim (1958), writing at the turn of the century, called this lack of values and norms "anomie," and demonstrated that under anomic conditions, suicide rates rise dramatically.

The sociologist Ferdinand Tönnies (1963), describing the changes in society that took place at the time of the Industrial Revolution, described two basic kinds of social organization. Modern American sociologists still often call them by the German words, *Gemeinschaft* and *Gesellschaft*, or literally, "community" and "society."

The *Gemeinschaft* form of social organization is the preindustrial form. It is characterized by group cohesiveness and coherent social order, but little freedom. In communal cultures, status is ascribed and jobs, wealth, and marriage are determined on the basis of who a person is, rather than what he or she can do. *Gemeinschaft* contains small social units (e.g., family, small village) and diffuse relationships in which various social roles, such as family member, boss, friend, teacher, healer, and church member, are extensively intermixed within the same small group of individuals.

In contrast, the *Gesellschaft* form encourages individual freedom and ambition, but at the price of social isolation and anomie. It is characterized by achieved rather than ascribed statuses. Units of social organization are large, so that even many of the people in a particular congregation or factory work force, let alone in a neighborhood or town, may not be known to each other. This form is also distinguished by role specificity. Thus we pray with one group of people, work with another, and socialize with a third. Few, if any, formalized activities take place within the extended family. The extended family all but disappears, and even the nuclear family is weakened. Social isolation and anomie are significant sources of stress in this more modern form of society (Nisbet, 1973). People often seek to recreate a sense of community by joining authoritarian cults, but these are often unstable, and they often isolate their members from the few social and familial ties that contemporary culture does permit.

In our increasingly individualistic and materialistic world, individuals are constantly thrown back upon themselves and their own resources. The German sociologist and philosopher Arnold Gehlen (1980) has written that one of the functions of society is to protect the individual from the burden of excessive choice. If that be so, contemporary industrialized societies are less than completely successful in that function. Never before has such a large percentage of the population been without durable and dependable social support.

The loss of community is related to the lack of meaning that is so often described by sociologists and existential philosophers as a concomitant of contemporary life. The premodern world view was communal and spiritual, as contrasted with the individualistic and materialistic consciousness of contemporary times. Premoderns felt themselves to be useful and necessary elements of a cosmological order that had inherent purpose and meaning (Taylor, 1975). But the replacement of religion by science as the ultimate source of epistemological authority; the desacralization of nature; the preeminence of rationality; and the relativization of values have disrupted the human security that emanated from a sense of belonging and the confidence that each individual life had some larger purpose and meaning. Existential writers have described this shift in human self-perception in compelling terms:

In a universe suddenly divested of illusions and lights, man feels an alien, a stranger. His exile is without remedy since he is deprived of the memory of a lost home or the hope of a promised land. (Camus, 1960, p. 5)

Such writers as Kobasa and Antonovsky have indicated and demonstrated the deleterious effects of alienation upon the ability to cope with stress. We have reviewed the evidence suggesting that people who find some purpose in existence, who believe that their activities are meaningful, and who view life as possessing coherence and lawfulness are less vulnerable to stress. Antonovsky's (1979) concept of a "sense of coherence" brings to mind the writings of the great sociologist Max Weber and his concept of "theodicy." "Theodicies" are elements of a cultural world view, explanations that confer meaning on experiences of suffering and wrongfulness. Berger, Berger, and Kellner (1973) have pointed out that, despite the great changes that have accompanied modernization, the "finitude, fragility, and mortality" of the human condition is essentially unchanged; but those previous definitions of reality that made life easier to bear have been seriously weakened by modernization. As becomes clear in the next section, some psychologists have suggested that the client's world view is the proximate cause of emotional distress, and that effective treatment of stress disorders requires the client to develop a world view that serves to counteract many psychologically debilitating aspects of living.

THE REALM OF BELIEFS

Some cognitively oriented therapists have addressed the issue of the client's world view directly. Most of their efforts have focused on specifying those beliefs and attitudes that generate emotional distress. Alfred Adler (1932), the precursor of modern cognitive therapy, wrote very eloquently about the need to correct the client's "mistaken" beliefs and erroneous modes of thought and perception. Beck and his colleagues (see Beck, Chapter 9, this volume; Beck, 1976; Bedrosian & Beck, 1980) have identified what they characterize as "cognitive distortions" that increase stress and emotional discomfort. Many of these distortions bear more than a passing resemblance to informal fallacies of logic (Copi, 1961). Among these are overgeneralization (the inductive fallacy), polarized thinking (black–white, dichotomous reasoning), magnification and exaggeration (overemphasis of the most negative possibilities in a given situation), and personalization (falsely self-referent ideation).

Ellis (1962) believes that much behavior pathology stems from demonstrably false and irrational cognitions that must be replaced by a "saner" world view if the client is to diminish excessive levels of emotional arousal. The Ellisonian *Weltanschauung* expunges perfectionism and moralism (Horney's tyranny of the "shoulds"), and replaces them with the following goals of living (Ellis, 1973):

1. Self-interest (rational egoism and long-range hedonism).
2. Self-direction (assumption of responsibility for one's own life).
3. Tolerance (acceptance of human fallibility and suspension of blaming others).
4. Acceptance of uncertainty (acknowledgment of the contingent nature of human existence).
5. Flexibility (openness to change and novel circumstances).
6. Scientific thinking (objective, rational patterns of thought).
7. Commitment (involvement in something outside oneself).

8. Risk taking (willingness to attempt new behavior, to chance failure in the pursuit of important goals).

9. Self-acceptance (inner-directedness).

Woolfolk and Richardson (1978) have described a "practical philosophy of living," derived from various modern psychological theories and ancient sources of wisdom, regarding the cognitive set most likely to promote effective coping and a sense of relatedness to the world. What follows is a partial listing of their recommended guidelines for a life style of minimal unnecessary stress:

1. A focus on cognitive appraisal. (Our emotional reactions to the world stem largely from our appraisals of the world, and these appraisals can be modified.)

2. Values that extend beyond mere self-interest.

3. A benevolent sense of humor.

4. Self-responsibility.

5. Tolerance, forgiveness, and the abandonment of blame.

6. Empathy and concern for others.

7. Establishment of priorities and the effective management of time in accordance with those priorities.

8. Acknowledgment, philosophical integration, and acceptance of the difficult, arbitrary, and capricious character of fate.

Barber (Chapter 6, this volume) notes that his clinical experience has indicated the necessity of "gently guiding" clients "to develop a broader philosophy of life" in order to teach them how "to meet the major and minor problems of life with equanimity." His "philosophical" approach for coping with life's difficulties has four major tenets:

1. Acceptance of the tragic and undesirable aspects of life.

2. A focus on amelioration of the negative aspects of life, rather than the more customary pattern of magnifying their impact by protesting their very happening.

3. Acknowledgment of our limited ability to influence many unfavorable circumstances and events.

4. An emphasis on improving one's life by anticipating predictable negative events, becoming less judgmental and more compassionate, emphasizing the positive potential of ourselves and others, and influencing others by example.

Various existential writers have addressed similar questions related to the development of a coherent and viable world view in the face of the uncertainties of the modern predicament. Many of their speculations strike to the heart of the issues raised in the cognitive therapy of stress management and are convergent with the viewpoints cited above. "Authenticity" is a multidimensional construct in existential philosophy that refers to the individual's acceptance of responsibility for the creation of his or her own experience of the world. We can choose and act on the basis of our choices. Existence is not a fact but a task. To attribute our experience of the world to the influence of circumstance or the acts of other individuals is an act of "bad faith" (Sartre, 1956). Alienation, the preeminent modern condition, is overcome through some passionate commitment to a direction in life. The primary developmental task of each individual is to make his or her life meaningful.

There are clearly many convergences among the various theoretical attempts to specify a salutary world view. The kind of personal philosophy most favorable to the mental and physical well-being of the client would seem to be one that provides some balance between individual needs for self-development and communal needs of relatedness. Such a *Weltan-schauung* would include a recognition and acceptance of the inevitable misfortunes and limitations of life, tolerance for the imperfections of oneself and others, an involvement in the *process* of one's life rather than its outcomes, a commitment to something outside oneself, and a balance between effortful striving and passive, detached observation. Also required is some system of belief, whether it be of the religious or secular humanistic variety, that makes the world intelligible and meaningful.

There are, of course, limits to this kind of instrumental psychophilosophical analysis. Determining those beliefs that reduce the stress of life is not the same as establishing the truth or value of those beliefs. Any world view that is advanced on the basis of its instrumental benefits to health and happiness will be subject to various forms of legitimate criticism. One such criticism is the ethical rejoinder suggesting that many individuals believe that some values are worth being stressed for—indeed, worth dying for. Another is that values or beliefs that are adopted purely for self-service, as a means to an end of greater health and happiness, can never supply the kind of meaning and purpose that belief systems such as science or religion, which are perceived to be based on absolute authority of some kind, can supply. Hence a world view whose only claim to legitimacy is its salutary effect is inherently self-limiting and self-defeating. A careful examination of these positions takes us beyond the scope of this book and into the realm of philosophy.

RELIGION AND STRESS REDUCTION

In other times and in other societies, many of the forms of stress described in this chapter have been reduced systematically by religious practice, which often has embedded within it many of the stress management methods described in this book. Thus Patel (Chapter 4, this volume) introduces us to the notion that many stress reduction methods have originated in Hindu religion and philosophy. Many are also contained in Jewish and Christian religious practice. Meditation originated in Hindu prayer. Reciting, singing, or chanting prayer in Western religions may also have mantra-like qualities, despite the emphasis of Western religion on analytical rationality. This may be most obvious in the rituals of the various mystical sects, but is present also in prayers that are recited weekly or daily in most other religions. One of us (Lehrer) recently treated a very religious young Jewish man who was under severe stress on his job. The young man was advised to join a daily prayer meeting that met at lunchtime at his plant. The client reported a general decrease in on-the-job stress symptoms after doing this, much as other people report similar experiences after meditating.

Religious groups also serve to obviate anomie and social isolation by teaching morality and by encouraging networks of friendship and mutual help. They further provide a forum for organizing a belief system, in which human experience and scientific knowledge are integrated into a system of cosmology, philosophy, and ethics. Some religions are authoritarian, while others are more democratic; but the major religions all remain stable forces, having endured for centuries. Their effects, to be sure, are weakened by the complexity and role specificity of our society. We can disbelieve and remain totally outside any religious community, without affecting our other social roles. Similarly, we can (and often do) pray among people with whom we otherwise have little in common. Prescribed values can be essentially disregarded once the religious service is over. Also, the strict and uncompromising moral standards of some religious denominations may foster stress by creating high levels of guilt and discomfort. Nevertheless, some correlational data suggest (although they cannot prove) that being part of an organized religious group may protect people from some forms of stress-related disease. Regular church attendance has been found to be related to lower blood pressure (Grahm, Kaplan, Cornoni-Huntley, James, Becker, Hames, & Heyden, 1978); to lower rates of heart disease (Kaplan, 1976); and to good general physical and mental health (Comstock & Partridge, 1972).

CASE EXAMPLE[1]

Bob was a 46-year-old post-myocardial-infarction patient who had been referred by his cardiologist to receive adjunctive treatment in stress management. He had suffered a mild coronary 6 months previously and, following a short convalescence, had resumed normal activities. According to his cardiologist, those "normal" activities included a pattern of excessive hours on the job, many acrimonious exchanges with subordinates, and a weekly golf game that was contested by the client in a highly competitive manner. For the initial interview, I requested that both the client and his wife attend.

I met alone with Bob first. He described himself as "aggressive" and a "winner." He attributed his rather considerable successes in business (he owned a small company) to great drive and determination and to an ability to "really bear down when the going gets rough." Bob recognized that there might be some problems with his approach to life. He reported frequent episodes of frustration, irritation, and tension. He believed, along with his cardiologist, that emotional factors might have contributed to his coronary heart disease and expressed the wish to do "anything he could to avoid another heart attack." Bob indicated that since his coronary he had adhered to a rigid low-fat diet and to a five-times-a-week program of aerobic exercise supervised by his cardiologist. He reported a weight loss of 15 pounds since his heart attack.

After speaking with Bob, I met alone with his wife for a few minutes. She described him as "tense," "angry," and "overly competitive." She felt that he pushed both himself and his two sons "much too hard." She suggested that his hard-driving style was probably a mixed blessing, at best, in his current business, having been responsible for the loss of some customers and an inordinately high rate of employee turnover. She recalled the loss of a major account, following a heated argument between Bob and his customer, several months prior to his coronary. In her view, their marriage was sound and satisfying. She corroborated Bob's description of his diet and pattern of exercise and offered to do anything she could to aid my work with her husband.

My initial assessment of Bob was that he would be a reasonably good candidate for training in stress management. His history was one of completing what he started. He had adhered faithfully to a program of exercise

---

[1]Treated by Woolfolk.

and diet for the previous 5 months. His family was supportive. On the negative side was what seemed to be deeply ingrained patterns of tense striving and relentless self-pressure. In my notes recorded after our initial interview, I speculated that this man had probably never been relaxed in his life. I wrote that I wished I had questioned him about this.

During our second session, I began relaxation training with Bob. He had never been exposed to any systematic method of relaxation, but understood and accepted the rationale that I explained to him. He expressed some doubts about the prospect of spending 40 minutes per day "doing nothing but lying around," but said he was willing to give it a try. Because I felt it important that Bob experience an unqualified sense of relaxation, I decided to use a combined procedure that produces a very powerful initial effect. Using the modified progressive relaxation procedure (see Bernstein & Given, Chapter 3, this volume), I put Bob through two tension–release cycles with the following muscle groups: lower arms, upper arms, shoulders, chest, abdomen, thighs, and calves. Following this, I had Bob engage in abdominal breathing (see Patel, Chapter 4, this volume) for 5 minutes followed by some suggestions of relaxation (see Barber, Chapter 6, this volume), and had him imagine some peaceful scenes. During the exercise Bob moved around quite a bit. His breathing did not become slow and rhythmical, nor did it deepen substantially. He did not seem relaxed.

> *Therapist*: Bob, I noticed that you were moving about quite a bit during the exercise. Were you having any difficulties with it?
>
> *Client*: I don't know. It was hard to stay still. I had some trouble concentrating on what you were saying. It seemed like you were moving too slow. I kept wanting to get on with it, you know, to get where we were going.
>
> *Therapist*: Bob, I find myself wondering if you ever do anything analogous to relaxation training in your daily life. For example, do you ever just sit around doing nothing? Do you ever watch a sunset, listen to relaxing music, or sunbathe?
>
> *Client*: Not really. I feel like if I'm not accomplishing something I'm just wasting my time. Sometimes I'll sit and listen to Sinatra, but usually only if I'm really beat, you know, too tired to do anything else. Then I'll have a couple of Scotches, kick my shoes off, and really relax.
>
> *Therapist*: It sounds as though you may not give yourself permission to relax until you are almost totally exhausted. Is that correct?
>
> *Client*: Yeah, I guess you might say that.

Therapist: This may be the first obstacle for us to overcome in our work together. I believe that a first step in your learning to be able to turn off the tension, to develop some control over how emotionally aroused you become, is to learn what it means to be really relaxed and to give yourself permission to enter this state at times other than when you are completely spent. More than that, I think we are going to have to help you cultivate a taste for relaxation, to begin to value it. I wonder if you may have some misgivings about becoming a more relaxed individual?

Client: What do you mean?

Therapist: I'm thinking of your earlier somewhat derogatory characterization of relaxation. You haven't spent much of your life lying around, have you?

Client: Listen, Doc, I'm willing to give it a try.

Therapist: That's all anyone can ask of you.

I was not, however, willing to risk having Bob practice the exercise he had learned, given its rather weak effects during the session. Instead, I gave him the assignment of listening to Sinatra records after having relaxed by consuming no more than 2 ounces of 90-proof spirits for a half hour a day, immediately upon arrival at home from work. Because the relaxation exercise he had learned in the session had produced such weak effects, I chose to establish a daily pattern of relaxation with a device that seemed destined to produce more positive initial effects and less frustration in the client.

During our third session, in which I readministered the procedure utilized in the second session, it became clear that one aspect of the method that troubled Bob was the closing of his eyes. He reported that he had difficulty keeping his eyes closed and found that preoccupation over this distracted him from listening to my voice. On the more positive side, he found the abdominal breathing to be very soothing.

At this point, I had Bob attempt an eyes-open meditation with a breathing focus (see Patel, Chapter 4, this volume; Carrington, Chapter 5, this volume). I instructed the client to direct his awareness to the sensations of his abdomen and chest as he breathed in and out, using abdominal breathing. I directed his gaze to a Monet print hanging on my office wall. Somewhat surprisingly, this procedure appeared to be quite effective. We arranged for Bob to practice a version of this procedure once daily at home in the morning before work, while sticking with Sinatra in the afternoon.

With the passage of 3 more weeks, Bob had learned to meditate upon his breathing with his eyes closed. He came to find the experience peaceful and reported that he looked forward to most meditation sessions. He also indicated that he felt generally less tense. Having established a regular routine of meditation, we turned to using meditation on a stress-contingent basis (see Carrington, Chapter 5, this volume). The client came to be able to engage in a minimeditation on many occasions when he found himself angry or irritated. He stated that he felt he was gaining some control over his temper.

Although treatment was progressing smoothly after 6 weeks, my discussions with Bob began to reveal just what a thoroughly hostile individual he was and to uncover some cognitions central to that hostility:

> *Client*: I guess you're right that just about anything can piss me off.
> *Therapist*: From what you are saying I conclude that you think most people are assholes who are constantly screwing up, and that if they just exercised a decent amount of care and consideration that they wouldn't get in your way.
> *Client*: Look, I'm really not asking for that much. I work my butt off. I go out of my way to help people. I'm straight with everybody. And what do I get in return? A lot of crap.

It became clear that Bob's anger stemmed, rather predictably, from the sense that other people were not living up to what he felt were legitimate expectations of them. Continual violations of what he believed to be fair and just treatment enraged him. Following Beck (1976; see also Chapter 9, this volume) and Ellis (1962, 1973), I set about to challenge these cognitions and to help him rethink many of his "irrational" assumptions and alter some of his distorted thought processes.

> *Therapist*: Bob, you keep telling me about all the assholes in the world and their constant wrongdoing. But let me ask you this: How were you appointed as the interpreter of universally correct morality? How is it that you are so certain that your views on these matters are self-evidently true?
> *Client*: I'm not sure what you mean.
> *Therapist*: Well, let's take a look at some of these transgressions that disturb you so greatly and see if we can place a somewhat different interpretation on them.

A rather close examination of anger-provoking incidents revealed that Bob reacted to these with a high degree of moral indignation and was possessed with a notable lack of empathy for other parties involved, a complete lack of any sense of tolerance or inclination toward forgiveness, and no broader philosophical perspective that allowed him to take these insults less personally. He was also entirely devoid of a sense of humor in such matters. Helping the client fashion a reappraisal of the anger-precipitating events was no easy project. He accepted the notion that one's view of a stressor, in large part, determined the reaction to it; however, he had difficulty imagining that his own rather rigid standards for others' conduct could be altered via our dialogues.

Working directly on Bob's cognitions was having minimal impact. He did try to substitute less moralistic and pejorative internal statements for his customary litany, and found this process somewhat helpful. But I sensed no real commitment in Bob to a change in his views. At this point, we embarked upon a more general discussion of values. I asked Bob to list in order of importance the five most important things to him in the world, and to bring the list to the next session. He arrived with the following list:

1. My Sons
2. My Wife
3. My Health
4. My Happiness
5. My Business

Therapist: It is interesting to me that you place your business fifth on the list.

Client: Why is that?

Therapist: Because I would estimate that you spend at least 10 times as many hours on your business as you do on all the other items combined.

Client: What are you getting at?

Therapist: Let's take your boys [aged 12 and 9], for example. How much time did you spend with them this past week? Now I'm talking about quality time actually engaged in some activity like throwing a ball around, talking with either of them, doing homework with them, going shopping with them, that sort of thing.

Client: I made a couple of their baseball games, but I guess that's about it.

Therapist: How about your wife? How much attention have you been giving her lately? How well do you know her? Do you know how she feels about being married to you? Are you aware of her personal hopes and aspirations? Do you talk to her about these things?

Client: I guess I may come up short in that area.

Therapist: If something happened to you tomorrow, do you think your family would know how important they are to you?

Client: I think so. I hope so.

Therapist: You don't sound certain.

Client: I don't know. I guess I'm not certain.

Therapist: There's something wrong here. You say your family is the most important thing in the world to you, but you're not convinced that they know that. It's clear you don't invest in these people that you care for so greatly anything like the time that you spend in your business. Most of your emotional energy seems to go into being pissed off at a world that is just not perfect enough to live up to your lofty standards. Maybe you're so angry so much of the time that you don't have anything positive left to give anyone.

Client: Jesus, I'd hate to think that.

Therapist: So would I. So would I.

Bob appeared for his next appointment more subdued than usual. He reported having tried to talk to his elder son and discovering that he did not know how. A conversation with his wife had unleashed a torrent of complaints about his "workaholic" habits and his neglect of his family. Fortunately, his wife's complaints were balanced by some expressions of her love for him and her admiration of many of his attributes.

Client: I guess some of the things you were saying last week really hit home. I'd like to make some changes.

Therapist: It won't be easy and it won't be free. It will cost you something. You'll have to give something up.

Client: What's that?

Therapist: Your anger.

Client: I don't know if I can do that. I think I have been angry for a lot of my life.

Therapist: It is true that we cannot perform an operation that removes your anger in the way that a surgeon removes a tumor. Coping with anger involves not only understanding the kinds of beliefs that lead to anger, but also attempting to cultivate a set of beliefs and attitudes that lead to other, more positive kinds of emotions.

Client: What did you have in mind?

Therapist: Oh, I was thinking of tolerance, forgiveness, flexibility, empathy, and humor. How does that sound to you?

Client: To tell you the truth, it sounds a little too saintly. Couldn't we shoot for something a little more down to earth?

Therapist: Why not? It's your life; I think it ought to be up to you to decide.

I saw Bob for another 4 months after this pivotal session. During that time, we worked much more successfully on his excessive anger. Our success came, I believe, from the development in Bob of a positive vision of himself toward which he was working, rather than an exclusive focus upon the maladaptive habits and cognitions that were in need of change. Greater clarification of Bob's values and our joint effort to make his actions more consistent with those values seemed to supply Bob with a feeling that he reported not having experienced previously—the belief that he was doing something worthwhile with his life. Within the context of that effort, the stress management treatment produced very satisfactory results.

REFERENCES

Ader, R., Kreutner, A., & Jacobs, H. L. Social environment, emotionality and alloxan diabetes in the rat. *Psychosomatic Medicine,* 1963, *25*, 60–68.

Adler, A. *What life should mean to you.* New York: Basic Books, 1932.

Alcoholics Anonymous. *Twelve steps and twelve traditions.* New York: AA World Services, 1975.

Antonovsky, A. *Health, stress and coping.* San Francisco: Jossey-Bass, 1979.

Beck, A. T. *Cognitive therapy and the emotional disorders.* New York: International Universities Press, 1976.

Beck, A. T., Rush, A. J., Shaw, B. F., & Emery, G. *Cognitive therapy of depression.* New York: Guilford Press, 1979.

Bedrosian, R. C., & Beck, A. T. Principles of cognitive therapy. In M. J. Mahoney (Ed.), *Psychotherapy process.* New York: Plenum, 1980.

Berger, P. L., Berger, B., & Kellner, H. *The homeless mind.* New York: Random House, 1973.

Berkman, L. F., & Syme, S. L. Social networks, host resistance, and mortality: A nine-year follow-up of Alameda County residents. *American Journal of Epidemiology,* 1979, *109*, 186–204.

Blackwell, B. Treatment adherence. *British Journal of Psychiatry,* 1976, *129*, 513–531.

Borkovec, T. D., & Sides, J. K. Critical procedural variables related to the physiological effects of progressive relaxation: A review. *Behaviour Research and Therapy,* 1979, *17*, 119–126.

Calhoun, J. B. Population density and social pathology. *Scientific American,* 1962, *206*, 139–148.

Camus, A. *The myth of Sisyphus and other essays.* New York: Vintage, 1960.

Caplan, R. D., Cobb, S., French, J. R. P., Jr., Harrison, R. V., & Pinneau, S. R., Jr. *Job demands and worker health* (DHEW Publication No. (NIOSH) 75-160). Washington, D.C.: U.S. Government Printing Office, 1975.

Carrington, P., Collings, G. H., Benson, H., Robinson, H., Wood, L. W., Lehrer, P. M.,

Woolfolk, R. L., & Cole, J. W. The use of meditation–relaxation techniques for the management of stress in a working population. *Journal of Occupational Medicine,* 1980, *22,* 221–231.

Cassel, J. Psychosocial processes and "stress": Theoretical formulation. *International Journal of Health Services,* 1974, *4,* 471–482.

Christenson, W. N., & Hinkle, L. E. Differences in illness and prognostic signs in two groups of young men. *Journal of the American Medical Association,* 1961, *177,* 247–253.

Cobb, S. Social support as a moderator of life stress. *Psychosomatic Medicine,* 1976, *38,* 300–314.

Comstock, G. W., & Partridge, K. B. Church attendance and health. *Journal of Chronic Diseases,* 1972, *25,* 665–672.

Cooley, E. J., & Keesey, J. Moderator variables in life stress and illness relationship. *Journal of Human Stress,* 1981, *7,* 35–40.

Copi, I. M. *Introduction to logic.* New York: Macmillan, 1961.

Davidson, R. J. Specificity and patterning in biobehavioral systems: Implications for behavioral change. *American Psychologist,* 1978, *33,* 430–436.

Davidson, R. J., & Schwartz, G. E. The psychobiology of relaxation and related states: A multi-process theory. In D. I. Mostofsky (Ed.), *Behavior control and modification of physiological activity.* Englewood Cliffs, N.J.: Prentice-Hall, 1976.

Dohrenwend, B. S., & Dohrenwend, B. P. (Eds.). *Stressful life events: Their nature and effects.* New York: Wiley, 1974.

Dunbar, J. M., & Stunkard, A. J. Adherence to medical regimen. In R. Levy, B. Rifkind, B. Dennis, & N. Ernst (Eds.), *Nutrition, lipids, and coronary heart disease.* New York: Raven Press, 1979.

Durkheim, E. *Suicide.* Glencoe, Ill.: Free Press, 1958.

Ellis, A. *Reason and emotion in psychotherapy.* New York: Lyle Stuart, 1962.

Ellis, A. *Humanistic psychotherapy: The rational–emotive approach.* New York: McGraw-Hill, 1973.

Eyer, J. Hypertension as a disease of modern society. *International Journal of Health Services,* 1975, *5,* 539–558.

Friedman, M., Rosenman, R. H., & Carroll, V. Changes in serum cholesterol and blood clotting time in men subjected to cyclic variation of occupational stress. *Circulation,* 1958, *17,* 852–861.

Gehlen, A. *Man in the age of technology.* New York: Columbia University Press, 1980.

Gelenberg, A. J., & Klerman, G. L. Maintenance drug therapy in long-term treatment of depression. In J. P. Brady & H. K. H. Brodie (Eds.), *Controversy in psychiatry.* Philadelphia: W. B. Saunders, 1978.

Glueck, B. C., & Stroebel, C. F. Biofeedback and meditation in the treatment of psychiatric illness. *Comprehensive Psychiatry,* 1975, *16,* 303–321.

Gore, S. The effect of social support in moderating the health consequences of unemployment. *Journal of Health and Social Behavior,* 1978, *19,* 157–165.

Grahm, T. W., Kaplan, B. H., Cornoni-Huntley, J. C., James, S. A., Becker, C., Hames, C. G., & Heyden, S. Frequency of church attendance and blood pressure elevation. *Journal of Behavioral Medicine,* 1978, *1,* 37–43.

Haynes, S. G., Feinleib, M., & Kannel, W. B. The relationship of psychosocial factors to coronary heart disease in the Framingham Study. *American Journal of Epidemiology,* 1980, *111,* 37.

Johnson, J. H., & Sarason, I. G. Life stress, depression and anxiety: Internal–external locus of control as a moderator variable. *Journal of Psychosomatic Research,* 1978, *22,* 205–208.

Kaplan, B. H. A note on religious beliefs and coronary heart disease. *Journal of the South Carolina Medical Association,* 1976, 60–64.

Kobasa, S. C. Stressful life events, personality and health: An enquiry into hardiness. *Journal of Personality and Social Psychology,* 1979, *37,* 1–11.

Kobasa, S. C., Maddi, S. R., & Courington, S. Personality and constitution as mediators in the stress–illness relationship. *Journal of Health and Social Behavior,* 1981, *22,* 368–378.

Kraus, A., & Lilienfeld, A. Some epidemiologic aspects of the high mortality rate in the young widowed group. *Journal of Chronic Diseases,* 1959, *10,* 207–217.

LaRocco, J. M., House, J. S., & French, J. R. P., Jr. Social support, occupational stress and health. *Journal of Health and Social Behavior,* 1980, *21,* 202–218.

Lazarus, R. S., & Cohen, J. B. Environmental stress. In I. Altman & J. F. Wohlwill (Eds.), *Human behavior and environment* (Vol. 2). New York: Plenum, 1977.

Lehrer, P. M. How to relax and how not to relax: A re-evaluation of the work of Edmund Jacobson. *Behaviour Research and Therapy,* 1982, *20,* 417–428.

Levi, L. *Stress and distress in response to psychosocial stimuli.* New York: Pergamon Press, 1972.

Lin, N., Simeone, R. S., Ensel, W. M., & Kuo, W. Social support, stressful life events, and illness: A model and an empirical test. *Journal of Health and Social Behavior,* 1979, *20,* 108–119.

Luthe, W., & Schultz, J. H. *Autogenic therapy* (Vol. 2, *Medical applications).* New York: Grune & Stratton, 1969.

Matthews, K. A., Glass, D. C., Rosenman, R. H., & Bortner, R. W. Competitive drive, pattern A, and coronary heart disease: A further analysis of some data for the Western Collaborative Group Study. *Journal of Chronic Diseases,* 1977, *30,* 489–498.

Minter, R. E., & Kimball, C. P. Life events and illness: A review. *Psychosomatics,* 1980, *19,* 334–339.

Nisbet, R. *The social philosophers: Community and conflict in Western thought.* New York: Crowell, 1973.

Nuckolls, K. B., Cassel, J., & Kaplan, B. H. Psychosocial assets, life crisis and the prognosis of pregnancy. *American Journal of Epidemiology,* 1972, *95,* 431–441.

Pinneau, S. R. *Effects of social support on occupational stresses and strains.* Paper presented at the annual meeting of the American Psychological Association, Washington, D.C., 1976.

Rahe, R. Epidemiological studies of life change and illness. *International Journal of Psychiatry in Medicine,* 1975, *6,*133–146.

Sartre, J. *Being and nothingness.* New York: Philosophical Library, 1956.

Smith, R. E., Johnson, J. H., & Sarason, I. G. Life change, the sensation-seeking motive, and psychological distress. *Journal of Consulting and Clinical Psychology,* 1978, *46,* 348–349.

Suls, J., & Mullen, B. Life events, perceived control and illness: The role of uncertainty. *Journal of Human Stress,* 1981, *7,* 30–33.

Syme, S. L., Hyman, M. M., & Enterline, P. E. Cultural mobility and the occurrence of coronary heart disease. *Health and Human Behavior,* 1965, *6,* 173–189.

Taub, E. Self-regulation of human tissue temperature. In G. E. Schwartz & J. Beatty (Eds.), *Biofeedback: Theory and research.* New York: Academic Press, 1977.

Taylor, C. *Hegel.* Cambridge, England: Cambridge University Press, 1975.

Toffler, A. *Future shock.* New York: Random House, 1970.

Tönnies, F. *Community and society.* New York: Harper & Row, 1963.

Turner, R. J. Social support as a contingency in psychological well-being. *Journal of Health and Social Behavior,* 1981, *22,* 357–367.

Vaillant, G. E. Natural history of male psychologic health. *New England Journal of Medicine,* 1979, *301,* 1249–1254.

Williams, A. W., Ware, J. E., & Donald, C. A. A model of mental health, life events, and social supports applicable to general populations. *Journal of Health and Social Behavior,* 1981, *22,* 324–336.

Williams, R. B., Haney, T. L., Lee, K. L., Kong, Y., Blumenthal, J. A., & Whalen, R. E. Type A behavior, hostility, and coronary atherosclerosis. *Psychosomatic Medicine,* 1980, *42,* 539–549.

Woolfolk, R. L., Lehrer, P. M., McCann, B. S., & Rooney, A. J. Effects of progressive relaxation and meditation on cognitive and somatic manifestations of daily stress. *Behaviour Research and Therapy,* 1982, *20,* 461–468.

Woolfolk, R. L., & Richardson, F. C. *Stress, sanity and survival.* New York: Simon & Schuster, 1978.

12 EVALUATING EXPERIMENTAL DESIGNS IN RELAXATION RESEARCH

THOMAS D. BORKOVEC, MARK C. JOHNSON, AND
DEBORAH L. BLOCK

The purpose of the present chapter is to outline the current consensus among scientists on the methodological rules for drawing conclusions from scientific experiments on relaxation techniques, so that experimental research can become a useful source of knowledge. Much of what is described here can be found in more elaborate sources pertaining to the design and methodology of therapy outcome research (cf. Campbell & Stanley, 1963; Gottman & Markman, 1978; Kiesler, 1971). We have attempted to translate these rules into examples from the relaxation area and have appended a summary checklist that can be used to evaluate any particular research article on relaxation.

Research on relaxation ordinarily comes in one of two forms: efficacy research and theoretical research. "Efficacy" refers to the therapeutic effectiveness of a technique, and an efficacy study may bear on a variety of issues, including the effectiveness of procedure or variation of a procedure; the types of problems for which a technique is effective; and the characteristics of the subjects with a particular problem for whom the procedure is effective. Theoretical research, while sometimes conducted in the context of an efficacy design, focuses on questions of mechanism (of the presenting problem, of the therapy technique, or of their interaction) and aspires to the generation of general laws of behavior. Even though each type of study may have its own particular problems to circumvent, scientific requirements in terms of designs and methodology do not really vary. Scientific method attempts to support or disconfirm, through empirical evidence and following specifiable rules, certain statements or hypotheses about relaxation techniques, regardless of whether those statements refer to their effectiveness (Does it work?) or their mechanisms (How does it work?).

INTERNAL VALIDITY

Evaluation of any relaxation study requires a basic judgment about its "internal validity," or the extent to which the methods and design of the study allow us to conclude unambiguously that relaxation treatment caused a change in the client's behavior. Let us assume that a therapist has interviewed and assessed a client reporting general anxiety, and has applied over a 2-month trial a basic stress reduction procedure to that client. At the end of this period, the client is reporting a much more relaxed life style, less intense reactions to environmental stressors, and more rapid recovery from stress events. Anxiety and tension are no longer reported as problems, and significant others validate the client's statements by their own observations. Blood pressure readings and self-reported anxiety measures taken before and after each session indicate progressive improvements. As clinicians, we are likely to conclude that the stress reduction treatment caused these significant improvements, and we may well be correct in that conclusion. The problem from the scientific point of view is that although the data argue in favor of that conclusion, several other rival explanations for the change are equally plausible and equivalently supported by the observed outcome. The goal of an *experimental* study of the effects of a stress reduction procedure is to eliminate, or rule out, the most likely alternative explanations of change, leaving only the treatment factor supported as a cause of improvement. These alternative explanations have been called "threats" to the internal validity of an experiment (cf. Campbell & Stanley, 1963; Cook & Campbell, 1979). We briefly review below the eight primary threats and note ways in which researchers have attempted to control for, or to rule out, their effects. It should be kept in mind that experimental studies failing to control for these potentially confounding factors do not provide adequate evidence to support the efficacy of the therapy employed.

HISTORY

Our client may have experienced many other events during the 2-month treatment trial. Therapy as an historical event has made up only a small fraction of his or her life experiences. The observed improvement may have been due to any number of those unknown, undocumented events (e.g., reduction in life stressors, positive events that have changed the client's overall attitude, the reading of a fictional story that gave the client a new and adaptive perspective on life). Probably a good number of "spontaneous remissions" among psychological disorders (Eysenck, 1952) are due to the countless possible historical events that occur to the person independent of any treatment.

MATURATION

Passage of time allows for the operation of basic maturational processes that may facilitate improvement. Brief treatment trials with adults seem unlikely to involve this factor, but maturation is a likely explanation for change with children. Moreover, since adult maturational processes are not well understood, we are wise not to ignore this potential threat to our conclusions.

REPEATED TESTING

Reduced anxiety scores over the treatment trial may simply reflect a repeated-testing effect. If we employ objective methods of assessing whether our client is showing improvement (e.g., making physiological recordings; presenting mild or imaginary stressors in the therapy office and measuring degree of stress reaction; periodically administering anxiety questionnaires), the improvement revealed even in these objective measures may simply reflect practice effects or decreasing novelty of the assessment situation.

MEASUREMENT ERROR

Our measurement method for observing clients' improvement may change over time, irrespective of clients' behavior. For example, as therapists we have the goal of helping clients, and our observation of their behavior may be biased in the direction of seeing improvement. Significant others may be similarly influenced if they know that these persons are undergoing therapy. Indeed, even research assistants employed as "objective observers" may yield biased ratings if they know which observation samples are occurring prior to therapy and which are occurring after therapy.

STATISTICAL REGRESSION

If clients or subjects are selected on the basis of extreme scores on psychological tests (e.g., high anxiety scores), their pretherapy-to-post-therapy improvement on those measures may occur solely on the basis of a statistical artifact. Unless a measure possesses perfect test–retest reliability (and no psychological test does), extreme scores will "regress" toward the group mean upon second administration. Thus, clients high on anxiety will seem improved on test scores, even though no actual change in anxiety level has occurred. (See Campbell & Stanley, 1963, for an excellent discussion of this artifact.)

With an individual client, any of the five explanations above may contribute to some degree of observed improvement. They are just as likely to have been the cause of observed change as the administration of stress reduction procedures is. In an experimental group study, the current method for ruling out or eliminating these threats to our conclusion that treatment has caused improvement is to include a "no-treatment" condition. If we measure anxiety before and after treatment among clients, half of whom by random assignment receive treatment and half of whom do not over the same period of time, any differences we observe in degree of improvement between these two groups can be attributed to the presence of treatment. We can draw this conclusion unambiguously, because the no-treatment group is just as susceptible to the effects of history, maturation, repeated testing, instrumentation, and statistical regression as the treated group is. The only difference between the two groups is the administration of therapy, and thus any difference in outcome observed between the two groups can be due only to treatment. We have reduced the reasonableness of attributing differential change to these five threats.

Once we begin to discuss the use of experimental and control groups, three further threats to the study's internal validity need to be addressed:

SELECTION

Even using a no-treatment condition, we may falsely conclude that the treatment has caused the change on the basis of differential outcome. If by chance assignment the treatment condition was composed of those clients who would have changed the most even without treatment—or, alternately, the no-treatment condition contained those clients who would show the least change—our conclusion that treatment caused the improvement would be erroneous.

ATTRITION

Even if our treatment and no-treatment groups were totally equivalent on all variables related to change before treatment, differential dropout rates during treatment may destroy that equivalence and thus invalidate our conclusions. For example, some treatment clients may terminate the treatment prematurely because they are not being helped by the therapy; this results in outcome data for this group that is biased in the direction of improvement. Alternately, no-treatment clients may drop out due to "spontaneous remission," leaving data on the control condition that reflect the most disturbed and unchanged individuals. When large or differential attrition occurs, outcome comparisons are suspect.

INTERACTIONS WITH SELECTION AND OTHER THREATS

Treatment and no-treatment groups may differ in numerous ways related to the first five threats (i.e., one group is more influenced than the other by history, maturation, repeated testing, instrumentation, and/or statistical regression). For example, let us assume that an experimenter compares a group of experienced, middle-aged meditators to a group of college students who have never practiced meditation. Any differences that are found favoring the meditation group cannot be interpreted as unambiguous support for the value of meditation, because the treatment groups differ not only on meditation experience, but also on possible maturational influences and past history of experience, attitudes about meditation, and so on.

While the first five threats to internal validity are generally addressed by inclusion of a no-treatment control group, the last three threats are dealt with via *random assignment* of subjects to experimental conditions. Again, if these rival factors are in operation, random assignment will equally distribute their probabilities of influencing the treatment and control groups. It is important to realize that this is an assumption that we anticipate will work in the long run. That is, randomization will create equivalent groups, given the repeated assignment of subjects to groups. In the short run (i.e., in a single study), randomization may fail due to chance. This statistical assumption inherent in random assignment indicates two requirements. First, in any individual study, the researcher must produce evidence of group equivalence prior to treatment on variables related to change. Thus, well-reported studies will present analyses showing that experimental conditions did not differ on pretest status (e.g., initial severity, age, sex, medication status). Unfortunately, we do not always know how many other variables relate to improvement, so the second requirement is that we cannot place too much confidence in the outcome of a single study. Thus, the scientific accumulation of knowledge is based on replications—the demonstration of the same outcome in more than one study before we feel confident in drawing a cause-and-effect conclusion.

FURTHER SPECIFICATION OF THE INDEPENDENT VARIABLE

The explication of cause-and-effect relationships within the clinical research literature cannot stop after addressing only the basic validity issues just discussed. In order to appreciate more fully the scientific approach for evaluating therapy outcome studies, we must consider a variety of further design issues. In this section, we discuss how we can advance our goal of demonstrating unambiguous cause-and-effect relationships through employing heuristic experimental designs. By relating these to validity considerations, it is possible to show how sophisticated research designs may provide increasing specification of independent (therapy/treatment) variables. The goal is the same as that presented above: ruling out further rival hypotheses concerning what specific aspect of treatment is causing outcome improvement.

The demonstration that a relaxation technique is effective in some way, relative to a no-treatment condition, actually tells us little about the technique's efficacy and represents only the beginning of its investigation. In terms of internal validity, several rival hypotheses implicating extra-therapeutic variables unrelated to the therapy procedure remain viable and must be ruled out before we can draw conclusions about the specific effects of the technique. For example, as clinicians we are aware that the therapies we employ are more than simply techniques or procedures, and that in order to understand what happens in any given therapy situation, we must be cognizant of the impact of the client's and the therapist's expectancies. The credibility of both the clinician and the treatment, the demand characteristics of the experimental situation, and the contribution of placebo effects on any outcome we obtain—all of these factors need to be addressed experimentally by incorporating specific control groups or other methodological devices that go beyond the no-treatment comparison design.

PLACEBO CONTROL DESIGNS

Just as the use of no-treatment control groups and the randomization of clients' assignment to groups minimize several threats to internal validity, the addition of placebo groups allows even further specification of the treatment's putative claim to have caused a positive outcome. Without such groups, we are left in the dark about the role of extratherapeutic aspects of our treatment, and consequently have no sure basis for concluding that the technique itself has caused the improvement. Likely rival hypotheses about the causes of improvement include client expectation of improvement and the contact, support, suggestion, and attention of the therapist—factors common to most therapeutic interventions. Thus, a comparison condition that includes those elements but lacks an ingredient thought to be actively effective for influencing the disorder represents one way of ruling out the placebo hypothesis.

The mere inclusion of a "placebo" condition in an outcome study does not guarantee that we have controlled for these characteristics (Kazdin & Wilcoxon, 1976). Empirical investigation has revealed that some commonly employed placebo conditions either are not believable or do not generate therapeutic expectancies equivalent to therapy procedures. Recent attempts to solve this problem have included the following:

1. *Methods to insure equivalent credibility among treatment and control conditions.* With increasing frequency, outcome investigators are assessing via self-report scales the believability and expectancy-inducing quality of each condition employed in a study. Ordinarily, participants rate their respective treatment on such scales after the first session of administration. Equivalent ratings across conditions increase our confidence that the placebo group shares beliefs about treatment and expected outcome to a degree equal to that of the group receiving therapy. To maximize the likelihood of such equivalence, it is wise to employ, as placebos, procedures nearly identical in content, length, amount of therapist contact, and other factors to the therapy condition to which they will be compared, without including any theoretically active procedures. In the ab-

sence of reported credibility ratings, this can be used as a partial basis for judging the quality of a placebo condition in any given study.

2. *The search for alternative methods of controlling for placebo effects* (cf. O'Leary & Borkovec, 1978). Because of a variety of conceptual, methodological, and ethical problems inherent in the use of placebo-group designs, alternative ways of ruling out placebo influence are being explored. None is totally satisfactory (e.g., some have ethical problems, while others do not rule out therapist contact factors), but it may be hoped that further developments will be stimulated by their suggestion:

a. *"Best available" control group.* A substitute for the placebo group can involve the use of whatever therapy procedure is viewed as the best technique currently available for treating the problem. Creation of equivalent expectancies between this procedure and the one of interest to the investigator is not guaranteed and must be assessed.

b. *Component control group.* A single procedural element or inert combination of several elements of a multicomponent therapy can be employed as a placebo condition, and can also provide important information for the isolation of the therapy's active ingredients (see further discussion of component control designs, below). Some degree of procedural similarity between conditions is guaranteed.

c. *Neutral expectancy.* An experimenter may present treatment under the guise of experimental study, with no reference to therapy or expected changes in behavior. Change via a technique in the absence of therapeutic expectancy would provide compelling evidence ruling out a good portion of the placebo factor as an explanation of improvement. The disadvantages of this approach include the complete removal of a potentially important source of clinical improvement and the use of deceptive instructions.

d. *Counterdemand instructions.* Subjects can be informed that they should not expect any improvement until the last treatment session; outcome is then evaluated just before that session. Any treatment effects observed during this counterdemand period can be viewed as relatively independent of the influence of demand characteristics and therapeutic expectancy. Disadvantages include a requirement of knowing how many sessions are necessary to generate improvement and possible changes in subject expectancy prior to the last session.

e. *Informed consent.* The ethical problem of uninformed placebo administration can be circumvented by telling all subjects that they may be assigned initially to a placebo condition. Frustration of subjects and an accurate or inaccurate belief that they are in the placebo group represent potential problems with this approach.

Obviously, researchers will struggle for some time to resolve the dilemma between the required elimination of the placebo hypothesis and the difficulty in doing so. Future developments, however, may solve the problem and at the same time lead to specifying the "active ingredients" of the placebo, so long recognized as a powerful agent for change in medicine and psychology (cf. Shapiro & Morris, 1978).

It should be apparent by this point that the traditional outcome question (i.e., "Does therapy work?") is deceptively framed, and that through increasing specification of independent (treatment) variables, we can isolate whether or not a specific treatment is responsible for a therapeutic effect (Paul, 1969). The no-treatment control group will allow us to rule out traditional threats to internal validity (e.g., history, maturation, statistical regression). Randomization of clients' assignment to compared groups further strengthens our confidence in interpreting an experiment's results by controlling (in the long run) for selection, mortality, and interactions with selection. Finally, the placebo condition allows the elimination of therapy factors not specific to a particular procedure's specific operations. In the rest of this section, we briefly mention three other designs that provide increasing clarification of the specific elements of any given treatment that are producing change.

COMPONENT CONTROL DESIGNS

Whereas placebo designs attempt to control for conditions that are purportedly common across all therapies, component designs represent an attempt to identify the active ingredient(s) specific to a particular treatment procedure. For instance, if a clinical researcher wanted to know more about how progressive relaxation produces changes in clients, he or she could test the separate components of this treatment and then compare their efficacy in isolation and combination. Abbreviated progressive relaxation involves two basic operations: tension and release of muscle groups, and focused attention to the resultant physiological sensations. An investigator could create a 2×2 design involving the presence and absence of each element, with the combined operations representing the typical relaxation package and the absence of both components defining a placebo condition. Subjects would be randomly assigned to each of the four procedures, and the outcomes would provide information on the critical elements necessary for any given effect and whether or not the components are additive in influence. Such studies are very useful for pursuing questions of mechanism, not only of the techniques but also of the disorder so treated (e.g., for insomnia; cf. Borkovec, 1979). This design approach, along with the parametric designs discussed below, has the potential of providing the greatest degree of specification of independent variables, especially if the research program continues to break up identified, active elements and to apply analogous designs to each subelement. While these designs are primarily devoted to theoretical questions, the likelihood of applied by-products is obvious: Technique components or parameters irrelevant to outcome can be discarded.

PARAMETRIC DESIGNS

Any technique has numerous dimensions along which it can vary in application. For example, in abbreviated progressive relaxation, the amount of time a muscle group is tensed or the duration between the tensing of muscle groups can be short or long; therapists can employ indirect verbal suggestions of warmth, calmness, and relaxation that are stated frequently or infrequently, with a conversational tone and volume or a soft tone of voice; training sessions can be brief or lengthy, occurring once a week or more often; and so forth. Research on such parameters can indicate what values are optimal for outcome effectiveness, but it also can lead to statements of theoretical value. Whereas little parametric investigation of relaxation techniques has been conducted, the literature on phobic anxiety provides a useful illustration. Parametric manipulations of the duration of exposure to a phobic stimulus during a single session yield a curvilinear extinction curve (cf. Eysenck, 1979). Short- and long-exposure conditions produce decrements in fear, whereas midrange durations (about 15 minutes) result in a paradoxical *increase* in fear. Such empirical evidence has led to the pursuit of the phenomenon of anxiety incubation, whose eludication will contribute to our knowledge of the nature of fear.

CONSTRUCTIVE DESIGNS

The last design we discuss here is the constructive design. It too helps clinical researchers build a greater understanding of the process and mechanisms whereby therapeutic changes can occur. Unlike the component control designs, which dismantle a treatment package in search of its active ingredients, constructive designs *add* components to an existing treatment to increase its effectiveness. A good example of the fruits of such research is provided by Patel and her colleagues in their research on relaxation and hypertension (Patel, 1975; Patel & North, 1975). By combining yoga and biofeedback, they were able to provide a much more effective intervention. Evaluation of such designs generates questions such as which combination(s) prove most effective, and whether the contribution of any two components are simply additive or are more complexly interactional. If the latter is the case, future component control designs may further tease out the cause-and-effect relationship involved in the combined approach.

There is one remaining design that we do not describe here. Comparative designs contrast two or more active techniques (e.g., progressive relaxation vs. meditation). Because Lehrer and Woolfolk have devoted an entire chapter of this book to this topic (see Chapter 13), we do not duplicate here their comments on design and methodological considerations in this area.

Our hope in this rather cursory discussion of design issues has been to acquaint the reader with some of the ways in which researchers can approach the question of treatment effectiveness and treatment mechanisms. The alternatives discussed here by no means exhaust the methods available to clinical researchers. We have obviously focused on group designs, to the neglect of single-subject designs and case histories. Our intention is not to downgrade these approaches, but merely to familiarize the reader with the most commonly employed designs in the relaxation literature and the most powerful designs currently available for explicating cause-and-effect relationships.

Our focus in this section has generally been on specification of independent variables and threats to internal validity (i.e., on aspects of the treatment itself that result in change). As clinicians, it is important for us to know not only which types of treatments work best with which types of disorders, but also *how* these treatments work when they do. Research employing placebo (or alternative) designs begin to address the efficacy question, whereas the component control, parametric, and constructive designs further establish efficacy and begin to address questions of mechanism. As the latter phase continues, results bearing on the nature of the therapy, the nature of the disorder, and their interaction provide increasingly significant knowledge about human behavior, from which further technique development for clinical application can occur.

Before proceeding to a discussion of external validity, or the generalizability of a research conclusion, two additional methodological aspects relating to both internal and external validity need to be addressed: the effects of therapist variables, and the representativeness of the relaxation technique employed.

THERAPIST EFFECTS

The effects of therapist bias and therapist characteristics represent an important, often ignored, and only partially resolvable problem. If a study employs only a single therapist conducting both therapy and placebo conditions, differential outcome may be attributable solely to a therapist effect or to interaction of this unique therapist with the study's particular procedures. For example, the single therapist may prefer or be better trained in one technique over another, such that differential outcome is a function of bias or experience, rather than of the therapies themselves. External validity similarly suffers in the sense that we cannot generalize the study's findings to other therapists differing in personality characteristics, style, sex, age, level of experience, and other factors. A partial solution is provided by including multiple therapists, each treating an equal number of subjects in each condition. If the same outcome results from the treatment of each therapist, we are in a stronger position to rule out their characteristics as the cause of change and to generalize the results beyond any unique therapist characteristic. Ideally, the investigator would randomly sample therapists from a heterogeneous set of characteristics. Because this is never practical, use of multiple therapists is only a partial attempt at solution. Moreover, bias may still be a factor in the results. If all therapists in a study prefer the same technique or are aware of the placebo status of the control condition, therapist bias remains a strong rival hypothesis. Further steps taken by investigators to rule out bias have included (1) choosing therapists experienced in and biased toward the therapy procedure that is predicted by the investigator to be inferior to the comparison therapy (e.g., Paul, 1966); (2) having therapists with different biases treat a portion of subjects in both the preferred and nonpreferred treatment conditions, and (3) obtaining pretherapy ratings by therapists of expected outcomes for each condition in the study. If results fail to reflect or are opposite to therapists' preferences, a conservative estimate of the efficacy of the nonpreferred technique is thus provided. Unfortunately, this approach does not solve the problem when undisguised placebo conditions are employed, and therapist bias in placebo designs remains a methodologically unsolved problem. The most serious problem, however, is the use of a single therapist, and studies so designed are nearly uninterpretable.

One method of circumventing the therapist effect is to use automated tape-recorded treatments. Unfortunately, direct comparisons of taped versus "live" abbreviated relaxation training (e.g., Paul & Trimble, 1970) indicate significant inferiority of the physiological effects of standardized, taped procedures. Whether this is due to the absence of a supportive therapist or to the absence of subject control of session progress remains unanswered. However, we must view with suspicion the outcome of any study employing taped treatments.

None of the above is meant to imply a disregard for therapist variables. If multiple therapists are used, our efficacy conclusions are strengthened in terms of both internal and external validity. If a main or interactive effect involving the therapists factor is found in the analyses, the potential exists for pursuing the nature of therapist behavior that facilitates or retards the efficacy of a given technique. Such further research can contribute significantly to our knowledge about relaxation process in particular and therapist variables influential to human change processes in general. Unfortunately, as in many areas of therapy research (cf. Parloff, Waskow, & Wolfe, 1978), little is known about therapist effects in relaxation training, and this topic remains a high-priority area for further investigation.

FAITHFULNESS TO TECHNIQUE REPRESENTATION

The development of a therapy technique is routinely couched in an originator's theoretical view of human behavior, as well as in his or her experience during its development. Experimental evaluations of the procedure require operational specificity, which in one way or another translates the original procedure into a sharply defined, replicable set of observable operations. To the extent that the investigator's procedure deviates from that of the developer, the study will not provide a true representation of the technique. Consequently, we must evaluate the study's section on methods to determine whether sufficient details are offered to judge the faithfulness of that representation. For example, some studies have simply stated that "Jacobsonian relaxation" was administered. Such an operational definition is inadequate to allow us to assess what exactly was done and how closely the procedures did indeed meet the theoretical and procedural requirements of the Jacobson technique. Similarly, "abbreviated progressive relaxation" is not the same as "Jacobsonian progressive muscular relaxation," although some articles have blurred this distinction. Finally, a recent review (Borkovec & Sides, 1979) has indicated the implications of deviating from prescribed procedure. Studies on the physiological effects of abbreviated progressive relaxation were divided into those showing significant effects relative to appropriate control conditions and those that did not. The two sets of studies differed significantly on the number of training sessions administered and on whether or not "live" versus taped instructions were used, and a tendency was found for a difference in whether or not the subjects employed had a target problem hypothesized to relate to physiological hyperactivity. Progressive relaxation is designed to be a learned skill requiring practice, a procedure necessarily under the subject's control through its graduated progression; it is useful primarily for clients who can benefit from reduced physiological activity. We do not wish herein to discourage research assessing the effects of alternate procedures with novel problems. However, it is logically (and now empirically) clear that certain deviations destroy certain types of relaxation effects, and we cannot draw conclusions about a technique on the basis of poor representation of its procedures.

EXTERNAL VALIDITY

"External validity" refers to the extent to which the cause-and-effect conclusions of an internally valid experiment can be generalized beyond the specific circumstances of the particular experiment. We are not interested in a specific result obtained by a particular therapist with a unique sample of clients under particular laboratory and measurement conditions. Rather, we wish to make general statements about the laws of behavior exemplified by the results. Rarely in science do we actually discover a general law of behavior applicable to all people and all settings in a single or even in several studies, although such laws may ultimately be derived from an accumulation of scientific studies over a long period of time.

Ordinarily, we are limited to more restricted statements of relationships among specific independent and dependent variables. For example, a general law concerning "the relaxation response" may eventually emerge from many experimental studies of relaxation, including its behavioral, cognitive, autonomic, biochemical, and neurophysiological effects, and may be found applicable to all people. At the present time, however, we are limited in our conclusions to a subset of relationships. For example, experimental data now conclusively indicate that relaxation techniques are effective in treating a specifiable subset of the insomnias. Such a finding obviously does not allow us to assume that relaxation would be effective with other subsets of sleep disturbance, much less with schizophrenia, organic brain syndrome, or alcoholism. We may develop a theory that provides a logical framework for hypothesizing a therapeutic relaxation effect for aspects of these latter disorders, or by chance trial we may empirically discover that relaxation can play a significant role in their treatment. However, the research finding that insomnia is reduced by relaxation does not, in and of itself, justify our generalizing this therapeutic conclusion to other disorders. In fact, we can never logically generalize any empirical finding to any sample or setting beyond those employed in the study in question. Ultimately, a generalization must be empirically tested under the conditions to which we wish to generalize.

Science, however, could never proceed if we did not make good guesses about generalization based on specific studies. Thus, somewhere between the uniqueness of a specific study and a general law of human behavior lies an area of good guesses regarding the generalizability of a particular study. Whereas we cannot eliminate threats to external validity with control conditions, as is done for internal validity, we can take steps to increase the likelihood that a result from a particular study is generalizable to some degree. Two general guidelines are useful in this regard. First, to the extent that the setting, clients, therapists, procedures, and measures are similar to those to which we wish to generalize, we are on safer ground in assuming that the relationships found in the original study will be maintained in the new situation. Secondly, theory and other research may guide the reasonableness of our generalizations. For example, if inexperienced therapists or automated treatment techniques are found to be effective in treating some disorder, we would feel confident in generalizing such an effect to experienced therapists. If middle-aged, chronic insomniacs are found in several studies to respond well to relaxation treatment, we might reasonably assume that college-aged insomniacs would also benefit. Of course, we might be wrong, and empirical testing is the only ultimate resolution, but it should be noted that we do have some basis for evaluating the generality of some conclusions on the basis of the investigator's methodological choices.

The exact replication exemplifies the safest test of generalizability. We would reasonably assume that a study conducted on the same relaxation technique, using the same measures, similar laboratory conditions, similarly trained therapists, and clients selected for the same degree of severity on the same disorder, should produce results similar to those of a previous study. Such replications represent the backbone of science. A single experiment may by chance alone produce a unique outcome having no generality at all. Replication on a separate sample markedly increases our confidence that some law of behavior is being expressed and is worthy of further pursuit. In a real sense, an *exact* replication of conditions never occurs, because there will always be some variation in the characteristics of the people involved and the procedures used. It should be noted, therefore, that if a cause-and-effect relationship continues to emerge despite a little, a moderate degree, or a great deal of variation of these variables, the generality of the relationship increases accordingly. It should be noted also that as these variables diverge greatly from the original study, the likelihood of observing the same relationship declines unless our originally documented relationship represents a very general law of behavior. In a real sense, then, issues of external validity represent two sides of the same question: Under what conditions does a specific relationship occur, and under what conditions does it not occur? Data that bear on either aspect of this question help to identify the range of applicability of a given relationship en route to a statement of a law of behavior.

A parallel process exists in our clinical work. If a particular treatment strategy is useful for a client with particular problems and a particular set of characteristics, we are likely to try the technique with a later client with similar problems and characteristics. Similarly, when we hope that our client's more relaxed demeanor in therapy is indicative of a more adaptive style in his or her natural environment, or when we trust that our client's therapeutic gains will be maintained a year after successful termination, we are assuming generalization. These three examples represent generalizations regarding treatment efficacy across people, across settings, and across time, respectively. Clinically, we make guesses on the basis of experience and of our implicit or explicit theories of human behavior that these generalizations are correct, but we will not know for certain unless evidence is obtained that would justify our assumption—a process very much akin to that of the scientist.

In reading reports of research, we can evaluate the extent to which its findings are generalizable. Beginning with points raised by Campbell and Stanley (1963), we describe below some common threats to the external validity of experiments and some methods that, if employed in the study, increase the likelihood of the generality of its findings. In each case, the question raised is whether the treatment effects observed are due solely to an interaction of treatment with some unique characteristic of the study, or whether they are indeed reflective of relationships of some enduring, generalizable value.

INTERACTION OF SELECTION, HISTORY, OR MATURATION AND TREATMENT

A treatment effect found in an experiment may be limited to a particular type of presenting problem and the particular characteristics (e.g.,
age, history, sex, socioeconomic status, chronicity of disorder, severity
of disorder) of the subjects employed. A relaxation effect on primary insomnia may not reasonably be generalizable to the sleep disturbance of
a schizophrenic inpatient; the relaxation reduction of general anxiety
among college students may not be generalizable to psychiatric anxiety
disorders; and successful treatment of young anxiety disorder clients may
not imply successful treatment of middle-aged or elderly clients with
anxiety disorders. One very important requirement in a report is that it
define and specify the characteristics of the population sampled, in order
to allow the reader to judge the sample's similarity to other groups. A way
of maximizing generality in a single study is to sample a very heterogeneous population with regard to several client characteristics other than
the presenting problem. There is a tradeoff here, however. The greater
we make the heterogeneity of the sample, the less likely we will find a
treatment effect unless we have tapped into a fairly general law of behavior.
The more likely resolution of this problem occurs through the accumulation of several studies wherein heterogeneity across studies validates the
generality of the treatment effect. The point to remember is that the outcome of a specific study may not be relevant to subjects or clients who
differ considerably from the sample employed in that investigation.

Certainly the most often cited criticism of outcome research on the
basis of external validity involves that class of studies known as "therapy
analogues." Usually, the term "analogue studies" refers to the employment of college students with mild problems, from which generalizations
to clinical samples are often made. Use of such subjects is a matter of
pragmatic considerations. Plentiful supplies of such subjects are con-
veniently obtainable for large, factorial studies, and ethical issues, while
certainly not absent, tend to be less severe. In evaluating the results of
an analogue study, however, three points should be kept in mind:

1. No study is generalizable in the logical sense, and statements
of generalization must ultimately be empirically tested. This is true
even if we desire to generalize from one clinical sample to another.
2. Similarity of characteristics between samples is a good basis
for the likelihood of valid generalization. College-student insomniacs
can be selected for severe latency problems and long chronicity. Over
the past 10 years, it is now clear that outcome results are quite compar-

able between such samples and those involving referred patients with insomnia. Poor examples of analogue research include studies which use weak selection criteria (in terms of problem severity) or samples of subjects for whom there is no evidence that the targeted behavior is indeed a problem.

3. Every therapy investigation, even when clients and experienced therapists are involved, is an "analogue" in the sense that the situation (measures, setting, standardization of technique application) differs from that customary in nonexperimental clinical work.

Thus, while we should be cautious in drawing implications from analogue studies, by no means is it appropriate to rule out their relevance *a priori*.

PRETEST SENSITIZATION: INTERACTION OF PRETESTING AND TREATMENT

Outcome experiments typically begin with a variety of assessments prior to therapy, against which posttherapy measurements are contrasted in order to define degree of improvement. Our clients rarely undergo such elaborate, often laboratory-based, measurements, so one can question whether treatment effects would also occur in the absence of such pretherapy experiences, not customarily part of the operation of a clinical setting. For example, a study involving hypnotic relaxation may report significant therapeutic effects, but such training may have been effective because the prior administration of a hypnotic induction scale sensitized the subjects to respond to the treatment. The empirical solution to this possibility is to conduct a Solomon four-group design: Subjects are randomly assigned to experimental and control conditions, wherein half in each condition are pretested and half are not. If similar effects emerge regardless of pretest status, we can assume generality in settings where such pretesting is not possible or desirable.

REACTIVE ARRANGEMENTS: INTERACTION OF SETTING AND TREATMENT

Even more problematic for generalizing the results of many experimental investigations to the clinical situation is the reactive nature of an "experiment" per se, whether that experiment is in a clinical setting or a research laboratory. The mere fact that a subject or client knows that he or she is in an experimental therapy investigation, along with the presentation of ethically required information about the details of the study that is necessary for proper informed consent, may have unknown interactive influences on the person's reaction to treatment. A portion of this problem has been covered in the earlier discussions of placebo, demand, and expectancy effects, and relates more directly to issues of internal validity. That portion relevant to external validity involves the question of how closely the setting and procedures correspond to those found in the clinical situation. Although little can be done to circumvent the problem of subjects' knowing they are in an experiment, efforts to approximate the clinical setting within the context of an experiment may minimize its reactive effect and insure greater generality. This implies that we can evaluate to some extent how well the "methods" section of a report documents the employment of clinical skill, clinical office-like atmosphere, and the matching of general clinical operation as a background for the superimposition of an experimental design. A well-known cartoon exemplifies the problem we face when we are attempting to study the physiological effects of relaxation: A subject sits with numerous electrodes and other devices emanating from his body in a copper-screened room with computers and polygraphs humming and blinking away; the experimenter, wearing a stained white laboratory coat and carrying a clipboard, says, "Now just relax." The incongruity of the setting and the instruction indicates how reactive our arrangements can be as we pursue a sometimes elusive phenomenon.

MULTIPLE-TREATMENT INTERFERENCE: TREATMENT INTERACTION WITH TREATMENT

Anything that happens (or does not happen) before therapy begins can influence a client's reaction to the treatment. To the extent that whatever happens before therapy is different from what would ordinarily happen in other studies or in clinical settings, the results may not be generalizable to those situations. In abbreviated progressive relaxation, a demonstration of the muscle groups and ways of tensing and releasing them is clinically required. Without such pretraining, it is less likely that training will have a therapeutic effect. Conversely, some studies have preceded relaxation training with other events that may promote improvement in and of themselves or may interact with subsequent training. For example, Kahn, Baker, and Weiss (1968) provided an hour of Rogerian interviewing prior to treating insomniacs with autogenic relaxation training. As Eisenman (1970) pointed out, their favorable outcome may have been due not to relaxation, but to the interview or to a combination of the two. The component designs discussed earlier provide a method for evaluating the separate and combined influences of multiple or sequential treatment procedures. Alternately, sequential components can be counterbalanced across subjects (one group receives one order, while the other group receives the opposite order); this procedure controls for order of treatment component administration, although no independent assessment of the effects of each element is provided.

A tradeoff often exists between internal and external validity. As researchers, we often purchase high degrees of experimental control at the cost of lessened ecological ("real-life") validity. Aside from encouraging ourselves to allow systematic movement between laboratory and field research, we can also continue our efforts to develop internally valid designs for use in clinical settings and to evolve laboratory settings that increasingly match the clinical situation. Until then, we must evaluate any individual experiment on the basis of its internal and external validity, and must realize that some powerfully documented relationships may not exist outside the laboratory setting and that some effects observed in the field may be due to a number of variables unrelated to the treatment employed.

FURTHER SPECIFICATION OF THE DEPENDENT VARIABLE

We have previously discussed how experimental research can lead to an increasing specification of the independent variable (therapy) via the elimination of rival hypotheses regarding what is causing the observed improvement. A no-treatment condition allows the ruling out of history, maturation, and so forth, and provides support for the hypothesis that something about therapy has caused the change. Placebo groups and other controls for demand characteristics provide greater specificity of conclusion by further eliminating nonspecific factors and supporting the presence of some active ingredient in the therapy as the vehicle promoting change. Component control and parametric designs rule out elements or technique parameters of the active therapy and allow us to be quite specific about the particular aspects of a treatment that are causing therapeutic benefit. The increasing specificity of our conclusions about therapy that is reflected in such an approach has a parallel on the side of the dependent variable.

What we mean by "improvement" and the response changes by which improvement takes place can be increasingly defined, narrowed, or broadened as we systematically develop our methods of measurement further. As Gottman and Markman (1978) have noted, we may begin with a global definition of a targeted problem (e.g., "insomnia," "general anxiety"), but as we proceed with research we can become increasingly specific about measuring the construct and the organismic processes related to it. Cook and Campbell (1979) refer to a more general set of related issues by the term "construct validity." We can arbitrarily divide specification of dependent variables into two domains: outcome content and outcome context.

OUTCOME CONTENT

Specification of outcome content involves the isolation of what is being changed. This question has three aspects to it. The first is the outcome criterion problem. The second involves auxiliary outcome measures that can help elucidate change mechanisms or identify response processes mediating the cause-and-effect relationship between treatment and improvement. The third aspect entails a look at subject characteristics that are important due to individual differences in the change process.

The Outcome Criterion Problem

The term "outcome criterion problem" refers to how to choose to define improvement in the target problem operationally. Criteria for improvement in very few areas of clinical psychology have been standardized. Constructs such as "anxiety" or "relaxation" are elusive ones, having no agreed-upon meaning or measurement. Given this state of affairs the theoretical framework of the researcher and the values he or she holds all have an impact on this decision about measures to be employed. Until the outcome criterion problem is resolved, we will be unable to answer the question of whether or not therapy as practiced by the clinician is effective (Kiesler, 1971). In the meanwhile, research proceeds, with theory and past results guiding our efforts to define and measure meaningfully the constructs of interest. Certainly the area of anxiety has seen many decades of measurement development, reflective of the theoretical perspective of each period. The current, prevalent view is that "anxiety" is a label for a complex pattern of separate but interacting response systems: cognitive, physiological, and behavioral (cf. Lang, 1968). Consequently, its recommended measurement involves assessments via a combination of self-report, physiological, and behavioral measures. This notion of response indicators as separate but interacting is becoming increasingly pervasive in other areas of research as well. In relaxation research, we are ordinarily interested in assessing the targeted problem area via the subject's phenomenological experience (e.g., as assessed via anxiety and relaxation scales), the degree of sympathetic quieting (e.g., as measured by physiological recordings of heart rate, respiration, muscle activity, skin conductance), and the behavioral effects of relaxation (e.g., as assessed by increased performance, decreased overt signs of anxiety). Each of these measurement domains has a variety of reliability and validity problems, relating to the methods of administration and the meaning of the values in each case. The heart, for example, is not placed in human beings to show researchers how relaxed someone is; rather, its function is to move blood around the body in order to maintain life. Its indirect meaning as a reflection of emotional experience is superimposed on this more basic function. The conditions of its measurement may also cloud our interpretation, necessitating careful design controls to increase the validity of our conclusions based on the assessment. For example, it is well known that some "hypertensive" individuals show elevated blood pressure *only* in the physician's office; presumably this is indicative of anxiety associated with the assessment itself and not of chronically high blood pressure. To circumvent such problems, physiological researchers will ordinarily allow an adaptation period prior to sampling autonomic activity, will include no-treatment conditions to equate groups for such reactions, and so on. We cannot address all of the measurement problems inherent in relaxation assessment in the present chapter, but we do wish, in summary, to make two main points relevant to the outcome criterion problem in relaxation studies. First, multiple assessment of the target problems across the three measurement domains is necessary if we are to obtain a comprehensive picture of what is being changed by the application of a relaxation technique. Secondly, we need to be aware that the measurements customarily obtained in relaxation studies are used to make inferences about depth of relaxation, lessened anxiety, or decreased problem behavior, and those inferences may or may not be appropriate, depending on the reliability and validity of the measures as indicants of the inferred construct.

By way of example, a researcher may begin with an interest in the effects of relaxation on "insomnia." Operational definition may start with reports of latency to sleep onset of 60 minutes or more, and treatment effects are assessed via daily morning reports of sleep latency from the previous night. A single self-report measure does not provide a comprehensive view of what is being changed, although designs providing relatively valid phenomenological reports (e.g., treatment vs. placebo, counterdemand) could lead to cause-and-effect conclusions about the efficacy of relaxation in reducing the *subjective experience* of insomnia (e.g., Steinmark & Borkovec, 1974). Inclusion of behavioral observations by roommates (e.g., Nicassio & Bootzin, 1974) strengthens our conclusions by providing behavioral data in addition to self-reports, resulting in evidence of objective as well as subjective improvement. Electroencephalographic evaluations would allow conclusions about cortically defined improvement (e.g., Freedman & Papsdorf, 1976). Obviously, the combination of all three response domains results in highly specific as well as comprehensive statements about relaxation effects on "insomnia."

Researchers are becoming increasingly aware that the outcome criterion problem is broader than simply the identification of a single, satisfactory outcome measure—something clinicans have always realized. Kazdin and Wilson (1978) have delineated a variety of aspects of change that need to be evaluated before we can have comprehensive understanding of the value of a treatment procedure:

    1. Clinical significance of the change, as opposed to mere statistical significance.
    2. Proportion of clients who change, rather than only group mean comparisons.
    3. Breadth of change—the impact of the change on the client's social, marital, and occupational adjustment.
    4. Durability of change.
    5. Efficiency in terms of how therapy is administered and for how long treatment must be administered.
    6. Cost in terms of professional expertise of the therapists.
    7. Cost to the client, financial and emotional.
    8. Cost-effectiveness of the therapy.
    9. Acceptability of the therapy by the population served.

Within this context, we need to know more than whether a relaxation technique produces greater reductions in heart rate or in reported anxiety. For example, effective technique may be too costly, may influence too few clients, or may fail to produce clinically sufficient improvement.

Research that includes such evaluations will aid in increasingly specifying the breadth and significance of the changes emanating from the application of a particular relaxation technique. As in specification of independent variables, we can rule out aspects of change for any technique by including a variety of assessments.

Auxiliary Outcome (Pretest–Posttest) Measures

Improvement in the target problem is the major outcome content for any efficacy study. However, researchers and clinicians alike are also interested in the mechanisms and related response processes by which improvement takes place. Relaxation may reduce experienced daily tension, but obviously the technique has an influence on some process within the individual in order to effect such change. Our interest in these mechanisms has both theoretical and applied goals. Conceptually, we would like to learn more about how things work and what such conclusions imply about the operations of techniques, the nature of the disorder being treated, and indeed the nature of human behavior and experience. Pragmatically, elucidation of the processes by which therapy effects change will lead to the development of increasingly effective therapy techniques. Some researchers will include not only outcome measures central to their definition of the target problem, but also additional measures obtained before and after treatment that are designed to assess what other changes are taking place. The assumption is that a process that does not covary with improvement cannot be related to that improvement, and therefore can be ruled out as a hypothesized mediator. Processes correlated with target outcome, on the other hand, may be mediational or may point toward a mediational process. Correlational support cannot establish such a process as a causative mediator, but subsequent experimental manipulation of that process can lead to such support.

Referring back to our insomnia example, let us assume that a researcher has established the efficacy of relaxation training in reducing latency to sleep onset. Two of the major theories of psychological insomnia implicate physiological hyperactivity and cognitive intrusions in mediating the disorder. Although faster sleep onset is the outcome criterion, lowered physiological activity at bedtime or decreased frequency of uncontrollable thoughts would represent possible mechanisms by which relaxation might effect outcome. Measuring these two domains would provide disconfirmatory or supporting correlational evidence of their role.

Subject Characteristics

The specification of dependent varibles often leads us toward the role of subject characteristics. Characteristics of the client will influence the way in which the client reacts to a given technique. While the target problem itself might be homogeneous (e.g., a simple phobia), persons having this problem might be quite heterogeneous in terms of the mechanisms involved in the maintenance of the problem and/or the processes by which a technique has an influence. Kiesler (1971) refers to the notion of a treatment's being effective across all categories of clients as a "uniformity myth." The question is not whether a treatment is effective overall, but with what specific clients a given technique is effective and how such change takes place in each case.

A good example in the relaxation literature derives from Davidson and Schwartz's (1976) model. Self-report measures of anxiety obviously contained some items relevant to the anxious cognitions of the person (e.g., "I worry a lot"), whereas others reflected his or her somatic experience (e.g., "My heart pounds"). The inferred construct of "anxiety" was thus a composite of cognitive and physiological processes, as reflected in a total score over both self-report domains. No doubt benefiting from Lang's (1968) suggestion that some channels of response may be more relevant than others to the "anxiety" of a given subject, Davidson and Schwartz (1976) have argued that anxiety may be based primarily in the cognitive events of some people and in the somatic events of others. The natural, subsequent step was to argue that, because some relaxation techniques are more cognitive in nature (e.g., meditation) and others are somatically oriented (e.g., progressive relaxation), the different techniques may be especially effective for particular kinds of clients whose experience of anxiety is based more predominantly on one channel of response than on another. Previous (e.g., Lehrer, Schoicket, Carrington, & Woolfolk, 1980) and future pursuit of these ideas will obviously provide results of both theoretical and applied significance.

OUTCOME CONTEXT

We are interested in specifying not only the types of changes that take place in an outcome investigation, but also in the types that take place in the context of change measurement. This part of our discussion of specification of dependent variables overlaps considerably with topics considered previously in the discussion of external validity. The question of "context" refers principally to the generality of observed change over settings (transfer) and over time (maintenance). Specification is involved, because research that includes assessment in multiple settings and with long-term follow-up provides opportunities to isolate the degree of transfer and maintenance produced by a particular technique.

Transfer

Many laboratory studies focus on highly controlled assessments of the impact of relaxation. Whether or not a subject is able to reduce experienced tension and autonomic activity in a laboratory may or may not relate to such success in daily living circumstances. The laboratory measures, because of their likely greater reliability and validity, are useful for theoretical research, but without ecologically valid measures of a target problem in the natural setting in which it occurs, we cannot legitimately draw conclusions about therapeutic efficacy. Such ecologically valid approaches are exemplified by daily self-monitoring of the target problem, reports from significant others, observations and behavioral ratings in the natural environment by independent assessors, and telemetric physiological recordings.

In discussing further issues regarding the transfer of training effects, we wish to highlight what appears to be one of the major deficiencies in experimental studies of relaxation. Practice and application of relaxation are essential to most techniques. As a learned skill requiring learned application to daily living circumstances, relaxation training cannot be expected on any known theoretical grounds to influence target problems solely on the basis of two, or four, or 10 sessions of training. Yet studies exist in the literature, albeit rarely, wherein no practice is instructed. The majority of studies instruct subjects to practice twice a day between sessions. Even with such practice, we remain curious about how an investigator could assume that the effects of two 15-minute practice sessions per day will generalize throughout the day, will aid in reducing anxiety reactions to daily stressors, or will facilitate recovery from stressful events. With a few exceptions, wherein application practice has been taught and enforced in some detail (e.g., anxiety management training—Suinn & Richardson, 1971; stress inoculation—Meichenbaum, 1975), virtually no relaxation studies involve explicit and detailed instructions in how to apply the technique to daily life. While the inclusion of natural-setting outcome measures would allow us to draw conclusions regarding the transfer of training effects to the situations in which the targeted problem occurs, the presence or absence of practice and application instructions in a particular study will inform us about the likelihood that the technique will have a transfer effect.

Maintenance

For both theoretical and applied reasons, the question of how long therapeutic effects from relaxation training will last is of great importance. We have little interest in an effect of short duration. Yet the relaxation literature, like the body of research for many therapy techniques, has generally lacked long-term follow-up information. Moreover, similar to the transfer problem, we know very little about methods of maintaining improvement; we need to develop ways of guaranteeing the continuation of practice and application (e.g., booster sessions, gradually briefened relaxation procedures) and to evaluate their effects on the maintenance of improvement. Thus, a study with long-term follow-up data would receive high marks as we evaluate its results, as would a study attempting to develop maintenance procedures, if such a one is ever published.

Process Issues

While "follow-up" refers to assessment of temporal generalization subsequent to treatment, there are other measurement possibilities related to time during the process of therapy itself. "Process measurement" involves the assessment of client responses as therapy is taking place (cf. Kazdin & Wilson, 1978). Similar to auxiliary outcome measures, process assessment can provide information about what response processes are being influenced by treatment and whether these sites of effect are mediating outcome improvement. For example, physiological recordings during relaxation sessions can be correlated with outcome improvement. If the person's ability to reduce sympathetic activity during the treatment covaries with reductions in the target problem, we have evidence that (1) physiological hyperactivity may be maintaining condition of the disorder, and (2) relaxation produces improvement in that disorder via its capacity to reduce such activity. In the absence of such covariation, we would need to look elsewhere for the mechanism of change. Frequency of reported practice and application exemplifies another process measure. If such frequency does not relate to outcome improvement, serious questions can be raised about exactly how relaxation is influencing change. Again, such correlational data cannot provide cause-and-effect conclusions, but would point our attention toward or away from certain hypothesized mediators for further experimental pursuit. Thus, process measures provide additional methods of specifying dependent variables, and studies that include them generate valuable information lost in those studies without them.

STATISTICAL CONCLUSION VALIDITY

In addition to internal, external, and construct validity, another type of validity that must be considered in evaluating outcome studies is statistical conclusion validity. Almost all outcome studies rely on statistical methods to increase our ability to infer cause-and-effect relationships between independent (treatment) and dependent (outcome) variables. Cook and Campbell (1979) define "statistical conclusion validity" as "the ability to reasonably infer the presence and magnitude of covariation between cause and effect" (p. 39). At issue here is the validity of making inferences based on statistical evidence. In this section, we discuss threats to this form of validity and some methods of reducing their likelihood.

LOW STATISTICAL POWER

As researchers, we may infer that no real difference between experimental conditions exists when in fact one does. This is most likely to occur when sample sizes are small and when α levels are set low. Studies using a small number of subjects with less conservative statistical power tests (e.g., correlations) are thus susceptible to what is referred to as "Type II error." Thus, a clinical treatment study wherein only a few subjects participate (n per group < 10) increases the likelihood that we will misinterpret the treatment's effectiveness. A common way to decrease the likelihood of Type II error is to apply relatively stringent statistical tests on larger samples (see Cohen, 1970, for practical guidelines for making such choices).

VIOLATED ASSUMPTIONS OF STATISTICAL TESTS

We may draw invalid conclusions for a given study due to violations of the assumptions of the statistical tests used to interpret the data. For example, in order to interpret an analysis-of-variance design legitimately, we must assume homogeneity of variance between groups. While the possibility of heterogeneous variance is not a serious problem when the number of subjects in each group is equal (since the F-test is robust to such violations), this is a serious threat to validity when unequal numbers are found in compared groups. Researchers can deal with this either by using equal numbers per group or by pretesting for homogeneity of variance between groups of unequal numbers.

ERROR-RATE PROBLEM

We may infer that a real difference exists when it really does not ("Type I error"). The likelihood of such an invalid inference increases as the number of mean comparisons between group increases. A study that performs separate analyses of variance on every item of a long questionnaire would be guilty of such a violation, because chance would dictate that in at least one of 20 cases the results would prove significant. The cleanest way around this problem is to have specific *a priori* hypotheses regarding the anticipated outcome of a given study, to limit the number of comparisons performed (especially post hoc comparisons), and to employ multivariate analyses when many dependent measures are obtained.

RELIABILITY OF MEASURES

If we use measures that possess low reliability, our conclusions will be unreliable even when these are employed in an otherwise valid design. Since group means are more stable than individual means (given the same measurement devices), researchers commonly employ group rather than single-subject designs. Well-documented studies will provide evidence of the stability and reliability of the measures used, and the finest studies will administer several repeated assessments before and after therapy in order to maximize reliable measurement (Epstein, 1979).

We have reviewed in this chapter the various dimensions along which research studies on relaxation techniques can be evaluated. Broadly, we are concerned with (1) whether or not the investigator's conclusions are appropriate and valid, and how specific those conclusions can be in terms of what has caused change (internal validity); (2) the extent to which those conclusions can be reasonably applied to other subjects, settings, and conditions (external validity); (3) the degree to which the measures and methodology allow inferences about the central construct (e.g., relaxation, anxiety) investigated (construct validity); and (4) the appropriateness of statistical procedures employed upon which the conclusions are based (statistical validity). The appended checklist (see Appendix) can serve as a useful guide for evaluating a particular study on the dimensions relevant to each of these general areas. Very few studies will receive high marks on every dimension. Any study, even a poorly conducted one, allows some conclusions, although the conclusions may be so broad and unspecifiable that they lack any real importance. Some studies will allow certain, valid, and specific conclusions with varying degrees of generalizability, and it is this set of studies that contributes to an accumulation of scientifically based knowledge. Any single study in and of itself is relatively unimportant and gains importance only in the context of several investigations on the same topic. With each study complementing others by its own strengths and limitations, the conclusions based on the entire set have a greater likelihood of contributing in an enduring way to our knowledge base. Finally, it is also good to remember that the scientific approach to human behavior provides a unique source of knowledge best seen as an important but not a final authority among our numerous sources.

SOME CONCLUDING COMMENTS ON THEORETICAL RELAXATION RESEARCH

What exactly does relaxation training do? How does it influence human behavior, and by what mechanisms? Such fundamental questions about relaxation underlie all of our questions about therapeutic efficacy. The authors of earlier chapters in this volume have offered a variety of theoretical statements concerning the process of relaxation. The modern literature and our own speculations lead to a rather long list of possible relaxation effects:

    1. Reduced tension during the day and creation of a pleasant affective state.
    2. Reduced anxiety response in anticipation of stressors.
    3. Reduced anxiety response during stress presentation.
    4. More rapid recovery from stress events.

The possible mediators of those effects include the following:

    1. Ability to produce increased parasympathetic and decreased sympathetic activity.
    2. Increased awareness of muscle tension and autonomic activity.

3. Increased awareness of cognitive activity and stream of consciousness.

4. Increased control over autonomic and cognitive activity.

5. Increased control of attention to internal activity.

6. Increased concentration (attention focusing) on thoughts, images, physiological activity, affect, and environmental stimuli with an implied decrease in distractibility.

7. Increased ability to shut off inner dialogue.

These effects and mechanisms are neither mutually exclusive nor exhaustive. Several may be relevant to the efficacious treatment of some disorders or of some clients with a particular disorder, whereas others are relevant to other disorders or other persons. Some mechanisms may merely be by-products of others.

Modern experimental research on relaxation has primarily concerned itself with only a fraction of these possibilities: efficacy for rather gross definitions of a few targeted problems (e.g., insomnia, felt anxiety) and success at reducing physiological arousal. It seems to us that more profound changes, which have ramifications reaching beyond the reduction of sleep-onset latency or heart rate to something more fundamental to the nature of human experience, are possibly occurring through the extended practice of relaxation. As scientists, it is appropriate for us to view with caution claims made by some relaxation traditions. Attempts at experimental validation of such claims are one way of providing additional supporting or disconfirming evidence. On the other hand, we are curious about the facts that relaxation and meditation practices have been at the core of many philosophical and religious traditions for several centuries; that unusual and life-changing experiences reportedly emanate from their practice; and that there exists a certain amount of interobserver reliability in the words used to describe such experiences. Of course, a rigorous study of the esoteric relaxation literatures, complete with objective content analyses of such reports, might yield conclusions to the contrary. However, it does seem odd that a technique that simply reduces muscle tension and heart rate to some extent would be so central to so many traditions for so long a period of time. It is important that experimental research continues to pursue the issue of relaxation mechanisms in order to provide objective, communicable knowledge, while remaining open to numerous possible effects inherent in the procedures. Scientific progress on the issue will not occur by efficacy studies alone; theoretical research is necessary.

Let us take one speculative mechanism and see what types of researchable questions might evolve. Castaneda (1972) was instructed in a form of concentrated meditation by a Yaqui shaman, and, by his anecdotal report, he learned to shut off his "inner dialogue." Presumably via such a procedure, he left his "ordinary" way of viewing reality and became immersed in an entirely different reality. Now, of course, there is no way to document his experience. Yet recent theorizing and research in psychology suggests interesting possibilities analogous to the statements in Castaneda's report. Let us consider the following:

1. Much of our behavior and affect may relate to the things we say to ourselves ("self-statements"; see Meichenbaum, 1975).
2. Self-statements are partially conscious, partially controllable expressions of deeper belief systems (Ellis, 1958).
3. Psychological insomniacs may have trouble falling asleep because of uncontrollable thought intrusions, and effective relaxation treatment of insomnia appears to operate via its effect on reducing such intrusions (Borkovec, 1979).
4. Chronic worriers report inability to turn off worry-related cognitions, and a brief period of worry results in an increase in negative cognitive intrusions (Borkovec, 1982).

This set of statements, each with some limited empirical support, suggests interesting possibilities. First, cognition may often be automatic and relatively uncontrolled, even though much of what we consider to be "ourselves" is identified with that process. We are probably unaware of much of our stream of thoughts and images, despite the fact that they appear to contribute to feelings of depression and anxiety, to the creation of insomnia, and to our overall interpretation of our internal and external environment. Relaxation may indeed preclude the occurrence of cognitive intrusions. Self-statements derived from deeper-structure belief systems may preserve those beliefs via the distortion of new information and selective recall. To the extent that lasting change (in behavior, in attitudes, in world view) results from changes in deep structure, shutting off surface self-statements may remove the daily supports of old belief systems; provide access to new, less distorted information; and thus facilitate deep-structure change. Castaneda became more open to alternative beliefs once his ordinary inner dialogue ceased.

A research program could heuristically pursue several lines of research to address these notions, including, for example, the following:

1. The effects of relaxation training on attention and concentration ability could be assessed via pretherapy-to-posttherapy evalu-

ations with a variety of attentional capacity measures and performance tasks.

2. Thought-sampling procedures could be employed to assess the
effects of relaxation on reducing the "inner dialogue."

3. Assessment of the effects of cognitive restructuring under relaxed versus nonrelaxed conditions could be evaluated, using any
number of behavioral and self-report measures of change.

The combination of a variety of outcome, auxiliary outcome, and
process measures with component control and parametric designs would
yield a great amount of information on relaxation as it relates to attention, cognitive activity, and behavioral change. The fact that the stimulus
for such a focus derived from a Yaqui Indian and a sprinkle of suggestive
research and theorizing from cognitive–behavioral models should not
trouble us. As Neal Miller has suggested, scientific research must follow
its rules and be conservative in its conclusions, while being bold in its generation of testable propositions derived from any source.

APPENDIX

Below is a list of questions summarizing issues of design and methodology
relevant to evaluating outcome studies on relaxation techniques. The chapter page on which each point is discussed is indicated parenthetically. Every
investigation allows some conclusion, though studies vary in the specificity
and number of allowable conclusions. The listed questions are only a
guideline for making judgments about various aspects of experimentation
that have an impact on the types of conclusions that can be drawn.

CHECKLIST FOR EVALUATING RELAXATION STUDIES

Internal Validity and Degree of Specification of Independent
Variables

- Includes no-treatment condition? (p. 371)
- Uses random assignment? (p. 372)
- Differential attrition? (p. 372)
- Analyses for relevant pretest differences? (p. 373)
- Includes placebo group? (p. 374)
- Credible placebo group? (p. 374)
- Alternative methods controlling for client expectancy? (p. 375)
- Uses component control design? (pp. 376–377)

- Uses parametric design? (p. 377)
- Uses constructive design? (pp. 377–378)
- Uses comparative design? (p. 378)
- More than one therapist? (pp. 379–380)
- Controls for therapist bias? (pp. 379–380)
- Taped or "live" training? (p. 380)
- Sufficient description of technique to judge its faithfulness? (pp. 380–381)

External Validity and Specification of Dependent Variables

- Subject sample defined and specified in detail? (p. 384)
- Heterogeneous characteristics (e.g., age, sex, education) sampled? (p. 384)
- Is pretest sensitization a possibility? (p. 385)
- "Clinic"-like or "experiment"-like atmosphere? (pp. 385–386)
- Sequential treatments? (pp. 386–387)
- Multidimensional measurement of problem behavior? (pp. 388–390)
- Variety of aspects of outcome measured? (p. 390)
- Uses auxiliary outcome measures? (p. 391)
- Includes levels of a relevant subject characteristic? (p. 392)
- Assesses improvement in natural setting? (p. 393)
- Uses detailed practice and application instructions? (pp. 393–394)
- Follow-up data collected? (p. 394)
- Process measures obtained? (pp. 394–395)

Statistical Validity

- Stringent statistical tests? (p. 395)
- Sufficiently large sample? (p. 395)
- Equal n per condition or homogeneous variance? (pp. 395–396)
- Limited number of statistical tests or use of multivariate analyses? (p. 396)
- Information reported or demonstrated on stability and reliability of measures? (pp. 396–397)

REFERENCES

Borkovec, T. D. Pseudo (experiential)-insomnia and idiopathic (objective) insomnia: Theoretical and therapeutic issues. *Advances in Behaviour Research and Therapy,* 1979, *2,* 27–55.

Borkovec, T. D. *Relaxation techniques, anxiety, and worry: A search for effects and mechanisms.* Paper presented at the North American Society for the Psychology of Sport and Physical Activity, University of Maryland, May 1982.

Borkovec, T. D. & Sides, J. K. Critical procedural variables related to the physiological effects of progressive relaxation: A review. *Behaviour Research and Therapy,* 1979, *17,* 119–126.

Campbell, D. T., & Stanley, J. C. *Experimental and quasi-experimental designs for research.* Chicago: Rand McNally, 1963.

Castaneda, C. *Journey to Ixtlan.* New York: Simon & Schuster, 1972.

Cohen, J. *Statistical power analysis for the behavioral sciences.* New York: Academic Press, 1970.

Cook, T. D., & Campbell, D. T. *Quasi-experimentation: Design and analysis issues for field settings.* Chicago: Rand McNally, 1979.

Davidson, R. J., & Schwartz, G. E. The psychobiology of relaxation and related states: A multi-process theory. In D. I. Mostofsky (Ed.), *Behavior control and modification of physiological activity.* Englewood Cliffs, N.J. Prentice-Hall, 1976.

Eisenman, R. Critique of "Treatment of insomnia by relaxation training": Relaxation training, Rogerian therapy, or demand characteristics. *Journal of Abnormal Psychology,* 1970, *75,* 315–316.

Ellis, A. Rational psychotherapy. *Journal of General Psychology,* 1958, *59,* 35–49.

Epstein, S. The stability of behavior: I. On predicting most of the people much of the time. *Journal of Personality and Social Psychology,* 1979, *37,* 1097–1126.

Eysenck, H. J. The effects of psychotherapy: An evaluation. *Journal of Consulting Psychology,* 1952, *16,* 319–324.

Eysenck, H. J. The conditioning model of neurosis. *The Behavioral and Brain Sciences,* 1979, *2,* 155–199.

Freedman, R., & Papsdorf, J. D. Biofeedback and progressive relaxation treatment of sleep-onset insomnia: A controlled, all-night investigation. *Biofeedback and Self-Regulation,* 1976, *1,* 253–271.

Gottman, J. M., & Markman, H. J. Experimental designs in psychotherapy research. In S. Garfield & A. E. Bergin (Eds.), *Handbook of psychotherapy and behavior change.* New York: Wiley, 1978.

Kahn, M., Baker, B. L., & Weiss, J. M. Treatment of insomnia by relaxation training. *Journal of Abnormal Psychology,* 1968, *73,* 556–558.

Kazdin, A. E., & Wilcoxon, L. A. Systematic desensitization and nonspecific treatment effects: A methodological evaluation. *Psychological Bulletin,* 1976, *83,* 729–758.

Kazdin, A. E., & Wilson, G. T. Criteria for evaluating psychotherapy. *Archives of General Psychiatry,* 1978, *35,* 407–416.

Kiesler, D. J. Experimental designs in psychotherapy research. In A. E. Bergin & S. Garfield (Eds.), *Handbook of psychotherapy and behavior change.* New York: Wiley, 1971.

Lang, P. J. Fear reduction and fear behavior: Problems in treating a construct. In J. M. Shlien (Ed.), *Research in psychotherapy.* Washington, D.C.: American Psychological Association, 1968.

Lehrer, P. M., Schoicket, S., Carrington, P., & Woolfolk, R. L. Psychophysiological and cognitive responses to stressful stimuli in subjects practicing progressive relaxation and clinically standardized meditation. *Behaviour Research and Therapy,* 1980, *18,* 293–303.

Meichenbaum, D. A self-instructional approach to stress-management: A proposal for stress inoculation training. In I. Sarason & C. D. Spielberger (Eds.), *Stress and anxiety* (Vol. 2). New York: Wiley, 1975.

Nicassio, P., & Bootzin, R. A comparison of progressive relaxation and autogenic training as treatments of insomnia. *Journal of Abnormal Psychology,* 1974, *83,* 253–260.

O'Leary, K. D., & Borkovec, T. D. Conceptual, methodological, and ethical problems of placebo groups in psychotherapy research. *American Psychologist,* 1978, *33,* 821–830.

Parloff, M. B., Waskow, I. E., & Wolfe, B. E. Research on therapist variables in relation to process and outcome. In S. Garfield & A. E. Bergin (Eds.), *Handbook of psychotherapy and behavior change.* New York: Wiley, 1978.

Patel, C. H. 12-month follow-up of yoga and biofeedback in the management of hypertension. *Lancet,* 1975, *i,* 62–65.

Patel, C. H., & North, W. R. S. Randomised controlled trial of yoga and biofeedback in the management of hypertension. *Lancet,* 1975, *ii,* 93–95.

Paul, G. L. *Insight versus desensitization in psychotherapy.* Stanford, Calif.: Stanford University Press, 1966.

Paul, G. L. Behavior modification research: Design and tactics. In C. M. Franks (Ed.), *Behavior therapy: Appraisal and status.* New York: McGraw-Hill, 1969.

Paul, G. L., & Trimble, R. W. Recorded versus "live" relaxation training and hypnotic suggestion: Comparative effectiveness for reducing physiological arousal and inhibiting stress response. *Behavior Therapy,* 1970, *1,* , 285–302.

Shapiro, A. K., & Morris, L. A. Placebo effects in medical and psychological therapies. In S. Garfield & A. E. Bergin (Eds.), *Handbook of psychotherapy and behavior change.* New York: Wiley, 1978.

Steinmark, S., & Borkovec, T. D. Active and placebo treatment effects on moderate insomnia under counterdemand and positive demand instructions. *Journal of Abnormal Psychology,* 1974, *83,* 157–163.

Suinn, R., & Richardson, R. Anxiety management training: A non-specific behavior therapy program for anxiety control. *Behavior Therapy,* 1971, *2,* 498–510.

13 ARE STRESS REDUCTION TECHNIQUES INTERCHANGEABLE, OR DO THEY HAVE SPECIFIC EFFECTS?: A REVIEW OF THE COMPARATIVE EMPIRICAL LITERATURE

PAUL M. LEHRER AND ROBERT L. WOOLFOLK

THE SCOPE OF THIS CHAPTER

This chapter reviews the empirical literature on selected comparisons between treatments described in this book. We focus on the theme of differential effects of the various techniques, and we examine evidence for the "specific-effects" hypothesis. The specific-effects hypothesis was outlined in the greatest detail by Davidson and Schwartz (1976), who cited the frequent laboratory findings of desynchronies between behavioral, cognitive, and somatic measures of anxiety. Although sometimes these dimensions do vary together, usually they do not. Thus, the specific-effects hypothesis suggests that a treatment that is oriented to one of these modalities will have the greatest effect on symptoms of that modality: cognitive treatments on cognitive symptoms, behavioral treatments on behavioral symptoms, and so on. Lazarus (1973) suggested a similar scheme for categorizing psychological problems and for matching treatments to problems.

The antithesis of the specific-effects hypothesis was put forward by Benson (1975), who argued that all the relaxation techniques produce a single "relaxation response." A possible compromise position grew out of the research of G. E. Schwartz, Davidson, and Goleman (1978), who concluded that the specific effects of various relaxation techniques may be superimposed upon a general relaxation response.

Davidson and Schwartz classified Jacobson's relaxation technique (cf. McGuigan, Chapter 2, this volume) as a somatically oriented technique, because it focuses almost exclusively on muscular control. Some of the modified Jacobsonian procedures (cf. Bernstein & Given, Chapter 3) might also be thought of as primarily somatic techniques, but they contain more cognitive components, particularly suggestion. Similarly, biofeedback has a primarily somatic emphasis. Cognitive therapy is obviously a cognitive technique. Autogenic training has a combination of cognitive and somatic foci. It involves saying a formula (a cognitive activity) but paying attention to somatic processes. Davidson and Schwartz (1976) first classified mantra meditation as a somatic technique, but later reclassified it as a cognitive technique, because saying a verbal mantra might be expected to block verbal anxiety thoughts very directly (G. E. Schwartz *et al.*, 1978).

In this chapter, we review all studies we have found that directly compare one technique with another on a sufficiently large number of subjects to test for statistical significance. This is potentially a huge task. The number of possible comparisons would equal the factorial of the number of techniques described in this book. Fortunately for this enterprise, the empirical literature has not yet expanded to the point where all potential comparisons have been evaluated.

Because of the wide array of research procedures used, and because of various methodological inadequacies in virtually all of the studies in the literature, we emphasize statistical differences that *have* been found between techniques, rather than findings of no difference. The need to give standard treatment protocols to all subjects and to keep treatment time sufficiently brief to accommodate the needs of research and researchers could decrease therapeutic effectiveness, and also could obscure subtle differences between the effects of various treatments. Choice of subject population is also a problem in many of the studies we reviewed. Using college students as the subject population may have contributed to the small between-groups differences found in many of the studies. Lehrer (1978) found that normal subjects tend to show a "floor effect" in psychophysiological studies of relaxation. With little or no relaxation training, they are able to relax very deeply. Thus, in emphasizing studies that did find differences, we are assuming that problems of procedures and measurement did tend to obscure some differences, and that several replications of particular differences between techniques give us a more accurate picture of the effects of the techniques than do multiple findings of "no differences." Also, if all techniques do produce only a single "relaxation response," then, based on chance, we would expect to find no consistent pattern of differences among techniques across studies. Then all findings of specific effects of particular techniques would be contradicted by diametrically opposite findings in other studies. Studies with negative results for progressive relaxation have been compiled and cited elsewhere (Lehrer, 1982).

In fact, we cannot actually expect a compilation of methodologically imperfect studies to yield conclusive answers. There is still an "art" to doing any form of therapy for emotional disorders. The empirical literature cannot yet tell us exactly which technique to use when. However, a sufficient number of comparative studies have been done to give us some useful information on which to base our therapeutic art.

PROCEDURAL VARIABLES IN PROGRESSIVE RELAXATION: JACOBSON'S METHOD VERSUS VARIOUS "MODIFIED JACOBSONIAN PROCEDURES"

DIFFERENCES BETWEEN TECHNIQUES

In Chapter 1 we outline some of the major differences between Jacobson's original technique, as described by McGuigan (Chapter 2), and the modified progressive relaxation procedures, as described by Bernstein and Given (Chapter 3). We believe that the two are sufficiently distinct for us to consider them to be two separate techniques. So far, there are only two studies that compare Jacobson's technique *in toto* with some of the modified techniques *in toto*. One provided some support for the use of Jacobson's original technique. P. E. Turner (1978) studied college students and compared Jacobson's technique to two of the modified Jacobsonian methods, the methods described by Wolpe (1969) and by Paul (1966). Fewer sessions were devoted to the latter two techniques than to Jacobson's technique (seven and three sessions, respectively, in contrast with 16 sessions for the Jacobson technique). Also, the latter two techniques made much greater use of suggestion, and they emphasized relatively large muscle flexions in order to achieve a state of relaxation. Turner also included an electromyographic (EMG) biofeedback condition, a self-relaxation control, and a no-treatment control. He found marginally superior results for Jacobson's original technique. Jacobson's technique was the only one found to be superior to his control conditions (self-relaxation and no treatment) in reducing scores on Spielberger's State–Trait Anxiety Inventory. On this measure, differences between Jacobson's technique and the others were significant. The same pattern of results was obtained for the Taylor Manifest Anxiety Scale and for subjective ratings of emotional discomfort. In these cases, however, the results only approached statistical significance or were not significant at all. No significant between-groups differences emerged for heart rate or skin conductance. It is possible, of course, that all differences found in this study result simply from the greater number of therapy sessions in Jacobson's technique. This possibility, and the relative smallness of the differences between groups, are reasons to be rather cautious about making sweeping conclusions from this study. In a similar study, Snow (1977) studied female college students and found no physiological differences between Jacobson's and Wolpe's relaxation methods, either during a period of relaxation or during exposure to a stress film. The fact that both of these studies examined college students rather than a population of clinically anxious individuals may have rendered them insensitive to treatment effects. It is known that normal college students can be induced to relax very easily, with practically no training at all (cf. Lehrer, 1972).

LIVE VERSUS TAPED PROGRESSIVE RELAXATION TRAINING

At first blush, the literature on progressive relaxation in general looks rather equivocal. Approximately half the studies find that progressive relaxation produces greater decreases in various measures of physiological arousal than do various control conditions. The other studies show no differences between groups (Lehrer, 1982). The picture looks markedly different when we examine only the studies that measured *generalized* effects of training—that is, the ability of people to use their relaxation skills *outside* the training session. Actually, this is the most important test for a relaxation technique. We need our relaxation skills most when we are faced with stressful situations. These situations rarely occur at times when we can stretch out on a reclining chair and listen to a relaxation tape —or, even less likely, at a time when we can arrange a quick session with a relaxation therapist. Table 13-1 shows the studies that have found significant generalized physiological effects for live and for taped relaxation instructions. Six studies found significant physiological effects for live progressive relaxation instruction, but only one study (Sime & DeGood, 1977) found significant effects for taped instruction. The latter study used a relaxation procedure that was very different from the one used in other studies. All four progressive relaxation sessions were devoted to training of the frontalis muscle alone—and the frontalis muscle was the only measure to show significant physiological effects. Even at that, the effects were not very powerful. An EMG biofeedback condition showed stronger effects.

The importance of live training is even more graphically illustrated when we examine reports of comparisons between live and taped progressive relaxation *within a single study.* Although a number of studies found no differences between these two approaches, those studies that did find differences between live and taped training all favored live training. These studies are summarized in Table 13-2.

Why is live training more effective psychophysiologically? Paul and Trimble (1970) hypothesize that immediate feedback to the subject and response-contingent training (i.e., advancing the pace of training when the skill is being learned rapidly and giving additional instruction when some problems in learning take place) are the critical ingredients in the advantage of live training. The reasons for the advantages of live training become self-evident when we think about the training of other analogous muscular skills. Could anyone doubt that live training in (say) learning to play tennis, to dance, or to play the piano would be more effective than taped training?

Data from studies by Quayle (1979) and Godsey (1979) show that the advantage of live training in producing physiological effects is not simply due to the repetition of instructions when subjects have difficulty feeling tension in a particular muscle group. Both of these studies examined subject-contingent versus program-contingent repetitions of instructions. In the subject-contingent condition, instructions were repeated when a subject appeared to be having difficulty locating a sensation of tension or difficulty relaxing a particular muscle. In the program-contingent condition, instructions were presented at a predetermined pace, regardless of the progress of individual subjects. No consistent differences between conditions emerged. Quayle (1979) found that subject-contingent instructions produced greater decreases in EMG levels and skin temperature than did program-contingent instructions; but that program-contingent instructions were more effective in reducing self-report measures of anxiety. Similarly, Godsey (1979) found no significant differences between subject-contingent and program-contingent instructions on heart rate or skin conductance. (In both studies, live training produced greater decreases than taped training in the physiological measures mentioned above.)

Thus factors other than simple repetition of instruction must account for the greater effectiveness of live instruction. One possibility is that the results are accounted for by "nonspecific" factors in the relationship between client and therapist. The warmth displayed by the therapist may be critical for success. Taub (Taub, 1977; Taub & School, 1978) has shown that even the relatively mechanical procedure of hand temperature warming through biofeedback cannot be learned from an instructor with an aloof, matter-of-fact style, although it is readily learned from an instructor who is interpersonally warm. Another factor might be the amount of feedback that the live instructor is able to give to the learner during training. When the subject is unable to feel tension, the instructor may point it out, or try to illustrate it kinesthetically by passive flexion of a muscle, by putting resistance against an attempted limb movement, and so forth. Relaxation instruction involves teaching the trainee to be his or her own biofeedback machine. This is done using all possible methods of effective communication, demonstration, and reinforcement.

DIFFERENCES BETWEEN TECHNIQUES: EVALUATION OF THE SPECIFIC-EFFECTS HYPOTHESIS

BIOFEEDBACK AND PROGRESSIVE RELAXATION

Studies of EMG biofeedback combined with taped relaxation instructions do suggest that feedback may be one of the important ingredients in live progressive relaxation training. Under some circumstances, EMG biofeedback appears to render taped relaxation training an effective technique for reducing at least one measure of physiological arousal: EMG from the muscle under the biofeedback electrodes. These data are summarized in Table 13-3. By itself, EMG biofeedback appears to be a more effective technique than taped relaxation instruction. As can be seen in Table 13-4, seven studies show greater effects for EMG biofeedback than for taped progressive relaxation, whereas only one (Sheridan, Vaughan, Wallerstedt, & Ward, 1977) found the opposite.

Although EMG biofeedback may potentiate the effects of taped relaxation training, it appears to add little to the effectiveness of live progressive relaxation instruction. Chesney and Shelton (1976) found that, in relieving symptoms of tension headaches, the combination of live progressive relaxation training and EMG biofeedback did not differ from live progressive relaxation instructions, although only in the combined group did the results differ from no treatment. Comparisons between EMG biofeedback and live relaxation instruction generally have shown that, on a variety of measures, the latter has more powerful stress-reducing effects (see Table 13-5). LeBoeuf and Lodge (1980) did find larger effects for EMG biofeed-

TABLE 13-1.   Studies Finding Generalized Psychophysiological Effects for Live PMR

Authors	Results	Comments
Beiman, Israel, & Johnson (1978)	Reductions in RR, frontalis EMG, Anxiety Differential scores: Live PMR > taped PMR, EMG BFK, ROM.	Testing was done at a separate posttest session. Five sessions of training
Jacobson (1934a, 1934b)	EMG levels from various muscles among trained Ss were lower than those attained by untrained Ss.	Trained Ss were mostly patients in treatment for neuromuscular tension states. Control Ss were normal volunteers.
Lehrer, Woolfolk, Rooney, McCann, & Carrington (1983)	1. Forearm EMG during stressful scenes in movie: PMR < MED = NT. 2. Frontalis EMG during stressful scenes in movie: PMR < MED < NT. 3. Decreases in SCL-90–R (Obsessive–Compulsive, Depression, general severity index, positive symptom total): PMR > MED > NT. 4. Decreases in IPAT Anxiety scale on covert anxiety and low self-control were significant for PMR, not MED or NT. Between-groups ANOVA n.s.	Five sessions of live group training. Ss were high in anxiety. Testing was done at a separate posttest session.
Miller, Murphy, & Miller (1978)	1. a. Frontalis EMG decreases during training sessions: BFK = PMR > SR. b. Pretest-to-posttest decreases were significant for PMR and BFK, not for SR (groups × treatment ANOVA n.s.). 2. Decreases in an *ad hoc* dental anxiety scale: BFK = PMR > SR. 3. STAI State Anxiety decreases: BFK = PMR > SR. 4. STAI Trait Anxiety decreases: No differences between groups.	Ss were dental phobics. Ten sessions of live training; testing was done during dental appointments as well as during training sessions.
Lehrer (1978)	1. Occipital alpha increased by PMR in anxiety neurotics, decreased in normals. 2. Cardiac accelerations to noxious tones decreased	Four to five sessions of individual training; testing was done at a separate posttest session.

TABLE 13-1. *(Continued)*

Authors	Results	Comments
	by PMR in anxiety neurotics.	
	3. Skin conductance decreased by PMR in anxiety neurotics.	
	4. STAI State Anxiety decreased by PMR.	
Southam (1981)	1. Decreases in DBP at clinic visits and in work site: PMR > NT; maintained at 6-month follow-up.	Eight sessions live individual training plus taped home training. Ss were hypertensive.
	2. Decreases in SBP at clinic visits: PMR > NT.	

Note: Explanation of abbreviations: *Treatments*—BFK, biofeedback; CCR, cue-controlled relaxation; FF, false biofeedback control; CSM, clinically standardized meditation; MED, meditation; NT, no-treatment control; PMR, progressive relaxation; ROM, Benson's "relaxation response," or "respiratory one meditation"; S, subject; SD, systematic desensitization; SR, self-relaxation control; TM, transcendental meditation; WL, waiting list. *Measures*—ANOVA, analysis of variance; DBP, diastolic blood pressure; HR, heart rate; MACL, Mood Adjective Check List; POMS, Profile of Mood States; RR, respiration rate; SBP, systolic blood pressure; STAI, State–Trait Anxiety Inventory; SUDs, Subjective Units of Discomfort; TMAS, Taylor Manifest Anxiety Scale.

back than for progressive relaxation in reducing frontalis EMG during a training session, but the advantage of EMG biofeedback did not generalize to heart rate or to anxiety levels.

AUTOGENIC TRAINING VERSUS OTHER METHODS

The six standard exercises in autogenic training emphasize sensations involving the autonomic nervous system (e.g., warm hands, slow heart rate, cool forehead, warm solar plexus). Thus, according to the specific-effects hypothesis, the technique might be expected to have greater effects on autonomic activity than those of progressive relaxation and/or EMG biofeedback. The latter two techniques should have their greatest effects on the musculoskeletal system.

Autogenic training does appear to have greater effects on autonomic measures than either progressive muscle relaxation or EMG biofeedback does. Lehrer, Atthowe, and Weber (1980) found greater decreases in heart rate during autogenic training than during progressive relaxation in subjects who initially scored high on the IPAT Anxiety Inventory (Krug, Scheier, & Cattell, 1976). Both groups showed decreases in anxiety and

TABLE 13-2.   Studies Finding Differences between Live and Taped PMR

Authors	Results	Comments
Beiman, Israel, & Johnson (1978)	Reductions in RR, frontalis EMG, Anxiety Differential scores: Live PMR > taped PMR, EMG BFK, ROM.	Five sessions of training in each condition; testing was done at a separate posttest.
Godsey (1979)	1. Live PMR produced lower skin conductance levels during rest and lower HR variability during stressful imagery than taped PMR. 2. Similar differences, but n.s. for HR variability during rest and for self-reported anxiety during stressful imagery.	Measures were taken during the 3rd session of training. Both subject-contingent and program-contingent instructions were used.
Paul & Trimble (1970)	Decreases in forearm EMG, HR, RR, Anxiety Differential: Live PMR > taped PMR = SR.	Two sessions of group training. Measures were taken during training sessions. Ss were college students.
Quayle (1979)	1. Decreases in EMG and skin temperature: Live PMR > taped PMR. 2. No differences between taped and live PMR in changes in subjective anxiety.	Five sessions of training. Ss were volunteers.
Russell, Sipich, & Knipe (1976)	1. Live PMR training in 16 muscle groups produced decreases in EMG and Anxiety Differential. 2. Live PMR training in four muscle groups produced no effects. 3. Taped PMR training in 16 muscle groups produced decreases in Anxiety Differential, not in EMG. 4. SR produced decreases in EMG, not in Anxiety Differential.	Three sessions of training. Ss were respondents to ads for tense people.
Israel & Beiman (1977)	1. On MACL, STAI, and Anxiety Differential, live PMR > taped PMR = SR. 2. No differences between groups in HR, RR, frontalis EMG.	Measures were taken during the last 3 minutes of the three training sessions.

Note. For explanation of abbreviations, see footnote to Table 13-1.

TABLE 13-3.   Taped PMR plus EMG BFK

Authors	Results	Comments
Townsend, House, & Addario (1975)	1. Frontalis EMG: Decreased over treatment sessions, and generalized to self-practice session in PMR + BFK group, not in "group therapy" group. Between-groups effect was significant. 2. POMS and STAI: Decreased across sessions in PMR + BFK, but not in group therapy. Between-groups effect was n.s.	Ss were anxious psychiatric inpatients. Twelve sessions of treatment.
Feely (1978)	1. State anxiety: PMR + BFK < control.	Nine sessions; Ss were narcotics addicts.
Chesney & Shelton (1976)	1. Reductions in headache frequency: PMR = PMR + BFK > BFK alone = NT. 2. Reductions in headache duration: PMR = PMR + BFK > BFK alone. 3. Reductions in headache severity: PMR + BFK (only) > NT.	Ss had tension headaches. PMR: Three sessions of live group training, plus home taped practice. BFK: Four times weekly for 2 weeks.
Miller, Murphy, & Miller (1978)	1. a. Frontalis EMG decreased during training sessions: BFK = PMR > SR. b. Pretest-to-posttest decreases were significant for PMR, BFK; not for SR (groups × treatment ANOVA n.s.). 2. Decreases in an *ad hoc* scale of dental anxiety: BFK = PMR > SR. 3. STAI State Anxiety decreases: BFK = PMR > SR. 4. STAI Trait Anxiety decreases: No differences between groups.	Ss were dental phobics. Ten sessions of live training. Testing was done during dental appointments as well as during training sessions.
Reed & Saslow (1980)	1. Achievement Anxiety Test (Alpert & Haber, 1960), decreases in debilitating anxiety, and increases in facilitative anxiety: Significant for EMG BFK + taped PMR, not for taped PMR alone or for NT.	Ss were college students high on test anxiety.

(continued)

TABLE 13-3. *(Continued)*

Authors	Results	Comments
	2. STAI State Anxiety decreases: Significant for EMG BFK + taped PMR and for taped PMR alone, not for NT. 3. STAI Trait Anxiety decreased in taped PMR and at $p<.1$ in EMG BFK + taped PMR; not in NT. 4. Frontalis EMG: EMG BFK + taped PMR and taped PMR alone decreased within and across sessions; not NT.	
Reinking & Kohl (1975)	The following conditions were studied: (a) PMR; (b) frontalis EMG BFK; (c) EMG BFK plus monetary reward; (d) EMG BFK + PMR; (e) NT. 1. Frontalis EMG: Decreases over sessions in all groups. Toward last sessions, BFK groups > PMR. 2. SUDs scores: All groups decreased over sessions. No between-groups differences.	Ss were psychology students; 15 1-hour sessions.
Hutchings & Reinking (1976)	1. Decreases in headache scores: BFK alone, BFK + PMR > PMR. 2. Frontalis EMG: Decreases earlier in training for BFK and BFK + PMR than for PMR.	Ten sessions. Ss had tension headaches. PMR training was combined with autogenic suggestions.

Note. For explanation of abbreviations, see footnote to Table 13-1.

in various other self-report measures of psychological distress. Subjects undergoing autogenic training also experienced more sensations relevant to autonomic effects than did subjects in the progressive relaxation group, while the latter reported more sensations of muscular relaxation. Similar verbal reports, but with no significant physiological findings, were reported by Shapiro and Lehrer (1980) from a population of normal volunteers. In another study, Fray (1975) found autogenic training to be superior to EMG biofeedback in maintaining blood pressure reductions at follow-up. The effects of the two techniques immediately after treatment, however, were not different.

TABLE 13-4.   Studies Finding Differences between Taped PMR and EMG BFK

Authors	Results	Comments
Sime & DeGood (1977)	Reductions in frontalis EMG activity, pretraining to posttraining: Frontalis BFK > PMR > placebo (listening to music).	Four sessions of training. In the PMR tape, *all* the instructions were devoted to the frontalis area.
DeBerry (1979)	1. Lowest-level frontalis EMG in training session: BFK > NT, PMR = NT, treatment groups > NT. 2. Pretraining-to-posttraining changes in EMG: No differences between groups. 3. Decreases in STAI State Anxiety: BFK > PMR > NT.	Ss were college students. Three 25-minute sessions.
Haynes, Moseley, & McGowan (1975)	Frontalis EMG decreases: 1. BFK > PMR, FF, SR. 2. PMR without tensing = FF, BFK but > PMR, SR.	Only one session of training. Data were collected during the training session. Ss were college students.
Sheridan, Vaughan, Wallerstedt, & Ward (1977)	1. Frontalis EMG dropped over training sessions for PMR, not for BFK or SR. Also, within-session decreases in PMR, BFK. Groups did not differ at posttest session. 2. Women *reported* relaxing better under PMR than BFK. Differences were in the opposite direction for men, but were n.s.	Four sessions of training followed by one posttest session.
Fee & Girdano (1978)	1. Frontalis EMG decreases pretraining to posttraining in frontalis EMG BFK and in taped MED; not in taped PMR, NT, placebo. 2. RR decreases only in taped PMR and MED, but treatments × pre–post ANOVA interaction n.s.	Ten sessions of training. Ss were college students.
Reed & Saslow (1980)	See Table 13-3.	
Reinking & Kohl (1975)	See Table 13-3.	
Hutchings & Reinking (1976)	See Table 13-3.	

Note. For explanation of abbreviations, see footnote to Table 13-1.

TABLE 13-5.   Studies Finding Differences between Live PMR Training and EMG BFK

Authors	Results	Comments
Chesney & Shelton (1976)	1. Reductions in headache frequency: PMR = PMR + BFK > BFK = NT. 2. Reductions in headache duration: PMR = PMR + BFK > BFK. 3. Headache severity: PMR + BFK (only) > NT.	PMR: Three sessions of live group training plus home taped practice. Ss had tension headaches. BFK: Four times weekly for 2 weeks.
P. E. Turner (1978)	1. STAI State and Trait Anxiety: Jacobson's PMR > Wolpe's PMR = Paul's PMR = EMG BFK = SR = NT. 2. The same pattern was obtained for HR, skin conductance levels, TMAS, and SUDs, but n.s.	
Beiman, Israel, & Johnson (1978)	Reductions in RR, frontalis EMG, Anxiety Differential scores: Live PMR > taped PMR, EMG BFK, ROM.	Five sessions of training in each condition; testing was done at a separate posttest.
Canter, Kondo, & Knott (1975)	By the end of training: 1. Frontalis EMG: BFK > "PMR" 2. Patients' and therapists' ratings of decreases in symptoms: BFK > "PMR"	From 10 to 15 sessions, as determined by patient needs, hospital stay. Ss were psychiatric inpatients. Measures taken before, during, and after sessions. "PMR" group got suggestions to relax *without* tension–release training.
Haynes, Sides, & Lockwood (1977)	Improvement in self-reported sleep-onset latency: Live PMR > BFK at 1-year follow-up.	*Immediately* after treatment the groups did not differ.
LeBoeuf & Lodge (1980)	Frontalis: 1. EMG reductions during last training sessions: EMG BFK > PMR. 2. HR reduction during last training session: EMG BFK = PMR. 3. Self-rated anxiety (TMAS and STAI), and clinician-rated anxiety (Hamilton Anxiety Inventory): EMG BFK = PMR.	Sixteen sessions of training. Ss were anxiety neurotics.

Note. For explanation of abbreviations, see footnote to Table 13-1.

The effects of autogenic training on autonomic activity may be quite similar to those of biofeedback for autonomic variables. Surwit, Pilon, and Fenton (1978) found no differences between finger temperature biofeedback and the combination of finger temperature biofeedback and autogenic training on physiological or self-report measures of symptoms associated with Raynaud's disease.

Conversely, there is evidence that progressive relaxation and EMG biofeedback produce greater decreases in muscular tension and associated symptoms than does autogenic training. A study by Staples, Coursey, and Smith (1975) found lower frontalis EMG levels during the last of 10 sessions of taped training in progressive relaxation and in EMG biofeedback than in taped autogenic training. There were no EMG differences between groups at follow-up, however; nor were there any differences in anxiety between groups at any time. All groups showed anxiety reductions. Detrick (1977) studied people suffering from muscle contraction headaches. He compared autogenic feedback training (cf. Norris & Fahrion, Chapter 8, this volume), consisting of a combination of peripheral skin temperature biofeedback and autogenic training, with a combination of EMG biofeedback and progressive relaxation. He found the combination of EMG biofeedback and progressive relaxation to be more effective than was the autogenic feedback training in reducing self-reported headache activity and frontalis EMG levels. Subjects in the group receiving EMG biofeedback plus progressive relaxation also reported lower levels of anxiety than subjects in the autogenic feedback group. One might expect the opposite findings to occur among migraine sufferers, whose problem primarily involves autonomic activity rather than muscular activity. A study by Sloan (1977), however, failed to find differences in therapeutic effects between autogenic feedback training and progressive relaxation plus EMG biofeedback. The only significant between-groups difference in this study was on frontalis EMG. Subjects in the group receiving relaxation plus EMG biofeedback showed greater decreases in this measure than did subjects in the autogenic feedback condition—a finding that is consistent with the specific-effects hypothesis.

There also are some completely negative findings. A study by Byasse (1975) failed to find any differences among progressive relaxation, autogenic training, and self relaxation in blood pressure readings among hypertensives. All groups improved during treatment, but treatment effects did not persist at a 4-month follow-up.

As mentioned above, Davidson and Schwartz (1976) hypothesize that autogenic training should have more cognitive effects than such purely somatically oriented techniques as biofeedback or progressive relaxation, because it contains a mixture of cognitive and somatic elements. We have found no evidence for this (Lehrer, Atthowe, & Weber, 1980; Shapiro & Lehrer, 1980; Staples *et al.,* 1975). Indeed, the opposite was found by Detrick (1977), who observed greater decreases in self-reported anxiety (a cognitive measure) for the combination of progressive relaxation and EMG biofeedback than for autogenic feedback training.

The literature on autogenic training reports a phenomenon called "autogenic discharges" (cf. Schultz & Luthe, 1969). No equivalent observations are reported in the literature on progressive relaxation. Autogenic discharges are described as emotional or physical discharges, often unpleasant, consisting sometimes of pain, anxiety, palpitations, muscle twitches, and so forth. Crying is also often experienced. Although these events must be treated carefully during therapy, they are usually not considered to be countertherapeutic. Autogenic discharges are thought to reflect the body's process of achieving homeostasis. Sometimes, however, they may make the technique too unpleasant to practice, thus leading to dropout; or, alternatively, they may produce effects that are medically dangerous (e.g., increases in blood pressure among hypertensives). Thus subjects must be carefully monitored to be sure that they do not experience intolerable autogenic discharges. Also, the length of autogenic exercises is purposely kept very short (often 30 seconds to 3 minutes at the beginning), in order to avoid autogenic discharges. One study that specifically examined autogenic discharges in several techniques (Lehrer, Atthowe, & Weber, 1980) found that subjects in an autogenic training group experienced sensations of palpitations when they were first introduced to the autogenic formula, "My heartbeat is calm and regular." No analogous phenomena occurred during progressive relaxation. This was a transient experience, and was not associated with a negative outcome of autogenic training. Indeed, subjects in the autogenic training group achieved lower heart rates than subjects in other groups during a posttraining stress test. Progressive relaxation appeared to have had somewhat more motivating effects than autogenic training, however. Subjects in the progressive relaxation group reported having done more home practice than subjects in the autogenic training group.

RELAXATION VERSUS MEDITATION

Because he believes that all relaxation techniques have approximately the same effects, Benson (1975) argues that the best technique would be the one that is simplest to teach and to learn. He has devised a very simple form of meditation, which requires a person simply to say the word "one" with each exhalation. Benson calls his method the "relaxation response," but for the purposes of this review, we are renaming it, more descriptively, "respiratory one meditation" (ROM). Because of its simplicity, ROM can be taught in one session. Benson argues that the effects of ROM are at least equivalent to those of more complex techniques (cf. Greenwood & Benson, 1977). Further, because of the relative ease of administering it, Benson argues that ROM is preferable to other techniques.

G. E. Schwartz et al. (1978), in contrast to Benson, describe some evidence that transcendental meditation (TM) produces specific cognitive effects. They compared people who meditate regularly with people who exercise regularly, and found that the meditators had fewer self-reported cognitive symptoms of stress than did exercisers, while exercisers had fewer self-reported somatic symptoms of stress than did meditators. This finding was inconclusive, however, because subjects had not been randomly assigned to the two groups. It is therefore possible that preexisting individual differences between groups may have accounted for the findings.

Some evidence has accumulated that progressive relaxation and meditation have very different effects on muscle tension and tonic heart rate (see Table 13-6). Warrenberg, Pagano, Woods, and Hlastala (1980) found that resting heart rates are lower among long-term practitioners of progressive relaxation than among long-term practitioners of TM. This is not surprising, in view of the fact that progressive relaxation is specifically directed at the skeletal muscles, and that heart rate is directly affected by muscle tension. This result is consistent with the Davidson and Schwartz (1976) hypothesis. A similar study of long-term practitioners of progressive relaxation and TM by Curtis and Wessberg (1980) failed to find any differences between the groups on heart rate, skin conductance, or respiration rate. Warrenburg et al. (1980), however, note that the levels of arousal in these subjects were unusually high; this perhaps suggests a problem in the experimental method.

The effects of meditation appear to be rather variable. There is some evidence that mantra meditation may, under some circumstances, produce a desynchrony between cortical and somatic indices of arousal. One study (Lehrer, Schoicket, Carrington, & Woolfolk, 1980) found more electroencephalographic (EEG) alpha but higher heart rate and muscle tension in a testing session after training in mantra meditation than after either progressive relaxation or a control condition (see Table 13-6). Thus

TABLE 13-6. Studies Finding Differences between PMR and Mantra MED in Lowering Somatic Arousal

Authors	Measures	Comments
Studies finding PMR to be superior		
Lehrer, Woolfolk, Rooney, McCann, & Carrington (1983)	Forearm EMG, frontalis EMG.	During stressful scenes in film, forearm: PMR < MED = NT; frontalis: PMR = MED < NT.
Bradley & McCanne (1981)	HR during practice.	Four taped sessions: PMR > ROM > NT, but only under condition of positive expectancy.
Warrenberg, Pagano, Woods, & Hlastala (1980)	HR.	Long-term PMR practitioners < long-term TM practitioners both before and during practice of technique in lab.
Heidi & Borkovec (1983)	Increases in HR, RR, frontalis EMG during practice. ("Relaxation-produced anxiety")	All Ss received both techniques. MED > PMR (note opposite results for skin conductance).
Studies finding mantra MED to be superior		
Lehrer, Schoicket, Carrington, & Woolfolk (1980)	HR decelerations to loud tones augmented more in MED than in PMR. EEG alpha higher in MED than in PMR. Significant for frontal, not occipital.	Measures taken at posttest session. Ss were volunteers recruited from ads. EEG alpha results not replicated in later study. Four sessions of live group training.
Lehrer, Woolfolk, Rooney, McCann, & Carrington (1983)	HR decelerations to loud tones.	Volunteer Ss high on IPAT Anxiety Inventory. Five sessions of live individual or small-group training.
Parker, Gilbert, & Thoreson (1978)	Blood pressure decreased among alcholics. Both MED and PMR produced decreases in DBP, although decreases in MED occurred sooner in the 3-week, nine-session training. SBP decreased only in MED.	Relaxation instructions were tape-recorded.
Fee & Girdano (1978)	See Table 13-4.	

Note. For explanation of abbreviations, see footnote to Table 13-1.

meditation appeared to produce cortical relaxation with simultaneous somatic arousal. The EEG results in this study are consistent with other studies finding EEG effects for meditation, but must be treated with caution, because they were not replicated in a subsequent study (Lehrer, Woolfolk, Rooney, McCann, & Carrington, in press). Actually, various EEG effects are reported in the meditation literature. States of meditative ecstasy often appear to be accompanied by increases in beta activity and suppression of alpha; while alpha appears to be enhanced in some states of meditative relaxation (cf. reviews by West, 1980; Woolfolk, 1975). We have hypothesized that frontal EEG alpha may be a physiological marker for diminished cognitive activity (Lehrer, Schoicket, Carrington, & Woolfolk, 1980), thus making our own results consistent with the Davidson and Schwartz (1976) hypothesis. Progressive relaxation, on the other hand, has not been found to have any consistent effects on EEG activity. Lehrer (1978) found that progressive relaxation produced increases in occipital alpha among anxiety neurotics, but borderline-significant *decreases* in alpha among normal subjects. Lindholm and Lowry (1978) found that prior training in progressive relaxation did not facilitate learning in an alpha biofeedback experiment. Lehrer (1978) found no effects for progressive relaxation training on the sensory–motor rhythm (approximately 13 Hz, recorded from near the motor cortex).

Given these findings, how may we evaluate the studies suggesting that meditation may be an effective treatment for psychosomatic disorders, such as hypertension (Benson, 1977; Benson, Rosner, Marzetta, & Klemchuk, 1974)? Although the effects of meditation on tonic muscle tension and heart rate may be quite variable, the effects on cardiac reactivity are more consistent. Indeed, in two studies, we found greater cardiac decelerations in meditation than in progressive relaxation in response to noxious stimuli (Lehrer, Schoicket, Carrington, & Woolfolk, 1980; Lehrer *et al.,* in press). The relation between this result and the EEG findings is unclear. Perhaps both reflect cognitive relaxation. The augmented cardiac accelerations to noxious stimuli may reflect a tendency to react to changes in the environment with curiosity, acceptance, and interest rather than with threat. Thus the cardiac decelerations evoked by the noxious stimulation in our studies may be interpreted as "orienting" rather than as "defensive" reflexes (cf. Graham & Clifton, 1966, Sokolov, 1963). Similar results were reported by Goleman and Schwartz (1976), who found greater autonomic responsivity to stressful scenes in a movie among meditators than among nonmeditators, but found faster autonomic recovery among meditators. It is possible that such a set, over a long period of time, might diminish tonic cardiovascular activity—and thus may be helpful in overcoming psychosomatic disease.

The effects of meditation on paper-and-pencil measures of anxiety, stress, and tension are much less consistent, and do not unequivocally support the Davidson and Schwartz (1976) hypothesis (see Table 13-7). Some studies find progressive relaxation to produce more self-reports of diminished muscle tension and increased feelings of relaxation, and find meditation to produce self-reports of reduced worrying, anxiety, and similar states. However, other studies report exactly the opposite (see Table 13-8). Not only do these data fail to confirm that meditation has more cognitive effects than progressive relaxation; but they even indicate that meditation may, under some circumstances, produce perceptions of muscular relaxation that equal or exceed those produced by progressive relaxation.

Other interesting differences between meditation and progressive relaxation are summarized in Table 13-9. Several studies, including two of ours (Carrington, Collings, Benson, Robinson, Wood, Lehrer, Woolfolk, & Cole, 1980; Lehrer et al., 1983), found that subjects reported enjoying meditation more than progressive relaxation and practicing it somewhat more. The differences between groups on these measures are not large, but they are significant and consistent across studies. Zuroff and

TABLE 13-7.   Studies Finding Differences between PMR and Mantra MED on Self-Report of Muscle Tension plus Relaxation

Authors	Measures	Comments
Lehrer, Schoicket, Carrington, & Woolfolk (1980)	Posttesting session and posttherapy session questionnaire items about feelings related to muscle tension.	PMR < CSM, WL.
Woolfolk, Lehrer, McCann, & Rooney (1982)	Spouse or roommate reports of tension and calmness.	Before training versus after five sessions of training: PMR Ss showed decreased tension but not MED or NT Ss.
Lehrer, Woolfolk, Rooney, McCann, & Carrington (1983)	1. Home practice questionnaire measure of tension. 2. Fenz's (1967) Muscle Tension Scale; Lehrer & Woolfolk (1982) Hyperventilation Scale.	1. Tension was reduced in PMR but not MED over five weekly sessions of live training. 2. MED decreased tension but PMR did not. ANOVA was n.s.

Note. For explanation of abbreviations, see footnote to Table 13-1.

Schwarz (1978) also reported that college-student subjects (at least at their university in the late 1970s) had higher expectancies for meditation than for progressive relaxation.

On the other hand, there is also some evidence from our work (Carrington *et al.*, 1980; Lehrer *et al.*, in press) that meditation may produce more negative side effects than progressive relaxation. Specifically, more people report sensations of transient anxiety during practice of meditation than during practice of progressive relaxation. This is consistent with the heightened physiological arousal and physiological reactivity that is sometimes found in meditation. Heidi and Borkovec (1983) call it "relaxation-produced anxiety," and also report more frequent occurrences of it in meditation than in progressive relaxation. Carrington (1977) interprets it as a "destressing" phenomenon, reflecting a state of relatively high tension prior to meditation. It appears to be similar to the phenomenon of "autogenic discharges" referred to in the literature on autogenic training. Such anxiety reactions may be less common in progressive relaxation because of its more direct effects in lowering heart rate and muscle tension. If the problem of relaxation-produced anxiety becomes troublesome in the training of particular individuals, the research literature thus suggests that progressive relaxation may be somewhat easier for the person to tolerate. The phenomenon probably results from an increased somatic awareness that often occurs during deep relaxation, coupled with an anxiety-producing interpretation of the meaning of the remaining perceptions of somatic arousal. It is known that anxious individuals are more sensitive to these perceptions and are more likely to interpret them as anxiety. Thus, among anxiety neurotics, the heightened physiological arousal produced by an injection of lactate can produce a full-fledged panic attack, whereas in other people it produces only the *somatic* sensation of being anxious without the "mental fear" (cf. review by Ackerman & Sachar, 1974). The person's interpretation of the meaning of the somatic sensations and his or her interpretation of the threat content in the situation appear to be critical to the development of the mental fear in this situation. Patients who do not experience the fear tend to credit the reassuring presence of the doctor for their calmness.

There have been a number of studies finding no differences between meditation and progressive relaxation. Table 13-10 summarizes the studies finding that the techniques are both effective in lowering various indexes of stress; Table 13-11 summarizes the studies showing neither technique to be effective. Because of the methodological problems described earlier as inherent in all research on relaxation methods, the findings of "no dif-

TABLE 13-8. Studies Finding Differences between Mantra MED and PMR in Measures of Cognitive Anxiety or Arousal

Authors	Measures	Comments
Studies finding mantra MED to be superior		
Warrenberg, Pagano, Woods, & Hlastala (1980)	Rating of tension in two testing sessions.	Measures were taken during the first testing session. Ss were long-term PMR practitioners and long-term TM practitioners.
Lehrer, Schoicket, Carrington, & Woolfolk (1980)	1. Ratings of worry activity during practice. 2. Decreases in IPAT Anxiety Inventory Overt Anxiety, and STAI State and Trait Anxiety.	1. CSM < PMR during 4 weeks of practice (live group training). 2. CSM > PMR, WL.
Woolfolk, Lehrer, McCann, & Rooney (1982)	1. SCL-90–R: Hostility, Obsessive–Compulsive. 2. Somatic and cognitive arousal on daily home questionnaire. 3. Lehrer & Woolfolk (1982) scale of cognitive, behavioral, and somatic anxiety. 4. Spouse or roommate reports of tiredness, annoyance, grouchiness, irritation, intensity. 5. IPAT Anxiety Inventory: full-scale, Tension, Overt Anxiety.	Improvement in MED, not in PMR or NT. Between-groups ANOVA $p < .06$ for SCL-90–R Hostility, $p < .05$ for IPAT Tension, n.s. for other measures. Five sessions of training.
Carrington, Collings, Benson, Robinson, Wood, Lehrer, Woolfolk, & Cole (1980)	1. SCL-90–R: Depression, Phobic Anxiety, Psychoticism, general severity index, positive symptom total. 2. Reported improvements on social relationships.	1. Improvement at 5.5 months: ROM = CSM > NT. PMR did not differ from any other group. 2. At 5.5 months: CSM > ROM, PMR.
Zuroff & Schwartz (1978)	Total score and Distress factor of S-R Inventory of Anxiousness.	Decreases for TM, not PMR or NT. Note that there were no differences on autonomic factor. One live individual session followed by three large-group sessions.
Studies finding PMR to be superior		
Lehrer, Woolfolk, Rooney, McCann, & Carrington (1983)	1. SCL-90–R: Obsessive–Compulsive, Depression, general severity index, positive symptom total.	1. Decreases from pretraining to posttraining: PMR > MED > WL.

TABLE 13-8.   *(Continued)*

Authors	Measures	Comments
	2. IPAT Anxiety Inventory.	2. Decreases from pretraining to posttraining in Covert Anxiety and Low Self-Control are significant for PMR, not WL or MED. Between-groups ANOVA n.s.
Heidi & Borkevec (1983)	MANOVA on multiple self-report tests of anxiety and tension.	Decreases in PMR > MED. All Ss received one session of taped instruction on each technique.
Gilbert, Parker, & Clairborn (1978)	Self-rated increases in vigor and decreases in depression.	One session of taped training. Pretraining versus posttraining: PMR > ROM = SR.

Note. For explanation of abbreviations, see footnote to Table 13-1.

ferences" are presented only for the reader's information. We do not emphasize them when other studies do find consistent differences.

Thus progressive relaxation and mantra meditation do appear to have some important differences in effects. The cognitive–somatic differences are measurable, but—especially in the case of cognitive effects—this distinction is neither reliable nor strong. It is doubtful that these differences have any clinical implications. Differences in motivational effects and in relaxation-produced anxiety are stronger and do appear to have clinical implications. Both techniques have powerful somatic and cognitive effects; and, as outlined below and elsewhere in this book, both are clinically very useful.

MEDITATION VERSUS BIOFEEDBACK

The G. E. Schwartz *et al.* (1978) hypothesis predicts that biofeedback for various somatic functions would produce relatively more somatic effects and meditation more cognitive effects. A study by Cuthbert, Kristeller, Simons, Hodes, and Lang (1981) provides some slight support and some contrary evidence for this hypothesis. Self-report measures of anxiety (i.e., cognitive measures) were reduced more by Benson's meditation technique (ROM) than by heart rate biofeedback. However, ROM also was found to be more effective than heart rate biofeedback in reducing skin

TABLE 13-9.   Studies Finding Other Differences between MED and PMR

Authors	Measures	Comments
Zuroff & Schwarz (1978)	Expectancy of positive results.	College students had more positive expectancies of MED.
Heidi & Borkovec (1983); Lehrer, Woolfolk, Rooney, McCann, & Carrington (1983); Lehrer, Schoicket, Carrington, & Woolfolk (1980)	Increases in arousal or anxiety produced by MED or PMR.	Happened much more in MED than in PMR.
Lehrer, Woolfolk, Rooney, McCann, & Carrington (1982); Carrington, Collings, Benson, Robinson, Wood, Lehrer, Woolfolk, & Cole (1980)	Ss report of liking technique more and/or practicing it more.	MED > PMR.

Note. For explanation of abbreviations, see footnote to Table 13-1.

TABLE 13-10.   Studies Finding Both PMR and MED to Be Effective, but with No Differences between Them

Authors	Measures	Comments
Woolfolk, Carr-Kaffashan, McNulty, & Lehrer (1976)	Improvement in self-rated sleep-onset latency and difficulty falling asleep.	PMR = MED > WL.
Cangelosi (1980)	1. EMG decreased from presession to postsession. 2. Increases in self-rated ability to relax.	PMR = ROM = combined > attention placebo.
Comer (1977)	Performance measures.	MED = applied MED = PMR = applied PMR > WL after 4 weeks of training and also at 3-week follow-up.
Wood (1978)	1. Trait anxiety. 2. State anxiety.	1. Decreases in PMR, MED, HR: BFK > SR. 2. Reduced in PMR and MED before exam, not reduced in other groups.
Hendricksen (1978)	Confusion and bewilderment on POMS.	PMR and MED showed decrease but placebo did not among alcoholic inpatients.
Raskin, Bali, & Peeke (1980)	TMAS, Current Mood Check List, social ratings, frontalis EMG, situational anxiety.	EMG BFK = "PMR" (i.e., without tensing during training) versus TM. All groups improved.

Note. For explanation of abbreviations, see footnote to Table 13-1.

TABLE 13-11.   Studies Finding Neither MED nor PMR to Be Effective

Authors	Measures	Comments
Boswell & Murray (1979)	Trait anxiety.	Decreases: PMR = MED = NT = "antimeditation" control. Tape-recorded home training.
Bridgewater (1979)	HR, RR, STAI State Anxiety during and after stress film.	MED = PMR = SR. Training consisted of four lectures and 5 weeks of home practice. Ss were tested during stress film.
Greff (1979)	Not specified in dissertation abstract.	PMR versus ROM versus EMG BFK versus SR studied in a clinical situation.
S. Turner (1978)	Skin conductance; EEG alpha; frontalis EMG; HR; STAI State and Trait Anxiety; POMS Anxiety and Depression; bidirectional (cognitive vs. somatic) questionnaire.	PMR = MED = SR.
Curtis & Wessberg (1980)	HR, RR, skin resistance.	Long-term practitioners of PMR and TM were studied. There were no differences between practice and control conditions during testing session. Level of arousal was high.
Cauthen & Prymak (1977)	HR, skin temperature, skin conductance levels.	No significant differences between short-, medium-, and long-term meditators or between these and Ss given brief taped PMR training. NT group differed from a pseudomeditation control.

Note. For explanation of abbreviations, see footnote to Table 13-1.

conductance and heart rate. The latter finding is distinctly contrary to the specific-effects hypothesis. EMG biofeedback was found to have effects similar to those of heart rate biofeedback. It is possible that this contrary finding is due to the rather brief training (three sessions) in biofeedback. Learning heart rate control may be a more difficult task than mediation and thus may require longer training. Strong findings consistent with the specific-effects hypothesis were reported by Sedlacek, Cohen, and Boxhill (1979). Twenty sessions of combined training in peripheral temperature and EMG biofeedback were compared with the same number of training sessions in ROM. The effects for biofeedback in lowering blood pressure were dramatically greater than for meditation. Here, however, the large number of sessions devoted to ROM may have hurt the technique. ROM can be learned easily in only one or two sessions. It is difficult to imagine how people could be kept from being bored during 20 sessions of training. At the very least, subjects may have wondered why so much training was needed. This may have hurt the credibility of the procedure, and hence its effectiveness. Two other studies (Fee & Girdano, 1978; Zaichkowsky & Kamen, 1978) found no differences between EMG biofeedback and ROM in reducing frontalis EMG. Although these studies are somewhat supportive of the specific-effects hypothesis, further research is needed to determine how stable these results are.

RELAXATION THERAPY VERSUS COGNITIVE THERAPIES

The hypothesis of specific effects should be even more applicable to the distinction between cognitive therapies and relaxation therapies than to that between different forms of relaxation therapy. Cognitive therapies do not necessarily teach people to reduce physiological arousal directly, and most relaxation therapies teach little about cognitive control. Lazarus (1977) has argued the opposite, however. He suggests that even biofeedback—the least cognitive of relaxation therapies—is mediated by cognition. He contends that the critical effect of biofeedback is cognitive: It occupies the client's attention with somatic processes, so that he or she will become less concerned with stressful thoughts or events; or, alternatively, the self-knowledge gained about stress responses and the events that produce it lead people to rethink the meaning of these events, and to change their behavior accordingly. A similar argument was made by Holroyd (1979). Similarly, Beck argues in Chapter 9 of this volume that psychophysiological reactions are controlled by cognitions about the meaning of various stressors, and thus suggests that cognitive therapy should lower physiological arousal quite directly.

There is considerable evidence for specific effects of cognitive interventions. Mitchell and White (1977) gave a sample of subjects suffering from "severe predormital insomnia" initial taped training in progressive relaxation, and followed this with training either in mental relaxation or in a self-monitoring control. The mental relaxation condition involved the subjects' imagining themselves doing relaxing things. Improvements in latency of sleep onset were greater in the mental relaxation group than in the self-monitoring group. Also, some subjects received mental relaxation training simultaneously with progressive relaxation instruction, while others received the mental relaxation instruction afterward. Progressive relaxation alone (i.e., the control condition) appeared to reduce ratings of presleep tension, but not of intrusive cognitions. The addition of mental relaxation reduced presleep tension still further, and also reduced intrusive cognitions. Woolfolk and McNulty (1982) found some evidence that sleep-onset insomnia is largely mediated by presleep cognitive instrusions. They also found that cognitive components of an insomnia treatment had greater impact on measures of sleep disturbance than did somatic aspects of the procedure.

In some instances, the greater cognitive effect of cognitive therapy may manifest itself in greater decreases on self-report measures of anxiety than those produced by more somatic interventions. Baither and Godsey (1979) found that rational–emotive therapy reduced scores on the Anxiety Differential (Alexander & Husak, 1962) among underachieving college students, whereas progressive relaxation had no measurable effect. The treatment and the testing were done in the classroom situation. Groups were found to differ at a borderline level of significance ($p < .06$).

Cognitive therapy may even have greater effects than relaxation therapies on self-report measures of *somatic* symptoms. The process of self-observation and self-report obviously requires similar kinds of mental activity to other cognitive tasks (i.e., all require verbal and analytic skills, those that are commonly associated with dominant-hemisphere brain function). Self-report of stress symptoms involves both interpretation of the environment as stress-producing, and interpretation of somatic perceptions as indicating pain or stress. Thus, when we review data below on treatment of tension headaches, we find evidence that cognitive therapy adds significantly to the effects of relaxation or biofeedback therapy, and may even be superior to the latter. We do not consider this to be contrary to the specific-effects hypothesis, because the measures of improvement used in these studies of otherwise somatic disorders are cognitive (i.e., self-reports of pain and discomfort).

Studies with more equivocal findings include one by Lent (1979), who found rational–emotive therapy to be inferior to cue-controlled desensitization (a combination of cue-controlled relaxation and desensitization) in reducing self-reported public-speaking anxiety. The cue-controlled desensitization condition may have produced greater effects because the procedure includes major cognitive as well as somatic components, as we outline below. Kantor (1979) found stress inoculation training, systematic desensitization, and speaking skills training to be equally effective in reducing public-speaking anxiety.

In summary, there is considerable evidence for greater cognitive effects for cognitive therapy than for relaxation therapy, but much less evidence for greater somatic effects for relaxation therapy. Additional research is needed, using purely somatic dependent measures.

APPLIED TRAINING IN RELAXATION: COMBINING SOMATIC AND COGNITIVE TRAINING

For all the treatments described in this book, generalization to everyday life is of critical importance. One approach to generalization of skills has been "cue-controlled relaxation." This procedure involves training a person to think of a word such as "relax" or "calm" while in the relaxed state, thus, by association, giving the word the characteristics of a cue that might *elicit* relaxation. Grimm (1980), however, in reviewing the empirical outcome literature on cue-controlled relaxation, found that the method does not appear to have particular advantages over progressive relaxation alone. Indeed, some studies have found superior results for progressive relaxation (cf. Holstead, 1978). It is difficult to explain why, in this instance, one part of a training package might be more effective than the whole package. One possible reason is that, in the studies of cue-controlled relaxation that have been done so far, the relaxation training has been greatly truncated because of the need to fit cue-controlled training into the therapy program within allowable time limits. The number of training sessions given to people in studies of cue-controlled relaxation has typically not been greater than the number given to people that used progressive relaxation alone. The relaxation training thus probably was not as intensive or effective as in studies of progressive relaxation alone.

Another therapy package that combines relaxation therapy and cognitive interventions is called "anxiety management training" (Deffenbacher & Suinn, 1982; Suinn, 1975, 1977; Suinn & Richardson, 1971). This approach combines training in live progressive relaxation with deep breathing and imagining a relaxing scene. In addition, clients are trained to imagine anxiety-provoking scenes and to use their relaxation skills in order to reduce the anxiety elicited by the scenes. Clients also are trained to recognize "early warning" signs of stress; to use their relaxation skills when these occur; and to relax *while* they are imagining the anxiety scene, without avoiding it. One study (Shoemaker, 1976) found anxiety management training to be more effective than progressive relaxation training alone in reducing self-reported general anxiety among anxiety neurotics.

A number of studies have compared relaxation therapy with various other combinations of cognitive and behavioral interventions aimed at helping people to apply their relaxation skills in daily life. Goldfried and Trier (1974) found that specific training in applying progressive relaxation skills to public-speaking anxiety potentiated the effects of progressive relaxation. Chang-Liang and Denney (1976) found their technique of applied relaxation training (progressive relaxation training, plus instructions on how to use it in daily life) to be more effective than systematic desensitization in reducing trait anxiety and test anxiety. However, progressive relaxation training alone and a no-treatment control condition did not differ from either of the other two training conditions. Mitchell and Mitchell (1971) compared the combination of relaxation, desensitization, and assertive training to each of the components individually, and found the combination to be more effective for treatment of migraine headaches than any of the individual treatments. Another study, however, found no differences between relaxation therapy and applied relaxation training (Comer, 1977).

Results of studies comparing progressive relaxation with systematic desensitization suggest that desensitization is altogether a more powerful technique, probably because it combines good training in progressive relaxation with an additional technique. Several studies have found this to be true on measures of self-report or behavioral assessment of phobic behavior (Aponte & Aponte, 1971; Cooke, 1968; Freeling & Shemberg, 1970; Johnson & Sechrest, 1968). One study also found desensitization to have greater effects on a physiological measure than progressive relaxation. Moore (1965) found greater decreases in respiratory resistance for desensitization than for progressive relaxation among asthmatics.

In summary, despite the relatively weak effects found in studies of cue-controlled relaxation, most combinations of relaxation and cognitive training are more effective than is either therapy alone. Specific training in how to apply relaxation skills in daily life is an advisable addition to relaxation therapy. Also, relaxation therapy may be a useful accompaniment to cognitive approaches in treatment of stress-related problems.

BEHAVIORAL INTERVENTIONS VERSUS
RELAXATION THERAPIES

Although they are not reviewed in a separate chapter in this book, behavioral interventions are often used in stress reduction. The specific-effects hypothesis suggests that these interventions would be most effective among individuals manifesting behavioral deficits (e.g., lack of social skills, learning skills, or other situational skills), or among phobic individuals who show avoidance behavior. The large literature on assertion training and social skills training has been reviewed extensively (Alberti, 1977; Twentyman & Zimering, 1978). Generally, these behavioral techniques have been found to reduce anxiety as well as to improve behavioral functioning. Indeed, Marks (1981) strongly argues that exposure to phobic situations is by far the most effective component in treatment of phobias. He argues that relaxation therapy contributes little more than a placebo effect in treatment of obsessive–compulsive conditions while directly preventing such individuals from engaging in obsessions and/or compulsions can produce dramatic reductions in symptoms.

Before reviewing studies relevant to the specific effects of behavioral therapies, we should point out that, behavioral measures often do not correlate well with cognitive and somatic measures. For example, Lang (1971) reviewed evidence that, in snake phobics, the correlations are very small among three variables: autonomic response to a snake, performance on a behavioral approach test, and self-ratings of anxiety. Similarly, Lehrer and Leiblum (1981) found only moderate correlations between behavioral, somatic, and self-report measures of nonassertiveness and assertion anxiety. Each kind of measure may be valid, however. In the latter study, nonassertive female clients at a community mental health center were differentiated from normal women by each of the three kinds of measures. We (Lehrer & Woolfolk, 1982) presented data showing that self-reported social avoidance is less closely related to self-reported cognitive and somatic symptoms of anxiety than the latter two are to each other. Which of the three kinds of symptoms is the most important to treat? In our opinion, this depends on which is most debilitating to the particular individual.

Behavioral treatments do appear to have specific effects on behavioral measures. For example, Biran and Wilson (1981) found greater effects for a form of exposure therapy than for rational–emotive therapy in an approach test among individuals afraid of heights or of elevators. Some cognitive effects, however, were greater for rational–emotive therapy.

Also, the specific effects of behavioral versus relaxation interventions appear to interact with the particular symptoms or response style a person has. Oest, Jerremalm, and Johansson (1981) classified a group of 40 psychiatric outpatients by whether they were primarily physiological reactors or behavioral reactors in a test situation involving social interaction under conditions of stress. They compared applied relaxation training with social skills training. Subjects who were treated according to their primary symptoms showed greater decreases than others did on a combined measure of change in anxiety and stress. Heart rate during the posttest exposure to the social stressor decreased in physiological reactors, but not behavioral reactors. There was a nonsignificant tendency for heart rate to decrease more in applied relaxation training among the physiological reactors and more in social skills training among the behavioral reactors. Similarly, self-reported social activity increased among behavioral reactors during and after social skills training. This did not happen for applied relaxation training, or among physiological responders. Self-ratings of anxiety during the test situation decreased more in applied relaxation training than in social skills training.

A more dramatic finding of specific effects was obtained in a study of the treatment of asthma in children (Hock, Bramble, & Kennard, 1977). Relaxation therapy was found to improve airway resistance and asthmatic symptoms, while assertion therapy made the symptoms worse.

Thus there is substantial evidence for specific behavioral effects for behavioral treatments, when compared with treatments that are clearly somatic or cognitive—although social skills training may produce effects that generalize to heart rate among people who have specific social–behavioral problems.

HYPNOSIS VERSUS OTHER METHODS

Much of the literature comparing hypnosis with other relaxation methods is difficult to interpret. As discussed in this book by Barber (Chapter 6), the hypnotic state is difficult to define, and the procedures for inducing it are rather varied. One can perhaps consider all the techniques included in this book to be—or, at least, to involve—some form of suggestion. Another problem is that most of the investigators comparing hypnosis with other methods have been interested primarily in immediate effects during the hypnotic situation, and have tended to give very cursory training in *all* the techniques that were used. Finally, only very few of the studies used random assignment, a sufficiently large *n,* and adequate controls for expectancy or therapist contact.

Nevertheless, some tentative evaluation can be made that bears on the specific-effects hypothesis. Hypnosis must, at the very least, include a cognitive (or, at least, a conscious mental) component. The *sine qua non* of the hypnotic experience is a focusing and/or narrowing of attention.

It also usually involves taking a more compliant mental set. Although theoretically some hypnotic procedures could include important somatic suggestions or training comparable to that contained in biofeedback or Jacobson's relaxation procedure, none of the comparative studies we found did so in the hypnosis condition.[1] We thus would expect hypnosis to have more powerful effects on cognitions and, perhaps, on overt behaviors (because the latter are under very direct and overt conscious control) than on somatic activity.

In evaluating these studies, we consider all self-report measures to be cognitive, even when the reports are about somatic activity or overt behavior. We are classifying the acts of self-observation, self-conceptualization, and self-report as essentially cognitive processes. All involve verbal behavior. Thus the dramatic hypnotic effects on pain perception, smoking, obesity, or anxiety may be considered to be cognitive.

The earliest of the comparative studies were done in Gordon Paul's laboratory, and they confirmed the physiological predictions of the specific-effects theory. They found that live training in progressive relaxation had more powerful effects than hypnotic suggestion to relax had in reducing levels of physiological arousal and in diminishing physiological reactivity to stressful imagery. Both methods were superior to an elaborate placebo procedure (Paul, 1969a, 1969b). When the procedures were delivered via tape recording, however (Paul & Trimble, 1970), the conditions did not differ. Similarly, Crosson (1980) found greater skin temperature effects during temperature biofeedback than during hypnosis; and Fernandez-Abscal and Miguel Tobal (1979) found greater decreases in respiration rate with progressive relaxation or autogenic training than with hypnotic relaxation or a no-treatment control. The effects of hypnosis did not differ from those of the control condition on this measure.

Not all the studies showed such clear results, however. Significant but equivalent reductions in blood pressure were obtained for both progressive relaxation and hypnosis by Deabler, Fidel, Dillenkoffer, and Elder (1973). Borkovec and Fowles (1973) found no differences between three sessions of progressive relaxation and three sessions of hypnotic relaxation on measures of frontalis EMG, respiration rate, heart rate, and skin conductance.

---

[1]Many hypnotic procedures do involve a relaxation induction. We do not consider this to be training in somatic relaxation, because the person is not specifically trained to control a physiological function. Rather, suggestions of warmth, heaviness, relaxation, and so forth, are most commonly used in these inductions.

Some clearly negative findings were also reported. Barabasz and McGeorge (1978) found significantly greater increases in skin temperature for relaxation instructions plus hypnotic hand-warming suggestions than for continuous hand temperature biofeedback, a false feedback control, or relaxation instructions alone. Measurement was done during a single training session. There is some doubt, however, about the efficacy of the biofeedback and relaxation procedures used in this study. The biofeedback and the relaxation conditions did not differ from the false feedback condition. Use of only a single session of biofeedback probably biased the study in favor of hypnosis, because a single session of temperature biofeedback or relaxation training is rarely sufficient to produce reliable physiological effects, while hypnotic effects may be achieved more readily in a single session.

Combining hypnosis with biofeedback does not appear to enhance the somatic effects of hypnosis. Friedman and Taub (1977) reported greater diastolic blood pressure reductions during seven sessions of hypnosis than during a no-treatment control condition, or than during a combination of hypnosis and biofeedback. Only the hypnosis group and a group receiving biofeedback without hypnosis showed significant decreases in blood pressure over the course of the study. If the results of this study are found to hold up in subsequent studies, we would be forced to conclude that, in combination, the two techniques weaken rather than potentiate each other. The unrelenting truth of the biofeedback machine may undermine the more flexible "suggested truth" that must be believed if one is to enter a hypnotic trance; and the hypnotic set may detract from learning the biofeedback task. The latter effect, in fact, is implicitly assumed by Jacobson when he deliberately avoids using suggestion as an aid to learning muscle relaxation (Jacobson, 1938, 1970). This study is plagued with methodological difficulties, however, so such conclusions cannot yet be firmly drawn. The biofeedback-only group was not found to differ significantly from any of the other groups, including the control groups. This raises questions about the manner in which the biofeedback treatment was administered. Also, subjects were not randomly assigned to groups, and the groups differed at pretest on the major dependent variable. Subjects in the hypnosis groups were screened for high hypnotizability, while the other groups were not; and subjects in the biofeedback-only group had initially higher blood pressures than subjects in the other groups.

One study of self-report and behavioral measures produced generally more powerful effects for hypnosis than for progressive relaxation—a result consistent with the specific-effects hypothesis. It also illustrates the complexity of stress-related somatic problems. In a study of dental phobia, hypnotic relaxation and suggestions of pain reduction were found to be more effective than progressive relaxation in reducing self-reported pain caused by an injection (McAmmond, Davidson, & Kovitz, 1971). Hypnosis was also more effective in convincing subjects that the treatment was effective, and in inducing subjects to visit a dentist within 5 months after treatment. The results were not unequivocal, however. In a test of pain tolerance, hypnosis was superior to progressive relaxation only for subjects with initially "medium" levels of skin conductance. There were no between-groups differences for subjects who initially had low skin conductance levels, and progressive relaxation appeared to be the more effective treatment among subjects with initially high skin conductance levels. These latter results suggest that somatic arousal may indeed be related to the experience of pain, and that reduction of arousal may be a particularly important intervention among people with initially high levels of arousal (cf. studies by Sternbach, 1968, and Mersky & Spear, 1967, showing relationships between pain and anxiety). Among persons with lower arousal, however, pain perception may be affected by cognitive factors more than by physiological arousal. Some doubt may be cast on the interpretability of this study by the fact that hypnotic subjects were given live inductions, while progressive relaxation instructions were delivered via tape recording.

Several other studies found no significant differences between hypnosis and various somatically oriented therapies. Andreychuk and Skriver (1975) found that alpha biofeedback, hypnotic induction, and hand temperature biofeedback all produced decreases on a self-reported headache index among migraine headache sufferers. The decrease was greatest for hand temperature biofeedback, but subjects in this group also had the highest initial headache index scores. Another problem with this study is that it failed to test for changes in alpha, finger temperature, or depth of trance; so it is possible that the lack of differences might have been caused by poor teaching or induction technique in one or more groups. Schlutter, Golden, and Blume (1980) studied sufferers from tension headaches, and found no differences between hypnotic suggestion, EMG biofeedback, and a combination of biofeedback and progressive relaxation in responses to experimentally induced pain. The measures included self-rated pain and tolerance for pain. Spies (1979) studied test-anxious college students, and compared hypnosis with a combination of taped progressive relaxation and frontalis EMG biofeedback as components of systematic desensitization. Both conditions produced decreases in self-rated test anxiety, with no significant differences between groups. Finally, Graham, Wright, Toman, and Mark (1975) found decreases in self-reported symptoms of insomnia among subjects told they were receiving relaxation instructions, but not among subjects told they were being hypnotized. Actually, all subjects were given a procedure similar to autogenic training. Differences between groups were not found to be significant.

In summary, there is some evidence that cognitively or behaviorally oriented hypnotic suggestions have greater cognitive and behavioral effects and smaller somatic effects than do specifically somatically oriented techniques. Most of these studies, however, have major methodological problems.

We have found two studies comparing meditation with hypnosis. Baermark and Gaunitz (1979) found a lower respiration rate during meditation than during hypnosis. Also, subjects reported experiencing more vivid imagery during hypnosis than during meditation. Both groups showed lower heart rate and respiration rate and higher skin temperature while practicing their techniques than during a control condition of quiet rest. In this study, however, the groups were not comparable. The meditation group consisted of experienced meditators, while the hypnosis group consisted of inexperienced but highly hypnotizable subjects. In a complex within-group study, Morse, Martin, Furst, and Dubin (1975) found no significant differences between meditation and hypnosis on a variety of physiological measures. Meditation was judged to have a less effortful induction than autohypnosis, but no differences were found on this measure between meditation and heterohypnosis. In summary, meditation and cognitively oriented hypnotic inductions appear to have similar effects. This is consistent with the classification of both as cognitive techniques.

DRUG THERAPY VERSUS AND COMBINED WITH OTHER STRESS REDUCTION THERAPIES

There are relatively few studies that systematically compare drug therapies with relaxation therapies or other stress reduction therapies, or that measure the specific effects of each kind of therapy when they are combined in a treatment package. In this section we are influenced by the arguments presented by Lader (Chapter 10, this volume) and Ganguli and Detre (1982), who have reviewed most of these studies in detail. We are reviewing only the studies on anxiety or stress here; we are not reviewing the literature on psychosis or on depression. Drug therapy clearly has an important role in treating the latter conditions.

Several studies have evaluated the use of drug therapy in helping phobic individuals to expose themselves to situations that produce fear. Two studies found that diazepam reduces anxiety in agoraphobics during exposure therapy (Hafner & Marks, 1976; Marks, Viswanthan, Lipsedge, & Gardner, 1972). Neither of these studies, however, evaluated the effect of the drug on the willingness of agoraphobics to undergo exposure therapy; and exposure to the phobic situation appears to be the most critical component in effective treatment for phobias. Similarly the comparative effectiveness of the drug versus exposure therapy was not evaluated. Whitehead and Blackwell (1979) report studies showing that minor tranquilizers and short-acting barbiturates can, under some circumstances, facilitate desensitization or flooding therapy, but they indicate that findings of "no effects" have also occurred. None of these studies assessed long-term effects of drug-aided versus nondrug desensitization.

Some evidence exists for the usefulness of antidepressant medications for treatment of phobias or obsessive–compulsive disorders—but only when these problems are accompanied by depression or by panic attacks. Zitrin, Klein, and Woerner (1978) studied agoraphobics who had panic attacks versus those who did not, and found that imipramine facilitated treatment among the former. In a similar study using a related drug, clomipramine, Marks, Stern, Mawson, Cobb, and McDonald (1980) found that clomipramine and exposure therapy had additive effects among those obsessive–compulsives who had depressive symptoms, but not among those without depression. Studies of monoamine oxidase inhibitors suggest that they are not helpful as adjuncts or substitutes for behavior therapy in treatment of phobias (cf. review by Whitehead & Blackwell, 1979).

Ganguli and Detre (1982) report having found several studies that show no effects for β-adrenergic blocking drugs (e.g., propranolol) in facilitating exposure in agoraphobic patients. They criticize these studies on methodological grounds. Among these studies, however, was one by Hafner and Milton (1977) which found that propranolol *impeded* progress with exposure therapy.

Drug therapies, particularly those involving minor tranquilizers, appear to be prone to higher relapse rates than do behavior therapies for anxiety-related conditions. The only study we have found comparing drug therapy with relaxation therapy per se for anxiety was by Lavallée, Lamontagne, Pinard, Annable, and Tétreault (1977). These investigators conducted a two-way factorial experiment on chronically anxious psychiatric patients. The factorial dimensions were EMG biofeedback relaxation therapy versus a self-relaxation control; and diazepam (5 mg, three times a day) versus placebo. Treatment was conducted over an 8-week period. Although EMG levels were reduced during treatment in both drug and bio-feedback therapies, there were no differences between groups in self-ratings or psychiatric ratings of anxiety during that time. All groups showed decreases in anxiety. The authors interpret the relatively good showing of the placebo–self-relaxation group as indicating the power of regular rest in decreasing anxiety symptoms. During the course of a 6-month follow-up, however, subjects who had received diazepam showed increases in anxiety, whereas the anxiety levels in the placebo groups remained low. During this time the authors also found that diazepam-treated subjects were taking more drugs and were doing less relaxation practice than were subjects who had been given the placebo. Thus, it appeared that diazepam reduced the motivation to try to cope with anxiety through relaxation, and thereby led to a resurgence of symptoms.

Similar results were obtained from a study of migraine sufferers by Mitchell and Mitchell (1971), described above. They found that their combined behavioral treatment (consisting of relaxation, desensitization, and assertive training) was more effective among people who had not previously received drug therapy than among those who had. In this study, however, subjects were not selected randomly for the two groups. It is thus possible that subjects who had been taking medication and who later referred themselves for a relaxation study had the kind of problem that cannot be effectively treated by any known form of treatment. A better study by Solyom, Heseltine, McClure, Solyom, Ledwidge, and Steinberg (1973) compared an array of behavioral interventions with phenelzine and with brief psychotherapy. The phenelzine group also received the psychotherapy. Although the effects of behavior therapy and of phenelzine were equivalent at the end of the treatment period, the relapse rate was substantially greater in the drug group. Finally, Tyrer and Steinberg (1975) compared phenelzine with a package of behavioral techniques for treating agoraphobia, and found no differences in treatment effectiveness between the two. The group who received the drug, however, showed a greater tendency to relapse after drug therapy was discontinued.

The problems of high relapse rates, increased dependence upon drugs, and failure to develop effective coping skills reflect generally poor long-term outcome of drug therapy for many stress-related disorders. Wooley, Blackwell, and Winget (1978) review evidence that medical treatment, by itself, makes some psychosomatic disorders worse.

Thus, with the possible exception of tricyclic antidepressants among people with panic attacks and/or with underlying depressive symptomatology, we do not have convincing evidence that drug therapy has better effects than behavioral approaches in reducing anxiety—or, in fact, that it can even significantly facilitate behavioral treatment of this problem. There is some evidence that drug therapy may produce higher dropout rates and may make people with chronic stress-related symptoms more reliant upon drugs, and thereby more resistant to behavioral treatment. This may bode ill for long-term effects of combined drug therapy and behavioral therapy for anxiety. On the other hand, some individuals are unwilling to undertake purely psychological treatment, and many individuals (and, indeed, clinics) are financially unable to offer such treatment. Pharmacological treatment is a faster and usually much less costly alternative.

Much research remains to be done in the area of pharmacological treatments for stress. The promise of β-blockers has not been sufficiently evaluated. Also, we do not have enough empirical knowledge of the effects of anxiolytic drugs in making agoraphobics more willing to undergo exposure therapy—which appears to be the most important form of therapy for that condition. We have found no studies comparing drug therapy and stress-reduction therapies for transient anxiety or for most other stress-related disorders, and we have found no data on personality predictors for good responses to medication as opposed to some other form of therapy. The empirical literature on the interaction between drug therapy and psychological treatment is also paltry, despite the often advertised rationale that pharmacological treatment facilitates psychotherapy. Whitehead and Blackwell (1979) suggest that differences in professional backgrounds and interests between investigators interested in psychopharmacology and those interested in behavior therapy may explain why so few collaborative studies have been done comparing the interactive effects of the two treatments.

OTHER PROCEDURAL AND PREDICTIVE FACTORS: EXPECTANCY AND LOCUS OF CONTROL

Expectancy for success is an important ingredient in success of any psychological treatment. Thus Beiman (1976) found that, when negative expectancies are deliberately given, the within-session effects of a single session of progressive relaxation are negligible. Wilson (1979) gave subjects a session of relaxation training, and then exposed them to a social interaction. They had been told that the effects of relaxation would last more than a half hour. Subjects in the relaxation group rated the person with whom they were interacting as more attractive than did subjects who were in a control condition. Brown (1977) found that positive expectancy is important in treating hyperkinesis with relaxation therapy.

Borkovec, Johnson, and Block (Chapter 12, this volume) describe an ingenious "counterdemand" procedure, whereby subjects expect poor success for a limited time (e.g., the first four sessions). This manipulation does not appear to interfere with willingness to practice, and it successfully differentiates the effects of training from those of a willingness to believe that the method works. Generally, active treatments are found to produce positive effects during the counterdemand periods, although further improvement is usually obtained after that period is over (Borkovec & Hennings, 1978; Borkevec & Weerts, 1976; Carr-Kaffashan & Woolfolk, 1979).

Expectancies do not appear to account for whatever differences there are between various techniques. Although some of the studies comparing meditation and relaxation show slightly higher expectancies produced by the meditation, the effects of most of the techniques have been to raise expectancies by an equivalent amount.

The effect of expectancy may interact with internal locus of control in making training more effective with internally oriented clients. If a person does not believe that a treatment method will work, or if the person does not believe that various symptoms of stress can be overcome by his or her own effort, then the person probably will not practice the relaxation method consistently, thus weakening its effects. Lewis, Biglan, and Steinbock (1978) found that subjects high in internal control also had high expectancies for success and practiced their relaxation instructions more at home. Consequently, they showed greater reduction in trait anxiety than others did.

Having an internal locus of control does not necessarily make progressive relaxation more powerful within a given training session, however. In a single-session study, Ollendick and Murphy (1977) found that progressive relaxation produced greater reductions in heart rate and state anxiety among those with external locus of control than among those with internal locus, while cognitive relaxation training (focusing on pleasant thoughts and feelings) had greater effects for those with internal locus of control.

There have been two studies that found greater effects among those with external than among those with internal locus of control. Prager-Decker (1978) found that individuals high on external locus of control learned to reduce EMG activity more quickly during EMG biofeedback sessions than did high-internal subjects. These findings may be explainable by the fact that subjects were not asked to practice the technique at home between sessions, so individuals' belief in their own ability to control the symptoms had no chance to affect their practice behavior. Also, all biofeedback instruction was given from an external source (i.e., the biofeedback machine), thus making this treatment particularly appealing to externally oriented subjects. No such differences between those with internal and those with external locus of control were found for progressive relaxation in this study. More difficult to explain are the findings of Hendricksen (1978) that meditation, progressive relaxation, and a placebo all produced greater decreases in state anxiety among inpatient alcoholic subjects with external (vs. internal) locus of drinking control. The fact that this measure did not show differences between placebo and treatment conditions perhaps indicates that external subjects were merely being more sensitive to demand characteristics of the situation (i.e., they may have thought that the experimenters were most interested in producing changes in their anxiety levels). Changes on a measure that did show differences between treatment and control conditions—the Confusion–Bewilderment scale on the Profile of Mood States—were not related to internality–externality. Also, external–internal locus of drinking control may be quite different from other forms of externality–internality. External subjects may perhaps have felt able to control their anxiety levels, but not their drinking, so this study does not necessarily contradict previous findings of greater relaxation effects on anxiety among those with internal than among those with external locus of control. Finally, external subjects had manifested higher pretest (and posttest) anxiety than had internal subjects, thus raising the possibility of a floor effect in the latter group, and raising further questions about the interpretability of these results.

SUMMARY

Unquestionably the various therapeutic approaches described above have highly specific effects, as well as general stress-reducing effects. The somatic–cognitive–behavioral distinction appears to be useful in this regard. Therapies directed to one of these modalities appear to have their greatest and most consistent effects on that particular modality.

Thus, autogenic training appears to have specific effects on the particular autonomic functions included in the autogenic exercises, despite the fact that both autogenic training and progressive relaxation produce general decreases in physiological arousal. Similarly, progressive relaxation appears to have specific effects on the musculoskeletal system, and biofeedback on the various particular response systems addressed in the training.

In comparisons between meditation and either progressive relaxation or biofeedback, the latter techniques have slightly more powerful somatic effects. Meditation, however, does not appear to have consistently stronger cognitive effects, thus throwing some doubt on G. E. Schwartz *et al.*'s (1978) characterization of mantra meditation as a cognitive technique.

Hypnosis does appear to have a more consistent effect on cognitive processes than on somatic processes, and *training* to relax generally produces greater somatic effects than do *suggestions* to relax. Hypnosis is not, however, a strictly cognitive technique. In some reports hypnosis has greater somatic effects than biofeedback, and there are a number of findings of no differences between hypnosis and various somatically oriented self-control techniques. The apparent anomalies might be explained by methodological difficulties in some of the latter studies. Also, hypnosis is more than one simple technique. In all the studies we reviewed, the hypnotic technique emphasized the focusing of attention and the control of thoughts and overt behavior; hence, perhaps, the relatively greater cognitive effect. The additive contribution of hypnotic suggestion to more somatically oriented techniques, such as progressive relaxation or biofeedback, has not been studied.

Cognitive therapy does have specific effects on various cognitive measures of stress. Comparisons between cognitive therapy and various relaxation therapies have revealed some of the clearest examples of somatic–cognitive specificity. Cognitive measures appear to be affected more by cognitive than by other kinds of therapies, just as physiological measures show the greatest changes in response to somatic therapies.

To be sure, some generalization does take place from one modality to another. In most of the studies we reviewed, all the treatments produced significant decreases on a broad array of measures. This particularly appears to happen when a modality-specific treatment is applied to a focal problem. Even in these cases, however, the specific effects are not obscured. We thus agree with G. E. Schwartz *et al.*'s (1978) conclusion that specific effects are superimposed upon a more global relaxation response.

The specific-effects hypothesis remains viable, even though some studies found no differences between the effects of various contrasting stress reduction techniques. In most of these studies, the methods themselves contain elements of more than one treatment modality. Thus, for example, mantra meditation may contain verbal and somatic components, and hypnosis may include behavioral or somatic suggestions and training as well as a manipulation to alter attention and cognition. Also, many of the studies are poorly controlled, and particular treatments have often been compared in only very few studies.

We have also discussed at length the distinction between Jacobson's progressive relaxation and the modified progressive relaxation techniques. Since the former technique is singularly and intensely somatic, we would expect it to have specific somatic effects, while the latter may have greater cognitive and behavioral effects. No such differences have been revealed, however. We have seen one unreplicated finding of a small *general* advantage for Jacobson's technique, but no evidence for specific effects. The amount of data relevant to this question is rather paltry, however, so definite conclusions cannot be drawn. No studies of this problem have been done on a clinical population. Also, we should add that only a handful of the studies reported in this chapter used Jacobson's original technique. The modified techniques are so widely accepted as equivalent to Jacobson's that they are routinely described as "Jacobsonian relaxation." The evidence reviewed here does indicate that the modified techniques have some therapeutic effects, especially when they are administered live and in an individualized fashion. Although some of the components that sometimes differentiate the two techniques have been studied (e. g., taped vs. live training, length of training, use of EMG biofeedback, cue-controlled training), the contributions of most of the critical elements that distinguish the two techniques (e.g., the use of "tension–release cycles" as a method of relaxing; training in all muscle groups vs. only a few during a single training session; presentation of the technique completely as a muscular skill) have not been systematically investigated.

Related to the issue of distinctions between Jacobson's technique and the modified techniques is the issue of suggestion. Although differences between progressive relaxation and pure suggestion have been studied, there is little information about how relaxation training and suggestion may add to each other. All the techniques, including Jacobson's, necessarily include some elements of suggestion. Merely paying money and spending time learning to relax produces a suggestive effect. Thus a more cogent question may be as follows: What specific forms of suggestion are most powerful (or harmful) in particular circumstances? We know surprisingly little about this.

Motivational effects of the various techniques are also important in our evaluating them. If people stop practicing a technique, it will have little therapeutic effect. Our own work has suggested that subjects enjoy meditating more than they do practicing progressive relaxation, and they enjoy progressive relaxation more than they do autogenic training. However, these are only group differences. Techniques do differ in their appeal to particular individuals. Given the serious problem of dropout, the motivational effects of various techniques on particular individuals may be among their most important differential characteristics. Some people prefer to meditate, some to relax their muscles, some to talk about their thoughts and feelings, and others to use machines. A sensitive therapist will take these factors into account in designing a treatment.

What, then, is known about individual differences in responses to the various techniques? The comparative literature on this subject is rather scanty. The dimension of internal–external locus of control appears to point to a preliminary conclusion that internally oriented subjects will master relaxation techniques better than will externally oriented subjects. This only appears to be the case where subjects must practice their techniques between sessions—but all effective techniques require this in the clinical situation. Internal locus of control makes people value and practice their techniques more, although it is possible that biofeedback has special appeal to high-external subjects. Internality versus externality may help to predict differential response to cognitive therapy, biofeedback, and progressive relaxation. More studies need to be done on this topic before any such conclusions can be drawn with confidence. Other personality predictors also may prove to be of some value.

DIFFERENTIAL TREATMENT EFFECTS ON
SPECIFIC DISORDERS

In this section, we review the literature on comparisons between stress reduction techniques as applied to specific disorders. This section is not meant to be an exhaustive review of the entire literature on applications of these techniques. Many disorders that have been found to respond to one or more of these therapies are not included, because the relevant comparative studies have not been done.

HEADACHES

The literature comparing progressive relaxation and EMG biofeedback for treatment of tension headaches has been reviewed by Silver and Blanchard (1978). They concluded that EMG biofeedback and progressive relaxation both have substantial therapeutic benefits, but that neither technique has a therapeutic advantage over the other. Belar (1979) criticized this conclusion because of design flaws in the studies that were reviewed, and called for further research on the subject. Blanchard, Andrasik, and Silver (1980) responded by reviewing additional evidence to bolster their conclusion, and by offering evidence that the design flaws cited by Belar should not appreciably affect the results. They raised an alternative issue for future research. Citing a previous review of theirs (Blanchard, Ahles, & Shaw, 1979) showing that relaxation of biofeedback training helps only 40–80% of randomly assigned tension headache sufferers, they called for research using the alternative treatment available for those who fail with one, and for research on individual difference variables that would predict positive response. Other literature reviews have reached similar conclusions to those of Blanchard *et al.* A review by Beaty and Haynes (1979) concluded that both progressive relaxation and EMG biofeedback are helpful for relief of tension headaches and have equivalent effects.

Literature reviews that have disagreed with Blanchard *et al.*'s conclusions, thus far, are unconvincing. For example, Pinkerton, Hughes, and Wenrich (1982, p. 279) conclude in their literature review that EMG biofeedback plus relaxation training is more effective than is either treatment alone. However, this review included several studies that used only taped relaxation instruction, or *suggestions* to relax versus actual *training* in relaxation. Their conclusions do not appear to apply to live relaxation training.

One possible conclusion from these findings is that relaxation therapies are preferable to biofeedback because they do not require expensive equipment. If they have equivalent effects, why invest the additional money? Recently, however, it has become possible to use the same argument to draw the opposite conclusion. The price of clinically useful biofeedback equipment has been reduced to less than that of three to five sessions with a professional therapist, and a month's rental of more elaborate equipment costs as little as two therapy sessions. Under these conditions, it may be more economical to have a technician administer biofeedback or to have the client do much of the biofeedback training at home than it is to have a highly trained professional administer relaxation therapy.

Conversely, the combination of autogenic training and biofeedback treatment for peripheral temperature warming is often considered to be the best psychological treatment for vascular, particularly migraine, headaches. However, no differences have been consistently found between skin temperature biofeedback and various forms of relaxation therapy for this problem (cf. review by Beatty, 1982). Similarly, no consistent differences have been reported between EMG biofeedback and finger temperature biofeedback in the treatment of migraine headaches (cf. review by Pinkerton *et al.,* 1982). It is thus possible that general relaxation training is more critical than is specific vascular control in treatment of this problem.

Recent studies using crossover designs have suggested that biofeedback machines may have therapeutic as well as financial advantages. Blanchard, Andrasik, Neff, Arena, Ahles, Jurish, Pallmeyer, Saunders, Teders, Barron, and Rodichok (1982) first administered 10 sessions of live training in progressive relaxation to a subject population consisting of sufferers from migraine headches, tension headaches, and a combination of the two. All kinds of headaches improved with this treatment, although improvement among tension headache sufferers was greatest. All subjects whose symptoms had not improved by at least 60% were then administered biofeedback. Tension headache sufferers received frontalis EMG biofeedback, and migraine headache sufferers and sufferers from both kinds of headaches received biofeedback for increasing peripheral skin temperature. All groups improved further during biofeedback therapy, with the combined migraine and tension headache sufferers showing the greatest improvement. Another study from the same laboratory, using the same research design with migraine headache sufferers, found very similar results (Blanchard, Andrasik, Neff, Teders, Pallmeyer, Arena, Jurish, Saunders, & Rodichok, 1982). Thus biofeedback may have a critically important treatment role for some individuals, even when relaxation therapy is also used.

Other comparisons in the literature have been between muscularly oriented and autonomically oriented therapies. The effects of muscularly oriented therapy appear to be greater than those of an autonomically oriented therapy in treatment of muscle tension headaches. As cited above, the combination of EMG biofeedback and progressive relaxation has been found to be more effective than autogenic feedback training in the treatment of tension headaches (Detrick, 1977).

Cognitive and environmental factors play a large role in causation of tension headaches, and some evidence has been reported that cognitive therapy should play a commensurately large role in treatment. Beaty and Haynes (1979) call our attention to such variables as home practice, the credibility of the various placebo conditions, "nonspecific intervention variables such as therapist contact, instructions, subject expectancies, and the reactive effects of self-monitoring." They also note that muscle tension has been found to be only a modest predictor of tension headaches. They cite such other known contributors as degree of exposure to environmental stressors, general autonomic arousal, social contingencies, and variability in pain tolerance and threshold. They hypothesize that the most effective treatment package would address all these factors individually. Also, as we have argued above, research studies measure headaches entirely by self-report measures. Thus, not only is symptom formation affected by stress-inducing cognitive interpretations of stressors in the environment, but it is also influenced by the interpretations given to the physiological effects of the stressors. It is thus not surprising that cognitive therapies might have particularly beneficial effects. Holroyd and Andrasik (1982) found greater effects for cognitive therapy than for biofeedback therapy in treatment of tension headaches. These results persisted through a 2-year follow-up. Similarly, a partial-crossover-design study by Huber and Huber (1979) found that the combination of rational–emotive therapy and autogenic training provided relief to migraine sufferers who previously had been unsuccessfully treated by medication and relaxation therapy. An intriguing study on two subjects by Kremsdorf, Kochanowicz, and Costell (1981) found that cognitive therapy reduced self-reported headache activity but not EMG levels, while EMG biofeedback reduced EMG levels but not self-reported headache activity.

In summary, cognitive, relaxation, and biofeedback therapies all appear to have a role in the treatment of headaches. Muscularly oriented therapies have a greater effect than do autonomically oriented therapies for tension headaches. Temperature biofeedback appears to help some individuals with migraine or mixed headaches. Cognitive therapy, either alone or in combination with relaxation therapy, can play a particularly important treatment role.

HYPERTENSION

Most reviews of the literature on treatment of hypertension have found no difference between blood pressure biofeedback and progressive relaxation instruction, or between various forms of relaxation treatment (cf. Agras & Jacob, 1979; Frumkin, Nathan, Prout, & Cohen, 1978; Goldstein, 1982; Seer, 1979; Tarler-Benlolo, 1978). The amount of decrease varies among studies but averages about 10–20 mm Hg; usually the decrease is slightly greater in systolic than in diastolic blood pressure.

There have, however, been differences of opinion about the effectiveness of meditation compared to other relaxation methods. Pinkerton *et al.* (1982, p. 150) comment that studies of meditation have had less consistent positive effects than studies of progressive relaxation have had. On the other hand, Parker, Gilbert, and Thoreson (1978) found greater effects for meditation than for progressive relaxation among alcoholics. It is possible that meditation is much more motivational for this particular population (alcoholics), or that the form of progressive relaxation instruction used (tape-recorded) was particularly ineffective. Also, the effects were measured only during a single session. In our experience, meditation can be taught effectively in a single session, while progressive relaxation, being a more complex skill, takes more time. Thus the results of this study do not give convincing evidence for the superiority of meditation. Nevertheless, the relative *limitations* of meditation are not universally agreed upon among those who have reviewed the literature. Henry (1978) suggests that meditation methods may prove to be more effective than biofeedback methods.

Cognitive methods and suggestion have also been used in the treatment of hypertension. An interesting study by Minsky (1978) found that suggestions to direct imagery toward expanding the arteries produces greater reductions in diastolic blood pressure among hypertensives than does general relaxation imagery (e.g., lying in a hammock). Similarly, Redmond, Gaylor, McDonald, and Shapiro (1974) found that suggestions to "make your heart beat slower and less forcefully, and your vessels less resistant to the flow of blood" had effects equivalent to those of three sessions of live instruction in progressive relaxation. The effects of the latter, however, are minimal, because of the brevity of the training. Although Pinkerton *et al.* (1982) reported having found one unpublished report on successful treatment of hypertension by cognitive therapy, we have found no comparisons between comprehensive cognitive therapy and intensive relaxation therapy.

There are some suggestions in the literature that combinations of relaxation therapies have greater effects than do single treatments (Agras & Jacob, 1979; Pinkerton *et al.*, 1982, p.152). However, the value of combinations of techniques for treating hypertension has not been proven. Pinkerton *et al.* indicate that studies using combinations of treatments also studied patients with initially higher pressures than did studies using only a single technique. They also assert that the combination of progressive relaxation and blood pressure biofeedback has been definitively shown to be no more effective than is either of those two techniques individually (Pinkerton *et al.*, 1982, p. 156).

In summary, most relaxation methods produce moderate but clinically useful decreases in blood pressure. Under most circumstances, the effects of meditation may be slightly less than those of progressive relaxation, biofeedback, or autogenic training; however, this disadvantage may be offset in some populations by the greater motivational properties of meditation. Cognitive therapy and suggestion have also proven helpful, but these methods have not yet been systematically compared with relaxation methods. Similarly, psychological methods have not been systematically compared with pharmacological methods. Investigators have generally assumed that psychological methods should be used to supplement pharmacological methods. All reviews have cited numerous studies showing that hypertensive patients can safely decrease antihypertensive medication intake after some form of psychological treatment. In view of the unpleasant and occasionally harmful side effects of this medication, psychological treatments may become increasingly more prominent in the treatment of this common but serious disorder.

ASTHMA

Pinkerton *et al.* (1982), in their review of the literature on psychological treatment, concluded that progressive relaxation has significant effects on improving asthmatic symptoms and on improving various measures of respiratory functioning in asthmatics. They also report that the combination of relaxation and systematic desensitization has greater beneficial effects than does progressive relaxation alone. In most of the studies in this review, people were desensitized to the bodily feelings associated with asthmatic symptoms and/or to situations that typically elicit asthmatic attacks.

Erskine-Milliss and Schonell (1981), on the other hand, conclude that progressive relaxation has no effect on asthma, whereas other methods of relaxation are effective. In our opinion, Erskine-Milliss and Schonell are in error. The progressive relaxation studies they reviewed were done only on children with severe asthma. However, Davis, Saunders, Creer, and Chai (1973) dramatically demonstrated that relaxation therapy (in this case, the combination of progressive relaxation and EMG biofeedback) was effective only with children suffering from mild asthma.

INSOMNIA

Insomnia also appears to be helped by many behavioral methods approximately equally. Woolfolk *et al.* (1976) found equivalent improvements in self-reports of predormital insomnia for meditation and progressive relaxation; Nicassio and Bootzin (1974) found equivalent effects for progressive relaxation and autogenic training; R. M. Turner and Ascher (1979) found equivalent effects for progressive relaxation training, paradoxical intention, and stimulus control procedures; and Haynes, Sides, and Lockwood (1977) found equivalent effects for taped progressive relaxation and EMG biofeedback. All the methods were found to be superior to control treatments. Gershman and Clouser (1974) found taped progressive relaxation training and systematic desensitization to be equally effective in improving self-reported ability to fall asleep. Both were more effective than a no-treatment control condition on this measure; but only progressive relaxation improved subjects' self-reported ability to go back to sleep after having been awakened. This possibly results from the relatively greater amount of time devoted to relaxation training in the relaxation condition than in the desensitization condition, of which relaxation is one component. Borkovec and Fowles (1973), on the other hand, found no differences between hypnotic relaxation, progressive relaxation, and a self-relaxation control in sleep improvement. It is possible, however, that the self-relaxation condition included important components of active treatment—regular relaxation during the day and focus on internal bodily states. All three treatments were more effective than a no-treatment control. When, in another study, an adequate control for expectancy and demand characteristics was used, progressive relaxation and desensitization were found to be more effective than a pseudodesensitization placebo (Steinmark & Borkovec, 1974). (See our longer discussion of expectancy and demand effects, above.) Using similar procedures in other studies, Borkovec, Kaloupek, and Slama (1975) and Borkovec and Hennings (1978) found progressive relaxation to be more effective than suggestions to relax (i.e., without training). When EEG rather than self-report was used as the criterion for improvement in sleep onset, progressive relaxation was found to be clearly superior to no treatment and to a placebo (Borkovec & Weerts, 1976). In a literature review, Knapp, Downs, and Alperson (1976) concluded, "Almost any variant of relaxation training produces statistically significant reductions in latency to sleep onset and a reduction in number of awakenings" (p. 623).

In a review of the research on insomnia, Borkovec (1979) draws the distinction between "idiopathic insomnia" (i.e., insomnia that is evidenced in all-night EEG recordings) and "pseudoinsomnia" (i.e., insomnia that is revealed only in self-report measures). He describes data indicating that progressive relaxation is an effective treatment for the former, but not for the latter, when compared with appropriate placebo conditions. Similarly, Woolfolk and McNulty (1983) found greater improvement in self-reported insomnia for treatments based on use of imagination than for progressive relaxation. In this study, they compared four relaxation-based treatments. All were found to be more effective than a no-treatment control.

Combinations of treatments may be more effective than individual treatments. Mitchell and White (1977), in the study described above, found that the combination of mental relaxation and taped progressive relaxation instruction reduced self-reported latency to sleep more than did progressive relaxation alone. In the group that was given mental relaxation after progressive relaxation training, decreases in latency to sleep were noted both after progressive relaxation training *and* after mental relaxation training. Similarly, only subjects receiving training in the combination of treatments showed increases in ratings of sleep satisfaction after training. At a 1-month follow-up, however, both groups showed improvement. We have found no studies on whether progressive relaxation adds any strength to the effects of imaginal or cognitive techniques.

The results may be explained by the nature of psychologically produced insomnia. It may include elements of somatic and cortical arousal, worry, conditioned anxiety to the bed situation, and operant reinforcement (secondary gain). Since each technique probably works on a different aspect of the problem, it is not surprising that various psychological treatments have similar effects, and that combinations of treatments are better than individual treatments.

ANXIETY

All of the relaxation methods reported in this book appear to produce changes in clinical and self-reported manifestations of anxiety. Despite the wide use of relaxation methods for treating anxiety, however, the methods all appear to have some limits. For example, Raskin, Johnson, and Rondesvedt (1973) showed that severe panic attacks in anxiety neurotics were not prevented by daily practice in the combination of progressive relaxation instruction and frontalis EMG biofeedback. They did show that these methods improved situational anxiety, insomnia, headaches, and other symptoms associated with anxiety. Similarly, LeBoeuf and Lodge (1980) found that EMG biofeedback and progressive relaxation each had only marginal effects on anxiety neurosis.

Studies comparing live progressive relaxation training with biofeedback have found no advantages for biofeeback (cf. reviews by Gatchel, 1982; Wilkinson, 1977). Progressive relaxation and meditation also appear to have equivalent effects in the treatment of anxiety. Some studies have found greater anxiety-reducing effects for meditation than for relaxation instructions (Carrington et al., 1980; Lehrer, Schoicket, Carrington, & Woolfolk, 1980; Woolfolk, Lehrer, McCann, & Rooney, 1982) but other studies have found the opposite (Lehrer et al., 1983; Gilbert, Parker, & Clairborn, 1978). Still other studies have found no differences between the two techniques (Boswell & Murray, 1979; Greff, 1979; S. Turner, 1978; Wood, 1978). These effects remain equivalent even when we examine the effects of live versus taped training separately. In his review of the literature, Mathews (1982) concludes that various relaxation strategies do not differ in their effects on clinical anxiety. Similarly, progressive relaxation and autogenic training have been found to produce equivalent decreases in self-reported anxiety. This was found for the SCL-90 (Shapiro & Lehrer, 1980) and for the IPAT Anxiety Inventory (Lchrer, Atthowe, & Weber, 1980). Finally, anxiety management training was, as reported above, found in one study to be more effective than was progressive relaxation training alone in reducing self-reported general anxiety (Shoemaker, 1977). Thus the combination of cognitive and relaxation strategies appears to have some advantages in treating chronic anxiety—which itself obviously has a combination of cognitive and somatic characteristics. Traditional group therapy, however, has not been found to be as effective as the combination of EMG biofeedback and progressive relaxation has been in reducing anxiety (Townsend, House, & Addario, 1975). Shacket (1979) compared two techniques that both have a strong cognitive component: systematic desensitization and rational–emotive therapy. Although no differences were found between groups on the full-scale IPAT Anxiety Inventory, desensitization appeared to reduce scores on the Apprehension subscale more than did rational–emotive therapy.

ANGER AND AGGRESSIVE BEHAVIOR

There have also been a few studies of the effect of relaxation training on anger or aggressive behavior. Two of our studies showed decreases in self-rated (SCL-90–R) symptoms of hostility produced by various relaxation techniques, including progressive relaxation, meditation, and autogenic training (Carrington et al., 1980; Lehrer et al., 1983). Although differences were found between active treatment groups and no-treatment control groups, no differences were found between the various active treatment methods. In another study, however, mantra meditation was found to reduce self-rated hostility more than progressive relaxation, at a marginally significant level (Woolfolk et al., 1982). No group maintained a significant decrease on this measure at a 6-month follow-up. Shapiro and Lehrer (1980), using five sessions of live individual training, found that neither progressive relaxation training nor autogenic training produced any significant changes in self-rated hostility, compared with a no-treatment control group. Woolfolk (in press) reported the successful treatment of a case of chronic hostility by methods of meditation.

Cognitive approaches to coping with stress have also been used as treatments for excessive anger (Green & Murray, 1975; Novaco, 1975). A few studies comparing cognitive stress management techniques with relaxation therapy have also appeared. Bott (1979) compared progressive relaxation (including training in deep breathing and in situational use of relaxation) with a verbal discussion group that taught alternative coping strategies to retarded individuals. A combined treatment group was also included. All groups showed improvements in staff ratings of aggressiveness, but the most significant improvement was noted in the combined group. In several post hoc measures, the verbal discussion group and the combined group showed greater decreases than did the relaxation group. Similarly, Schlichter (1978) found that stress inoculation training was more effective than any one of the elements that make it up (i.e., progressive relaxation and behavior rehearsal), and also more effective than a no-treatment condition in reducing verbal anger in a role-playing situation. However, no differences were found between the treatment elements and the complete package either in verbal aggressiveness reported from imaginary scenes or in self-reported anger. These measures were reduced more in the treatment groups than in the no-treatment control.

PHOBIAS

The literature on behavioral treatment of phobias is very large and has been reviewed a number of times (e.g., Borkovec & O'Brien, 1976; Marks, 1975; Mathews, 1971, 1978). Although some methodological criticisms have been made of the state of the empirical literature on the subject, the general conclusion appears to be that desensitization is effective. The contribution of progressive relaxation as a component of desensitization has, however, not been established. If relaxation instruction does contribute at all to the effectiveness of desensitization, the type of training does not seem to matter. The most important effect of relaxation training on phobias may be as a component of *in vivo* desensitization. It may convince the person that an approach can be made to the phobic situation without much risk, because of the belief that panic can always be controlled by relaxation. Indeed, the critical variable for improvement appears to be mental or, preferably, *in vivo* exposure to the anxiety-provoking situation. This may be because phobias are usually defined in terms of their cognitive or behavioral components (i.e., they are usually assessed in terms of how fearful a person reports being in the phobic situation, or how much the person is willing to expose himself or herself to it). We have discussed the literature pertinent to this issue above, in the section "Behavioral Interventions versus Relaxation Therapies."

Cognitive therapy also has been found helpful in treatment of phobias—perhaps even more so than desensitization. We have found no studies comparing combined cognitive and relaxation–desensitization therapies with either of the individual components. The effect of cognitive therapy on approach behavior is not, however, as great as that of direct behavioral exposure (cf. Biran & Wilson, 1981).

TEST ANXIETY

Various methods of relaxation instruction appear to be equally effective in treatment of test anxiety and significantly better than no-treatment controls. Differences between relaxation procedures and placebo conditions are minimal, however. Where significant differences do occur, the previously mentioned superiority of EMG biofeedback over taped relaxation instruction manifests itself. Cognitive methods appear to be more effective than relaxation methods, and the addition of cognitive methods to relaxation methods may produce greater therapeutic improvements than the addition of relaxation to cognitive methods. (In these generalizations, we are considering systematic desensitization to be a cognitive technique that also includes a relaxation component. Systematic desensitization does not appear to be as powerful as cognitive therapy, but it has been found to be slightly and inconsistently superior to progressive relaxation.) Differences between active treatments are more pronounced on self-report measures of test anxiety, but are also occasionally found among measures of performance on tests. The studies are summarized in Table 13-12.

DEPRESSION

Although much attention has been given to the use of cognitive therapies for treatment of depression (cf. Beck *et al.,* 1979), relatively little attention has been given to treatment of depression by relaxation therapies. However, the few studies that have been done have generally shown some positive results. Wheeler (1977) studied psychiatric inpatients scoring high on the Beck Depression Inventory, who also were anxious and scored high on external locus of control. The subjects were divided among a progressive relaxation group, a group receiving an attention placebo, and a no-treatment group. Compared to the two control groups, the progressive relaxation group produced the greatest decreases in self-rated depression and anxiety. Similarly, Carrington *et al.* (1980), using taped training, found significantly greater decreases in the SCL-90 Depression scale in a meditation condition than in a no-treatment control. Progressive relaxation did not differ from either of the other groups. Lehrer *et al.* (1983), on the other hand, using live training, found greater decreases on the SCL-90 Depression scale among subjects given progressive relaxation than among those given meditation—although both active treatments showed greater decreases than did the no-treatment control group. Similarly, Shapiro and Lehrer (1980) found significantly greater decreases on the SCL-90 Depression scale among normal volunteers after training in progressive relaxation or autogenic training than in a no-treatment control. No differences were found between the two active treatments. Finally, Gilbert *et al.* (1978), in a single taped training session with hospitalized alcoholics, found greater increases in self-reported vigor and decreases in self-reported depression with progressive relaxation than with Benson's meditation or with a self-relaxation control.

On the other hand, in a study of depressed outpatients, McLean and Hakstian (1979) found progressive relaxation to be less effective than cognitive-behavior therapy, and no more (or less) effective than psychotherapy or tricyclic antidepressant therapy. This study did not use a control group, so it is not possible to tell if the latter treatments were equally effective or equally *in*effective. Woolfolk *et al.* (1982), using a procedure almost identical to that used by Lehrer *et al.* (1983), found no differences among relaxation, meditation, and the no-treatment control group on the SCL-90–R Depression scale.

RAYNAUD'S DISEASE

In Raynaud's disease, a potentially serious ailment, blood flow to the periphery of the body is severely restricted because of spasms in the peripheral blood vessels. Medical treatment for this condition often involves major surgery (e.g., a sympathectomy) or medication to dilate the blood vessels—medication that often has rather severe side effects. Raynaud's disease appears to be effectively treated in a significant number of cases by various relaxation techniques (cf. reviews by Blanchard, 1979; Pinkerton *et al.*, 1982, pp. 163–165; Sappington, Fiorito, & Brehony, 1979; Surwit, 1982). The latter two reviews emphasize, however, that no differences have been found between finger temperature feedback training and various relaxation techniques, including autogenic training.

LOWER BACK PAIN

Kravitz (1978) compared progressive relaxation with the combination of progressive relaxation and EMG biofeedback. Equivalent improvements were found with both approaches. This study also found that patients suffering from lower back pain do not differ from normal subjects in EMG activity from the back muscles during rest, although patients' EMG levels are much higher than those of normals when they are asked to engage in various isometric contractions not directly connected with movement of the back. Thus it appears that such people tend to involve their back muscles unnecessarily in various muscular activities. Paralumbar

TABLE 13-12. Summary of Findings on Test Anxiety

Authors	Decreases in test anxiety	Improvement in test performance
Studies finding differences between techniques		
Johnson & Sechrest (1968)	PMR > SD > NT (but individual comparisons were n.s.).	SD > PMR = NT on final exam scores.
Freeling & Shemberg (1970)	SD > PMR = visual imagery.	SD = PMR = visual imagery on an anagrams test.
Counts, Hollandsworth, & Alcorn (1978)	CCR = CCR + EMG BFK = placebo > NT.	CCR + EMG BFK > CCR = placebo = NT.
Pesta & Zwettler (1977)	Cognitive methods > PMR = combined.	
Chang-Liang & Denney (1976)	1. Applied relaxation training > NT. 2. PMR and SD did not differ from either group.	Applied relaxation training > PMR = SD = NT on Wonderlink Personnel Test.
Baither & Godsey (1979)	Rational–emotive therapy > NT. PMR differed from neither.	
Reed & Saslow (1980)	1. EMG BFK > taped PMR, NT on debilitating anxiety. 2. EMG BFK = PMR > NT on STAI State Anxiety during test.	
Studies finding that techniques are equivalent, but more powerful than control conditions		
Rothman (1979)	PMR + SD = EMG BFK + SD > NT.	PMR + SD = EMG BFK + SD = NT on academic performance.
Snyder & Deffenbacher (1977)	Relaxation as self-control = SD > placebo (SD produced the greatest *increases* in facilitative anxiety).	
Comer (1977)	MED = applied MED = PMR = applied PMR > NT (on performance measure only). On self-report measures, no differences between groups.	
Thompson, Griebstein, & Kuhlenschmidt (1980)	Live administration of anxiety management training (AMT; Suinn & Richardson, 1971) or stress management training (SMT; Budzynski, 1974), each crossed with forearm EMG BFK or taped supplemental instruction in AMT or SMT. All > NT in STAI	Treatment groups > NT.

TABLE 13-12.   *(Continued)*

Authors	Decreases in test anxiety	Improvement in test performance
	State Anxiety, and a somatic–cognitive trait anxiety questionnaire.	

Other studies

Authors	Decreases in test anxiety	Improvement in test performance
Maxwell (1979)	PMR + deep breathing + cognitive restructuring = cognitive restructuring alone = placebo.	PMR + deep breathing = cognitive restructuring alone = placebo on diagnostic reading test.
Dawson & McMurray (1978)	Random-item SD without relaxation = SD.	
Khan (1978)	EMG BFK = EMG BFK + relationship therapy.	EMG BFK = EMG BFK + relationship therapy on the WISC–R.
Schuchman (1978)	EMG BFK + SD = PMR + SD = nondirective counseling.	
Deffenbacher & Michaels (1980)	PMR = SD.	
Bernthal (1977)	PMR = EMG BFK = temperature BFK. All groups were given visualization and coping imagery.	
Finger & Galassi (1977)	Suggestions to relax = suggestions to pay attention to test materials.	Suggestions to relax = suggestions to pay attention to test materials on Wonderlink Personnel Test and Digit Symbols Test.

Note. For explanation of abbreviations, see footnote to Table 13-1.

EMG levels during isometric exercises were reduced more in those receiving biofeedback plus progressive relaxation than in those receiving the simple progressive relaxation. However, interpretation of this finding is clouded somewhat, because control subjects also reduced their EMG levels more than did progressive relaxation subjects. No differences between groups were found under rest conditions. In a similar study by Jerome (1978), progressive relaxation therapy was also found to be effective in reducing lower back pain and paraspinal muscle tension. This study also examined electrocautery and injections of Facet, and found that the treatment combining relaxation with one of the physical techniques had the best effects. Barlow (1977) reported several cases of low back pain successfully treated by the Alexander technique. This method involves training in less stressful use of the body while doing things. In general, although the literature contains some promising suggestions, there is little adequately controlled research on self-control treatment of this problem.

DYSMENORRHEA

Several studies of relaxation treatment for dysmenorrhea have appeared. Duson (1976) found six sessions of progressive relaxation and desensitization to be just as effective as cognitive restructuring in reducing symptoms. Both were more effective than a control condition, and treatment gains were maintained at a 1-month follow-up. Relaxation therapy was found to be more effective with spasmodic dysmenorrhea (i.e., due to muscle cramping) than with congestive dysmenorrhea (i.e., due to fluid retention). No such difference occurred for cognitive restructuring. Similarly, Chesney and Tasto (1975) found a relaxation–desensitization procedure to be effective in treating spasmodic but not congestive dysmenorrhea, compared to pseudotherapy and waiting-list control groups. Treatment gains were maintained at a 2-month follow-up.

One might expect that congestive dysmenorrhea might respond better to treatments that emphasize blood flow. No comparative studies, and only one controlled study, are reported thus far in the literature. None of these reported whether subjects suffered from congestive or from spasmodic dysmenorrhea. Several case studies have reported improvement in symptoms following hand temperature biofeedback (Adler & Adler, 1979). Sedlacek & Heczey (1977) reported using a combination of EMG biofeedback, hand temperature biofeedback, and vaginal temperature biofeedback. In a controlled study, Heczey (1977) found vaginal temperature biofeedback to be more effective than autogenic training, and found both treatments to be more effective than a no-treatmentt control group. Improvement in the treatment groups ranged from 64% in group-administered autogenic training to 92% in biofeedback. There was no improvement in the control condition.

A negative finding of sorts was reported by Rosenthal (1978), who found no differences among five sessions of progressive relaxation, systematic desensitization, and nondirective therapy, either in self-reported symptoms of dysmenorrhea or in trait anxiety. The results of this study, however, are difficult to interpret because no true control group was used. All the training conditions could have been either equally effective or equally ineffective.

In summary, the literature suggests that muscle relaxation may be more effective with spasmodic dysmenorrhea. Adequate comparative studies of congestive dysmenorrhea have not been done. Additional comparative studies using cognitive therapies also must be done.

OTHER CONDITIONS

Comparison studies have found the combination of biofeedback training and Lamaze training more effective than Lamaze training alone on a variety of measures of emotional lability of the infant, as well as on reduction of labor time (R. A. Schwartz, 1979). Feely (1978) found a better relapse rate after narcotics detoxification for the combination of taped progressive relaxation and biofeedback than for biofeedback alone, despite the fact that there were no differences between groups in the initial response to treatment. Similarly, Rosenberg (1980) found that progressive relaxation training was more effective than alcoholism education in reducing use of alcohol among alcoholics—but only among those alcoholics who used alcohol primarily to reduce emotional tension. In their extensive literature review on the subject, however, Nathan and Goldman (1979) argued that tension reduction is inadequate as an explanation for most cases of alcoholism. Thus therapies that focus only on tension reduction probably would not be sufficient to ameliorate this condition. Kazdin and Wilson (1978) noted that comparatively few controlled studies have been done on behavioral treatment of drug addiction. This is still the case. Most widely used treatments, however, emphasize treating overt behavior and self-concept rather than tension.

RELAXATION THERAPY WITH CHILDREN

Children can learn relaxation techniques at least as well as adults can, and they seem to be better able than adults to master some methods. For example, it is widely known that preadolescent children usually have the highest scores on tests of hypnotizability (Hilgard, 1965). Although many children can be treated with the standard relaxation techniques described in this book, modifications in the techniques have been devised to cater to children's particular needs, abilities, and motivational levels (cf. Koeppen, 1974).

A pediatric disorder that has been widely treated with stress reduction techniques is childhood hyperactivity. Rivera (1978) found that progressive relaxation can be taught effectively to hyperactive children, and that it shows some generalization to cognitive testing conditions. Subjects given relaxation training showed greater decreases than did those given a placebo in impulsivity scores on the Matching Familiar Figures test. Dunn (1980) found significant behavioral improvement and decreased muscle tension in hyperactive boys given 10 sessions of progressive relaxation training. The same boys showed no improvement during 10 weeks of placebo sessions. Similarly, Brown (1977) studied the combination of task-motivational instructions (encouraging participation and outlining expected positive outcomes) and relaxation instructions, and compared this with a condition in which subjects received only relaxation instructions. Both treatments produced greater increases in self-esteem than did a placebo condition among hyperkinetic children. Only the combined treatment, however, was more effective than the placebo in reducing hyperkinetic behaviors. Thus, making specific suggestions about expected changes appears to be a critical factor in making relaxation useful for treating hyperkinetic behavior. Unfortunately the effects of task-motivating instructions *without* relaxation instructions was not assessed. Klein (1976) found no differences between relaxation training and an exercise program in measures of reflectivity–impulsivity or on tests of coding. Both treatments improved reflectivity, but neither affected coding ability. This study had no control group. Bhatara, Arnold, Lorance, and Gupta (1979) review the scanty published literature on the effects of progressive relaxation on hyperactivity. They conclude that " the extra effort involved in the EMG biofeedback training is not justifiable in hyperkinesis, but muscle relaxation training might have a place in the multimodality treatment of hyperactivity" (p. 182).

Relaxation therapies have also been used for the treatment of anxiety-related academic difficulties. Padawer (1977) found that relaxation was more effective than classroom activities were in improving attention, memory, and concentration among poor readers in an inner-city school. Khan (1978) found that EMG biofeedback alone and the combination of EMG biofeedback and relationship therapy both produced decreases in state anxiety (although not trait anxiety), and produced increases in Wechsler Intelligence Scale for Children—Revised (WISC–R) scores among elementary-school children who had been diagnosed as having problems with high anxiety levels. Palmari (1980) found that the combination of cue-controlled relaxation and cognitive therapy was more effective than was either cognitive therapy alone or standard educational treatment in improving scores on the Peabody Individual Achievement Test and teachers' ratings of aggressiveness and attentiveness. Robertin (1980) found that progressive relaxation training and a procedure emphasizing right-hemisphere learning both improved scores on mathematics tests among special education students. Right-hemisphere learning, on the other hand, was superior to progressive relaxation in improving vocabulary scores and in decreasing state anxiety during the testing situation. Thus modes of thinking and working may, as specific coping devices in school, be the treatment of choice in such situations. On the other hand, Paull (1980) found 4 weeks of daily stress management training followed by 7 weeks of weekly training to have no effect on a rote learning task or on a test of social maturity. Thus, although not all studies find significant effects for relaxation in improving behaviors associated with learning, most of the studies show that it can make a contribution in some populations. This is probably because poor learning ability is often accompanied by feelings of anxiety in the learning situation. Relaxation cannot be considered a substitute for good remedial teaching, but it may serve as a useful adjunct.

CONCLUSION

This literature review allows us to conclude, along with G. E. Schwartz *et al.* (1978), that various relaxation techniques do have some distinguishing differences in their effects, but that these effects are superimposed upon a large (and often clinically much more significant) global relaxation response. This is of more than just theoretical interest. Although most stress reduction treatments produce decreases in a broad array of stress-related symptoms, there is some evidence for greater reductions in muscular problems (e.g., tension headaches) following muscular interventions (EMG biofeedback or progressive relaxation) as opposed to autonomic interventions (e.g., autogenic feedback therapy). Also, disorders that primarily involve cognitive processes (e.g., test anxiety, insomnia, anxiety, phobias, depression, anger) tend to respond particularly well to cognitive therapies, and, in some instances, to respond better to cognitive than to relaxation therapies. Cognitive therapy may also be particularly effective with tension headaches, thus suggesting that cognitions, as well as muscle tension, might play a critical role in the development of this problem. Other psychosomatic conditions might also respond well to cognitive therapy, but few relevant comparative studies have been done. Despite the probable importance of cognitive factors in the development and maintenance of psychosomatic symptoms, we nevertheless have sufficient evidence to argue for the specific use of relaxation or biofeedback therapies for these conditions.

For most psychosomatic problems, combinations of techniques appear to produce better cumulative effects than one technique alone. An exception to this rule seems to occur when using a combination of techniques means administering one or all of the component techniques only superficially. One research method that appears to hold promise for factoring out specific effects of various techniques is the use of sequential or crossover designs, in which those individuals who do not benefit from one technique are offered another.

In comparisons between various biofeedback therapies and various relaxation therapies, we generally find equivalent effects. Thus, the economics of equipment expenses versus expenses in staff time may be important factors in deciding which approach is better. However, therapist contact is necessary even in biofeedback therapy, as is therapist warmth. Thus the economic advantages of using a machine-administered treatment may not be as great as they may seem. Preliminary results from crossover studies on treatment of headaches also suggest that particular individuals not helped by relaxation therapy may benefit from use of the machines. Thus both relaxation therapies and biofeedback may remain with us for some time to come.

Many issues remain unresolved. What is the most effective combination of roles for relaxation therapy and cognitive therapy in treatment of psychosomatic problems? More studies are needed on the incremental effects of combining one therapy with another. Even the comparative literature on specific effects of relaxation *versus* cognitive techniques is woefully small for psychosomatic problems. Similarly, we still have few notions about personality predictors of response to specific techniques.

Despite the unresolved issues, however, we are impressed with the scope and consistency of the literature to date. These techniques are effective; they have slightly different effects. Combinations of techniques, if training is intensive and properly tailored to the individual, are more effective than is the application of single techniques.

REFERENCES

Ackerman, S. H., & Sachar, E. J. The lactate theory of anxiety: A review and reevaluation. *Psychosomatic Medicine,* 1974, *36,* 69–81.
Adler, C. S., & Adler, S. M. Biofeedback and psychosomatic disorders. In J. V. Basmajian

(Ed.), *Biofeedback: Principles and practice for clinicians*. Baltimore: Williams & Wilkins, 1979.

Agras, S., & Jacob, R. Hypertension. In O. F. Pomerleau, & J. P. Brady (Eds.), *Behavioral medicine: Theory and practice*. Baltimore: Williams & Wilkins, 1979.

Alberti, R. E. *Assertiveness: Innovations, applications, issues*. San Luis Obispo, Calif.: Impact Publishers, 1977.

Alexander, S., & Husak, T. The anxiety differential: Initial steps in the development of measures of situational anxiety. *Educational and Psychological Measurement*, 1962, *22*, 325–348.

Alpert, R., & Haber, R. N. Anxiety in academic achievement situations. *Journal of Abnormal and Social Psychology*, 1960, *61*, 207–215.

Andreychuk, T., & Skriver, C. Hypnosis and biofeedback in the treatment of migraine headaches. *International Journal of Clinical Hypnosis*, 1975, *23*, 172–183.

Aponte, J. F., & Aponte, C. E. Group programmed desensitization without the simultaneous presentation of aversive scenes with relaxation training. *Behaviour Research and Therapy*, 1971, *9*, 337–346.

Baermark, S., & Gaunitz, S. Transcendental meditation and heterohypnosis as altered states of consciousness. *International Journal of Clinical and Experimental Hypnosis*, 1979, *27*, 227–239.

Baither, R. C., & Godsey, R. Rational emotive education and relaxation training in large group treatment of test anxiety. *Psychological Reports*, 1979, *45*, 326.

Barabasz, A., & McGeorge, C. Biofeedback, mediated biofeedback, and hypnosis in peripheral vasodilation training. *American Journal of Clinical Hypnosis*, 1978, *21*, 28–37.

Barlow, W. *The Alexander technique*. New York: Knopf, 1977.

Beatty, J. Biofeedback in the treatment of migraine: Simple relaxation or specific effects? In L. White & B. Tursky (Eds.), *Clinical biofeedback: Efficacy and mechanisms*. New York: Guilford Press, 1982.

Beaty, E. T., & Haynes, S. N. Behavioral intervention with muscle-contraction headache: A review. *Psychosomatic Medicine*, 1979, *41*, 165–179.

Beck, A. T., Rush, A. J., Shaw, B. F., & Emery, G. *Cognitive therapy of depression*. New York: Guilford Press, 1979.

Beiman, I. The effects of instructional set on physiological response to stressful imagery. *Behaviour Research and Therapy*, 1976, *14*, 175–179.

Beiman, I., Israel, E., & Johnson, S. A. During training and posttraining effects of live and taped extended progressive relaxation, self-relaxation, and electromyogram biofeedback. *Journal of Consulting and Clinical Psychology*, 1978, *46*, 314–321.

Belar, C. D. A comment on Silver and Blanchard's (1978) review of the treatment of tension headaches by EMG feedback and relaxation training. *Journal of Behavioral Medicine*, 1979, *2*, 215–220.

Benson, H. *The relaxation response*. New York: Morrow, 1975.

Benson, H. Systemic hypertension and the relaxation response. *New England Journal of Medicine*, 1977, *296*, 1152–1156.

Benson, H., Rosner, B. A., Marzetta, B. R., & Klemchuk, H. P. Decreased blood pressure in pharmacologically treated hypertensive patients who regularly elicited the relaxation response. *Lancet*, 1974, *1*, 289–291.

Bernthal, J. R. EMG biofeedback, thermal biofeedback, and progressive relaxation in the treatment of examination anxiety of adult education students (Doctoral dissertation, University of Michigan, 1977). *Dissertation Abstracts International*, 1977, *38*, 1292A–1293A. (University Microfilms No. 77-17, 952)

Bhatara, V., Arnold, L. E., Lorance, T., & Gupta, D. Muscle relaxation therapy in hyperkinesis: Is it effective? *Journal of Learning Disabilities*, 1979, *12*, 182–186.

Biran, M., & Wilson, G. T. Treatment of phobic disorders using cognitive and exposure methods: A self-efficacy analysis. *Journal of Consulting and Clinical Psychology,* 1981, *49,* 886–899.

Blanchard, E. B. Biofeedback: A selective review of clinical applications in behavioral medicine. In R. McNemara (Ed.), *Behavioral approaches to medicine: Application and analysis.* New York: Plenum, 1979.

Blanchard, E. B., Ahles, T. A., & Shaw, E. R. Behavioral treatment of headaches. In M. Hersen, R. M. Eisler, & P. M. Miller (Eds.), *Progress in behavior modification* (Vol. 8). New York: Academic Press, 1979.

Blanchard, E. B., Andrasik, F., Neff, D. F., Arena, J. G., Ahles, T. A., Jurish, S. E., Pallmeyer, T. P., Saunders, N. L., Teders, S. J., Barron, K. D., & Rodichok, L. D. Biofeedback and relaxation training with three kinds of headache: Treatment effects and their prediction. *Journal of Consulting and Clinical Psychology,* 1982, *50,* 562–575.

Blanchard, E. B., Andrasik, F., Neff, D. F., Teders, S. J., Pallmeyer, T. P., Arena, J. G., Jurish, S. E., Saunders, S. L., & Rodichok, L. D. Sequential comparisons of relaxation training and biofeedback in the treatment of three kinds of chronic headache, or, the machines may be necessary some of the time. *Behaviour Research and Therapy,* 1982, *20,* 469–481.

Blanchard, E. B., Andrasik, F., & Silver, B. V. Biofeedback and relaxation in the treatment of tension headaches: A reply to Belar. *Journal of Behavioral Medicine,* 1980, *3,* 227–232.

Borkovec, T. D. Pseudo(experimental)-insomnia and idiopathic (objective) insomnia: Theoretical and therapeutic issues. *Advances in Behaviour Research and Therapy,* 1979, *2,* 27–55.

Borkovec, T. D., & Fowles, D. C. Controlled investigation of the effects of progressive relaxation and hypnotic relaxation on insomnia. *Journal of Abnormal Psychology,* 1973, *82,* 153–158.

Borkovec, T. D., & Hennings, B. L. The role of physiological attention-focusing in the relaxation treatment of sleep disturbance, general tension, and specific stress reaction. *Behaviour Research and Therapy,* 1978, *16,* 7–19.

Borkovec, T. D., Kaloupek, D. G., & Slama, K. M. The facilitative effect of muscle tension–release in the relaxation treatment of sleep disturbance. *Behavior Therapy,* 1975, *6,* 301–309.

Borkovec, T. D., & O'Brien, G. T. Methodological and target behavior issues in analogue therapy outcome research. In M. Hersen, R. M. Eisler, & P. M. Miller (Eds.), *Progress in behavior modification* (Vol. 3). New York: Academic Press, 1976.

Borkovec, T. D., & Weerts, T. C. Effects of progressive relaxation on sleep disturbance: An electroencephalographic evaluation. *Psychosomatic Medicine,* 1976, *38,* 173–180.

Boswell, P. C., & Murray, E. J. Effects of meditation on psychological and physiological measures of anxiety. *Journal of Consulting and Clinical Psychology,* 1979, *47,* 606–607.

Bott, L. A. An investigation of the use of verbal discussion and relaxation training to control aggression in mildly and moderately retarded adults (Doctoral dissertation, The Ohio State University, 1979). *Dissertations Abstracts International,* 1979, *40,* 1864B.

Bradley, B. W., & McCanne, T. R. Autonomic responses to stress: The effects of progressive relaxation, the relaxation response, and expectancy of relief. *Biofeedback and Self-Regulation,* 1981, *6,* 235–251.

Bridgewater, M. J. The relative efficacy of meditation in reducing an induced anxiety reaction. (Doctoral dissertation, New Mexico State University, 1979). *Dissertation Abstracts International,* 1979, *40,* 903B. (University Microfilms No. 79-18, 222)

Brown, R. H. An evaluation of the effectiveness of relaxation training as a treatment modality for the hyperkinetic child (Doctoral dissertation, Texas Tech University, 1977). *Dissertation Abstracts International,* 1977, *38,* 2847B. (University Microfilms No. 77-

25, 502)

Budzynski, T. H. *Relaxation training program.* New York: BMA Audio Cassettes, 1974.

Byasse, J. E. Progressive relaxation and autogenic training in the treatment of essential hypertension (Doctoral dissertation, University of Louisville, 1975). *Dissertation Abstracts International,* 1977, *37,* 452B. (University Microfilms No. 76-16, 329)

Cangelosi, A. The differential effects of three relaxation techniques: A physiological comparison (Doctoral dissertation, University of Iowa, 1980). *Dissertation Abstracts International,* 1981, *42,* 418B. (University Microfilms No. 81-14, 239)

Canter, A., Kondo, C. Y., & Knott, J. R. A comparison of EMG biofeedback and progressive muscle relaxation training in anxiety neurotics. *British Journal of Psychiatry,* 1975, *127,* 470–477.

Carr-Kaffashan, L., & Woolfolk, R. L. Active and placebo effects in the treatment of moderate and severe insomnia. *Journal of Consulting and Clinical Psychology,* 1979, *47,* 603–605.

Carrington, P. *Freedom in meditation.* New York: Doubleday, 1977.

Carrington, P., Collings, G. H., Jr., Benson, H., Robinson, H., Wood, L. W., Lehrer, P. M., Woolfolk, R. L., & Cole, J. W. The use of meditation–relaxation tedchniques for the management of stress in a working population. *Journal of Occupational Medicine,* 1980, *22,* 221–231.

Cauthen, N. R., & Prymak, C. A. Meditation versus relaxation: An examination of the physiological effects of relaxation training and of different levels of experience with meditation. *Journal of Consulting and Clinical Psychology,* 1977, *45,* 496–497.

Chang-Liang, R., & Denney, D. R. Applied relaxation as training in self-control. *Journal of Counseling Psychology,* 1976, *23,* 183–189.

Chesney, M. A., & Shelton, J. L. A comparison of muscle relaxation and electromyographic biofeedback treatments for muscle contraction headaches. *Journal of Behavior Therapy and Experimental Psychiatry,* 1976, *7,* 221–225.

Chesney, M. A., & Tasto, D. The effectiveness of behaviour modification and spasmodic and congestive dysmenorrhea. *Behaviour Research and Therapy,* 1975, *13,* 240–253.

Comer, J. F. Meditation and progressive relaxation in the treatment of test anxiety (Doctoral dissertation, University of Kansas, 1977). *Dissertation Abstracts International,* 1978, *38,* 6142B. (University Microfilms No. 78-09, 340)

Cooke, G. Evaluation of the efficacy of the components of reciprocal inhibition psychotherapy. *Journal of Abnormal Psychology,* 1968, *73,* 464–467.

Counts, D. K., Hollandsworth, T. D., & Alcorn, J. D. Use of electromyographic biofeedback and cue-controlled relaxation in the treatment of test anxiety. *Journal of Consulting and Clinical Psychology,* 1978, *46,* 990–996.

Crosson, B. Control of skin temperature through biofeedback and suggestion with hypnotized college women. *International Journal of Clinical and Experimental Hypnosis,* 1980, *28,* 75–87.

Curtis, W. D., & Wessberg, H. W. A comparison of heart rate, respiration, and galvanic skin response among meditators, relaxers, and controls. *Journal of Altered States of Consciousness,* 1980, *2,* 319–324.

Cuthbert, B., Kristeller, J., Simons, R., Hodes, R., & Lang, P. J. Strategies of arousal and control. Motivation, meditation, and biofeedback. *Journal of Experimental Psychology: General,* 1981, *110,* 518–546.

Davidson, R. J., & Schwartz, G. E. Psychobiology of relaxation and related states. In D. Mostofsky (Ed.), *Behavior modification and control of physiological activity.* Englewood Cliffs, N.J.: Prentice-Hall, 1976.

Davis, M. H., Saunders, D. R., Creer, T. L., & Chai, H. Relaxation training facilitated by biofeedback apparatus as a supplemental treatment in bronchial asthma. *Journal of*

Psychosomatic Research, 1973, *17,* 121–128.

Dawson, R. W., & McMurray, W. E. Desensitization without hierarchical presentation and concomitant relaxation. *Australian Journal of Psychology,* 1978, *30,* 119–132.

Deabler, H. L., Fidel, E., Dillenkoffer, R. L., & Elder, S. T. The use of relaxation and hypnosis in lowering high blood pressure. *American Journal of Clinical Hypnosis,* 1973, *16,* 75–83.

DeBerry, S. The effect of EMG biofeedback, progressive muscle relaxation and cognitive style on muscle tension and anxiety (Doctoral dissertation, Long Island University, 1979). *Dissertation Abstracts International,* 1979, *40,* 1357B. (University Microfilms No. 79-18, 482)

Deffenbacher, J. L., & Michaels, A. C. Two self-control procedures in the reduction of targeted and nontargeted anxieties: A year later. *Journal of Counseling Psychology,* 1980, *27,* 9–15.

Deffenbacher, J. L., & Suinn, R. M. The chronically anxious patient. In D. M. Doleys, R. L. Meredith, & A. R. Ciminero (Eds.), *Behavioral medicine: Assessment and treatment strategies.* New York: Plenum, 1982.

Detrick, P. F. Demonstration and comparison of the efficacy of EMG biofeedback assisted relaxation versus autogenic feedback training for the treatment of tension headaches (Doctoral dissertation, University of Southern Mississippi, 1977). *Dissertation Abstracts International,* 1978, *38,* 5009B. (University Microfilms No. 78-02, 902)

Dunn, F. M. Relaxation training and its relationship to hyperactivity in boys (Doctoral dissertation, Brigham Young University, 1980). *Dissertation Abstracts International,* 1980, *41,* 348B. (University Microfilms No. 80-16, 079)

Duson, B. M. Effectiveness of relaxation–desenitization and cognitive restucturing in teaching the self-management of menstrual symptoms to college women (Doctoral dissertation, University of Texas at Austin, 1976). *Dissertation Abstracts International,* 1977, *37,* 6322B. (University Microfilms No. 77-11, 508)

Erskine-Milliss, J., & Schonell, M. Relaxation therapy in asthma: A critical review. *Psychosomatic Medicine,* 1981, *43,* 365–372.

Fee, R. A., & Girdano, D. A. The relative effectiveness of three techniques to induce the trophotropic response. *Biofeedback and Self-Regulation,* 1978, *3,* 145–157.

Feely, T. M. The effects of electromyographic biofeedback training and EMG biofeedback with progressive relaxation training on narcotics addicts during medical detoxification (Doctoral dissertation, St. Louis University, 1978). *Dissertation Abstracts International,* 1978, *39,* 1474B–1475B. (University Microfilms No. 78-14, 556)

Fenz, W. D. Specificity in somatic responses to anxiety. *Perceptual and Motor Skills,* 1967, *24,* 1183–1190.

Fernandez-Abscal, E. G., & Miguel Tobal, J. J. Breathing styles in different relaxation methods. *Informes del Departmento de Psicología General, University of Madrid,* 1979, *2,* 127–141.

Finger, R., & Galassi, J. P. Effects of modifying cognitive versus emotional responses in the treatment of test anxiety. *Journal of Consulting and Clincal Psychology,* 1977, *45,* 280–287.

Fray, J. M. Implications of electromyographic feedback for essential hypertensive patients (Doctoral dissertation, Texas Tech University, 1975). *Dissertation Abstracts International,* 1975, *36,* 3036B. (University Microfilms No. 75-26, 839)

Freeling, N. W., & Shemberg, K. M. The alleviation of test anxiety by systematic desensitization. *Behaviour Research and Therapy,* 1970, *8,* 293–299.

Friedman, H., & Taub, H. A. The use of hypnosis and biofeedback procedures for essential hypertension. *International Journal of Clinical and Experimental Hypnosis,* 1977, *27,* 335–347.

Frumkin, K., Nathan, R. J., Prout, M. F., & Cohen, M. C. Nonpharmacological control of essential hypertension in man: A critical review of the experimental literature. *Psychosomatic Medicine,* 1978, *40,* 294–320.

Gatchel, R. J. EMG biofeedback in anxiety reduction. In L. White, & B. Tursky (Eds.), *Clinical biofeedback: Efficacy and mechanisms.* New York: Guilford Press, 1982.

Ganguli, R., & Detre, T. Psychopharmacology and behavior therapy. In L. Michelson, M. Hersen, & S. M. Turner (Eds.), *Future perspectives in behavior therapy.* New York: Plenum, 1982.

Gershman, L., & Clouser, R. A. Treating insomnia with relaxation and desensitization in a group setting by an automated approach. *Journal of Behavior Therapy and Experimental Psychiatry,* 1974, *5,* 31–35.

Gilbert, G. S., Parker, J. C., & Clairborn, C. D. Differential mood changes in alcoholics as a function of anxiety management strategies. *Journal of Clinical Psychology,* 1978, *34,* 29–232.

Godsey, R. L. Efficacy of response contingent and program contingent progression in live and taped progressive relaxation training (Doctoral dissertation, Texas A & M University, 1979). *Dissertation Abstracts International,* 1980, *40,* 3928B. (University Microfilms No. 80-03, 135)

Goldfried, M. R., & Trier, C. S. Effectiveness of relaxation as an active coping skill. *Journal of Abnormal Psychology,* 1974, *83,* 348–355.

Goldstein, I. B. Biofeedback in the treatment of hypertension. In L. White & B. Tursky (Eds.), *Clinical biofeedback: Efficacy and mechanisms.* New York: Guilford Press, 1982.

Goleman, D. J., & Schwartz, G. E. Meditation as an intervention in stress reactivity. *Journal of Consulting and Clinical Psychology,* 1976, *44,* 456–466.

Graham, F. K., & Clifton, R. K. Heart-rate change as a component of the orienting response. *Psychological Bulletin,* 1966, *65,* 305–320.

Graham, K., Wright, G., Toman, W., & Mark, C. Relaxation and hypnosis in the treatment of insomnia. *American Journal of Clinical Hypnosis,* 1975, *18,* 39–42.

Green, R. A., & Murray, E. J. Expression of feeling and cognitive reinterpretation in the reduction of hostile aggression. *Journal of Consulting and Clinical Psychology,* 1975, *43,* 375–383.

Greenwood, M. M., & Benson, H. The efficacy of progressive relaxation in systematic desensitization and a proposal for an alternative competitive response. *Behaviour Research and Therapy,* 1977, *15,* 337–343.

Greff, C. H., Jr. Comparative effectiveness of three methods for effecting client relaxation in a clinical setting (Doctoral dissertation, California School for Professional Psychology, San Diego, 1979). *Dissertation Abstracts International,* 1980, *40,* 3929B–3930B. (University Microfilms No. 80-04, 336)

Grimm, L. G. The evidence for cue-controlled relaxation. *Behavior Therapy,* 1980, *11,* 283–293.

Hafner, R. J., & Marks, I. M. Exposure *in vivo* of agoraphobics: Contributions of diazepam, group exposure, and anxiety evocation. *Psychological Medicine,* 1976, *6,* 71–88.

Hafner, R. J., & Milton, F. The influence of propranolol on the exposure *in vivo* of agoraphobics. *Psychological Medicine,* 1977, *7,* 419–425.

Haynes, S. N., Moseley, D., & McGowan, W. Relaxation and biofeedback training in the reduction of frontalis muscle tension. *Psychophysiology,* 1975, *12,* 547–552.

Haynes, S. N., Sides, H., & Lockwood, G. Relaxation instruction and frontalis electromyographic feedback intervention with sleep-onset insomnia. *Behavior Therapy,* 1977, *8,* 644–652.

Heczey, M. D. Effects of biofeedback and autogenic training on menstrual experiences: Relationships among anxiety, locus of control and dysmenorrhea (Doctoral dissertation,

The City University of New York, 1977). *Dissertation Abstracts International,* 1978, *38,* 5571B. (University Microfilms No. 78-05, 763)

Heidi, F. J., & Borkovec, T. D. Relaxation-induced anxiety: Paradoxical anxiety-enhancement due to relaxation training. *Journal of Consulting and Clinical Psychology,* 1983, *51,* 171–182.

Hendricksen, N. E. The effects of progressive relaxation and meditation on mood stability and state anxiety in alcoholic inpatients (Doctoral dissertation, University of Missouri–Columbia, 1977). *Dissertation Abstracts International,* 1978, *39,* 981B. (University Microfilms No. 78-14, 120)

Henry, J. P. Relaxation methods and the control of blood pressure. *Psychosomatic Medicine,* 1978, *40,* 273–275.

Hilgard, E. R. *Hypnotic susceptibility.* New York: Harcourt, Brace, 1965.

Hock, R. A., Bramble, J., & Kennard, D. W. A comparison between relaxation and assertive training with asthmatic male children. *Biological Psychiatry,* 1977, *12,* 593–596.

Holroyd, K. A. Stress, coping, and the treatment of stress-related illness. In J. R. McNamara (Ed.), *Behavioral approaches to medicine: Application and analysis.* New York: Plenum, 1979.

Holroyd, K. A., & Andrasik, F. Do the effects of cognitive therapy endure? A two-year follow-up of tension headache sufferers treated with cognitive therapy or biofeedback. *Cognitive Therapy and Research,* 1982, *6,* 325–333.

Holstead, B. N. Cue-controlled relaxation: An investigation of psychophysiological reactions to a stressor film (Doctoral dissertation, University of Mississippi, 1978). *Dissertation Abstracts International,* 1978, *39,* 2987B. (University Microfilms No. 78-05, 763)

Huber, H. P., & Huber, D. Autogenic training and rational–emotive therapy for long-term migraine patients: An explorative study of a therapy. *Behavior Analysis and Modification,* 1979, *3,* 169–177.

Hutchings, D. F., & Reinking, R. H. Tension headaches: What form of therapy is most effective? *Biofeedback and Self-Regulation,* 1976, *2,* 183–190.

Israel, E., & Beiman, I. Live versus recorded relaxation training: What form of therapy is most effective? *Biofeedback and Self-Regulation,* 1977, *8,* 251–254.

Jacobson, E. Electrical measurements concerning muscular contraction (tonus) and the cultivation of relaxation in man: Relaxation times of individuals. *American Journal of Physiology,* 1934, *108,* 573–580. (a)

Jacobson, E. Electrical measurements concerning muscular contraction (tonus) and the cultivation of relaxation in man: Studies in arm flexors. *American Journal of Physiology,* 1934, *107,* 230–248. (b)

Jacobson, E. *Progressive relaxation.* Chicago: University of Chicago Press, 1938.

Jacobson, E. *Modern treatment of tense patients.* Springfield, Ill.: Charles C Thomas, 1970.

Jerome, J. A. Decreasing musculoskeletal tension via biofeedback and relaxation training procedures for the treatment of chronic low back pain (Doctoral dissertation, Michigan State University, 1978). *Dissertation Abstracts International,* 1979, *40,* 969B. (University Microfilms No. 79-17, 721)

Johnson, S. M., & Sechrest, L. Comparison of desensitization and progressive relaxation in treating anxiety. *Journal of Consulting and Clinical Psychology,* 1968, *32,* 280–286.

Kantor, L. E. Stress inoculation as a means of teaching anxiety management skills: An evaluation of stimulus generalization (Doctoral dissertation, Bowling Green State University, 1979). *Dissertation Abstracts International,* 1980, *40,* 3401B. (University Microfilms No. 80-00, 043)

Kazdin, A., & Wilson, G. T. *Evaluation of behavior therapy.* Cambridge, Mass.: Ballinger, 1978.

Khan, M. A. The effects of EMG biofeedback assisted relaxation training upon problem-solving abilities of anxious children (Doctoral dissertation, Western Michigan University, 1978). *Dissertation Abstracts International,* 1978, *39,* 2476B. (University Microfilms No. 78-21, 838)

Klein, S. A. Relaxation and exercise for hyperactive impulsive children. (Doctoral dissertation, Colorado State University, 1976). *Dissertation Abstracts International,* 1977, *37,* 6334B. (University Microfilms No. 77-12, 044)

Knapp, T. J., Downs, D. L., & Alperson, J. R. Behavior therapy for insomnia: A review. *Behavior Therapy,* 1976, *7,* 614 & 625.

Koeppen, A. S. Relaxation training for children. *Elementary School Guidance and Counseling,* 1974, *9,* 14–21.

Kravitz, E. A. EMG biofeedback and differential relaxation training to promote pain relief in chronic low back pain patients (Doctoral dissertation, Wayne State University, 1977). *Dissertation Abstracts International,* 1978, *39,* 1485B–1486B. (University Microfilms No. 78-16, 047)

Kremsdorf, R. B., Kochanowicz, N. A., & Costell, S. Cognitive skills training versus EMG biofeedback in the treatment of tension headaches. *Biofeedback and Self-Regulation,* 1981, *6,* 93–102.

Krug, S. E., Scheier, I. H., & Cattell, R. B. *Handbook for the IPAT Anxiety Scale.* Champaign, Ill.: Institute of Personality and Ability Testing, 1976.

Lang, P. J. The application of psychophysiological methods to the study of psychotherapy and behavior change. In A. E. Bergin & S. L. Garfield (Eds.), *Handbook of psychotherapy and behavior change: An empirical analysis.* New York: Wiley, 1971.

Lavallée, Y. J., Lamontagne, G., Pinard, G., Annable, L., & Tétreault, L. Effects of EMG biofeedback, diazepam and their combination on chronic anxiety. *Journal of Psychosomatic Research,* 1977, *21,* 65–71.

Lazarus, A. A. Multimodal behavior therapy: Treating the BASIC ID. *Journal of Nervous and Mental Disease,* 1973, *156,* 404–411.

Lazarus, R. S. A cognitive analysis of biofeedback control. In G. E. Schwartz & J. Beatty (Eds.), *Biofeedback: Theory and research.* New York: Academic Press, 1977.

LeBoeuf, A., & Lodge, J. A comparison of frontalis EMG feedback training and progressive relaxation in the treatment of chronic anxiety. *British Journal of Psychiatry,* 1980, *137,* 279–284.

Lehrer, P. M. Psychophysiological effects of relaxation in a double-blind analog of desensitization. *Behavior Therapy,* 1972, *3,* 193–208.

Lehrer, P. M. Psychophysiological effects of progressive relaxation in anxiety neurotic patients and of progressive relaxation and alpha feedback in nonpatients. *Journal of Consulting and Clinical Psychology,* 1978, *46,* 389–404.

Lehrer, P. M. How to relax and how not to relax: A re-evaluation of the work of Edmund Jacobson: I. *Behaviour Research and Therapy,* 1982, *20,* 417–428.

Lehrer, P. M., Atthowe, J. M., & Weber, E. S. P. Effects of progressive relaxation and autogenic training on anxiety and physiological measures, with some data on hypnotizability. In F. J. McGuigan, W. Sime, & J. M. Wallace (Eds.), *Stress and tension control.* New York: Plenum, 1980.

Lehrer, P. M., & Leiblum, S. L. Physiological, behavioral, and cognitive measures of assertiveness and assertion anxiety. *Behavioral Counseling Quarterly,* 1981, *1,* 261–274.

Lehrer, P. M., Schoicket, S., Carrington, P., & Woolfolk, R. L. Psychophysiological and cognitive responses to stressful stimuli in subjects practicingg progressive relaxation and clinically standardised meditation. *Behaviour Research and Therapy,* 1980, *18,* 293–303.

Lehrer, P. M., & Woolfolk, R. L. Self-report assessment of anxiety: Somatic, cognitive, and behavioral modalities. *Behavioral Assessment,* 1982, *4,* 167–177.

Lehrer, P. M., Woolfolk, R. L., Rooney, A. J., McCann, B., & Carrington, P. Progressive relaxation and meditation: A study of psychophysiological and therapeutic differences between two techniques. *Behaviour Research and Therapy,* 1983, *21,* 651–662.

Lent, R. W. A comparison between cue-controlled desensitization, cognitive restructuring, and a credible placebo in alleviating public speaking anxiety (Doctoral dissertation, Ohio State University, 1979). *Dissertation Abstracts International,* 1979, *40,* 1899B. (University Microfilms No. 79-22, 513)

Lewis, C. E., Biglan, A., & Steinbock, E. Self-administered relaxation training and money deposits in the treatment of recurrent anxiety. *Journal of Consulting and Clinical Psychology,* 1978, *46,* 1274–1283.

Lindholm, E., & Lowry, S. Alpha production in humans under conditions of false feedback. *Bulletin of the Psychonomic Society,* 1978, *11,* 106–108.

Marks, I. M. Behavioral treatments of phobic and obsessive–compulsive disorders: A critical appraisal. In M. Hersen, R. M. Eisler, & P. M. Miller (Eds.), *Progress in behavior modification* (Vol. 1). New York: Academic Press, 1975.

Marks, I. M. *Cure and care of neuroses: Theory and practice of behavioral psychotherapy.* New York: Wiley, 1981.

Marks, I. M., Stern, R. S., Mawson, D., Cobb, J., & McDonald, R. Clomipramine and exposure for obsessive–compulsive rituals: I. *British Journal of Psychiatry,* 1980, *136,* 1–25.

Marks, I. M., Viswanthan, R., Lipsedge, M. S., & Gardner, R. Enhanced relief of phobias by flooding during waning diazepam effect. *British Journal of Psychiatry,* 1972, *121,* 495–505.

Mathews, A. M. Psychophysiological approaches to the investigation of desensitization. *Psychological Bulletin,* 1971, *76,* 73–91.

Mathews, A. M. Fear reduction research and clinical phobias. *Psychological Bulletin,* 1978, *85,* 390–404.

Mathews, A. M. *Anxiety and its management.* Unpublished manuscript, Department of Psychology, St. George's Hospital Medical School, London, England, 1982.

Maxwell, M. S. Experimental evaluation of theoretically differentiated treatments of test anxiety (Doctoral dissertation, University of Texas at Austin, 1979). *Dissertation Abstracts International,* 1979, *40,* 1363A. (University Microfilms No. 79–20, 167)

McAmmond, D., Davidson, P., & Kovitz, D. A comparison of the effects of hypnosis and relaxation training on stress reduction in a dental situation. *American Journal of Clinical Hypnosis,* 1971, *13,* 233–242.

McLean, P. D., & Hakstian, A. R. Clinical depression: Comparative efficacy of outpatient treatments. *Journal of Consulting and Clinical Psychology,* 1979, *47,* 818–836.

Mersky, H., & Spear, F. G. *Pain: Psychological and psychiatric aspects.* London: Balliere, Tindall, & Cassell, 1967.

Miller, M. P., Murphy, P. J., & Miller, T. P. Comparison of electromyographic feedback and progressive relaxation. *Journal of Consulting and Clinical Psychology,* 1978, *46,* 1291–1298.

Minsky, P. J. High blood pressure and interpersonal disengagement: A study of maladaptive coping styles and ameliorative treatments (Doctoral dissertation, Loyola University, 1978). *Dissertation Abstracts International,* 1978, *38,* 5580B. (University Microfilms No. 78-07, 075)

Mitchell, K. R., & Mitchell, D. M. Migraine: An exploratory treatment application of programmed behavior therapy techniques. *Journal of Psychosomatic Research,* 1971, *15,* 137–157.

Mitchell, K. R., & White, R. G. Self-management of severe predormital insomnia. *Journal* of *Behavior Therapy and Experimental Psychiatry,* 1977, *8,* 57–63.

Moore, N. Behavior therapy with bronchial asthma: A controlled study. *Journal of Psychosomatic Research,* 1965, *9,* 257–274.

Morse, D., Martin, J., Furst, M., & Dubin, L. A physiological and subjective evaluation of meditation, hypnosis, and relaxation. *Psychosomatic Medicine,* 1975, *39,* 304–374.

Nathan, P. E., & Goldman, M. S. Problem drinking and alcoholism. In O. F. Pomerleau & J. P. Brady (Eds.), *Behavioral medicine: Theory and practice.* Baltimore: Williams & Wilkins, 1979.

Nicassio, P., & Bootzin, R. A comparison of progressive relaxation and autogenic training as treatment for insomnia. *Journal of Abnormal Psychology,* 1974, *83,* 235–260.

Novaco, R. W. *Anger control: The development and evaluation of an experimental treatment.* Lexington, Mass.: D. C. Heath, 1975.

Oest, L. G., Jerremalm, A., & Johansson, J. Individual response patterns and the effects of different behavioural methods in the treatment of social phobias. *Behaviour Research and Therapy,* 1981, *19,* 1–16.

Ollendick, T. H., & Murphy, M. J. Differential effectiveness of muscular and cognitive relaxation as a function of locus of control. *Journal of Behavior Therapy and Experimental Psychiatry,* 1977, *8,* 223–228.

Padawer, D. D. Reading performance of relaxation trained children. (Doctoral dissertation, University of Pennsylvania, 1977). *Dissertation Abstracts International,* 1977, *38,* 1306A. (University Microfilms No. 77-19, 903)

Palmari, J. J. Relaxation and cognitive coping statements as supplemental remedial interventions for learning problems in children (Doctoral dissertation, Hofstra University, 1980). *Dissertation Abstracts International,* 1980, *40,* 5796B. (University Microfilms No. 80-12, 855)

Parker, J. C., Gilbert, G. S., & Thoreson, R. W. Reduction of autonomic arousal in alcoholics: A comparison of relaxation and meditation techniques. *Journal of Consulting and Clinical Psychology,* 1978, *46,* 879–886.

Paul, G. L. *Insight versus desensitization in psychotherapy.* Stanford, Calif.: Stanford University Press, 1966.

Paul, G. L. Inhibition of physiological response to stressfu imagery by relaxation training and hypnotically suggested relaxation. *Behaviour Research and Therapy,* 1969, *7,* 249–256. (a)

Paul, G. L. Physiological effects of relaxation training and hypnotic suggestion. *Journal of Abnormal Psychology,* 1969, *74,* 425–437. (b)

Paul, G. L., & Trimble, R. W. Recorded versus "live" relaxation training and hypnotic suggestion: Comparative effectiveness for reducing physiological arousal and inhibiting stress response. *Behavior Therapy,* 1970, *1,* 285–302.

Paull, R. C. The effect of relaxation training on a rote learning task and the psychosocial maturity of inner city black seventh graders: A program in holistic education (Doctoral dissertation, University of Southern California, 1980). *Dissertation Abstracts International,* 1980, *41,* 602A.

Pesta, K., & Zwettler, S. Influence of cognitive desensitization in test anxiety in school children: A therapeutic comparison. *Zeitschrift für Klinische Psychologie,* 1977, *6,* 130–143.

Pinkerton, S., Hughes, H., & Wenrich, W. W. *Behavioral medicine: Clinical applications.* New York: Wiley, 1982.

Prager-Decker, I. J. The relative efficacy of progressive muscle relaxation, EMG biofeedback and music for reducing stress arousal of internally versus externally controlled individuals (Doctoral dissertation, University of Maryland, 1978). *Dissertation Abstracts International,* 1979, *39,* 3177B. (University Microfilms No. 79-00, 924)

Quayle, C. M. The relative effectiveness of audio-taped and live therapist presented relaxation in terms of physiological parameters (Doctoral dissertation, Utah State University, 1979). *Dissertation Abstracts International,* 1980, *40,* 3961B. (University Microfilms No. 80-05, 114)

Raskin, M., Bali, L. R., & Peeke, H. V. Muscle biofeedback and transcendental meditation. *Archives of General Psychiatry,* 1980, *37,* 93–97.

Raskin, M., Johnson, G., & Rondesvedt, J. W. Chronic anxiety treated by feedback-induced muscle relaxation: A pilot study. *Archives of General Psychiatry,* 1973, *28,* 263–266.

Redmond, D. P., Gaylor, M. S., McDonald, R. H., & Shapiro, A. P. Blood pressure and heart rate response to verbal instructions and relaxation in hypertension. *Psychosomatic Medicine,* 1974, *36,* 285–297.

Reed, M., & Saslow, C. The effects of relaxation instructions and EMG biofeedback on test anxiety, general anxiety, and locus of control. *Journal of Clinical Psychology,* 1980, *36,* 683–690.

Reinking, R. H., & Kohl, M. L. Effects of various forms of relaxation training on physiological and self-report measures of relaxation. *Journal of Consulting and Clinical Psychology,* 1975, *43,* 595–600.

Rivera, E. An investigation of the effects of relaxation training on attention to task and impulsivity among male hyperactive children (Doctoral dissertation, University of Southern California, 1978). *Dissertation Abstracts International,* 1978, *39,* 2841A.

Robertin, H. Anxiety reduction and academic progress (Doctoral dissertation, Union Graduate School, Ohio, 1979). *Dissertation Abstracts International,* 1980, *40,* 4500A. (University Microfilms No. 80-02, 948)

Rosenberg, S. D. Relaxation training and a differential assessment of alcoholism (Doctoral dissertation, California School of Professional Psychology, San Diego, 1979). *Dissertation Abstracts International,* 1980, *40,* 3963B. (University Microfilms No. 80-04, 362)

Rosenthal, R. L. Differential treatment of spasmodic and congestive dysmenorrhea (Doctoral dissertation, Washington University, 1978). *Dissertation Abstracts International,* 1978, *39,* 1498B. (University Microfilms No. 78-16, 421)

Rothman, H. S. Electromyographic biofeedback training versus progressive muscle relaxation training in the treatment of test anxiety (Doctoral dissertation, Washington State University, 1979). *Dissertation Abstracts International,* 1979, *40,* 463B. (University Microfilms No. 79-15, 148)

Russell, R., Sipich, J., & Knipe, J. Progressive relaxation training: A procedural note. *Behavior Therapy,* 1976, *7,* 566–568.

Sappington, J. T., Fiorito, E. M., & Brehony, K. A. Biofeedback as therapy in Raynaud's disease. *Biofeedback and Self-Regulation,* 1979, *4,* 155–169.

Schlichter, K. J. An application of stress inoculation training in the development of anger-management skills in institutionalized juvenile delinquents (Doctoral dissertation, Pennsylvania State University, 1977). *Dissertation Abstracts International,* 1978, *38,* 6172B. (University Microfilms No. 78-08, 420)

Schlutter, L., Golden, C., & Blume, H. A comparison of treatments for prefrontal muscle contraction headache. *British Journal of Medical Psychology,* 1980, *53,* 47–52.

Schuchman, M. C. A comparison of three techniques for reducing Scholastic Aptitude Test anxiety (Doctoral dissertation, Hofstra University, 1977). *Dissertation Abstracts International,* 1978, *38,* 2010A. (University Microfilms No. 77-20, 673)

Schultz, J. H., & Luthe, W. *Autogenic therapy* (Vol. 1, *Autogenic methods*). New York: Grune & Stratton, 1969.

Schwartz, G. E., Davidson, R. J., & Goleman, D. T. Patterning of cognitive and somatic processes in the self-regulation of anxiety: Effects of meditation versus exercise. *Psychosomatic Medicine,* 1978, *40,* 321–328.

Schwartz, R. A. Biofeedback relaxation training in obstetrics: Its effect on the perinatal and neonatal states (Doctoral dissertation, California School of Professional Psychology, San Diego, 1979). *Dissertation Abstracts International,* 1980, *40,* 3967B. (University Microfilms No. 80-04, 364)

Sedlacek, K., Cohen, J., & Boxhill, C. *Comparison between biofeedback and relaxation response in the treatment of hypertension.* Paper presented at the annual meeting of the Biofeedback Society of America, San Diego, 1979.

Sedlacek, K., & Heczey, M. *A specific biofeedback treatment for dysmenorrhea.* Paper presented at the annual meeting of the Biofeedback Society of America, Orlando, Florida, March 1977.

Seer, P. Psychological control of essential hypertension: Review of the literature and methodological critique. *Psychological Bulletin,* 1979, *86,* 1015–1043.

Shapiro, S., & Lehrer, P. M. Psychophysiological effects of autogenic training and progressive relaxation. *Biofeedback and Self-Regulation,* 1980, *5,* 249–255.

Sheridan, C. L., Vaughan, K. S., Wallerstedt, M. J., & Ward, L. B. *Electromyographic biofeedback and progressive relaxation compared: Interactions with gender and type of dependent measure.* Paper presented at the annual meeting of the Biofeedback Society of America, Orlando, Florida, March 1977.

Shacket, R. W. The relative effectiveness of rational–emotive therapy and systematic desensitization in the treatment of anxiety (Doctoral dissertation, University of Missouri–Columbia, 1979). *Dissertation Abstracts International,* 1980, *40,* 4508B–4509B. (University Microfilms No. 80-07, 192).

Shoemaker, J. Treatments for anxiety neurosis (Doctoral dissertation, Colorado State University, 1976). *Dissertation Abstracts International,* 1977, *37,* 5377B. (University Microfilms No. 77-68, 13)

Silver, B. V., & Blanchard, E. B. Biofeedback and relaxation training in the treatment of psychophysiological disorders: Or, are the machines really necessary? *Journal of Behavioral Medicine,* 1978, *1,* 217–239.

Sime, W. E., & DeGood, D. E. Effect of EMG biofeedback and progressive muscle relaxation training on awareness of frontalis muscle tension. *Psychophysiology,* 1977, *14,* 522–530.

Sloan, P. E. A comparison of the effectiveness of autogenic feedback training versus electromyogram feedback assisted relaxation for the treatment of migraine headaches (Doctoral dissertation, University of Southern Mississippi, 1977). *Dissertation Abstracts International,* 1978, *40,* 3458B.

Snow, W. G. The physiological and subjective effects of several brief relaxation training procedures (Doctoral dissertation, York University, Canada, 1977). *Dissertation Abstracts International,* 1978, *40,* 3458B.

Snyder, A. L., & Deffenbacher, J. L. Comparison of relaxation as self-control and systematic desensitization in the treatment of test anxiety. *Journal of Consulting and Clinical Psychology,* 1977, *45,* 1202–1203.

Sokolov, E. N. *Perception and the conditioned reflex.* New York: Macmillan, 1963.

Solyom, L., Heseltine, G. F. D., McClure, D. J., Solyom, C., Ledwidge, B., & Steinberg, G. Behaviour therapy versus drug therapy in the treatment of phobic neurosis. *Canadian Psychiatric Association Journal,* 1973, *18,* 25–32.

Southam, M. A. Generalized effects of relaxation training in essential hypertensives (Doctoral dissertation, Stanford University, 1981). *Dissertation Abstracts International,* 1981, *42,* 553B. (University Microfilms No. 81-15, 833)

Spies, G. Desensitization of test anxiety: Hypnosis compared with biofeedback. *American Journal of Clinical Hypnosis,* 1979, *22,* 108–111.

Staples, R., Coursey, R., & Smith, B. *A comparison of EMG biofeedback, autogenic, and progressive training as relaxation techniques.* Paper presented at the annual meeting of the Biofeedback Research Society, Monterey, California, February 1975.

Steinmark, S., & Borkovec, T. D. Active and placebo treatment effects on moderate insomnia under counterdemand and positive demand instructions. *Journal of Abnormal Psychology,* 1974, *83,* 157–163.

Sternbach, R. A. *Pain: A psychophysiological analysis.* New York: Academic Press, 1968.

Suinn, R. M. Anxiety management training for general anxiety. In R. Suinn & R. Weigel (Eds.), *The innovative therapies: Creative and critical contributions.* New York: Harper & Row, 1975.

Suinn, R. M. *Manual: Anxiety management training.* Unpublished manuscript, 1977. (Available from Rocky Mountain Behavioral Science Institute, P.O. Box 1066, Fort Collins, Colo. 80522.)

Suinn, R. M., & Richardson, F. C. Anxiety management training: A nonspecific behavior therapy program for anxiety control. *Behavior Therapy,* 1971, *2,* 498–510.

Surwit, R. S. Biofeedback and the behavioral treatment of Raynaud's disease. In L. White & B. Tursky (Eds.), *Clinical biofeedback: Efficacy and mechanisms.* New York: Guilford Press, 1982.

Surwit, R. S., Pilon, R. N., & Fenton, C. H. Behavioral treatment of Raynaud's disease. *Journal of Behavioral Medicine,* 1978, *1,* 323–335.

Tarler-Benlolo, L. The role of relaxation in biofeedback training: A critical review of the literature. *Psychological Bulletin,* 1978, *85,* 727–755.

Taub, E. *Self-regulation of human tissue temperature.* In G. Schwartz & J. Beatty (Eds.), *Biofeedback: Theory and research.* New York: Academic Press, 1977.

Taub, E., & School, P. J. Some methodological considerations in thermal biofeedback training. *Behavior Research Methods and Instrumentation,* 1978, *10,* 617–622.

Thompson, J. G., Griebstein, M. G., & Kuhlenschmidt, S. L. Effects of EMG biofeedback and relaxation training in the prevention of academic underachievement. *Journal of Counseling Psychology,* 1980, *27,* 97–106.

Townsend, R. E., House, J. F., & Addario, D. A comparison of biofeedback-mediated relaxation and group therapy in the treatment of chronic anxiety. *American Journal of Psychiatry,* 1975, *132,* 598–601.

Turner, P. E. A psychophysiological assessment of selected relaxation strategies (Doctoral dissertation, University of Mississippi, 1978). *Dissertation Abstracts International,* 1978, *39,* 3010B. (University Microfilms No. 78-24, 063)

Turner, R. M., & Ascher, L. M. Controlled comparison of progressive relaxation, stimulus control, and paradoxical intention therapies for insomnia. *Journal of Consulting and Clinical Psychology,* 1979, *47,* 500–508.

Turner, S. *A comparison of muscle relaxation, meditation, and self-relaxation in anxious patients.* Unpublished master's thesis, Somerville College, Oxford University, 1978.

Twentyman, C. T., & Zimering, R. T. Behavioral training of social skills: A critical review. In M. Hersen, R. M. Eisler, & P. M. Miller (Eds.), *Progress in behavior modification* (Vol. 7). New York: Academic Press, 1978.

Tyrer, P. J., & Steinberg, D. Symptomatic treatment for agoraphobias and social phobias: A follow-up study. *British Journal of Psychiatry,* 1975, *127,* 163–168.

Warrenberg, S., Pagano, R. R., Woods, M., & Hlastala, M. A comparison of somatic relaxation and EEG activity in classical progressive relaxation and transcendental meditation. *Journal of Behavioral Medicine,* 1980, *3,* 73–93.

West, M. A. Meditation and the EEG. *Psychological Medicine,* 1980, *10,* 369–375.

Wheeler, M. C. Relaxation training as a prescriptive therapy for anxious and external depressives (Doctoral dissertation, Syracuse University, 1976). *Dissertation Abstracts International,* 1977, *37,* 5849B. (University Microfilms No. 77-99, 13)

Whitehead, W. E., & Blackwell, B. Interactions between drugs and behavior therapy. In R. McNamara (Ed.), *Behavioral approaches to medicine.* New York: Plenum, 1979.

Wilkinson, M. A critical view of the current use of electromyographic biofeedback in general relaxation training. *Canadian Counsellor,* 1977, *11,* 182–184.

Wilson, M. L. The effects of relaxation and cognitive expectancy on attraction in a social interaction (Doctoral dissertation, University of North Carolina at Chapel Hill, 1979). *Dissertation Abstracts International,* 1979, *40,* 2442B. (University Microfilms No. 79-25, 981)

Wolpe, J. *The practice of behavior therapy.* New York: Pergamon Press, 1969.

Wood, D. T. The effects of progressive relaxation, heart rate biofeedback, and content-specific meditation on anxiety and performance in a class situation (Doctoral dissertation, University of Toledo, 1978). *Dissertation Abstracts International,* 1978, *39,* 3458A. (University Microfilms No. 78-24, 531)

Wooley, S., Blackwell, B., & Winget, C. A learning model of chronic illness behavior: Theory, treatment and research. *Psychosomatic Medicine,* 1978, *40,* 379–401.

Woolfolk, R. L. Psychophysiological correlates of meditation. *Archives of General Psychiatry,* 1975, *32,* 1326–1333.

Woolfolk, R. L. Self-control meditation applied to a case of chronic anger. In D. S. Shapiro (Ed.), *Meditation: Appraisal and status.* Chicago: Aldine, in press.

Woolfolk, R. L., Carr-Kaffashan, L., McNulty, T. F., & Lehrer, P. M. Meditation training as a treatment for insomnia. *Behavior Therapy,* 1976, *7,* 359–365.

Woolfolk, R. L., Lehrer, P. M., McCann, B. S., & Rooney, A. J. Effects of progressive relaxation and meditation on cognitive and somatic manifestations of daily stress. *Behaviour Research and Therapy,* 1982, *20,* 461–468.

Woolfolk, R. L., & McNulty, T. F. Treatment of insomnia: A component analysis. *Journal of Consulting and Clinical Psychology,* 1983, *51,* 495–503.

Zaichkowsky, L. K., & Kamen, R. Biofeedback and meditation: Effects on muscle tension and locus of control. *Perceptual and Motor Skills,* 1978, *46,* 955–958.

Zitrin, C. M., Klein, D. F., & Woerner, M. G. Behavior therapy, supportive psychotherapy, imipramine and phobias. *Archives of General Psychiatry,* 1978, *35,* 307–316.

Zuroff, D. C., & Schwarz, J. C. Effects of transcendental meditation and muscle relaxation on trait anxiety, maladjustment, locus of control and drug use. *Journal of Consulting and Clinical Psychology,* 1978, *46,* 264–271.

AUTHOR INDEX

Italicized page numbers indicate author citations in tables.

478

Basmajian, J. V., 222, 252*n*.
Beary, J. F., 79, 103*n*., 149, 181*n*., 250, 252*n*.
Beatty, J., 447, 465*n*.
Beaty, E. T., 446, 448, 465*n*.
Beck, A. T., 255–304, 262, 264, 265, 266*n*., 269, 272, 273, 275–277, 291, 292, 295, 304*n*., 305*n*., 339, 354, 361, 364*n*., 456, 465*n*.
Becker, C., 357, 365*n*.
Bedrosian, R. C., 354, 364*n*.
Beiman, I. H., 119, 139*n*., *410*, *412*, *416*, 440, 465*n*., 470*n*.
Belar, C. D., 446, 465*n*.
Bell, C., 15
Benson, H., 7, 11*n*., 45, 68*n*., 76–79, 103*n*., 104*n*., 106*n*., 107*n*., 109, 110, 116, 117, 119, 126, 127, 130–134, 139*n*., 141*n*., 149, 156, 176, 181*n*., 250, 252*n*., 342, 364*n*., 404, 418, 419, 421, 422, *424*, *426*, 453, 454, 456, 465*n*., 467*n*., 469*n*.
Berger, B., 353, 364*n*.
Berger, F. M., 312, 332*n*.
Berger, P. L., 353, 364*n*.
Berkman, L. F., 347, 364*n*.
Bernheim, H., 149, 182*n*.
Bernstein, D. A., 5, 11*n*., 43–68, 44, 47, 48, 49*n*., 51, 62, 66, 68*n*., 69*n*.
Bernthal, J. R., *459*, 465*n*.
Berrenberg, J. L., 198, 219*n*.
Besseghini, I., 78, 107*n*.
Bevan, A. T., 100, 103*n*.
Bhatara, V., 462, 465*n*.
Bickford, A. F., 74, 104*n*.
Biglan, A., 441, 472*n*.
Bihldorf, J. P., 153, 182*n*.
Biran, M., 432, 455, 465*n*.
Blackwell, B., 102, 103*n*., 307, 312, 317, 332*n*., 337, 364*n*., 438, 439, 440, 477*n*.
Blanchard, E. B., 156, 157, 176, 182*n*., 223, 252*n*., 446, 447, 466*n*., 475*n*.
Block, D. L., 368–401
Bloomfield, S., 102, 103*n*.
Blume, H., 436, 474*n*.
Blumenthal, J. A., 348, 367*n*.
Boller, J. D., 223, 252*n*.
Bond, A. J., 316, 333*n*.

Bootzin, R. R., 169–172, 182*n*., 185*n*., 187*n*., 390, 402*n*., 451, 473*n*.
Borkovec, T. D., 5, 11*n*., 49*n*., 51, 62, 67, 68*n*., 171, 172, 175, 182*n*., 186*n*., 336, 364*n*., 368–401, 375, 377, 390, 399, 401*n*.-403*n*., *420*, 423, *425*, *426*, 434, 441, 451, 452, 455, 466*n*., 470*n*., 476*n*.
Bortner, R. W., 348, 366*n*.
Bostem, F., 249, 250, 252*n*.
Boswell, P. C., *427*, 453, 466*n*.
Bott, L. A., 454, 466*n*.
Bowlby, J., 258, 305*n*.
Boxhill, C., *427*, 475*n*.
Boyd, J. R., 96, 103*n*.
Boylan, M., 171, 185*n*.
Bradley, B. W., *420*, 466*n*.
Brady, J., 223, 252*n*.
Braid, J., 142, 182*n*.
Bramble, J., 433, 470*n*.
Breckenridge, A., 72, 103*n*.
Brehony, K. A., 457, 474*n*.
Bridgewater, M. J., *427*, 466*n*.
Bristol, J., 131, 140*n*.
Brod, J., 74, 104*n*.
Brown, B., 248, 252*n*.
Brown, D. A., 156, 182*n*.
Brown, E. A., 168, 182*n*.
Brown, R. H., 441, 462, 466*n*.
Brunton, P., 72, 73, 104*n*.
Budzynski, T. H., 188–217, 189–193, 201–203, 205, 208, 210, 213, 217, 217*n*.-219*n*., 228, 252*n*., *458*, 467*n*.
Burish, T. G., 243, 252*n*.
Byasse, J. E., 417, 467*n*.

Calhoun, J. B., 346, 364*n*.
Campbell, D. T., 368, 369, 371, 383, 388, 395, 402*n*.
Camus, A., 353, 364*n*.
Cangelosi, A., *426*, 467*n*.
Cannon, W. R., 74, 104*n*.
Canter, A., 191, 218*n*., *416*, 467*n*.
Capla, G., 96, 105*n*.
Caplan, G., 265, 305*n*.
Caplan, R. D., 350, 364*n*.
Carlson, A.J ., 12, 13
Carol, M. P., 79, 103*n*., 149, 181*n*., 250, 252*n*.

480

AUTHOR INDEX

Carrington, P., 7, 11*n*., 78, 104*n*.,
108–139, 109, 111, 115, 117–119,
122, 124, 126, 130–134, 139*n*.,
342, 364*n*., 392, 402*n*., *410*, 419,
420, 421–423, *424*, *426*, 453, 454,
456, 457, 467*n*., 471*n*.
Carr-Kaffashan, L., 7, 11*n*., 78,
107*n*., 116, 141*n*., 171, 187*n*.,
426, 441, 451, 467*n*., 477*n*.
Carroll, V., 350, 365*n*.
Carruthers, M., 78, 100, 101, 106*n*.
Case, D. B., 177, 182*n*.
Cassel, J., 346, 347, 365*n*., 366*n*.
Castaneda, C., 399, 402*n*.
Cattell, R. B., 411, 471*n*.
Cautela, J. R., 48, 68*n*.
Cauthen, N. R., *427*, 467*n*.
Cazort, R. J., 318, 332*n*.
Chai, H., 168, 180*n*., 183*n*., 451,
467*n*.
Chang-Liang, R., 431, *458*, 467*n*.
Chave, S., 308, 333*n*.
Chaves, J. F., 144, 145, 181*n*.
Chesney, M. A., 157, 182*n*., 409,
413, *416*, 460, 467*n*.
Children of the Center for Attitudinal
Healing, 245, 252*n*.
Chiu, J. T., 78, 107*n*., 168, 187*n*.
Christenson, W. N., 346, 365*n*.
Chudzek, G. M., 96, 104*n*.
Claghorn, J. L., 251, 254*n*.
Clairborn, C. D., *425*, 453, 456,
469*n*.
Clancy, J., 308, 332*n*.
Clements, G., 250, 254*n*.
Clifton, R. K., 421, 469*n*.
Clinite, J. C., 96, 104*n*.
Clouser, R. A., 451, 469*n*.
Coates, T. J., 174, 186*n*.
Cobb, J., 438, 472*n*.
Cobb, S., 347, 350, 364*n*., 365*n*.
Coe, W. C., 146, 186*n*.
Cohen, I. M., 312, 332*n*.
Cohen, J., 395, 402*n*.
Cohen, J., *427*, 475*n*.
Cohen, J. B., 347, 366*n*.
Cohen, M. C., 449, 469*n*.
Cole, J. W., 78, 104*n*., 117, 119,
130–134, 139*n*., 342, 365*n*., 422,
423, *424*, *426*, 453, 454, 456,
467*n*.

Collings, G. H., 78, 104*n*., 117, 119,
130–134, 139*n*., 342, 364*n*., 422,
423, *424*, *426*, 453, 454, 456,
467*n*.
Collison, D. R., 167, 182*n*.
Comer, J. F., *426*, 431, *458*, 467*n*.
Comstock, G. W., 357, 365*n*.
Cook, T. D., 369, 388, 395, 402*n*.
Cooke, G., 431, 467*n*.
Cooley, E. J., 349, 365*n*.
Cooper, M. J., 116, 139*n*.
Copi, I. M., 354, 365*n*.
Cornoni-Huntley, J. C., 357, 365*n*.
Costell, S., 448, 471*n*.
Counts, D. K., *458*, 467*n*.
Courington, S., 348, 366*n*.
Coursey, R., 417, 418, 476*n*.
Coussons, R. T., 96, 103*n*.
Covi, L., 321, 332*n*.
Covington, T. R., 96, 103*n*.
Cox, D. J., 157, 182*n*.
Crawford, P. L., 168, 186*n*.
Creer, T. L., 168, 183*n*., 451, 467*n*.
Creighton, J., 245, 254*n*.
Crisp, A., 96, 104*n*.
Crofton, K., 217, 218*n*.
Cropp, G. J. A., 168, 180*n*.
Crosson, B., 434, 467*n*.
Cullen, T. D., 197, 219*n*.
Curry, S., 315, 333*n*.
Curtis, W. D., 419, 427, 467*n*.
Cuthbert, B., 425, 467*n*.

Dalton, R., 154, 172, 173, 180*n*.,
181*n*.
Dalvi, C. P., 78, 104*n*.
Daniels, L. K., 157, 182*n*., 183*n*.
Das, N. N., 110, 139*n*.
Datey, K. K., 78, 104*n*.
Davidson, P., 436, 472*n*.
Davidson, R. J., 67, 68*n*., 120, 139*n*.,
141*n*., 179, 183*n*., 340, 365*n*.,
392, 402*n*., 404, 405, 417, 419,
421, 422, 425, 443, 444, 463,
467*n*., 474*n*.
Davies, J., 131, 139*n*.
Davis, M. H., 168, 183*n*., 451, 467*n*.
Davison, G. C., 45, 68*n*.
Dawson, R. W., *459*, 468*n*.
Day, J. H., 168, 186*n*.
Deabler, H. L., 176, 183*n*., 434, 468*n*.

SUBJECT INDEX

Italicized page numbers indicate material in tables.